New Directions in Contemporary Sociological Theory

New Directions in Contemporary Sociological Theory

Edited by
Joseph Berger
and
Morris Zelditch Jr.

ROWMAN & LITTLEFIELD PUBLISHERS, INC.
Lanham • Boulder • New York • Oxford

Dedicated, with love, to Theory and Renée

ROWMAN & LITTLEFIELD PUBLISHERS, INC.

Published in the United States of America
by Rowman & Littlefield Publishers, Inc.
A Member of the Rowman & Littlefield Publishing Group
4720 Boston Way, Lanham, Maryland 20706
www.rowmanlittlefield.com

PO Box 317, Oxford, OX2 9RU, United Kingdom

British Library Cataloguing in Publication Information Available

Library of Congress Cataloging-in-Publication Data

New directions in contemporary sociological theory / edited by Joseph Berger and Morris Zelditch Jr.
p. cm.
Includes bibliographical references and index.
ISBN 0-7425-0868-4 (cloth : alk. paper) —ISBN 0-7425-0869-2 (pbk. : alk. paper)
1. Sociology. I. Berger, Joseph, 1924- II. Zelditch, Morris, Jr.
HM585 .C665 2002
301—dc21

2002002038

Printed in the United States of America

∞™ The paper used in this publication meets the minimum requirements of American National Standard for Information Sciences—Permanence of Paper for Printed Library Materials, ANSI/NISO Z39.48-1992.

Contents

Figures

Tables

I

INTRODUCTION

1

Theory Programs, Teaching Theory, and Contemporary Theories

Joseph Berger and Morris Zelditch Jr.

THE PLACE OF THEORETICAL RESEARCH PROGRAMS IN COURSES ON SOCIOLOGICAL THEORY

This book assesses the growth of sociological theory at the turn of the millennium. Its purpose is to expose students in courses on sociological theory to a useful and important addition to the more standard books in the subject. The more standard books in the subject tend to take one of three approaches. One approach is organized around major thinkers, like Marx, Weber, Durkheim, Simmel, Mead, and Parsons. A second is organized around major schools of thought, like structural functionalism, historical materialism, human ecology, rational choice theory, the theory of action, and symbolic interactionism. A third is organized around major sociological concepts—of social organization, like norms, values, beliefs, and institutions; of stratification, like class, status, and power; of social processes, like socialization, deviance and social control, and social conflict; of group process and social psychology, like roles, identities, power, exchange, and justice.

While all of these approaches are important and necessary, they typically neglect an important feature of sociological theory—that it is continually changing, continually evolving new theories. Such continual growth can be seen not only in the theories presented in the thirteen chapters in this book but in many others, such as the theory of power-dependence relations (growth of which is described in Cook, Molm, and Yamagishi 1993), bargaining and conflict (Lawler and Ford 1993), microdynamics (Turner 1993); in network theories such as the resource dependency theory of interorganizational relations (Pfeffer 1981) and the theory of structural holes (Burt 1992); in macro theories ranging from Riess's theory of sexual behavior (1986) to Rule's theory of civil disorder (1988).

Theory Growth and Theoretical Research Programs

Each chapter analyzes the growth of a particular program of theoretical research. *Theoretical research programs*, such as expectation states theory (chapter 3) or network exchange theory (chapter 5), are made up of: (1) working theoretical and methodological strategies; (2) sets of interrelated theories embodying these strategies; and (3) sets of theory-based empirical models applying these theories to concrete instances (Berger and Zelditch 1998). Analysis of such programs differs from the analysis of individual theoretical arguments, or unit theories, such as Davis and Moore's theory of stratification or Emerson's theory of power. It also differs from the analysis of overarching metatheoretical strategies orienting the construction of unit theories, such as structural functionalism or exchange theory. Theoretical research programs are more dynamic than orienting strategies, because more oriented to theory growth, and more complex than unit theories, because more concerned with networks of theory-theory relations. But in some respects theoretical research programs have elements of both: From overarching metatheoretical strategies they derive working theoretical strategies that guide how problems are formulated, how unit theories are constructed, how research testing them is carried out, and how empirical findings are assessed. At the same time, though a theoretical research program grows over time into a network of interrelated theories, it typically begins as a single, unit theory. It acquires its distinctive character by the elaboration of this initial theoretical formulation, by proliferation of it into other theories in order to explain other phenomena, by its integration with related or competing theories, and by multiplying models of the particular, concrete, empirical instances to which the theory is applied (Berger and Zelditch 1993, 1998; Wagner and Berger 1985).

Theoretical research programs are the level of analysis best suited to studying issues that involve the growth and change of theories over time. Overarching metatheoretical strategies are important to orienting the growth of theories but they do not, in themselves, grow very much. Unit theories grow, but focusing on a unit theory obscures the larger context of its relations to other theories that play an important role in its growth.

In our view, therefore, in order to understand the current state of sociological theory, students need to be exposed to major theoretical research programs as well as major thinkers, major schools, and major concepts. But this is difficult for theory courses to do. The difficulty is partly that theory programs are continually changing. It is also due partly to the fact that journals publish strategies, unit theories, or applications, not expositions of how a theory evolves. Finally, it is also partly because, whether strategies, unit theories, or applications, what the journals publish is written for specialists and is often technical and inaccessible to students.

This book was especially constructed to deal with each of these difficulties. Its chapters look at the development of theory programs over time. They are as nontechnical as their authors are able to make them and have been written to be accessible to a wide audience of sociologists. Furthermore, each is written by either the creator(s) of the program's original theoretical formulation or a leading theorist working in the program.

This book is not meant to substitute for any of the more standard books on sociological theory. Rather, it has been conceived of as a natural addition to them. Whether a theory course is primarily organized around thinkers, schools, or concepts, such a course is more complete and comprehensive if it directly assesses the ongoing work in contemporary theory. This study has been specifically designed to provide students with an understanding of ongoing contemporary theory as it is actually being developed by sociological theorists today.

RECENT DEVELOPMENTS AND NEW DIRECTIONS IN CONTEMPORARY SOCIOLOGICAL THEORIES

The chapters in this book represent a wide range of substantive and methodological concerns. Ours is a diverse field and the book reflects the field. It includes chapters concerned with affect and status, with norms, exchange, and networks, with social movements and revolutions, and with institutional structures. It also includes reflections of some notable contemporary theorists on theory construction, theory integration, and careers in theory.

Affect and Status

Theories of identity are concerned with conceptions of the self derived from roles—for example, family or occupational roles, and membership in social categories or groups—for example, gender and race, and with the effects of such identities on behavior. Affect Control theory, developed by David Heise and his colleagues and described in chapter 2, "Understanding Social Interaction with Affect Control Theory," is one such formulation. Unlike most of them, however, Affect Control theory conceptualizes identity as a set of fundamental sentiments—that is, enduring affective meanings. The basic principle of the theory is that behavior is driven by a propensity to confirm fundamental sentiments: particular events generate transient sentiments, in a process of impression formation; deflection of transient from fundamental sentiments creates a tension that is resolved by identity-restoring perceptions or behavior. If not, reidentification occurs. One implication of the theory is that negative self-conceptions are self-maintaining; they seek and find self-confirmation.

This program has grown rapidly since it originally appeared through the elaboration of its initial formulation and applications of it to many concretely different instances, through proliferation, that is, its extension to the explanation of other phenomena, and through integration of elements of other theories. Elaborations include reformulation of "reidentification," incorporation of "modifiers" and "settings," and the construction of a mathematical model of the identity process; among many applications, a notable one is to organizational behavior, where it is assumed that executives act to maintain organizational identities, and hence also to interorganizational behavior across culture. Proliferations have been concerned with explanations of the sociology of emotions, stigmatized subcultures, and identity movements. Finally, throughout the course of its development, Affect Control theory has sought to integrate elements from other, competing theories such as linguistic theory.

A major focus of the program described by David Wagner and Joseph Berger in chapter 3, "Expectation States Theory: An Evolving Research Program," has been on constructing theories of status characteristics and expectation states and other related status theories. These theories describe the behavior of actors working in goal-oriented collective situations who are operating within a common cultural framework that includes generalized social beliefs and established social categories such as status characteristics. These theories describe the conditions under which status characteristics and cultural beliefs become activated. But activated cultural beliefs may be multiple and contradictory and activated status characteristics may lead to status consistencies or inconsistencies. Thus these theories further explain how actors organize such complex and often contradictory cultural information in forming expectations for self and others. These expectations in turn determine actual social behavior. An important recent concern in the Expectation States program has been with the problem of how status characteristics and generalized cultural beliefs—which are major macrostructures—come to be socially constructed out of interactive microprocesses.

This program has grown through elaborations, proliferations, and integrations. Earlier formulations of status characteristics theory have been replaced by later formulations that are broader in scope, account for a greater body of relevant empirical findings, and are analytically more powerful—that is, are formalized. The program has also grown through proliferations. Working within the same family of concepts and principles as well as employing auxiliary concepts, different theories have been developed for different domains, including the study of interaction hierarchies, distributive justice, and social evaluation processes. In addition, different branches of the program have been integrated using the graph theoretical formulation that was originally developed for the status characteristics theory.

There now also exists an extensive body of research concerned with applying these theories to explain the operation of major status distinctions, such as race and gender, and with using these theories as bases for social interventions.

Norms, Exchange, and Networks

Chapter 4 by Douglas Heckathorn, "Development of a Theory of Collective Action: From the Emergence of Norms to AIDS Prevention and the Analysis of Social Structure," describes the development of a relatively new research program that is concerned with the emergence of social norms and compliant behavior. "Primary incentives" are seen as rewards and punishments based on an actor's performances. "Secondary incentives" are rewards and punishments administered to a group based on the performances of one of its members. The theory describes how the two kinds of incentives operate to produce norms and actors' compliance with norms. Two major conclusions are that secondary incentives are more effective and efficient in social control processes than primary incentives, and reactions to sanctions depend on the networks in which individuals are embedded.

This formulation has been elaborated through a number of theoretical extensions and proliferation. Elaborations include an extension of the theory that deals with the effects of group heterogeneity on norms and one that enables Heckathorn to specify conditions under which different types of social norms will arise. Proliferation includes a theory that explains the emergence of selective incentives for collective action.

Of particular interest in this chapter is the information it provides on how the growth of a theoretical research program can occur in the context of important research on social interventions. The theory developed by Heckathorn has been the basis for developing a major program for AIDS intervention. Heckathorn describes how work on this intervention program has not only been highly effective but has also generated critical substantive and methodological problems whose solutions play an important role in the growth of theory.

"Network Exchange Theory," described in chapter 5 by David Willer and colleagues, is a major theoretical research program growing out of the work by David Willer and Bo Anderson on Elementary Theory (Willer and Anderson 1981). Network Exchange Theory (NET) is concerned with power processes as they occur in mixed-motive bargaining situations. These are situations where actors have to cooperate with each other to reach bargaining agreements and simultaneously compete with each other to gain maximum benefit from the bargaining arrangement.

A primary concern of this research has been with the effect of different types of network structures—for example, exclusive networks, inclusive networks, and both inclusive and exclusive networks on the emergent power processes. In addition, as reported in this chapter, there has been theoretical and experimental research that deals with the emergence and changes in network structures under different social rules that govern task activities.

Over the past twenty years this program has undergone extensive growth. Its scope has been continually expanded to encompass new and different types of network structures. It has built up an impressive body of empirical research on the actual operation of power processes in these networks. Its domain has been expanded to include, in addition to bargaining behaviors, network change dynamics and coalition behaviors. Most recently it has sought to establish theoretical and empirical linkages to other research programs. These include linkages to the status characteristics theory (Berger et al. 1977; see chapter 3) and the Zelditch and Walker Legitimation theory (Zelditch and Walker 1984; Zelditch 2001).

Social Movements and Revolutions

In chapter 6, "The Resource Mobilization Research Program: Progress, Challenge, and Transformation," Mayer Zald and John McCarthy are concerned with theories of social movements. Resource mobilization theory (RMT) is a family of theoretical research programs with multiple sources in the sixties. All of its variants understand movements to be the rational application of means to ends. The amount of movement activity depends on the means rather than ends—not because ends, such as remedying grievances, make no difference, but because ends are ineffectual without resources. Zald and McCarthy describe two RMTs in some detail. Their own, the "entrepreneurial-organizational" variant of RMT, emphasizes social movement organizations (SMOs), professional, paid cadres of issue entrepreneurs, interorganizational dynamics (such as cooperation and competition), and the role of exogenous as well as endogenous resources, which are provided by "conscience" constituencies, such as churches, private foundations, even government agencies. The "political opportunity" variant gives more emphasis to the costs and benefits of the behavior of states and regimes: behavior such as repression, on the one hand, support by allies in divided regimes on the other. It also gives more emphasis to networks of relations among participants than to movement organizations and studies protest events rather than organizations.

Zald and McCarthy describe considerable elaboration of the entrepreneurial-organizational variant of RMT due to competition with the political opportunity variant—hence challenges by other theorists as well as their own empirical research. Among other reformulations, they refined their conceptualization of resources, taking symbolic resources into account, and elaborated the mobilization of SMOs by umbrella organizations. But they also give a good deal of attention to rivals that do not share the same family of concepts and principles as RMT but, Zald and McCarthy argue, complement it.

Theories of social movements are concerned with the mobilization of collective action oriented to social change. Collective action is a problem because the ends of such action are a "public good," a good that, once provided, is available to anyone, whether or not they contributed to providing it (Olson 1965). Hence, whether an individual demands social change or not, contribution to collective action that might make such a change is not automatic: it must be explained. One explanation is Oliver and Marwell's "critical mass theory" of collective action.

Pamela Oliver and Gerald Marwell describe their program in chapter 7, "Recent Developments in Critical Mass Theory." This is an abstract and general theory concerned with the factors that affect the likelihood that actors will contribute their resources to obtain a public good and therefore the likelihood of collective action occurring. The initial statement of the theory by Oliver and Marwell describes the ways in which the distribution of interests and resources in a group (group heterogeneity) and the nature of the production function associated with a particular collective good affects collective action. A production function is a function that describes the specific relation between contributions that are made to attain a collective good and the amount of the collective good realized, given the level of contribution. In their chapter Oliver and Marwell also emphasize the highly conditional nature of results that derive from their formulation—that is, the dependence of these results on the nature of specific empirical parameters in a given situation.

Elaboration has been the primary mode of this program's growth. Following the initial formulation, subsequent theoretical statements have been developed within the same family of concepts and principles that have expanded the initial formulation to cover the effects of other major factors on collective action. These include the effects of size and the structure of social ties that exist in a group. Oliver and Marwell also trace the impact of their formulation on subsequent work by other scholars in what is an evolving area of research in sociology today.

Jack Goldstone, an eminent scholar in the study of revolutions, describes the history of the growth of sociological theories of revolutions from their founding fathers—Tocqueville, Marx, and Weber—to the present in chapter 8, "Theory Development in the Study of Revolutions." The primary form of theory growth, as Goldstone describes it, appears to be that of elaboration, but in this case elaboration is *across* families of different concepts and principles. To begin with, there is the attempt over time to make these theories more comprehensive so as to cover a greater range of different types of revolutions. Further, there is an effort to increase the analytic power of these theories so that they are able to account for more of the elements that are involved in the causation, development, and outcome of revolutions. And third, there is the attempt to make these theories more empirically adequate so that they better account for the known empirical facts concerning revolutions.

However, as Goldstone sees it, the actual path of development is not simple. Rather, "progress in one area often leads to regress in another." For example, at times theories are formulated that are very comprehensive but say less about the various elements in the causation, development, and outcome of revolutions or are more vulnerable with regard to their empirical accuracy. In addition, Goldstone argues that in trying to expand revolutionary theory so that it covers ever more cases, it becomes increasingly difficult to identify "a short and consistent list of causes that lead to revolution."

In the end, Goldstone proposes a major shift in theoretical perspective from a focus on the causative conditions that lead to revolutions to a focus on the major conditions of social and political stability that he describes. He argues that an infinite number of historical events can undermine these major conditions,

Furthermore, when these conditions are undermined a revolutionary situation obtains and continues to obtain until efforts to restore the major conditions of stability succeed.

Institutional Structures

In chapter 9, "The Development and Application of Sociological Neoinstitutionalism," Ronald Jepperson describes a research program that takes an institutional approach to accounting for social behavior. The core ideas of the program emphasize collective level and cultural processes in explaining social phenomena—as, for example, in the argument that "institutionalized demography creates demographers, and makes demographic control reasonable."

This program has been concerned with national states, organizations, and individuals. Rather than treating these entities as bounded, autonomous, or rational actors in explaining their characteristics, the emphasis has been on the social environments within which these entities operate and the impact of these environments: for the national states this is the world polity and culture, for organizations their institutional environments, and for individuals the doctrine of individualism that is part of the culture that these individuals enact.

Through the years, this program has grown through a combination of theory elaboration and proliferation. Early formulations have been refined and extended in response to ongoing empirical research and theoretical problems—for example, detailing the linkages between institutional environments and organizational forms. Simultaneously, the research areas that have been dealt with in this program have become extremely broad as its core ideas and logic have been applied, through an extensive body of theoretical and empirical research, to the diverse domains of national states, organizations, and individuals.

In sharp contrast to the neoinstitutionalist approach described by Jepperson, Bueno de Mesquita and his colleagues use game-theoretic concepts and principles to explain the operation of social institutions. In chapter 10, they present in a nontechnical manner an important example of their work: "The Selectorate Model: A Theory of Political Institutions."

Working with the concepts of a "selectorate" and a "winning coalition," Bueno de Mesquita, Morrow, Siverson, and Smith develop a theory of how political institutions shape the incentives of political leaders and thereby determine their political behavior. The "selectorate" is that set of citizens who can exercise political influence. The "winning coalition" is that subset of the selectorate whose members' support is necessary for an incumbent to stay in office.

Among the important results that are derived from this theory is the prediction that the greater the size of the winning coalition in a given political structure, the greater the likelihood that the political leader will invest available resources in public goods—such as prosperity and peace—as against private goods. This and other theoretical predictions are tested against an extensive body of historical data.

This program is growing through theoretical elaborations that are concerned with increasing its generality and with expanding its scope. The theory is being generalized so that its arguments do not depend only on a specific class of utility functions and expanded so as to incorporate an explanation of revolutions. The program has also grown by theoretical proliferations to other major areas of concern. These proliferations have dealt with international conflicts and domestic politics as well as foreign policy.

Theory Construction and Theory Integration

Sociologists have long been concerned with issues that are involved in the construction of theories, the evaluation of theories, and their application in empirical research. The literature on these issues includes research on the scope conditions of theories (Berger 1974; Walker and Cohen 1985; Foschi 1997; Tootell, Bianchi, and Munroe 1998), research on different types of theoretical structures and their growth (Berger and Zelditch 1993, 1998; Wagner and Berger 1985; Webster and Whitmeyer 2001), and the nature of formal theorizing (Fararo 2000; Willer 1996). For recent collections that deal with issues involved in theory construction, see Szmatka, Skvoretz, and Berger 1997 and Szmatka, Lovaglia, and Wysienska 2002.

Guillermina Jasso's discussion in chapter 12, "Seven Secrets for Doing Theory," is within the theory construction tradition. Using as examples her own extensive work in developing a theory of distributive justice and some recent work on status processes, she describes the various tasks a theorist faces in constructing a theory. To Jasso a theory is a hypothetical-deductive structure. As such, it consists of assumptions that are embedded in a formal or mathematical structure and of logical derivations from these assumptions that have empirical import—are testable and refutable. As Jasso sees it, one of the primary goals of the theorist is to develop as small a set of fruitful assumptions as is possible that can lead to the broadest set of novel and important empirical consequences. She argues, as do many others, that the ultimate test of a theory is how well it accords with empirical evidence. But she further claims that even if a given theory is eventually rejected, the theorist learns much from the theory building enterprise.

We have argued throughout that the basic unit for analyzing theoretical growth is the theoretical research program. It is in the context of theories interrelated through similar concepts and principles that theory elaboration, theory proliferation, and theory integration typically occur. But what of concepts, principles, and theories that exist in different programs? How can they be related to each other? This is the type of problem that Thomas Fararo and John Skvoretz have dealt with in their extensive research across different substantive areas.

In chapter 11, "Theoretical Integration and Generative Structuralism," Fararo and Skvoretz present three examples of their work on interrelating different theoretical research programs: developing a formal representation for institutional behavior, interrelating concepts and principles from expectation states theory (see chapter 3) with concepts in social network analysis, and unifying Blau's macrostructural theory (see chapter 13) with Granovetter's theory of weak ties.

In particular, Fararo and Skvoretz present a detailed and nontechnical description of their integration of the work of Blau and Granovetter. This integration is seen to involve three theories where Blau's differentiation theory and Granovetter's weak ties theory are each represented as a third, biased net theoretical model. This in turn has led to the construction of a more comprehensive formal theory in which Blau and Granovetter's are special cases. Furthermore, they go on to show how their formalization is *essential* in the empirical testing of Blau's theoretical arguments.

Throughout their chapter, Fararo and Skvoretz emphasize the logic of their theoretical activities. The result is a deeper understanding of theoretical growth *across* different theoretical research programs.

Reflections on Careers in Theory

Peter Blau and Immanuel Wallerstein are two of the most influential social scientists of our day. In chapter 13, "Reflections on a Career as a Theorist," and chapter 14, "The Itinerary of World-Systems Analysis; or, How to Resist Becoming a Theory," each in turn examines his long and productive career in sociology. These careers have followed distinctive but contrasting paths of development.

In the case of Blau, this path has led from research on work groups in bureaucracy to a theory of social exchange to research on the American occupational structure and social mobility to a study of Employment Security Agencies to a theory of population structures. But as he has moved from one research area to another, his basic orientation has been fundamentally the same. Specifically, it has been to try to develop abstract and general principles that as a set constitute a theory. The objective is to use such a theory to explain the social phenomena under investigation. Thus, although his research focus has shifted dramatically over the years, his career throughout has been fundamentally that of a social theorist.

Wallerstein describes in detail the development of his research from his original interests in the political structure of postcolonial African states to his conceptualization of world-systems analysis. As a consequence, this chapter provides a unique introduction to the substantive, methodological, and philosophical issues that have been dealt with within this program of sociological research. In sharp contrast to the position of Blau, Wallerstein rejects the idea of describing his work as involving the construction of a theory. In his own words, the construction of a theory often implies premature closure and thus can be counterproductive. This he thinks is particularly true when studying, as he does, historical systems that are large-scale and long-term. Thus in the approaches of Blau and Wallerstein, we see markedly different views on the role and use of sociological theory in research.

AFTERWORD

The chapters in this volume cover a broad range of topics involving different theoretical perspectives and different types of research methods. They also exhibit different types of theory growth, realized to a different extent. In these respects they reflect the diversity that exists along many dimensions in our field today. But it is important to recognize that they also reflect the richness in resources—in theoretical interests, in theoretical perspectives, and in the variety of theoretical and methodological tools—that are available to the sociologist today in developing contemporary sociological theories.

NOTE

Most of the chapters in this book were originally papers commissioned for a major conference on sociological theory at the turn of the millennium sponsored by the Theory Section of the American Sociological Association in the year 2000. It was because the purpose of the conference was to assess the growth of, and recent developments and new directions in, sociological theory that the conference chose to focus on theoretical research programs.

REFERENCES

Berger, Joseph. 1974. "Expectation States Theory: A Theoretical Research Program." Pp. 3–22 in *Expectation States Theory: A Theoretical Research Program*, edited by Joseph Berger, Thomas L. Conner, and M. Hamit Fisek. Cambridge, MA: Winthrop. Reprinted Lanham, MD: University Press of America, 1982, pp. 3–22.

Berger, Joseph, M. Hamit Fisek, Robert Z. Norman, and Morris Zelditch Jr. 1977. *Status Characteristics and Social Interaction: An Expectation States Approach*. New York: Elsevier.

Berger, Joseph, and Morris Zelditch Jr. 1993. "Orienting Strategies and Theory Growth." Pp. 3–22 in *Theoretical Research Programs: Studies in the Growth of Theory*, edited by Joseph Berger and Morris Zelditch Jr. Stanford, CA: Stanford University Press.

———. 1998. "Theoretical Research Formulations: A Reformulation." Pp. 71–93 in *Status, Power, and Legitimacy*, edited by Joseph Berger and Morris Zelditch Jr. New Brunswick, NJ: Transaction Publishers.

Burt, Ronald. 1992. *Structural Holes*. Cambridge, MA: Harvard University Press.

Cook, Karen S., Linda D. Molm, and Toshio Yamagishi. 1993. "Exchange Relations and Exchange Networks: Recent Developments in Social Exchange Theory." Pp. 296–322 in *Theoretical Research Programs: Studies in the Growth of Theory*, edited by Joseph Berger and Morris Zelditch Jr. Stanford, CA: Stanford University Press.

Fararo, Thomas J. (ed). 2000. "Symposium on Formal Theory." *Sociological Theory* 18:473–523.

Foschi, Martha. 1997. "On Scope Conditions." *Small Group Research* 28:535–555.

Lawler, Edward J., and Rebecca Ford. 1993. "Metatheory and Friendly Competition in Theory Growth: The Case of Power Processes in Bargaining." Pp. 172–210 in *Theoretical Research Programs: Studies in the Growth of Theory*, edited by Joseph Berger and Morris Zelditch Jr. Stanford, CA: Stanford University Press.

Olson, Mancur. 1965. *The Logic of Collective Action*. Cambridge, MA: Harvard University Press.

Pfeffer, Jeffrey. 1981. *Power in Organizations*. Marshfield, MA: Pittman.

Riess, Ira L. 1986. *Journey into Sexuality: An Exploratory Voyage.* Englewood Cliffs, NJ: Prentice Hall.

Rule, James B. 1988. *Theories of Civil Violence.* Berkeley and Los Angeles, CA: University of California Press.

Szmatka, Jacek, Michael Lovaglia, and Kinga Wysienska (eds). 2002. *The Growth of Social Knowledge: Theory, Simulation, and Empirical Research in Group Processes.* Westport, CT: Praeger.

Szmatka, Jacek, John Skvoretz, and Joseph Berger (eds). 1997. *Status, Network, and Structure: The Development of Group Processes.* Stanford, CA: Stanford University Press.

Tootell, Geoffrey, Alison Bianchi, and Paul Monroe. 1998. "Understanding the Nature of Scope Conditions: Some Considerations and Consequences, Including Hybrid Theories as a Step Forward." *Advances in Group Processes* 15:213–235.

Turner, Jonathan H. 1993. "A 'Pure Theory' Research Program on Microdynamics." Pp. 104–135 in *Theoretical Research Programs: Studies in the Growth of Theory,* edited by Joseph Berger and Morris Zelditch Jr. Stanford, CA: Stanford University Press.

Wagner, David G., and Joseph Berger. 1985. "Do Sociological Theories Grow?" *American Journal of Sociology* 90:697–728.

Walker, Henry A., and Bernard P. Cohen. 1985. "Scope Statements: Imperatives for Evaluating Theory." *American Sociological Review* 50:288–301.

Webster, Murray, and Joseph M. Whitmeyer. 2001. "Modeling Second-Order Expectations." *Sociological Theory* 19:250–270.

Willer, David. 1996. "The Prominence of Theory in Sociology." *Sociological Forum* 11:319–331.

Willer, David, and Bo Anderson (eds). 1981. *Networks, Exchange, and Coercion.* New York: Elsevier.

Zelditch, Morris, Jr. 2001. "Processes of Legitimation: Recent Developments and New Directions." *Social Psychology Quarterly* 64:4–17.

Zelditch, Morris, Jr. and Henry A. Walker. 1984. "Legitimacy and the Stability of Authority." Pp. 1–25 in *Advances in Group Processes,* vol. 1., edited by Edward J. Lawler. Greenwich, CT: JAI.

II

AFFECT AND STATUS

2

Understanding Social Interaction with Affect Control Theory

David R. Heise

Professionals at a collegial gathering engage in a variety of social actions like talking to one another, confiding, consulting, toasting, treating, complimenting, congratulating, and so on. These actions are rational in the sense that just such behaviors are required of professionals as they go about their work with each other. Yet professionals rarely are involved in structural- functional or cost-benefit analyses while engaging in these behaviors. Their actions emerge from their hearts. This anomaly—that individuals' sensible actions usually are unfolded intuitively rather than by rational analysis—might be called the principle of affective rationality. Rational actions often are affectively generated.

Affectively generated actions are a central focus of affect control theory (Heise 1979, 1999; Smith-Lovin and Heise 1988; MacKinnon 1994). This theory elaborates three basic ideas.

1. Individuals create events to confirm the sentiments that they have about themselves and others in the current situation.
2. If events don't work to maintain sentiments, then individuals reidentify themselves and others.
3. In the process of building events to confirm sentiments, individuals perform the social roles that operate society—the principle of affective rationality.

Nothing in this formulation is concerned with rational choice or functional analysis. Instead, humans are viewed as meaning-maintainers who continually reconstruct the world to fit intuitive knowledge generated from sentiments, within cognitive and logical constraints. In this perspective, rational analysis is rare rather than routine. When successful problem solving does occur, it quickly is assimilated into the affective meaning system and replayed thereafter as intuitive knowledge.

AFFECTIVE MEANING[1]

A psychologist, Charles Osgood, laid the foundation for studies of affective meaning with cross-cultural research substantiating three universal dimensions of affective response (Osgood, May, and Miron 1975). Indigenes in more than two dozen societies were presented with a list of concepts that exist in every culture—like father, mother, girl, water, moon—and asked to respond to each concept with a modifier. Later, indigenes were asked to name the opposite of each modifier, the modifier opposites were formed into rating scales, and indigenes used the scales to rate the concepts. Pan-cultural correlations were computed comparing mean ratings of the concepts, on scales administered in the same society and in different societies. For example, one pan-cultural correlation compared mean ratings of the concepts on a sweet-sour scale used in the United States and on a *bueno-malo* scale used in Mexico.

Statistical analysis of the pan-cultural correlations showed that scales clustered into three major groups—Evaluation, Potency, Activity—and every culture contributed scales to each group. For example, concepts rated as sweet by Americans tended to be rated good by Americans and *bueno* by Mexicans, so all three of these scales—sweet-sour, good-bad, and *bueno-malo*—contributed to the Evaluation cluster.

Evaluation concerns a sense of approval or disapproval that can elaborate into judgments of morality, aesthetics, functionality, hedonism, or other standards. *Potency* relates to an entity's impact and might elaborate into assessments of physical magnitude, strength, forcefulness, social power, expansiveness, and the like. *Activity* indexes an entity's spontaneity, which can elaborate into judgments of animation, speed, perceptual stimulation, age, propensity to be an agent, and so on.

An entity's affective meaning is measured by averaging judgments from multiple respondents on bipolar rating scales assessing Evaluation, Potency, and Activity (EPA).

SENTIMENTS

Fundamental sentiments are the enduring affective meanings prevailing in a society that allow individuals to orient quickly and automatically in different situations. For example, most Americans feel that doctors are helpful, powerful, and reserved—that's the fundamental sentiment about doctors. Americans' sentiment about children is quite different: good, weak, and lively. Gangsters provoke still another sentiment: bad, powerful, and active.

An individual's sentiment about an object is a result of private encounters with the object and interactions with others. For example, an individual's own experiences with children are one source of the individual's sentiment about children. The individual expresses her sentiment in public actions toward children and in talking about children with her associates. These public acts influence others' sentiments. Others' public behavior and talk—both face-to-face and in mass media exposures—also influence her sentiments. A shared sentiment toward child emerges. That shared sentiment affects the individual's private experiences with children in the future, whereupon even her private experiences will tend to support the shared sentiment toward child.

Public interaction and discourse cause an individual's sentiments to be almost the same as another individual's sentiments, so each individual's sentiment is an indicator of the shared cultural sentiment, and averaging over a few individuals to get rid of effects of each individual's recent private experiences provides a good estimate of the cultural sentiment. This "ethnographic simplification" contrasts with the sampling procedures required to assess uncorrelated characteristics in a population. For example, an individual's age does not influence anyone else's age, so we cannot take any one person's age as a reliable indicator of other individuals' ages or of the population mean age.

In affect control theory, a cultural sentiment about an entity is measured as the average EPA rating of the entity outside of the context of any event, typically by fifty to sixty indigenous raters, split evenly between males and females. These numbers are small by survey-research standards, but the numbers are substantially larger than the minimum number of informants required to assess cultural norms according to mathematical analyses of the ethnographic simplification by Romney, Weller, and Batchelder (1986).

Cross-culture Variations

Empirical studies show that sentiments in different cultures are both similar and different. As an example, consider sentiments for father, mother, and child as measured among indigenes of the United States, Canada, Japan, China, Germany, and Northern Ireland. Raters in all six cultures agree that fathers, mothers, and children are not bad, and mothers are the nicest of the three. Additionally, all agree that parents are powerful and children are powerless. However, aside from these general agreements, major differences arise.

1. Japanese evaluate family members less positively than people in the other cultures, and a child actually is felt to be neither good nor bad in Japan.
2. Chinese evaluate family members most positively; and the Chinese are different from people in the other five cultures in feeling that mothers are more powerful than fathers.
3. Generally, parents are evaluated more positively than children, but not in Germany, where fathers are felt to be less good than either children or mothers.
4. Mothers generally are felt to be nicer than fathers, but this difference is negligible in the United States. The power difference between fathers and mothers also is negligible in the United States.

In general, people in these six cultures largely agree about what kinds of individuals are relatively good or relatively bad, and they agree about who is relatively powerful and who is relatively powerless. Feelings about who is relatively active or passive—who is likely to exercise agency—are moderately shared across the cultures. The six cultures also largely agree about what kinds of actions are relatively right or wrong, while being quite diverse in assessing the weightiness and spontaneity of social actions. Of course, even where there are substantial correlations across cultures, each culture does maintain some unique meanings, as was the case with father-mother-child.

IMPRESSION-FORMATION PROCESSES

An event changes pre-event feelings about actor, behavior, object, and setting into new feelings. For example, suppose an employer cheats an employee. Previously we might have felt positive toward the employer and employee. However, cheating the employee makes the employer seem very bad, and the event detracts from the employee, too, as if we allow that this employee might have earned victimization. Cheating is palliated as a workplace happening: it is bad, but not as bad as usual. The office or factory where cheating occurred is defiled, fostering suspicions that the place might house other iniquities.

Social psychologists have developed equations for accurately predicting post-event impressions from the set of EPA profiles for pre-event feelings (Heise 1979, 1985; Smith-Lovin and Heise 1988; Britt and Heise 1992). Each of the many terms in these equations represents a mental process that occurs while interpreting events. Three terms are especially notable.

Every equation has a *stability* term. That fact means that the mind always transfers some pre-event feeling toward an event element to the post-event feeling involving the same event element. For example, actors are likely to seem good after events if the actors were good to begin with, and actors may continue to seem bad after events if they were bad beforehand. In the *morality* effect, evaluation of an actor's behavior strongly influences the impression of the actor's goodness or badness. For example, anyone rescuing another gets evaluative credit for engaging in a noble act. Anyone killing another is discredited for engaging in a horrible act. At the same time, though, we also are influenced by how evaluatively *consistent* the behavior is with the object of action. For example, an actor who performs a bad action on a good person violates a consistency principle—that good people deserve good treatment—so the actor seems bad not only because of the morality effect but additionally because of behavior-object inconsistency.

These three processes—stability, morality, and behavior-object evaluative consistency—influence evaluation of an actor in all cultures that have been examined so far: the United States, Ireland, Lebanon (Smith-Lovin 1987),

Canada (MacKinnon 1985/1988/1998), and Japan (Smith, Matsuno, and Umino 1994). In fact, research results indicate considerable cross-cultural similarity overall in forming impressions of an actor's goodness and activity. On the other hand, research indicates that there may be fairly substantial differences in how people in different cultures interpret the potency of an event's actor.

Similarities across cultures notwithstanding, on every dimension of impression formation, each different culture weights the processes differently and brings in a few unique considerations, thereby creating subtle cross-cultural differences in the interpretations of events.

Likelihood

Expected events create impressions confirming sentiments (Heise and MacKinnon 1987). For example, a mother hugging her baby creates impressions of mother and baby that are very close to sentiments about mothers and babies, and the affective meaning of hugging is sustained as well. So this event seems likely, to the point of being an action that is normative for mothers. On the other hand, a mother abandoning her baby creates impressions that depart substantially from basic sentiments. The mother seems much less good, less powerful, and more active than she should be; abandoning gains aberrant significance in this context, and an abandoned baby seems less good and lively than a baby should be. With impressions of mother, abandoning, and baby deflected so far from their fundamental affective meanings, this event seems unusual, to the point of being a form of deviance for mothers.

Occasionally an event wrenches impressions so far from sentiments that individuals have trouble believing such an event really could happen, as in a mother murdering a baby. Some events undermine sentiments still more and seem literally impossible. For example, a beloved leaving an individual through death creates an impression of the loved one and of the individual so far from fundamental sentiments that the event doesn't seem credible; so when it happens, the loved one may be conceived as living on, supernaturally.

In affect control theory, an event's likelihood is predicted from the degree to which the event generates impressions that deviate from sentiments. A difference between the fundamental sentiment and the transient feeling about an entity, cumulated over all three EPA dimensions, is a deflection. Cumulating over all entities involved in an event yields a total deflection, and values of total deflection translate to assessments of event likelihood. Total deflection is small in the case of likely events, whereas a large total deflection implies an unlikely event.

Total deflection also is an indicator of the psychological stress produced by an event. Experience that undermines fundamental affective meanings, creating a sense of strangeness, is stressful—even experiences that may be emotionally pleasant.

States of Being

Impression formation research focuses on action events, as just discussed, and also on copular assertions about an individual's state of being (e.g., the father is angry), mainly in the form of modifier-identity combinations (the angry father). Modifier-identity combination in the United States averages the preexisting impressions, with the modifier having about twice the impact of the identity. For example, in the case of Evaluation, noticing that a person has a good attribute like gentleness makes the person seem more pleasant, and noticing a bad attribute like surliness makes the person seem less pleasant. Characterized people also seem more pleasant if they have valued identities, and they seem more unpleasant if they have stigmatized identities—compare a gentle father with a gentle drunk. Moreover, evaluative consistency between attribute and identity makes a person seem more pleasant, and inconsistency makes a person seem more unpleasant. The net impact of all three factors together is that people with good attributes and good identities seem pleasant, but someone with a bad attribute or a bad identity seems unpleasant.

Copular impressions have been studied in the United States (Averett and Heise 1987; Heise and Thomas 1989) and Japan (Smith, Matsuno, and Ike 2000), and, overall, Americans seem to process states of being more simply than Japanese. For instance, Americans do not distinguish between trait modifiers (like irascible) and emotion modifiers (like angry), whereas Japanese are prone to stigmatize someone characterized by an unpleasant emotion more than someone characterized by an unpleasant trait.

EMOTIONS

In affect control theory, emotions manifest emergent affective meanings of an individual and also indicate how emergent meanings relate to the fundamental affective meanings of the individual (Averett and Heise 1987; Heise and Thomas 1989; Heise and Weir 1999; Smith-Lovin 1990, 1991, 1994). On the whole, an individual who seems bad as a result of an event should have unpleasant emotions, and an individual who seems good should have pleasant emotions. An individual who seems powerless as a result of an event should experience vulnerable emotions, and an individual who seems powerful should experience dominance emotions. An individual who seems passive as a result of an event should have tranquil emotions, and an individual who seems animated should have activated emotions. However, emotions also result from comparing impressions with sentiments associated with one's identity. For example, an individual who seems somewhat favored in a situation nevertheless should have an unpleasant emotion if the impression of the individual is not as good as the individual's very positive identity warrants.

A characteristic emotion is the emotion that would be experienced were an individual's identity confirmed perfectly. For example, a gangster getting perfect confirmation should experience anger and contempt. A heroine getting perfect confirmation should experience cheerfulness and friendliness. A minister should experience generosity and compassion. A prostitute should experience impatience and aggravation.

The characteristic emotion for an identity is only partly achieved in real relations because individuals with the identity interact with people in other identities, and there has to be some trade-off in maintaining one's own identity as opposed to others'. Others' identities tug emotions in different directions, and this process gives emotional character to different kinds of relationships. For example, a minister interacting with a sinner does not achieve perfect confirmation of self but instead is deflected such that expected emotions include apprehension and feeling overwhelmed. On the other hand, gratefulness and relief are the kinds of emotions a minister should enjoy in his or her personal relationship with God.

Recurrent emotions experienced in different relationships—structural emotions (Kemper 1978)—allow interactants to perceive the social structure within which they are situated. Norms for structural emotions may be imposed as a way of producing desired social structures (Hochschild 1983).

Most commercial and professional transactions are expected to be emotionally charged in orderly ways (Heise and Calhan 1995). Emotional control, masking emotional displays, and denial of felt emotions occur in social situations not to remove emotions from social life, but to achieve conformity with emotion norms (Heise and Calhan 1995) or in response to social control (Hochschild 1983; Staske 1996; Heise and Weir 1999).

Affect control theory's model of emotions leads to a nonintuitive hypothesis about how emotions arising from unexpected events relate to subsequent actions. A subsequent action will be designed to undo the uncharacteristic emotion that precedes it. For example, a husband theoretically would follow a flicker of jealousy with solicitous behavior rather than vindictiveness, in order to reclaim the positivity of himself and his spouse. Such a prediction goes against the commonsense notion that an emotion is a motive, producing behavior that is consistent with the emotion. In affect control theory, behavior is driven and controlled not by emotions but by the propensity to confirm fundamental affective meanings.

Making an emotion into a motivational state requires incorporating emotion into a person's fundamental affective meaning as an identity modifier defining a mood. For example, a man might turn himself into a "jealous husband" as a way of understanding a situation where his wife seems aroused and raunchy but is trying to escape him. Attributing jealousy to himself expresses his predicament, and being jealous sets a mood generating behavior and feelings that are generally consistent with the mood, though the tenor of behavior and feeling can vary with different partners, just as role behavior varies from one partner to another.

Whereas an individual generates experiences that eliminate uncharacteristic emotions, the individual acts to maintain a mood, because a mood is a fundamental—though temporary—aspect of self that the individual is actualizing. Cessation of a mood occurs by relinquishing the temporary definition of self, as when a series of happenings contradicts the mood identification.

Another hypothesis deriving from affect control theory's model of emotions is that emotions swing wildly between pleasant and unpleasant for individuals with extremely negative identities—a prediction that accords with clinical observations of emotional lability in individuals with very negative self-concepts. The affect control theory explanation is this. Variations in emotionality—sighing, smiling, frowning, and the like—have diminished impact on the self-experience of individuals who understand themselves as being fundamentally bad. So when events warrant a positive impression of themselves, individuals with negative selves have to overreact emotionally and work themselves into emotional beatitude. When circumstances warrant an impression of themselves as extra bad, they have to evoke an emotional hell internally in order to experience their downward deviation. Numbed in negativity, they have to magnify their feelings in order to experience an affected self.

CONSTRUCTING EVENTS

According to affect control theory, individuals seek experiences that confirm fundamental affective meanings. During a social interaction individuals intuit behaviors that would produce impressions validating fundamental affective meanings, and they are inclined to enact such behaviors, or ask others to enact them, in order to obtain confirming experiences.

Affect control theory's mathematical model (Heise 1987) delineates how an individual selects interpersonal behaviors that best confirm fundamental affective meanings. The model utilizes sentiment measurements, impression-formation equations, and mathematical minimization procedures to identify the EPA profile for ideal behaviors that would least deflect emergent affective meanings from fundamental affective meanings in a social situation. The EPA profile can be used to select behaviors that could be performed in the social interaction. The following example, based on analyses with affect control theory's mathematical model implemented in a computer simulation program called *Interact* (Schneider and Heise 1995), portrays the minded processes simulated by the model.

Suppose an individual sees herself as a doctor and her interaction partner as a patient. In U.S. culture, this definition of the situation leads her to feel that she is fundamentally quite good and powerful and neither lively nor still, and the patient is fundamentally neither good nor bad, quite weak, and slightly quiet. Suppose that the interaction is just beginning so nothing has happened to deflect transient meanings away from the fundamental meanings.

Now what behavior should the doctor perform to best confirm the fundamental meanings of both individuals in the situation? She might perform a behavior that is neutral in goodness, powerfulness, and liveliness (like *study* or *evaluate*), and such a behavior is not too bad a choice because it confirms the meaning of patient almost perfectly. However, such a behavior makes a doctor seem less good and potent than she really is. So the doctor increases the niceness of her behavior to quite good to get around that problem. A behavior that is quite good and neutral on potency and activity—like *talk to*, or *understand*—confirms the meaning of patient well, and it almost perfectly confirms the evaluation and activity aspects of a doctor's fundamental meaning. This behavior still leaves the doctor seeming not quite as powerful as she is supposed to be, but a more powerful behavior would detract from the goodness she is trying to confirm. So she reasonably settles on talking to the patient and understanding the patient's problems.

Doing so produces a transient meaning of the doctor as quite good, slightly powerful, and neither lively nor still. This emergent meaning is less powerful than a doctor should be, so her next action has to be somewhat more potent to avoid straying too far from the fundamental meaning of doctor. She needs to perform a behavior that is quite good, slightly powerful, and neutral on activity—like *console*, or *soothe*.

Consoling and soothing the patient leaves the doctor's emergent meaning still lacking the ideal level of potency, and meanwhile the patient begins to seem excessively indulged. In fact, the doctor's consideration of the patient, creating an excessively high evaluation of the patient, provides a context in which the doctor now can be more domineering. Now the doctor can employ behaviors that are only slightly nice, more powerful, and slightly quiet—like *direct*, or *counsel*.

As the interaction continues, the doctor seems somewhat less good and powerful than ideal, and the patient seems better and less powerless than a patient is in general. These emergent meanings of doctor and patient combine with sentiments about doctors and patients to produce the structural emotions of the relationship—the doctor feeling secure and compassionate and the patient feeling at ease and grateful.

Affect control theory offers some interesting hypotheses about the actions of individuals who operate with stigmatized selves. One such possibility is an individual who acquires a transient self-impression that is much more negative than the individual's identity—say, as a result of being derogated in public. Affect control theory predicts that the stigmatized individual will engage a valued other in an especially positive action in an effort to pull the transient impression of self up to a more positive value. This prediction was confirmed in a behavioral experiment designed to test the prediction (Wiggins and Heise 1987).

On the other hand, individuals with negative self-sentiments—especially those who are too submissive and passive to depend on active behavioral strategies—need assurance from others that their low opinion of themselves is justified. They seek others who criticize them, even when the derogations are emotionally painful, because being criticized is an experience that confirms their negative self-sentiments. This influences their choices for relationships.

> Because affect control theory suggests that only alters who view themselves in a fundamentally negative way will be likely to engage consistently in such negative behaviors, we predict that people with low self esteem will choose one another as interaction partners. This homophily principle leads to a perversely stable social structure: people who think negatively of themselves are locked into dissatisfying, unpleasant relations with similar others, whereas alters with high self esteem have little incentive to intrude into these persistently negative interactions. (Robinson and Smith-Lovin 1992:27)

Experiments by Robinson and Smith-Lovin (1992) substantiated these hypotheses among people with varying self-sentiments who had to decide whether critics or appreciators would be their future interaction partners. Individuals with low self-esteem associated with criticizers.

REIDENTIFICATIONS

Some interactions persistently produce impressions of participants that are far from fundamental affective meanings. This can happen when interactants have different definitions of the situation or when some interactants have special sentiments that others do not share. When interactants are trying to confirm different sentiments, they get caught in a conflict: the more one individual achieves sentiment confirmation, the more the others feel that emergent meanings are diverging from fundamental meanings. Disconfirming interactions also can arise structurally, when interactants' identities cannot be confirmed simultaneously, such as a lady with a mugger.

Sometimes the stress and strangeness of a disconfirming event can be resolved by interpreting a behavior in a way that makes the event less disturbing—for example, viewing a derogatory comment as just a joke. Another way to recover a sense that one understands what is going on is to redefine the situation, inferring interactants' identities from events that are happening, rather than trying to anticipate behaviors from presumed identities. That is, to cope with a breakdown in understanding, an individual can assign interactants new identities that explain their anomalous conduct.

Reidentification of an individual may involve assigning an entirely new identity in order to account for recent events in terms of revised role expectations. This is the concern of labeling theory in sociology. Alternatively, an individual may be reidentified by combining a personal characteristic with the individual's current identity, interpreting recent peculiarities in terms of the individual's personality or character. This is the concern of trait attribution research in psychology. Affect control theory provides a model of both kinds of reidentification.

Here is an example of how reidentification processes work, according to affect control theory. Suppose an individual is identified as a doctor and her interaction partner as a patient, and suppose the doctor insults the patient. This event stigmatizes both interactants, rather than confirming the doctor as fundamentally good and the patient as fundamentally neither good nor bad. An observer might wish to redefine the situation in order to understand this event better.

Redefining the doctor requires answering the question: What kind of individual would insult a patient? The transient impression of a doctor who insults a patient is slightly bad, slightly potent, and slightly active, so the observer might try an identity with that fundamental affective meaning (e.g., *fanatic, bigshot*). Such a reidentification works—a fanatic insulting a patient does maintain the meaning of patient and also confirms the potency and activity meanings of a fanatic. However, with such a bad actor identity, the transient impression of the actor insulting the patient is worse, so an even more negative identity like *quack* or *lunatic* provides a better solution: someone who insults a patient behaves like a quack or a lunatic. Such an identity explains the focal happening well, and once assigned, the new identity might be used to interpret other events involving that same actor.

Alternatively, an observer can try to understand the event as the action of a doctor with a peculiar personality. An actor who insults a patient is fundamentally quite bad, a bit potent, and slightly active. So what kind of personality trait would make a doctor into such a person? A trait that is quite bad, neutral on potency, and slightly lively—like *self-centered* or *spiteful*. The doctor who is insulting a patient could be expressing her self-centeredness or her spitefulness. Such a trait explains her peculiar behavior in the doctor role, and should explain her peculiar behavior in other roles, too. A related alternative is that the observer might choose to understand the doctor's unexpected behavior in terms of a mood, like *tormented* or *hostile*. A mood attribution would account for the uniqueness of the doctor's behavior in this one situation, while allowing that she usually acts normally.

Another avenue to understanding the event is redefinition of the patient, asking the question: What kind of person would a doctor insult? Such a person would be quite bad, neutral on potency, and active. Among the identities with fundamental meanings like this are *bigot* and *faultfinder*, so the doctor's insult is more understandable if the recipient is a bigot or faultfinder. Alternatively, an observer could attribute a trait like *bossy* or *manipulative* to the patient to explain the doctor's behavior.

A reidentification has to be logically connected to the identity of the interaction partner, the setting, and the nature of the act performed. Many identities that are affectively appropriate may not fit the context logically. For example, a doctor who insults a patient logically can be reidentified as a quack because a quack is a kind of doctor. However, without a major reframing, the doctor cannot logically be reidentified as a burglar, traitor, or bigamist, even though these identities are just as affectively appropriate as quack.

A reidentification also has to accord with features of the person being reidentified—especially the individual's sex. The feminist movement in industrialized societies has made gender less of an issue for workplace identities—for example, by substituting *chair* for *chairman.* However, gender still is important in labeling with some informal identifications, such as *beauty, stud, bitch,* and *bastard.*

Reidentification processes get another complication when an observer notices the emotions of interactants during unexpected conduct (Heise 1989). In general, an actor who displays a sustained emotion that fits the positiveness or negativeness of the actor's actions can be reidentified relatively positively. Notably, negative emotions like guilt or shame accompanying deviant actions suggest that the actor generally operates with a positive self-identification, and therefore the individual's future behavior probably will be normal. On the other hand, maintaining a positive mood while engaged in deviant conduct suggests that the actor is maintaining a negative identity, because only wicked individuals can engage in deviant behavior while feeling good, so observers should acknowledge the individual's negative self with a stigmatization, thereby preparing themselves to expect more negative behavior from that person in the future.

Emotions displayed by recipients of action also can influence reidentifications of an actor. For example, observing a woman speaking to a man and noticing that the man is embarrassed might cause an observer to guess that the woman has a grand identity in the man's eyes. Actors who are smarter, more authoritative, more famous make the objects of their attention feel quieter, less comfortable, more vulnerable; so an object person's embarrassment can warrant an inference about the actor's high status.

Because emotion links so closely to possession of identities and traits, emotion is a prime focus of negotiation among interactants maneuvering for relational position (Staske 1996; Heise and Weir 1999). The process can be involuted, as when one sweetheart tries to amplify a mild negative emotion displayed by the partner over forgetting an appointment: "Sorry! You're just sorry?" The underlying worry may be that the partner is insufficiently committed to the sweetheart identity, and indeed, the partner may be emoting with little intensity precisely to signal that the relationship is waning.

APPLICATIONS

Law

Robinson, Smith-Lovin, and Tsoudis (1994) proposed that affect control theory derivations relating emotions and reidentifications explain why journalists stress emotional reactions in reporting crimes, why lawyers advise clients about appropriate emotional conduct in the courtroom, why deference and demeanor enter into sentencing and probation recommendations, and why judges attend to perpetrators' emotions when considering reductions of sentences. In all of these cases, the presumption is that one cannot know what kind of person an offender really is unless one knows whether or not the offender's emoting in the context of the crime is appropriately negative.

In their research, Robinson, Smith-Lovin, and Tsoudis (1994) presented subjects with transcribed manslaughter confessions, including parenthetical descriptions of appropriate moods (e.g., "sad/unhappy, sits with eyes downcast") or inappropriate moods (e.g., "relaxed facial expressions"). Subjects in the experiment then rated the likelihood that the perpetrator was a habitual offender likely to repeat the offense in the future, and they recommended a sentence in terms of number of years of imprisonment. Emotional distress on the part of the perpetrator strongly reduced the perception of the perpetrator as a habitual offender, and seeing the perpetrator as a nonhabitual offender dramatically reduced the recommended years of imprisonment.

Tsoudis and Smith-Lovin (1998) extended the scope of the experiment to include the emotions of the victim in a study similar to the first, except that subjects read two passages with embedded emotion cues: the perpetrator's confession and the victim impact statement. Results replicated the first study with regard to perpetrator emotion—inappropriate emotion made the perpetrator and his crime seem worse. Additionally, the victim's emotion also had a major impact on the recommended sentence, as predicted. Victims who were sad and depressed by their victimization, as opposed to relaxed about it, were perceived as more positive characters, so the act that hurt them seemed worse, and the perpetrator deserved a longer sentence. Thus emotions of perpetrator and victim indirectly affect the seriousness of the offense, by changing the situated identities of perpetrator and victim. This fits earlier work (Smith-Lovin and Heise 1982) demonstrating that impression formation is a dynamic feedback process, with actor and object impressions influencing the impression of the behavior, even as the behavior shapes impressions of the actor and object.

Another study by Tsoudis and Smith-Lovin (2001) verified that perpetrator and victim emotions influence construals of a crime—how vicious it was, how justified, how premeditated, and so on—and these construals in turn influence sentencing. In terms of affect control theory, the affective meanings of the interactants determine the affective meaning of the criminal behavior, then the behavior's affective meaning supports inferences to fill in information about the crime, in the same way that affective meanings of identities permit inferences about the stereotypical traits of individuals with those identities (MacKinnon and Bowlby 2000).

Another potential courtroom application of affect control theory emerges from Goodwin's (1994) discussion of how five Los Angeles police officers won an acquittal in their trial for excessive violence, despite a video showing them bludgeoning a black man named Rodney King forty-seven times as he lay on the ground. The acquittal was accomplished through testimony from an expert on violence who actually turned the video into evidence for the defense by arguing that police were responding to King's aggressive moves. The problem for the prosecutor was that no equivalent expert was available to legitimize laypeople's perceptions, including King's on the night he was beaten. "No expert witnesses are available to interpret these events and animate the images on the tape from King's perspective. . . . [W]ithin the discourse of the courtroom, no one can speak for the suspect. His perception is not lodged within a profession and thus publicly available to others as a set of official discursive procedures" (Goodwin 1994:625).

Yet affect control theory analyses of the events do simulate laypeople's perceptions. Defining Rodney King as a villain (since he was apprehended after a dangerous chase), moderate deflection is produced the first time a police officer clubs him, indicating that a single use of a steel baton seems a little unusual but not remarkable: at worst, the officer seems *hotheaded* or *reckless* (affect control theory predictions are italicized). However, deflection grows with each additional clubbing, reaching high levels by the tenth blow, and the high deflection corresponds to a sense that something extraordinary is happening. The lay observer, in a state of shocked incredulity, seeks a redefinition of the situation so it makes sense. Those are not officers of the law but *brutes*, *bullies*, perhaps *vigilantes*, even *outlaws*! Thus, affect control theory analyses legitimate the interpretations of laypeople, and provide scientific evidence that the officers' behavior was outside cultural norms.

Commerce

On the basis of an empirical analysis of occupations, MacKinnon and Langford (1994) argued that the study of occupations requires a redirection of attention away from occupational prestige to EPA measurements of work identities. "[I]t is the affective associations of social identities—their social sentiments—that generate role behavior and those situationally specific and ephemeral affective experiences we recognize as emotions; and it is these affective dynamics at the micro-interactional level that give rise to social structure. Because prestige scores are inadequate measures of the social sentiments of occupational identities, they are of limited utility in studying the micro-interactional basis of social stratification" (MacKinnon and Langford 1994:234).

Work activity cannot be predicted from measurements of occupations on traditional dimensions like occupational prestige, or average education and income. However, EPA measurements of an occupational identity and of the identities in that occupation's role set do support analyses of the interactional aspects of work. Other analytic possibilities also emerge from measurements of work roles on EPA dimensions, such as the following.

According to Scher and Heise (1993), justice-related emotions (those believed to have inequity as their initiating condition) are gateways to deliberations about whether economic or political exchanges are fair or not, and eliminating justice-related emotions often precludes deliberations about injustice. They employed affect control theory simulations to reveal how the justice-related emotion of anger can arise in the workplace, and how this ordinarily is prevented.

> [The employee's] action of working for the employer can take on a variety of affective meanings, depending on the nature of the work. . . . By changing the affective meaning of work (i.e. by experimenting with different EPA profiles), we found that anger will arise if the work is even a little unpleasant . . . and if it is at least slightly active. . . . The potency of the work, which might be interpreted as its importance, is not crucial—people can get fed up with important work as well as unimportant work. . . . Affect control theory predicts that an employee repetitively engaging in such work comes to see the self as . . . substantially less good, more potent, and more lively than should be the case. Such a disconfirmation of identity rouses the emotion of anger.
>
> If the employer understands the work in the same way as the employee, then the employer is just as stressed by the situation as the employee. And the employer is able to do something about it within the rules of a transaction. Paying the employee helps bring the employee's self impression back to where it is supposed to be and greatly dissipates the propensity to anger. Making the payment more positive by paying well can wipe out the negative impression of the employee and the negative emotion. On the other hand, failing to pay or paying poorly while continuing to demand arduous work leaves anger and primes the employee to begin deliberating over the fairness of the transaction. (Scher and Heise 1993:238–239)

Another kind of organizational dysfunction can occur when workers in international corporations ignore local cultural differences (Schneider and Heise 1995). Smith (1995) indicated that American executives might conflict with Japanese civil servants by giving Japanese civil servants less respect than is appropriate for their high status in Japan. Schneider (2002) pointed out that behavior prescriptions developed in a foreign central office might prevent employees from confirming the affective meanings of their professional identities within their own cultures, putting them at risk of stress and deviant labeling.

Affect control theory predicts organizational activity under the assumption that executives produce such activity in order to maintain sentiments about organizations and organizational actions. Lerner (1983) had a panel of international decision makers measure sentiments associated with actions used by political leaders in the conduct of international relations (e.g., breaking diplomatic relations, extending economic aid). The EPA measurements were used to convert over three hundred qualitative events among Middle Eastern states into a quantitative network of interstate relations. Fundamental identities of the states then were estimated by seeking the EPA profile for each state that would best predict the EPA relations of that state with others, under the assumption that affect control theory accounts for the relations. Lerner demonstrated that nation identities could be inferred like this, and he showed that simulations based on the inferred identities and the EPA measurements of political actions predicted a significant proportion of the actual events that took place between Middle Eastern states. His work supports the idea that national leaders use political actions to maintain fundamental sentiments about their own nation and other nations.

Equivalent studies of interactions between business firms are yet to be done, but the basic idea seems equally relevant. That is, officers of business firms interact with officers of other firms, using the legal, financial, sales, and other departments of their organizations to implement macroactions (Heise and Durig 1997) that maintain affective meanings in the business world. For example, the computer wars at the turn of the century among Microsoft, Sun, IBM, and others seemed to be such affectively based processes.

Resocialization

Thomas and Heise (1995, figure 1) showed the impact of a subculture on sentiments about behaviors. In anonymous reports, university students evaluated "smoking marijuana, hash" and "sniffing cocaine," and also reported their experience with recreational drugs. Individuals having no experience with recreational drugs viewed both kinds of drug use as wicked. Those who had tried marijuana but nothing else felt that smoking marijuana was evaluatively neutral, and they viewed sniffing cocaine somewhat less negatively than nonusers. Those who had tried both marijuana and cocaine felt that using these drugs was a positive act. Those far enough into the drug subculture to have tried LSD as well as the other two drugs felt that using marijuana actually was virtuous!

In general, deviants who form subcultures acquire positive sentiments about the subculture's special identities and actions, whereupon those identities elicit the behaviors, not because the identities and behaviors are negative, but because they are positive. Smith-Lovin and Douglass (1992) documented this in a study of two Christian congregations in South Carolina during the 1970s. Members of a Unitarian church rated homosexuals as negative in evaluation and potency and positive in activity. Members of a nearby gay church congregation saw the goodness and potency of homosexuals as literally the opposite of what it was among the nongays. Affect control theory analyses suggested that homosexuals would behave negatively and produce little in the way of pleasant emotions for each other if they accepted the negative views of the Unitarians. However, sentiments held in the gay church congregation would permit them to be positive interaction partners, feeling emotions of affection and joy with each other. A second survey of the two church congregations revealed that the Unitarians actually did have the expectations deduced from their sentiments by affect control theory, while the gay Christians saw their interactions in the positive manner deduced from their positive sentiments.

Alcoholics Anonymous converts mainstream sentiments to subcultural sentiments for therapeutic reasons. For instance, AA transforms the meaning of *drunkard* from a rude, disgusting slob to a sensitive individual of great potential, as long as alcohol is avoided. Thomas (1996) obtained longitudinal data over a six-month period from individuals mandated to attend AA meetings by a treatment facility, counseling agency, or court order. She found that 85 percent of the sentiments she measured converged toward AA positions in the case of alcoholism-related stimuli, compared to 33 percent convergence on general stimuli. Surprisingly, mere attendance at AA meetings was enough to achieve the convergence toward subcultural norms; variations in commitment and participation did little to explain whose sentiments changed more.

Francis (1997a, 1997b) studied social support groups dealing with loss of spouse through death or divorce and was able to identify a general strategy used by such groups to metamorphose a support-seeker's negative self-sentiments to positive self-sentiments. First, these groups get the support-seeker to villainize the departed spouse and interpret the spouse's departure as an abandonment. This tactic changes the support-seeker's negative feelings about self from a fundamental sentiment that continues to be maintained into a transitory victimization that can be repaired and forgotten. Additionally, these groups provide an esteemed and powerful interaction partner—God or a healer—who the support-seeker can turn to in order to build a new sense of self-esteem and self-significance.

Britt and Heise (2000), examining the gay rights and black rights social movements, educed some social processes involved in metamorphosing a shameful identity into one that engenders pride. Historically, many gays and blacks accepted their stigmatization and withdrew from conventional society in shame. Social movement organizations turned the shame to fear through propaganda emphasizing the violence of oppressors, and then turned the fear to anger through further propaganda emphasizing the militancy of the social movement organizations. Finally, public demonstrations turned the activated and empowered selves into individuals who pridefully valued their identities.

THEORY GROWTH

Affect control theory's development illustrates several different strategies of theory growth. The strategies are listed at the end of the following résumé of the research program.[2]

Affect control theory focused initially on norms and roles, addressing the question of how individuals can acquire massive knowledge of their society during just a few years of socialization. The theoretical answer was that individuals learn the value, impact, and spontaneity (EPA) of entities, and this information generates complex social behavior as individuals construct events to maintain their sentiments. The viability of this theory was demonstrated first via computer simulations, and later by empirical studies.

An expansion of the theory quickly became obvious. The original quantitative model had individuals maintaining affective meanings by choosing an ideal behavior for a given actor and object. However, an alternative mathematical solution was to have individuals select an ideal actor for an observed action. Simulations confirmed the viability of this approach to reidentification, or labeling. The overall theory then was expanded by linking the two modes of meaning control in the context of meta-theoretical ideas from general systems theory: when behavioral control of meanings fails, individuals resort to higher order control through reidentification of interactants.

Linguistic case-grammar theory inspired the representation of events as actor-behavior-object combinations, and the linguistic theory suggested that representation of events could be improved by including social settings in the specifications of events. EPA data on settings were collected and the quantitative model was elaborated, whereupon simulations confirmed that controlling sentiments about settings modifies behavior predictions in sensible ways. Interestingly, implausible results from additional simulations indicated that settings probably do not get reidentified to fit actions that occur in them, which curtailed a conceivable expansion of the theory to explain how people reframe settings for different kinds of activity.

Linguistic theory also emphasizes the importance of state-of-being modifiers in representing actors and objects. Accordingly, EPA data on modifiers were collected and a quantitative model of modification was developed, whereupon simulations showed that behavior predictions responded sensibly to modifier specifications of individuals' personality traits, moods, or status characteristics.

Examining the quantitative model of modification suggested another expansion of the theory. Instead of forming an impression from an individual's identity and particular state of being, the individual's state of being might be inferred from the impression the individual has created and from knowledge of the individual's identity. Such an inference can be accomplished in two different ways mathematically, which led to affect control theory's models of attribution and emotion. Simulations and empirical tests demonstrated that these models function in sensible ways.

Affect control theory ordinarily is used to predict events from EPA ratings of identities and behaviors. However, some researchers interested in substantive problems instead pursued the implications of interpreting recorded events in terms of affect control. This was the approach taken in developing the ideas that international relations are grounded in the affective processes of political leaders, that support groups generally try to instill a particular sentiment structure in members' minds, and that social movement organizations involved in identity politics proceed through standard phases as they transmute shameful identities into identities engendering pride.

Affect control theory's ongoing cross-cultural elaborations begin empirically. First, a dictionary of EPA profiles is acquired to identify how a new culture's sentiments differ from the sentiments of previously studied cultures. Then, the quantitative model of impression formation is reestimated with data from indigenes in the new culture, in order to compare their thought processes with the thinking of indigenes in previously studied cultures. Third, the new materials are incorporated into the computer program, *Interact*, in order to support simulations of indigenous social interactions. The dictionaries, quantitative models of impression-formation, and simulations of social encounters enable rich interpretations of culturally specific processes and offer many explicit points of reference for comparative analyses.

This review of the affect control theory research program evidences the following strategies of theory growth.

1. Adopt ideas from other fields—like general systems theory or linguistics—in order to expand or integrate sociological formulations.
2. Reformulate a quantitative model mathematically, so as to solve additional sociological problems.
3. Interpret recorded events within the framework of an existing sociological theory in order to infer structures and processes that must exist in the domain of the events.
4. Measure a sociological theory's structural and processual parameters somewhere new in order to identify the theoretic model's permissible variations and the consequences of those variations.
5. Pursue, or discard, an idea depending on how hypotheses derived from the idea test out in computer simulations or in experiments. Computer simulations can be used this way when analysts (e.g., indigenes from the culture being studied) can assess the validity of simulation results.

Directions of future growth in affect control theory depend on interests of new researchers, which cannot be predicted. However, the five strategies above are such robust ways of gaining sociological knowledge that these strategies undoubtedly will be applied over and over as future sociologists augment affect control theory to address new issues.

CODA

Affect control theory expands Goffman's (1967:9) view that social interactants maintain an expressive order. "By entering a situation in which he is given a face to maintain, a person takes on the responsibility of standing guard over the flow of events as they pass before him. He must ensure that a particular expressive order is sustained—an order that regulates the flow of events, large or small, so that anything that appears to be expressed by them will be consistent with his face." Affect control theory broadens the notion of expressive order to relate to more than the face, or situational identity, of a focal person. In affect control theory, an individual behaves not just to maintain the meaning of self, but to maintain understandings generally—humans are meaning-maintainers.

Affect control theory helps us see how microsociological processes underpin other sociological phenomena, and how cultural diversity in sentiments and interpretive processes leads to different rationalities and emotional responses in different societies.

GLOSSARY OF TERMS USED IN AFFECT CONTROL THEORY (ACT)

activity A dimension of affect relating to arousal versus languor, initiative versus passivity, commotion versus quiescence.

affect Human processes that are mindful but not primarily cognitive and that have a somatic component but are not primarily behavioral. Examples are emotions, sentiments, impressions, motivations.

affective meaning Assessment of an object in terms of how good or bad the object is, how powerful or powerless, how active or inactive, along with the substantial social knowledge that can be generated from these judgments.

amalgamation Production of a new meaning by pairing a modifier with a noun, as in "rich professor" or "angry admiral."

attribution The process of accounting for an individual's involvements in events by means of a descriptive modifier. Personality traits, moods, status characteristics, or moral dispositions may be attributed.

behavior A process focused by an actor on an object, thereby creating an event and generating transient affective meanings, among other products.

cognitive constraints Categorizations and logical entailments of categories that underlie understanding of events. For example, a "son" is male, a "daughter" is female, and usage of either term presupposes a parent.

control In general systems theory, any process in which an agent acts in order to resist changes from the environment or to attain a particular goal state. In ACT, the focus is on control processes in which an individual resists changes in affective meanings or attempts to actualize affective meanings.

copular An assertion linking an entity to a state, either with a state-of-being verb like "seems" or by grammatical positioning, as in "happy camper."

culture Shared meanings regarding people, processes, and nonhuman objects. ACT focuses on the part of culture involving affective meanings regarding different kinds of people, interpersonal actions, and social settings.

deflection Deviation of an emergent affective meaning from a fundamental affective meaning. ACT proposes that individuals try to confirm fundamental affective meanings with emergent affective meanings, or, in other words, individuals seek experiences that minimize deflections.

denotative meaning The classification rules for applying a concept to some entity. These rules may include logical linkages that define relationships with other entities.

dictionary A database of words and their meanings. ACT dictionaries consist of words for identities, behaviors, modifiers, or settings. Each word is defined by average EPA profiles from males and females and by classification in social institutions (e.g., religion, academia).

distance The difference between two EPA profiles, measured quantitatively.

emergent meaning Synonymous with transient affective meaning in ACT.

emotion A transient affective state involving a particular physical countenance and a transient affective meaning for the self.

EPA dimensions *Evaluation,* measured on a scale from infinitely good to infinitely bad; *Potency,* measured on a scale from infinitely powerful to infinitely powerless; and *Activity,* measured on a scale from infinitely active to infinitely passive. These are the three universal aspects of affective meaning.

EPA profile A set of three numbers quantitatively defining an entity's affective meaning. The first number is an Evaluation measurement, the second is Potency, the third Activity.

Evaluation A dimension of affect indexing acceptance or rejection with regard to morality, beauty, usefulness, pleasure, and so on.

event The combination of an actor, a behavior, and an object of action within a setting. Events influence the affective meanings of their components, and according to ACT, individuals create events so as to produce transient affective meanings that will confirm fundamental affective meanings.

feeling Synonymous with transient affective meaning in ACT.

fundamental affective meaning The persistent, culturally grounded affective meaning of an entity that serves as a reference for individual experience.

identity A culturally defined category of person. An individual takes on an identity in each situation, actualizing the identity's fundamental affective meaning and thereby defining the individual's appropriate levels of status, power, and agency in the situation.

impression Synonymous with transient affective meaning in ACT.

impression formation The process by which an event combines affective meanings of actor, behavior, object, and setting, and forms new emergent meanings for each element. ACT uses empirically derived impression formation equations to predict the outcomes of this process.

inconsistency A case of colliding meanings. In ACT, inconsistencies arise when an event makes an entity seem both good and bad, or powerful and powerless, or active and inactive.

institution Associated social settings, identities, and behaviors. These associations set cognitive constraints in ACT analyses of social interaction.

Interact A computer program for analyzing sequences of social interaction, starting with interactants' definitions of the situation in verbal terms. The program incorporates dictionaries to represent cultures, impression-formation equations to describe emergence of new meanings, and mathematically derived equations to identify events that optimally confirm sentiments.

interactant A participant in a social interaction.

label An identity that accounts for an individual's involvement in an event. ACT specifies labels in terms of affective meaning, and this criterion has to be combined with cognitive constraints in order to get labels that are both affectively and logically appropriate.

likelihood A subjective assessment of frequency in the circumstances. High-deflection events that disconfirm sentiments seem unlikely, whereas low-deflection events seem likely unless they violate cognitive constraints.

logical meaning Knowledge of Y obtained from X with the premise that Ys invariably are Xs, or require an X. The supposition in ACT is that interpersonal behavior arises largely by maintaining both affective and logical meanings.

mood A nonpermanent fundamental affective meaning of the self obtained by amalgamating an emotion with one's situational identity.

optimal solution Completion of a partially specified event with the behavior or identity that will generate impressions of event elements as close as possible to the elements' fundamental affective meanings.

Potency A dimension of affect registering an entity's impact in terms of being big versus little, powerful versus powerless, consequential versus immaterial.

reidentification Changing an individual's fundamental affective meaning to better fit the individual's manner of participating in a situation. Reidentifications can be accomplished through labeling or attribution.

role A complex of behaviors expected of an individual with a particular identity in a particular institutional setting. ACT predicts role as the behaviors optimally maintaining the identity's fundamental affective meaning.

self-directed action A behavior focused on the self rather than on an external object.

sentiment Synonymous with fundamental affective meaning in ACT.

setting A culturally defined category of place or time in which certain kinds of interpersonal encounters occur. Events have to be constructed so as to confirm the fundamental affective meaning of the setting if the setting is salient in a situation.

simulations Analyses of social interaction obtained with *Interact.*

situation The web of meanings, especially about interactants' identities, that controls interactants' behaviors in a social encounter and that allows the interactants to understand what is going on. Defining the situation is a prerequisite for meaningful social interaction.

subculture Distinctive meanings maintained by a subgroup of a population for a realm of people, processes, and nonhuman objects that are of special significance within the subgroup. For example, drug users maintain a subculture in which drug users, drug experiences, and drug paraphernalia are more positively evaluated than in the general culture.

trait A culturally defined personality type that may be attributed to an individual and thereafter is available for adjusting the fundamental affective meaning of the individual in any situation.

transient affective meaning An entity's momentary affective meaning resulting from events. Transient affective meanings change to new transient affective meanings after the next event, as predicted by impression-formation equations.

NOTES

1. A glossary of terms used in affect control theory is provided in the appendix.
2. Retrospections with alternative emphases are available. MacKinnon and Heise (2000) focus on the buildup of intellectual resources in the research program; Heise (2000) emphasizes the contributions of mathematical analysis.

REFERENCES

Averett, C. P., and D. R. Heise. 1987. "Modified Social Identities: Amalgamations, Attributions, and Emotions." *Journal of Mathematical Sociology* 13:103–132.

Britt, Lory, and D. R. Heise. 1992. "Impressions of Self-Directed Action." *Social Psychology Quarterly* 55:335–350.

_____. 2000. "From Shame to Pride in Identity Politics." Pp. 252–268 in *Self, Identity, and Social Movements,* edited by Sheldon Stryker, Timothy J. Owens, and Robert W. White. Minneapolis: University of Minnesota Press.

Francis, Linda. 1997a. "Emotion, Coping, and Therapeutic Ideologies." *Social Perspectives on Emotion* 4:71–101.

_____. 1997b. "Ideology and Interpersonal Emotion Management: Redefining Identity in Two Support Groups." *Social Psychology Quarterly* 60:153–171.

Goffman, Erving. 1967. *Interaction Ritual: Essays on Face-to-Face Behavior.* Garden City, NY: Anchor Books.

Goodwin, Charles. 1994. "Professional Vision." *American Anthropologist* 96:606–633.

Heise, D. R. 1979. *Understanding Events: Affect and the Construction of Social Action.* New York: Cambridge University Press.

_____. 1985. "Affect Control Theory: Respecification, Estimation, and Tests of the Formal Model." *Journal of Mathematical Sociology* 11:191–222.

_____. 1987. "Affect Control Theory: Concepts and Model." *Journal of Mathematical Sociology* 13:1–33.

_____. 1989. "Effects of Emotion Displays on Social Identification." *Social Psychology Quarterly* 52:10–21.

_____. 1999. "Controlling Affective Experience Interpersonally." *Social Psychology Quarterly* 62:4–16.

_____. 2000. "Thinking Sociologically with Mathematics." *Sociological Theory* 18:498–504.

Heise, D. R., and Cassandra Calhan. 1995. "Emotion Norms in Interpersonal Events." *Social Psychology Quarterly* 58:223–240.

Heise, D. R., and Alex Durig. 1997. "A Frame for Organizational Actions and Macroactions." *Journal of Mathematical Sociology* 22:95–123.

Heise, D. R., and Neil MacKinnon. 1987. "Affective Bases of Likelihood Perception." *Journal of Mathematical Sociology* 13:133–151.

Heise, D. R., and Lisa Thomas. 1989. "Predicting Impressions Created by Combinations of Emotion and Social Identity." *Social Psychology Quarterly* 52:141–148.

Heise, D. R., and Brian Weir. 1999. "A Test of Symbolic Interactionist Predictions about Emotions in Imagined Situations." *Symbolic Interaction* 22:129–161.

Hochschild, Arlie Russell. 1983. *The Managed Heart: The Commercialization of Human Feeling.* Berkeley: University of California Press.

Kemper, T. D. 1978. *A Social Interactional Theory of Emotion.* New York: Wiley.

Lerner, Steven Jay. 1983. "Affective Dynamics of International Relations." Ph.D. Dissertation. University of North Carolina, Chapel Hill.

MacKinnon, Neil J. 1985/1988/1998. Final Reports to Social Sciences and Humanities Research Council of Canada on Projects 410-81-0089, 410-86-0794, and 410-94-0087. Guelph, Ont.: Department of Sociology and Anthropology, University of Guelph.

_____. 1994. *Symbolic Interactionism as Affect Control.* Albany: State University of New York Press.

MacKinnon, Neil J., and Jeffrey W. Bowlby. 2000. "The Affective Dynamics of Stereotyping and Intergroup Relations." *Advances in Group Processes* 17:37–76.

MacKinnon, Neil J., and D. R. Heise. 1993. "Affect Control Theory: Delineation and Development." In *Theoretical Research Programs: Studies in the Growth of Theory*, edited by Joseph Berger and Morris Zelditch Jr. Stanford, CA: Stanford University Press.

MacKinnon, Neil J., and Tom Langford. 1994. "The Meaning of Occupational Prestige Scores: A Social Psychological Analysis and Interpretation." *Sociological Quarterly* 35:215–245.

Osgood, Charles H., W. H. May, and M. S. Miron. 1975. *Cross-Cultural Universals of Affective Meaning.* Urbana: University of Illinois Press.

Robinson, Dawn T., and Lynn Smith-Lovin. 1992. "Selective Interaction as a Strategy for Identity Maintenance: An Affect Control Model." *Social Psychology Quarterly* 55:12–28.

Robinson, Dawn T., Lynn Smith-Lovin, and Olga Tsoudis. 1994. "Heinous Crime or Unfortunate Accident? The Effects of Remorse on Responses to Mock Criminal Confessions." *Social Forces* 73:175–190.

Romney, A. Kimball, Susan C. Weller, and William H. Batchelder. 1986. "Culture as Consensus: A Theory of Culture and Informant Accuracy." *American Anthropologist* 88:313–338.

Scher, Steven J., and D. R. Heise. 1993. "Affect and the Perception of Injustice." *Advances in Group Process* 10:223–252.

Schneider, Andreas. 2002. "Computer Simulation of Behavior Prescriptions in Multi-cultural Corporations." *Organization Studies* 23:105–131.

Schneider, Andreas, and D. R. Heise. 1995. "Simulating Symbolic Interaction." *Journal of Mathematical Sociology* 20:271–287.

Smith, Herman W. 1995. "Predicting Stress in American-Japanese Business Relations." *Journal of Asian Business* 12:79–89.

Smith, Herman W., Takanori Matsuno, and Shuuichirou Ike. 2000. "The Affective Basis of Attributional Processes among Japanese and Americans." *Social Psychology Quarterly* 64:180–194.

Smith, Herman W., Takanori Matsuno, and Michio Umino. 1994. "How Similar Are Impression-Formation Processes among Japanese and Americans?" *Social Psychology Quarterly* 57:124–139.

Smith-Lovin, Lynn. 1987. "Impressions from Events." *Journal of Mathematical Sociology* 13:35–70.

_____. 1990. "Emotion as the Confirmation and Disconfirmation of Identity: An Affect Control Model." Pp. 238–270 in *Research Agendas in the Sociology of Emotions*, edited by T. D. Kemper. Albany: State University of New York Press.

_____. 1991. "An Affect Control View of Cognition and Emotion." Pp. 143–169 in *The Self- Society Dynamic: Cognition, Emotion, and Action*, edited by Judith A. Howard and Peter L. Callero. New York: Cambridge University Press.

_____. 1994. "The Sociology of Affect and Emotion." Pp. 118–148 in *Sociological Perspectives on Social Psychology*, edited by K. Cook, G. Fine, and J. House. New York: Allyn and Bacon.

Smith-Lovin, Lynn, and William Douglass. 1992. "An Affect-control Analysis of Two Religious Groups." Pp. 217–247 in *Social Perspectives on Emotion*, Vol. 1, edited by V. Gecas and D. Franks. Greenwich, CT: JAI Press.

Smith-Lovin, Lynn, and D. R. Heise. 1982. "A Structural Equation Model of Impression Formation." Pp. 195–222 in *Multivariate Applications in the Social Sciences*, edited by N. Hirschberg and L. G. Humphreys. Hillsdale, NJ: Lawrence Erlbaum.

_____. 1988. *Analyzing Social Interaction: Advances in Affect Control Theory.* New York: Gordon and Breach. (Reprint of a special issue of the *Journal of Mathematical Sociology*, Vol. 13, 1987.)

Staske, Shirley A. 1996. "Talking Feelings: The Collaborative Construction of Emotion in Talk Between Close Relational Partners." *Symbolic Interaction* 19:111–135.

Thomas, Lisa, and D. R. Heise. 1995. "Mining Error Variance and Hitting Pay-dirt: Discovering Systematic Variation in Social Sentiments." *Sociological Quarterly* 36:425–439.

Thomassen, Lisa. 2002. "An Alcoholic Is Good and Sober: Sentiment Change in AA." *Deviant Behavior* 23:177–200.

Tsoudis, Olga, and Lynn Smith-Lovin. 1998. "How Bad Was It? The Effects of Victim and Perpetrator Emotion on Responses to Criminal Court Vignettes." *Social Forces* 77:695–722.

_____. 2001. "Criminal Identity: The Key to Situational Construals in Mock Criminal Court Cases." *Sociological Spectrum* 21:3–31.

Wiggins, Beverly, and D. Heise. 1987. "Expectations, Intentions, and Behavior: Some Tests of Affect Control Theory." *Journal of Mathematical Sociology* 13:153–169.

3

Expectation States Theory: An Evolving Research Program

David G. Wagner and Joseph Berger

Consider any of the following questions:

- How do actors develop a social structure in an unfamiliar, initially undefined situation?
- How and under what conditions do invidious status distinctions like race and gender come to affect behavior—and exactly what behaviors do they affect?
- What are the consequences of status inconsistency?
- How do actors evaluate the justice of their situations and with what consequences?
- In what ways do the evaluations of significant others affect one's self-conception?

All these issues have been the subject of sociological interest and investigation from the beginnings of the discipline. Simmel, Park, Mead, Cooley, Homans—these and many other sociologists have explored one or more of these questions. In more recent years *all* of them have been pursued extensively within a single program of investigation called *expectation states theory*.

Expectation states theory is a *theoretical research program*. A theoretical research program actually comprises a *set* of interrelated theories, along with basic and applied research testing and employing those theories. The basis for relationship among these theories is a *core set* of ideas implemented throughout the program. These ideas may then be developed in any of a variety of ways to provide explanations of social processes in new theoretical and empirical domains or to improve the accounts already developed in old ones. (For a more thorough account of the features and implications of theoretical research programs, see Wagner and Berger 1985; Berger and Zelditch 1997.)

The core of expectation states theory centers on the notion of an *expectation state*: What is it? How and under what conditions does it form? What behavioral consequences follow from its formation? An expectation is a social actor's stable anticipation of relative behavioral capacity among two or more actors. Thus, one actor *p* may see another actor *o* as less talented than herself. Or, *p* may believe actor *o* deserves a higher level of reward than does a third actor, *q*. Propositions in each of the basic theories in the program then explain either (1) how actors use information from the world around them (e.g., status, reward, or performance differences) to generate expectations; or (2) how these expectations affect actors' behavior toward one another (e.g., participation in or influence over task decisions).

A BRIEF HISTORY OF EXPECTATION STATES THEORY

These ideas were initially formulated in Berger's research in the 1950s (see especially Berger 1958). In this work Berger focused on informal problem-solving groups like those studied by Bales and his associates (see, e.g., Bales 1950, 1953; Bales et al. 1951; Bales and Slater 1955; Heinecke and Bales 1953). Bales had shown that actors in such groups who were initially similar in status (and strangers to one another) nevertheless rapidly developed inequalities in their interaction. They differed in the frequency of opportunities they had to contribute to solution of the group's problem, their actual level of participation in solving the problem, the evaluations group members made of their contributions, and influence over decisions made by the group regarding the problem. Moreover, these inequalities correlated quite highly with each other, forming a single hierarchy of power and prestige differences in the group. Once this hierarchy emerged, it was generally quite stable.

Berger argued that these phenomena reflect an underlying structure of expectations for performance of the task that emerges from the interaction of the group members. He argued that differences in the evaluations the actors make of specific task performances are sufficient (though not necessary) to generate such expectation states. In turn, these expectations determine the future course of interaction—in particular, the distribution of power- and prestige-related behaviors among the actors. Since these behaviors are all functions of the same underlying expectations, inequalities in their distribution should be highly correlated. Further, it was argued, power and prestige behaviors operate to maintain expectations. If power and prestige differences are functions of differences in expectations and they also maintain expectations, then these power and prestige differences should be stable absent change in the group's personnel or task conditions.

Branches of the Program

Over the next fifteen years, four different branches of the program developed from this initial set of ideas. Each branch focused on a different kind of substantive issue. The first branch was *power and prestige theory* (e.g., Berger 1958; Berger and Conner 1969). This branch retained the initial concern with the emergence and maintenance of power and prestige differences. Subsequent formulations in this branch (Berger and Connor 1974) were developed primarily to account in more detail and with greater complexity for the way in which the task interaction process itself generates expectation states. For example, how does the occurrence of differential participation rates in the group generate expectations that determine differences in the power and prestige order in the group?

The second—and certainly the most thoroughly developed—branch generated *status characteristics theory* (e.g., Berger, Cohen, and Zelditch 1966, 1972; Berger and Fisek 1974). Theories in this branch were developed to account for the processes by which (and the circumstances under which) external status information like gender and race would come to affect the distribution of power and prestige. The basic structure of these arguments has been to show when and how status information is likely to lead to the formation of expectation states. A version of Berger's original ideas could then be used to show how expectations (generated now by a different *status-organizing* process) would affect power and prestige. Foremost to emerge in this branch was the question of *status* inconsistency: what are the implications of multiple status differences with inconsistent implications for behavioral capacities? Will expectations form at all? If they do, what status information will be included in them?

A third branch of the program concerned the *status value theory of distributive justice* (e.g., Berger et al. 1968, 1972). Here the focus was on how actors use referential comparisons to develop expectations for reward allocation and, in turn, how these expectations are used in evaluating the justice and injustice of various reward situations. In these theories the kind of expectation formed would be different—concerned with reward allocation rather than with task performance. However, the basic structure of the argument remained the same. Under specific conditions and in specific ways, referential comparisons would generate expectations for reward, which would in turn dictate behavior (e.g., dissatisfaction with and rebellion against a collectively unjust under-reward). In this branch much of the original focus was on demonstrating differences in the predictions (and in the predictive ability) of status value theory over a competing account based on exchange principles called *equity theory* (Homans 1961, 1974; Adams 1965). How, in particular, does one distinguish over-reward from under-reward, self injustice from other injustice, and individual injustice from collective injustice?

Finally, *source theory* (e.g., Webster 1969; Webster and Sobieszek 1974) was concerned with how and when significant others come to have an effect on expectations. In this theory significant others, *sources*, were individuals with the right to evaluate actors, for example, teachers, whose evaluations affected actors' expectations. Work in this branch of the program also focused on an issue similar to the status inconsistency issue in status characteristics theory. Specifically, how do inconsistent evaluations by significant others affect expectations? Does it make a difference if the significant others have different status positions?

Patterns of Growth

Over the next fifteen years the program grew considerably. At least three different patterns of growth emerged. In some cases already-established theories were *elaborated.* Later formulations considered the same basic substantive questions as in earlier theory, but expanded its scope of application, or its deductive capacities, or increased its corroborated empirical consequences. In other cases new theories *proliferated* to deal with previously unexplored explanatory domains. These theories still made use of the core ideas but adapted or modified them to deal with issues unique to the new domain. This was done by introducing new concepts and assumptions auxiliary to the core set. In still other cases theories were developed that *integrated* previously disparate concerns from theories in different branches in the program. Sometimes, two or more of these growth patterns appeared in the same branch of the program. (See Wagner and Berger 1993 for a more comprehensive description of these developments.)

Over the last ten years work in the expectation states program has continued to increase. Elaborations, proliferations, and integrations continue to appear, and even at an accelerating pace. Table 3.1 provides a current summary of some of the major theories of the program and the primary issue with which each is concerned.

Table 3.1. Expectation States Theory

Theory	*Phenomenon of Concern*
Power and Prestige	The emergence and maintenance of differentiated power and prestige orders in groups not initially differentiated in status.
Status Characteristics and Expectation States	The formation of expectation states based on socially established status characteristics and the maintenance of power and prestige orders in status differentiated groups.
Distributive Justice	The creation of normative reward expectations and the meanings of different types of social justice and injustice that arise from the relation of these expectations to the actual allocation of rewards.
Sources of Evaluation	The formation of expectations and its effects on behavior based on the evaluations of actors who possess legitimated rights to evaluate others.
Reward Expectations	The interrelations of status, task, and reward expectations and the inequalities created by these interrelations. Partially integrates research from distributive justice and status characteristics branches.
Evolution of Status Expectations	The evolution of actors' status expectations as they move through different task situations with different others. Generalizes the status characteristics theory.

Status Cues	The processes and conditions under which verbal and nonverbal cues are used in attributions of performance capacities and status categories, and how they depend on actors' established status positions.
Legitimation	The process and conditions under which power and prestige orders are legitimated or delegitimated. Based on research from reward expectations and status characteristics branches.
Multiple Standards	The processes and conditions under which multiple standards are used to maintain prevailing status distinctions.
Behavior-Status	Theories and models integrating research from the power and prestige and the status characteristics branches.
Evaluations-Expectations	Integrates research from status characteristics and source theory branches.
Sentiments and Status	The interrelation of affect and sentiment processes with status and expectation state processes.
Status Construction	The processes and conditions under which institutionalized status characteristics are socially constructed and diffused through society.

A few other features of this history should be noted. First, techniques for experimentally manipulating expectations were developed very early in the program. This was very important in making it possible to separate the different processes by which expectations are formed from the processes governing the behavioral consequences of expectations.

Second, partly as a consequence of the development of these experimental techniques, a standardized experimental situation for testing expectation states ideas gradually emerged (see Berger et al. 1977: chapter 5; Cook, Cronkite, and Wagner 1974; Wagner and Harris 1995). The standardized nature of the research setting made it possible to compare results across empirical studies to a much greater degree than is commonly the case in sociology and experimental research generally. The cumulative effect of comparable research findings has been particularly important in the growth of the program.

Third, programs of applied and intervention research have been directly associated with several branches of the program (see especially Cohen 1993; Entwisle and Webster 1974; Lovaglia et al. 1998; Jackson, Hunter, and Hodge 1995; Wagner and Berger 1998).[1] This work has provided an important arena for the practical application of many of the theoretical developments within the program. It has also generated problems ideas that have been developed in subsequent theoretical formulations. (See also Webster and Whitmeyer 2001.)

Finally, as we develop, test, and apply various ideas in the program, a metatheoretical strategy for theoretical and empirical work *in status organizing processes* has gradually emerged. This metatheoretical frame of reference helps us to identify important areas for investigation and important issues to be resolved. It enables us to select the appropriate conceptual and empirical tools for constructing and testing new theories that address these areas and these issues. (These elements of the program are discussed most thoroughly in Berger, Wagner, and Zelditch 1992.)

THE DEVELOPMENT OF STATUS CHARACTERISTICS THEORY

By far the greatest amount of progress in the expectation states program has occurred in the status characteristics branch. Several theoretical formulations have been developed. Empirical evidence supporting these formulations has been extensive. And a profusion of application and intervention research has both guided and supported these formulations.

Background in Power and Prestige Theory

Status characteristics theory emerged from earlier work in the power and prestige branch of the program. The Bales research (and power and prestige theory) concerned situations in which actors were similar with respect to status distinctions like gender, race, or education. Status characteristics theory deals with situations in which actors are *not* similar with respect to such status distinctions.

In the absence of status differences, power and prestige theory argues, actors draw upon their experiences in the interaction situation itself to determine how they should behave toward each other. Berger's original formulation thus considered how consistent differences in the evaluations of task performance would lead to the emergence of expectation states, which would then guide all the power and prestige behaviors that in turn reinforced these expectations. A later power and prestige formulation (Berger and Conner 1974) then demonstrated how consistent differences in *any* of the power and prestige behaviors—such as participation rates—would lead to an underlying structure of expectations, the distribution of power and prestige behavior among the actors, and the reinforcing effect on the established structure of expectations. The hierarchy would be stable, regardless of which behavioral difference initially generated it.

In addition, specific models of the process by which expectations emerge from evaluations of specific performances have been constructed. These mathematical models (see Berger and Snell 1961; Conner 1965; Berger, Conner, and McKeown 1969; Fararo 1973) sought to detail the process by which differential evaluations of performances lead to differentiated expectation states. Once these expectations are formed they determine subsequent behavior consistent with the expectations. Thus, unless other structural factors intervene (e.g., new members or new information is introduced or the task focus changes), these differentiated expectations remain stable for the course of the interaction.

These models provide a rigorous representation of the core idea that observable power and prestige behaviors are determined by an underlying structure and that inferences about the unobservable states in the structure are made on the basis of behaviors that lead to their formation and that also are determined by them.

In a series of related studies, Foschi (1970, 1971, 1972; Foschi and Foschi 1976, 1979) considers how objective evaluations from external sources may help to generate and to overcome established expectation states. Using Bayesian models, she shows that the relative frequency of different evaluations of specific performances (i.e., unit evaluations) determines the structure of expectations established. Consequently, the establishment of expectations depends on achieving a threshold value of consistent evaluations. Moreover, changing those expectations depends on the number and extremity of evaluations that contradict the established expectations.

Research on Particular Status Characteristics

Aside from research on the power and prestige theory, status characteristics theory has also drawn heavily on prior research on the effects of particular status differences on task behavior. Basically, this research shows that external status distinctions *also* generate stable differences in power and prestige behavior, whether or not the status distinction is relevant to the group's task. For example, Torrance's (1954) study of Air Force bomber crews showed that the crew member's rank determined his level of influence on a variety of group tasks, even when rank had nothing to do with the task the crew was performing. Perhaps equally important, these results do not seem to depend on which concrete status distinctions are present. Strodtbeck, James, and Hawkins (1958), for example, showed that both gender and occupation determined selection of a foreman and rates of participation and influence. Investigations involving other status distinctions showed similar results. (See Caudill 1958; Croog 1956; Hurwitz, Zander, and Hymovitch 1960; Mishler and Troop 1956; Strodtbeck and Mann 1956; Torrance 1954; Zander and Cohen 1955; Ziller and Exline 1958. For a summary and analysis of some of this research see Cohen, Berger, and Zelditch 1972.)

In summary, this research showed that external status distinctions determined the distribution of power and prestige in task groups whether or not these distinctions were explicitly related to the task. Further, this generalization held for a wide range of different status distinctions. The initial theoretical task was to construct an abstract and general formulation that, among other things, could account for this generalization.

Initial Formulation

The first version of status characteristics theory laid the conceptual and propositional groundwork. Key to this formulation (in Berger, Cohen, and Zelditch 1966, 1972) was the conceptualization of the notion of a *diffuse status characteristic.* A diffuse status characteristic is an invidious distinction an actor draws between two or more states of a social characteristic in such a way that the states are differentially evaluated in terms of social worth and in terms of general and specific expectations associated with each state. Thus, if actor *p* believes that "male" is a better or a more highly valued state than "female," and that males are both generally more capable than females and specifically more capable at identifiable tasks, then gender is a diffuse status characteristic for *p*. These status beliefs, of course, need not be objectively accurate. In the first instance, they are social constructions that have been built up over time and have become part of the actor's basic cultural beliefs. As such, they appear to the actor to be widely shared, relatively stable representations of reality: "this is the way men and women are."

Let us suppose a male *p* does hold such a belief system with respect to gender and is working on a task with another actor who is a female. The theory argues that this is sufficient for *p* to activate his/her status evaluations and beliefs about general and specific task abilities. This *activation* (or salience) principle applies to any status characteristic that differentiates the actors or that is believed to be relevant to the task. Thus, gender would be activated or made salient in any mixed-sex task group; it would also be activated even in single-sex groups if the characteristic is culturally associated with the group's task (e.g., the task is gender-typed).

Further, the theory argues, once these status beliefs are activated, *p* will act as if they are relevant to task performance unless *p* has some reason for challenging their relevance. The burden of proof is on demonstrating that the characteristic *is not* relevant to performance rather than on demonstrating that it is relevant. Given this *burden of proof* principle, salient diffuse status characteristics become task relevant, and activated status distinctions and status advantages are generalized to new tasks and to new situations as a part of normal interaction. Thus, when gender is salient, it will be treated as relevant even in situations where there are no gender-based beliefs specific to the task at hand, provided it is not defined as irrelevant or dissociated from that task.

Given task relevance, *p* will *assign expectations* for task performance to self and other that are consistent with *p*'s status beliefs. The actor with a status advantage is expected to perform more capably at the task than the actor with a status disadvantage. If *p* has adopted the culturally dominant beliefs about gender, then *p* will assume that male actors in the situation will be more capable at the task than female actors.

As in power and prestige theory, once expectations are assigned to actors, these expectations determine their behavior toward each other. The *basic expectation assumption* states simply that the distribution of each of the observed power and prestige behaviors is a direct function of the difference in expectations. An actor whose expectations are relatively high in comparison to a second actor will initiate more interaction and exercise more influence, for example, than will the actor whose expectations are low relative to the first actor. This relationship between differences in expectations and power and prestige behaviors holds no matter what the process is by which task expectations are generated (e.g., by differences in status characteristics or performance evaluations or participation rates).

It is important to emphasize that this theory, like its elaborations and other theories in this program, is an abstract and general formulation. As such, it is not a theory about gender relations or racial distinctions or ethnic differences, although under appropriate conditions it is potentially applicable to *all* these social distinctions and many more. If for a population at a given time, gender is a diffuse status characteristic (i.e., its different states are associated with differences in general and specific expectations and differences in status evaluations), then the status characteristics theory is applicable to gender and can be used to describe status organizing behavior in a task situation involving gender. If gender is not a diffuse status characteristic, the theory is not applicable to it. And the same is true for other concrete social distinctions such as age, educational or occupational positions, and physical attractiveness. Thus, whether any particular social distinction is a diffuse status characteristic is a factual matter, not a theoretical issue.

Tests of the initial formulation were conducted by Berger, Cohen, and Zelditch (1972) and Moore (1968), using Air Force rank and educational attainment respectively as the diffuse status differences. The first study showed that the power and prestige ordering emerges consistent with the status distinction regardless of the amount of information the actor has about the situation provided that the information itself is consistent. *Minimally structured* situations (in which actors are aware only that the status characteristic discriminates between them) create consistent behavioral differences, as do *maximally structured* situations (in which actors are seen to possess task-relevant performance capacities that are aligned with their status difference). Moore, then, showed that status distinctions affect task behavior regardless of whether the salient status is initially defined as relevant to the task or not, thus providing support for the burden of proof principle.

Other studies refined and extended the initial formulation. The results from Berger, Fisek, and Freese (1976) suggest that information from *specific status characteristics* (i.e., those involving only the ability to perform specific, defined tasks—say mathematical ability or artistic ability) is used in establishing task expectations given that they are directly or indirectly related to the task. And the results from a study by Freese (1970) suggested that task expectations could be formed on the basis of two specific characteristics not initially related to the task provided that they had consistent performance implications.

The Revised Formulation

A revised formulation of status characteristics theory was presented by Berger and Fisek in 1974. This expanded the scope of the original status characteristics theory. A significant constraint on the applicability of the original theory was its restriction to situations involving only a single diffuse status characteristic. This restriction in scope was strategic; it enabled us to understand how a single diffuse status difference might operate to generate expectations before moving on to consider more complex multicharacteristic situations. In addition, the revised theory was expanded to incorporate the status-organizing effects of specific status characteristics.

The operation of multiple status characteristics was a primary concern of this formulation: How would actors deal with the salience of more than one status distinction, especially if the implications of some were inconsistent with the implications of others (say when a white but poorly educated male interacts with a black but highly educated female)? Many sociologists at the time assumed that actors would find status inconsistency inherently stressful and that therefore they would try to *eliminate or ignore* at least some of the status information to make the situation more consistent (or balanced). The most common form of the elimination (or balancing) argument was based on a *maximization* principle, according to which actors would retain status definitions that reflected positively on them and would eliminate information that reflected negatively (see, e.g., Lenski 1966).

However, based on experiments already performed in the program (see Berger and Fisek 1970; Berger, Fisek, and Crosbie 1970), the revised theory argues that actors *combine* the information from all salient status characteristics in forming expectation states, even in inconsistent situations. More specifically, the theory assumes each salient status characteristic in the situation comes to be related to the group's task through a *path of task relevance.* Each path defines an expectancy for task performance based on the status characteristic the actor possesses, and such paths also represent the task significance of that characteristic. Paths with positive task significance (i.e., ones that imply successful task performance) are combined with those with negative task significance (i.e., ones that imply poor task performance) in the formation of *aggregated expectation states.* An actor's *expectation advantage* (or disadvantage) relative to another actor then is equal to the difference between the aggregated expectations for self and the aggregated expectations for the other. Finally, according to an updated version of the basic expectation assumption, the distribution of power and prestige in the group is a direct probabilistic function of expectation advantage. The larger the expectation advantage, the greater the differentiation in power and prestige behaviors. Thus, for example, the difference in task influence between a white male and a black female working together should be greater than the difference between a white male and female (or a black female and a white female), assuming that they accept the dominant cultural definitions of race and gender. Different status situations generate different levels of task inequality.

Subsequent research has borne out many of these arguments. Kervin (1972) showed that the number, length, and consistency of paths of task relevance all directly affect the degree of differentiation in power and prestige. Wagner and Berger (1974, 1982) determined that paths of relevance worked similarly whether they linked consistent or inconsistent status elements. Webster and Berger (1975) found that *equating characteristics* (i.e., statuses that do not differentiate actors and are not defined as task relevant) appear to have no effects on the situation. Status theories make *no* predictions on status effects for situations involving equating characteristics. (For a recent discussion of the issue of equating characteristics, see Walker and Simpson 2000.)

Several studies tested direct implications of the combining argument. Zelditch, Lauderdale, and Stublarec (1980) established that actors combined status elements even in situations where eliminating seemed most likely (when one of the characteristics was the ability instrumental to success or failure at the task). The results of a study by Parcel and Cook (1977) that involved specific status characteristics not initially related to the task also suggests that actors combine information from these characteristics in determining status behavior. On the other hand, Freese and Cohen (1973) found evidence for elimination when two specific statuses are inconsistent with a single diffuse status. However, a partial replication by Webster and Driskell (1979) challenged this result, their results suggesting that combining occurs in this situation. (For a detailed review and analysis of a body of research that deals with the issue of elimination versus combining, see Balkwell 1991a.)

The Graph Theoretical Formulation

The next version of the theory—the graph formulation—was published in Berger et al. 1977. It involved far more extensive changes in the theory. This version expanded consideration to deal with any number of actors in the situation, any two of which would be involved in the interaction at one time. Different kinds of actors were identified. *Interactants* are those who are working directly with others to resolve a task problem. Thus, male and female attorneys working together on a legal brief would both be interactants. *Referent actors* are those to whom interactants relate themselves. Information about referent actors can affect the expectations that interactants form. If the female attorney in the previous example compared herself with a highly competent female law partner in the firm, such information could elevate her expectations on the immediate task. This formulation also allowed for sequences of interaction that involved changes: new actors could enter the situation, interactants could leave (possibly becoming referents), and referents could become interactants. The theory enables us to describe how such *sequencing* changes modify the expectations of interactants in the situation.

The graph formulation further develops the idea of a path of task relevance. Paths are connections between status characteristics possessed by actors and the outcome states of the group's tasks (i.e., "success" or "failure"). They may be based on information already existing in the situation, such as cultural beliefs that assert that males (or females) are particularly qualified on a given type of task. Or they may be induced in the situation on the basis of the burden of proof process that establishes the task relevance of status characteristics possessed by actors.

Paths of different length have different levels of strength in determining expectations. The longer the path connecting an actor to a task outcome, the weaker the contribution of that path to the actor's expectations. An inverse mathematical function is developed to derive values that define the *degree of task relevance* for paths of different length. They represent the strength of the actor's expectancy that a certain outcome will be attained ("success" or "failure") given the status information incorporated in a particular path.

The theory assumes that actors combine all status information made task relevant through these paths in forming expectations. Although the combining process probably occurs outside the actor's general awareness, we have been able to formulate a specific model to describe this process, based on a *principle of organized subsets.* This principle argues that actors process paths leading to successful task outcomes (positive information) and those leading to unsuccessful outcomes (negative information) in separate subsets. Within each subset status information is combined to determine, respectively, a value of positive expectations and a value of negative expectations. In this combining process an *attenuation* principle operates: that is, the more status information within a particular subset, the weaker the impact of each additional piece of like-signed status information on the aggregation of expectations. The actor's aggregated expectations are given by summing the positive and negative expectation values. An actor's *expectation advantage* relative to a second actor is equal to the aggregated expectations for self less that formed for the other. Finally, an actor's power and prestige position relative to an other is a direct continuous function of the actor's expectation advantage (or disadvantage) relative to that other.

A specific function for translating expectation advantage into specific task behaviors (specifically measures of influence) was developed in the graph formulation. In the first instance this function is applicable to the standardized experimental situation for which it was devised. Later work by Fisek, Berger, and Norman (1991) generated a second translation function that permitted behavioral predictions in groups of different sizes involved in open interaction. And Balkwell (1991b) has proposed a more general and powerful translation function that can be applied to groups of different sizes and in different types of experimental settings.

The graph formulation has proven to be much more than a simple elaboration of the earlier theories. Much work (though not all) in the program since 1977 has drawn extensively on the ideas presented in the 1977 theory, including work in branches *outside* status characteristics theory.

Why has this formulation had such an important impact on the program? The answer, we believe, lies primarily in the graph formalization that this theory incorporates. Actors, status elements, and task outcomes become points in the graph. Relations among these entities become signed lines linking points on the graph. The status structure of the situation can therefore be represented as a series of paths in the signed graph linking actors directly or indirectly with task outcomes.

The formalization has made for an analytically more powerful theory. Concepts such as the number, length, strength, and task significance of paths of task expectancy are formally developed. The principles of organized subset combining and the translation of expectations into behavior are rigorously formulated. The result is a formalized theory with far greater inferential capabilities than previous status theories. First, it allows us to formally represent an extremely wide range of status situations that actors may encounter. Second, given estimations of the appropriate parameters in the theory, we can derive specific predictions for the behavior of actors in these status situations. Third, because all of these status situations are represented using the same formal concepts and principles, we can derive general predictions in behavior across very broad classes of status situations. Humphreys and Berger (1981), for example, in a set of general theorems, show how the degree of task relevance of status differences, the degree of status consistency, and the number of status characteristics actors possess are related to the differentiation in power and prestige orders. They also show that quite different types of status structures may nevertheless be behaviorally equivalent (i.e., they can generate the same power and prestige differences). These results are all derived from the same fundamental principles of the graph theory of status organization.

There exist empirical tests of the graph theory. Originally, the theory was evaluated with respect to data from twelve studies, all of which were completed prior to its development. This, therefore, is better understood as an assessment of the consistency of the theory with its base rather than as an independent test of its predictions. Nevertheless, using parameter estimates from a small number of these studies, Berger et al. (1977) found that the fit of the theory to the data was good. Fox and Moore (1979), reanalyzing the same data plus additional data and using regression analysis, found an even better fit than originally reported by Berger and his colleagues.

Wagner, Ford, and Ford (1986) provided an important early test of the attenuation principle. Their study showed that information about task performance capabilities that confirms existing gender-based status distinctions (i.e., is *consistent* with prior status information) has a small but statistically significant impact on actors' task performance; a male actor's influence is increased somewhat, while a female actor's influence is decreased somewhat. In contrast, information about capabilities that disconfirms existing status distinctions (i.e., is *inconsistent* with prior status information) has a much larger (and obviously statistically significant) effect on behavior; a male actor's influence is decreased dramatically, while a female actor's influence is increased dramatically. The effect is so dramatic in the Wagner, Ford, and Ford study that the power and prestige order is *inverted*; when status expectations are disconfirmed as in this study, females are more influential than males. For further research that demonstrates the operation of status attenuation effects, see Rashotte and Smith-Lovin (1997).

Norman, Smith, and Berger (1988) and Berger et al. (1992), in a direct experimental test of different status organizing principles, pitted that of organized subsets against the elimination argument described above and a status cancellation argument where actors are seen to "cancel" opposite signed items of status information in forming expectations. The results were consistent with the principle of organized subsets and inconsistent with the alternative principles. These results also provide empirical support for the existence of status *positivity* (and *negativity*) *effects*—that is, the accentuated impact on expectations of minority positive (or negative) status information against a background of predominantly oppositely signed status information. These status effects are derivable from the principle of organized subsets.

Many additional studies that are relevant to the graph formulation have been conducted. Fisek, Norman, and Nelson-Kilger (1992) analyze the results of twelve of these studies, in addition to reviewing the evidence from the original twelve studies. Their analysis suggested a good fit between the experimental data and theoretical predictions.

RELATED DEVELOPMENTS

The graph formalization of status characteristics theory has provided the foundation for further development across a wide variety of additional social processes. Extensive work has been done in all of the areas listed in table 3.1. We will review the work in four of those areas here and then identify a number of others.

Reward Expectations

Reward expectations theory (see Berger et al. 1985) combines ideas from status characteristics theory and the status value theory of distributive justice. This theory deals with the formation of reward expectations in status situations in which differential rewards are to be allocated. Central to this formulation is the idea of a *referential structure*—basically a set of commonly held cultural beliefs describing how the states of a valued characteristic are typically associated with differences in reward levels. Three different types of referential structure are distinguished, depending on the kind of characteristic that is associated with rewards. *Categorical* structures relate diffuse characteristics with rewards; they invoke criteria of "who you are" in determining rewards. *Ability* structures connect specific task abilities with rewards; they invoke criteria of "what you can do" in determining rewards. *Outcome* structures associate task outcomes or achievements with rewards; they invoke criteria of "what you have done" in determining rewards. Status situations differ in the pattern of referential structures that govern the allocation of rewards. There are situations where only performance capacities matter, situations where capacities, achievements, and status categories matter, and situations where only status categories matter in the allocation of rewards—for example, in a seniority system.

Aside from introducing concepts and assumptions unique to this formulation—the notion of different types of referential structures and assumptions on the activation of these structures—the theory uses concepts and principles in the graph version of the status theory. The concept of path of relevance and degree of relevance are applied to reward expectations as well as task expectations. In addition, the assumption about processing multiple items of status information (the principle of organized subsets) is generalized to apply to the formation of reward expectations as well as task expectations in the same status situation.

The theory then enables us to derive general theorems that describe:

1. How activated reward standards (referential structures) are *combined* in the formation of aggregated reward expectations.
2. How an increase in the number or relevance of status characteristics possessed by actors in the group *increases* the inequality in reward expectations.
3. How an increase in the inconsistency of status characteristics possessed by actors in the group *reduces* the inequality in reward expectations.
4. How task and reward expectations are *interrelated*: changes in task expectations (by adding or eliminating status distinctions) produce changes in reward expectations, and changes in reward expectations (by adding or deleting referential structures) produce changes in task expectations.
5. How rewards *directly affect* performance expectations: the allocation of rewards generates performance expectations that determine task behaviors.

Research exists that is relevant to some of the major arguments in the reward expectations theory. Webster and Smith (1978) demonstrate the importance of referential structures in creating reward expectations. Studies by Jasso and Rossi (1977) and Alves and Rossi (1978) identify multiple referential structures in American society and demonstrate that the effects of these structures are combined in generating reward expectations. Parcel and Cook (1977) provide evidence on the interrelations between task and reward expectations. Studies by Lerner (1965), Cook (1970, 1975), Harrod (1980), Bierhoff, Buck, and Klein (1986), and Stewart and Moore (1992) all present evidence on how the allocation of rewards generates performance expectations. In addition, Ridgeway (1997) reports the results of an experiment in which she successfully uses this rewards-performance expectation relation to create differences in group identification in high- and low-rewarded status groups. Finally, pursuing a different line of research, Wagner (1995, 2000) reports the results of studies that suggest that male and female allocation preferences for rewards are the outcome of the *same* status-based processes, a result based on the reward expectation theory.

The Evolution of Status Expectations

The graph version of status characteristics theory is formulated only to deal with single-task situations in which most status and performance information is available at the beginning of the interaction. However, individuals often interact with the same or different others across a *sequence of tasks* where new status, performance, and evaluational information is acquired at different stages. To address this issue, Berger, Fisek, and Norman (1989) generalized the original graph theory by introducing auxiliary concepts and assumptions—such as the "relevance of tasks" assumption. This argues that on the completion of a task in a sequence of tasks, the outcome states of successive tasks come to be connected to each other in a consistent manner. This occurs unless the tasks are culturally dissociated or inversely related to each other. Using auxiliary concepts and assumptions in conjunction with the core concepts of the graph formulation, we are able to derive theoretical consequences that describe:

1. How expectations that emerge in one task situation affect those of a subsequent task situation (e.g., how expectations developed for a particular other on one task transfer to a second other on a new task).
2. How new information external to the group affects the evolution of expectations and behaviors across tasks (e.g., how evaluations by external authorities of achievements on past tasks affect the degree of status differentiation that emerges on current tasks).
3. How and under what conditions status interventions (such as efforts to reduce status inequalities) transfer across tasks (e.g., how status interventions can have a diminished yet lasting effect when interaction is closed to additional information from outside the group).

Some research exists that is relevant to this formulation. A study by Lockheed and Hall (1976) supports the theory's predictions regarding the transfer of expectations across tasks. Results of experiments by Pugh and Wahrman (1983) show that actors do transfer expectations to others with similar status characteristics (e.g., from one male to a second male) within a task, and those by Markovsky, Smith, and Berger (1984) show that this transfer of expectations to similar others can also occur when actors move from one task to a second. In addition, Prescott's (1986) results suggest that this transfer of expectations to new actors and to new tasks can occur even when the new actor introduces a new status characteristic into the situation. Further, in research concerned with a different consequence of this theory, an experiment by Nelson-Kilger (1992) indicates that changes in actors' behavior across successive task situations are related to the degree that the status structures of these situations are consistent or inconsistent with each other. While the results of existing research are promising, clearly more is needed in this area. In particular, we are in need of research that will allow us to assess the long-term and stable-state predictions of this theory.

Status Cues

In many task situations verbal and nonverbal social cues (e.g., patterns of speech, posture, direct references to background or experience, styles of dress) help actors form expectations. Berger et al. (1986) extended status characteristics theory to consider the role such cues play in generating status expectations.

The extension identifies several different kinds of status cues. *Indicative* cues (e.g., "I'm a doctor") directly lay claim to the actor's status state while expressive cues (e.g., a woman's style of dress) provide information from which status states can be inferred. *Task* cues (e.g., fluency of speech, looking while speaking rates) provide information about the actor's capacities on the immediate task, while *categorical* cues (e.g., vocabulary, language syntax) provide information about states of status characteristics that actors possess. The distinction between task and categorical cues crosscuts the distinction between indicative and expressive cues.

Berger et al. argue that, if no prior status differences exist in the group, then differences in task cues will be used to form expectations for self and other and that these performance expectations in turn will determine the distribution of power and prestige in the group. If, instead, status differences based on status characteristics exist from the outset of the group, then status characteristic difference will produce corresponding differences in expectations that in turn generate corresponding differences in the rates of task cue behaviors.

These arguments are developed to provide a status expectation account for two empirically documented relations that are known to exist between status differences and task cues: In homogeneous situations, differences in levels of task cues are correlated with differences in power and prestige behaviors and task evaluations; and in heterogeneous situations, differences in levels of task cues coincide with the status differentiation in the situation. (See Berger et al. 1986 for a review of relevant research.)

Berger and colleagues derive further arguments from this formulation that provide the bases of independent tests of their theory:

1. If, at the outset of the interaction, the differentiation in task cues is inconsistent with the differentiation in categorical cues (e.g., an apparently low-category individual displaying high task cues), then information from both types of cues will be combined in the formation of expectations. Further, since task cues provide immediate information about task capabilities, while categorical cues provide information about status characteristics that *become* relevant to the task, the strength of relevance of task cues is greater than that of categorical cues. Consequently, the effect of task cues will be greater than that of categorical cues when they are inconsistent (the combining argument).
2. If the status expectation arguments in this extension are correct, task cue levels should be strictly dependent upon expectation advantage. That is, different levels of expectation advantage should lead to different levels of task cues; an increase (or decrease) in expectation advantage should lead to an increase (or decrease) in task cue differentiation (the strict dependence argument).

There now exists research that is relevant to this extension. With respect to the combining argument, the current picture is a mixed one. In studies by Mohr (1986) and Sev'er (1989), both task and categorical cues affect, respectively, subjects' evaluations and influence behaviors. In the latter study, task cues show the principal effect and the pattern of responses by subjects is as predicted by the combining argument. In a study by Rainwater (1987), the results on the combining argument were not statistically significant; however, the direction of subject's responses is as expected. Further, Foddy and Riches (2000) in their study find that only task cues have the predicted effect on influence behaviors, although there is clear evidence for the effects of categorical cues on subjects' evaluations. Finally, in an experiment by Tuzlak and Moore (1984), both categorical and task cues are shown to affect influence behaviors in the early phases of their study, with task cues having substantially less effect in later phases. (See also Tuzlak 1988 on this study. For a further analysis of studies on status cues, see Fisek, Berger, and Norman 2002.)

Clearly, further research is needed in this area. However, one of the problems confronting such research is knowing how to "equate" contrasting cues of different types. This requires knowing the intensity levels and/or frequency rates at which tasks cues are maximally effective in creating task expectations, and categorical cues are maximally effective in the identification of status categories. Such knowledge is essential to further research on the combining argument.

A study by Dovidio et al. (1988) that investigates task cues such as looking while speaking, looking while listening, and gesturing provides evidence on the strict dependence argument. They examine behavior on gender-neutral, masculine, and feminine tasks. According to status theory, the male has an expectation advantage in the gender-neutral task; this advantage is increased on the masculine task and is decreased (it actually becomes a disadvantage) on the feminine task. Dovidio et al. find that when the task is gender-neutral, males look while speaking more frequently than females. When the task is masculine, the differences in looking while speaking between males and females is increased. However, when the task is identified as feminine, the usual ordering of these behaviors is reversed. Females look while speaking more frequently than males. The same pattern is true for the other task cue behaviors. (See also Balkwell and Berger 1996.) These results provide direct support for the strict dependence argument.

The status cues extension in part responds to arguments from dominance theories (see Mazur 1985; Lee and Ofshe 1981). Generally, these theories argue that dominance behaviors are the primary means by which status differences are established in groups. Expectation state researchers argue that is necessary to distinguish high and low task cue behaviors and dominating and propitiating behaviors. The former represent claims about competency at the task; the latter represent attempts to exercise control over others in the group. These behaviors are often confounded in the literature (especially in dominance theories). Task cue behaviors are effective to the extent that they have an impact on the actor's performance expectations in the situation. However, dominating and propitiating behaviors are effective to the extent that they reflect a legitimated power and prestige order. (See Ridgeway 1984; Ridgeway and Berger 1986.) Of particular relevance to the challenge from dominance theories is research by Ridgeway (1987). Ridgeway shows that in a situation in which we can assume there is no legitimated power and prestige order, high dominance behaviors are no more effective than low dominance behaviors in determining influence in groups. However, high task cue behaviors are more effective than low task cue behaviors; they are also more effective than either type of dominance behaviors. Research reported by Driskell, Olmstead, and Salas (1993) corroborates and further extends the findings by Ridgeway. (For additional research that supports other arguments in the status cues extension, see Ridgeway, Berger, and Smith 1985; Riches and Foddy 1989.)

Arguments such as those presented above have led to the development of still another extension of status characteristics theory, one concerned with the processes by which the power and prestige order is legitimated. We turn to this next.

Legitimation

Legitimation is often an important factor in status-organizing processes. For example, legitimacy is essential for leaders with traditionally low statuses (e.g., women or minorities) if they are to successfully engage in the directive behaviors ordinarily expected of a leader (see Eskilson and Wiley 1976; Fennell et al. 1978). More generally, legitimacy is important in determining the effectiveness of controlling (i.e., dominating and propitiating) behaviors.

Ridgeway and Berger (1986, 1988) developed an extension of the status characteristics theory that considers how and when a group's power and prestige order is likely to become legitimated. This theory applies to task situations where there is the allocation of differentially valued status positions. Ridgeway and Berger begin with the assumption (based on reward expectation theory) that the actor's cultural framework may include consensual beliefs (i.e., referential structures) that associate possession of differentially valued status positions with the possession of different states of diffuse status characteristics, or different levels of task capacities, or different levels of task achievement. For example, actors may believe that males ordinarily occupy higher-valued status positions than females in American society.

These beliefs (valid or not) about what is true in the larger social environment, when activated, generate expectations about who is to occupy high- and low-valued status positions in the immediate task situation. These expectations then determine differences in generalized deferential behaviors—respect, esteem, and importance granted to others. If this behavior is validated by others and task expectations are consistent with those for status positions, then the probability exists that the power and prestige order in the group becomes legitimated. Behavior is validated if others engage in similar behavior or at least engage in no behavior that contradicts the original behavior.

Legitimation establishes "what ought to be" in the immediate situation. Expectations become normative with the presumption that there will be collective support for these norms. A high-status actor has a right to expect a higher degree of esteem, respect, and generalized deference than does a low-status actor. At the same time, others have the right to expect more valued contributions from that actor than from the low-status actor. In addition, high-status actors come to have rights to exercise, if necessary, controlling behaviors—dominating and propitiating behaviors—over the actions of others.

This theory has been formalized and also extended to deal with conditions under which a legitimated order may be delegitimated (Berger et al. 1998). This formalization yields consequences that describe how the number, relevance, and consistency of status distinctions associated with referential beliefs *increase* the likelihood that a power and prestige order is legitimated, conditions under which a highly differentiated power and prestige order is *less likely* to be legitimated than one that is less differentiated, and conditions under which task success or failure can affect the likelihood of the legitimation or delegitimation of a power and prestige order.

This theory explains why low-status group members generally encounter resistance when they engage in power and prestige and task cue behaviors that are above their rank. (See Meeker and Weitzel-O'Neill 1977; Ridgeway 1982 regarding gender and Katz 1970; Katz and Cohen 1962; Cohen et al. 1970 regarding race.) It also explains the resistance that women and minorities encounter in mixed-gender and biracial groups when they engage in directive, assertive behaviors even though they are task leaders. Such resistance occurs because low external status members who have become task leaders are more likely to be operating from positions in a power and prestige order that is not a legitimated order. See also the study by Ridgeway, Johnson, and Diekema (1994), which provides direct support for the argument that the likelihood of legitimation is related to the consistency of status characteristics possessed by actors.

Finally, we observe that, like other theories in the expectation states program, the legitimation theory is a multilevel formulation. Cultural beliefs begin the process by affecting the likelihood that one actor treats another with honorific deference. But to result in legitimacy, this process depends on the contingent reactions of others who can provide consensual validation, and who can collectively construct a local reality that makes the power and prestige order normatively prescriptive.

Other Theoretical Extensions

The Theory of Multiple Standards

In general, behavioral outcomes tend to be consistent with status distinctions. Thus, for example, high-status actors succeed and low-status actors fail. However, outcomes that are inconsistent do occur; high-status actors fail and low-status actors succeed.

In a theory on *multiple standards,* Foschi (1989, 1992) argues that multiple standards act as filters between success and failure outcomes and the assignment of performance expectations to actors who differ in status. They provide different criteria for assessing performance outcomes. In the case of gender, for example, a double standard is activated along with the male/female distinction.

Several studies generally support Foschi's analysis of the double standard as applied to gender. Foddy and Graham (1987) found that in opposite-sex dyads women tended to set stricter standards for ability for themselves than did men, especially when they believed they had performed worse than their male partner. These differences appeared when the task was identified as masculine or gender-neutral. There was no evidence of the double standard when the task was identified as feminine.

Foschi (1996) showed that double standards are activated on masculine tasks regardless of the target of application of the standard (self or other) or the level of advantage the standard confers (large and small). And Foschi, Lai, and Sigerson (1994) demonstrated that the double standard operated even more strongly, at least for men, when the actor applying the standard was not a participating member of the group (and therefore not subject to an assessment of performance). An interesting consequence from Foschi's formulation is the argument that the greater an actor's status advantage relative to others, the greater the likelihood of maintaining that status advantage by activating (if necessary) multiple standards. In Foschi's theory, multiple standards are mechanisms that play a critical role in maintaining established status distinctions.

The Behavior-Status Theory

Fisek, Berger, and Norman (1991) have proposed two new integrations in the expectation states program. The first of these, the *behavior-status* theory, seeks to integrate research in initially homogeneous status situations (as in power and prestige theory) with that in initially status-differentiated situations (as in status characteristics theory) for multiple-actor open interaction settings. The key new idea in Fisek, Berger, and Norman (1991) is that of a *behavioral interchange pattern,* which is a set of interaction cycles or unit sequences between two or more actors that are consistent in their power and prestige significance. Berger (1958) and Berger and Conner (1969, 1974) conceptualize interaction sequences or cycles as being both decision making and expectation forming. If an actor *a* gives *b* an action opportunity to which *b* responds with a performance that *a* accepts, this interchange is a decision-making unit and at the same time a sequence that can result in *a* and *b* forming higher performance expectations for *b* than *a.* A *behavioral interchange pattern* is a set of unit sequences in which all the sequences have the same ordering in terms of expectation differences for the actors involved. Once these expectation differences have been created from interchange patterns, they are processed along with information from other relevant status characteristics in the formation of aggregated expectations.

Using this extension, the authors construct a specific model that predicts participation rates in open interaction settings for initially status differentiated groups (Skvoretz 1988; Lohman 1972; Morris 1977; Rosenholtz 1977; Lockheed 1976) and initially status homogeneous (Bales 1970) groups. (For a critical exchange on this model, see Robinson and Balkwell 1995; Fisek, Berger, and Norman 1997. See also Balkwell 1991.)

Within this formulation, and building on prior work by Fisek (1974) and Balkwell (1995), Skvoretz and Fararo (1996) have developed a structure formation model that is applicable to status heterogeneous as well as homogeneous open interaction groups. The model describes the development of power and prestige orders and treats such orders as probabilistic functions of an emerging underlying expectation structure (see also chapter 11). Initial results from experimental tests by Skvoretz, Webster, and Whitmeyer (1999) show support for this open interaction expectation states model. (For other recent expectation states research in open interaction settings, see especially Shelly and Webster 1997; Shelly and Munroe 1999.)

The Evaluations-Expectations Theory

In the second of these integrations, Fisek, Berger, and Norman (1995), in a theory on *evaluations and expectations,* seek to relate status characteristics theory to the theory of sources of self-evaluation (Webster 1969; Webster and Sobieszek 1974). The key new concept in this theory is the notion of *imputed possession,* which represents the performance capacities attributed to actors by evaluating sources. In this theory a *source* is an evaluator for whom actors hold positive performance expectations. The authors argue that the strength of these performance imputations by a source is a function of the expectations held for that source. Fisek, Berger, and Norman assess this formulation against data reported by Webster and Sobieszek (1974) and Ilardi and McMahon (1988) and find a good fit between predictions and observed data. Since the data existed prior to the formulation, this again is an assessment of the consistency of a theory with the available data. Independent tests of this formulation are still to be carried out.

Most recently, Webster and Whitmeyer (1999) have proposed an alternative model that relates expectations held for the source and the strength of imputed possession. Experimental tests to discriminate between these alternatives are presently under way.

STATE ORGANIZING PROCESSES

At the most general level, expectation state theories are concerned with processes that arise from the interaction that occurs within the context of a larger social framework. This cultural framework may inform, shape, and constrain the interaction situation. These theories are neither "micro" nor "macro." Rather, they are multilevel *interactor* theories (see Berger, Eyre, and Zelditch 1989, 1998).

Interactor theories distinguish between the immediate *situation of action* itself and the larger *social framework* (see figure 3.1). The situation of action is goal-focused and subject to significant variation, depending on who is involved in the interaction, the status and performance characteristics they possess, and the nature of the interaction in which they engage. The elements of a social framework are consensual, objectified, and enduring relative to the action situation. In status characteristics theories, the social or cultural framework may include different types of established status characteristics that are based, say, on gender, race, educational and occupational positions, and different types of commonly held cultural beliefs—categorical, ability, and outcome referential structures.

Status categories and cultural beliefs that are elements in the actor's social framework do not automatically come into play. In fact, they are *not* always significant. We therefore must formulate *salience* principles for the status characteristics theory that describe when different types of status characteristics are likely to become significant, and *activation* principles for the reward expectations and the legitimation theory that specify when basic cultural beliefs (referential structures) become important to the interaction.

Actors have to act upon and further process these cultural inputs in creating different types of behavioral expectations. In the status characteristics theory this involves the formation of expectations for performances, in the distributive justice and rewards theory expectations for rewards, and in the legitimation theory expectations for valued status positions. Theoretical principles govern these processes. In the status characteristics theory these include the *burden of proof* principle and *sequencing* principle, and in the legitimation theory, there is also the contingent action and reaction behavior that is involved in the *social validation* process.

Actors typically possess multiple status characteristics, and reward systems typically involve multiple reward standards. But cultural frameworks rarely (if ever) provide categories for the large number of possible combinations of social categories that individuals can possess and the cultural beliefs they can hold. Theoretical principles are required to describe how actors organize such information when applying them to specific individuals. The *principle of organized subsets* is that principle in the different status theories. In the status characteristics theory it describes how actors process multiple items of status information in forming aggregated expectations for performances. In the reward expectations theory and in the legitimation theory it describes how actors organize multiple items of cultural belief (referential structures) in forming, respectively, aggregated expectations for rewards and aggregated expectations for valued status positions.

Once expectation states have formed, they govern the behaviors of actors toward each other in the task situation. In status characteristics theory, the *basic expectation assumption* specifies how the actor's *expectation advantage* (or dis-

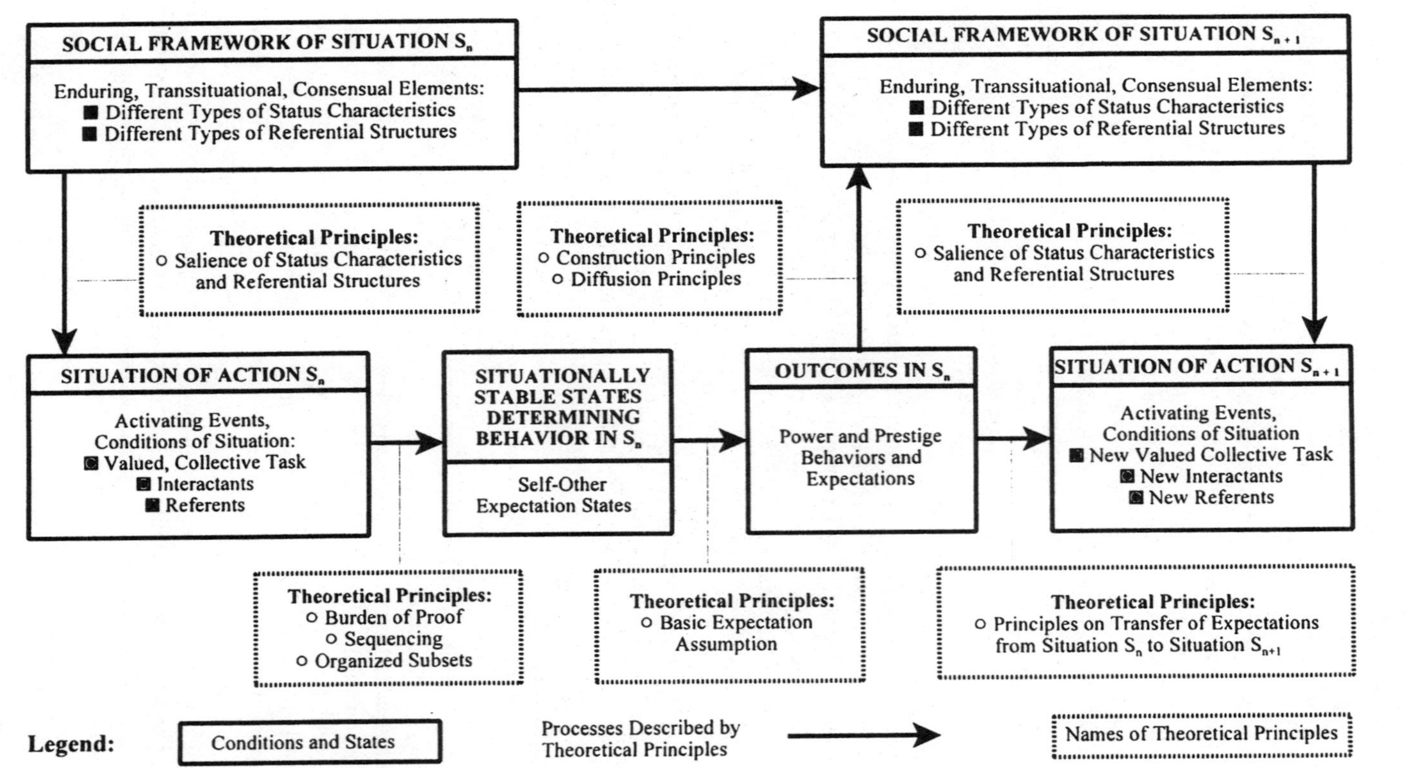

Figure 3.1. **Status Characteristics Theory as a State Organizing Process**

advantage) in performances with respect to another determines the distribution of power and prestige behaviors. In the reward theory, expectation differences in rewards determines the allocation of rewards and reward preferences; and in the legitimation theory, expectation differences in valued status positions determine the distribution of generalized deferential behaviors.

Once an interaction episode has been completed—for example, the group's goal has been achieved—the organizing processes may deactivate. Salient status differences can become latent and there may be a reduction in the differences in the power and prestige order. Other outcomes may occur. First, as described above in the theory of the evolution of status expectations, expectations that have emerged in one situation of action may be *transferred* to new situations and new actors. Second, as described in the *status construction* theory (Ridgeway 1991; see below), behavioral outcomes may become the bases on which new consensual and enduring status characteristics are created. New status beliefs can be *constructed* that become part of the actor's social framework. These status beliefs can then be activated in subsequent situations of action.[2]

RECENT DEVELOPMENTS

With the growth of research based on expectation states theory (and especially status characteristics theory), there has been an expansion of concern for issues in new explanatory domains. Two important recent developments have concerned *sentiment processes* and the *social construction of status characteristics.*

Sentiments and Status

There are, of course, other processes aside from status-organizing ones that affect the behavior of social actors, such as power, social control, sentiment, and affect processes. Each of these is important in its own right and each of these is likely to affect the character of status organization. It has long been known, for example, that the level of familiarity, degree of intimacy, and the particular pattern of sentiments affect status processes (see Strodtbeck et al. 1958; Hurwitz, Zander, and Hymovitch 1960; Heiss 1962; Leik 1963). At present, the most work on these other processes within the program has been on the effects of sentiment relations. This work deals with such questions as: Under what conditions are patterns of sentiment relations (patterns of interpersonal likes and dislikes) among actors likely to affect status organization? Are there different types of effects? And most important, what are the mechanisms that relate sentiment to status?

Recent research by Shelly (1993), Lovaglia and Houser (1996), and Driskell and Webster (1997) has demonstrated experimentally that sentiment relations directly affect status relations. But more importantly, this research leads us to believe that depending upon the type of sentiment patterns that emerge in a group, sentiment relations may either *dampen or accentuate* the effects of status difference on actors' behavior. The outcome depends on the nature of the sentiment pattern that develops and the degree to which it is consistent with or inconsistent with the status structure.

Lovaglia and Houser (1996), for example, have argued that if in a two-person group the high-status actor likes the low-status actor, who in turn dislikes the high, differences in power and prestige behavior between the two will be *reduced* in comparison to the situation where no sentiment relations were involved in their relationship. In this case the pattern of sentiments is inconsistent with that of status. In contrast, if the sentiment pattern is reversed—the high-status actor dislikes the low, who likes the high, then differences in power and prestige will be *increased* as compared to the situation where sentiment relations are absent. In this case the pattern of sentiments is consistent with that of status. In either case, this research and that of others suggest that sentiment relations *combine* with status relations to determine the degree of differentiation in power and prestige that occurs in a group.

Fisek and Berger (1998) identify at least two ways in which these relations might be combined. One involves a *constitutive* mechanism, the other a *mediational* mechanism. The constitutive mechanism assumes that actors' sentiments behave very much like other status elements. Therefore, the same organizing principles—salience, burden of proof, sequencing, organized subsets—apply to sentiments in the same manner that they apply to other status elements. As a consequence, positive and negative sentiment elements are aggregated along with other positive and negative status elements in the formation of expectation states. In this sense sentiments are constitutive components of these expectations.

In contrast, the mediational mechanism assumes that an actor's sentiments behave differently from other status elements. Whatever principles govern their salience and organization in the situation, they are *not* the same as those that govern status organization. Sentiment elements are therefore not aggregated with status elements in the formation of expectations. Instead, sentiment elements intervene in the translation of status-based expectations into power and prestige behaviors.

Which mechanism is involved? At present, we do not have a definitive answer to this question. However, current independent research by Bianchi (2000) and by Shelly (2001) may enable us to discriminate between these mechanisms. Once we know which mechanism it is, or whether each of these mechanisms operates but under different conditions, we will have the information we need to develop a *theoretical* formulation that interrelates sentiment and status processes.

The Construction of Status Characteristics

Traditionally, status characteristics theories have treated status differences (especially diffuse ones) as part of the established and enduring social or cultural framework within which interaction occurs. Their existence antecedes the interaction situation, endures through the status organization process, and persists after the interaction has ended. As with most elements of the social framework, status characteristics are usually *consensual, enduring,* and *transsituational.*

But not all characteristics that might be used to describe actors have these qualities. What is it about such characteristics as race, gender, and physical attractiveness that has made them so commonly part of actors' social frameworks? More important, *how* did they come to be part of these frameworks? How and under what conditions do previously neutral characteristics come to be status characteristics? How are institutionalized status characteristics constructed?

Recently, in an important set of papers, Ridgeway (1991, 1997) has focused on this emergence question. She starts with the notion of a diffuse status characteristic as that idea is conceptualized in status characteristic theories and argues that these are particularly likely to emerge in what she calls *doubly dissimilar situations.* Such situations involve the following properties:

1. Actors possess different states of a *discriminating characteristic.* That is, the characteristic distinguishes between them, but the states are not differentially status valued, nor are they associated with specific or general expectations.
2. Actors also possess different levels of resources in the situation; one therefore is relatively *resource rich* and the other is *resource poor.*
3. The difference in resources is correlated in a consistent manner with the different types of states on the discriminating characteristic.

In such doubly dissimilar situations, Ridgeway argues, the differences in resources are likely to generate differences in expectations and therefore in power and prestige behaviors; resource-rich actors will be expected to perform more capably than resource-poor actors. (Prior experiments in the expectation states program already provides considerable support for this argument; see research previously described on reward expectations above.) If this same double dissimilarity appears across a range of situations involving different tasks and different others, the differences in performance expectations will come to be attributed to the states of the characteristics the actors possess; actors who possess one state of the characteristic (i.e., the one associated with resource richness) will be expected to perform more capably than actors who possess the other state (i.e., the one associated with resource poorness). By this process, then, an initially nonvalued characteristic may come to have generalized performance expectations associated with it, and become a *diffuse status characteristic* for an actor.

For such a characteristic to become part of the social framework for actors generally (as with characteristics like race and gender), these status beliefs must be diffused through a social population. Ridgeway and Balkwell (1997) have described this diffusion process in some detail, drawing on arguments from the work of Blau (1977).

Other work has extended these ideas. Webster and Hysom (1998), for example, have shown how differences in properties other than resources can lead to the same sort of double dissimilarity. Ridgeway herself (2000) considers how the social validation process (as developed in the legitimation theory above) may also play a key role in the construction of status characteristics. Existing experimental research in general supports the analysis provided by status construction theory (see Ridgeway and Erickson 2000; Ridgeway et al. 1998), and further research is currently underway (see also Berger et al. 2002).

One implication of the development of this theory is particularly worth noting. It is common among sociologists to assume that social constructions are solely the outcome of idiosyncratic historical processes. We agree that such entities as status characteristics and referential beliefs are socially constructed and that there may be historically particular events involved in specific constructions. But as this research makes clear, we also believe that there are *general principles* that operate in these construction processes, and that it is possible to formulate these theoretical principles and assess them empirically.

CONCLUSION

The expectation states program is an evolving theoretical research program. It started with a single theory concerned with how interaction comes to generate stable differences in power and prestige. Over time the program has come to address first four and then more than a dozen different substantive concerns. It continues to evolve, but it still faces important tasks. There is the need to extend and formalize other branches of the program; there is the need to develop more theoretical interrelations between the different parts of the program; and there is generally still the need for more empirical research concerned with testing and applying the theories in the program. Some of this work is already under way, while new theoretical issues are emerging. Different social processes are being explored: for example, those concerned with social control (Berger 1988; Wagner 1988) and those concerned with affect processes (Berger 1988; Ridgeway 1994; Turner 1998). And research already is under way to relate the expectations state program to other major research programs being developed in sociology, particularly those concerned with power relations and power processes (Thye 2000; Willer et al. 1997; and see chapter 5).

Considered overall, the work in this program has been *cumulative*; we believe that we know much more about each of the processes we have studied than we did when we started. But there is still much to be done in developing the program. In this sense, expectation states theory is a program in progress.

NOTES

We gratefully acknowledge the research support to Joseph Berger by the Hoover Institution, Stanford University. An earlier version of this chapter was presented at the 95th annual meeting of the American Sociological Association in Washington, D.C., August 2000.

1. The research by E. G. Cohen and colleagues and that by Webster and Entwisle, in particular, has served to identify different concrete social distinctions as status characteristics, and has led to the development of highly effective interventions aimed at overcoming invidious status effects resulting from differentiation on status characteristics (see Cohen 1982, 1993; Cohen and Lotan 1995, 1997; Entwisle and Webster 1972, 1973, 1974; Webster and Entwisle 1974).

2. In the course of our work on expectation states theory, we have developed still other metatheoretical ideas that have shaped our work. These include the idea of distinguishing between generalizing and historical orientations in research (see Berger, Zelditch, and Anderson 1972), the idea of formulating scope conditions as part of the explicit structure of a theory (see Berger 1974; Walker and Cohen 1985), and the idea of distinguishing orienting strategies, theoretical research programs, and unit theories as different types of theoretical structures while conceptualizing research programs as the unit of analysis in theoretical growth (see Wagner and Berger 1985; Berger and Zelditch 1993, 1997).

REFERENCES

Adams, J. Stacy. 1965. "Inequality in Social Exchange." Pp. 267–99 in *Advances in Experimental Social Psychology*, vol. 2, edited by Leonard Berkowitz. New York: Academic.

Alves, W., and Peter Rossi. 1978. "Who Should Get What? Fairness Judgments of the Distribution of Earnings." *American Journal of Sociology* 84:561–64.

Bales, Robert F. 1950. *Interaction Process Analysis.* Reading, MA: Addison Wesley.

———. 1953. "The Equilibrium Problem in Small Groups." Pp. 111–61 in *Working Papers in the Theory of Action*, edited by Talcott Parsons, Robert F. Bales, and Edward H. Shils. Glencoe, IL: Free Press.

———. 1970. *Personality and Interpersonal Behavior.* New York: Holt, Rinehart, and Winston.

Bales, Robert F., and P. Slater. 1955. "Role Differentiation in Small Decision Making Groups." Pp. 259–306 in *Family, Socialization, and Interaction Process*, edited by Talcott Parsons and Robert F. Bales. Glencoe, IL: Free Press.

Bales, R. F., F. L. Strodtbeck, T. M. Mills, and M. E. Roseborough. 1951. "Channels of Communication in Small Groups." *American Sociological Review* 16:461–68.

Balkwell, James W. 1997a. "Status Characteristics and Social Interaction: An Assessment of Theoretical Variants." Pp. 135–76 in *Advances in Group Processes*, vol. 8, edited by Edward J. Lawler, Barry Markovsky, Cecilia Ridgeway, and Henry Walker. Greenwich, CT: JAI Press.

———. 1991b "From Expectations to Behavior: An Improved Postulate for Expectation States Theory." *American Sociological Review* 56:355–69.

———. 1995. "Strong Tests of Expectation-States Hypotheses." *Social Psychology Quarterly* 58:44–51.

Balkwell, James W., and Joseph Berger. 1996. "Gender, Status, and Behavior in Task Situations." *Social Psychology Quarterly* 59:273–83.

Berger, Joseph. 1958. "Relations between Performance, Rewards, and Action-Opportunities in Small Groups." Ph.D. dissertation, Harvard University.

———. 1974. "Expectation States Theory: A Theoretical Research Program." Pp. 3–22 in *Expectation States Theory: A Theoretical Research Program*, edited by Joseph Berger, Thomas L. Conner, and M. Hamit Fisek. Cambridge, MA: Winthrop Press.

———. 1988. "Directions in Expectation States Research." Pp. 450–74 in *Status Generalization: New Theory and Research*, edited by Murray Webster Jr. and Martha Foschi. Stanford, CA: Stanford University Press.

Berger, Joseph, Bernard P. Cohen, and Morris Zelditch Jr. 1966. "Status Characteristics and Expectation States." Pp. 29–46 in *Sociological Theories in Progress*, vol. 1, edited by Joseph Berger, Morris Zelditch Jr., and Bo Anderson. Boston: Houghton Mifflin.

———. 1972. "Status Characteristics and Expectation States." *American Sociological Review* 37:241–55.

Berger, Joseph, and Thomas L. Conner. 1969. "Performance Expectations and Behavior in Small Groups." *Acta Sociologica* 12:186–98.

———. 1974. "Performance Expectations and Behavior in Small Groups: A Revised Formulation." Pp. 85–109 in *Expectation States Theory: A Theoretical Research Program*, edited by Joseph Berger, Thomas L. Conner, and M. Hamit Fisek. Cambridge, MA: Winthrop.

Berger, Joseph, Thomas L. Conner, and William L. McKeown. 1969. "Evaluations and the Maintenance of Performance Expectations." *Human Relations* 33:481–502.

Berger, Joseph, Dana Eyre, and M. Zelditch Jr. 1989. "Theoretical Structures and the Micro-Macro Problem." Pp. 11–34 in *Sociological Theories in Progress: New Formulations*, edited by Joseph Berger, Morris Zelditch Jr., and Bo Anderson. Newbury Park, CA: Sage.

———. 1998. "Theoretical Structures and the Micro-Macro Problem." Pp. 55–70 in *Status, Power, and Legitimacy: Strategies and Theories*, edited by Joseph Berger and Morris Zelditch Jr. New Brunswick, NJ: Transaction.

Berger, Joseph, and M. Hamit Fisek. 1970. "Consistent and Inconsistent Status Characteristics and the Determination of Power and Prestige Orders." *Sociometry* 33:287–304.

———. 1974. "A Generalization of the Theory of Status Characteristics and Expectation States." Pp. 163–205 in *Expectation States Theory: A Theoretical Research Program*, edited by Joseph Berger, Thomas L. Conner, and M. Hamit Fisek. Cambridge, MA: Winthrop.

Berger, J., M. H. Fisek, and P. V. Crosbie. 1970. "Multi-Characteristic Status Situations and the Determinations of Power and Prestige Orders." *Technical Report No. 35*, Laboratory for Social Research, Stanford University.

Berger, J., M. Hamit Fisek, and Lee Freese. 1976. "Paths of Relevance and the Determination of Power and Prestige Orders." *Pacific Sociological Review* 19:45–62.

Berger, Joseph, M. Hamit Fisek, and Robert Z. Norman. 1989. "The Evolution of Status Expectations: A Theoretical Extension." Pp. 100–30 in *Sociological Theories in Progress: New Formulations*, edited by Joseph Berger, Morris Zelditch Jr., and Bo Anderson. Newbury Park, CA: Sage.

Berger, Joseph, M. Hamit Fisek, Robert Z. Norman, and David G. Wagner. 1985. "The Formation of Reward Expectations in Status Situations." Pp. 215–61 in *Status, Rewards, and Influence: How Expectations Organize Behavior*, edited by Joseph Berger and Morris Zelditch Jr. San Francisco: Jossey-Bass.

Berger, Joseph, M. Hamit Fisek, Robert Z. Norman, and Morris Zelditch Jr. 1977. *Status Characteristics and Social Interaction.* New York: Elsevier.

Berger, Joseph, Robert Z. Norman, James W. Balkwell, and Roy F. Smith. 1992. "Status Inconsistency in Task Situations: A Test of Four Status Processing Principles." *American Sociological Review* 57:843–55.

Berger, Joseph, Cecilia L. Ridgeway, M. Hamit Fisek, and Robert Z. Norman. 1998. "The Legitimation and Delegitimation of Power and Prestige Orders." *American Sociological Review* 63:379–405.

Berger, Joseph, Cecilia Ridgeway, and Morris Zelditch Jr. 2002. "Construction of Status and Referential Structures." *Sociological Theory* 20:157–79.

Berger, Joseph, and J. Laurie Snell. 1961. "A Stochastic Theory for Self-Other Expectations." *Technical Report No. 1*, Laboratory for Social Research, Stanford University.

Berger, Joseph, David G. Wagner, and Morris Zelditch Jr. 1992. "A Working Strategy for Constructing Theories: State Organizing Processes." Pp. 107–23. In *Studies in Metatheorizing in Sociology*, edited by George Ritzer. Newbury Park, CA: Sage.

Berger, Joseph, Murray Webster Jr., Cecilia L. Ridgeway, and Susan Rosenholtz. 1986. "Status Cues, Expectations,and Behavior." Pp. 1–22 in *Advances in Group Processes*, vol. 3, edited by Edward J. Lawler. Greenwich, CT: JAI Press.

Berger, Joseph, and Morris Zelditch Jr. 1993. "Orienting Strategies and Theory Growth." Pp. 3–19 in *Theoretical Research Programs: Studies in the Growth of Theory*, edited by Joseph Berger and M. Zelditch Jr. Stanford, CA: Stanford University Press.

———. 1997. "Theoretical Research Programs: A Reformulation." Pp. 29–46 in *Status, Networks, and Structure: Theory Development in Group Processes*, edited by Jacek Szmatka, John Skvoretz, and Joseph Berger. Stanford, CA: Stanford University Press.

Berger, Joseph, Morris Zelditch Jr., and Bo Anderson. 1972. "Generalizing and Historical Orientations in Sociology." Pp. ix–xxi in *Sociological Theories in Progress*, vol. 2, edited by Joseph Berger, M. Zelditch Jr., and B. Anderson. Boston: Houghton Mifflin.

Berger, Joseph, Morris Zelditch Jr., Bo Anderson, and Bernard P. Cohen. 1968. "Distributive Justice: A Status Value Formulation." *Technical Report No. 28*, Laboratory for Social Research, Stanford University.

———. 1972. "Structural Aspects of Distributive Justice: A Status Value Formulation." Pp. 119–46 in *Sociological Theories in Progress*, vol. 2, edited by Joseph Berger, Morris Zelditch Jr., and Bo Anderson. Boston: Houghton Mifflin.

Bianchi, Alison J. 2000. "Sentiment and Status Processes: A Test between Constitutive and Mediative Models in the Expectation States Tradition." Paper presented at the annual meeting of the American Sociological Association, Washington, D.C., August.

Bierhoff, Hans W., Ernst Buck, and Renate Klein. 1986. "Social Context and Perceived Justice." Pp. 165–85 in *Justice in Social Relations*, edited by Hans W. Bierhoff, Ronald L. Cohen, and Jerald Greenberg. New York: Plenum.

Blau, Peter M. 1977. *Inequality and Heterogeneity: A Primitive Theory of Social Structure.* New York: Free Press.

Caudill, William. 1958. *The Psychiatric Hospital as a Small Society.* Cambridge: Harvard University Press.

Cohen, Bernard P., Joseph Berger, and Morris Zelditch Jr. 1972. "Status Conceptions and Interaction: A Case Study of the Problem of Developing Cumulative Knowledge." Pp. 449–83 in *Experimental Social Psychology*, edited by Charles G. McClintock. New York: Holt, Rinehardt, and Winston.

Cohen, Elizabeth G. 1982. "Expectation States and Interracial Interaction in School Settings." *Annual Review of Sociology* 8:209–35.

———. 1993. "From Theory to Practice: The Development of an Applied Research Program." Pp. 385–415 in *Theoretical Research Programs: Studies in the Growth of Theories*, edited by Joseph Berger and Morris Zelditch Jr. Stanford, CA: Stanford University Press.

Cohen, Elizabeth G., M. Lohman, Katherine P. Hall, and D. Lucero. 1970. "Expectation Training I: Altering the Effects of Social Status Characteristics." *Technical Report No. 3,* School of Education, Stanford University.

Cohen, Elizabeth G., and Rachel A. Lotan. 1995. "Producing Equal-Status Interaction in the Heterogeneous Classroom." *American Educational Research Journal* 32:99–120.

———, eds. 1997. *Working for Equity in Heterogeneous Classrooms.* New York: Columbia University Teachers College Press.

Conner, Thomas L. 1965. "Continual Disagreement and the Assignment of Self-Other Performance Expectations." Ph.D. dissertation, Department of Sociology, Stanford University.

Cook, Karen S. 1970. "Analysis of a Distributive Justice Experiment: Goal Objects and Task Performance Expectations." M.A. apprenticeship paper, Department of Sociology, Stanford University.

———. 1975. "Expectations, Evaluations, and Equity." *American Sociological Review* 40:372–88.

Cook, Karen S., Ruth Cronkite, and David G. Wagner. 1974. "Laboratory for Social Research Manual for Experiments in Expectation State Theory." Laboratory for Social Research, Stanford University.

Croog, S. H. 1956. "Patient Government: Some Aspects of Participation and Social Background on Two Psychiatric Wards." *Psychiatry* 19:203–7.

Dovidio, John F., Clifford E. Brown, Karen Heltmann, Steve L. Ellyson, and Caroline F. Keating. 1988. "Power Displays between Women and Men in Discussions of Gender-Linked Tasks: A Multichannel Study." *Journal of Personality and Social Psychology* 55:80–587.

Driskell, James E., and Murray Webster Jr. 1997. "Status and Sentiment in Task Groups." Pp. 179–200 in *Status, Network, and Organization*, edited by Jacek Szmatka, John Skvoretz, and Joseph Berger. Stanford, CA: Stanford University Press.

Driskell, James F., B. Olmstead, and E. Salas. 1993. "Task Cues, Dominance Cues, and Influence in Task Groups." *Journal of Applied Psychology* 78:51–60.

Entwisle, Doris R., and Murray Webster Jr. 1972. "Raising Children's Performance Expectations." *Social Science Research* 1:147–58.

———. 1973. "Status Factors in Expectation Raising." *Sociology of Education* 46:115–26.

———. 1974. "Expectations in Mixed-Racial Groups." *Sociology of Education* 47:301–18.

Eskilson, A., and Mary Glenn Wiley. 1976. "Sex Composition and Leadership in Small Groups." *Sociometry* 39:183–94.

Fararo, Thomas J. 1973. "An Expectation-States Process Model." Pp. 229–37 in *Introduction to Mathematical Sociology*. New York: Wiley.

Fennell, Mary L., Patricia Barchas, Elizabeth G. Cohen, Anne M. McMahon, and Polly Hildebrand. 1978. "An Alternative Perspective on Sex Differences in Organizational Settings: The Process of Legitimation." *Sex Roles* 4:589–604.

Fisek, M. Hamit. 1974. "A Model for the Evolution of Status Structures in Task-Oriented Discussion Groups." Pp. 53–84 in *Expectation States Theory: A Theoretical Research Program*, edited by Joseph Berger, Thomas L. Conner, and M. Hamit Fisek. Cambridge, MA: Winthrop.

Fisek, M. Hamit, and Joseph Berger. 1998. "Sentiment and Task Performance Expectations." Pp. 23–40 in *Advances in Group Processes*, vol. 15, edited by John Skvoretz and Jacek Szmatka. Greenwich, CT: JAI Press.

Fisek, M. Hamit, Joseph Berger, and Robert Z. Norman. 1991. "Participation in Heterogeneous and Homogeneous Groups: A Theoretical Integration." *American Journal of Sociology* 97:114–42.

———. 1995. "Evaluations and the Formation of Expectations." *American Journal of Sociology* 101:721–46.

———. 1997. "Two Issues in the Assessment of the Adequacy of Formal Sociological Models of Human Behavior." *Social Science Research* 26:153–69.

———. 2002. "Status Cues and the Formation of Expectation." Unpublished manuscript, Bogazici University, Bebek, Istanbul.

Fisek, M. Hamit, Robert Z. Norman, and Max Nelson-Kilger. 1992. "Status Characteristics and Expectation States Theory: *A Priori* Model Parameters and Test." *Journal of Mathematical Sociology* 16:285–303.

Foddy, Margaret, and H. Graham. 1987. "Sex and Double Standards in the Inference of Ability." Paper presented at the annual meeting of the Canadian Psychological Association, Vancouver, BC, June.

Foddy, Margaret, and Phoebe Riches. 2000. "The Impact of Task and Categorical Cues on Social Influence: Fluency and Ethnic Accent as Cues to Competence in Task Groups." Pp. 103–130 in *Advances in Group Processes*, vol. 17, edited by Shane R. Thye, Edward J. Lawler, Michael W. Macy, and Henry A. Walker. Stamford, CT: JAI Press.

Foschi, Martha. 1970. "Contradiction of Specific Performance Expectations: An Experiment Study." Ph.D. dissertation, Department of Sociology, Stanford University.

———. 1971. "Contradiction and Change of Performance Expectations." *Canadian Review of Sociology and Anthropology* 8:205–22.

———. 1972. "On the Concept of Expectations." *Acta Sociologica* 15:124–31.

———. 1989. "Status Characteristics, Standards, and Attributions." Pp. 58–72 in *Sociological Theories in Progress: New Formulations*, edited by Joseph Berger, Morris Zelditch Jr., and Bo Anderson. Newbury Park, CA: Sage.

———. 1992. "Gender and Double Standards for Competence." Pp. 181–207 in *Gender, Interaction, and Inequality*, edited by Cecilia L. Ridgeway. New York: Springer-Verlag.

———. 1996. "Double Standards in the Evaluation of Men and Women." *Social Psychology Quarterly* 59:237–54.

Foschi, Martha, and Ricardo Foschi. 1976. "Evaluations and Expectations: A Bayesian Model." *Journal of Mathematical Sociology* 4:279–93.

———. 1979. "A Bayesian Model for Performance Expectations: Extension and Simulation." *Social Psychology Quarterly* 42:232–41.

Foschi, Martha, Larissa Lai, and Kirsten Sigerson. 1994. "Gender and Double Standards in the Assessment of Job Applicants." *Social Psychology Quarterly* 57:326–39.

Fox, John, and James C. Moore Jr. 1979. "Status Characteristics and Expectation States: Fitting and Testing a Recent Model." *Social Psychology Quarterly* 42:126–34.

Freese, Lee. 1970. "The Generalization of Specific Performance Expectations." Ph.D. dissertation, Stanford University.

Freese, L., and B. P. Cohen. 1973. "Eliminating Status Generalization." *Sociometry* 36:177–93.

Harrod, Wendy J. 1980. "Expectations from Unequal Rewards." *Social Psychology Quarterly* 43:126–30.

Heinecke, C., and R. F. Bales. 1953. "Developmental Trends in the Structure of Small Groups." *Sociometry* 16:7–38.

Heiss, Jerald S. 1962. "Degree of Intimacy and Male-Female Interaction." *Sociometry* 25:197–208.

Homans, George C. 1961. *Social Behavior: Its Elementary Forms.* New York: Harcourt Brace and World.

———. 1974. *Social Behavior: Its Elementary Forms,* rev. ed. New York: Harcourt Brace Jovanovich.

Humphreys, Paul, and Joseph Berger. 1981. "Theoretical Consequences of the Status Characteristics Formulation." *American Journal of Sociology* 86:953–83.

Hurwitz, J. I., Alvin. F. Zander, and B. Hymovitch. 1960. "Some Effects of Power on the Relations among Group Members." Pp. 448–56 in *Group Dynamics,* edited by Dorwin P. Cartwright and Alvin Zander. New York: Harper and Row.

Ilardi, Barbara, and Anne M. McMahon. 1988. "Organizational Legitimacy and Performance Evaluation." Pp. 217–44 in *Advances in Group Processes,* vol. 5, edited by Edward J. Lawler and Barry Markovsky. Greenwich, CT: JAI Press.

Jackson, Linda A., John E. Hunter, and Carole N. Hodge. 1995. "Physical Attractiveness and Intellectual Competence: A Meta-Analytic Review." *Social Psychology Quarterly* 59:108–22.

Jasso, Guillermina, and Peter H. Rossi. 1977. "Distributive Justice and Earned Income." *American Sociological Review* 42:639–51.

Katz, I. 1970. "Experimental Studies in Negro-White Relationships." Pp. 71–117 in *Advances in Experimental Social Psychology,* vol. 5, edited by Leonard Berkowitz. New York: Academic Press.

Katz, I., and M. Cohen. 1962. "The Effects of Training Negroes upon Cooperative Problem Solving in Biracial Teams." *Journal of Abnormal and Social Psychology* 64:319–25.

Kervin, John B. 1972. "An Information Processing Model for the Formation of Performance Expectations in Small Groups." Ph.D. dissertation, Johns Hopkins University.

Lee, M. T., and R. Ofshe. 1981. "The Impact of Behavioral Style and Status Characteristics on Social Influence: A Test of Two Competing Theories." *Social Psychology Quarterly* 44:73–82.

Leik, Robert K. 1963. "Instrumentality and Emotionality in Family Interaction." *Sociometry* 26:131–45.

Lenski, Gerhard. 1966. *Power and Privilege.* New York: McGraw-Hill.

Lerner, M. 1965. "Evaluation of Performance as a Function of Performer's Reward and Attractiveness." *Journal of Personality and Social Psychology* 1:355–60.

Lockheed, M. E. 1976. "Modification of Female Leadership Behavior in the Presence of Males." ETS-PR-76-28. Princeton: Educational Testing Service.

Lockheed, M. E., and K. P. Hall. 1976. "Conceptualizing Sex as a Status Characteristic: Applications to Leadership Training Strategies." *Journal of Social Issues* 32:111–24.

Lohman, M. R. 1972. "Changing a Racial Status Ordering—Implications for Desegregation." *Journal of Education and Urban Society* 4:383–402.

Lovaglia, Michael J., and Jeffrey A. Houser. 1996. "Emotional Reactions and Status in Groups." *American Sociological Review* 61:867–83.

Lovaglia, Michael J., Jeffrey W. Lucas, Jeffrey A. Houser, Shane R. Thye, and Barry Markovsky. 1998. "Status Processes and Mental Ability Test Scores." *American Journal of Sociology* 104:195–228.

Markovsky, Barry, Roy F. Smith, and Joseph Berger. 1984. "Do Status Interventions Persist?" *American Sociological Review* 49:373–82.

Mazur, A. 1985. "A Biosocial Model of Status in Face-to-Face Primate Groups." *Social Forces* 64:377–402.

Meeker, Barbara F., and P. A. Weitzel-O'Neill. 1977. "Sex Roles and Interpersonal Behavior in Task-Oriented Groups." *American Sociological Review* 42:91–105.

Mishler, E. G., and A. Tropp. 1956. "Status and Interaction in a Psychiatric Hospital." *Human Relations* 9:187–205.

Mohr, P. B. 1986. "Demeanor, Status Cue, or Performance?" *Social Psychology Quarterly* 49: 228–36.

Moore, James C. Jr. 1968. "Status and Influence in Small Group Interactions." *Sociometry* 31:47–63.

Morris, R. 1977. "A Normative Intervention to Equalize Participation in Task-Oriented Groups." Ph.D. dissertation, School of Education, Stanford University.

Nelson-Kilger, Max. 1992. "Status Gains and Status Losses: The Case of Gender." Ph.D. dissertation, Department of Sociology, Stanford University.

Norman, Robert Z., Roy F. Smith, and Joseph Berger. 1988. "The Processing of Inconsistent Status Information." Pp. 169–87 in *Status Generalization: New Theory and Research*, edited by Murray Webster Jr. and Martha Foschi. Stanford, CA: Stanford University Press.

Parcel, T. L., and K. S. Cook. 1977. "Status Characteristics, Reward Allocation, and Equity." *Sociometry* 40:311–24.

Prescott, W. S. 1986. "Expectation States Theory: When Do Interventions Persist?" Unpublished manuscript, Dartmouth College.

Pugh, Meredith D., and Ralph Wahrman. 1983. "Neutralizing Sexism in Mixed-Sex Groups: Do Women Have to Be Better Than Men?" *American Journal of Sociology* 88:736–62.

Rainwater, Julie A. 1987. "Status Cues: A Test of an Extension of Status Characteristics Theory." Ph.D. dissertation, Department of Sociology, Stanford University.

Rashotte, Lisa S., and Lynn Smith-Lovin. 1997. "Who Benefits From Being Bold? The Interactive Effects of Task Cues and Status Characteristics on Influence in Mock Jury Groups." Pp. 235–55 in *Advances in Group Processes*, vol. 14, edited by Barry Markovsky, Michael J. Lovaglia, and Lisa Troyer. Greenwich, CT: JAI Press.

Riches, P., and M. Foddy. 1989. "Ethnic Accent as Status Cue." *Social Psychology Quarterly* 52:197–206.

Ridgeway, Cecilia L. 1982. "Status in Groups: The Importance of Motivation." *American Sociological Review* 47:76–88.

———. 1984. "Dominance, Performance, and Status in Groups: A Theoretical Analysis." Pp. 59–93 in *Advances in Group Processes: Theory and Research*, vol. 1, edited by Edward J. Lawler. Greenwich, CT: JAI Press.

———. 1987. "Nonverbal Behavior, Dominance, and Status in Task Groups." *American Sociological Review* 52:683–94.

———. 1989. "Understanding Legitimation in Informal Status Orders." Pp. 131–59 in *Sociological Theories in Progress: New Formulations*, edited by Joseph Berger, Morris Zelditch Jr., and Bo Anderson. Newbury Park, CA: Sage.

———. 1991. "The Social Construction of Status Value: Gender and Other Nominal Characteristics." *Social Forces* 70:367–86.

———. 1994. "Affect." Pp. 205–30 in *Group Processes: Sociological Analyses*, edited by Martha Foschi and Edward J. Lawler. Chicago: Nelson-Hall.

———. 1997. "Where Do Status-Value Beliefs Come From? New Developments." Pp. 137–58 in *Status, Networks, and Structure: Theory Development in Group Processes*, edited by Jacek Szmatka, John Skvoretz, and Joseph Berger. Stanford, CA: Stanford University Press.

———. 2000. "The Formation of Status Beliefs: Improving Status Construction Theory." Pp. 77–103 in *Advances in Group Processes*, vol. 18, edited by Shane Thye, Edward J. Lawler, Michael W. Macy, and Henry A. Walker. Stamford, CT: JAI Press.

Ridgeway, Cecilia L., and James W. Balkwell. 1997. "Group Processes and the Diffusion of Status-Beliefs." *Social Psychology Quarterly* 60:14–31.

Ridgeway, Cecilia L., and Joseph Berger. 1986. "Expectations, Legitimation, and Dominance Behavior in Task Groups." *American Sociological Review* 51:603–17.

———. 1988. "The Legitimation of Power and Prestige Orders in Task Groups." Pp. 207–31 in *Status Generalization: New Theory and Research*, edited by Murray Webster Jr. and Martha Foschi. Stanford, CA: Stanford University Press.

Ridgeway, Cecilia L., Joseph Berger, and Roy Smith. 1985. "Nonverbal Cues and Status: An Expectation States Approach." *American Journal of Sociology* 90:955–78.

Ridgeway, Cecilia L., Elizabeth H. Boyle, Kathy J. Kuipers, and Dawn T. Robinson. 1998. "How Do Status Beliefs Develop? The Role of Resources and Interactional Experience." *American Sociological Review* 63:331–50.

Ridgeway, Cecilia L., and Kristan G. Erickson. 2000. "Creating and Spreading Status Beliefs." *American Journal of Sociology* 106:579–615.

Ridgeway, Cecilia L., Cathryn Johnson, and David Diekema. 1994. "External Status, Legitimacy, and Compliance in Male and Female Groups." *Social Forces* 72:1051–77.

Robinson, Dawn T., and James W. Balkwell. 1995. "Density, Transitivity, and Diffuse Status in Task-Oriented Groups." *Social Psychology Quarterly* 58:241–54.

Rosenholtz, Susan J. 1977. "The Multiple Ability Curriculum: An Intervention against the Self-Fulfilling Prophecy." Ph.D. dissertation, School of Education, Stanford University.

Sev'er, A. 1989. "Simultaneous Effects of Status and Task Cues: Combining, Eliminating, or Buffering?" *Social Psychology Quarterly* 52:327–35.

Shelly, Robert K. 1993. "How Sentiments Organize Interaction." Pp. 113–32 in *Advances in Group Processes,* vol. 10, edited by Edward J. Lawler et al. Greenwich, CT: JAI Press.

———. 2001. "How Performance Expectations Arise from Sentiments." *Social Psychology Quarterly* 64:72–87.

Shelly, Robert K., and Paul Munroe. 1999. "Do Women Engage in Less Task Behavior Than Men?" *Sociological Perspectives* 42:49–67.

Shelly, Robert K., and Murray Webster Jr. 1997. "How Formal Status, Liking, and Ability Status Structure Interaction: Three Theoretical Principles and a Test." *Sociological Perspectives* 40:81–107.

Skvoretz, John. 1988. "Models of Participation in Status Differentiated Groups." *Social Psychology Quarterly* 51: 43–57.

Skvoretz, John, and Thomas Fararo. 1996. "Status and Participation in Task Groups: A Dynamic Model." *American Journal of Sociology* 101:1366–414.

Skvoretz, John, Murray Webster Jr., and Joseph Whitmeyer. 1999. "Status Orders in Task Discussion Groups." Pp. 199–218 in *Advances in Group Processes,* vol. 16, edited by Shane R. Thye, Edward J. Lawler, Michael W. Macy, and Henry A. Walker. Stamford, CT: JAI Press.

Stewart, Penny, and James C. Moore. 1992. "Wage Disparities and Performance Expectations." *Social Psychology Quarterly* 55:78–85.

Strodtbeck, F. L., R. M. James, and C. Hawkins. 1958. "Social Status in Jury Deliberations." Pp. 379–88 in *Readings in Social Psychology,* 3d ed., edited by Eleanor E. Maccoby, Theodore M. Newcomb, and E. L. Hartley. New York: Holt.

Strodtbeck, Fred L., and R. D. Mann. 1956. "Sex-Role Differentiation in Jury Deliberations." *Sociometry* 19:3–11.

Thye, Shane. 2000. "A Status Value Theory of Power in Exchange Relations." *American Sociological Review* 65:407–32.

Torrance, E. Paul. 1954. "Some Consequences of Power Differences on Decision Making in Permanent and Temporary Three-Man Groups." *Research Studies* (State College of Washington, Pullman) 22:130–40.

Turner, Jonathan H. 1998. "Cecilia Ridgeway's and Joseph Berger's Expectation States Theories of Affect." Pp. 437–39 in *The Structure of Sociological Theory,* 6th ed. Belmont, CA: Wadsworth.

Tuzlak, A. 1988. "Boomerang Effects: Status and Demeanor over Time." Pp. 261–74 in *Status Generalization: New Theory and Research,* edited by Murray Webster Jr. and Martha Foschi. Stanford, CA: Stanford University Press.

Tuzlak, A., and James C. Moore. 1984. "Status, Demeanor, and Influence: An Empirical Assessment." *Social Psychology Quarterly* 47:178–83.

Wagner, David G. 1988. "Status Violations: Toward an Expectation States Theory of the Social Control of Deviance." Pp. 110–22 in *Status Generalization: New Theory and Research,* edited by Murray Webster Jr. and Martha Foschi. Stanford, CA: Stanford University Press.

———. 1995. "Gender Differences in Reward Preference: A Status-Based Account." *Small Group Research* 26:353–71.

———. 2000. "Status Inconsistency and Reward Preference." Unpublished manuscript, Department of Sociology, SUNY, Albany.

Wagner, David G., and Joseph Berger. 1974. "Paths of Consistent and Inconsistent Status Information and the Induction of Relevance." *Technical Report No. 53*, Laboratory for Social Research, Stanford University.

———. 1982. "Paths of Relevance and the Induction of Status-Task Expectancies." *Social Forces* 61:575–86.

———. 1985. "Do Sociological Theories Grow?" *American Journal of Sociology* 90:6972728.

———. 1993. "Status Characteristics Theory: The Growth of a Program." Pp. 23–63 in *Theoretical Research Programs: Studies in the Growth of Theories*, edited by Joseph Berger and Morris Zelditch Jr. Stanford, CA: Stanford University Press.

———. 1998. "Gender and Interpersonal Task Behaviors: Status Expectation Accounts." Pp. 229–61 in *Status, Power, and Legitimacy: Strategies and Theories*, edited by Joseph Berger and Morris Zelditch Jr. New Brunswick, NJ: Transaction.

Wagner, David G., Rebecca S. Ford, and Thomas W. Ford. 1986. "Can Gender Inequalities Be Reduced?" *American Sociological Review* 51:47–61.

Wagner, David G., and Robert O. Harris. 1995. "A Handbook for Expectation States Research." Unpublished manuscript, University at Albany (SUNY) Group Processes Laboratory, Department of Sociology.

Walker, Henry A., and Bernard P. Cohen. 1985. "Scope Statements: Imperatives for Evaluating Theory." *American Sociological Review* 40:288–301.

Walker, Henry A., and Brent T. Simpson. 2000. "Equating Characteristics and Status-Organizing Processes." *Social Psychology Quarterly* 63:175–85.

Webster, Murray, Jr. 1969. "Sources of Evaluations and Expectations for Performance." *Sociometry* 32:243–58.

Webster, Murray, Jr., and Joseph Berger. 1975. "Equating Characteristics and Social Interactions." Unpublished manuscript, Department of Sociology, Stanford University.

Webster, Murray, Jr., and James E. Driskell Jr. 1979. "Status Generalization: A Review and Some New Data." *American Sociological Review* 43:220–36.

Webster, Murray, Jr., and Doris R. Entwisle. 1974. "Raising Children's Expectations for Their Own Performance: A Classroom Application." Pp. 211–43 in *Expectation States Theory: A Theoretical Research Program*, edited by Joseph Berger, Thomas L. Conner, and M. Hamit Fisek. Cambridge, MA: Winthrop.

Webster, Murray, Jr., and Stuart J. Hysom. 1998. "Creating Status Characteristics." *American Sociological Review* 63:351–78.

Webster, Murray, Jr., and Roy F. Smith. 1978. "Justice and Revolutionary Coalitions: A Test of Two Theories." *American Journal of Sociology* 84:267–92.

Webster, Murray, Jr., and Barbara I. Sobieszek. 1974. "Sources of Evaluations and Expectation States." Pp. 115–58 in *Expectation States Theory: A Theoretical Research Program*, edited by Joseph Berger, Thomas L. Conner, and M. Hamit Fisek. Cambridge, MA: Winthrop.

Webster, Murray, Jr., and Joseph M. Whitmeyer. 1999. "A Theory of Second-Order Expectations and Behavior." *Social Psychology Quarterly* 62:17–31.

———. 2001. "Applications of Theories of Group Processes." *Sociological Theory* 19:250–70.

Willer, David, Michael Lovaglia, and Barry Markovsky. 1997. "Power and Influence: A Theoretical Bridge." *Social Forces* 76:571–603.

Zander, Alvin, and A. R. Cohen. 1955. "Attributed Social Power and Group Acceptance: A Classroom Experimental Demonstration." *Journal of Abnormal Social Psychology* 51:490–92.

Zelditch, Morris, Jr., Patrick Lauderdale, and Steve Stublarec. 1980. "How Are Inconsistencies between Status and Ability Resolved?" *Social Forces* 58:1025–43.

Ziller, R. C., and R. V. Exline. 1958. "Some Consequences of Age Heterogeneity in Decision-Making Groups." *Sociometry* 21:198–201.

III

NORMS, EXCHANGE, AND NETWORKS

4

Development of a Theory of Collective Action: From the Emergence of Norms to AIDS Prevention and the Analysis of Social Structure

Douglas D. Heckathorn

When beginning a research program it is impossible to know where the journey will lead. This chapter describes an ongoing research program of three phases. It began as a study of social norms—the informal standards of conduct that people impose on their family members, friends, and themselves—focusing on special situations in which social norms emerge extremely quickly, even literally over night. The study then broadened to focus on collective action, including not only normative control, but also social movements and broader systems of social cooperation.

The second phase began when, in collaboration with Robert Broadhead, this theory of collective action became the basis for a new form of AIDS-prevention intervention (Broadhead and Heckathorn 1994; Heckathorn et al. 1999). The intervention operates by harnessing peer pressure that creates and strengthens AIDS-prevention norms. Initially tested in several small towns in Connecticut (Broadhead et al. 1998), the intervention has subsequently been implemented in a number of other sites, including Yaroslavl, Russia (Sergeyev et al. 1999); and the principles upon which the intervention is based have been adapted to address other public health issues, including controlling high blood pressure and increasing adherence to AIDS therapy (Broadhead et al. forthcoming).

The third phase developed as an unanticipated by-product of the AIDS-prevention intervention, leading both to improved means for sampling hard-to-reach populations, such as drug injectors and the homeless, and for studying social structure, which, following Pareto, is conceived as structured patterns of affiliation.

COLLECTIVE ACTION

The research program began as a study of the emergence of norms (Heckathorn 1988). A problem faced in any such study is that the origins of most norms lie deep in the inaccessible past. For example, all societies have norms regulating theft, interpersonal violence, and deception. Though these norms are subject to contextual variations, as when higher-status people are granted privileges denied their social inferiors, and they change over time, as when new technologies such as the Internet create new opportunities for theft and deception, changes tend to be slow and are heavily influenced by established conventions. Examples of pristine norm emergence are rare.

As I was searching for contexts where norm emergence could be studied, I recalled a story told by a friend's father (Will Brothers) concerning his experiences as a drill instructor in a U.S. army boot camp during World War II. Discipline in U.S. boot camps is based on collective punishment; if one recruit breaks a rule, all recruits in the barracks are punished. Recruits whose violations have provoked the punishment of their peers are sometimes beaten in an institution known as the "blanket party." The speed with which these norms emerge is remarkable—they literally emerge and are vigorously enforced overnight. Whereas recruits might otherwise enjoy watching peers challenge the authority of the drill instructor, much as class clowns earn the esteem of their peers by tormenting teachers, norms prohibiting challenges to authority emerge quickly and are fiercely enforced in boot camps. Further investigation revealed that use of collective punishment in boot camps has been discussed both by sociologists (Gilham 1982) and by playwrights (e.g., Neil Simon in *Biloxi Blues*).

Collective Sanctions and Norm Emergence

Norm emergence based on collective punishment is explicable as purposive behavior. When the actions of others can provoke collective punishment, this creates a *regulatory interest*, that is, an incentive to regulate the actions. Described in economic terms, the action generates *externalities* (i.e., costs resulting from the collective punishment triggered by the action). Thus, the creation and enforcement of norms occurs when individuals act based on regulatory interests, which in turn are based on externalities. Similarly, norms can be created by collective rewards, as when members of a team earn rewards based on the team's success. The recognition that collective sanctions, either collective punishment or collective rewards, could trigger norm creation suggested that settings in which these were used could serve as a real-world laboratory for studying norm emergence.

Note that here norms are not seen merely as constraints on behavior, but rather as something that social actors *do*, that is, as a form of social action. Some actions affect only the actor. Other actions have consequences for others, especially the exercise of social influence, in which the aim of the action is to affect others' behavior. Social influence can take many forms, including persuasion intended to make others want to act in the intended way, incentives such as promises and threats, and even physical compulsion. By whatever means, individuals have considerable ability to influence one another's behavior. This is one of the consequences of mutual interdependence, that all of us are dependent in myriad ways upon those around us. An especially important form of social influence is based on social approval, a form of sanction that is important in all human societies. Though exercise of some social influence is idiosyncratic, much social influence is based on widely shared regulatory interests. When a widely shared regulatory interest leads to a consistent and coordinated exercise of social influence—that is, to *collective action*—a social norm can be said to exist. Thus, social norms are a form of collective social action. For example, the preference for physical safety is the regulatory interest underlying norms limiting violence, and the preference for security in one's possessions is the regulatory interest underlying norms prohibiting theft. These are regulatory interests that are, in a sense, built into the human condition, so all societies have norms limiting violence and defining property rights. The origins of these norms are therefore lost in antiquity. In contrast, when regulatory interests are created by collective sanctions, either collective reward or collective punishment, this creates a sort of real-world laboratory for the study of norm emergence.

The next step in the project was a survey of the literature on collective sanctions, which turned out to be voluminous. However, it was also fragmented, divided into a number of unrelated literatures. For example, there is a large anthropological and historical literature. Most traditional legal systems are based on a principle of corporate responsibility, in which the extended family is jointly responsible for each member's actions. In nineteenth-century Albania, if a person from one village killed someone from another's village, anyone from the victim's village was entitled to kill anyone from the culprit's village within twenty-four hours of the offence, and to kill anyone from the extended family of the culprit within forty-eight hours (Heckathorn 1988). Obviously, this strengthened incentives to regulate behavior within one's village and within one's household. Similarly, in traditional China, capital punishment for especially serious offences was extended to the culprit's father, brothers, and son; and women from the family were sold into slavery. As in the U.S. boot camp, the effect of such a system of collective sanctions was to strengthen the incentives of family members to regulate one another. Other literatures focus on collective sanctions in schools, firms, and prisons. Each documents cases in which collective sanctions create compliance norms, thereby co-opting informal norms, making them into an extension of the system of legal or organizational authority. When collective sanctions are successful, the norms that reinforce the authority of the agent controlling the sanction are termed *compliance norms.*

However, collective sanctions are not always successful, as illustrated by the Algerian revolution. According to Heggoy (1972:235), the French army overreacted to terrorism in Algiers:

> the terrorist cells were dismantled and most of the members were arrested or killed. The strategic victory, however, belonged to the nationalists, who reaped immense political gains from the high-handed military tactics. [The French] created isolated

> Algerian ghettos whose occupants grew increasingly united in their hatred of France. . . . The difference between Algerians and Europeans living in Algeria became markedly clearer. . . . This development forced the two communities to drift further and further apart. The nationalists capitalized on the social fault thus created and undertook the leadership of the Algerian population as a whole.

In essence, the nationalists used terror tactics to provoke the French colonial government to punish collectively and withhold collective rewards from the Algerian middle class and native Algerians in general. The result was to increase the incentives for previously procolonial Algerians to throw in their lot with the nationalists. This use of polarizing tactics based on terror is a time-honored tactic for fomenting revolution. Classic examples are the Sicarri and Zealots who opposed the Roman Empire's rule of Judea starting in the year A.D. 4. Public assassinations of Roman soldiers provoked the Romans into reprisals against civilians, which in turn increased public opposition to the Romans, eventually resulting in revolt (see Rapoport 1984).

Thus, collective sanctions create *ambivalent* incentives: incentives both to create and enforce compliance norms, and also opposite incentives to attack the source of the sanctions, to destroy its ability to dispense collective punishment or withhold collective rewards.

A formal mathematical model was constructed to explain when collective sanctions would either result in compliance norms or provoke revolt and to unify the diverse literatures in which collective sanctions were analyzed (see Heckathorn 1988). Consistent with the conception of norm emergence and enforcement as a form of purposive action, the first step in constructing the model was to define the actors composing the system. This included both the group of individuals subject to the collective sanction and the agent controlling the sanction. The second step was to define the options available to each actor and the costs of choosing each option. The agent was assumed to have issued some form of dictate, it had a specified ability to monitor behavior within the group to determine the degree of compliance with the dictate, and it could choose a threshold level of noncompliance that would trigger sanctions of specified severity. No prejudgment was made regarding either the extent of the agent's monitoring capacity or the severity of the collective sanction. These served as variables in the model, because one of the aims was to study the effects of changes in these terms. The members of the group made two interrelated choices. First, they were assumed to be able to choose whether to comply with the dictate. Second, they could choose to employ whatever social influence they possessed to encourage others to comply, thereby supporting a compliance norm, they could revolt, by seeking to deny the agent the ability to dispense collective punishment or withhold collective rewards, or they could do neither and remain passive. No prejudgment was made regarding the costs of complying with the agent's dictate, the extent to which each individual could control the behavior of others (i.e., group cohesion), the costs of exercising that control, the vulnerability of the agent to revolt, the cost of participating in a revolt, and the size of the group subject to collective sanctions. These also served as variables in the system, because the aim was to understand the consequences of changes in such factors as group size and cohesion. Third, mathematical analyses were carried out to determine how each of the model's variables affected the strength of the incentive to either create compliance norms or revolt.

The analyses revealed that controlling a group through collective incentives is rather like walking a tightrope. For the same factors that encourage members to choose compliance over passivity, such as employing a strong collective sanction, may also induce them to revolt. Similarly, moderately stringent demands for group compliance are most effective in producing compliance norms, because too stringent demands for group compliance tend to provoke revolt because sanctions come to be seen as inevitable, and too lenient demands cause the agent's dictate to be ignored. Another conclusion was that moderately cohesive groups are most effectively controlled by collective sanctions, because highly cohesive groups tend to revolt, and atomized groups lack the capacity to create effective compliance norms. In general, collective sanctions are most effective when used by a strong agent to control a small and relatively cohesive group, as in the example of the boot camp. Collective sanctions fail when used by vulnerable agents against a large and dispersed group, as in the example of the French in Algeria.

The analyses also lead to the recognition of institutional means that have evolved to reduce the revolt-inducing potential of collective sanctions. For example, when criminal punishment extends from the culprit to the culprit's family, the effect is not merely to strengthen incentives to encourage family members to behave lawfully, but also to encourage family members to assist and even join in criminal pursuits. To invert the usual phrase: if one will do the time, one might as well do the crime. To avoid such problems, the Chinese legal system permitted parents to divorce a child by making a payment to the emperor in anticipation of any damage the child might do. This helped to ensure that an incorrigible family member would not pull the entire family into complicity with or active participation in wrongdoing. The question of the effectiveness of the Israeli policy of blowing up the family homes of accused terrorists has been much debated. Whereas it may deter some measure of terrorism, it may also foster hostility toward the Israeli government, and thus may increase rather than reduce resistance. According to this model, the ultimate effectiveness of this policy would depend upon the stringency of sanctions, the perceived vulnerability of the Israeli government, and the cohesiveness of the Arab families involved, especially whether the person whose actions triggered sanctions continued to live in the household, and hence was under the potential control of household members.

Network-Mediated Social Control

The literature on collective sanctions focuses on special settings, including total institutions and revolutionary systems. However, after studying these sanctions, it became apparent that they are less rare and exotic than had been previously recognized (Heckathorn 1990). For virtually all individuals are members of groups with which they are interdependent. These include groups of family members, friends, neighbors, coworkers, and others with whom they interact regularly. To the extent that members of a group are interdependent, events that impact on any individual have consequences that extend to other group members. For example, when one person is promoted on the job or fired, the sanction spills over and affects family members and friends. Therefore, except in the limited case of social isolates, almost all social sanctions targeted at an individual generate collective rewards or punishments that impinge on his or her primary group. Imprisonment is an example of a punishment that spills over to others. It is not merely a personal calamity; it frequently drives whole families into poverty. Similarly, rewards spill over when a family's major breadwinner earns an important promotion because it improves the entire family's circumstances. Due to the spillover of rewards and punishments from individuals to others, social sanctions are virtually never individualized. Instead, they give rise to collective rewards or collective punishments.

Given that most social sanctioning includes both an individual and a collective component, behavioral compliance can arise from either of two theoretically distinguishable sources (see figure 4.1). First, it can arise from individual sanction-based control directed at an actor by an agent such as a teacher, parent, neighbor, or AIDS-prevention counselor. For example, an agent may target an actor with the promise of a reward or a threat of punishment. The result is a dyadic relation of the sort presumed in most analyses of influence relations. This is represented by the hollow arrow in figure 4.1. Second, compliance can also arise from network-mediated control, as when students obey teachers because punishment administered by the school would be augmented by parents, or when workers hold onto

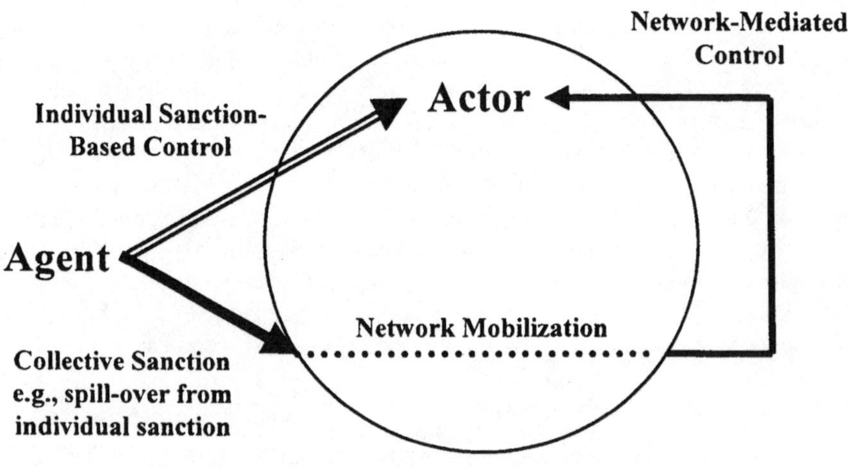

Figure 4.1. Network Embeddedness of Social Influence

disagreeable jobs because unemployment would inflict hardship on their families. In these cases, control occurs through a two-step process. First, the actor's group is promised a collective reward or threatened with a collective punishment based on whether the actor complies. Second, the group responds to that incentive by controlling the actor. In this way, the agent's influence is amplified through the group in which the target of control is embedded. This two-step process is represented by the solid arrows in figure 4.1.

Control based on individual sanctions works by altering peoples' *inclinations*, that is, their preferences regarding their own personal behavior (see table 4.1). It does this by using what may be termed *primary incentives*, such as performance-specific rewards or punishments. In contrast, network-mediated social control works by altering peoples' *regulatory interests*, that is, their preferences regarding how others behave. Network-mediated social control does this by using what may be termed *secondary incentives*, such as rewards or punishments based on the performance of peers. In other words, secondary sanctions create externalities—costs or benefits that are contingent on the behavior of others. Thus, secondary sanctions alter the externalities upon which regulatory interests are based.

Building on the previous analysis of collective sanctions, a formal model was constructed to analyze systems that include both primary and secondary incentives. In many respects, the setup for the model resembled the previous model. The system included both an agent and a group subject to the agent's sanctions. However, the sanction had not merely a collective sanction, but also individual

Table 4.1. Network-Mediated Control: Basic Terms

Two Type of Preferences

Inclination—A person's preferences regarding his or her own personal behavior.
Regulatory Interest—A person's preferences regarding how others should behave.

Two Types of Incentives

Primary Incentive—A reward or punishment that targets a specific individual based on his or her performance. If sufficiently strong, this changes the individual's inclinations.
Secondary Incentive—A reward or punishment administered to a group based on the performance of one of the group's members. If sufficiently strong, this changes the members' regulatory interests.

Two Types of Behavioral Control

Individual Sanction-Based Control—Behavioral control based on primary incentives that alter inclinations, thereby motivating compliance.

This is the type of control typically assumed in studies of organizational power and in theories of deviance and crime.

Network-Mediated Control—Behavioral control in which a secondary incentive alters group members' regulatory interests and thereby motivates them to exert control over one another.

According to the theory of network-mediated control, this is the type of social control that accounts for most compliance within organizations and communities.

sanctions, sanctions that could be targeted to individuals. Consistent with the recognition that when members of a group are interdependent, something that affects one individual thereby affects all of them, each individual sanction was assumed to spill over to other group members, thereby generating a collective sanction. The magnitude of that spillover served as a variable in the model. Members of the group could choose among multiple options. First, as in the previous model, they could choose whether to comply with the agent's dictates. Second, again as in the previous model, they could choose whether to use their influence to pressure others into compliance, or they could remain passive. Because the focus was on the relationship between primary and secondary incentives, the option of revolt was dropped from the model, and replaced with the option to oppose the emergence of compliance norms. This option involved exercising social influence to prevent others from creating and enforcing compliance norms. Variables in this model included the strength of the individualized sanction, the amount of spillover, which in turn determines the strength of the collective sanction, the cost of exercising compliant control (i.e., the cost of participating in enforcing compliance norms), the strength of the control, the cost of oppositional control, and the strength of that form of control. The interpretation of this basic model was broader than in the previous collective sanction analysis. For the agent could represent not merely purposive agents, such as supervisors, teachers, or police officers, but also a natural process, as in what game theorists term a "game against nature." For natural processes can also have both individualized and collective effects. For example, fire can spread to threaten neighbors' homes or fields, and unsanitary conditions can trigger epidemics. Thus, the "agent" could represent a collective bad, such as fire or disease, or a collective good, such as agricultural land or a fishery. With this expanded interpretation, the analysis was broadened to apply to collective action systems in general. The analysis of this model was based on a view of actors as purposive in the sense that their behavior was incentive driven (Heckathorn 1990).

A central conclusion from the theory was that secondary incentives could be both more efficient and more effective than primary incentives (Heckathorn 1990). This occurs when the means for intragroup control are both cheap and effective, as occurs in cohesive groups where peer approval is an important sanction. These conditions fit many primary groups such as family and friendship groups. In the case of individualized sanctions, compliance costs are internal. The targeted actor either complies or refuses to comply with the directive, and thereby bears whatever costs are involved. In contrast, in the case of secondary incentives, compliance costs are external. The targeted actor either succeeds or fails in inducing another actor to comply, so the costs of compliance are borne by that other actor, and the targeted actor bears merely the typically minimal cost of exercising social influence. It is usually easier to tell others what to do than to do it oneself. In extreme cases, one might urge others to endure great suffering to avoid minor inconvenience or embarrassment to oneself. As a result of the externalization of the costs of compliance, secondary incentives can produce a state termed "overcontrol" (Heckathorn 1990, 1991), in which compliance occurs even though its costs exceed those of noncompliance. This produces a social dilemma in which collective gains result not from strengthening but from weakening normative controls (Heckathorn 1990). To the extent that this occurs, secondary incentives can be so effective that they can produce superoptimal levels of compliance, and thereby create "zealots" in Coleman's (1990) sense.

A second reason for the exceptional effectiveness of secondary incentives concerns monitoring. Monitoring for primary incentives is undertaken by the agent controlling the sanctions. Police, teachers, and supervisors typically can observe only a small portion of behavior, so monitoring is difficult when activities cannot be geographically confined. In contrast, secondary incentives operate through peer influence, and peers tend to be far more effective monitors of behavior (Heckathorn 1990).

A third reason for the exceptional effectiveness of secondary incentives concerns what is termed the "hidden cost of reward." Material rewards may undermine intrinsic motivation when they are framed as "pay" rather than as "recognition" for achievement (Deci and Ryan 1985). This creates a dilemma for organizations that rely on primary incentives, because if their ability to reward symbolically is limited, they must rely on material rewards. In contrast, secondary incentives harness peer pressure, so they rely on nonmaterial rewards such as peer approval to secure compliance. Thus, whatever intrinsic motivation exists will be preserved, and even strengthened, because of peer support. Secondary incentives do, however, present a potential problem. If the secondary incentives employ material rewards, might they undermine intrinsic motivations to engage in peer influence? That is, might they weaken preexisting peer norms? According to the formal model, this does not occur because the exercise of peer influence entails a *commitment.* When a person urges peers to act in a certain way, that person publicly affirms the special value of that behavior. If that person then attempts to retreat from the commitment, he or she risks appearing opportunistic or hypocritical. Thus, inducing individuals to affirm publicly the value of acts serves as a means to strengthen their commitment to them. Indeed, public affirmations of commitment to particular ways of behaving are a fundamental and powerful social mechanism for creating and maintaining social cohesion.

The implication of this analysis is that treating relationships of power and authority as a set of dyadic relationships between superordinate and subordinate is a mistake, for reactions to sanctions depend on the networks in which the individuals are embedded. These groups can either amplify the effects of sanctions—and thereby enhance authority—or counter the effects of the sanctions—and thereby undermine the authority. Furthermore, the analyses suggest that much legal and organizational control derives not from the dyadic relationship between controller and target of control, but rather from the circuitous process described as network-mediated control. The implication is that some of the literature on legal and organizational control must be rethought to take into account the embedding of control relationships within larger social systems.

This theory of collective action resolved a problem that afflicted Olson's (1965) theory. According to Olson, the manner in which collective action is organized depends on group size. In small groups, each individual's stake in collective action is so strong that participants are not tempted to free ride. Each individual's net gain from his or her own participation exceeds its cost. These groups are termed "privileged." In medium sized groups, a temptation to free ride exists that is controlled through strategic interaction, in which each individual's contribution is conditional upon the contribution of others. Thus, collective action is based on reciprocity. In large groups Olson argued that collective action required selective incentives, such as punishment for noncontributors (e.g., criminal penalties for tax evasion) or rewards for contributors. Individuals then contribute, not because they value the collective good, but merely because of the sanctions. Thus, contribution is a *by-product of the sanctions.* Thus, the decision to contribute to the collective good is decoupled from any valuation of the collective good. This *by-product theory of collective action* has been criticized, because by explaining too much, it explains too little. It explains contribution in terms of selective incentives, but it does not explain the origins of those incentives.

A system of selective incentives, including a normative system, is itself a collective good. For the norms confer benefits even on those who did not contribute to their production, that is, those who did not participate in norm enforcement. Therefore, a free-rider problem arises, termed the *second-order free-rider problem* (for an analysis, see Heckathorn 1989). The problem with Olson's by-product theory is that it does not explain how this problem is resolved. Yet, the above model provides a resolution. Recall that in the model, regulatory interests govern the exercise of social influence, and the cost of exercising that influence is generally low. It is almost always easier to tell someone else what to do, than to do it oneself. When a collective good is valued, this creates a regulatory interest, an incentive to encourage others to contribute to its production. Regulatory interests are strengthened based on the number of persons one can control, the effectiveness of that control, and valuation of the outcome of that control. Though this regulatory interest can be weak in large groups, if the costs of exercising influence are correspondingly low, even weak regulatory interests can shape the exercise of influence. Therefore, in large groups, where the significance of any individual's contribution is small, norms mandating contribution can nonetheless arise. Thus, regulatory interests provide the link that was missing in Olson's theory, between valuation of the collective good, and selective incentives.

The model was further extended to analyze the effects of group heterogeneity on norms (Heckathorn 1993). In a series of papers, Marwell, Oliver, and associates (Oliver, Marwell, and Teixeira 1985) had argued that contrary to conventional wisdom (Olson 1965), increases in both group size and heterogeneity promote collective action. This occurred, they argued, because the larger and more diverse a group, the greater would be the number of individuals with an especially strong interest in promoting collective action. This group would then serve as a "critical mass" that would trigger the emergence of collective action. This analysis considered only a single way in which collective action could be organized, voluntary cooperation in which each individual chooses independently whether to contribute to the collective endeavor. They therefore ignored selective incentives.

To evaluate the Marwell-Oliver analysis, the network-mediated control model was extended to include three forms of heterogeneity, variation in the extent to which the collective good was valued, variations in the cost of contributing to the collective good, and variations in the size of the contribution the individual could make. More specifically, each of these terms was assumed to be normally distributed. For example, whereas in the previous analysis (Heckathorn 1990), all group members were assumed to value the collective good equally, in this new analysis (Heckathorn 1993), valuations varied around a specified mean and standard deviation.

The conclusions from this analysis differed from those of Marwell and Oliver. For the analysis (Heckathorn 1993) showed that depending on the circumstances, heterogeneity can either promote collective action, or it can cause the group to fragment into mutually antagonistic factions. The latter can occur when what is for some a collective good is for others a collective bad, or when costs of contribution vary. Such cases are common in real-world collective action problems. For example, when environmentalists promote regulations to protect what they see as valuable and fragile ecosystems, the affected industries often complain about loss of jobs. The analysis further showed that polarization is especially likely when collective action is organized through selective incentives. For selective incentives compel even those who lack any interest in the collective good to contribute, and thereby provide those individuals with an incentive to mobilize in opposition. This was an issue Marwell and Oliver did not consider, because they considered only voluntary contributions. However, public policies reflect recognition of the potentially divisive nature of selective incentives. Politicians are frequently reluctant to support use of public funds for controversial programs. For example, in New York, state-sanctioned needle exchanges do not receive public funds. They operate through private donations. This ensures that individuals who oppose these exchanges will not be taxed to support a program they do not support, and thereby weakens their incentive to mobilize in opposition to the exchanges.

INSTITUTIONAL DESIGN

The second phase of this research program was based on a chance meeting. After having concluded that collective incentives were potentially more effective than the individualized incentives upon which most of the literature on organizational and social control was based, I began seeking ways to test this proposition. At that time, I met a medical sociologist, Robert Broadhead, and we began discussing a process evaluation he had conducted of AIDS-prevention projects targeting active injection drug users in San Francisco and New York. He was struck by an apparent paradox. The interventions worked quite well in reducing AIDS risk behavior such as sharing syringes. Yet the outreach workers who carried out the community education performed poorly. Broadhead suggested that the solution to this paradox lies in the role of injectors—they played a highly active role in passing along what they had learned from the outreach workers to their peers, thereby amplifying the impact of the intervention.

Over a series of lunches, Broadhead and I discussed the question of whether my work on collective action could be used as the basis for a new form of AIDS-prevention intervention that would create and strengthen prevention norms among injectors. More specifically, the idea was to base the intervention on secondary rather than primary incentives, so that the target of the intervention, active injectors, would take over many of the roles typically performed by full-time professionals. Broadhead's evaluation of outreach worker–based interventions demonstrated that injectors were capable of playing an energetic and constructive role in a prevention intervention, so the idea seemed promising.

Some background on traditional approaches to AID prevention may be useful. Traditional AIDS-prevention efforts for injection drug users (IDUs) have been based on a "provider-client" model called "street-based outreach" (Brown and Beschner 1993). The model involves hiring a small number of community members, usually ex-addicts or people with street credentials, to contact and work with members of their own community as clients. They do this by going into neighborhoods as "outreach workers" (OWs) to distribute AIDS-prevention materials and information, and to recruit injection drug users (IDUs) to various programs and services, including research interviews conducted by social scientists.

Outreach projects operate under conditions that cause hierarchical supervision to break down. First, moral hazard problems abound because of the opportunities to gain illicitly from working in active drug scenes. For example, Broadhead and Fox (1990) reported cases where outreach workers used their jobs as a cover for drug dealing and fencing stolen goods. Second, adverse selection problems are severe. Being streetwise is an essential qualification for an OW. Such individuals are generally accomplished hustlers, so distinguishing those with a sincere desire to work to prevent AIDS from those who simply wish to hustle a project is virtually impossible; projects can only find out they have been conned *ex post* (Broadhead and Heckathorn 1994). Finally, monitoring of performance is necessarily limited because AIDS-prevention outreach occurs on the street, in single-room-occupancy hotels, public housing projects, public parks and so on. In sum, moral hazard and adverse selection problems are unusually severe, and monitoring of OWs' performance is limited. The result is an array of organizational problems that invite and allow poor performance by OWs to go on virtually unnoticed, and that push outreach projects toward inertia (Broadhead and Heckathorn 1994).

In contrast, IDUs responded impressively to the outreach services they received; IDUs adopted many risk reduction measures, and they volunteered and substantially augmented the efforts of OWs. Put simply, IDUs went well beyond the role of being mere clients; their response to traditional outreach was far more robust and far-reaching than were the efforts of outreach projects themselves.

In light of users' responsiveness, an AIDS-prevention intervention that relied on IDUs as active collaborators seemed feasible. Such an intervention would contrast with the traditional model that turns IDUs into clients of, and makes them dependent on, paid staffs of OWs. The model would also draw upon and strengthen the sharing rituals and norms of reciprocity that already underlie and sustain drug user networks in the first place (Preble and Casey 1969). It would do so by enhancing the mutual opportunities and incentives for IDUs to work with their own peers, and to invest themselves in their own intervention.

A Peer-Driven Intervention

Based on the theory of network-mediated social control (Heckathorn 1990), we designed such a model, called a "Peer-Driven Intervention" (PDI), that began operating in March, 1994 in eastern Connecticut (Broadhead and Heckathorn 1994). The PDI was compared to a traditional outreach intervention operating in a separate but demographically similar community. The PDI uses secondary incentives to harness the potentially enormous power of peer-pressure as a means for altering behavior.

The PDI design employed a two-step process. First, the essential activities of traditional outreach were identified. Second, a structure of secondary incentives was implemented that offers IDUs recognition and modest material rewards for encouraging their drug-using peers to carry out prevention activities in their own community.

The first task of traditional outreach is recruiting IDUs into prevention programs. As in traditional programs, the nexus of the PDI is a storefront facility within which AIDS testing and counseling services are offered, as well as risk reduction education and materials such as bleach kits and condoms. In the PDI, IDUs are motivated to recruit other users for the above services via a coupon system: for each IDU recruited bearing a coupon, the user who recruited him or her receives a monetary reward. Only modest rewards are required, because the cost involved in exercising influence over peers is small,

Table 4.2. Incentive Structures in Two Types of Interventions

Task	*Traditional Outreach Intervention*	*Peer-Driven Intervention*
Recruit users for interviews, AIDS education, and HIV antibody test counseling.	Outreach Workers (OWs) are assigned the task of accessing and recruiting injection drug users (IDUs) in the community. Continued employment is conditional on satisfactory job performance. The reward structure relies on primary incentives to motivate OWs to provide services to their IDU clients.	Each IDU is given three recruitment coupons. She is then told that if a peer she has recruited comes to the program for an interview with her coupon, she will be rewarded. The monetary reward structure is mixed, because it combines a primary incentive (the reward for being interviewed), and secondary incentives (the rewards for recruiting peers). Project staff also strongly emphasize altruistic motivations for recruiting peers.
Educate users about AIDS, harm reduction, and other health measures.	OWs are assigned the task of educating users in the community. Continued employment is conditional on satisfactory job performance. The reward structure relies on primary incentives to motivate OWs to provide education to their IDU clients.	Each IDU-recruiter who educates a peer about AIDS prevention, as measured by a brief eight-item knowledge test administered before each interview, earns an additional reward. Because a reward is earned from eliciting a positive response from a peer, education is motivated by a secondary incentive. Project staff also strongly emphasize altruistic motivations for educating peers.
Distribute AIDS prevention materials.	OWs are assigned the task of distributing prevention materials in the community.	Before leaving the storefront, each IDU is given prevention materials for her personal use and for distribution to peers. Prevention materials are valued by users, so no exogenous incentives are required for their distribution.

and there now exists widespread concern about AIDS within the injection community—which is to say that *regulatory interests among IDUs concerning AIDS prevention already exist.* Furthermore, recruiting and educating peers involves a public commitment to AIDS prevention that reinforces those regulatory interests. Each recruit, in turn, is also given a small number of coupons to recruit still other IDUs within their drug-using network. Thus, the mechanism coopts user networks to serve as a medium to recruit further IDUs.

This approach has several advantages. First, it puts the burden of identifying recruits on those with the best current information: active users. Second, the PDI's pay-for-performance design recognizes and rewards the most productive recruiters. As a result, subjects are rewarded in direct proportion to the success of their recruitment efforts, and those who recruit no one receive nothing.

Third, a PDI offers a built-in accommodation to the cultural diversity in the user population: with IDUs accessing their peers, the recruitment effort is always couched in culturally appropriate terms for each user subgroup. Thus, built into a PDI is a performance-based reward system that continuously adapts to cultural and other subgroup differences.

Another central task of outreach is distributing AIDS-prevention information. Traditional programs educate IDUs both in the field, and at a storefront, van, or similar space. In a PDI, IDUs are given the training, and incentives to educate their peers in the community. The extent to which IDUs pass on information to those they recruit is measured through questions added to standard interview schedules, and the reward to the recruiter depends on the knowledge of the recruit. This approach has several advantages. First, it puts the responsibility for educating IDUs on those who are most likely to be influential: their peers. Second, it entails considerable repetition. Subjects are first educated by their peer-recruiter, then by project staff, then subjects rehearse what they have learned when educating and recruiting several of their peers. Third, its pay-for-performance design recognizes and rewards the most effective educators.

When the PDI was compared with the traditional outreach project, several findings were notable. The data were based on an initial interview and one six-month follow-up interview that assesses health status and behaviors that put people at risk for AIDS, sexually transmitted diseases, and other drug and sex-related health problems. The first finding was that IDUs can indeed be motivated by secondary incentives to recruit their peers. When compared to the traditional outreach control site, the PDI succeeded in recruiting 50 percent more IDUs during the first calendar year of operation, as well as a sample that was more heterogeneous in drug preference, and drawn from a wider geographic area (Broadhead et al. 1995).

Second, IDUs can be motivated, and are able, to provide effective AIDS-prevention education to their peers in the community. They respond favorably, and sometimes enthusiastically, to the opportunity to acquire potentially life-saving information and share that information with their peers. Some recruiters reported that they went over the lesson several times with their recruits. In anticipation of their role as a peer educator, some IDUs have even taken notes during the education they received from project staff, and some have also called the project to ask for further clarification. Scores on the knowledge assessment test show that peers can educate as effectively as professional OWs, and after IDUs have recruited and educated several peers, recruiters' own knowledge level significantly exceeds that of subjects in the control intervention (Broadhead et al. 1995).

Third, and most significantly, the PDI produces reductions in AIDS risk behaviors, including reductions in estimated injection frequency and syringe sharing. Figure 4.2 summarizes the effects of PDIs on syringe sharing behaviors in New London (Heckathorn et al. 1999), Middletown and Meriden, Connecticut (Broadhead et al. 1998), and Yaroslavl, Russia (Sergeyev et al. 1999). These are compared with the one- and two-year impact results from the project's control

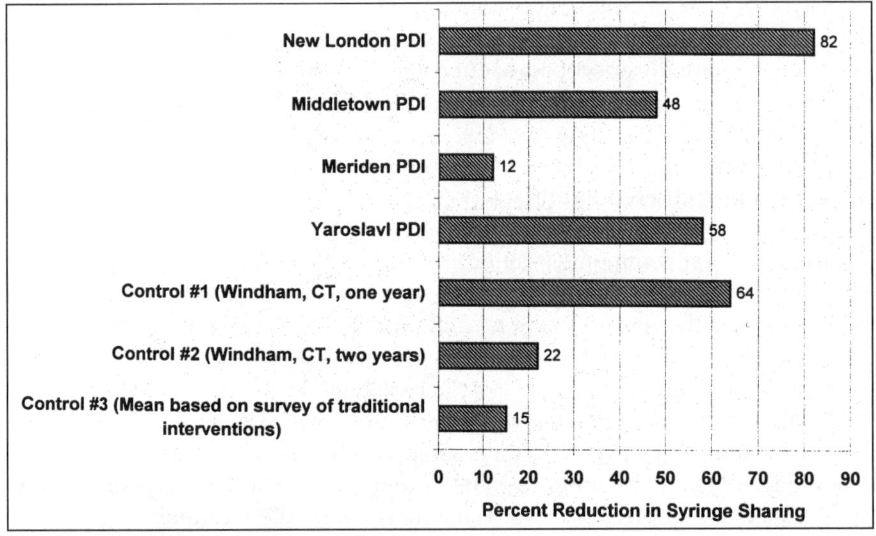

Figure 4.2. Changes in Syringe Sharing by Intervention

site, a traditional intervention implemented in Windham, Connecticut. PDI impact results can also be compared with impact results from the dozens of traditional interventions that have been implemented and evaluated in the U.S. Needle and Coyle (1997) surveyed studies assessing these traditional outreach interventions, and they provide a national benchmark against which PDI impact can be compared.

All interventions reduced syringe sharing, but to varying degrees. Three of the four PDIs produced substantial reductions, from 48 percent in Middletown, 58 percent in Yaroslavl, to 82 percent in New London. The fourth PDI's impact was substantially lower, only 12 percent. Though further research will be required to confirm this hypothesis, this difference appeared to result from a "proximity effect" (Broadhead et al. 1998:52). The three more effective PDIs were located near the center of each city's drug scene. In contrast, subjects in Meriden had less ready access to the PDI, in most cases requiring a twenty-minute bus ride, and then walking a mile. This disadvantaged them in several ways, for example, making it difficult for them to return to the intervention's storefront for prevention materials during which prevention messages could be reinforced.

The impact results from the three controls are also variable. In a survey of dozens of standard interventions conducted by Needle and Coyle (1997), reductions in syringe sharing ranged from 13 percent to 43 percent, with a mean of 15 percent. The one-year and two-year impact results from our project's control site were also variable, with substantially stronger reductions during the first year than for two years. The reasons for this reduction remains unclear, though it may be related to a volunteerism effect, in which the most educable and tractable subjects made themselves available for recruitment by the traditional intervention's professional outreach workers, and after the first year, this especially tractable pool of subjects had been exhausted.

Overall, when the PDI impact results are compared with that from traditional interventions, most of the PDIs perform respectably. Specifically, three of the four PDIs not only exceeded the mean for previously published evaluations of standard interventions, but also exceeded the maximum reduction reported in these studies. These benchmarks were also exceeded during the control intervention's first year, though these results were not sustained. The variability in these results suggests the need for more research to better identify the determinants of intervention impact, but what is clear is that under suitable conditions the PDI can serve as an effective means for reducing AIDS risk behavior.

Fourth and finally, because of its greatly reduced reliance on professional staff, the PDI is far less expensive than traditional outreach. At our control site, the full-time salaries and fringe benefits paid to the OWs resulted in recruitment and education costs that averaged $623 per recruit, as compared to only $14 per recruit in the PDI. Hence there is more than a forty-fold differential in cost. This is an important issue for any public health intervention, because budgets for public health are always limited.

Our approach to AIDS prevention was supported in a report from the Institute of Medicine (1995) of the National Academy of Sciences. The report's aim was "assessing the social and behavioral science base for HIV/AIDS prevention and intervention," and it was "targeted primarily to policy-makers who will be making decisions for the HIV/AIDS research agenda in the next decade." The PDI was described as "the state of the art of preventive intervention."

SAMPLING AND SOCIAL STRUCTURE

The third phase of this research program began as an unanticipated spin-off of the AIDS project. Recall that the PDI's recruitment mechanism was based on a chain-referral process, where the initial respondents (i.e., the "seeds") each recruited several peers, who each recruited several more peers, and so forth as the interventions expanded wave by wave. When designing the intervention, Broadhead and I had concluded that recruitment quotas were necessary to prevent the emergence of professional recruiters, who might then seek to monopolize recruitment rights and even battle for turf. The question was, how should the quota be established? If the quota was too small, recruitment would die out; and if too large, professional recruiters might emerge.

To provide a principled means for exploring these questions, I constructed a mathematical model with which to simulate the recruitment process (Heckathorn 1997). For simplicity in constructing the model, the population was assumed to be indefinitely large, to correspond to an intervention drawing from a large population of potential participants. This model provided the means for simulating the effects of alternative quotas, including exploring the ability of the recruitment process to reach groups who were socially distant from the seeds with which recruitment began. That is, the simulated population was divided into distinct groups, corresponding to race/ethnicity or other social categories, with differential connections among groups. Based on these analyses, the quota was ultimately set at three recruits per respondent.

These simulations produced an unexpected result, the finding that after a modest number of recruitment waves, the composition of the sample became the same, irrespective of the choice of initial seeds. That is, whether all the seeds were drawn from a single category, or dispersed among all the categories, the sample composition ultimately converged upon a single equilibrium. Furthermore, unless population groups were nearly totally socially isolated from one another, this finding was unaffected by the network structure of the population. A bit of checking confirmed that when the recruitment process was modeled as a form of stochastic process called a "Markov chain" (Kemeny and Snell 1960), this result corresponded to a well-known theorem, the law of large numbers for regular Markov chains.

The equilibrium result suggested a new extension of the research program, because it suggested that the AIDS intervention's recruitment process could serve as a sampling process that was *reliable*. That is, were the sampling to be repeated (e.g., starting with a different set of seeds), the sample composition would be the same. Further analysis addressed the issue of *validity*, that is, whether the sample would correspond to the population from which the sample was drawn.

This phase of the project began as an effort to develop better means for sampling hard-to-reach populations such as injectors, and evolved into a new approach to studying social structure. Let us first consider sampling. Great attention has been devoted recently to the problems involved in sampling hidden populations because of two recent events, the AIDS epidemic (Watters and Biernacki 1989; Laumann et al. 1989) and decreases in the accuracy of the U.S. census (Brown et al. 1999). Efforts to address both problems have focused attention on problems in sampling hidden populations. The primary focus has been on injection drug users, men who have sex with men, and the homeless.

Given its small size, using traditional methods to sample a hidden population would be prohibitively expensive. Furthermore, when a hidden population has privacy concerns, it cannot be reached by methods such as household surveys or random digit dialing, nor can these methods reach those with unstable living arrangements as when several families live in an apartment although only one's name appears on the lease (Sudman and Kalton 1986).

Three methods currently dominate studies of hidden populations. First, location sampling involves identifying locations where members of the population can be found, and then deploying interviewers. A problem is that location sampling is practical only for locations that are large and public. However, such large public scenes tend not to draw a representative sample of any hidden population. For example, not all injectors buy their drugs on the street.

Institutional samples are a second method for sampling hidden populations. In the case of drug injectors, samples are drawn from drug-treatment programs and prisons. Here, the researcher relies on the institution to draw the sample. The problem is that only a select group of subjects enter drug treatment programs, prisons, and other institutional settings.

The third method for sampling hidden populations is chain-referral sampling, the best-known form of which is snowball sampling (Goodman 1961). This has traditionally been considered a form of convenience sampling about which no claims of representativeness can be made. In a now-classic article, Erickson (1979:299) argued that the sample begins with a bias because when sampling a hidden population the choice of initial subjects cannot be random, and further biases of an unknown nature are added as the sample expands during subsequent waves. Subsequent to Erickson's analysis, additional biases have been identified, so sources of bias in chain-referral samples include: (1) nonrandom choice of initial subjects, that is, the choice of "seeds"; (2) volunteerism, in which more cooperative subjects agree to participate in larger numbers or masking in which less cooperative subjects are under represented; (3) differentials in recruitment, in which some groups recruit more peers into the study than others; (4) differentials in network size, because referrals occur through network links so groups with larger personal networks will be over sampled; and (5) differentials in homophily, or tendency toward in-group recruitment, because groups with greater homophily will be over sampled. Because of these problems, chain-referral samples have traditionally been seen merely as a form of convenience sample, suitable only for pilot studies and formative research.

Despite this recognition of bias, there has been a resurgence of interest in chain-referral methods because of their unique ability to reach those who would be missed by other methods, including those who shun public gatherings and institutional affiliations. Research on the "small world problem" suggests that any two people in the country are connected by no more than six network links, the now-famous "six degrees of separation." The implication is that everyone could be reached by a maximally expansive chain-referral sample after only a handful of waves.

A prerequisite for the use of chain-referral samples to study hidden populations is that the population be linked by a "contact pattern." That is, members of the population must know one another. These contact patterns are robust in the populations upon which AIDS-prevention research has focused. Injectors form contacts when they buy drugs, and these are strengthened because regular users cultivate multiple sources to ensure continuity of supply. These bonds are further strengthened because drugs are often purchased jointly and shared. The robustness of its contact patterns makes this population ideally suited to chain-referral sampling. Therefore, the best sources of information about injectors in any community are the injectors.

Respondent-Driven Sampling

The design principle of respondent-driven sampling (RDS) is simple. If the biases associated with chain-referral methods are understood, it is possible to redesign the sampling process to eliminate those biases that are not inherent in the method, and to quantify and control those that are inherent in the method. Therefore, RDS includes both a specific method for structuring the chain-referral process to reduce one set of biases, and analytic procedures to weight the sample to compensate for others. In this way, chain-referral sampling can be made into a statistically valid sampling method.

The first source of bias is due to the selection of initial subjects. Figure 4.3 depicts the recruitment tree generated by RDS beginning with a single seed. Over the course of many waves, the sample expanded to include more than one hundred recruits.

An examination of recruitment patterns by ethnicity confirms that the choice of initial subjects does indeed introduce a bias into the sample (see table 4.3). Recruitment reflects *homophily*, a tendency to recruit persons like oneself. For

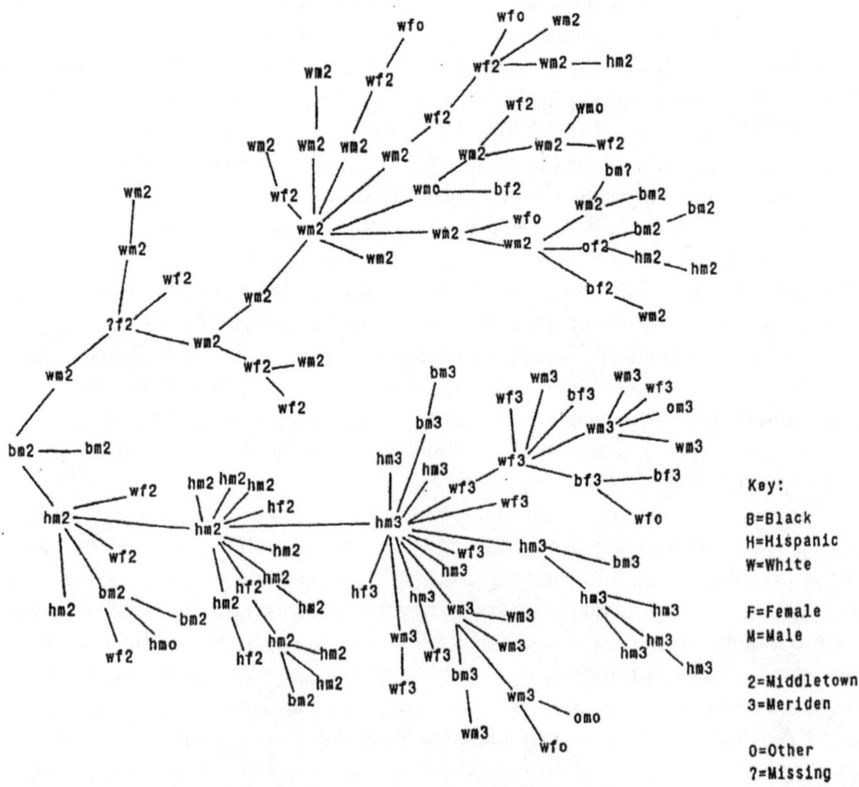

Figure 4.3. Peer Recruitment Network Beginning from a Single Seed

Table 4.3. Race and Ethnicity of Recruits, by Race and Ethnicity of Recruiter (New London)

Race/Ethnicity of Person who Recruited	*Race/Ethnicity of Recruit*				
	W	B	H	O	Total
Non-Hispanic White (W) (n = 65)	73.9%	13.9%	7.7%	4.6%	100%
Non-Hispanic Black (B) (n = 39)	33.3%	51.3%	10.3%	5.1%	100%
Hispanic (H) (n = 19)	31.6%	10.5%	57.9%	0%	100%
Other (O) (n = 7)	28.6%	42.9%	28.6%	0%	100%

example, in a study of injectors in New London, Connecticut, non-Hispanic white injectors recruited, on average, 74 percent other non-Hispanic whites; Hispanics recruited 58 percent Hispanics; and non-Hispanic blacks recruited 51 percent blacks. Only the very small group in the Other category failed to recruit differentially from within.

It might seem that homophily would make chain-referral samples irrevocably biased. For example, a group that had been over represented among the seeds with which recruitment began might seem as though it would remain over represented in the sample. However, as noted above, the manner in which homophily affects recruitment as the chain-referral sample expands from wave to wave can be identified by modeling the process as a form of stochastic model known as a Markov chain (see figure 4.4). A Markov chain consists of a set of two or more states (e.g., subject characteristics such as gender or ethnicity), and transition probabilities from state to state (i.e., probabilities that a subject with a given set of characteristics will recruit a subject with each other possible set of characteristics). As an illustration of a Markov chain, see figure 4.4A, which depicts table 4.3's data on recruitment by race and ethnicity. The four states correspond to the recruiter's race and ethnicity (i.e., Hispanic, non-Hispanic black or white, and other), and the double line arrows depict the transition probabilities within and single line arrows depict transition probabilities across states. Recruitment is a stochastic process and can be visualized as a point whose location corresponds to the state of the most recent recruit, cross-state recruitment moves the point to a different state by following the arrows, and within-state recruitment keeps the point at the same location.

The conclusion from modeling the recruitment process as a Markov chain is that biases introduced by the selection of initial respondents are progressively *weakened* with each recruitment wave. The manner in which this occurs is illustrated in figure 4.5, which depicts the results of two simulations showing how the composition of each wave would have changed had recruitment begun from either Hispanic injectors (figure 4.5A) or non-Hispanic white injectors (figure 4.5B), based on projections from figure 4.4A's recruitment patterns. The vertical axes represents the percentage of injectors of each type, and the

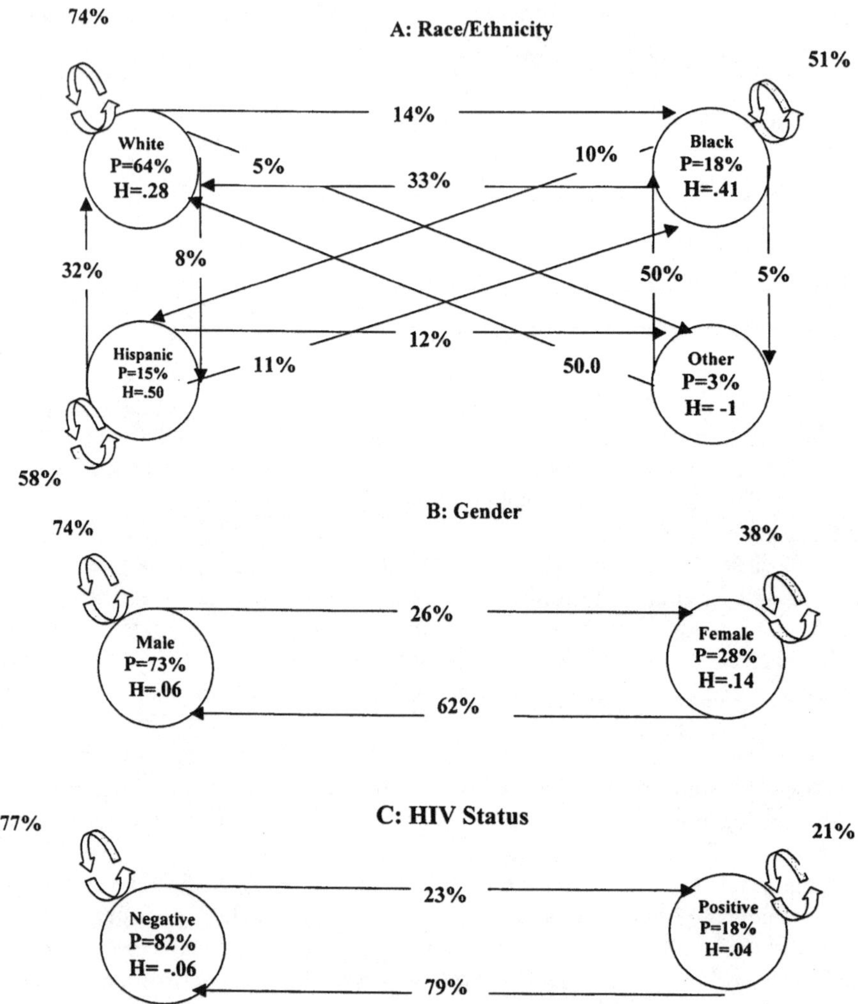

Note: "P" is estimated population; H is estimated homophily

Figure 4.4. Network Structures of Drug Injectors—Patterns of Association Show Varying Degrees of Homophily (New Longdon, CT)

horizontal axes represent the number of recruitment waves, where wave 0 refers to the seed or seeds, which in this exercise were assumed to be ethnically homogeneous. Wave 1 refers to the seeds' recruits; wave 2 refers the recruits' recruits, and so forth. Had recruitment begun with only Hispanic seeds the percentage of Hispanics in each wave decreases from the initial value of 100 percent, to 58 percent in the first wave, 37 percent in the second wave, eventually stabilizing at 18 percent. This stable point is termed the *equilib-*

rium, because it does not change with later waves. When equilibrium is reached, the composition of that and each additional wave is 22.9 percent non-Hispanic blacks, 55.2 percent non-Hispanic whites, 18.2 percent Hispanics, and 3.7 percent other.

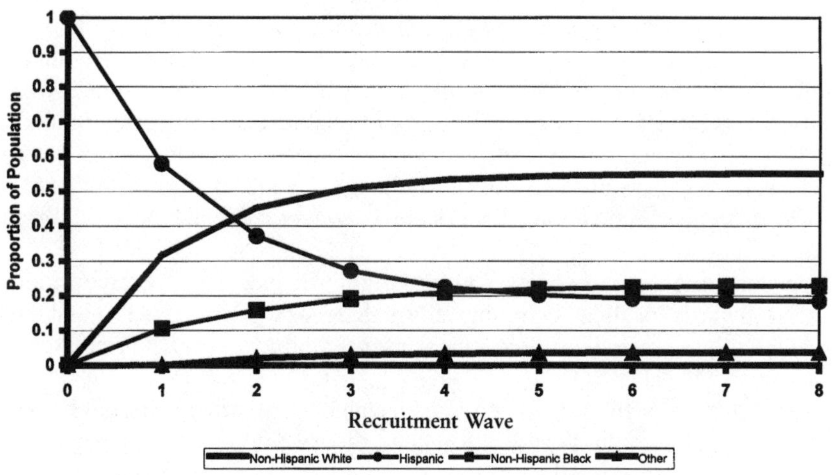

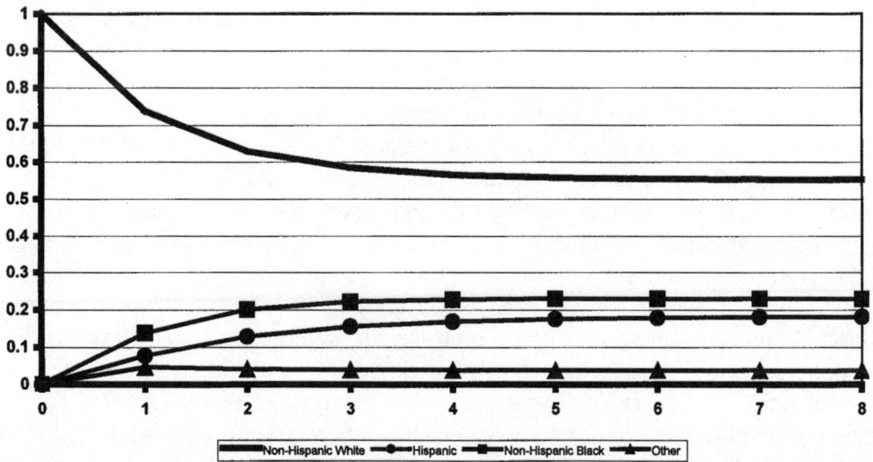

Figure 4.5. Two Simulations of Recruitment in a Respondent-Driven Sample—Race and ethnicity of recruits in a respondent-driven sample, beginning with all Hispanic or non-Hispanic white seeds.

In contrast, in the simulation where recruitment began with only non-Hispanic white seeds (figure 4.5B), the percentage of Hispanics in each wave increases, from the initial value of 0 percent, to 8 percent in wave 1, 13 percent in wave 2, and stabilizes at 18 percent in wave 5 and subsequent waves. Note that after equilibrium is attained, the composition by wave in figure 4.5B is the same as in figure 4.5A. This convergence reflects an important characteristic of RDS. If sampling is allowed to proceed through a minimum number of waves, it will attain an equilibrium that is *independent of the characteristics of the respondents from which sampling began* (Heckathorn 1997). Thus, it does not matter whether all seeds were drawn from the same group or from any mix of groups, the ultimate composition of the sample will be the same. Hence, whatever bias was introduced by the selection of initial respondents is eliminated if sampling is continued through enough waves. After the desired number of subjects is recruited, computations can be performed (see Heckathorn 1997:186) to confirm that the composition of the sample converged with the equilibrium sample composition.

To ensure that referral chains will be lengthy, respondents receive modest financial rewards for their recruiting efforts. A second means used to lengthen referral chains is a quota on recruitment rights, a limit of three recruits per respondent.

A second form of bias arises when especially cooperative respondents volunteer for recruitment in disproportionate numbers. In previous applications of RDS, several measures were employed to reduce this bias. The first was a combination of material and social incentives. Subjects were paid for the interview. A second and more consequential incentive was social, the exercise of influence by the peer recruiter. Using this dual system, even respondents for whom the material reward from the interview was irrelevant could be induced to participate through the social influence of the peer recruiter. In addition to harnessing peer pressure, another means for reducing this source of bias was to ensure that the interview site was located conveniently and in neutral turf. Otherwise, subjects would be under represented for whom the location was accessible only with difficulty, or for whom the location was threatening. Third, the interview staff was trained to treat all subjects respectfully and nonjudgmentally. In addition, amenities such as free coffee were provided. This is crucial for a sampling method that relies on peer recruitment; subjects cannot be expected to recruit peers unless their own experience was positive. To assess this potential source of bias, subjects were asked about the composition of their networks, this was compared to their recruitment patterns, and no significant discrepancies were found (Heckathorn 2002).

Thus, the use of material and social incentives to produce long referral chains serves to reduce the first two sources of bias, those due to the choice of initial subjects and volunteerism. The other three biases associated with chain-referral methods are inherent in the manner in which subjects are recruited into the sample. However, this does not mean that chain-referral sampling need be either invalid or unreliable. For based on a sufficiently detailed understanding of these sources of bias, the sample can be weighted to compensate exactly for them, thereby producing an unbiased sample. The procedure for compensating for each of the three source of bias relies on the same logic. Information gathered during the recruitment process provides the means for quantitatively measuring this bias, and then controlling it through a weighting process.

The third source of bias derives from differential recruitment. This bias occurs when a group recruits especially effectively, because its distinctive recruitment pattern is thereby over represented in the sample—for example, if this group tends to recruit more of another group's members, the latter will be over represented in the sample. The recruitment quotas reduce this form of potential bias, but given that not all subjects fulfill their quotas, variation remains. Previous applications of RDS provide evidence for recruitment differentials. For example, in a study of injectors in Meriden, Connecticut, it was found that HIV positive respondents recruited 69 percent more than HIV negative respondents. Of course, this greater involvement of HIV positive subjects in an AIDS-prevention intervention is easily understandable. Similarly, in that town, injectors aged 26 and more recruited 20 percent more than did injectors aged 18–25, so the older injectors were more energetic. RDS weights the sample to compensate for these differentials, by mathematically projecting what the sample composition would have been had all groups recruited with equal effectiveness (Heckathorn 2002).

Biases due to differentials in network size are controlled in a logically similar manner. When network sizes are unequal, the better-connected group is over sampled. For example, in the study of several small cities in Connecticut, New London, Middletown, and Meriden, HIV positive injectors were found to have consistently larger personal networks by amounts ranging from 28 percent to 36 percent. Therefore, they were reachable by a larger number of potential recruitment chains, and were hence recruited in somewhat greater numbers. The procedure for compensating for differentials in network size is based on the recognition that in RDS, the relationship between recruiter and recruit is almost always reciprocal, where this means that a tie in one direction implies a tie in the opposite direction (Heckathorn forthcoming). For example, if A is a friend to B, then B is typically also a friend to A. In previous applications of RDS, the relationships between recruit and recruiter involved some form of ongoing personal relationship in 97 percent to 99 percent of cases depending on the site. For example, in New London, the recruiter was most commonly a friend (64 percent), followed by an acquaintance (19 percent), or spouse or other sex partner (9 percent), and only 3 percent reported having been recruited by a stranger. The presence of preexisting social relationships between recruit and recruiter results from the combination of a quota on recruitment coupons and the rewards for recruiting. If recruitment coupons were available in unlimited numbers, impersonal forms of recruiting would be possible, for example, placing piles of coupons in locations were potential recruits might gather. However, given that coupons are given out only in very modest numbers, the overwhelming majority of respondents recruit persons with whom they already have a relationship rather than approaching strangers. The RDS method weights the sample to compensate for these differentials, by mathematically projecting what the sample composition would have been had all groups had equal network sizes (Heckathorn 2002). Similarly, biases due to differentials in homophily are controlled through mathematically projecting what the sample composition would have been had all groups had equal homophily. Finally, standard errors are computed based on a variant of boot-strapping (Heckathorn 2002).

Using RDS to Study Social Structure

An advantage of RDS over standard probability sampling is that it provides information not only about the respondents, but also about their social structure. For when respondents recruit their peers they provide information about the social network in which they are embedded, where, as in the works of Simmel, social structure is defined in terms of the structure of affiliations. Furthermore, this information is based not on self-reports, as in network sampling (Granovetter 1976), in which respondents are asked to report on their peers. In contrast in RDS, information on network links is behavioral, having been derived from recruitment records. This is significant, not only because of issues of validity and reliability, but also because analyses need not be limited to information respondents have regarding their peers. Consider, for example, figure 4.4C's depiction of structure by HIV status, which shows that HIV positive respondents are thoroughly integrated in the injector community. That is, both HIV positive and negative respondents have near zero homophily. Such an analysis would not have been possible based only on self-reports, because many injectors do not know the HIV status of their peers, and even if they did have that information, its disclosure without the permission of the peer would be a violation of the Connecticut HIV Confidentiality Law. Such problems do not arise for RDS, because respondents need only provide information regarding themselves, and network links are established behaviorally.

This approach to studying social structure is consistent with social network-based quantitative definitions (Blau 1977; Rapoport 1979). A system is said to lack structure if social relationships are formed randomly. In that case, individuals are indifferent between ties formed within and outside the group. Therefore, the proportion of within-group ties equals the proportional size of the group. As thus defined, structure can take either of two basic forms. First, *homophily* refers to a tendency to form within-group ties. Homophily in the formation of friendships was recognized before the turn of the century by Galton, and it has been found based on age, education, prestige, social class, and race and ethnicity (McPherson and Smith-Lovin 1987). Alternatively, *heterophily* or equivalently, *negative homophily*, refers to a tendency to form out-group ties, for example, tribes with exogamous marriage systems require that marriages occur outside one's clan. As thus defined, a system is *structured* if it reflects either homophily or heterophily. Thus, homophily and heterophily are the elements out of which social structures are built. Figure 4.4 provides graphic depictions of the social structure of injectors in New London, Connecticut, with respect to race/ethnicity, gender, and HIV status.

As thus defined, structure depends both on the form of relationship considered and the type of group. If a basis for group identification is socially irrelevant, it does not serve as a basis for structural differentiation, and homophily is zero. For example, whether one is born in an odd or even month is socially irrelevant, so homophily is zero based on this status. Similarly, in the United States, blood type is socially irrelevant, so homophily is presumably zero. In contrast, in Japan where blood type is widely believed to determine interpersonal compatibility, if that belief comes to shape the formation of relationships, structure will emerge. In contrast, race and ethnicity, and other basic demographic variables, are strongly structuring. Thus, determining whether an attribute affects homophily is a way of determining its social significance. This approach to the analysis of social structure is now being employed to study jazz musicians in four cities, New York, New Orleans, Detroit, and San Francisco (Heckathorn and Jeffri 2001). The aims include determining the extent to which affiliation patterns are determined by musical form (e.g., fusion, classical, or contemporary jazz), rather than the demographic factors, such as race and class, around which affiliation patterns are structured in the larger society.

CONCLUSION

This brief summary of an ongoing research program offers a couple of lessons. One is that the stark separation traditionally existing in sociology between theoretic and applied work need not exist. James Coleman (1990) emphasized the extent to which modern societies are increasingly the product of purposive design. Most of us spend our lives embedded in markets and organizations whose guiding principles are defined by laws and regulations. Politicians play an especially important role in institutional design, at levels ranging from the halls of congress to local zoning boards, and from heads of interest groups to community activists. Decisions made within firms are no less important, particularly because, under the impact of globalization, some firms dwarf in economic power all but the largest countries. Therefore, fundamental institutions are being designed and redesigned, frequently without any systematic assessment of the consequences of those decisions. For example, in the case of AIDS prevention, the traditional approach was not adopted after an exhaustive assessment of available alternatives; it merely borrowed a design from the antipoverty programs of the 1960s. Institutional design is a process to which sociologists should be able to contribute. Indeed, after having made a profession of studying social phenomena, it would bode ill for the future of the profession if sociologists had no useful advice to offer. Many prominent sociologists have combined theoretic and applied work (e.g., James Coleman and Peter Rossi), however this remains the exception. As the example of AIDS-prevention intervention illustrates, even apparently highly abstract theory can have important practical implications.

A second lesson from the research program concerns the inherently uncertain nature of the research enterprise. It is inherent in research that one does not know what the result will be. Otherwise, one would be an engineer. When conducing research, one must remain open to unanticipated results, whatever they may be. This involves not only the obvious requirement that one act with integrity, by accepting disappointing results when a favored theory fails an empirical test. Equally important, it involves remaining alert to opportunities to expand the project, even into wholly unanticipated directions. For example, when I began the study of norm emergence, I had no idea this would become relevant to AIDS prevention; and when beginning the design of the AIDS-prevention intervention, I had no idea that this would lead to improved means for sampling hidden populations and studying social structure. This experience is by no means atypical, even in other research programs in which I have been involved. For example, a study of bargaining resulted in my development of a formal model, resistance theory (Heckathorn 1980,1983), that serves as both an element of network exchange theory (Markovsky, Willer, and Patton 1988), and also provided the basis for a transaction resource theory that was used to analyze negotiation during the U.S. Constitutional Convention of 1787 (Heckathorn and Maser 1987a), the history of regulation of business in the United States (Heckathorn and Maser 1987b), disclosure rules and default provisions in contract law (Coleman, Heckathorn, and Maser 1989), congressional decision making (Heckathorn and Maser 1990), and the debate from 1787 to 1789 over ratification of the U.S. Constitution (Anthony, Heckathorn and Maser 1994). As a researcher, one must remain alert to unanticipated opportunities to move the project into a new direction. Wherever the path leads, one must be prepared to follow.

NOTE

This research was made possible by grants from the Centers for Disease Control and Prevention (U62/CCU114816-01) and the National Institute on Drug Abuse (RO1 DA08014).

REFERENCES

Anthony, Denise L., Douglas D. Heckathorn, and Steven M. Maser. 1994. "Rational Rhetoric in Politics: The Debate over Ratifying the U.S. Constitution." *Rationality and Society* 6:489–518.

Blau, Peter M. 1977. *Inequality and Heterogeneity*. New York: Free Press.

Broadhead, Robert S., and Kathryn J. Fox. 1990. "Takin' It to the Streets: AIDS Outreach as Ethnography." *Journal of Contemporary Ethnography* 19:322–48.

Broadhead, Robert S., and Douglas D. Heckathorn. 1994. "AIDS Prevention Outreach among Injection Drug Users: Agency Problems and New Approaches." *Social Problems* 41:473–95.

Broadhead, Robert S., Douglas D. Heckathorn, Frederick Altice, Yael van Hulst, Michael Carbone, Gerald Friedland, Patrick O'Connor, and Peter Selwyn. Forthcoming. "Increasing Drug User's' Adherence to HIV Theropeutics." *Social Science and Medicine.*

Broadhead, Robert S., Douglas D. Heckathorn, Jean-Paul C. Grund, L. Synn Stern, and Denise L. Anthony. 1995. "Drug Users versus Outreach Workers in Combating AIDS: Preliminary Results of a Peer-Driven Intervention." *Journal of Drug Issues* 25:531–64.

Broadhead, Robert S., Douglas D. Heckathorn, David Weakliem, Denise Anthony, Heather Madray, Robert Mills, and James Hughes. 1998. "Harnessing Peer Networks as an Instrument for AIDS Prevention: Results from a Peer-Driven Intervention." *Public Health Reports* 113, supplement 1:42–57.

Brown, B., and G. M. Beschner. 1993. *Handbook on Risk of AIDS: Injection Drug Users and Sexual Partners.* Westport, CT: Greenwood Press.

Brown, Lawrence D., Morris L. Eaton, David A. Freedman, Stephen P. Klein, Richard A. Olshen, Kenneth W. Wachter, Martin T. Wells, and Donald Ylvisaker. 1999. "Statistical Controversies in Census 2000." *Technical Report 537*, Department of Statistics, U.C. Berkeley.

Coleman, James S. 1990. *Foundations of Social Theory.* Cambridge, MA: Belknap Press.

Coleman, Jules L., Douglas D. Heckathorn, and Steven M. Maser. 1989. "A Bargaining Theory Approach to Default Provisions and Disclosure Rules in Contract Law." *Harvard Journal of Law and Public Policy* 12:639–709.

Deci, Edward L., and Richard M. Ryan. 1985. *Intrinsic Motivation and Self-Determination in Human Behavior.* New York: Plenum.

Erickson, Bonnie H. 1979. "Some Problems of Inference from Chain Data." *Sociological Methodology* 10:276–302.

Gilham, Steven A. 1982. "The Marines Build Men: Resocialization in Recruit Training." Pp. 231–41 in Reid Luhman (ed.), *The Sociological Outlook.* Belmont, CA: Wadsworth.

Goodman, L. A. 1961. "Snowball Sampling." *Annals of Mathematical Statistics* 32:148–70.

Granovetter, Mark. 1976. "Network Sampling: Some First Steps." *American Journal of Sociology* 83:1287–1303.

Heckathorn, Douglas D. 1980. "A Unified Model for Bargaining and Conflict." *Behavioral Science* 25:261–84.

———. 1983. "Extensions to Power-Dependence Theory: The Concept of Resistance." *Social Forces* 61:1206–31.

———. 1988. "Collective Sanctions and the Emergence of Prisoner's Dilemma Norms." *American Journal of Sociology* 94:535–62.

———. 1989. "Collective Action and the Second-Order Free-Rider Problem." *Rationality and Society* 1:78–100.

———. 1990. "Collective Sanctions and Compliance Norms: A Formal Theory of Group-Mediated Social Control." *American Sociological Review* 55:366–84.

———. 1991. "Extensions of the Prisoner's Dilemma Paradigm: The Altruist's Dilemma and Group Solidarity." *Sociological Theory* 9:34–52.

———. 1993. "Collective Action and Group Heterogeneity: Voluntary Provision versus Selective Incentives." *American Sociological Review* 58:329–50.

———. 1997. "Respondent Driven Sampling: A New Approach to the Study of Hidden Populations." *Social Problems* 44:174–99.

———. 2002. "Respondent Driven Sampling II: Deriving Valid Population Estimates from Chain-Referral Samples of Hidden Populations." *Social Problems* 49:11–34.

Heckathorn, Douglas D., Robert S. Broadhead, Denise L. Anthony, and David L. Weakliem. 1999. "AIDS and Social Networks: Prevention through Network Mobilization." *Sociological Focus* 32:159–79.

Heckathorn, Douglas D., and Joan Jeffri. 2001. "Finding the Beat: Using Resondent-Driven Sampling to Study Jazz Musicians." *Poetics* 28:307–29.

Heckathorn, Douglas D., and Steven M. Maser. 1987a. "Bargaining and Constitutional Contracts." *American Journal of Political Science* 31:142–68.

———. 1987b. "Bargaining and the Sources of Transaction Costs: The Case of Government Regulation." *Journal of Law Economics and Organization* 3:69–98.

———. 1990. "The Contractual Architecture of Public Policy: A Critical Reconstruction of Lowi's Typology." *Journal of Politics* 52:1101–23.

Heggoy, Alf Andres. 1972. *Insurgency and Counterinsurgency in Algeria.* Bloomington: Indiana University Press.

Institute of Medicine. 1995. *Assessing the Social and Behavioral Science Base for HIV/AIDS Prevention and Intervention.* Washington, D.C.: National Academy Press.

Kemeny, John G., and J. Laurie Snell. 1960. *Finite Markov Chains.* Princeton, NJ: Van Nostrand.

Laumann, Edward O., John H. Gagnon, Stuard Michaels, Robert T. Michael, and James S. Coleman. 1989. "Monitoring the AIDS Epidemic in the United States: A Network Approach." *Science* 244:1186–89.

Markovsky, Barry, David Willer, and Travis Patton. 1988. "Power Relations in Exchange Networks." *American Sociological Review* 53:220–36.

McPherson, J. Miller, and Lynn Smith-Lovin. 1987. "Homophily in Voluntary Organizations: Status Distance and the Composition of Face-to-Face Groups." *American Sociological Review* 52:370–79.

Needle, Richard H., and Susan Coyle. 1997. "Community-Based Outreach Risk Reduction Strategy to Prevent HIV Risk Behaviors in Out-of-Treatment Injection Drug Users (IDUs)." Paper presented at the National Institutes of Health Consensus Development Conference on Interventions to Prevent HIV Risk Behaviors, Bethesda, MD, Feb. 11–13.

Oliver, Pamela E., Gerald Marwell, and Ruy Teixeira. 1985. "A Theory of the Critical Mass. I. Interdependence, Group Heterogeneity, and the Production of Collective Action." *American Journal of Sociology* 91:522–56.

Olson, Mancur. 1965. *The Logic of Collective Action.* Cambridge: Harvard University Press.

Preble, Ed, and J. J. Casey. 1969. "Taking Care of Business—The Heroin User's Life on the Street." *International Journal of Addictions* 4:1–24.

Rapoport, Anatol. 1979. "A Probabilistic Approach to Networks." *Social Networks* 2:1–18.

Rapoport, David C. 1984. "Fear and Trembling: Terrorism in Three Religious Traditions." *American Political Science Review* 78:658–77.

Sergeyev, Boris, Tatyana Oparina, Tatyana P. Rumyantseva, Valerii Volkanevskii, Robert S. Broadhead, Douglas Heckathorn, and Heather Madray. 1999. "HIV Prevention in Yaroslavl, Russia: A Peer-Driven Intervention and Needle Exchange." *Journal of Drug Issues* 29:777–804.

Sudman, Seymour, and Graham Kalton. 1986. "New Developments in the Sampling of Special Populations." *Annual Review of Sociology* 12:401–29.

Watters, John K., and Patrick Biernacki. 1989. "Targeted Sampling: Options for the Study of Hidden Populations." *Social Problems* 36:416–30.

5

Network Exchange Theory

David Willer, Henry A. Walker, Barry Markovsky, Robb Willer, Michael Lovaglia, Shane Thye, and Brent Simpson

Power is one of the most important phenomena in sociology and social psychology for it affects many aspects of social life. Power processes affect a couple's resolution of disputes about where to spend a summer vacation. Power relations also influence the behavior of employees vying for promotions and the negotiations between auto salesmen and prospective clients.

What is power? What processes create it? What are its effects on social behavior? This chapter discusses new directions in the development of Network Exchange Theory (Markovsky, Willer, and Patton 1988; Willer 1999a). Network Exchange Theory describes structural power conditions and the mechanisms that produce power advantages and disadvantages among positions in exchange networks. The roots of Network Exchange Theory can be traced to Elementary Theory, which describes the relationship between several types of social structures (including exchange structures) and behavior in social relations (Willer and Anderson 1981; Willer 1987). The line of inquiry in Elementary Theory that focuses on exchange structures and power relations eventually acquired the label, Network Exchange Theory or "NET."[1]

The first section of this chapter reviews NET's approach to power. The theory identifies seven structural power conditions including basic network connections, combinations of network connections, and structural variants that mimic basic connection types. The section ends with suggestions for new research on the interrelation of structural conditions. The second section uses several NET procedures to investigate "dynamic networks." By design, previous work has focused on fixed-structure networks. Dynamic networks are structures in which actors may open or close exchange relations. The study of dynamic networks calls for new experimental investigations.

NET research has expanded understandings of power structures and processes and the theory is poised to address a variety of social phenomena that interact with power. We include in this chapter analyses that connect NET to several other major theories. The third section of the chapter connects NET to Game Theory as a way of addressing collective action problems in social structures. The fourth and fifth sections combine ideas from NET and Status Characteristics Theory to address the conversion of power to status and of status to power, respectively. The sixth section begins the integration of NET and Legitimacy Theory to explain and predict the stability of social structures. Despite extensive investigation of exchange structures over the years, very little has been learned about the processes that make them stable. The chapter concludes by considering issues of complexity as we apply NET to larger networks under increasingly natural conditions. All of these issues are at the cutting edge of sociological theory and all have important implications for future research.

THE NETWORK EXCHANGE THEORY OF POWER: A BRIEF REVIEW

NET analyzes structural determinants of power as benefit and power as control. In this section, we describe seven structural power conditions and show how they generate power events. NET researchers use exchange ratios as indicators of power events. An exchange ratio that benefits *i* at *j*'s expense shows that *i* is exercising power over *j*. Power can also establish control. An exchange ratio that benefits *i* at *j*'s expense shows that *i* controls *j* more than *j* controls *i*.[2]

A fundamental assumption of NET (and of all exchange theories) is that actors seek benefit and control and resist cost and subordination. We begin our exposition by explicating a model of *resistance*, that is, the extent to which social actors resist accepting particular exchange ratios. On one hand, the resistance model helps to show how each structural power condition affects actors in relations. On the other, we use the idea to generate predictions for the power conditions. We apply the model to dyads and seven structural power conditions and use simple structures to illustrate power effects.

Resistance and Equipower Dyads

Exchange network researchers have been most interested in applying their theories to *mixed-motive* situations. Actors negotiating exchanges must *compete* with their potential exchange partners in order to garner higher payoffs. At the same time they must *cooperate* with their partners to make agreements. The resistance model uses these dual motives to predict exchange ratios.

Consider a situation in which two actors, A and B, can negotiate the division of 24 units of a valued resource. Let P_i be actor *i*'s payoff from a given exchange offer, for example, $P_A = 20$ and $P_B = 4$. $P_i max$ represents *i*'s best possible outcome (P_A max = 23, P_B max = 23), while $P_i con$ is *i*'s payoff at confrontation when *i* and *j* cannot agree (P_A con = 0, P_B con = 0). $P_i max - P_i$, is then *i*'s interest in gaining a better payoff, and $P_i - P_icon$ is *i*'s interest in avoiding confrontation. For A and B, resistance to exchange is weakest when $P_i = 23$ and strongest when $P_i = 1$. Stated formally, resistance, R_i, is given as

$$\frac{P_i \max - P_i}{P_i - P_icon} \tag{5.1}$$

In an A-B dyad, actors are assumed to make agreements at the point of equal resistance (Willer 1981, 1999a):

$$R_A = \frac{P_A\max - P_A}{P_A - P_Acon} = \frac{P_B\max - P_B}{P_B - P_Bcon} = R_B \tag{5.2}$$

When A and B are negotiating the division of 24 units of some resource, and both gain nothing when they cannot agree,

$$R_A = \frac{23 - P_A}{P_A - 0} = \frac{23 - P_B}{P_B - 0} = R_B$$

Solving equation 5.2, the resistance model predicts an even exchange, that is, $P_A = P_B = 12$. A and B gain numerically equal benefit from the exchange—dyads are equipower structures.

Exclusive Connections

Consider the B-A-C network. The network is *exclusively connected* at A if A can exchange with B or C but not both. More generally, *i* is exclusively connected when the number of *i*'s exchange partners, *Ni*, is greater than the number with whom *i* can exchange, *Mi*. Exchanges in the exclusively connected B-A-C network must always include A but either B or C must be excluded. A's structural position provides advantages in negotiated exchanges. Examples include overfull labor markets in a capitalist economy and dating networks among the very attractive.

Exclusively connected networks like B-A-C are strong power structures in which high power actors who cannot be excluded exchange with partners who can be excluded. For example, let B offer A the 12-12 division predicted in equipower dyads. C hopes to avoid exclusion and begins negotiations with A but B's offer affects A's payoff at confrontation in the A-C negotiation. P_Acon had been zero in the dyad but here it increases to 12 because A will gain 12 from B if A and C do not reach agreement. To avoid exclusion, C must better B's offer; thus $P_Cmax < 12$. The result is that the exclusively connected structure provides A with higher benefit, that is, greater power, than B or C.

More generally, let P_A^{t-1} be the payoff to A from one of A's exclusive alternatives at time t - 1. Then $P_Acon = P_A^{t-1}$, the cost of confrontation for A at t, is the alternative payoff already offered at t - 1. The *Pmax* for C now has an upper bound: $P_Cmax < P_C^{t-1}$, which is the payoff to C of an offer just better for A than

A's alternative payoff. Thus, the general resistance expression where R^H_A is the resistance of the high power A, and R^L_C is the resistance of the low power C, is:

$$R^H_A = \frac{P_A max - P_A}{P_A - P^{t-1}_A} = \frac{P^{t-1}_C - P_C}{P_C - P_C con} = R^L_C \tag{5.3}$$

For the example, A and C's negotiation is constrained by

$$R_A = \frac{23 - P_A}{P_A - 12} = \frac{11 - P_C}{P_C - 0} = R_C$$

from which we find that $P_A = 18$ and $P_C = 6$. These values signal a step in an iterative bargaining process. Now B reopens negotiations at t+1, and plugging in new values of $P_A con = 18$ and $P_B max = 5$ gives $P_A = 21$ and $P_B = 3$. At the end point of negotiations $P_A = P_A max = 23$ and $P_B = 1$, with power maximally favoring A.[3]

Hierarchy/Mobility

NET suggests a power condition called *hierarchy/mobility* when it is applied to organizational hierarchies. It is analogous to exclusive connection and identical in its effects on benefit and control. NET allows the theorist to explain when organizational hierarchies have centralized control and when they do not. It also explains why control is associated with two conditions: (1) salary differentials from bottom to top, and (2) promotion systems in which higher positions are filled from below.

To illustrate, A—the Director of Widget, Inc.—is considering B and C for a promotion and will choose the more obedient of the two. In a pyramidal hierarchy, either B or C, but not both, can be promoted. The salaries of higher positions exceed those of lower positions and both B and C prefer promotion to staying in place. However, when either B or C is promoted, the other is *excluded* from promotion. As rivals for promotion, the two compete to offer higher and higher levels of obedience to A. NET's analysis shows that opportunities for hierarchical mobility create structural power conditions and the condition is reproduced for mobility between every pair of levels in the hierarchy (Willer 1987).

NET's analysis of hierarchy/mobility explains the hostility between bureaucratic and traditional statuses that Weber ([1918] 1968) referred to as the "leveling of social differences" (983). Imagine a hierarchy in which only half the officials will be promoted. Call that half "men" and the other half "women." With no prospects for promotion, women have no reason to offer higher levels of productivity. For men, the competition for promotion and thus the motive to offer more and more obedience is less than it would have been had all officials been considered for promotion. At some levels, a man will have only women colleagues and need not compete at all. Therefore, any policy that uses distinctions like gender to favor some officials over others will reduce obedience.

By contrast, a hierarchical organization practicing "equal opportunity" as a promotion policy will have greater power differences.

Inclusive Connection

The B-A-C network is *inclusively connected* at A if A must exchange with both B and C to benefit. More generally, *i* is exclusively connected when three values are equal: (1) N_i, the number of *i*'s exchange partners; (2) M_i, the number with whom *i* can exchange; and (3) Q_i, the number with whom *i* needs to exchange to benefit.[4] Examples include the manufacturer who must buy an array of parts from single suppliers and the boss whose irreplaceable subordinates have highly interdependent jobs. In the inclusively connected B-A-C network, A loses the value of its first exchange if it fails to complete a second exchange. Let A exchange first with B at equipower for P_{Ab}.[5] Then $P_{Ac}con = -P_{Ab}$ and,

$$R_A^I = \frac{P_A max - P_A}{P_A - (-P_{Ab})} = \frac{P_C max - P_C}{P_C - 0} = R_C \quad (5.4)$$

with $R_A{}^I$ being A's resistance as affected by inclusion.

As in the example of exclusive connection, assume there are 24 resource units available in each of the two relations in B-A-C. If A exchanges first with B, $P_{Ac}con = P_{Ab} = -12$ and

$$R_A^1 = \frac{23 - P_A}{P_A - (-12)} = \frac{23 - P_C}{P_C - 0} = R_C$$

$P_A = 9.72$ and $P_C = 13.97$. More generally, the effect of inclusive connection increases with the number of relations an actor has (its "degree") but at a decreasing rate. For example, let A be inclusively connected to a third partner D who exchanges last. With A-B and A-C exchanges completed, $P_{Ad}con = 12 + 10.03 = 21.72$. Therefore, $P_A = 8.47$ when exchanging with D.

Ordering

The order in which exchanges occur can also be a source of power. Ordering conditions help explain the benefits of "gatekeeping" and why corrupt officials receive bribes. The B-A-C structure is ordered when A must exchange with B *before* exchanging with C. The resistance model implies that A and B are not power equals. B is more powerful than A because B acts as a gatekeeper controlling A's access to payoffs from C. Since A cannot negotiate with or profit from C until the exchange with B is completed, A's cost of confrontation with B is the loss of payoffs from exchanging with C.

Ordering does not affect A's second exchange in this case, and so A-C will function as an equipower dyad. Furthermore, A's disadvantage in the first relation is loss of payoffs from the second. Thus, $P_{Ab}con = -P_{Ac}$. The quantitative effect of ordering is exactly the same as the effect of inclusive connection, and equation 5.4 is used for predictions. For example, in B-A-C, A expects to gain 12 when exchanging later with C, but loses that 12 if agreement with B is not reached. Thus $P_{Ab}con$ = -12 and, using equation 4 for A-B, P_A = 9.72 and P_B = 13.97. Like inclusive connection, the effect of ordering increases with degree. If A must exchange with B, then C, and finally D, the resistance model predicts P_A = 8.47 for the first exchange. That value is exactly the same as the resistance prediction for A's last exchange in the inclusively connected 3-branch.[6] Although their effects are quantitatively identical, the two structural power conditions are distinct. The ordering effect is greatest in the *first* exchange and declines to zero in the last, but inclusive connection's effect is nil in the first exchange and maximal in the last.

Ordering and hierarchy/mobility are structural power conditions but, unlike exclusive and inclusive connections, they are not connection types. Nevertheless, they are similar in that (1) exclusive connection and hierarchy/mobility produce extreme power differences while inclusive connection and ordering produce less extreme differences; and (2) inclusive connection and ordering are affected by degree, the number of *i*'s exchange partners, *Ni*. NET considers hierarchy/mobility and ordering *variants* of exclusive and inclusive connection respectively.

Null Connection

The B-A-C network is null connected if A can exchange with and benefit from either or both partners. More generally, *i* is null connected when *i* can exchange with all partners and need exchange with only one to benefit ($N = M > Q = 1$). Assume Widget, Inc. has two positions to fill, and B and C are candidates. Further, A, the personnel director of Widget, Inc., knows that only B and C are qualified to fill the positions. Then negotiations in the B-A and A-C relations are independent and there are no power differences in either. The two relations can be treated as independent dyads, and so exchange ratios are predicted using equation 5.2. With B-A-C null connected, the salaries that B and C negotiate will be substantially better than if the connection had been exclusive. Experimental results show no power differences in null connected networks (Brennan 1981; Willer and Skvoretz 1999). Early social exchange theories fostered the notion that centralization always creates power differences (e.g., Homans 1974; Emerson 1972a, 1972b). The fact that null connected networks are equipower counters the claim. In fact, NET shows that, depending upon the type of structural power condition, the central actor can be higher, lower, or equal in power with those at the periphery.

Inclusive-Null Connection

If A is the central position in a 3-branch, A is inclusive-null connected if three exchanges are possible and at least two must be completed for A to benefit.

More generally, i is inclusive-null connected when (1) i is connected to N others, (2) i can exchange with all ($M = N$), and (3) i needs to exchange with at least one fewer than M to benefit ($M > Q > 1$). Combining inclusive connection with null connection eliminates the effect of the former (see Willer and Skvoretz 1999). In the 3-branch, A benefits when exchanging only twice. Because A has one exchange which need not be completed, A's first exchange is not affected by inclusive connection. With the completion of that exchange, A still has one exchange which need not be completed; thus inclusive connection does not affect A's second exchange. With the completion of the second exchange, the two exchanges that A needs are completed and inclusive connection cannot affect the third exchange.

The effects of inclusive connections are frequently masked in natural settings because null connection eliminates them. For example, a manufacturing firm that needs all of a very large number of different parts to build its product is inclusively connected. If the firm has two suppliers for each part, however, it is inclusive-null connected and is not disadvantaged by inclusive connection.

Mixing Null Connection and Ordering

The theoretical similarity of inclusive connection and ordering implies that null connection can eliminate the effect of ordering—an implication recently verified experimentally (Corra 2000). An example is B and C acting as gatekeepers controlling A's access to exchange with D. The B-A-C subnetwork is null connected because A can gain access to D by exchanging with either B or C or both. Because A need exchange with only one other to access D, A has one exchange that need not be completed and the effect of ordering is entirely eliminated. This implies that gatekeepers must monopolize their control of access to benefit from that control. The Chamberlain could become rich if he alone controlled access to the king. We return to mixed ordering and null connection below in our discussion of research on an exception to monopolization.

Inclusive-Exclusive Connection

A 3-branch, such as A linked to B, C, and D, is the smallest network in which inclusive-exclusive connection can occur. A is inclusive-exclusively connected when at most two exchanges with A's three partners are possible and both must be completed for A to benefit. More generally, i is inclusive-exclusively connected when i is connected to N others, can exchange with fewer ($M < N$), and needs to exchange with no more than M to benefit ($M \geq Q > 1$). Mixing exclusive and inclusive connection eliminates the effect of inclusive connection. For example, in the 3-branch, A benefits when exchanging twice, but has three opportunities. Thus A's first exchange is not affected by inclusive connection. With the completion of that exchange, A still has one exchange that need not be completed, so inclusive connection does not affect A's second exchange. But exclusive connection threatens all three exchanges, putting A into a position of high power. In fact, experiments show that A gains exactly the same payoffs when inclusive-exclusively connected as when exclusively connected (Willer and Skvoretz 1999).

Mixing Exclusion and Ordering

A 3-branch mixes exclusive connection and ordering when A must exchange with either B or C, but not both, to reach D. Without exclusive connection A would be lower in power in the first exchange. But exclusive connection eliminates the effect of ordering while reversing the power exercise. Now A exercises power over B and C.

The Future of Research on Structural Power Conditions

There is yet much to be learned about structural power conditions. To illustrate we pose two questions. First, does hierarchy/mobility eliminate the effect of inclusive connection? If it does, we can explain how power is centralized in organizations even when tasks are interdependent. The similarity of hierarchy/mobility and exclusive connection strongly suggests that mixing hierarchy/mobility and inclusive connection will eliminate the effect of inclusive connection, but there is no supportive experimental evidence.

Second, are there conditions under which either exclusive or null connection does not eliminate the effects of ordering? The relevant research has not been done, but related work hints at an answer. Recent experiments show that coalitions of low power actors can countervail and even reverse power in branch networks where the central position is inclusive-exclusively connected. Power is reversed because coalition formation eliminates the effect of exclusive connection and uncovers the effects of inclusive connection, which favor peripheral actors (Willer 1999b). Those experiments suggest that ordering effects will also be uncovered when multiple gatekeepers form a coalition.

As this brief review shows, NET is a well-developed theory of power in social structures. The theory has been subjected to experimental tests as extensive as any in sociology. In natural settings where there are no theoretically pure structures, structural power conditions will be mixed. Theories like NET have an advantage over other formulations because they offer predictions for a variety of structural power conditions and combinations of conditions. It is time for those who investigate historical and contemporary structures and institutions to put this cutting-edge knowledge to use.

NETWORK DYNAMICS

Tests of exchange network theories have been limited to fixed-structure exchange networks. Naturally occurring exchanges are not limited to fixed network structures and this observation leads some to assume that theories of exchange networks are limited to static structures (Macy and Flache 1995). Although only two papers connect actors' interests to changes in exchange networks (Leik 1992; Willer and Willer 2000), NET applies to dynamic configurations as well.

We use two ideas in the discussion that follows. The first is the distinction between strong, equal, and weak power networks developed by Simpson and Willer (1999). Strong power networks contain two and only two types of positions: one or more high power positions that are never excluded and two or more low power positions, at least one of which must be excluded. Strong power networks are bipartite; low power positions are connected only to high power positions. In equal power networks, either there is an even numbers of positions and no position is ever excluded or there is an odd number and all are excluded with exactly the same likelihood. All other exchange networks are weak power. In Type 1 weak power networks, like the Stem (figure 5.1a), at least one position is never excluded, but other positions face exclusion with some likelihood. In Type 2 weak power networks, like the Kite (figure 5.1b), all positions face the possibility of exclusion, but not with the same likelihood.

The second idea is the assumption of rationality. Actors seeking to maximize their payoffs from exchange, alter the network by adding and deleting links to others; links are added or deleted only in ways expected to produce higher payoffs. In most cases higher payoffs will mean that the actor's power position is improved. In other cases, higher payoffs will mean that the actor is excluded less frequently. Space limitations require us to restrict our analysis to 1- exchange networks where power is based in exclusive connection. Furthermore, the discussion will focus only on *adding* of links. Deleting links is discussed elsewhere (Willer and Willer 2000).

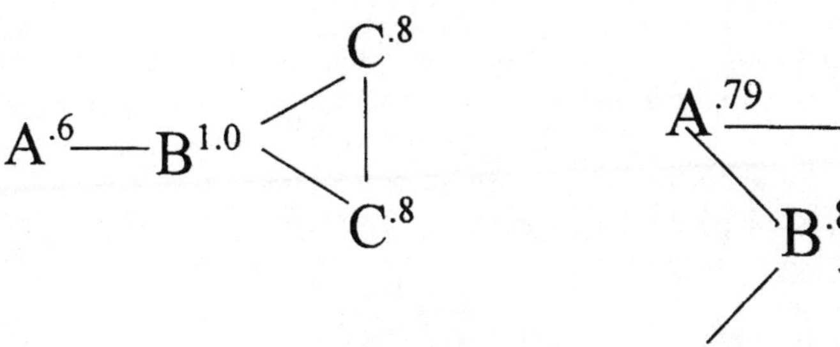

Figure 5.1. Two Weak Power Networks

In what follows, the term "prefers to" expresses a strict preference for the changed network over the initial network. An actor prefers to add a link to the initial network only if the resulting network is more advantageous to that actor than the initial one. For this analysis, the links which actors add must connect their own position to another and are assumed to be free of cost to the position initiating them. When the hypotheses below make reference to the quality of a network, such as "strong power," the reference is only to the *initial* state of the network. After adding a link, the network may stay strong power, become weak, split, etc. Finally, the hypotheses refer only to links added between nodes of the specified network. Links added between networks are excluded from this analysis.

Hypothesis 1: In a strong power network, any low power position will prefer to add links.

If a low power position in a strong power network is free to add a link to any position, it will add a link to another low power position. If the network is the simplest strong power network—the three-actor line—then the addition of a link between the two low power positions results in a fully connected, equal power network. In all other strong power networks, adding a link between two low-power actors either (1) motivates the two low power positions to break away from the network to create an equal power dyad; or (2) transforms the network from strong to weak power. Since weak power exchanges do not approach the maximal divisions of strong power networks, low power positions prefer either outcome. When there is a single high power position, all low power positions are connected to the high power position. The only connections that can be added are to others low in power.

Consider the "L5" structure A-B-C-D-E. There are multiple high power positions (B and D are high power), and some high and low power positions are not connected. Interestingly, low power positions like A prefer to add connections to high power positions like D because doing so reduces the likelihood of exclusion. Assume that B exchanges first with C. Instead of becoming an isolate, A's new connection to D gives A the .5 likelihood of being included in the A-D-E subnetwork that remains after the B-C exchange.

Hypothesis 2: In strong power networks with multiple high power positions, any high power position will prefer to add any link that is not a "break."

A break is an exchange relation that is never used. Because high power positions prefer to exchange with those low in power, relations connecting high power positions to each other are never used. They are breaks. Thus Hypothesis 2 asserts that high power positions will add links to low power positions, but not to each other.

Because singular high power positions are fully connected, only multiple high power positions can add links. In the A-B-C-D-E network, D prefers to be connected to A because of "decay effects." Decay effects occur when some positions exchange first, leaving a residual network. For example, when B exchanges first with C, the residual network is the D-E dyad, where D is no longer high power. But when D adds the connection to A and exchanges second, D will have two low power positions, A and E, and will still be high power. Though low power actors like E prefer to exchange in the D-E dyad, not E, but A and D determine whether E will ever have that opportunity. And we already know that A will exchange with D because, as discussed under Hypothesis 1, A prefers a link to D to its absence.

Hypothesis 3: In a Type 1 weak power network, any position will prefer to add links.

Consider the "Stem" of figure 5.1a. The highest power position, B, cannot add links. Thus Hypothesis 3 does not apply. Both A and the Cs can add links, and each prefers adding at least one. If either C connects to A, that C cannot be excluded and joins B as a higher power position. The result is a weak power network consisting of a box with a diagonal connecting one C and B.

A also prefers to add the C-A connection because A's likelihood of being included increases from .6 in the Stem to .85 in the new structure. The lower likelihood of exclusion implies that A gains power. In fact, A prefers to connect to both Cs, for then the network is fully connected. A cannot be excluded and is equal in power to every other position. The same line of reasoning follows for other Type 1 weak power networks. For example, the B position in A-B-C-D is less powerful than B in the Stem. Thus B in the line network prefers to add a connection to D, converting the network into the Stem.

Hypothesis 4: In a Type 2 weak power network, any position will prefer to add links.

All positions in Type 2 weak power networks potentially are excludable, e.g. the "Kite" in figure 5.1b. Excludable weak power positions always prefer additional links connecting them to other positions. New links increase their likelihood of being included and they gain higher payoffs when they exchange.

Hypothesis 5: In equal power networks, any position will prefer to add any link.

When the density of any equal power network is less than maximal, the addition of a link changes the network to weak power, where the two positions just connected become the higher power positions. As the higher power positions, both will exchange with others for higher payoffs than are possible in the equal power network. Therefore, all positions prefer to add a link.

Hypothesis 6: Any position in any network that can add a link will prefer to add at least one.

Following Hypothesis 2, a necessary condition for Hypothesis 6 is that the added link is not a break. That condition is not particularly restrictive, however. As links are added, power is rapidly attenuated such that strong power conditions are soon eliminated. With strong power eliminated, breaks can no longer occur.

Hypothesis 6 has very general and important implications for historical and contemporary power structures. If any position that can add a link will do so, then, having added that link, if another link can be added, it will be added and similarly to full connection. Therefore, all networks will go to maximum density and become equal power. This implies that, when positions are free to add links, power differences will dissolve. Nevertheless, power structures have existed for millennia, suggesting that, for power structures to persist across time, lower power positions must be prevented from adding new links. The foregoing hypotheses also have important implications for new directions in NET research. Though all are indirectly supported by research on static network configurations, they have yet to be tested under conditions that permit actors to change their relations. Those tests will add important depth to our understanding of how power structures are sustained over time.

GAMES, STRUCTURE, AND COLLECTIVE ACTION

Recent work extends NET to provide a method for identifying games—in the "game theoretic" sense—embedded within network exchange structures (Willer and Skvoretz 1997). *Strategic analysis* attributes strategies to some positions so that games can be derived for others. To illustrate we use Br32, a "branch" network with a central A position and three peripheral positions, B, C, and D. A can exchange with two of the peripherals and excludes the third. Br32 is a strong power structure. For the following examples, 24 valued resources are divided in each relation.

Let A follow the strategy of accepting the best offer, and selecting randomly among tied offers. Students of game theory will recognize the payoffs displayed at t = 1 of figure 5.2 as those of a prisoners' dilemma game. In fact, these are the payoffs to A's three peripherals. (To keep the display compact, only two payoffs are shown. The discussion explains which payoff goes to each of the three peripherals.) We determine payoffs as follows. If the three peripherals cooperate with each other and send the equipower offer of 12-12, A will randomly choose two of three possible exchanges and the expected payoff to each peripheral is 12 x 2/3 = 8 as shown in the upper left cell at t = 1. If one peripheral cooperates and two defect to make the 11-13 offer more favorable to A, A will accept both defection offers, both defectors receive 11, and the cooperator receives zero. These payoffs are shown in the upper right and lower left cell of n = 1. Finally, if all three defect and offer 11-13, two of three offers will be accepted and the expected payoff is 11 x 2/3 = 7.33 as displayed in the lower right cell at t = 1.

Looking beyond t = 1, figure 5.2 gives the process of power development for Br32. Because each instance of joint defection produces a new game, the payoffs for joint defection (D) at t and cooperation (C) at t + 1 are identical. That is, the power process is a defection chain where the payoffs for joint defection at t = 1 are the payoffs for joint cooperation at t = 2, the payoffs for defection

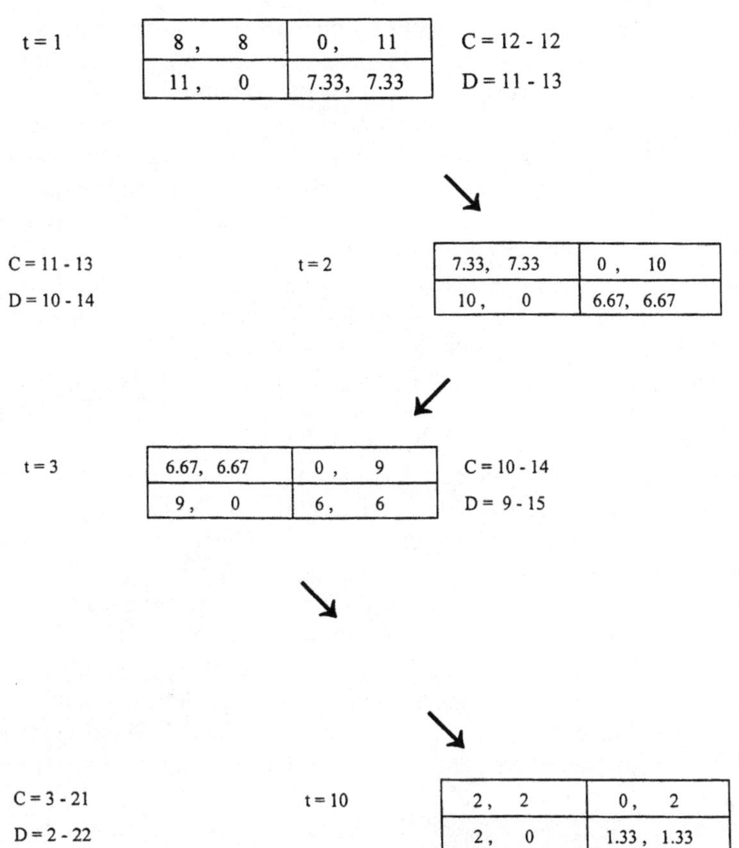

Figure 5.2. Power Development in Br32 as a Defection Chain

Note: After Willer and Skvoretz (1997)

at t = 2 are the payoffs for cooperation at t = 3, and similarly to t = 10. All games to t = 10 are prisoners' dilemmas. Because defection is the dominant strategy, defection down the chain to t = 10 is predicted. After t = 10, the game is no longer a prisoners' dilemma and lacks a dominant strategy. Nevertheless, the t = 10 game has a "best response" which is defection. Any peripheral should defect if s/he believes that others will do so. Given the prior series of defections, we predict defection to t = 11 where the power process ends at offers of 2-22 favoring the central position.

The power process of figure 5.2 occurs because the dominant strategy in a prisoners' dilemma is joint defection, which is *Pareto suboptimal.* As the low-power actors bid against each other, their payoffs diminish *and* the central A's payoffs increase. Thus, as peripherals defect down the chain, A exercises more and more power and A's payoffs increase. Experiments pitting human subjects against a computer that selected its best offer and chose randomly from tied offers find a mean payoff of 2.65 for humans at the periphery. The value stands midway between the payoffs predicted for t = 10 and t = 11. More generally, only strong power structures contain prisoners' dilemma games (Willer and Skvoretz 1997). Therefore, strategic analysis predicts correctly that only strong power structures have power processes such as those outlined in figure 5.2.

Identifying games in structures is a first step toward understanding how power can be blocked when peripherals form coalitions. The next step was taken by Simpson and Macy (2001). They point out that, if at least two of the three peripherals of Br32 defect, defection will continue until at least t = 10 where the payoff is 1.33. If only one peripheral defects, however, each of the two cooperators will gain 12 half the time, averaging 6. Both cooperators prefer 6 to the payoff of 1.33 at the end of the chain. These observations allow construction of the *supergame* of figure 5.3.

The payoff matrix of the figure 5.3 supergame is the *chicken game,* which has no dominant strategy. Nevertheless, cooperation is the best response for any peripheral who believes that only one other will defect. Cooperation for two is the best response because, as just noted, they will each gain 6, which is preferred to 1.33. In fact, cooperating peripherals in Simpson and Macy's experiment shared resources equally. As a result, when A accepts the offer of either, both gained 6 for the round. Further, given the belief that two others will cooperate, the best response for the third peripheral is to defect, gaining 11 which is preferred to 8 (see figure 5.3). Interestingly, the research found evidence that both two- and three-person coalitions were stable enough to reduce power exercised by the central A.

The many possible ties between NET and game theory suggest an array of future projects. For example, the application of game theory to structures not only

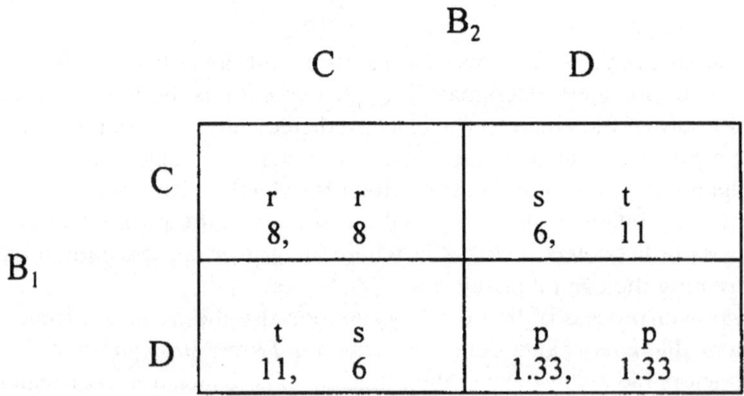

Figure 5.3. Payoff Matrix for Low Power Actors in Br32 as a Chicken Game: One B Defecting on the Diagonal

predicts when power will and will not develop, but also sets out design parameters for effective coalitions. From the existence of the defection chain it follows that fully countervailing power will require suppression of all defections (free riding). Therefore, coalitions seeking power equality must be able to sanction free riders. A second example: Coalitions allow low power actors to countervail the effects of power due to exclusion; but coalitions have no effect on inclusion. This offers the possibility of power reversal. When a network is inclusive-exclusively connected and peripherals have organized an effective coalition, the only operative power condition remaining is inclusion and it favors the coalition. Therefore, NET predicts that the coalition will reverse power such that exchange ratios will come to favor the peripherals.

FROM POWER TO STATUS

Power and status are fundamental dimensions of social relations (Kemper and Collins 1990), yet it is unlikely that they are entirely independent. Homans (1974) considered power to be the ultimate source of status in society. A person wielding power consistently over a period of time gains prestige and influence, at least to some degree. While this is an intuitive explanation of the relationship between power and status, until very recently the causal connection from power to status has proven difficult to demonstrate. We review theory and research that supports the existence of that causal connection.

Status characteristics theory (SCT) explains status in terms of shared expectations for contributions in collective task settings (Berger, Cohen, and Zelditch 1972; Berger et al. 1977, Berger, Rosenholtz, and Zelditch 1980). Group members who are expected to make contributions valuable to the achievement of group goals are accorded high status and influence by other group members. To the extent that status and influence are associated, if power exercise produces status, then it also will produce influence. An interesting research question follows: "Do powerful people maintain their influence in situations where they lack the capacity to reward or punish?" Reward expectations theory, a branch of SCT, suggests that they do (Berger et al. 1985; Moore 1985). Rewards have been shown to carry status value (Stewart and Moore 1992). If power confers the ability to obtain rewards and accumulate resources, it follows that powerful people who amass resources through power exercise will attain high status as a result (Lovaglia 1994).

The proposition that power confers status was first experimentally investigated in a setting where subjects initially competed with a powerful partner in an exchange network (Lovaglia 1995). Next, subjects worked on a series of tasks with the same partner but the partner had no power over the subject. However, the partner could suggest a correct answer to a problem the two faced together. Lovaglia used the number of times the participant changed her or his mind to agree with the partner as a measure of the partner's influence over the participant. Influence is a generally accepted indicator of status differences in task groups (Berger et al. 1977).

If rewards have status value, then the greater rewards amassed by the partner in the network exchange setting should lead to greater influence for the partner when the two work together. Results, however, were mixed. While participants reported higher expectations for the competence of powerful partners, the powerful partners achieved no advantage in influence (Lovaglia 1995).

Lovaglia (1995) surmised that participants experience strong negative emotions when exchanging with powerful partners. Subsequent research demonstrated that negative emotions block the influence of high-status partners (Lovaglia and Houser 1996). In a gift exchange setting, participants either exchanged gifts with a partner, thereby producing positive emotion, or they were confronted by a partner who refused to reciprocate a gift. Participants who exchanged gifts with their partner reported positive emotions while those whose partner refused to reciprocate reported negative emotions. Then when participant and partner worked together to solve a series of problems, the influence of the partner was lower when the partner had failed to reciprocate and the participant felt negative emotions. Thus negative emotions experienced by less-powerful actors as the result of unfavorable exchanges may well block the influence of high power people.

To complete the argument that negative emotions block the influence effects of status based in power differences, it is necessary to show that power use in exchange settings induces negative emotions in those low in power (Lovaglia 1997). Willer, Lovaglia, and Markovsky (1997) conducted another experiment on a strong power network. Participants assigned to low-power positions reported significant negative emotions directed toward their high power partners. Furthermore, the negative emotions expressed by low-power participants were similar to those associated with reduced influence in the Lovaglia and Houser (1996) task situation. Thus, findings of the three studies taken together (Lovaglia 1995; Lovaglia and Houser 1996; Willer, Lovaglia, and Markovsky 1997) are consistent with the proposition that high power can increase status and influence, but increases in status and influence can be blocked by the negative emotional reactions produced by the exercise of power.[7]

Given experiments that show that the influence of the powerful can be blocked, how is it that, in the larger society, the powerful are often highly influential as well? One explanation is that power and influence are exercised over different people. In a large and complex economic system, a person can exercise power in one domain, amassing resources from one set of people, and subsequently use those resources to gain influence over another set of people in a different societal domain. For example, Donald Trump amassed a great fortune through real estate transactions but his success is often attributed to some special ability—"the art of the deal," as he calls it. In one instance, an elderly Atlantic City woman refused to sell her home to Trump to make way for construction of a new casino. Trump used economic and political pressure on Atlantic City officials to get the property condemned. The woman expressed extreme negative emotions toward Trump and his status-based influence over her is undoubtedly nil. She would be unlikely to follow his advice on any matter. However, millions of people in the United States are aware only of Trump's successful deals and great fortune. His success and resources have increased his status considerably. His public stature has grown so great that he seriously considered running for president of the United States.

The line of reasoning we described inspired new research that examines whether those who observe the exercise of power accord status to the powerful. In one experiment (R. Willer 2000), subjects first observed several exchange rounds in one of two networks: either the A-B-A strong power structure, or the A-B-B-A weak power structure. Subsequently, subjects interacted on a task with a partner who had been in either a high power or a low power position in the observed network. No structural power differences were imposed in the task setting. The indicator of influence was the number of problems in which the participant changed her initial answer to agree with the partner's suggestion. Occupants of high power positions in strong power networks were significantly more influential than their low power exchange partners in the task situation. If observing the exercise of strong power against others produces negative emotions, those emotions do not seem to affect the influence powerful people have over observers.

Interestingly, for the weak power network, there were no differences in the influence observers accepted from higher and lower power participants. However, it is possible that the difference in resources gained by the high and low power actors in weak power structures are not large enough for observers to attribute status differences. Alternatively, qualitative data gathered from participants indicates that, because the weak power network has two higher power positions, it may be easier to detect a network advantage there than in the A-B-A network with its lone high power position. Subjects may have attributed the success of the weak power Bs to a structural advantage, and the success of the strong power Bs to the individuals. To test this possibility, R. Willer and Lovaglia are now comparing the influence on observers resulting from extreme and moderate resource divisions, while holding network structure constant at A-B-A.

Future research will investigate whether philanthropy affects the status of those who exercise power. Turn-of-the-century industrialist Andrew Carnegie became one of the best-known philanthropists in the United States by endowing public libraries. Before then, Carnegie had alienated segments of American society by his extreme anti-labor activities, particularly the killing of the Homestead strikers. Perhaps philanthropy is an effective way to overcome negative reactions to power exercise, increasing the influence and status of the wealthy and powerful. As did Lovaglia (1995), R. Willer and Lovaglia will begin with subjects competing in a power structure, assigned to either high or low power positions. After several exchange rounds, those in high and low power positions will be paired to work on a series of problems. Success on the problems, from which they mutually benefit, will determine a substantial portion of their pay. The problems must be paid for with resources gained in the power structure. Because the subject from the high power position has significantly greater resources with which to purchase task problems compared to the subject from the low power position, there is an opportunity for the high power subject to be philanthropic. The design will allow experimenters to control information on levels of philanthropy that subjects receive.

Because philanthropic contributions can be public goods, they can solve collective action problems. If research demonstrates that people are motivated to contribute in order to increase status and influence, then a new path toward solving collective action problems is opened. For that demonstration, R. Willer and Lovaglia will manipulate levels of generosity shown by the high power partners in purchasing opportunities for mutual success and check for different levels of influence. Also investigated is whether high power partners choose to be philanthropic.

FROM STATUS TO POWER

Another developing line of work addresses fundamental connections between status and power in social exchange. Consider the following illustration. Imagine that you would like to purchase a good quality retro sports car for a reasonable price. An advertisement purports to have just what you are looking for: a 1980 Camaro with bucket seats and low mileage. Perfect! You go to examine the car and are greeted by a rugged gentleman with a warm handshake. In the course of conversation you learn he is a military general and winner of the prestigious Congressional Medal of Honor. He explains further that until recently he was the Pentagon's leading authority on hostage negotiations. The car, he tells you, was a gift he received from a wealthy American hostage whose release he had negotiated. How do his personal traits (occupation, gender, race) affect your perceptions of him? More importantly, how do they affect your perceptions of the car? Would you view the car differently if it were owned by someone less notable? Would you negotiate differently with that person than with the general?

This section reviews two theories that address issues of status and power in bargaining. Both theories draw formal connections between NET and SCT. The first is the Status Value Theory of Power developed and tested by Thye in a series of papers (1999a, 1999b, 2000). The theory connects status to power by describing how valued status traits (like race or occupation) affect perceptions of related goods, and consequently, the power of individuals in exchange. The second is the Theory of Status Influence (Willer, Lovaglia, and Markovsky 1997; Thye 1999a). It asserts that status characteristics alter beliefs and performance expectations, which, in turn, produce influence and power in negotiations. We summarize the theories' arguments and report on the experimental evidence to date.

The Status Value Theory of Power

The Status Value Theory of Power links perceptions of value to power in negotiations. Three kinds of value are demarcated in the theory:

1. *Monetary value* refers to the amount of money an object is worth as determined by prevailing market conditions.
2. *Consummatory value* refers to the subjective utility an individual places on an object as a function of intra-personal or situational needs. For example, although tap water is of little monetary value, it has substantial consummatory value to one who is thirsty.
3. *Status value* refers to the honor or esteem that comes from possessing certain characteristics or objects (Thye 1997, 1999b; Berger, Cohen, and Zelditch 1972; Veblen 1899). For example, individuals who hold prestigious jobs or Congressional Medals of Honor are generally more honored or esteemed than those who do not. The theory claims that a person's social status will affect the status value of objects related to that person. In turn, the status value of objects is predicted to affect the way such objects are distributed in exchange.

Next we describe the kinds of situations to which the theory applies, and present the core theoretical ideas as a series of related propositions.

The theory applies to settings in which individuals of different status seek to exchange nominally distinct resources. At least one of these resources must be explicitly *relevant* to the status of the actors.[8] When relevant, the resources serve as "status markers" that are distinguished by the differential status they convey. Real world examples of status markers include the title "Distinguished Professor," an Olympic gold medal, or a private parking space. The theory explains what kinds of exchangeable items acquire status value, and how this affects power in such relations.

The first assumption describes the spread of status value from people to objects (Berger, Cohen, and Zelditch 1972). It claims that objects *relevant* to an actor's status will acquire value consistent with the actor's status. As such, the first assumption claims that actors inflate or deflate the status value of objects in accord with the status of those possessing them. Expressed formally,

Assumption 1: If actor *i* assigns relevance to states of valued status characteristics SC*i*+ or SC*i*- and to objects X*i*, then *i* assigns status value to the objects consistent with values of the characteristics.

The second assumption connects the possession of valued goods to power. It claims that actors with highly valued resources have power over others. This is a standard assumption in exchange theory that has received much empirical support over the years (Thibaut and Kelley 1959; Homans 1974; Emerson 1981; Willer and Anderson 1981). Yet, ironically, few exchange theorists have discussed the dimensions and determinants of value in systems of exchange (Emerson 1987 is an exception). When the status value of goods is high, independent of other types of value, the goods themselves should be more valuable than when status value is low. In this way the theory claims that the status value of goods will confer power over and above that generated by the monetary or consummatory value of the goods.

Assumption 2: If actors *i* and *j* believe that resources controlled by *i* are of greater value than those possessed by *j*, then *i* has power over *j*.

The final assumption connects power to behavioral outcomes:

Assumption 3: If actor *i* has power over actor *j*, then *i* receives more favorable outcomes than *j* in exchanges between the two.

Thye (2000) tested the theory with a series of experiments wherein status differentiated subjects exchanged resources via networked personal computers. The subjects were assigned randomly to distinct network locations and told that their partners were higher-, equal-, or lower-status relative to themselves. Next, each subject was assigned a distinct commodity on the basis of the status information. Each was given blue poker chips, whereas higher status partners were awarded purple chips and lower status partners were given orange chips. Following the status manipulation and chip assignments there were 60 rounds in which subjects negotiated exchanges of the colored chips, with a maximum of one deal per round. The theory is supported if (1) purple poker chips are perceived to be most valuable; and (2) the subjects with the purple poker chips earn higher profits from others.

The theory fared well on both predictions. First, subjects' estimation of the status value of objects was measured via a number of questionnaire items. Figure 5.4 shows the results. Overall, the chips held by higher status partners were viewed as more important, more worthy of acquisition, and preferable compared to those of lower status partners in the same network location. Only three of 30 subjects (10 percent) indicated that orange chips associated with low-status partners were more important than purple chips associated with the higher status partner. The last pair of columns indicate that, given the choice of earning 100 orange or 100 purple chips, a full 70 percent of subjects indicated they would prefer the "higher status" purple chips.

The exchange data indicate that status value effects also translated into power for the high-status actor. Figure 5.5 shows that status confers power in all three of the structures tested to date. For example, the left two bars of figure 5.5 indicate that when a total of 30 poker chips could be exchanged, the higher status member of a dyad earned 19.05 units, leaving the lower status member with only 10.95. The same pattern was observed in a status differentiated triangle where the highest status member again earned the greatest share of profit (see Thye 2000 for details). A third test found that status value effects reduce the

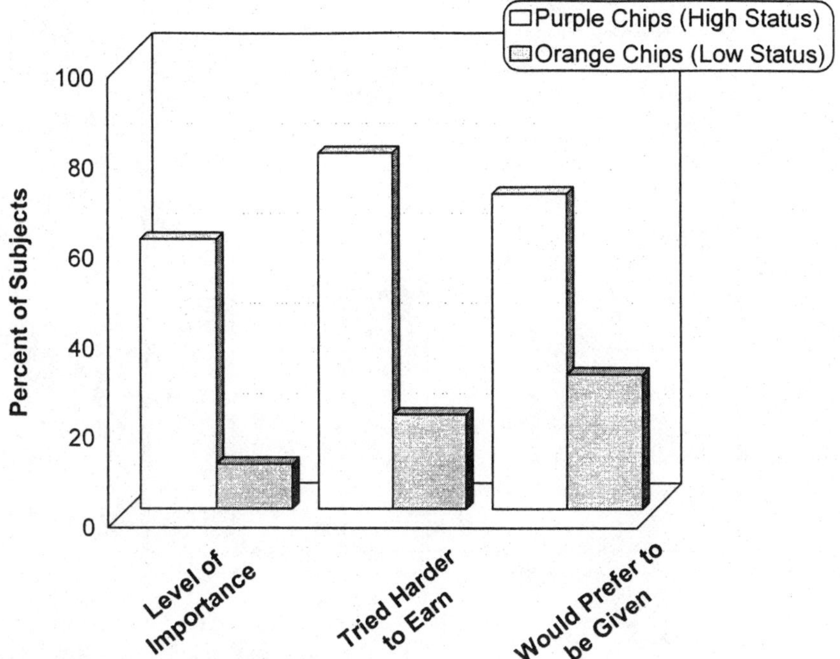

Figure 5.4. Results from Status Value Questions
Note: Adapted from Thye 2002.

exercise of power in the weak power L4 structure (A1-B1-B2-A2). Compared to a baseline condition of relatively higher status actors, when the subjects in position B1 and B2 were lower status they exercised significantly less power (see Thye 2000 for details).

To summarize, the status value theory of power prescribes conditions under which high-status actors' goods will be perceived as more valuable than those of low-status actors. This phenomenon, called the spread of status value, is predicted to give higher status individuals an advantage in exchange with lower status partners. The experimental evidence to date has shown that (1) status value transfers from people to related objects; and (2) subjects take the status value of objects into consideration when negotiating exchanges. In terms of the questions posed for our hypothetical car buyer, there are two implications. First, the theory and evidence to date suggest that perceptions of the Camaro *are* affected by the status of the owner when the car is relevant to that person's status. Second, this perception gives high-status owners a significant advantage in exchanges with low-status buyers. Overall, the status value theory of power provides a rigorous account of the mechanism through which status is translated into power.

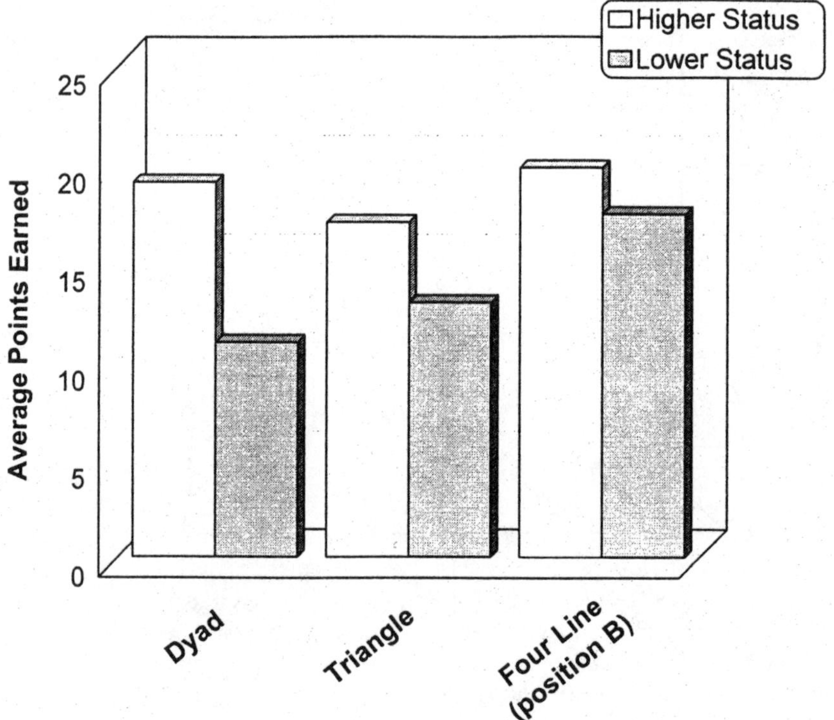

Figure 5.5. Status Differentiated Exchange Outcomes
Note: Adapted from Thye 2002.

The Theory of Status Influence

Readers familiar with SCT will recognize that status leads to influence in collectively oriented task groups (Ridgeway and Walker 1995). Social influence is not restricted to such groups, however, and exchange networks should provide fertile ground for studying influence processes. For example, assume the general asserts that another buyer is also interested in the Camaro and has made an offer that you must better. To the degree you believe this information is accurate, the original buyer-owner dyad is transformed into a buyer1-owner-buyer2 strong power structure, with the owner in the high power position. The claim of status influence theory is that, under such circumstances, higher status actors will be believed more readily than lower status actors. One measure of belief is the effect on exchange rates: High-status actors should again profit more than low-status actors. Experiments now under way are testing for status influence effects in exchange.

In sum, the intersection of power and status has proven to be a rich and fertile domain for theory development and testing. Two theories now exist that connect status and power through perceptions of value (e.g., Thye 1997, 2000) and social influence (e.g., Willer, Lovaglia, and Markovsky 1997; Thye 1999a). Both theories are young, and their projected growth curves are steep. For example, yet unpublished work on status value connects NET's resistance model with formal modeling procedures of SCT (Thye 1999b) to generate exact predictions of exchange ratios from status differences. Given empirical support already in place and new projects under way, there is little doubt that building links between power and status will continue to be at the cutting edge of theory and research.

LEGITIMACY, LEGITIMATION PROCESSES, AND NETWORK EXCHANGE

Network structures and connection types establish conditions for social exchange. Consequently, network structures affect the organization of power and status in exchange networks and the influence patterns that power and status differences produce. In turn, legitimacy and legitimation processes create powerful effects on the relationship between network structures and patterns of power, status, and influence. Previously, NET researchers devoted limited attention and resources to studies that explore the effects that legitimation processes have on behavior in exchange networks. (See Walker et al. 2000. For an exception, see Bell, Walker, and Willer 2000.) As evidence of awakened interest, this section charts new research on legitimation now planned by NET researchers.

Legitimation processes are fundamental components of social life (Zelditch and Walker 1984; Walker, Thomas, and Zelditch 1986).[9] In that regard, they share an essential similarity with other social processes. However, unlike processes that produce stratification, divided labor, and social control, legitimation processes do not stand alone. They accompany, overlay, or otherwise affect other social processes and the structures those processes establish (Zelditch 2001). As an example, all known societies have divisions of labor and systems of stratification. Both are routinely analyzed by sociologists. However, it is not particularly meaningful to refer to a society's system of legitimacy. Instead, the theoretical and empirical focus is on whether specific social structures or institutions—for example, politics, the economy, or religion—possess legitimacy.

Exchange networks are, as a matter of course, social structures. They include social positions or roles, relations between roles, and rules that govern interactions among role occupants. Consequently, we might expect that exchange networks and their various subunits vary in the degree to which they possess legitimacy. To date, neither NET nor any other exchange-theoretic conception has systematically analyzed the legitimacy of exchange networks or the way that legitimacy affects exchange processes. We begin our brief exploration of such issues with a short summary of ideas from legitimacy theory.

Legitimacy is at once a process and the outcome of a process. Social scientists use "legitimacy" and correlative terms, for example, "legitimation," "legitimize," to describe (1) the process through which some social element acquires legitimacy; (2) the condition or state of being legitimate; or (3) the grounds, that is, justifications or accounts, upon which some social process or structure lays claims to legitimacy. Our exposition employs terminology developed by Dornbusch and Scott (1975) and used extensively by Zelditch and Walker (1984); Walker, Thomas, and Zelditch (1986); and Walker, Rogers, and Zelditch (1988).

Dornbusch and Scott began with Weber's ([1918] 1968) seminal statement and identified a basic problem. Weber's discussion conflates two ideas about legitimacy, referring to (1) the belief that some social order or arrangement is desirable or proper; and (2) rules or other social arrangements that are binding on (or govern the actions of) all group members. Dornbusch and Scott labeled as propriety individual notions or evaluations of desirability and appropriateness.

They reserved Weber's term *validity* for the idea that social arrangements—for example, procedures, rules, or laws—govern all members of the relevant collectivity.

Zelditch and Walker use these ideas in their multiple-source, multiple-object conception of legitimacy. Sources of legitimacy—propriety, validity, endorsement, and authorization—confer legitimacy on objects of legitimation. Objects may include institutions, that is, social structures including roles, statuses, and the rules governing their relationships, persons (role occupants), and actions. As an example, a belief that the presidency is an appropriate governmental position is an expression of propriety. Validity refers to the collective and constitutive component of legitimacy. The U. S. Constitution establishes the validity of the executive, legislative, and judicial branches of government and provides rules that govern interactions among the three branches. All citizens are subject to constitutional provisions, that is, the government's validity, whether or not they imbue those provisions with propriety.

Legitimacy theorists argue that, *ceteris paribus*, propriety guides individual actions (Dornbusch and Scott 1975; Zelditch and Walker 1984). However, legitimation processes are inherently collective. Collective validation of social institutions establishes a framework for meaningful, socially sanctioned behavior. Validity establishes direct pressure on individuals to conform with established procedures, practices, and laws. Validity also creates indirect pressure through its effects on propriety. Collectively validated structures, practices, and procedures buttress and strengthen individual group members' sense that those elements are appropriate. Finally, the *endorsement* of ordinary group members, and the *authorization* of high-status authorities, reinforce conformity pressures. The Constitution is legitimate because the founding fathers authorized it and generations of citizens endorsed it.[10]

Legitimacy shapes and influences social interaction in a variety of settings including families, formal organizations, the community of nation states, and exchange networks—the focus of our attention here. Legitimacy effects are hidden in most NET studies of exchange behavior because the studies are conducted in legitimately constituted controlled laboratory situations. Indeed, we believe that studies confirming NET's predictions (and the predictions of other theories of exchange networks) depend to an important degree on legitimacy processes. Research participants typically presume the constitutive authority of the institution, e.g., a research university, which legitimizes the experimenter. The actions of legitimate experimenters legitimize the exchange situation in which they are placed. Furthermore, as shown by Zelditch and Walker (1984; Walker, Thomas, and Zelditch 1986), the failure of actors in low power network positions to rebel only serves to endorse the structurally based inequalities in such networks.

Legitimacy and Illegitimacy in Exchange

Consider the effects of varying legitimacy in a natural exchange setting like the following. Actor A possesses money, a valued resource, and is interested in purchasing a car from dealer B. A will pay up to $24,000 for the car that cost B $20,000. B is willing to sell the car at any price over $21,000. NET predicts an equipower exchange in which A and B complete an exchange at $22,500. NET also predicts that the exchange price will vary if A and B are members of an exchange network: The price declines when other Bs have similar cars to sell, and increases when other As wish to purchase B's car.

Consider an alternative scenario. Unbeknownst to A, B purchases some cars from a ring of thieves who "divert" new cars from various ports of entry. B *illegitimately* possesses the car A wants, and will sell it at a price lower than $22,500 but only if A negotiates wisely. In terms of the resistance model given earlier in this chapter, B's illegitimate possession of the car ensures that its Pcon is substantially lower than Pcon for legitimate owners. Because B will accept offers substantially below the car's "market value," A may actually buy the car for less than $21,000—the break-even point for honest Bs.

Finally, consider a third alternative. As before, B purchases some cars on the black market but in this instance, A knows B by reputation. That is, A attributes impropriety to B. A will begin bidding *lower* than $21,000 for several reasons. A knows that B possesses some autos illegitimately, i.e., A knows that $P_B$con is lower than that for honest Bs. A also knows that any purchase she makes from B may be an illegal, i.e., illegitimate, act and potential costs associated with that illegality increase A's resistance to exchanges with B as compared with exchange with an honest B. Finally, when A knows the price for a legitimate purchase, a substantially lower price is tainted by illegitimacy.

Legitimacy and Network Exchange Structures

The effect that illegitimacy and legitimacy have on the stability of exchange structures is a fertile area for new research. Consider the Br321 network in which three peripheral Bs are connected to a central A. The network is strong power because only two Bs can exchange with A, and one B must be excluded. Not being inclusively connected, A can profit if it completes a single exchange. We suggest that legitimacy stabilizes experimental exchange structures like

Br321 and contributes to power development even when substantial inequalities are generated. When A exercises power, the Bs would benefit by acting collectively to countervail that power. That they do not is due in part to the standard experimental protocol, which does not include mechanisms allowing coalition formation. Nevertheless, subjects could act collectively without those mechanisms but may not do so because that action would not be legitimate. By omitting mechanisms for coalition formation, the legitimacy of the experiment does not cover collective action directed against those high in power. That is to say, the institutional rules that govern, i.e., legitimize, the structure make collective action politically impossible (Friedrich 1958).

The Zelditch-Walker research program demonstrates that coalitions will not form when legitimacy processes impede collective action (Walker and Zelditch 1993). Thus granting less powerful network positions the mechanisms to form coalitions does not ensure that actors actually will form them (Walker, Rogers, and Zelditch 1988). The Zelditch-Walker research program has yet to study exchange networks. Nevertheless, the results of that program's research bear upon the power structures of NET.

We now show how to extend legitimacy theory to the domain of NET by examples that parallel Zelditch and Walker's early studies of the stability of authority such as Walker, Thomas, and Zelditch (1986). Consider again the Br321 network, but now with a mechanism for coalition formation. Before dealing with the central A, low power Bs may join a "group." In the group, resources gained from exchanges with Bs are shared equally. To coordinate activity, Bs vote on offers to be sent to A and then see the others' votes. When negotiations with the central A are completed, group members decide whether to sanction those who did not join. Low power subjects who are sanctioned receive no payoff regardless of deals they have made with A.

NET and Legitimacy Theory both predict that the low power Bs will form coalitions, but for different reasons. NET asserts that the Bs act out of self-interest to gain higher payoffs. Legitimacy theory asserts that the Bs form coalitions because the experimenter has legitimated coalition formation by *authorization*. In fact, experimental subjects do form effective coalitions as soon as they have the opportunity to do so (Willer 1999b). While that formation is consistent with predictions of both theories, more tests are needed to more fully evaluate the assertions of Legitimacy Theory.

For one future study, Legitimacy Theory will be tested by pitting authorization against self-interest. Thomas, Walker, and Zelditch (1986) show that authorities can *delegitimize* coalition formation. For the design, the experimenter will authorize coalition formation, but only for later rounds of the experiment. During the first 20 out of 30 bargaining rounds, coalition formation is *delegitimized* by the experimenter. Again, legitimacy theory implies that collective action will be less likely and occur later, that is, the power structure will be more stable, under such conditions than in situations that legitimize coalition formation unconditionally.

A second study will test the effect of *endorsement* on collective action. Again the object is to find the strength of the effect of legitimacy by pitting it against self-interest. As in Thomas, Walker, and Zelditch (1986), subjects are first queried about whether and when collective action should begin. The feedback of responses to those queries is experimentally controlled so that subjects are led to believe that others think collective action should be delayed. Again early coalition formation is delegitimized, but now by endorsement. As for authorization, legitimacy theory predicts that collective action will be less likely and will occur later, that is, the power structure will be more stable, than in situations where endorsement legitimizes immediate coalition formation.

Finally, consider the potential stabilizing effects of a "legitimizing frame." The example is a Br661 network in which six peripheral Bs all can exchange with a central A. The structure is equipower but, being centralized at A, it appears similar to strong power networks. In Br661, peripheral positions are not low power and coalition formation will not benefit them. But naive participants rarely understand that coalitions will not help before they begin bargaining. Following self-interest alone, subjects will form coalitions in early rounds of the experiment and attempt to act collectively. However, after finding that coalitions have no payoff, subjects in later rounds should dispense with coalitions and act individually.

Will subjects in such structures form coalitions because an experimenter *authorizes* them to do so? Will they be more likely to do so if earlier they participated in a strong power network? Conversely, when subjects learn that they gain nothing from coalitions in Br661, will they subsequently fail to form or delay forming coalitions in a structurally similar strong power network? Legitimacy theory implies hypotheses that address these questions. However, definitive answers await more theoretical analysis and empirical tests as we use legitimacy theory to extend NET to more complex and dynamic situations.

COMPLEXITIES AND OPPORTUNITIES

The new directions reviewed thus far indicate a theory in the process of rapid expansion. Each line of work involves straightforward integrations and additions to the theory, and each opens up broad and unexplored research domains. These new directions, especially when aimed at understanding network dynamics, richer conceptualizations of actors, and larger networks, evoke the qualities of an entirely separate emerging theory that may provide directions for solutions and even further developments. *Complexity theory* offers tools that should help to satisfy cravings to apply NET in more natural social settings. More accurately, complexity theory is both a general orientation toward understanding complex phenomena, and a set of concepts, models, and applications (Waldrop 1992). As discussed below, it would appear to be well suited for applications to networks that are more dynamic and more complex than either the early NET models or the networks we study in laboratories. In this section we illustrate several ways in which approaches to complexity may inform theoretical developments.

Dynamics and Agent-Based Systems

To date, NET most often is applied to sets of network positions in which ties represent fixed exchange opportunities, and the dependent variable of interest is equilibrated profit levels at the end of exchange sequences. There are some exceptions, however. First, the GPI approach introduced by Markovsky, Willer, and Patton (1988) anticipated the attrition of certain unused ties. The effect was to transform some networks into smaller, simpler, isolated substructures. Second, Leik (1992) and Willer and Willer (2000) studied situations in which actors choose to open or close network ties, given opportunities to do so. Both approaches entail primitive dynamics whereby a resultant structure follows from an initial structure.

In addition to relational structures, profit structures also manifest dynamics. For instance, Brennan (1981) applied a regression model to the time-paths of profit differentiation across network positions. Additionally, Marsden (1983) published a very sophisticated theoretical model for resource flows, however it has not been tested empirically and its scope appears not to intersect with that of NET. Since Brennan and Marsden's work, most research has concentrated on the stabilized, long-run pattern of exchange outcomes with only strategic analysis studying profit dynamics.

A dynamic approach to social networks would address one or more network *processes*. These may include events that generate or mark changes in gross network structures, in subsets of inter-actor relationships, in the internal states or overt behaviors of individual members of a network, or in virtually any other identifiable property of networks that can vary over time and is relevant to some theoretical purpose. Ironically, the success of prior NET research may partially account for the lack of dynamic analyses. Researchers have developed quite a thorough understanding of the networks that have been investigated. Most exhibit straightforward profit differentiations across time as they march toward their predicted equilibria. Until recently there have been no anomalies suggesting the need for dynamic approaches. Computer simulations built on very simple assumptions produce the same straightforward dynamics and outcomes (Markovsky 1992, 1995). NET researchers generally acknowledge the importance of dynamics, but have not had to confront and solve dynamic problematics. If intriguing questions about static and equilibrium phenomena have driven theoretical progress thus far, then what questions may demand answers of a more dynamic character?

The branch of complexity theory that may be most relevant to exchange network dynamics is the study of *agent-based systems* (Epstein and Axtell 1996; Sichman, Conte, and Gilbert 1998). Aside from its relatively limited use of computer simulations, NET has relied heavily on *analytic models* for generating its predictions. These are mathematical equations that take as their input a quantified representation of the network structure, enact what is essentially a one-step algebraic transformation, and generate an expected pattern of network power effects as output. This may be thought of as a "top-down" solution to predicting power in exchange networks. In contrast, our computer simulations exemplify the "bottom-up" approach characteristic of agent-based systems. That is, instead of employing a kind of master formula that solves the entire system, the simulations imbue each actor in each network position with certain information, processing methods, action proclivities, and behavioral repertoires. A "virtual" context is established with rules and constraints on interaction. That is, network connections limit the potential interaction partners, turn-taking norms establish negotiation sequences, bargaining rules define what constitute successful and unsuccessful exchanges, and so on.

Computer simulations of network exchange processes have been designed to reflect closely the conditions used in experimental tests of NET. The great benefit of this approach has been to aid in the planning of experiments and the interpretation of findings. However, the disadvantages are evident as soon as one begins to read the literature on agent-based systems. The very constraints that make our simulations so useful as an adjunct to our experimental work severely reduce their utility as tools for exploring network dynamics under less constrained conditions. Interestingly, even with the constraints imposed by the NET paradigm, we still have observed intimations of complex dynamics, as when Markovsky (1992) noted that some exchange networks manifest *sensitive dependence* on the outcomes of arbitrary exchange events early in a sequence. For example, in some structures, an actor in a certain position may choose between tied offers from two others, with that choice determining the irrevocable fate of entire substructures. Such processes are hallmarks of the chaotic dynamics at the heart of complex systems.

Agent-based simulation approaches still are a novel development in sociology.[11] Although this is not the appropriate place to review this research, we describe below some of the ways that key concepts from complexity theory in general, and agent-based systems in particular, may direct expansion of NET's scope and power.

Network Complexity

NET researchers often allude to the goal of applying their theories to more complex networks: more actors, more relations, more kinds of relations, and fewer scope restrictions on decision strategies and exchange rules. Today, researchers in other scientific disciplines associate "complexity" with a well-defined set of empirical problems and theoretical solutions. Loosely speaking, complex systems have relatively large numbers of mutually influential objects or agents, and emergent (often surprising) higher-level patterns and structures that arise from seemingly chaotic substrates. Thus, *complexity* refers to conditions and processes that pose challenges which existing theories cannot meet, i.e., many elements interacting over time with mutual feedback and changing environments. Additionally, complexity research points to a fairly well-circumscribed class of phenomena that emerge when conditions and processes are complicated in certain ways. Many of these phenomena are finally becoming more comprehensible through an integrative theoretical approach.[12]

If exchange networks can be shown to possess certain key properties associated with complex systems, then a framework for dynamic extensions of NET could be discovered among complexity concepts and theories. One such property is *self-organization*—the emergence of spontaneous structure or pattern without guidance from the outside environment (Barton 1994). Self-organization appears in surprisingly diverse phenomena including self-synchronizing chemical reactions, current-formation in fluids, role differentiation in insect colonies, automobile traffic patterns, the growth of cities, and the evolution of celestial bodies (Prigogine and Stengers 1984). In NET research, the consistently observed macro-orders of power differentials qualify as emergent, self-organized phenomena. They are neither purposively created from within by subjects, nor imposed from outside by researchers. They arise out of a combination of exchange rules, network structures, and locally oriented actions. However, so far only the simplest combinations have been investigated.

Adaptation is another property that typifies complex systems. System behaviors and properties react dynamically to external and internal perturbations or threats. NET experiments control such contingencies experimentally. Thus, another research direction may involve relaxing such controls and introducing environmental variability. This could entail manipulating resources available within different sectors of the exchange network, or perhaps introducing competition for exchanges from exogenous sources.

Feedback is another critical component of complex systems. As long as components of the system are coupled neither too loosely nor too tightly, their mutual responsiveness may have unintended, self-sustaining outcomes that reverberate throughout the system, for example, nuclear fission or runaway economic inflation. In the network context, this may suggest that the most theoretically interesting phenomena might be found in networks of moderate density, that is, moderate "coupling."

Not only should complexity theory orient NET researchers toward self-organization, adaptation, and feedback, it should suggest directions for solving otherwise intractable problems. It is probably safe to project that networks larger than those studied in the published literature will pose severe problems for current theoretical models—if only due to the explosion of possible structural forms that occurs with small increments in the number of positions (Skvoretz 1996). Already the old analytic models are breaking down. For example, Lucas et al. (forthcoming) investigated linear networks from two to seven positions in length. Prior research suggested that large profit differentiations would emerge across connected positions in odd-length lines, whereas even-length lines would produce only small advantages and disadvantages. The results were not nearly so clear-cut, however. On average, the longer the line, the greater the reduction in inequality for more central positions—for even- *and* odd-length lines. Moreover, with increasing length, the overall pattern of outcomes seems to become increasingly sensitive to the random idiosyncrasies of individual actors.

Such findings may become clearer if we think in terms of larger exchange patterns self-organizing around interactions with random components. Subjects in laboratory networks have some leeway to explore their options. However, experimental controls and smaller network structures constrain whatever systematic profit differentials might accrue from such explorations. As a result, subjects tend not to stray far from the predicted path. However, slightly larger networks (e.g., 7-actor lines) provide more opportunity for the compounding effects of multiple subjects acting slightly "out-of-line." This leads the process to stray from NET predictions in directions from which backtracking is unlikely or impossible. Localized anomalies, such as those due to individual explorations, will crop up virtually at random, with the effect of switching the subsequent course of events to a track that leads to stable but nonpredicted macro patterns.

Thought experiments and computer simulations suggest further possibilities. For example, an actor in a disadvantaged position who takes an inordinately hard bargaining stance has an immediate and direct effect on neighboring positions. Even if this actor quickly returns to "normal" behavior, the local effect of the disruption may diffuse through the network in wave-like fashion. Depending on the peculiarities of a given network structure, and the state of the profit structure at a given moment, positions many steps removed from the deviant eventually may experience unexpected windfalls or losses of exchange opportunities. Conceptually it is a short step from identifying this positive feedback or "network-wave" phenomenon to specifying the conditions that would amplify or dampen such effects.

CONCLUSIONS

Legitimacy, status, and power may all interact in natural settings, further adding to the "complexification" of exchange networks and the potential avenues for theory and research. For instance, we argued that power processes create status differences and that status differences produce power effects. Explorations of dynamic exchange systems undoubtedly will encounter legitimacy effects as well (Walker and Zelditch 1993). NET researchers have not explored this issue empirically but Bell, Walker, and Willer (2000) discuss legitimacy effects on power processes in formal organizations. Legitimate power exercise ought to ensure that theoretically predicted resource flows *reduce* negative emotional reactions, and reduce collective action (e.g., coalition formation), under institutions that permit it. Similarly, we anticipate that *illegitimate* power exercise will introduce noise in studies of resource flows, increase negative emotional reaction, and enhance the likelihood of negative reactions (Walker and Zelditch 1993; Bell, Walker, and Willer 2000).

These and related complexities may presage the future of NET, especially if we take seriously our own call to study larger structures under relaxed scope conditions. Theories of complexity point out important aspects of exchange networks about which we may not have otherwise thought. Analysis of complexity directs us to stand at the edges of known structures and processes and to understand how uncertainty, exploration, and innovation help us grasp phenomena that until now seemed incomprehensible.

All successful theories have modest beginnings: small sets of concepts and assumptions apply under highly constrained, usually unrealistic conditions to explain and predict relatively simple phenomena. Although one cannot generally predict which theories will grow, evolve, and flourish or which will fall by the wayside, it is safe to assert that theories in a developing research field cannot remain static if they are to be viable. They must be the focus of concerted efforts to broaden their scope of application, and to expand, refine, and verify their predictions. The constraints that characterized early formulations must be relaxed over time in order to expose the theory to increasingly complex and natural conditions. Ideally, even while the phenomena covered by the theory become increasingly complex, the theory itself remains relatively simple. NET could be broadened and refined further, and it could be simpler. Work continues.

NOTES

The authors thank the National Science Foundation for grants testing the theoretical developments reported in this work.

1. Current usage can be confusing since many researchers use the term "network exchange theory" to describe a variety of exchange approaches to the study of power. This chapter focuses on Network Exchange Theory, the label Markovsky, Willer, and Patton 1988 gave to the unit theory that grew out of Elementary Theory. We use the term "exchange network theory" in lowercase to describe other exchange-theoretic ideas.

2. Power as benefit can be traced to Marx's idea of exploitation ([1867] 1967) and power as control to Weber's conception of domination ([1918] 1968). Two more recent definitions are offered by Dahl and Lukes: (1) "A has power over B to the extent that he can get B to do something which B would not otherwise do" (Dahl 1957:202–3); (2) "A exercises power over B when A affects B in a manner contrary to B's interests" (Lukes 1974:34). Dahl's definition, in the tradition of Weber, focuses on power as control whereas Lukes's definition, in the tradition of Marx, focuses on power as the distribution of benefits.

3. See Willer and Markovsky (1993) and Willer (1999a) for applications of resistance to other strong power structures.

4. With one qualification, previous studies of inclusive connection show that the second exchange, not the first, is affected (Patton and Willer 1990; Willer 1999a). The qualification is that exchanges are sequential, as they must be here. In some networks, the exchanges of an inclusively connected position can become effectively simultaneous. As exchanges approach simultaneity, the effect of inclusion becomes the same in all relations.

5. Our designation of the A-B exchange as the "first exchange" is arbitrary. NET predicts A's disadvantage no matter which exchange occurs "first."

6. An N-branch is a network with N positions connected only to a single central position.

7. It is intriguing to imagine that power use may have increased status while only influence was blocked by negative emotion, but our research uses influence as the indicator of status. In the future it may be useful to disconnect status and influence, however, the two were not separable in this research.

8. Following Freese and Cohen (1973:182), "an element e_i is relevant to an element e_j only if an actor who possesses e_i, is expected to possess e_j."

9. We use the plural because it is not clear that there exists a single legitimation process (Zelditch 2001).

10. In December 2000, the U.S. Supreme Court took actions that ensured George W. Bush's ascendancy to the office of President. However, their split decision (5 to 4) offers only a weak authorization. Furthermore, Bush's failure to win the popular vote and questions concerning voting and counting of ballots in Florida suggest that his presidency lacks endorsement. Legitimacy theory implies that he may encounter substantial difficulty governing the country.

11. Examples include Burke 1997; Carley and Lee 1998; Hanneman, Collins, and Mordt 1995; Macy and Skvoretz 1998; and Smith and Stevens 1999, and this list is not very far from exhaustive.

12. See Waldrop (1992) for examples in a broad range of disciplines; Holland (1998) who emphasizes emergent phenomena; Eve, Horsfall, and Lee (1994) for sociological applications; and Read and Miller (1998) for a social psychological focus.

REFERENCES

Barton, Scott. 1994. "Chaos, Self-organization, and Psychology." *American Psychologist* 49:5–14.

Bell, Richard S., Henry A. Walker, and David Willer. 2000. "Power, Influence, and Legitimacy in Organizations: Implications of Three Theoretical Research Programs." Pp. 131–77 in *Research on the Sociology of Organizations*, vol. 17, edited by Samuel Bacharach and Edward J. Lawler. Greenwich, CT: JAI Press.

Berger, Joseph, Bernard P. Cohen, and Morris Zelditch Jr. 1972. "Status Characteristics and Social Interaction." *American Sociological Review* 37:241–55.

Berger, Joseph, M. Hamit Fisek, Robert Z. Norman, and David G. Wagner. 1985. "Formation of Reward Expectations in Status Situations." Pp. 215–61 in *Status Rewards and Influence*, edited by Joseph Berger and Morris Zelditch Jr. San Francisco: Jossey-Bass.

Berger, Joseph, M. Hamit Fisek, Robert Z. Norman, and Morris Zelditch Jr. 1977. *Status Characteristics and Social Interaction*. New York: Elsevier.

Berger, Joseph, Susan J. Rosenholtz, and Morris Zelditch Jr. 1980. "Status Organizing Processes." *Annual Review of Sociology* 6:470–508.

Brennan, John S. 1981. "Some Experimental Structures." Pp. 188–204 in *Networks, Exchange and Coercion*, edited by David Willer and Bo Anderson. New York: Elsevier/Greenwood.

Burke, Peter J. 1997. "An Identity Model for Social Exchange." *American Sociological Review* 62:134–50.

Carley, Kathleen, and Ju-Sung Lee. 1998. "Dynamic Organizations: Organizational Adaptation in a Changing Environment." *Advances in Strategic Management* 15:269–97.

Corra, Mamadi. 2000. "Applying Resistance to Ordering in Exchange Networks: A Theoretical Extension." *Current Research in Social Psychology* 5:84–96, *www.uiowa.edu/~grpproc.*

Dahl, Robert. 1957. "The Concept of Power." *Behavioral Science* 2:201–18.

Dawes, Robyn M. 1988. *Rational Choice in an Uncertain World.* San Diego: Harcourt Brace Jovanovich.

Dornbusch, S. M., and W. R. Scott. 1975. *Evaluation and the Exercise of Authority.* San Francisco: Jossey-Bass.

Emerson, Richard M. 1972a. "Exchange Theory, Part I: A Psychological Basis for Social Exchange." Pp. 38–57 in *Sociological Theories in Progress*, vol. 2, edited by Joseph Berger, Morris Zelditch Jr., and Bo Anderson. Boston: Houghton-Mifflin.

———. 1972b. "Exchange Theory, Part II: Exchange Relations and Networks." Pp. 58–87 in *Sociological Theories in Progress,* vol. 2, edited by Joseph Berger, Morris Zelditch Jr., and Bo Anderson. Boston: Houghton-Mifflin.

———. 1981. "Social Exchange Theory." In *Social Psychology: Sociological Perspectives,* edited by Morris Rosenberg and Ralph H. Turner. New York: Basic.

———. 1987. "Toward a Theory of Value in Social Exchange." Pp.11–46 in *Social Exchange Theory,* edited by K. S. Cook. Newbury Park, CA: Sage.

Epstein, Joshua M., and Robert Axtell. 1996. *Growing Artificial Societies.* Washington, DC: Brookings.

Eve, Raymond A., Sara Horsfall, and Mary E. Lee. 1994. *Chaos, Complexity, and Sociology: Myths, Models, and Theories.* Newbury Park, CA: Sage.

Friedrich, C. J. 1958. "What Is Meant by 'Politically Impossible'?" *American Behavioral Scientist* 1 (5):3–5.

Freese, Lee, and Bernard P. Cohen. 1973. "Eliminating Status Generalization." *Sociometry* 36:177–93.

Hanneman, Robert A., Randall Collins, and Gabriele Mordt. 1995. "Discovering Theory Dynamics by Computer Simulation: Experiments on State Legitimacy and Imperialist Capitalism." *Sociological Methodology* 25:1–46.

Holland, John H. 1998. *Emergence: From Chaos to Order.* Reading, MA: Perseus Books.

Homans, George Caspar. 1974. *Social Behavior: Its Elementary Forms.* Rev. ed. New York: Harcourt Brace Jovanovich.

Kemper, Theodore D., and Randall Collins. 1990. "Dimensions of Microinteraction." *American Journal of Sociology* 96:32–68.

Leik, Robert K. 1992. "New Directions for Network Exchange Theory: Strategic Manipulation of Network Linkages." *Social Networks* 14:309–23.

Lovaglia, Michael J. 1994. "Relating Power to Status." *Advances in Group Process* 11:87–111.

———. 1995. "Power and Status: Exchange, Attribution, and Expectation States." *Small Group Research* 26:400–26.

———. 1997. "Status, Emotion, and Structural Power." Pp. 159–78 in *Status, Network, and Structure: Theory Development in Group Processes,* edited by Jacek Szmatka, John Skvoretz, and Joseph Berger. Stanford, CA: Stanford University Press.

Lovaglia, Michael, and Jeffrey Houser. 1996. "Emotional Reactions, Status Characteristics, and Social Interaction." *American Sociological Review* 61:867–83.

Lovaglia, Michael, John Skvoretz, David Willer, and Barry Markovsky. 1995. "Assessing Fundamental Power Differences in Exchange Networks." *Current Research in Social Psychology* 1:8–17, *www.uiowa.edu/~grpproc.*

Lucas, Jeffrey, C. Wesley Younts, Michael J. Lovaglia, and Barry Markovsky. Forthcoming. "Lines of Power Development in Exchange Networks." *Social Forces.*

Lukes, Steven. 1974. *Power: A Radical View.* London: Macmillan.

Macy, Michael W., and Andres Flache. 1995. "Beyond Rationality in Models of Choice." *Annual Review of Sociology* 21:73–91.

Macy, Michael W., and John Skvoretz. 1998. "The Evolution of Trust and Cooperation Between Strangers: A Computational Model." *American Sociological Review* 63:638–60.

Markovsky, Barry. 1992. "Network Exchange Outcomes: Limits of Predictability." *Social Networks* 14:267–86.

———. 1995. "Developing an Exchange Network Simulator." *Sociological Perspectives* 38:519–45.

Markovsky, Barry, David Willer, and Travis Patton. 1988. "Power Relations in Exchange Networks." *American Sociological Review* 53:220–36.

Marsden, Peter V. 1983. "Restricted Access in Networks and Models of Power." *American Journal of Sociology* 88:686–717.

Marx, Karl. [1867] 1967. *Capital.* New York: International Publishers.

Moore, James C., Jr. 1985. "Role Enactment and Self Identity." Pp. 262–315 in *Status, Rewards, and Influence,* edited by Joseph Berger and Morris Zelditch Jr. San Francisco: Jossey-Bass.

Patton, Travis, and David Willer. 1990. "Connection and Power in Centralized Exchange Networks." *Journal of Mathematical Sociology* 16:31–49.

Prigogine, Ilya, and Isabelle Stengers. 1984. *Order Out of Chaos.* Toronto: Bantam Books.

Read, Stephen J., and Lynn C. Miller. 1998. *Connectionist Models of Social Reasoning and Social Behavior.* Mahwah, NJ: Lawrence Erlbaum Associates.

Ridgeway, Cecilia L., and Henry A. Walker. 1995. "Status Structures." Pp. 281–310 in *Sociological Perspectives on Social Psychology,* edited by Karen S. Cook, Gary Alan Fine, and James S. House. Boston: Allyn and Bacon.

Sichman, Jaime S., Rosaria Conte, and Nigel Gilbert (eds.). 1998. *Multi-Agent Systems and Agent-based Simulation.* New York: Springer.

Simpson, Brent, and Michael W. Macy. 2001. "Collective Action and Power Inequality: Coalitions in Exchange Networks." *Social Psychology Quarterly* 64:88–100.

Simpson, Brent, and David Willer. 1999. "A New Method For Finding Power Structures." Pp. 270–84 in *Network Exchange Theory,* edited by David Willer. Westport, CT: Praeger.

Skvoretz, John. 1996. "An Algorithm to Generate Connected Graphs." *Current Research in Social Psychology* 1 (5):43–49, *www.uiowa.edu/~grpproc.*

Skvoretz, John, and David Willer. 1993. "Exclusion and Power: A Test of Four Theories of Power in Exchange Networks." *American Sociological Review* 58:801–18.

Smith, Thomas S., and Gregory T. Stevens. 1999. "The Architecture of Small Networks: Strong Interaction and Dynamic Organization in Small Social Systems." *American Sociological Review* 64:403–20.

Stewart, Penny A., and James C. Moore. 1992. "Wage Disparities and Performance Expectations." *Social Psychology Quarterly* 55:78–85.

Thibaut, John W., and Harold H. Kelley. 1959. *The Social Psychology of Groups.* New York: Wiley.

Thomas, George M., Henry A. Walker, and Morris Zelditch Jr. 1986. "Legitimacy and Collective Action." *Social Forces* 65:378–404.

Thye, Shane R. 1997. *From Status to Power: A Status Value Theory of Power in Exchange Networks.* Ph.D. dissertation, Department of Sociology, University of Iowa.

———. 1999a. "Status Influence and Status Value." Pp. 248–55 in *Network Exchange Theory,* edited by David Willer. Westport, CT: Praeger.

———. 1999b. "A Status Value Theory of Power: Ratio Level Predictions for New Exchange Structures." Paper presented at the annual meeting of the American Sociological Association, Chicago.

———. 2000. "A Status Value Theory of Power in Exchange Relations." *American Sociological Review* 65:407–32.

Veblen, Thorstein. 1899. *The Theory of the Leisure Class.* New York: Macmillan.

Waldrop, M. Mitchell. 1992. *Complexity.* New York: Simon and Schuster.

Walker, Henry A., Larry Rogers, and Morris Zelditch Jr. 1988. "Legitimacy and Collective Action: A Research Note." *Social Forces* 67:216–28.

Walker, Henry A., George M. Thomas, and Morris Zelditch Jr. 1986. "Legitimation, Endorsement, and Stability." *Social Forces* 64:620–43.

Walker, Henry A., Shane R. Thye, Brent Simpson, Michael J. Lovaglia, David Willer, and Barry Markovsky. 2000. "Network Exchange Theory: Recent Developments and New Directions." *Social Psychology Quarterly* 63:324–37.

Walker, Henry A., and Morris Zelditch Jr. 1993. "Power, Legitimacy, and the Stability of Authority: A Theoretical Research Program." Pp. 364–81 in *Theoretical Research Programs,* edited by Joseph Berger and Morris Zelditch Jr. Stanford, CA: Stanford University Press.

Weber, Max. [1918] 1968. *Economy and Society.* Berkeley: University of California Press.

Willer, David. 1981. "Quantity and Network Structure." Pp. 109–27 in *Networks, Exchange, and Coercion,* edited by David Willer and Bo Anderson. New York: Elsevier/Greenwood.

———. 1987. *Theory and the Experimental Investigation of Social Structures.* New York: Gordon and Breach.

———. 1999a. *Network Exchange Theory.* Westport, CT: Praeger.

———. 1999b. "The Power of Collective Action." Paper presented at the annual meeting of the American Sociological Association, Chicago.

Willer, David, and Bo Anderson. 1981. *Networks, Exchange, and Coercion.* New York: Elsevier.

Willer, David, Michael Lovaglia, and Barry Markovsky. 1997. "Power and Influence: A Theoretical Bridge." *Social Forces* 76:571–603.

Willer, David, and Barry Markovsky. 1993. "The Theory of Elementary Relations: Its Development and Research Program." Pp. 323–63 in *Theoretical Research Programs: Studies in Theory Growth,* edited by Joseph Berger and Morris Zelditch Jr. Stanford CA: Stanford University Press.

Willer, David, and John Skvoretz. 1997. "Games and Structures." *Rationality and Society* 9:5–35.

———. 1999. "Network Connection and Exchange Ratios: Theory, Predictions, and Experimental Tests." Pp. 195–225 in *Network Exchange Theory,* edited by David Willer. Westport, CT: Praeger.

Willer, David, and Jacek Szmatka. 1993. "Cross-National Experimental Investigations of Elementary Theory: Implications for the Generality of the Theory and the Autonomy of Social Structure." Pp. 37–81 in *Advances in Group Processes,* vol. 10, edited by E. J. Lawler, B. Markovsky, K. Heimer, and J. O'Brien. Greenwich CT: JAI Press.

Willer, Robb. 2000. "The Status Value of Power Use." Paper presented at the annual meeting of the American Sociological Association, Washington, DC.

Willer, Robb, and David Willer. 2000. "Exploring Dynamic Networks: Hypotheses and Conjectures." *Social Networks* 22:251–72.

Zelditch, Morris. 2001. "Processes of Legitimation: Recent Developments and New Directions." *Social Psychology Quarterly* 64:4–17.

Zelditch, Morris, Jr., and Henry A. Walker. 1984. "Legitimacy and the Stability of Authority." Pp. 1–25 in *Advances in Group Processes,* vol. 1, edited by E. J. Lawler. Greenwich, CT: JAI Press.

IV

SOCIAL MOVEMENTS AND REVOLUTIONS

6

The Resource Mobilization Research Program: Progress, Challenge, and Transformation

Mayer N. Zald and John D. McCarthy

Sociologists in the late 1960s and early 1970s began to develop a relatively new theoretical paradigm of social movements and protest that came to be called the Resource Mobilization (RM) perspective (Jenkins 1983). They were responding to changes in the larger society, to intellectual currents in the social sciences, and to theoretical critiques and empirical research. Their starting points were various. Some challenged the usefulness of "breakdown theory," which argued that both collective action and individual criminality were a result of the loosening of societal bonds and normative controls (Lohdi and Tilly 1973). Others reacted against deprivation and grievance based theories, which attempted to predict collective action directly from levels of grievances, with no regard to the costs of action (McCarthy and Zald 1973, 1977; Oberschall 1973). William Gamson (1968) saw social movements and disruptive protest as a tactical necessity for those excluded from access to and influence with authoritative decision makers. Since many scholars identified with the 1960s movements, they saw them as means to ends, rather than as an expression of irrational impulses, disorganization, or deviance.

These scholars differed among themselves in research style, their work ranging from laboratory studies, to case studies, to analyses of historical strike and protest data. They varied, as well, in their theoretical style, from formal modeling to substantive analysis. Nevertheless, by 1976 when a conference was convened at Vanderbilt University (Zald and McCarthy 1979), it was apparent that a new paradigm or framework had emerged. Shaped, but not bound, by the problem of collective action as described by Mancur Olson (1965), an approach emerged that saw collective action and social movements as normal extensions of everyday life. The new work probed how solidary action was achieved, how resources were gathered, how costs and benefits were weighed, and how social relations facilitated collective action.

A decade or so after its initial statements, the RM framework had come to dominate a much-enlarged field of social movement research (Morris and Herring 1988). The approach was widely seen as exhibiting two main variants. These were the political process or political opportunity one and the entrepreneurial organizational variant. They came to be labeled RMI and RMII respectively (Perrow 1979) and the distinction was widely perpetuated (Jenkins 1983). Now, almost three decades after the first statements appeared, and while social movement research is flourishing, it remains to be seen whether or not the several variants of the RM program will continue to dominate movement scholarship. We will return to this question below. Here we assess the growth and transformation of the RM program, especially the organizational entrepreneurial variant with which we are identified (McCarthy and Zald 1973, 1977; Zald and McCarthy 1987). Our assessment of the growth and transformation of the study of social movements includes attention to the critiques, theoretical developments, and research findings generated by the theory. Throughout our presentation we will draw upon research that chronicles the development of the U.S. environmental movement to illustrate central principles.

Section I focuses upon the background assumptions and orienting propositions of the organizational entrepreneurial version of RM theory with which we are associated. While section I develops the theoretical assumptions and scope conditions of the theory, section II reviews subsequent empirical research and several theoretical critiques that suggest a reformulation of some of the core concepts. Section III places the organizational entrepreneurial version of RM in the broader theoretical context developed by scholars of other variants of RM that have significantly increased the explanatory power of the RM research agenda. Brief attention is devoted to the Political Opportunity approach, and to the Strategic Framing approach. We conclude with a discussion of extensions of the RM program, unresolved issues, and recent research and conceptual trends that lead away from a focus on the research problems identified by the program.

I: ASSUMPTIONS, SCOPE CONDITIONS, AND ORIENTING PROPOSITIONS

Social movements (SMs) can be defined as mobilized or activated (effective) demand (preferences) for change in society (McCarthy and Zald 1977). This broad definition is not fully accepted in the larger community of scholars, nor even among the community of scholars that constitute the RM community, most of whom make the actions of social movement adherents the centerpiece of a definition (Diani 1992; Oliver 1989). Nevertheless, it is strategically useful to the organizational entrepreneurial version of RM to adopt such a definition, which focuses upon how and why social change demands are generated and how social movement organizations (SMOs), whether small and informal or large and more formal, are generated and organized. Central to our approach is the separation of increasing or decreasing demand for movement activity and social change from the possibility of the stimulation of demand by SMOs. Consequently the organizational growth, decline, or adaptation of SMOs may be more or less tightly linked to increases or decreases in preferences for changes (social movements). Casting the U.S. environmental movement into this conceptualization, strong preferences for environmental protection constitute the social movement, and the many organized environmental groups are the SMOs that may both reflect and create it. This approach separates both preferences and the size and vitality of SMOs from objective grievances. A nation with very low levels of environmental pollution, by international standards, for instance, could experience very high demand for environmental social change efforts as well as many highly organized SMOs.

Moreover, as demand increases and as a movement meets with responses from the larger society and polity, the possibilities for the expansion of the number of SMOs and differentiation among them increases. All the SMOs representing the preferences of an SM can be thought of as an industry (SMI). For instance, the U.S. environmental movement includes thousands of organized groups ranging from very large and highly professionalized national groups to very small, mostly volunteer local groups (Brulle 2000). SMIs typically display tactical differentiation and internal competition and conflict, which is especially common between the large national and small local SMOs in the U.S. environmental movement (Edwards 1995). There may be few or many SMs and SMIs in a society at any one point in time. All of the SMOs and SMIs may be considered a social movement sector (SMS). An important issue that flows from this conceptualization is what factors account for variation in the size and orientation(s) of a national SMS (Garner and Zald 1987).

Background Assumptions and Scope Conditions

Four background assumptions, embodied in key contrasts, set off the organizational entrepreneurial version of RM from earlier traditions or approaches in social movement theory.

1. Contrasted with theories that attempted to predict mobilization levels directly from "frustration" or deprivation, RM assumes that the amount of mobilization or movement participation that occurs cannot be predicted directly from the extent of deprivation or grievances among a group. Participation involves expenditures of time, energy, and money, and groups with few resources are less able to act on grievances or perceived injustices.
2. Some earlier theories had held that participation in movements was a form of irrational and pathological behavior: at the individual level it was an expression of personal alienation and/or pathology; at the societal level, a result of isolated, uprooted, and unattached groups. RM treats social

movement participation as "normal behavior," expecting that it emerges out of biographical circumstances, social supports, and immediate life situations.

3. Most prior theories located the resources (volunteer labor and financial support) that were mobilized for social change largely or completely within the aggrieved or beneficiary constituency. Our version of RM locates many of the resources available for supporting social change in the larger society. These include all levels of government, foundations, religious institutions, and conscience constituencies, groups that support the movement's goals, even though its members are not eligible to receive the direct output of the policy/political changes that the movement advocate. Supporters of action to protect rainforests are a particularly good example of conscience constituents, as were white supporters of the civil rights movement.
4. Prior theories of social movements focused largely upon the interaction between SMIs and authorities, with the activists attempting to raise costs for authorities or drawing attention to the legitimacy of their claims. The organizational entrepreneurial version of RM draws attention to the role of the media in mediating between the movement and bystander publics (those citizens with no strong preferences for social change). Bringing in the role of the media raises the possibility that movement activists and authorities are caught in a larger contest for the support of bystander publics that may include bystander elite groups.

Our theoretical formulation grew out of an empirical stock taking of trends in the dynamics of social movements in the United States (McCarthy and Zald 1973). Although it was stated in quite general terms, seemingly applicable to social movements in any society, it had implicit and explicit scope conditions that some have argued has limited its applicability. Among the most important of these scope conditions are these: It is intended to apply to societies that have

1. Voluntary association traditions. Individuals can choose to affiliate and participate in voluntary associations and knowledge of how to organize them is fairly widespread.
2. Freedom of speech and freedom of assembly laws that are normatively accepted, even if not universally applied.
3. A mass media that is fairly open to reporting grievances and protest.
4. An electoral system is so structured that small groups have little chance of gaining legislative office. Thus, mobilization for social change outside of the electoral system is encouraged.

This approach can and has been applied in situations where these scope conditions do not hold (e.g., Khawaja 1994). And, other versions of RM (e.g., Oberschall 1973; Tilly 1978) are not as dependent upon these scope conditions. Yet, it is clear that our version was formulated with these conditions in mind, and the propositions we developed and the objects of analysis that were chosen took these scope conditions as shaping the parameters in which analysis took place.

Orienting Propositions

The organizational entrepreneurial version of RM is a middle range theory that develops propositions about the interrelationship of demands for change (i.e., sentiments, preferences, tastes, values, grievances), costs and benefits of attempting to realize those demands, SMOs and technologies of mobilization and protest, SMIs, and the SMS. Here we present the core concepts of the theory and selected propositions.

Demands, Costs and Benefits, and Resources

SMOs draw on the sentiment or preference pool in the larger society. (Sentiment pools can be thought of as the distribution of attitudes for or against some proposed social change, broadly conceived.) Sentiment or preference pools vary in the number of people that share the sentiment and the intensity with which those sentiments for change are held. Over time the size and intensity of the preference pool changes as issues and problems succeed each other on the public agenda. Of course, for some parts of the population, the preference structure may be relatively stable, even while the size of the sentiment pool in the rest of the society may fluctuate. (For example, the grievances and preferences of the African American community may have relatively stable preferences on civil rights issues, while the rest of the society may experience dramatic fluctuations in the level of concern.) Issue entrepreneurs, (politicians, journalists, ministers, SMO leaders, public intellectuals, and so on) attempt to define the issues for specific and general audiences. If they are successful, they enlarge and intensify the sentiment pool, that is, they increase the number of people committed to a demand or preference for change and intensify the commitment to the issue of those who already share that preference.[1]

Having a preference for change, or a sense of injustice, does not automatically translate into taking action to rectify the feeling of injustice. Action occurs in the context of the life situation of the potential participant and in the context of competing commitments, social supports, costs, and resources. Competing commitments may include commitments to work, to family, and to educational goals that may inhibit participation. Individuals differ in the resources that they command relevant to a movement's tasks and the extent to which those resources (skills, money, time, and status) can be put in the service of the movement. Individuals with available discretionary time and money and with few competing commitments, are more likely to act on their preferences to participate in movement activities. Similarly, if others in one's life-space share values and grievances and already participate in movement related activities, the social costs of participation are lowered. Conversely, if there exist few supports for participation, we would expect a lower likelihood of acting on preferences.

The resources social movements draw upon come from many sources. Specific resources, such as labor, facilities, and money may be supplied by individuals who are part of the presumed beneficiary base of the movement—the group whose claims of injustice or deprivation are to be rectified. Or they may be derived from conscience constituencies—others in the society who believe in the rightness of the cause, even though they themselves and their friends and relatives will not directly benefit from the changes advocated. Monies, labor, facilities, and especially the conferral of legitimacy may also be made available through institutional channels, such as church bodies, philanthropic foundations, and government programs (Cress and Snow 1996). The major U.S. environmental SMOs have established ongoing funding relationships with some of the largest private foundations (e.g., Ford, Pew, and McArthur) that provide them stable sources of support that is not so subject to shifts in political opportunities (Jenkins and Halcli 1999; Brulle and Caniglia 1999). There are also societal infrastructural resources that may be available to movements that effect their ability to mobilize. The development of the mass media, of cheaper and more rapid transportation means, of postal systems, and of electronic communication systems, such as fax and the Internet, may affect mobilization costs.

Social Movement Organizations: Structure, Technologies, and Professionalization

SMOs are relatively formal organizations that develop to manage the interdependencies of adherents and activists committed to the movement. If a movement effort endures beyond a single event and links several networks of adherents and activists, a more or less formal organization (at a minimum a mailing list, a name, and a set of controllers of the mailing list and attendant resources) is likely to develop. Although many SMOs may be relatively small, enduring movements with a substantial number of adherents may develop larger SMOs that link adherents in different locales and even countries.[2]

Activists, acting on their own, as members of networks, or as self-identified agents of SMOs, attempt to transform bystander publics into sympathizers, and sympathizers into adherents (contributors of money and labor). Cadre, the activists who devote the most time, money, and energy to the organization are drawn from the ranks of adherents to an SM. They also may be drawn from the ranks of cadre and adherents of previous movements and ideologically compatible collective action streams. Thus, as a new focused movement emerges, it can draw on adherents of prior movements or ideologies that are less active and resonant at the present time.

As SMOs grow larger and command larger resource flows, they are likely to develop cadre and staff that devote considerable amounts of time to the SMO. Indeed, professionalization may occur in that cadre may develop skills specific to leading and managing SMOs and in that careers may develop in a specific SMI or related organizations and industries. A number of structural/institutional problems also present themselves as SMOs become larger and less transient. These include: the relationship between cadre and adherents; how choices are made about programs, tactics and goals; the relationships between central offices and chapters or local groups; and the extent to which SMOs operate in conformance with accounting and other standards that constrain organizations in general and the nonprofit/social movement sector.

SMOs combine resources to attempt to accomplish social change. Two interlinked set of repertoires or technologies can be thought to be employed (Oliver and Marwell 1992). *Technologies of mobilization* include techniques for recruiting adherents—members who contribute money through direct mail and telephone campaigns, participants in demonstrations and marches, recruits to "cells" for illegal and terrorist activities. *Technologies of protest* include relatively peaceful and legal activities, such as speaking to public gatherings, marches and demonstrations, and lobbying efforts. And they can also include more confrontational activities that may be legal or illegal, such as boycotts, sit-ins, and other blockades of "normal" civil activity, to clearly illegal activity such as property damage, murder, arson, and theft. The two kinds of technologies may be interlinked in that the protest or change activity, when visible, may affect bystanders' and sympathizers' readiness to become adherents. On the other side, the kinds of mobilization technologies that are utilized may serve to mobilize adherents with different kinds of commitments to protest activities, shaping the subsequent tactical repertoires of SMOs.

In large modern societies, with widely dispersed communities, the conditions and injustices that SMs wish to rectify are not directly experienced or perceived by most bystanders. Similarly, bystander publics do not directly perceive the actions of SMOs and SM activists. Instead, mass media firms (print, television, and radio) filter perceptions through their reporting routines and the images that they convey. The amount, substantive content, and biases of media coverage is a complex result of the range of events and newsworthy stories in the larger society, the competitive situation of the media organizations, and the professional commitments and expectations of media staff. Since enlarging sentiment pools depends at least in part on this indirect filtering, SMO and SM cadre are dependent upon and strategically attempt to shape the amount and nature of media coverage of the movement. Reference elite groups, such as business and religious leaders, and authorities, too, are affected by filtered perceptions of the movement and its causes. And authorities may also attempt to shape and limit media coverage.

Social Movement Industry (SMI) and Social Movement Sector (SMS)

As the sentiment pool expands, as more people support the movement and as more resources are available for mobilization, the number of SMOs may increase. As an SMI expands the SMOs within it are likely to become differentiated along lines that parallel the ideological constellation of their constituency as well as in terms of the functional niche that they occupy. If the sentiment pool was fully homogeneous, fewer SMOs might be founded, but SMOs are created to gather up the resources of segments of the pool that typically differ in the extremity of their diagnoses and in their commitments to different kinds of tactics and program. In turn, those SMOs are likely to encourage the segmenting and fragmenting of the sentiment pool.

All of the SMOs that share a general movement goal can be thought of as an industry. SMOs within an industry may cooperate, compete, and sometimes engage in conflict with one another. They come together for some shared purposes either of protest or of collective representation; they compete for resources from sympathizers and adherents; and they conflict over leadership of the movement as a whole, over who should represent the movement to authorities and the larger public. Moreover, as more resources become available, specialization of function may occur. Some SMOs may become information gathering organizations, others provide legal services, and still others lobbying services to other SMOs committed to the broad general goals of the movement.

There may be several social movements at varying degrees of mobilization at any one time in a society, or there may be none. Societies differ in the extent to which they encourage and facilitate social movements. All of the SMIs in a society can be conceived as the Social Movement Sector. The size and orientation of the SMS is a function of the amount of societal resources devoted to social change (whatever its content), the extent to which associational resources are provided by the larger society. It is also a function of the pluralistic or authoritarian orientation of the state, and the relationship of the movement sector to the political party space. The size and shape of the SMS therefore can be expected to vary between nation states and over time within a state.

These are the core conceptual elements of the organizational entrepreneurial version of RM theory. Over the past several decades an extensive body of scholarship has accumulated building upon these elements as well as sometimes challenging their usefulness. In the next section we briefly touch upon some of the, in our judgement, most important extensions and challenges to the elements.

II: EXTENSION AND CHALLENGE

The development of the resource mobilization paradigm altered the problematics of theory and the components of social movements to be studied. Testable hypotheses were developed, but probably more important was the redirection of the sociological gaze, such that aspects of movement phenomena that had been ignored previously subsequently came to the forefront of attention. In this section we revisit the conceptualization of resources, discuss the need for a demography of SMIs and the SMS, explore the ties between SMOs and public protest, ask how media processes shape sentiment pools, and conclude with a brief discussion of micro-mobilization. We do so with an eye toward how subsequent work has extended and challenged the founding conceptual elements of RMII.

What Are Resources and Where Do They Come From?

We began with fairly obvious categories of resources—the amount and kind of labor, money, contributions in kind, and legitimacy. Many scholars used some version of this same set of resources, but critics noted the unexamined use of these categories, calling for a more refined specification of resources. Several important attempts have been made to develop more fine-grained specifications (Oliver and Marwell 1992; Cress and Snow 1996). It is increasingly clear that symbolic and informational resources are central to SMOs, yet the problem remains of how to best think about and, especially to measure, symbolic resources. One study of peace movement SMOs in the United States found legitimacy more important to organizational survival than financial resources or members (Edwards and Marullo 1995). Another study found that the spread of ideas about the environment was one of the most important precursors of the founding of new environmental SMOs. SMOs use symbols and frames to attract support, and they deploy newly invented repertoires of action to bring about change, but these resources cannot be so easily controlled as can money and the labor of supporters.

Exogenous Resources

More than the other RM approaches, RMII focused on the supply of external resources. What have we learned recently about the funding of SMOs and SMIs by philanthropic foundations, churches, and government? National SMOs clearly depend heavily upon these institutional sources of support. Many local SMOs also receive support from these sources. In general, however, the more professionalized SMOs are, the more likely they are to receive them. Trends in the flow of exogenous resources suggest that they flow after indigenous protest rather than being responsible for fomenting it (Jenkins and Eckert 1986). A number of studies suggest that the more indigenous resources controlled by communities of social movement adherents, the greater the likelihood they will be mobilized (e.g., Khawaja 1994). The national organizations of the U.S. environmental SMI have been successful in raising large amounts of resources from their affluent constituents, and have also come to depend upon large resource flows from private foundations (Jenkins and Halcli 1999).

Demography of the U.S. SMS

RMII's focus upon cadre and leaders creating diverse organizations to mobilize supporters made clear a need for knowledge about the number and form of the SMOs across the number of SMIs making up the SMS. We do not yet have adequate studies of the whole sector,[3] but we do have several comprehensive studies of SMIs for the United States (the peace movement industry and the environmental movement industry). The national environmental SMI, for instance, is composed of thousands of SMOs. The majority of them are small local associations of individual members led by volunteers. But many local SMOs are led by paid staff, and many of them are coalitions of other organizations. And, many local SMOs are affiliated with networks of other SMOs. At the national level, SMOs are highly likely to be led by paid staff, and significant numbers of them have organizational members and many have no membership at all. It is clear that the professionalized national part of the U.S. SMS has grown rapidly over recent decades. This is especially true among national environmental organizations like the Sierra Club and the National Resources Defense Council which, in spite of large memberships, have become highly professionalized in management, lobbying, and knowledge production (Mitchell, Mertig, and Dunlap 1991). There is also a set of transnational environmental SMOs, many of which preceded the development of national environmental agencies (Frank et al. 1999). The difficulties in enumerating SMIs means that we have no systematic studies of the size and dynamics of the entire U.S. social movement sector.

The Impact of Organizational Capacity on Protest

The organizational entrepreneurial version of RM asserts that there ought to be a connection between the size and shape of the SMI and the size and shape of protest. This is not a well-developed research area but we can say something about how many protest events in fact have SMO sponsorship and involvement, about the consequences of SMO sponsorship, about how national protests are organized, and about the large scale trends in the organization of protest. Studies based on newspaper accounts of protest events show great variation in whether they have SMO sponsorship, but if they do, the events tend to be less confrontational unless the sponsors are student organizations (Van Dyke, Soule, and McCarthy 2001). Protest events in national political centers, such as Washington, D.C. and Bonn, Germany, are more likely to be formally permitted and, therefore, have SMO sponsors than are events outside of those centers. Large-scale protest events are typically organized by coalitions of organizations, through a process Gerhards and Rucht (1992) call meso-mobilization, whereby umbrella organizations mobilize sympathetic SMOs who in turn mobilize their members. And, finally, Minkoff (1997) shows in her study of ethnic-racial and women's SMOs that increases in the organizational capacity of those SMIs lead to subsequent increases in their protest mobilization.

Micro-mobilization

One of the major problematics of the broader RM program, as was the case with earlier approaches to social movements, has been the explanation of individual decisions to participate in movement activities. And while many scholars in the RM tradition did not and do not make solving Mancur Olson's paradox central to their analyses, there is no question that his argument was extraordinarily important for sharpening the agenda of social scientists wherever group interests are at stake. That argument claimed that collective action in pursuit of collective goods (and all social movements pursue collective goods in that what would be obtained would be obtained for all or many members of the group) is bound to be beset by free rider problems. In the first instance, Olson made problematic what had been assumed. Group interests do not automatically lead to action, since few will act if the good will be provided to them, whether or not they act. If interests do not automatically lead to action, and if many people with shared identities and values (interests) do not act, how do we account for the fact that some do?

Olson's work was subjected to extensive debate and refinement, among those scholars interested in the forms of collective action studied by social scientists interested in protest and social movements, and among political scientists and economists interested in interest groups, public choice, and public policy.[4] The upshot of much critique, research and theorization is that Olson's formulation has tautological elements, includes hidden assumptions, is over generalized, and ignores processes aside from selective incentives that contribute to collective action (see Oliver 1993:273–75). A social-psychological theory of micro-mobilization has been developed that utilizes subjective-utility theory, notions of personal efficacy, perceived costs and risks, network interdependence, and social and ideological incentives to explain individual participation in events and campaigns.[5]

RMII has been roundly criticized for adopting unrealistic psychological assumptions of rational choice (stemming importantly from taking Olson's free rider problem seriously), but a more compelling line of criticism has focused upon its lack of emphasis upon the collective nature of social movement participation. This line of analysis has yielded great theoretical dividends suggesting the crucial importance of reaching thresholds of critical masses of participants to waves of participation as well as the role of expectations of the success of collective efforts (see Oliver 1993). Of course, no special explanations are needed to account for the extensive paid participation of activists in SMOs.

Our approach focused upon organizational needs and the organizational provision of opportunities for participation and mobilization, what has subsequently been called a supply side explanation of individual participation. Subsequent research has shown that one of the best predictors of whether a social movement adherent participates is whether or not she is asked to do so, consistent with our supply side account of the process.

Organizational Rationality

Among the many critics of RM, only Ralph Turner (1981) recognized how explicitly lacking the early statements of RMII were in a theory of organizational action in spite of it having been perceived as a strongly organizational perspective (Jenkins 1983). The analysis of the emergence, structure, and dynamics of SMOs and SMIs, of course, could and can benefit from ideas about other kinds of organizations and populations of organizations. RMII was built upon the Weberian conception of organizational rationality that has been deeply ingrained in modern organizational analyses through the work of Herbert Simon and his colleagues. Organizational leaders operate with "bounded rationality." That is, within their cognitive and attitudinal biases, they attempt to make decisions based upon the best knowledge to which they have access in a manner that aims to insure their most efficient route to the desired outcomes. Thus, the logics of SMO leaders use as they choose strategies and tactics can be usefully, and should be, distinguished from the individual logics citizens use in choosing whether or not to take part in the activities that SMO leaders make available to them.

III: RESOURCE MOBILIZATION IN WIDER CONTEXT

We now have seen how theoretical critique and the findings of empirical research have extended some of the originating questions of RMII. That approach was also criticized deservedly for underemphasizing the role of political and cultural processes in understanding social movements. We now turn to the two variants of the larger RM program that have attended directly to these processes.

First we discuss the correspondence between the organizational entrepreneurial RM approach and the political process or political opportunity approach. We conclude that while they share many concerns, each exhibits greater power than the other in accounting for one or another social movement process. Nevertheless, the political process approach has become increasingly prominent, and may now represent the dominant RM variant. We then turn to a discussion of frame and script analysis that has provided powerful new tools for social movements analysis, supplementing both original RM approaches. Frame and script analysis provides a link between social movement analysis and the cultural and discourse analyses that have become prominent elsewhere in the social sciences and the humanities. We conclude the section with two contrasts between the three RM streams, first reviewing several empirical studies aimed at assessing the relative power of the three variants in explaining protest and SMO expansion and, second, contrasting citation patterns to the foundational pieces of scholarship within the three.

Political Process and Resource Mobilization

RMII and Political Process approaches are meso-level theories aimed at explaining more durable forms of collective action: How and when do movements emerge, grow, are sustained, and decline are the large questions that motivate them. The different emphases of the two approaches were apparent almost at the beginning. We have described RMII in some detail above. In contrast, RMI conceived protests and movements as instigated primarily by political processes and as directed mainly at political change. Quite correctly, state action was seen as creating the goals of collective action through its impositions of costs through unwanted policies, through repression of activity, and through promises of possible benefits to be derived by changes in policy. Moreover, changes in regimes and in political coalitions change the potential for attaining goals and thus the subjective utilities of action. It could be argued that political process approaches are but more narrowly specified resource mobilization theories. On the other hand, a political process theorist such as McAdam (1982) explicitly used demographic and social changes in the larger society as the explanation for the changes in political alignments and possibilities. In that sense, the approach displayed a broader scope than the organizational entrepreneurial approach.

As the two variants have developed other differences have emerged between them beyond simply the greater weight given to and specification of political structures, opportunities, and constraints in political process theory. RMII drew attention to the central role of organizations, professionals, and monetary resources in a way that the political process approach did not. As well, research in the political process tradition has typically focused more on the role of sustaining networks of activists and participants and on the analysis of protest events and their correlation with changes in political opportunity. These differences can be seen as coincidental and not inherent in fundamental differences in their assumptions. For instance, although researchers in the two traditions may differ in the extent to which they focus on networks or organizations as building blocks, none of them would deny that both of these can play an important role in the mobilization process. Similarly, writers in both traditions would acknowledge the theoretical importance of examining the sources and amounts of money used in movement campaigns. Yet, while analytically, both approaches can accommodate the potential importance of financial resources, one can read many studies by students of political process and almost never encounter the word money or the phrase financial contribution. And on the other hand, it is striking that writers in the tradition of the organizational entrepreneurial approach are still far less likely to elaborate the dimensions of political opportunity structure. During the last several decades the pace of scholarship more closely related to RMI has quickened considerably. This has led critics to conclude that it now "dominates the field of social movement research by powerfully shaping its conceptual landscape, theoretical discussion and research agenda" (Goodwin and Jasper 1999:28). This burst of scholarly activity has been accompanied by an increasingly detailed specification of the political factors (e.g., state repression, regime instability, elite allies, and the like)[6] that are expected to shape levels of collective action, typically protest activity.

Though not inherent in the theory, the political process approach early on focused more on protest events and cycles of protest and less on the SMOs that might provide continuity between events and cycles. As part of a comparative study of the timing of collective action episodes, Charles Tilly and his collaborators and students developed a methodology for using archives and newspaper reports as data sources for protest events.[7] (A parallel methodology was developed by Charles Perrow and his students to study the protests and movements of the 1960s and 1970s in the United States, but that project appears to have had less influence on the spread of the methodology). The advantages of developing the methodology were considerable. Collection of data on the details of many events stored in standardized formats vastly simplified the task of data collection and reduced the costs of studying protest. Easily disputable claims about the amount of protest then could be replaced with systematically derived quantitative measures. A research exemplar was created which facilitated the training of graduate students in research shops. In recent years, with the advent of electronic scanning techniques, the technology has been made even more efficient. A special issue of *Mobilization* (fall 1999) showcases the extent and variety of research programs in which the methodology is being deployed both in Europe and the United States.[8]

Yet the approach is not without its limitations. Oberschall has argued (2001) that while useful for describing trends and relationships, the technique is limited theoretically because it slights agency and the choices of activists. Moreover, the tendency to focus primarily upon protest events, and not claims-making such as lobbying and holding press conferences, may give a distorted view of the activities of activists and SMOs (Koopmans and Statham 1999). A methodological commitment to protest event measurement may to a great extent shape the questions asked about and the interpretation of social movement growth and dynamics. As a result, for instance, using only protest to study the environmental movement in the United States during recent decades would seriously misunderstand it since the major national environmental SMOs sponsored public protest only rarely, specializing rather in the use of "insider tactics" such as lobbying.

Framing and Culture

Practitioners of the two original branches of resource mobilization tended to treat values and beliefs as exogenous and outside of the sphere of analysis. Goals were treated as prior and exogenous to action and the valuation of the means to achieve them were treated as largely an issue in instrumental rationality. Such "belief blindness" is shared with most rational choice theories and much of structural sociology. Activists and leaders employ visual and verbal symbols to encourage participation and contributions and to make claims upon authorities. But these theories do not have much to say about how the words work; that is, how symbolic processes and discourse are bundled into frames and ideologies and why some are more successful than others.[9] The earlier Chicago School approach to collective behavior (Turner and Killian 1957) was rooted in symbolic interaction theory, but, given the conceptual tools available and the interactionist thrust of the times, except for the concept of emergent norms, short shrift was given by researchers to beliefs and ideology. The development of frame and script analysis provide tools for analysis that serve as powerful complements to the original branches of RM that had largely ignored how beliefs, frames, and ideologies operated.

Frame analysis was developed by David Snow, Robert Benford, and their collaborators, drawing on the work of Erving Goffman and others. Frames create expectancies and thus shape perceptions of possibilities. Snow, Benford, and others developed a number of subsidiary concepts, such as prognostic and diagnostic frames, frame resonance, frame amplification, and master frames, allowing analysis of how movements use signs and symbols to bind potential members to organizations and draw them into movement activity.

At roughly the same time, William Gamson and Andre Modigliani (1989) drew upon developments in cognitive psychology to analyze everyday ideologies. In particular they used script analysis to examine how metaphors and packages of related cognitive elements developed around objects of political contention (e.g., welfare reform, reproductive rights, and affirmative action). In each case parties were seen to develop more or less complex packages of metaphors and arguments. While these may be logically and tightly argued by intellectuals, Gamson (1992) eventually focused instead upon how these are deployed in the everyday talk of citizens from different walks of lives.

Snow and his collaborators are more likely to focus upon how SMOs use frames, while Gamson focuses on how the citizens package local ideologies. The techniques developed by Gamson are more labor intensive and not so easily standardized. It is clear that social movement scholars have subsequently employed frame analysis far more than script analysis. As we noted earlier, partly for the rhetorical purpose of sharpening the focus on resources and costs of action, RMII had downplayed the role of grievances in generating movements. Indeed, in an often-quoted statement we observed that there are always enough grievances available in a society to fuel social movements so, consequently, grievances can be ignored for purposes of social movement analysis. In the long run, however, while there is no simple and always direct connection between "objective conditions" and levels of movement mobilization, any complete account of movements must take into account how grievances and life conditions enter into mobilization. Frame analysis provides a window into how SMOs, activists, and leaders translate perceptions into actionable grievances and pathways.[10]

Neither script analysis nor frame analysis are competitors with the two original branches of RM, rather they are complements. Each is an approach that allows explication of a major component of claims making and mobilization. Indeed, we have argued elsewhere (McAdam, McCarthy, and Zald 1996) that framing and culture, when combined with political opportunity and mobilization, offers the possibility of a modern synthesis of approaches. Merely working across the boundaries of the three conceptual domains, however, represents a rather weak kind of synthesis. So far these conceptual domains have not been successfully integrated into a more general theoretical framework.

Theory Contests

Recently, the three streams of RM have been pitted against one another numerous times in what might be called loose "theory contests." In these contests variables and concepts derived from the three perspectives are compared in terms of their demonstrated empirical utility in accounting for collective action by U.S. suffragettes (McCammon 2001), Palestinians on the West bank (Khawaja 1994), U.S. environmentalists (McLaughlin and Khawaja 2000), Townsend movement activists (Amenta and Zylan 1991), homeless people and their supporters in the United States (Snow et al. forthcoming; Soule et al. 1999; Cress and Snow 1996), women and racial/ethnic activists in the United States (Minkoff 1995, 1999), and 1980s U.S. peace movement activists (Edwards and Marullo 1995). These studies have examined one of two forms of collective action, the temporal pattern of the likelihood of the occurrence of protest events or the vitality of SMOs. SMO vitality refers to either the rate of organization formation or the likelihood of SMO survival.

We cannot systematically review all of these detailed research reports here, but we briefly note two of them, and then summarize the pattern of results. Snow and his colleagues (forthcoming) crafted an empirical assessment of the relative utility of resource mobilization (RMII) and political opportunity (RMI) theories, among others. Using variables aimed at tapping each theory, they carried out an event history analysis of 519 protests around homelessness in 17 cities over a twelve-year period. They conclude, "the analysis reveals relatively strong support for resource mobilization perspective, . . . and weak support for the political opportunity perspective" (i). Similarly, in their assessment of the factors related to the rate of founding of environmental SMOs in the United States between 1895 and 1994, McLaughlin and Khawaja (2000) conclude that their "findings contradict recent theoretical claims concerning the importance of political opportunity structure to the dynamics of social movements" (426). It may well be that rates of organizational formation may depend upon more stable features of political systems such as freedom to form them than the shorter-term shifts in political opportunity that this research taps.

To summarize the results of these several studies, we think it is fair to conclude that, when credibly measured, (1) hard grievances are not useful in accounting for temporal variation in collective action; (2) the availability of financial and preexisting organizational resources are almost always shown to have a strong positive impact upon rates of collective action; (3) effective framing efforts enhance rates of collective action; and (4) there exists quite mixed support for the role of variation in political opportunities in explaining rates of collective action.

Yet, it is not clear that the variables measuring the concepts associated with one or another of the theoretical variants will always be more useful than those associated with the other. Rather than taking their findings as evidence for a generalized support of one variant of theory over another, Snow and his colleagues, for instance, argue that different perspectives will be more or less useful for different kinds of movements and levels of analysis. Too often, they argue, applications and critiques have proceeded as if they apply equally to all kinds of movements. Theory contests are certainly useful, but in understanding the range and complexity of social movement processes, it is unlikely that any one theory will be fully adequate. It may well turn out to be the case that social movements vary in the extent to which they are shaped by political processes. For instance, labor movement vitality is probably far more vulnerable to political opportunities than women's movement vitality (Soule et al. 1999).

Comparison of Citation Patterns

Another way to assess the relative impact of the several RM streams upon subsequent scholarship rests on an examination of the pattern of citations to the foundational works of each of them. We engaged in a quick review of citations to several of these works over the last fifteen years in the *Social Science Citation Index*. These included the two early McCarthy and Zald papers (1973, 1977), Tilly's major statement, *From Mobilization to Revolution* (1978), McAdam's now-classic work (1982), Oberschall's pathbreaking work (1973), and Snow, Rochford, Worden, and Benford's foundational piece on framing (1986). We can make three observations about the pattern of citations across these works. First, work from each of the three variants continues to be widely cited by a diverse range of scholars. The large number of cites (between thirty and fifty per year for each of the foundational pieces) reflects the recent vitality of the social movements research community more generally. It is among the handful of sociological subfields whose scholars' work is greatly over-represented in the top journals of the discipline (*American Sociological Review, American Journal of Sociology and Social Problems*) in contrast to their numbers (Karides et al. 2001). Second, each stream gains attention beyond the boundaries of sociology in different collateral scholarly fields. The work of RMI scholars is more widely cited by political scientists, especially those in Europe, while that of RMII scholars is more likely to be noticed by organizational scholars and sociologists of religion. The newer work of the framing RM variants is widely noticed among communication, media, and cultural studies scholars. And, third, the citation patterns bolster our sense that the RMI approach is now the dominant one even though RMII continues to be influential.

IV. THE FUTURE OF RM: LACUNAE, EXTENSIONS, AND INSURGENT APPROACHES

Fewer than thirty years ago a brash new way of thinking about protest and social movements began to emerge. The several variants of RM made problematic what had been unproblematic: interests do not directly translate into action and the task of theory was to develop concepts and explanations of how and when mobilization occurs, what forms it takes, with what consequences. Combined with an enormous growth of interest in protest and social movements stemming from the turbulence of the times, the several RM theories came to dominate a greatly enlarged field of study.

We have given a brief overview of the growth and transformation of the scholarship comprising this program, with a special focus on our own variant of RM, its close relative, the Political Process approach, and the synthesis of both of these with framing and cultural analysis. What issues or problems have been bypassed or left unresolved by the program? What are some possible extensions of the program to areas and topics that have remained outside of its scope? Are there ongoing or newly emergent research programs that offer some possibility of displacing the several intertwined branches of the RM program?

Lacunae and Extensions

Riots, Disruption, and Societal Breakdown

Thomas Kuhn convinced many scholars to assume that new theories may displace older ones, without actually disproving them or even dealing with many of their central claims. RM theorists of all stripes attacked grievance or deprivation theory, argued against societal breakdown as the impetus for the emergence of collective action, and proposed that social movements depended upon a more well-organized social base than earlier theories had posited. And, as we noted above, grievances have been reintegrated into RM through the conceptualization of framing processes.

But, what has become of the issue of the relationship of social movements to societal breakdown and the issue of how much SMOs dampen or enhance massive outbreaks of collective action? Frances Fox Piven and Richard Cloward (1979, 1992, 1997) deserve credit for struggling to keep these issues open to discussion and research. On the issue of organization, they pose the question of whether SMOs contribute to widespread mobilization and how SMOs may inhibit the pursuit of goals of radical transformation. Piven and Cloward are better, in our judgment, in describing the range of mobilization than in analyzing its infrastructural mechanisms. But they do highlight a critical lacuna in the RM theoretical program. The theory of emergent disorders, both of riots with little organizational coherence and of parallel episodes of collective action with few personnel or organizational linkages among them, is likely to have different sustaining structures. And it may call for a different theoretical analysis than the ones crafted for the more enduring movements that are the focus of RM.[11]

Piven and Cloward argue that the rejection of breakdown theory may have been premature. Breakdown theory argues that new and *nonroutine* forms of protest ought to be correlated with indicators of societal breakdown, yet some studies purporting to undermine breakdown theory were instead based upon the relationship between indicators of breakdown and more *routine* and *legal* forms of protest. Bert Useem (1998) has shown how aspects of breakdown theory can be used to improve and modify RM analyses.[12]

Religious Vitality

Before the advent of RM, sociologists of social movements made religious groups a central focus, but the recent work, dominated by RM approaches, has severely under emphasized religious movements. At the same time, a new perspective that accounts for variation in religious vitality has emerged (Warner 1993; Finke and Stark 1992). This theoretical approach is quite compatible with RMII, and offers the possibility of expanding both RMI and RMII's analytic power. These scholars claim that people are more likely to act religiously to the extent that they are asked to do so by a large number and a great variety of religious organizations. If this is so, then accounting for the extent and diversity of religious organizations in a society is the key to understanding rates of religious participation. The direct extension to activism implies that its vitality should be the result of the extent and diversity of SMOs that attempt to mobilize citizens. Both broader political processes, especially the role of states in regulating religious organizations, and organizational processes, especially the invention and spread of organizational forms, are factors affecting the extent and diversity of religious organizations. This approach has broad analytic sweep, and its basic principles provide the possibility for invigorating RMII. To this point, there seem to be fewer parallels between the political process approach and theorization of religious vitality.

Social Movement Processes and Firms

A more explicit extension of RM ideas can be seen in the very recent upsurge of interest in collective action and social movement theory to the behavior of corporations, both in external processes leading to changes in organizational policies and to internal processes of collective action. Gerald Davis and colleagues (Davis and Thompson 1994; Davis and McAdam 2000) have been most explicit in conceptualizing how collective action processes affect merger movements, the adoption of corporate policies and the like. Recently Rao and his colleagues (2000) have shown how social movements may shape larger organizational fields of firms. Further, several scholars (Creed and Scully 2000; Martin and Meyerson 1998; Katzenstein 1998) have traced how coaction, caucuses, and social movements emerge within organizations. Although Zald and Berger (1978) charted this territory two decades ago, their work languished. Closer ties between the vigorous organizational research community and scholars working within both variants of RM theory is likely to vitalize and extend the paradigm.

Contentious Politics

McAdam, Tarrow, and Tilly (1996, 2001) are working to extend RMI. They came to believe that it could be fruitful to refocus the political process model into a theory of contentious politics. They seek to broaden the domain of political events beyond the historical social movements to include, for instance, nationalism. Can a more inclusive collective action theory be useful across several domains of scholarship not ordinarily well linked, they ask. Their work may succeed in enriching subsequent scholarship in the RMI tradition, but it also, by its strong privileging of political processes, is likely to lead to further underemphasis of the role of organizational and resource aggregation processes that have been at the heart of the RMII agenda.

New Programs

There is no evidence that the scholarly interest in social movements is declining, and there are indications that a new cycle of public protest is beginning (Smith 2001). The processes of social change around the world continue to throw up instances of protest and collective action that demand explanation. The younger generation of scholars, often attracted to social science by their interests in the political and social questions of the day, will be drawn to social movement topics related to those questions. For instance, the emergence of the radical right and fundamentalist movements has led to a surge of scholarly interest. Similarly, the globalization of movements and the movement reactions to globalization processes demand scholarly attention.

What may change, however, is the resonance of the RM program to younger generations of scholars. For one, the pursuit of the new implies satiation with the old; it may simply be more exciting intellectually to advance the value of a new perspective rather than reworking and modifying the details of established paradigms. For another, as new substantive and theoretical issues that are not so easily integrated within the RM program come to intrigue scholars, the hegemony of the RM programs over social movement scholarship may be threatened.

New Social Movements Theory

An early instance of such a challenge occurred with the rise of New Social Movement theory (NSMT). Among other things, NSMT argued that postindustrial society had created the conditions for the emergence of movements based upon lifestyle and identity issues that were submerged or suppressed earlier. To the extent that these movements focused upon consciousness raising, within group solidarity, and identity/ideology work, the emphases of RM seemed misplaced and NSM theorists were reluctant to employ its conceptual tools. Of course, most, if not all, New Social Movements (the environmental, peace, and women's, for instance) also have strong political agendas and, as a result, all of the theoretical issues of mobilization and organization are relevant to them as well. Moreover, as Mary Bernstein (1997) shows, those aspects of identity and ideology that are emphasized by an NSM are shaped by political conflict. NSMT did articulate an analytic issue that most RM theorists had ignored: interests are based upon identities. RM had made problematic the relationship of interests to mobilization; NSMT makes problematic the relationship of interests to identities. The recent work of Alberto Melucci (1996), a prominent early exponent of NSMT, maintains the problematic of identity and consciousness while nesting those processes within ones identified by the several RM streams.

Culture, Emotions, and Movements

A more recent challenge to the dominance of the intersecting RM theoretical approaches is being mounted around claims that their de-emphasis of the role of culture undermines an understanding movement processes (Goodwin and Jasper 1997; Jasper 1998; Goodwin, Jasper and Polletta, 2000; Polletta, 1997). While this is not the place to review their several contributions, it can be said that they are not satisfied that the strategic framing approach successfully rescues the original RM streams from the difficulties associated with what earlier critics called a "blindness to culture." A key plank in their platform also is to make the role of emotion and its analysis again a central question for movement analysts. Judging from a perusal of recent citation patterns this challenge is finding wide resonance among social movement scholars.

Factors Affecting the Dominance of RM

We conclude by briefly alluding to what we believe are the important factors that help maintain the dominance of a theoretical approach like RM. First is the quality of the ideas. We have focused most of our attention in the foregoing upon the ideas that compose the several variants of RM, and pointed to the key ideas embodied in extensions and critiques of them. But the dominance of theoretical communities depends upon more than the strength of ideas (Shils 1968). It depends also upon commonly accepted and legitimated research templates and also institutionalized scholarly locations and must pay special attention to the institutionalization and resource flows surrounding research in the community (Mullins 1963). An assessment of the eventual success of challenges to RM theoretical hegemony then, we think, must pay special attention to these factors. Our own faith in the quality of the ideas of RMII, then, convinces us that its survival as an authoritative approach to the study of social movements depends most importantly upon resources and organizational processes.

Even if the Resource Mobilization paradigm, of both types, is eclipsed by the pursuit of the new, the paradigm focuses upon issues that are central to action of activists and cadre. In the dialectical processes of the social sciences, the issues and problems will return in new form, only reconfigured in the context of the emerging understandings. Thus, we expect the paradigm, its assumptions and problematics, to become part of the continuing dialectic about collective action and social movements in the future.

NOTES

We thank Martin D. Hughes for his research assistance and Sarah Soule and Bob Edwards for their helpful critiques of an earlier version of the manuscript. This chapter complements another of our recent papers (McCarthy and Zald, 2002). This discussion is broader than that one, placing our approach in the larger context of related theories of collective action and social movements; McCarthy and Zald (2002) provides a more extensive review of the evidence generated in relationship to our approach.

1. RMII originally included notions of the issue of entrepreneurship in the definition of grievances and the proffering of solutions and pathways of action. But we did not have available the language of framing to examine the ways in which symbols were used to package diagnoses and prognoses as was later developed by David Snow and his colleagues. We return to framing ideas below.

2. Zald and Ash (1966) first introduced the SMO acronym. Their analysis had used an organization-environment framework that was then current in organizational theory to explicate the dynamics of organizational adaptation. In particular they asked how and when SMOs were able to avoid the tendencies to bureaucratization in conservatism that had been predicted by Michels and Weber. Initially, RM tended to assume their analysis and did not pay much attention to organizational dynamics.

3. In contrast to small local businesses in labor unions, for instance, we have no official registry of SMOs. As a consequence, researchers have great difficulty in creating credible enumeration of the SMOs in an SMI.

4. See Hardin (1982) for a general review.

5. See McAdam, McCarthy, and Zald (1989); Oliver (1993); and especially Klandermans (1997) for reviews of research on determinant of individual participation and mobilization.

6. See McAdam (1996) for a review of this body of work.

7. Tilly's recent book about the emergence of national protest in Great Britain (1995) illustrates the mature deployment of the methodology.

8. See also Rucht, Koopmans, and Neidhardt (1999).

9. But see McAdam (1982), who argues that cognitive liberation is an important part of the process of delegitimation of the old order.

10. Just as concepts of resources and political opportunities have been subjected to extensive empirical use and critique, so, too, has the concept of frames. Robert Benford (1997) edited an issue of *Sociological Inquiry* devoted to a critique and extension of the framing literature. That represented a critique from the point of view of a friendly insider. Recently, Pam Oliver and Hank Johnston (2000) have argued that the focus upon frames borrows much from the analysis of ideologies, and, more importantly, misshapes the agenda for the analysis of important symbolic clusters.

11. In an effort to fill this gap Susan Olzak (1992), however, offers a compelling account of that subset of events that are primarily ethnic conflict ones that are based in group conflict over access to labor markets.

12. Historically, American sociologists had conflated the study of collective behavior—fads and fashions, riots, and public opinion—with social movements, rebellion and revolution. One consequence, in retrospect not entirely beneficial, of the development of the RM program was the separation of the study of social movements from the study of collective behavior. While the study of social movements has grown enormously, the study of collective behavior has languished.

REFERENCES

Amenta, Edwin, and Yvonne Zylan. 1991. "It Happened Here: Political Opportunity, the New Institutionalism, and the Townsend Movement." *American Sociological Review* 56:250–265.

Benford, Robert. 1997. "An Insider's Critique of the Social Movement Framing Perspective." *Sociological Inquiry* 67:4092430.

Bernstein, Mary. 1997. "Strategic Uses of Identity by the Gay and Lesbian Movement." *American Journal of Sociology* 103:531–65.

Brulle, Robert J. 1996. "Environmental Discourse and Social Movement Organizations: A Historical and Rhetorical Perspective on the Development of U.S. Environmental Organizations." *Sociological Inquiry* 66:58–83.

———. 2000. *Agency, Democracy and Nature: The U.S. Environmental Movement from a Critical Theory Perspective.* Cambridge, MA: MIT Press.

Brulle, Robert J., and Beth Schafer Caniglia. 1999. "Money for Nature: A Network Analysis of Foundations and Environmental Groups." Paper presented at the annual meeting of the American Sociological Association, Chicago.

Creed, W. E. Douglas, and M. A. Scully. 2000. "Songs of Ourselves: Employees' Deployment of Social Identity in Workplace Encounters." *Journal of Management Inquiry* 9:391–412.

Cress, Daniel M., and David A. Snow. 1996. "Mobilization at the Margins: Resources, Benefactors, and the Viability of Homeless Social Movement Organizations." *American Sociological Review* 61:1089–1109.

Davis, Gerald F., and Doug McAdam. 2000. "Corporations, Classes, and Social Movements." Pp. 195–238 in *Research in Organizational Behavior*, edited by Barry Staw and Robert Sutton. Oxford: Elsevier Science.

Davis, Gerald F., and Tracy Thompson. 1994. "A Social Movement Perspective on Corporate Control." *Administrative Science Quarterly* 39:143–173.

Diani, Mario. 1992. "The Concept of Social Movement." *Sociological Review* 40:1–25.

Edwards, Bob. 1994. "Semiformal Organizational Structure among Social Movement Organizations: An Analysis of the U.S. Peace Movement." *Nonprofit and Voluntary Sector Quarterly* 23:309–333.

———. 1995. "With Liberty and Environmental Justice for All: The Emergence and Challenge of Grassroots Environmentalism in the United States." Pp. 35–55 in *Ecological Resistance Movements: The Global Emergence of Radical and Popular Environmentalism*, edited by Bron Raymond Taylor. Albany, NY: SUNY Press.

Edwards, Bob, and Sam Marullo. 1995. "Organizational Mortality in a Declining Social Movement: The Demise of Peace Movement Organizations in the End of the Cold War." *American Sociological Review* 60:908–927.

Finke, Roger, and Rodney Starke. 1992. *The Churching of America, 1776–1990: Winners and Losers in Our Religious Economy*. New Brunswick, NJ: Rutgers University Press.

Frank, David John, Ann Hironaka, John Meyer, Evan Schofer, and Nancy Brandon Tuma. 1999. "Rationalization and Organization of Nature in World Culture." Pp. 81–99 in *Constructing World Culture: International Nongovernmental Organization Since 1875*, edited by John Boli and George M. Thomas. Stanford, CA: Stanford University Press.

Gamson, William A. 1968. *Power and Discontent*. Homewood, IL: Dorsey Press.

———. 1992. *Talking Politics*. New York: Cambridge University Press.

Gamson, William A., and Andre Modigliani. 1989. "Media Discourse and Public Opinion on Nuclear Power." *American Journal of Sociology* 95:1–38.

Garner, Roberta, and Mayer N. Zald. 1987. "The Political Economy of Social Movement Sectors." Pp. 293–318 in *Social Movements in an Organizational Society*, edited by Mayer N. Zald and John D. McCarthy. New Brunswick, NJ: Transaction Press.

Gerhards, Jurgen, and Dieter Rucht. 1992. "Mesomobilization: Organizing and Framing in Two Protest Campaigns in West Germany." *American Journal of Sociology* 98:555–595.

Goodwin, Jeff, and James M. Jasper. 1999. "Caught in a Winding, Snarling Vine: The Structural Bias of Political Process Theory." *Sociological Forum* 14:27–54.

Goodwin, Jeff, James M. Jasper, and Francesca Polletta. 2000. "Return of the Repressed: The Fall and Rise of Emotions in Social Movement Theory." *Mobilization* 5:65–84.

Hardin, Russell. 1982. *Collective Action*. Baltimore, MD: Johns Hopkins University Press.

Jasper, James M. 1997. *The Art of Moral Protest: Culture, Biography, and Creativity in Social Movements*. Chicago: University of Chicago Press.

———. 1998. "The Emotions of Protest: Affective and Reactive Emotions in and around Social Movements." *Sociological Forum* 13:397–424.

Jenkins, Craig. 1983. "Resource Mobilization Theory and the Study of Social Movements." *Annual Review of Sociology* 9:527–553.

Jenkins, J. Craig, and Craig M. Eckert. 1986. "Channeling Black Insurgency: Elite Patronage and Professional Social Movement Organizations in the Development of the Black Movement." *American Sociological Review* 51:812–829.

Jenkins, J. Craig, and Abigail Halcli. 1999. "Grassrooting the System? The Development and Impact of Social Movement Philanthropy, 1953–1990." Pp. 229–256 in *Philanthropic Foundations: New Scholarship, New Possibilities*. Bloomington: Indiana University Press.

Karides, Marina, Joya Misra, Ivy Kennelly, and Stephanie Moller. 2001. "Representing the Discipline: *Social Problems* Compared to *ASR* and *AJS*." *Social Problems* 48:111–128.

Katzenstein, Mary Fainsod. 1998. *Faithful and Fearless: Moving Feminist Protest inside the Church and Military*. Princeton, NJ: Princeton University Press.

Khawaja, Marwan. 1994. "Resource Mobilization, Hardship, and Popular Collective Action in the West Bank." *Social Forces* 73:191–220.

Klandermans, Bert. 1997. *The Social Psychology of Protest*. Cambridge, MA: Blackwell.

Koopmans, Ruud, and Paul Statham. 1999. "Political Claims Analysis: Integrating Protest Event and Political Discourse Approaches." *Mobilization* 4:203–222.

Lohdi, A. Q., and Charles Tilly. 1973. "Urbanization, Criminality, and Collective Violence in Nineteenth Century France." *American Journal of Sociology* 79:296–318.

Martin, J., and D. Meyerson. 1998. "Women and Power: Conformity, Resistance and Disorganized Coaction." Pp. 311–348 in *Power and Influence in Organizations*, edited by R. M. Kramer and M. A. Neale. Thousand Oaks, CA: Sage Publications.

McAdam, Doug. 1982. *Political Process and the Development of Black Insurgency, 1930–1970.* Chicago: University of Chicago Press.

———. 1996. "Political Opportunities: Conceptual Origins, Current Problems, Future Directions." Pp. 23–40 in *Comparative Perspective on Social Movements: Political Opportunities, Mobilizing Structures, and Cultural Framings,* edited by Doug McAdam, John D. McCarthy, and Mayer N. Zald. New York: Cambridge University Press.

McAdam, Doug, John D. McCarthy, and Mayer N. Zald. 1989. "Social Movements and Collective Behavior: Building Macro-Micro Bridges." Pp. 695–738 in *Handbook of Sociology,* edited by Neil J. Smelser. Newbury Park, CA: Sage Publications.

———. 1996. "Introduction: Opportunities, Mobilizing Structures, and Framing Processes—Toward a Synthetic, Comparative Perspective on Social Movements." Pp. 1–22 in *Comparative Perspective on Social Movements: Political Opportunities, Mobilizing Structures, and Cultural Framings,* edited by Doug McAdam, John D. McCarthy, and Mayer N. Zald. New York: Cambridge University Press.

McAdam, Doug, Sidney Tarrow, and Charles Tilly. 1996. "To Map Contentious Politics." *Mobilization* 1:17–34.

———. 2001. *Dynamics of Contention.* New York: Cambridge University Press.

McCammon, Holly J. 2001. "Stirring Up Suffrage Sentiment: The Formation of the State Woman Suffrage Organizations, 1866–1914." *Social Forces* 80:449–480.

McCarthy, John D., and Mayer N. Zald. 1973. *The Trend of Social Movements in America: Professionalization and Resource Mobilization.* Morristown, NJ: General Learning Press.

———. 1977. "Resource Mobilization and Social Movements: A Partial Theory." *American Journal of Sociology* 82:1212–1241.

———. 2002. "The Enduring Vitality of the Resource Mobilization Theory of Social Movements." Pp. 535–565 in *Handbook of Sociological Theory,* edited by Jonathan Turner. New York: Kluwer Academic/Plenum Publishers.

McLaughlin, Paul, and Marwan Khawaja. 2000. "The Organizational Dynamics of the U.S. Environmental Movement: Legitimation, Resource Mobilization, and Political Opportunity." *Rural Sociology* 65:422–439.

Melucci, Alberto. 1996. *Challenging Codes: Collective Action in the Information Age.* New York: Cambridge University Press.

Minkoff, Debra. 1995. *Organizing for Equality: The Evolution of Women's and Racial-Ethnic Organizations in America, 1955–1985.* New Brunswick, NJ: Rutgers University Press.

———. 1997. "The Sequencing of Social Movements." *American Sociological Review* 62:779–799.

———. 1999. "Bending with the Wind: Strategic Change and Adaptation by Women's and Racial Minority Organizations." *American Journal of Sociology* 104:1666–1703.

Mitchell, Robert Cameron, Angela G. Mertig, and Riley E. Dunlap. 1991. "Twenty Years of Environmental Mobilization: Trends among National Environmental Organizations." *Society and Natural Resources* 4:219–234.

Morris, Aldon D., and Cedric Herring. 1988. "Theory and Research in Social Movements: A Critical Review." *Annual Review of Political Behavior* vol. 2, edited by Samuel Long. Boulder, CO: Westview Press.

Mullins, Nicholas. 1963. *Theory Groups in American Sociology.* New York: Harper and Row.

Oberschall, Anthony.1973. *Social Conflict and Social Movements.* Englewood Cliffs, NJ: Prentice-Hall.

———. 2001. "The Theory of Collective Action versus the Dodo." *Angewandte Socialforschung* 22:74–80.

Oliver, Pamela. 1993. "Formal Models of Collective Action." *Annual Review of Sociology* 19:271–300.

———. 1989. "Bringing the Crowd Back In." *Research in Social Movements, Conflict and Change* 11:1–30.

Oliver, Pamela E., and Gerald Marwell. 1992. "Mobilizing Technologies for Collective Action." Pp. 251–272 in *Frontiers in Social Movement Theory,* edited by Aldon D. Morris and Carol McClurg Mueller. New Haven, CT: Yale University Press.

Olson, Mancur. 1965. *The Logic of Collective Action.* Cambridge, MA: Harvard University Press.

Olzak, Susan. 1992. *The Dynamics of Ethnic Competition and Conflict.* Stanford, CA: Stanford University Press.

Perrow, Charles. 1979. "The Sixties Observed." Pp. 192–211 in *The Dynamics of Social Movements*. Cambridge, MA: Winthrop.

Piven, Frances Fox, and Richard Cloward. 1979. *Poor People's Movements*. New York: Pantheon.

———. 1992. "Normalizing Collective Protest." Pp. 301–325 in *Frontiers in Social Movement Theory*, edited by Carol McClurg Mueller and Aldon D. Morris. New Haven, CT: Yale University Press.

———. 1997. *The Breaking of the American Social Compact*. New York: The New Press.

Polletta, Francesca. 1997. "Culture and Its Discontents: Recent Theorizing on the Cultural Dimensions of Protest." *Sociological Inquiry* 67:431–450.

Rao, Hayagreeva, Calvin Morrill, and Mayer N. Zald. 2000. "Power Plays: Social Movements, Collective Action, and New Organizational Forms." *Research in Organizational Behavior* 22:237–282.

Rucht, Deiter, and Ruud Koopmans. 1999. "Special Issue: Protest Event Analysis." *Mobilization* 4:123–255.

Rucht, Deiter, Ruud Koopmans, and Freidhelm Neidhardt. 1999. *Acts of Dissent: New Developments in the Study of Protest*. Lanham, MD: Rowman and Littlefield.

Shils, Edward. 1968. "Tradition, Ecology, and Institution in the History of Sociology." Pp. 165–256 in *The Calling of Sociology and Other Essays in Pursuit of Learning*, edited by Edward Shils. Chicago: University of Chicago Press.

Smith, Jackie. 1997. "Characteristics of the Modern Transnational Social Movement Sector." Pp. 42–58 in *Transnational Social Movements and Global Politics: Solidarity beyond the State*. Syracuse, NY: Syracuse University Press.

———. 1998. "Global Civil Society: Transnational Social Movement Organizations and Social Capital." *American Behavioral Scientist* 42:93–107.

———. 2001. "Globalizing Resistance: The Battle of Seattle and the Future of Social Movements." *Mobilization* 6:1–19.

Snow, David A., Daniel M. Cress, Sarah A. Soule, and Susan G. Baker. Forthcoming. "A Event History Analysis of Homeless Protest, 1980 to 1991: An Assessment of Strain, Resource Mobilization, Political Opportunity, and Threshold Theories." *American Sociological Review*.

Snow, David A., E. Burke Rochford, Steven K. Worden, and Robert D. Benford. 1986. "Frame Alignment Processes, Micromobilization, and Movement Participation." *American Sociological Review* 51:464–481.

Soule, Sarah A., Doug McAdam, John D. McCarthy, and Yang Su. 1999. "Protest Events: Cause or Consequence of State Action? The U.S. Women's Movement and Congressional Action, 1956–1979." *Mobilization* 4:239–255.

Tilly, Charles. 1978. *From Mobilization to Revolution*. New York: McGraw-Hill.

———. 1995. *Popular Contention in Great Britain, 1758–1834*. Cambridge, MA: Harvard University Press.

Turner, Ralph H. 1981. "Collective Behavior and Resource Mobilization as Approaches to Social Movements: Issues and Continuities." *Research in Social Movements, Conflict and Change* 4:1–24.

Turner, Ralph H., and Lewis M. Killian. 1957. *Collective Behavior*. Englewood Cliffs, NJ: Prentice-Hall.

Useem, Bert. 1998. "Breakdown Theories of Collective Action." *Annual Review of Sociology* 24:215–238.

Van Dyke, Nella, Sarah Soule, and John D. McCarthy. 2001. "Predicting Confrontational Tactic Use: Social Movement Actors and Organizations." Paper presented at the 2001 annual meeting of the American Sociological Association, Anaheim, CA.

Warner, Stephen R. 1993. "Work in Progress toward a New Paradigm for the Sociological Study of Religion in the United States." *American Journal of Sociology* 98:1044–1093.

Zald, Mayer N., and Roberta Ash. 1966. "Social Movement Organizations: Growth, Decay, and Change." *Social Forces* 44:327–341.

Zald, Mayer N., and Michael A. Berger. 1978. "Social Movements in Organizations: Coup d'Etat, Bureaucratic Insurgency, and Mass Movement." *American Journal of Sociology* 83:823–861.

Zald, Mayer N., and John D. McCarthy, eds. 1979. *The Dynamics of Social Movements*. Cambridge, MA: Winthrop.

———. 1987. *Social Movements in an Organizational Society*. New Brunswick, NJ: Transaction Press.

7

Recent Developments in Critical Mass Theory

Pamela E. Oliver and Gerald Marwell

It is now about a decade since we published *The Critical Mass in Collective Action* (Marwell and Oliver 1993), in which we (with the help of several graduate students) laid out the elements of what we called the "Theory of the Critical Mass," or what others have subsequently labeled "Critical Mass Theory." The purpose of publishing what is basically a theoretical analysis (besides the usual crass considerations) is to invite others into the game—into consideration of the issues that motivate the work in the first place, and the approach that characterizes the theory. In this chapter we are pleased to report that Critical Mass Theory did not fall entirely on deaf ears (blind eyes would probably be a better metaphor, but it is never used). The past decade has seen a number of adventurous and interesting uses, revisions, and extensions of the theory. The variety of these efforts means that, considered formally, Critical Mass Theory is no longer a single theory at all, although it is a deeply theoretical enterprise. It contains a solid core of interconnected and cumulative work that has built on our original postulations and analyses, and has developed some distinctive approaches and findings.

Our exposition of the growth and change in Critical Mass Theory begins by sketching the key ideas and insights that led us to start thinking about the critical mass, and by summarizing the major concepts and arguments that we developed. In the core of the chapter, we review the major work that has built upon and revised the theory over the past decade. Much of this work contains important and sustained intellectual attack on issues that we posed in our earlier analyses, and represents new theory that addresses the implications, limitations, or even failures of our writings.

BEGINNINGS

Like most early work in the resource mobilization/rational choice tradition, Critical Mass Theory began as a conversation with Mancur Olson's *Logic of*

Collective Action (1965). For students of social movements in the 1960s (including us: e.g., Demerath, Marwell, and Aiken 1965) the most compelling argument in *Logic* was Olson's assertion that "rational, self-interested individuals will not act to achieve their common or group interests" (1965:2) without private or selective individual incentives which reward cooperators or punish noncooperators. Prior to Olson, social scientists assumed that there was a natural tendency for people with shared interests (interest groups) to act together in pursuit of those interests. Economists, however, had long argued that coercive taxation is necessary because rational individuals in a competitive market would not voluntarily contribute money to pay for public goods such as armies, legislatures, parks, public schools, or sewage systems. Olson argued that all group goals or group interests were subject to the same dilemma. He defined a collective good as one which, if provided to one member of a group with an interest in that good, cannot be withheld from any other member. This is generally called nonexcludability or "impossibility of exclusion," (Hardin 1982:16). Collective action was thus defined as any action that provides a collective good. Olson argued that if the benefits of a collective good cannot be withheld from nonparticipants, rational members of interest groups are motivated to free ride on the contributions of others. Furthermore, he argued, this temptation would be greater the bigger the group, where the benefits of a contribution would have to be divided up among more people, and any one person's contribution would be less likely to make a noticeable difference in the outcome. Thus, he said, collective action is "irrational" unless people are given private or selective incentives as inducements to make contributions to collective goods. Olson's argument had a major influence on early resource mobilization theory in the study of social movements. He problematized collective action and, thus, opened the door to studying the conditions under which collective action can occur.

Ironically, Olson's theory arguing that collective action is irrational appeared in the midst of one of the great historical periods of social movements. The irony was lost on no one. The data and the theory seemed at least somewhat at odds. Marwell's experimental work, widely cited in Economics, added fuel to the fire, by showing that under a variety of conditions where Olson would predict no public goods production, groups in fact produced very substantial amounts of public goods (e.g., Marwell and Ames 1979, 1980, 1981). Everyone who seriously engaged Olson's arguments mathematically or experimentally (or both) rapidly recognized that his arguments were much too general and unconditional to be generally true, and research articles rapidly proliferated which either presented his core claims in a different mathematical format that could more unambiguously represent them, or used a different mathematical format to show why his claims were not correct, or provided experimental evidence that real people's behavior did not follow his claims. Early examples include Smith (1976); Schofield (1975); Hardin (1982); Frohlich (Frohlich, and Oppenheimer 1974; Frohlich, Oppenheimer, and Young 1971); Chamberlin (1974); and Bonacich (1976).

Marwell's experiments (1979) created real-life large-group collective dilemmas by setting up situations in which high school students, and other kinds of subjects in later work, were asked whether they wished to make contributions to a fund that would be doubled, but then distributed equally to all members of the group, whether they contributed to the fund or not. Marwell found that students did contribute much more in these experiments than economists' theories would predict, although their contributions were suboptimal. In fact, the only group of subjects studied whose behavior actually fit the economists' predictions were economics graduate students (Marwell and Ames 1981)!

Oliver (1980) joined these debates by focusing on the side-payments or incentive issue. It had quickly been recognized (by Frohlich, among others) that private or selective incentives could not logically "solve" the collective action problem, because paying for the incentive was itself a kind of "collective action" that merely created a second order public goods problem. Oliver's particular contribution to this issue (besides explaining it clearly in a venue where many sociologists saw the argument) was to show that rewards and punishments were structurally different as incentives because they would necessarily have different cost structures. She argued that rewards were more efficient when a small group could provide the good for everyone, while punishments were more efficient for enforcing unanimous cooperation. Even though our study of citations revealed that her particular contribution was rarely engaged, the "second order" problem of paying for incentive structures has been an important subsequent line of research that has merged with Critical Mass Theory. For Oliver, the selective incentives work involved engaging the issues that led to our later emphasis on production functions and structures of organizing. In particular, she encountered economists' critiques of their own standard "convexity" assumptions and the beginnings of the literature (now much more prominent and developed) on nonlinearities and increasing marginal returns or economies of scale.

CRITICAL MASS THEORY

Our intention in producing Critical Mass Theory was to develop a theory that would encompass both Olson's argument and the fact of collective action; one which would allow us to make predictions about the conditions under which collective action would and would not emerge. We began by confronting a basic assumption of Olson's that students of actual social movements find quite unrealistic. Like most economic theories of markets, Olson assumes that individual interest group members make their decisions *independently* of one another. Although they have complete information about the "game" they are "playing" or the decision they must make, they have essentially no information about each other. Since no social movement actually looks like this, our key decision was to try to model a situation in which decisions by group members are *inter*dependent. Experimentalists studying prisoner's dilemmas had rapidly established that subjects who could communicate with each other almost invariably locked into cooperative solutions.

The second issue we wanted to confront was the idea that there were different kinds of collective action, and extend and elaborate the initial recognition that sometimes a few can provide the good for many, while at other times unanimous action is needed. From this, and from economists' discussions of convexity assumptions, we developed our way of talking about accelerating and decelerating production functions as special cases of the economists' general S-shaped (convex) curves.[1] This permitted us to show that decelerating production functions fostered at least initial levels of action but created problems of optimization, strategic action, surpluses, and free riding. By contrast, accelerating production functions had daunting start-up costs and fostered inaction, but opened the door for contractual solutions or solutions in which actors could reasonably assume that their own actions would motivate later contributions by others. Subsequent authors, especially Heckathorn (1996), linked production functions to games, showing that the prisoner's dilemma occurs in a fairly small portion of a game space with linear production functions, while accelerating production functions create assurance games, and decelerating production functions create chicken games.

Putting production functions together with interdependence led us to one of our innovations. There are a variety of ways in which one can model interdependence. To talk about interdependence and production functions together, we postulated a situation in which group members made decisions *sequentially*, with full knowledge of what had been done previously and, in some cases, with the ability to calculate the effects of their actions on the action choices of subsequent actors. This way of modeling the decision process was, as far as we know, novel at the time, and gave us and subsequent researchers a way of addressing issues that had previously been ignored, partly for lack of tools. In subsequent work, we worked with the more common model of contractual solutions, but we never thought these would just "happen" and instead explicitly modeled how they would be created with organizer-centered theory. An "organizer," a figure we knew well from social movements, would incur costs to contact others and seek to form a contract.

Our fourth core insight was that the behavior of heterogeneous groups could not be predicted from models of one individual at a time, that heterogeneous groups would not generally behave the same way as homogeneous groups, and that larger groups could not be assumed to act like very small groups (dyads or triads). Thus, we insisted on incorporating group heterogeneity and larger groups into our models right from the outset, even though this often made them less elegant. Our emphasis on heterogeneity quickly led to an emphasis on the critical mass, the subset of highly interested and/or highly resourceful people who play a crucial role in the early phases of collective action. The idea of the critical mass in exactly this sense was common in social movements; in fact, "Critical Mass Bulletin" was (and is) the name of the newsletter of the Collective Behavior and Social Movements section of the American Sociological Association, which predated the formation of the section. We saw our attempts to formalize the decisions of the critical mass and the consequences of their actions for the total group's outcome as directly related to core issues in the study of social movements. Interestingly, one line of citations to our work treats it as a species of threshold models, and the "critical mass" as specifically the threshold. However, this conception holds only for the accelerative phases of collective action, where the critical mass overcomes the start-up costs and creates the conditions for others' involvement. Although we certainly talked about this kind of role of the critical mass, these citations ignore our own work, which explicitly argued that the early contributors play a very different role in the decelerating cases, where they provide the good and give everyone else the opportunity to free ride. In our models, interest heterogeneity generally improved group outcomes, and resource heterogeneity sometimes did, although extreme heterogeneity could be harmful under some conditions. We explicitly argued that the effects of heterogeneity depended heavily on the mean level of the variable in question and on the specific kind of collective action process, as well as the levels of other variables. Nevertheless, our emphasis on the critical mass definitely tended to stress the people who were different from the others.

Our rebuttal to Olson's "group size" argument was one of the most widely cited (and misunderstood) of our specific claims, even though our argument had been anticipated many times in the previous literature. To recapitulate, Olson simply *defines* a "large group" as one in which no individual makes a noticeable contribution to the collective good. We never disputed Olson's claim that actors assumed to be acting according to the principles of rational means-end decision making would not make contributions with no noticeable effects and, to our knowledge, no one else disputes this claim, either. However, Olson also advanced the empirical claim that groups with large numbers of individuals in them would generally be "large groups" in his sense, that is, would be groups in which no individual could make a noticeable difference in the collective good. It is with this empirical claim that we disagreed (and disagree). We have said, and still say, that the whole thing hinges on the production function, on the way in which contributions translate into units of the collective good. There are, in fact, many different "types" of production functions with many different properties, and the significance of individual contributions in each varies tremendously. The whole matter of collective action is a subset of the more general economic problem of externalities, in which individuals' actions affect other people. Our bottom line is that *there are no general principles of collective action*: you have to set some parameters of particular kinds of actions first, and then you can examine the effects of other factors such as group size. To make the point strongly, we showed that in cases of high jointness of supply and heterogeneous groups, a collective good could actually be provided by fewer contributors in a larger interest group than in a smaller one, assuming that the two groups have the same distributional properties.

We then investigated the effects of network centralization as well as network density on the prospects for collective action. Our unexpected finding was that, when groups are heterogeneous, network centralization increases the rate of collective action by increasing the probability that an organizer will be tied to the few large contributors. This finding is clearly specific to the particulars of this model, although it both encouraged further study of networks in collective action, and pointed to the way particular mechanisms affect the results. This result is particularly contingent on the assumption we made that organizers do not randomly choose from people in their networks, but rather choose those who will make the largest contributions to the contract, a process we called *selectivity*, and to which we devoted attention in subsequent analyses.

The remainder of our findings, one first published in the *Journal of Mathematical Sociology* and the other published only in our book (Marwell and Oliver 1993), have received very little play. This is probably mostly due to where they were published, but also because they have less sound bite value. In the first, Prahl, Marwell, and Oliver (1991) explored the tradeoffs between reach and selectivity in recruitment campaigns. Using an organizer-centered model of simultaneous coordinated action and an accelerating production function, they developed an equilibrium equation for the expected total contribution from a heterogeneous group with a given distributions of interest and resources, and show how this expected contribution varies as the parameters vary. The "reach" is the total number mobilized; the "selectivity" is the mean interest or resource level of those mobilized. (The "shape" of the distribution is held constant as a lognormal with standard deviation equal to the mean.) Both reach and selectivity have thresholds that must be achieved if any of the collective good is to be obtained. Once all the necessary thresholds are reached, further increases in reach or selectivity for resource are more efficacious than further increases in selectivity for interest.

In the other model, we assumed that organizers have finite resources that can be used in some mix of contacting people or in gaining information about who is likely to contribute more, and measured the cost of information as the decrease in the number of people who could be contacted. The question, then, is when is the information worthwhile. We explored the problem with two different models, each hinging on the fact that the mean of some top fraction of a distribution must be higher than the overall mean of the distribution. We found that information is worth more as group heterogeneity increases, that there is an optimum information level which increases as group heterogeneity increases, and that there is always a point at which it is more worthwhile to expand networks and gain information rather than mobilize more people from within the existing networks.

Apart from these "findings," and our development of sequential decision models as an approach to interdependence, it seems to us that our use of experimental design in simulation modeling has also been important. This was particularly evident in the analysis of network effects. We held constant an accelerating production function and the process of an organizer-centered mobilization of a contractual agreement. There were five independent variables: interest and resource heterogeneity, organizing cost, network density, and network centralization. The core of the analysis is an experimental design and a Monte Carlo simulation. There are 6 possible values each for the 2 heterogeneity terms, 10 for costs and density, and 19 for centralization, which taken together define a $6 \times 6 \times 10 \times 10 \times 19$ design with 68,400 cells. Since it was impossible to generate all possible combinations of parameters (2,794 cases were generated across several months' time), parameters were themselves randomly chosen from uniform distributions across the ranges of interest, thus yielding a representative random sample of the full design. A further random component is the generation of heterogeneous groups of size 400 with the indicated heterogeneity and network parameters. We analyzed output from the simulation with standard regression techniques. We found generally positive heterogeneity effects, and the expected negative effect of organizing costs and positive effect of network density.

In any complex mathematical model, anything that is part of the specification of the model could be material in generating its results. Seemingly minor variations in assumptions can often generate large differences in results. In our own work, we tried to ferret out all these ancillary assumptions to determine how consequential they were, but, of course, we did not always succeed. As we reviewed others' works, we often spotted seemingly minor operational differences that produce huge differences in the results. We will mention two. First, we assumed that organizers would select the "best" potential contributors, that is, those who would make the highest contributions. Models that make similar assumptions generate very different results regarding the effects of heterogeneity than those that assume that the selection of participants from a pool of eligibles is random. In particular, our findings about the beneficial effects of heterogeneity on collective action depend upon our assumption that organizers select whom to organize, rather than choosing randomly.

Secondly, our algorithms permitted individuals to contribute only some of their resources, so "resourceful" individuals with low or moderate interest levels would make partial contributions; this specification is the underlying reason for the generally positive effects we obtain from resource heterogeneity. Many other modelers have required that a contributor give all of her resources or none of them, regardless of interest level; such models often find a negative resource heterogeneity effect because highly resourceful persons with lower interest levels give zero, rather than the lower amount they would be willing to give based on their interest if partial contributions are permitted. This all-or-nothing assumption applies to movements which require recruits to give away all their worldly goods, and others' theoretical findings that the wealthy are less likely to join such movements (e.g., Kim and Bearman 1997) seem plausible, but such cases are obviously very different from the less-extremist secondary associations which permit partial contributions, as our models assumed. Despite the substantial sociological significance of these competing assumptions, few of the authors who used the all-or-nothing specification called attention to this difference when they contrasted their results with ours (an exception is Heckathorn 1993), nor did they recognize the substantive significance of the all-or-nothing assumption. We continue to believe that the assumption of partial contributions is more generally applicable.

DEVELOPMENTS IN CRITICAL MASS THEORY

For convenience, we divide recent work that we see as making substantial use of or building upon Critical Mass Theory into five groups: (1) Communication studies; (2) Adaptive learning models; (3) Sanctioning systems; (4) Influence models; (5) Network analyses.

Although we were generally aware of most of the work we describe below, we also decided to systematically examine all citations to Critical Mass Theory from the past decade, using the Web of Science (the on-line version of the Social Science Citation Index), which contains citations in articles published in the journals it tracks, but excludes all books and book chapters, as well as some journals. With this method, we identified 223 citations to the theory. We reviewed these citations and then attempted to locate copies of the articles to see how the theory was used. The exercise proved informative, but also somewhat humbling and frustrating. We recommend it only to those whose interest in the workings of the discipline is greater than their commitment to an exalted vision of themselves. However, some of the work we describe came to our attention only through this more thorough process.

Less than a tenth of the papers that cited our work was involved in serious applications or extensions of the theory. We suppose that the kind of gratuitous or passing reference to Critical Mass Theory that we found in about two-thirds of the citations is similar to most citations of most work. We have certainly used the technique of including a citation to some article in a long list that supports a general claim (e.g., "uses mathematical models" or "discusses collective action") ourselves. About one in four papers mentioned some specific claim in our work, but did not centrally relate that claim or idea to a larger theoretical structure.

One very general point about the reception of Critical Mass Theory in the wider literature does seem to us worth mentioning before we discuss the work that makes more elaborate use of the theory. In many ways, it seems that the most widely appreciated and copied aspect of our work is simply our use of the term "critical mass." Unfortunately, there is divergence in how even our use of this term has been interpreted. We tended to stress that the problem of collective action should be understood not as the problem of obtaining unanimous participation, but as the problem of getting enough people organized to contribute that some or much of the collective good could be provided. However, perhaps the majority of those who cite us seem to understand the "critical mass" as a species of threshold model, which is about getting enough initial cooperators so that a tipping point could be passed and unanimous cooperation can be achieved. And, of course, another group of those who cite the "critical mass" formulation do so to reject it entirely as a copout, believing that the only "real" solutions to collective action require that large numbers of individuals participate simultaneously and/or without knowledge of the behavior of others.

COMMUNICATION STUDIES

Perhaps the most interesting and widespread *applications* of Critical Mass Theory have been in an area quite outside our original domain of interest—communication. Communication scholars have really appreciated the core spirit of the theory, which is the need to analyze a particular situation rather than expect simple bivariate patterns to hold. They have recognized that information is a public good, and that different structures for sharing information have different properties that affect people's willingness to participate. One of the very interesting things about information as a public good is that no actor benefits from the contribution of her own information to the common pool; individuals benefit only from others' contributions. Some scholars might have taken this as a sign that our models could not possibly apply. But to the contrary, communication theorists have used our theory the way we would hope, as a framework pointing to the crucial factors to study. Three lines of research seem to us especially worth attention:

1. Markus (1987) develops an explicitly "critical mass" theory of *interactive media*, such as telephone, paper mail systems, electronic mail, voice messaging, or computer conferencing. The characteristics of interactive media are (a) widespread use creates universal access, so that people can use it who have not contributed to creating the system; and (b) there is reciprocal interdependence, so the benefits and costs of using the media are affected by those who adopt later as well as those who are prior adopters. Interactive media are thus subject to problems of start-up costs and discontinuance, and the problem of "who will go first," issues that "diffusion of innovations" theory does not handle well. In extending Critical Mass Theory into this new area, Markus argues that the production functions for interactive media are generally accelerating, and that there are only two stable states: everyone uses a medium, or no one. He predicts that our findings for accelerating production functions will generally hold, and thus expects that the costs of use will be critical, that heterogeneity will increase universal access, and that high interest/resource persons will be the early users.
2. Thorn and Connolly (1987) apply Critical Mass Theory to understand contributions of information to *databases*. Such contributions can only benefit other people, and not the contributor. Based on Critical Mass Theory, they predict that reduced contributions arise from higher contribution costs, larger groups, lower values of information to participants, and greater asymmetries in information value and benefits across participants. Although they explicitly cite our emphasis on nonlinear production functions, and their own arguments about information value seem to imply an accelerating production function, they operationalize their experiments with a linear production function in which everyone's dominant strategy is not to contribute, but there is the possibility of side payments or incentives. When they discuss heterogeneity, they argue that the people with the most or best information to give

will have no interest in worse information from others, so the early contributions will not attract later contributions, but this hinges on the assumption of a linear production function: the question would be what kind of database is being constructed. In their experiment, players acted as managers of a country's agricultural output, and also had information about demand in their country for all the products. They could pay a cost to contribute their demand information to a database accessible to all players. Some interesting results are: (a) contributions declined as costs increased; (b) asymmetries (heterogeneity) in either how useful the information was or how much they would benefit from the information lowered contributions; (c) bidding arrangements so players could compensate others for information raised contributions; (d) group size had no effect.

3. Monge et al. (1998) study the creation and maintenance of "*interorganizational communication and information systems*" (ICIs), in which different firms pool information. Such information goods include "*connectivity*, the ability of partners to directly communicate with each other through the information and communication system" and "*communality*, the availability of a commonly accessible pool of information to alliance partners" (411). They extensively quote Critical Mass Theory, but as a framework for analysis, not as a set of static propositions. Thus they examine the characteristics of the goods, of the participants, of the group, and of the action processes. They carefully distinguish the dimensions of connectivity and communality in ICIs and the ways these are produced, and then explicitly bring in the distinction between decelerating and accelerating production functions, quoting Markus's argument that connective goods generally have accelerating production functions. They carefully weigh the conditions under which this would be true, specifying particular conditions under which the production function would be decelerating. For participants, they begin with interests, quote Klandermans as well as us to argue that interests can change over time, and give explicit reasons as to why interest in the collective goods will rise as more and more people participate, as well as why participants will experience increasing net gains after the start-up costs have been paid. Our specific treatment of how heterogeneity works is used as the basis for a very careful discussion of the ways in which heterogeneity will affect the systems at issue. Size and coordination issues are similarly explicitly discussed. They specifically consider the possibility that the resource-rich members of a collectivity will share information only among themselves, and trace the conditions that will lead them to be willing to share with the resource-poor.

ADAPTIVE LEARNING MODELS

Like most rational choice approaches, Critical Mass Theory has begun by assuming that actors are not only rational but "forward-looking." Macy (1989,

1990, 1991a, 1991b) has greatly expanded the theory, and in a sense argued for an alternative, by postulating a quite different fundamental assumption; that is, that instead of being forward-looking, actors are best characterized as backward-looking adaptive learners. As accepted in most psychological theory, adaptive learners repeat behaviors that have had positive consequences in the past, and change behaviors that have had negative consequences. Although Macy's first articles stressed the superiority of his assumptions over rational decision assumptions, he and others now recognize that different decision models produce similar results under wide ranges of circumstances, and that, when they do not, the "best" model varies depending on circumstances.

We believe that assumptions about which way actors look are less important than two other elements of Macy's work. First, he treats actors' choices as probabilistic or stochastic, rather than determinate. In Macy's models, the probabilistic luck of multiple actors happening to do the same thing at the same time plays a crucial role in outcomes. At the cooperative equilibrium, populations divide into permanent contributors and permanent noncooperators. Secondly, Macy emphasizes the importance of an aversive privativistic baseline that leads actors to experiment with prosocial behavior. This is in contrast with rational action models that treat the baseline as a neutral or zero point. He stresses the very important point that the level of satisfaction or dissatisfaction with the status quo is an important motivator. Macy uses a general S-shaped production function and does not directly compare adaptive learning to rational decision models with the same production functions, nor does he identify where on the S-shaped curve the outcomes land, so it is very difficult from his published work to determine just how much difference adaptive learning makes in the final outcome of a process, and this problem is exacerbated when he addresses group heterogeneity and compares his results with ours. Despite our wish for more controlled comparisons, we think that Macy's work has offered major advances in our understanding of collective action.

SANCTIONING SYSTEMS

Heckathorn (1988, 1989, 1990, 1991, 1992, 1993, 1996) has built a complex formal model which takes off from Critical Mass Theory and combines it with the rather basic discussions of Oliver (1980) and Coleman (1988) about the "second order problem," to develop a broad-based theory of collective action. He adds sanctioning systems to a collective goods situation. In his basic case, an external agent imposes a collective punishment on the *group* if anyone defects, but the actors would otherwise prefer defection. The question is whether group members will impose internal sanctions on each other to force cooperation. The short answer is that sanctions can cut either way: group members may either enforce compliance or use their sanctions to enforce rebellion and resistance to the external control agent. Heckathorn's conclusions are complex and contingent. Interactions among sanction strength, group cohesion, and the mix of individual and collective sanctions determine whether a group is indifferent to the external agent, compliant, or rebellious. He finds divisions of labor within groups. Group cooperation often arises through "hypocritical compliance," using sanctions to make others comply while defecting oneself, until there are enough sanctions to make everyone cooperate. Many groups retain this division of labor in equilibrium: some members cooperate with the external agent, while others bear the cost of the sanctions to enforce their cooperation.

Heckathorn's sanctioning system has a particular production function, and he does not discuss its consequences for his results. However, when he tackles the question of group heterogeneity, he constructs careful controlled comparisons between "'voluntary" systems with no sanctions, "compliance" systems with sanctions to enforce cooperation, and "'balanced'" systems with sanctions both for and against cooperation. He finds that when the average/mean interest is low, heterogeneity increases cooperation in all regimes, most in the compliant control system, next in the oppositional control, and least in the voluntary system. However, there is a transitional range after which heterogeneity produces even higher cooperation for voluntary compliance systems, but lower cooperation for compliant control systems and drastically lower cooperation for oppositional control. Resource and cost heterogeneity improve voluntary compliance when conditions are otherwise unfavorable, but have little effect on systems with sanctions.

This line of work has been extremely productive and has influenced subsequent scholars. Macy (1993) has modified Heckathorn's model to add an adaptive learning component and to investigate the effects of sanctioning systems with different types of production functions. Flache and Macy (1996) show that actors in sanctioning systems can become more oriented toward exchanging bilateral approval than in coercing each other to contribute to the collective good. Heckathorn has also shown that his compliant control model can be an effective basis for an AIDS abatement program that uses group peer pressure to discourage needle sharing (Heckathorn and Broadband 1996; Heckathorn et al. 1999), while Brown and Boswell (1995) have used it to derive predictions concerning interracial solidarity versus strikebreaking in the 1919 steel strike.

We also want to mention, but cannot begin to summarize, Heckathorn's work in integrating collective action and game theory approaches, showing how payoff functions define a complex space in which, to quote Heckathorn, "In addition to the trust problem arising in the prisoner's dilemma, collective action also confronts the bargaining problem of the chicken game, the coordination problem of the assurance game, the overcooperation problem of the altruist's dilemma, and the absence of a problem in the privileged game. Hence, studies of collective action should explore the full range of possible games" (1996).

INFLUENCE MODELS

Sanctioning system models have shown one way in which people can shape other people's behavior, but a number of modelers argue that collective action is created and sustained less by attention to the collective good than by mechanisms through which cooperative action has a direct effect on others' future actions. Critical Mass Theory argued that actors would attend to their influence on others in accelerative cases, in which there were increasing marginal returns to contributions and high rates of participation were necessary to provide the collective good. All of the four influence models discussed below implicitly assume some sort of accelerative dynamic, at least insofar as they construct systems in which cooperation fosters more cooperation, and there is a general assumption that more collective action is better, although they are not necessarily grounded in our analysis of production functions.

1. Although we have several disagreements with the way that Kim and Bearman (1997) represent Critical Mass Theory,[2] they develop an interesting model that emphasizes opinion change as a key. Their model assumes that people respond to the decisions of others around them to whom they have a network tie, and that they assess the likelihood that their own actions will affect others. Actors increase their interest in a good if they are connected to others with higher interest levels who contribute toward its provision, and decrease their interest in the good if they are connected to others with lower interest levels who defect. The key result of the analysis of this model is that collective action occurs only if there is a positive correlation between interest and power/centrality, and that collective action cannot occur at all if interest and power/centrality are negatively correlated. Kim and Bearman also find that the degree of interest heterogeneity has positive effects on contributions (if the regime permits any action at all); but this effect doubtless arises because it leavens the population with some people with higher initial interest rates who can "pull up" others more effectively (if the network ties are in place).
2. The core of Lohmann's (1994) influence model is a "signaling" process. Others' actions signal the extent of dissent from the regime. People protest to influence others, not to bring the regime down directly. Lohmann uses a great deal of data on the timing and size of protests in Leipzig, as well as on the opinions of protesters and the general population at different points in time, to directly challenge our claim that extremists are important for the critical mass. She instead argues that protest accelerates when moderates are involved early in the process. Lohmann does not "test" her model with the data in any direct sense, but instead uses her model as a framework for discussing the data. Nevertheless, this kind of link between theorizing and empirical data has been very rare, and it would be interesting to take her findings back into the "collective action" modeling tradition.
3. Gould's (1993) work on collective action and networks introduces two different kinds of interdependence effects in a model of public goods provision. First, Gould suggests that norms of fairness play a role in determining collective outcomes. Since people do not like being exploited, Gould reasons, they also do not wish to be viewed as exploiters. Therefore any contribution to a collective good by one person is subject to some matching function where

others will contribute some fraction of the contribution made by the first person. When each person contributes, this changes the total contribution and the average contribution per person, which in turn invokes the norms of fairness again causing each individual to reevaluate his or her contribution level and move it up a fraction more. Thus, the provision of the public good results from an iterative, interdependent process, rather than a set of individual, independent decisions. He assumes that you will try to "match" your contribution to the average contribution everyone else has made. To model this, he assumes that people change their decisions over time. He has one person who starts contributing when no one else does. Everyone else starts at zero, but their subsequent behavior is determined by this equation:

$$c_i(t) = \frac{\lambda}{N-1} \sum_j^N c_j(t-1),\ i \neq j$$

This equation says that i's contribution at time t equals the average of everyone else's contributions at time t-1 multiplied by λ, a parameter that ranges between 0 and 1, where 1 means you match the average perfectly, and 0 means you stay at zero no matter what else others do. From this starting point, Gould derives an equation for the equilibrium contribution from a group.

Second, Gould examines the effects of network density and the position within the network of key (initial) contributors by assuming that the fairness equation above considers only the people to whom you have network ties. From there, he works deductively to derive a variety of network effects, and those effects are large. Generally speaking, the greater the network density (that is, the greater the number of ties between individuals), the greater the total contribution to the public good will be. However, this effect is conditioned on the position of the initial contributor within the network. If the first contributor is randomly positioned in the network structure, network density monotonically increased the level of total contribution. If the most central actor in the network is the initial contributor, then increases in network density through low levels of density increased the total contribution (to much higher levels than the random actor scenario), but continued increases in density beyond those low levels resulted in decreases in the total contributions because these ties would be to those who started as noncontributors, and thus would lower the average for the "fairness" equation. If the least central actor was the first to contribute, then network density also monotonically increased contribution levels, but at a much slower rate of increase.

4. Glance and Huberman (1993) develop a stochastic model in which someone intending to participate does so with probability p and may defect with probability 1-p; similarly, someone intending to defect does so with probability q. Benefits are linear with actual contributions, and each individual can estimate the number of other cooperators using the utility function, but

there will be errors in actual cooperation. The future expected utility of ongoing interactions affects decisions, but with time discounting. Actors assume their actions will affect others' future actions, with these effects decreasing with group size, and increasing with the overall level of cooperation. Then using mean field theory (assumptions that group is large, and that average value of a function of a variable is well approximated by the function at the average of the variable), they derive equilibria for this model. They take several other steps, including finding critical group sizes (all of which follows from the prior assumption that effects of actors' actions on others decrease with group size). This model produces a wide variety of outcomes, including persistence of nonoptimal outcomes, flip-flop strategies, and sharp transitions from cooperation to defection.

NETWORKS

Although quite a few authors have made passing references to our work on networks, or have briefly mentioned our finding that network centralization aided mobilization, we located only two works that drew on our broader theoretical perspective in their discussions of networks.

1. Ohlemacher (1996) works with networks, developing the concept of relays, which are mobilization-mediating social networks. The general context of this work is the importance of weak ties. His summary of Critical Mass Theory stresses importance of the critical mass, as well as homogeneity, heterogeneity, and our self-comparisons to Granovetter. His own contribution is to define a "social relay." Social relays connect previously unconnected networks, acting as brokers or transmitters of contacts between strangers or groups of strangers; form the immediate environment, organizational background, or institutional grounding of several face-to-face networks; and in some cases generate new networks by charging preexisting contacts in a new way. Social relays thus spread mobilization to networks outside themselves. Structurally, relays are heterogeneous, they generate subnetworks (the critical mass) that create new networks, and they need a rich body of weak ties that link as much of the population as possible. He has empirical data on citizens campaigns in Germany which demonstrate the importance of these distinctions. This work thus builds on and extends our initial work on network effects, but goes well beyond it in specifying the elements that are crucial in a rich empirical case.
2. In a recent work published after we wrote the first draft of this chapter, Jones and his colleagues (Jones et al. 2001) build directly on our critical mass arguments in developing their theory of coalition formation in examining the mobilization networks of a variety of protests. They argue that coalition forms are central to mobilization and draw on our work to stress that the critical mass in this process is the need for a few highly productive

organizers to be brought together. They stress the central importance of locating the few high-contributing individuals who can form a coalition. In discussing the factors that might impede organizers from working together, their essential point is that mobilization has a different production function from that of planning and framing. Our distinction between accelerative and decelerative production functions is central to their argument, as they contend that protest forms have accelerative production functions, while leadership functions have decelerative functions. They suggest that there are factors that can impede leadership, that is, that there are negative production functions in leadership. Framing also involves decelerative production functions. Thus they argue that the dynamic between mobilization, with its accelerative function, and framing with its decelerative function, is crucial in understanding coalition dynamics. Small groups are important in initial phases of mobilizing, but are important in all phases of framing. In addition to the critical mass, the authors also refer to our older work on mobilizing technologies (Oliver and Marwell 1992), which emphasizes the incompatibilities of mobilizing money and mobilizing personnel.

REFLECTIONS

If we were to pick the one possible contribution of Critical Mass Theory for which we would most like to take credit, it would be the change from simple mono-causal theorizing about "collective action," as if it were a unitary entity, toward a disciplined search for the distinctions among different types of collective action and the factors which distinguish them. The political scientist Elinor Ostrom has said about our work: "The kind of theory that emerges from such an enterprise does not lead to the global bivariate (or even multivariate) predictions that have been the ideal to which many scholars have aspired" (1998) and then quotes us as saying: "This is not to say that general theoretical predictions are impossible using our perspective, only that they cannot be simple and global. Instead, the predictions that we can validly generate must be complex, interactive, and conditional" (Marwell and Oliver 1993:25). More generally, Critical Mass Theory has helped social scientists move away from trying to develop "*the* theory of collective action" and to recognize instead that there are a lot of different issues and a lot of different kinds of collective action, and that one can shade into the other depending upon the structural characteristics of the situation.

Sociologists rarely use the term "response surface" but it is a very helpful concept for thinking about the complexities involved in collective action. A response surface is simply a k-dimensional graph of an outcome variable as predicted by k-1 independent variables. In the kinds of models we have been considering, the outcome is the total contribution to the collective good (or the total number of contributors), and the independent variables have included such factors as group size, the cost of the good, the degree of jointness of supply, the shape of the production function, the mean resource and interest levels, the degree of interest and resource heterogeneity, the presence or absence of sanctioning systems, and so on. There are large regions of the response surface in which a few variables are at levels that make collective action impossible, so that other variables have no effect, and other large sections in which collective action should never be problematic. All the other variables make a difference only in the regions of the response surface where cost/benefit relations do not overwhelm other factors. It is obviously impossible to study all possible independent variables at once, but when we write models, we should be envisioning the location of our model within the full response space, recognizing what is being held constant (and at what level), and what is being varied (and within what ranges). Simply by explicitly listing the factors held constant and comparing them to other models one might more readily call to attention seemingly unimportant operational decisions that turn out to make big differences in the results, for example the way whether actors must "spend" all their resources or can make partial contributions changes how "resource heterogeneity" affects collective action.

Envisioning the full response surface should be linked with a search for controlled comparisons and thoughtful experimental designs to clarify complex interdependencies. This is all too rare. Instead, most of us seem to approach modeling so we can say something like, "See, I can make my model do something different from what your model did." Our own work is as subject to this criticism as that of those who have followed us.

All of these various formal models should also be subjected to some empirical assessment. For example, Lohmann specifically argued that we, and most other formal modelers, are wrong to stress the importance of highly interested actors in the initial stages of action: she calls them "extremists," and says, to the contrary, that in the opinion data that form her empirical case it is the participation of moderates that is crucial. With the increasing amount of protest event data becoming available, it is possible to subject collective action models to very different kinds of tests, looking at whether they produce shapes and patterns of protest event distributions over time that look like empirical data.

Despite the lack of empirical data supporting the models of Critical Mass Theory in detail, we stand by many of the assumptions that animated them. We think that the claim that it is important to analyze the specific production function of a particular case has stood the test of time, although analysts often downplay this factor when they want to stress others. We believe the general argument that there are different kinds of or phases of collective action that have the properties we pointed to in our contrast between the decelerative and accelerative cases has stood up, although this contrast is often downplayed. We think that Heckathorn's further specification of the differing dynamics of collective action in different cases will further advance attempts to clarify the different kinds of dynamics of collective action. We stand by the empirical claim that relatively small groups of people are often at the core of action. Research also often reveals the importance of a small initial cadre even in protest waves that become very big. Whether we correctly identified the particular dynamic whereby the initial participants motivate future participants seems open to question, but we have seen very little empirical evidence that supports the idea that huge protests "come from nowhere." However, our proposed mechanism of the contractual solution does not seem to have garnered much empirical support. Instead, theory and data seem to point more to the creation of *implicit* contracts through signaling, or considerations of what we called "indirect production" through considering the effects of one's actions on the future actions of others.

Within the broader terrain of rational choice theory, there has been serious and illuminating discussion of the differences among forward-looking, backward-looking, and sideways-looking models, as well as discussions of the kinds of factors people attend to in their decisions. Empirically, it is quite clear that real people do all of these, although they do them in different circumstances, and do not necessarily follow the posited decision rules accurately. It is also clear that in many circumstances, different assumptions about individual decisions lead to essentially the same results at aggregate group levels. In our own work, we came increasingly to focus on the larger structural factors of the collective action problem itself that shaped action contexts, rather than individual decision rules. The shift from determinate to stochastic decision models seems to us to be a definite advance, and we are well aware that stochastic "matching rules" fit empirical behavior patterns much better than the kind of determinate decision models we developed. However, it should be said that it is not clear that we would have been able as easily to understand the dynamics of production functions and explore the effects of group heterogeneity and network centralization if we had not started with the simpler determinate decision rules. We suspect that the next wave of theorizing will move increasingly toward "statistical mechanical" approaches that treat behavior probabilistically, in which the underlying decision engine is less consequential.

Theory books tend to treat theory development subsequent to initial statements as if there were some kind of triumphal march to greater and greater clarity and/or generality and/or verification. Alternatively, the image presented is of a grand conflict with competing theories, and/or negative findings, either credible or mistaken. Our experience seems more mundane. It may be a comment either on the discipline or on our unclear exposition, to realize that we received so many essentially gratuitous citations to our work that either ignored its content completely or abstracted some single claim from its larger complex and interactive context. At the same time, we take no small amount of pride (and perhaps undeservingly claim some small share of the credit) in the work which has built on our beginnings and crafted elegant and complex models capable of integrating a large number of factors which built upon each other and truly expanded our understanding of the dynamics of collective action.

GLOSSARY

altruist's dilemma Term coined by Douglas Heckathorn: a game in which those who seek to maximize *others'* payoffs produce worse collective outcomes than those whose behavior is selfish. For example, "the tragedy of the lawns" occurs because suburbanites attempting to please their neighbors spend time and money to maintain neighborhood lawn standards that are higher than any resident actually cares about.

assurance game A game in which actors' payoffs are maximized if their actions are coordinated and there are no incentives to defect. A classic example is the problem of where to meet your friend if you agreed on a time to meet but forgot to specify a place.

chicken game The classic game is two teenagers driving toward each other: the one who swerves first is the "chicken" and the other wins. Similar to the prisoner's dilemma, except the payoff if both "defect" (do not swerve) is the worst outcome.

collective good A good which, if provided to one member of a group, cannot be withheld from any other member (a criterion known as "impossibility of exclusion").

contract A mechanism to reduce risk through an agreement that binds parties to make contributions if enough others make contributions.

convexity assumption A standard assumption in microeconomics that the payoff function of returns to expenses is convex, which means that the marginal returns to investment first rise and then fall. When this assumption is true, there is an optimum investment level.

critical mass The subset of highly interested and/or highly resourceful people who play a crucial role in the early phases of collective action.

externalities The effects of one actor's actions on other actors, called "external" because it is outside a given actor's calculation of her own costs and benefits. Examples include putting industrial pollutants or sewage into a river downstream from one's own business or home, or a building that blocks another's view or sunlight.

heterogeneous group A group that varies on some relevant characteristic, such as level of interest in a good or amount of resources.

homogeneous group A group in which all members are alike on relevant characteristics, such as their level of resources or interest in a collective good.

jointness of supply A good has jointness of supply when the cost of providing it does not vary with the number of people who enjoy or use it. A classic example is a bridge. The degree of jointness of supply can be thought of as variable, when the cost of a good rises less than proportionately with the number who will use it.

optimal The provision level of a collective good which maximizes the total net payoff to a group, where the total net payoff is the sum of the benefits to all group members minus sum of the costs to all group members.

- **suboptimal** The provision level of a collective good is suboptimal if less of it is provided than the optimal amount (i.e., group members have spent too little to maximize their net payoffs).
- **superoptimal** The provision level of a collective good is superoptimal if more of it is provided than the optimal amount (i.e., group members have spent too much to maximize their net payoffs).

organizer A group member who contacts possible contributors seeking agreement to the contract. He or she often absorbs the costs of organizing the collective action.

prisoner's dilemma The classic story is two accomplices are captured, and each is told that if they confess and turn "state's witness" against their partner, they will be let off with probation while the other will serve twenty years; if both confess, they will each serve five years, but if neither confesses, they will both be convicted of a lesser charge and serve only two years. A particular "mixed motive" game in which each actor's individual payments are maximized if she or he "defects," regardless of what the other actor does, but if both actors defect they are worse off than if they both cooperate.

privileged group A group in which some individual may have enough interest in the collective good to himself provide the entire group some level of the good.

production function An equation which specifies the relationship between how many resources are contributed to (or invested in) purchasing the collective good by the group, and the amount of the collective good that is realized or provided by that level of contribution.

accelerating production function A production function in which the marginal returns to investment are always rising. Generally arises when high start-up costs create a long initial period of low returns, and returns are highest at the maximum level of feasible contributions (i.e., when there is unanimous cooperation). The highest net payoff occurs at the maximum possible contribution level.

decelerating production function A production function in which the marginal returns to investment are always declining, so that initial expenditures produce the highest marginal benefits and each subsequent expenditure produces a smaller benefit. The highest net payoff occurs at some optimum provision level that is lower than the maximum possible.

public good See "collective good."

reach The total number of group members mobilized. See selectivity.

response surface A k-dimensional graph of an outcome variable as predicted by k-1 independent variables. The output or criterion variable is the dependent variable or "y" that sociologists are used to. If there is one independent variable or input ("x"), the standard two-dimensional graph of a line showing how y changes with x is a two-dimensional response surface. If there are two independent variables, the plot of the outcome as a function of the inputs is a surface in a three-dimensional graph. The general concept of the response surface simply extends this idea into n-dimensional space. The goal of response surface analysis is to understand how the output variable changes as a function of multiple inputs.

selectivity A concept relevant to organizing, when an organizer expends resources to mobilize others and the costs of mobilizing are proportional to the number mobilized. Selectivity occurs when the potential targets of mobilization are heterogeneous and the organizer chooses whom to mobilize so as to raise the mean interest or resource level of those mobilized. There may be a tradeoff with "reach," the pure number mobilized, so that organizers may choose whether to mobilize more people less selectively, or fewer people more selectively.

NOTES

1. In fact, the manuscript that was reviewed called these two types u-concave and u-convex functions. It was a fortunate insight that let us rename them to accelerating and decelerating in the copyediting stage.

2. They begin by stating they want to develop a collective good solution that is a large-group solution where no contribution is noticeable and they do not want implausible assumptions. They quote us as saying the critical mass triggers action without mentioning the accelerating production function, which we list as the condition for this result, then criticize us for saying that only a few provide the good, which is the predicted outcome of a steeply decelerating production function, thus entirely missing the key distinction in our work. They then get us exactly backward by saying that there are order effects in the accelerative case (it is the decelerative case that produces order effects), and say we argued that the most interested would necessarily go first. What we actually said was that contributions would be maximized if the *least* interested would go first, but this was a psychologically improbable scenario, and it would seem rather than that the most interested would tend to go first. Thus what we actually said is what Kim and Bearman also assume in their model. Finally, they ignore our discussion of projecting others' future contributions in the accelerative case, despite its close parallels with their own model.

REFERENCES

Bonacich, R., G. H. Shure, J. P. Kahan, and R. J. Meeker. 1976. "Cooperation and Group Size in the N-Person Prisoners' Dilemma." *Journal of Conflict Resolution* 20:687–706.

Brown, C., and T. Boswell. 1995. "Strikebreaking or Solidarity in the Great Steel Strike of 1919—A Split Labor-Market, Game-Theoretic, and Qca Analysis." *American Journal of Sociology* 100:1479–1519.

Chamberlin, John. 1974. "Provision of Collective Goods as a Function of Group Size." *American Political Science Review* 68:707–16.

Coleman, James S. 1988. "Free Riders and Zealots: The Role of Social Networks." *Sociological Theory and Methods* 6:52–57.

Demerath, N. J., III, Gerald Marwell, and Michael T. Aiken. 1971. *Dynamics of Idealism: White Activists in a Black Movement.* San Francisco: Jossey-Bass.

Flache, A., and M. W. Macy. 1996. "The Weakness of Strong Ties: Collective Action Failure in a Highly Cohesive Group." *Journal of Mathematical Sociology* 21:3–28.

Frohlich, Norman, and Joe A. Oppenheimer. 1974. "The Carrot and the Stick: Optimal Program Mixes for Entrepreneurial Political Leaders." *Public Choice* 19:43–61.

Frohlich, Norman, Joe A. Oppenheimer, and Oran R. Young. 1971. *Political Leadership and Collective Goods.* Princeton, N.J.: Princeton University Press.

Glance, N. S., and B. A. Huberman. 1993. "The Outbreak of Cooperation." *Journal of Mathematical Sociology* 17:281–302.

Gould, Roger V. 1993. "Collective Action and Network Structure." *American Sociological Review* 58:182–96.

Hardin, Russell. 1982. *Collective Action.* Baltimore: Johns Hopkins University Press.

Heckathorn, Douglas D. 1988. "Collective Sanctions and the Creation of Prisoners-Dilemma Norms." *American Journal of Sociology* 94:535–62.

———. 1989. "Cognitive Science, Sociology, and the Theoretic Analysis of Complex Systems." *Journal of Mathematical Sociology* 14:97–110.

———. 1990. "Collective Sanctions and Compliance Norms—A Formal Theory of Group-Mediated Social-Control." *American Sociological Review* 55:366–84.

———. 1991. "Extensions of the Prisoner's Dilemma Paradigm: The Altruist's Dilemma and Group Solidarity." *Sociological Theory and Methods* 9:34–52.

———. 1992. "Collective Action and Group Heterogeneity: Cohesion and Polarization in Normative Systems." *Advances in Group Process* 9:41–63.

———. 1993. "Collective Action and Group Heterogeneity—Voluntary Provision Versus Selective Incentives." *American Sociological Review* 58:329–50.

———. 1996. "The Dynamics and Dilemmas of Collective Action." *American Sociological Review* 61:250–77.

Heckathorn, Douglas D., and Robert S. Broadhead. 1996. "Rational Choice, Public Policy, and AIDS." *Rationality and Society* 8:235–60.

Heckathorn, Douglas D., Robert S. Broadhead, Denise L. Anthony, and David L. Weakliem. 1999. "AIDS and Social Networks: HIV Prevention through Network Mobilization." *Sociological Focus* 32:159–79.

Jones, Andrew W., Richard N. Hutchinson, Nella van Dyke, and Leslie Gates. 2001. "Coalition Form and Mobilization Effectiveness in Local Social Movements." *Sociological Spectrum* 21.

Kim, HyoJoung, and Peter S. Bearman. 1997. "The Structure and Dynamics of Movement Participation." *American Sociological Review* 62:70–93.

Lohmann, Susanne. 1994. "The Dynamics of Informational Cascades—The Monday Demonstrations in Leipzig, East-Germany, 1989–91." *World Politics* 47:42–101.

Macy, Michael W. 1989. "Walking Out of Social Traps: A Stochastic Learning Model for Prisoner's Dilemma." *Rationality and Society* 1:197–219.

———. 1990. "Learning-Theory and the Logic of Critical Mass." *American Sociological Review* 55:809–26.

———. 1991a. "Chains of Cooperation—Threshold Effects in Collective Action." *American Sociological Review* 56:730–47.

———. 1991b. "Learning to Cooperate—Stochastic and Tacit Collusion in Social-Exchange." *American Journal of Sociology* 97:808–43.

———. 1993. "Backward-Looking Social-Control." *American Sociological Review* 58:819–36.

Markus, M. L. 1987. "Toward a Critical Mass Theory of Interactive Media—Universal Access, Interdependence, and Diffusion." *Communication Research* 14:491–511.

Marwell, Gerald, and Ruth E. Ames. 1979. "Experiments on the Provision of Public Goods, I: Resources, Interest, Group Size, and the Free-Rider Problem." *American Journal of Sociology* 84:1335–60.

———. 1980. "Experiments on the Provision of Public Goods, II: Provision Points, Stakes, Experience, and the Free Rider Problem." *American Journal of Sociology* 85:926–37.

———. 1981. "Economists Free Ride, Does Anyone Else? Experiments on the Provision of Public Goods, IV." *Journal of Public Economics* 15:295–310.

Marwell, Gerald, and Pamela E. Oliver. 1993. *The Critical Mass in Collective Action: A Micro-Social Theory*. Edited by J. Elster and M. S. McPherson. Cambridge: Cambridge University Press.

Monge, P. R., J. Fulk, M. E. Kalman, A. J. Flanagin, C. Parnassa, and S. Rumsey. 1998. "Production of Collective Action in Alliance-Based Interorganizational Communication and Information Systems." *Organization Science* 9:411–33.

Ohlemacher, T. 1996. "Bridging People and Protest: Social Relays of Protest Groups against Low-Flying Military Jets in West Germany." *Social Problems* 43:197–218.

Oliver, Pamela E. 1980. "Rewards and Punishments as Selective Incentives for Collective Action: Theoretical Investigations." *American Journal of Sociology* 85:1356–75.

Oliver, Pamela E., and Gerald Marwell. 1992. "Mobilizing Technologies for Collective Action." In *Frontiers in Social Movement Theory*, edited by A. Morris and C. M. Mueller. New Haven: Yale University Press.

Olson, Mancur, Jr. 1965. *The Logic of Collective Action*. Cambridge, MA: Harvard University Press.

Ostrom, Elinor. 1998. "A Behavioral Approach to the Rational Choice Theory of Collective Action." *American Political Science Review* 92:1–22.

Prahl, R., G. Marwell, and P. E. Oliver. 1991. "Reach and Selectivity as Strategies of Recruitment for Collective Action—A Theory of the Critical Mass .5." *Journal of Mathematical Sociology* 16:137–64.

Schofield, Norman. 1975. "A Game Theoretic Analysis of Olson's Game of Collective Action." *Journal of Conflict Resolution* 19.

Smith, Jan. 1976. "Communities, Associations, and the Supply of Collective Goods." *American Journal of Sociology* 82:291–308.

Thorn, B. K,. and T. Connolly. 1987. "Discretionary Databases—A Theory and Some Experimental Findings." *Communication Research* 14:512–28.

8

Theory Development in the Study of Revolutions

Jack A. Goldstone

A common indictment of theory development in sociology is that it is often a matter of shifting fads—modernization, Marxism, feminism, postmodernism—with little cumulation or greater understanding of the empirical world. With regard to theories of revolution, the overthrow of the shah of Iran in 1979 and the collapse of communist regimes in the Soviet Union and Eastern Europe in 1989–1991, neither of which were predicted by then-current theories of revolution, further cast doubt on the value of theory. To this day, theorists of revolution cannot even agree on whether or not the era of revolutions is coming to an end (Goodwin 2001; Selbin 2001).

Nonetheless, I believe that theories of revolution have made remarkable progress in understanding the causes, processes, and outcomes of revolutions. Naturally, this progress involves controversies, the falsification and abandonment of some theories, and the supersession and incorporation of others. What is important, however, is that these shifts in theory have been driven by the confrontation of theory with empirical events. This confrontation has led to successive modification of theories, the introduction of new concepts, and the development of new approaches. The result is that theories of revolution today address more cases, with more fidelity to historical events, and with a greater grasp of the various elements that comprise revolutions, than ever before.

I believe it is possible to show that there has been a fairly continuous, cumulative advance in theories of revolution since the nineteenth century, with newer theories consciously building on older ones and seeking to overcome their limitations in explaining empirical events. There have been some notable failures, such as the inability to predict the collapse of communism. Yet these should not be taken to imply the failure of revolutionary theory, any more than such unanticipated phenomena as high-temperature superconductivity or quasars implied the failure of physical theory. Specific theories often need revision when confronted with unexpected discoveries; that is the context of progress in all scientific fields.

Revolutionary theory also has several successes to its credit. These include identifying the Philippines under Marcos, Zaire under Mobutu, and Indonesia under Suharto as the type of regimes (neopatrimonial or personalist dictatorships) that are prone to revolutionary overthrow, and pointing out that the revolutionary collapse of communism in the U.S.S.R. was likely to produce further violence, instability, and failures to institutionalize democracy in most former Soviet states, rather than the smooth transition to stable and prosperous democracy that was anticipated by more optimistic observers.

While revolutionary theory has made cumulative progress, this was not (nor is ever likely to be) a smooth, straight line of advance in regard to all areas of accuracy, scope, and detail.

Rather, the growth of revolutionary theory is like a spiral that expands while going up and down, backwards and forwards. For example, revolutionary theory may be expanded to cover additional cases, but this may at first require less attention to some of the details of specific cases. At other times, revolutionary theory may be sharpened to better explain one particular aspect of revolutions, such as outcomes or urban mobilization, but at the price of focusing on a smaller number of cases. What is important is that over an extended period of time the cumulative effect of all these efforts is the construction of a richer, more complex theory of revolutions that explains more cases, and more aspects of those cases, than previous theories.

In some respects, the growth of revolutionary theory closely follows the pattern outlined in Thomas Kuhn's (1996) classic study of scientific revolutions. At any one time, a particular perspective on revolutions tends to be dominant, with most researchers seeking to add details to that perspective and apply it to additional cases. Initially, these efforts are successful. Yet over time, anomalies emerge, as certain empirical aspects of revolutions prove difficult to incorporate into the dominant perspective. In addition, surprising empirical events—usually new revolutions—force theorists to reevaluate their theories. As a result, the dominant theory of revolutions becomes beleaguered, and faces extensive criticism. Eventually, a new perspective emerges that integrates key aspects of prior theories, while offering a new synthesis of concepts and empirical findings that researchers find does a better job of matching theoretical perspectives with historical facts.

This shift in dominant perspective has occurred three times in the twentieth century; we may now be on the verge of a fourth. I discuss each of these shifts below. First, however, it is necessary to make explicit the criteria used in discussing the progress of revolutionary theories.

CRITERIA OF PROGRESS IN THEORIES OF REVOLUTION

The issue of progress in science—even the physical sciences—remains controversial. Although the existence of a "real" world and of "objective" historical facts is debated by philosophers, and theorists of revolution are aware of these debates, practitioners in the field take for granted that events called "revolutions" actually did occur in history (and do occur in the present). They also believe that certain facts—such as when the old regime fell, which actors played important roles, what they did, and what kind of regime or interregnum followed—can be ascertained by historians with reasonable confidence. Of course, particular facts may be called into question by new discoveries, and biases can affect which facts are brought to attention (leading, for example, to a long neglect of the role of women in revolutions). Nonetheless, theorists of revolution are largely agreed that the goal of their theories is to answer such questions as: Why was the French monarchy overthrown in 1789? What actors were mainly responsible for the fall of the shah of Iran in the late 1970s? What is the likely outcome of the collapse of communism in the Soviet Union in 1991? Progress thus needs to be seen in terms of this accepted goal among the community of theorists and researchers on revolutions.

Within this context, we can specify several dimensions of progress in revolutionary theory. The following builds on the work of Berger and Zelditch (1993).

Range of Revolutions and Revolutionary Situations Covered

Although no two revolutionary situations are precisely alike, all revolutions and revolutionary situations share certain elements worthy of explanation. These are: a collapse of or attempt to overthrow political authority; formal or informal popular mobilization; and efforts to create new institutions and values to replace those that prevailed under the old regime. A recent authoritative source, the *Encyclopedia of Political Revolutions* (Goldstone 1998c), lists 165 revolutions and revolutionary situations in world history from 1500 to the present. Additional events in ancient and medieval history—from the fall of the Old Kingdom in Pharonic Egypt to the party struggles of Renaissance Italy—are also sometimes considered to have revolutionary characteristics. No theory of revolution has ever offered to explain all of these events.

Theories of revolution instead have been making slow progress in expanding the range of cases that they address. This is usually done by identifying subgroups of cases. Most theories of revolution in the last two centuries have begun by focusing on a small number of "great" revolutions. In these cases, popular uprisings helped to overthrow the rulers, change the established religious and government institutions, and undermine accepted status distinctions.

These cases include the English Revolution of the seventeenth century, the French and American Revolutions of the eighteenth century, the Russian Revolution of 1917, and the Chinese Revolutions of 1911 and 1949. Other subcategories of revolution include anticolonial revolutions (e.g., Algeria 1962, Vietnam 1954); revolutions in modern dictatorships (Iran 1979, Nicaragua 1979, Philippines 1986); and guerrilla wars in Latin America (Peru's Shining Path, Colombia's La Violencia, El Salvador's Farabundo Marti Liberation Movement).

At their current state of development, theories of revolution are often judged simply by how many events they encompass within one such subcategory of revolutions, taking for granted that we are still a long way from producing a theory that will satisfactorily account for all revolutions and revolutionary events.

Elements of Revolutions and Revolutionary Situations Addressed

Revolutions are complex phenomena, involving millions of actors and stretching across years or decades of time. Each revolution thus embraces dozens of distinct elements. These include background causes; immediate precipitating events; revolutionary leaders; different groups of followers; the leaders of the old regime and of counterrevolutionary movements; the revolutionary programs or ideologies of key actors; the battles and power shifts in the course of the revolution; and the outcomes of the revolution in the economy, the political structure, the status system, and international relations. A complete theory of revolutions would explain how each of these elements emerges, is involved in the development of the revolutions, and is related to other elements. Again, we are far from such a theory. Therefore, theories of revolution have usually focused on a few key elements and their interrelationships. Progress has lain in addressing more and more elements, and understanding their mutual influence, in the making of revolutionary events.

Correspondence or Accuracy of Explanation

Like any other scientific theories, theories of revolution are developed to answer questions about empirical observations. Thus we can ask of such theories how well their answers correspond to known, and to new, details regarding those observations. For example, Marx's theory of revolution explained the outbreak of revolutions by claiming that when class conflicts reach a critical level in society, the newly rising classes will grasp political power from the economically declining classes. This theory seemed to accord with the known facts of the English and French revolutions as they were understood from the mid-nineteenth through the mid-twentieth centuries. However, from the mid-twentieth century scholars undertook more detailed biographical analyses of the leaders and followers of these revolutions, and made it clear that representatives of economically rising and falling classes were to be found almost equally among both revolutionaries and supporters of the old regime. The failure of Marx's theory to accord with these facts led researchers to abandon, or seek to massively alter, Marx's theory of revolutions to obtain a new theory that better corresponded to the (now) known facts.

Theories of revolution are constantly being tested by new facts, both newly emerging facts about old revolutions and facts regarding new and recent revolutions. Together, the assaults of history and the unfolding present pose a double-barreled challenge to the empirical accuracy of revolutionary theory.

Relationship to Similar Events

Theories of revolution often treat revolutions as isolated, special events. However, sociology and history recognize that revolutions are but one form of collective action, along with riots and social protest movements; political science recognizes revolutions as but one form of political change, along with reform movements, coups d'etat, and democratic transitions. Theories of revolution thus need to place revolutions within this broader constellation of related events. One form of recurrent progress in the theory of revolutions lies in reformulating the way in which revolutions resemble or differ from, and are causally related or unrelated to, other forms of collective action and political change.

Integration of Diverse Theories and Methods

Because revolutions are such complex events, different theoretical approaches are often used to examine particular elements. Thus, for example, theories of leadership may be used to account for the emergence and success of revolutionary leaders; structural theories of institutions may be used to account for the stability or overthrow of particular institutions; and theories of individual motivation may be used to account for the recruitment of particular groups to revolutionary activity. These theories are often different in their formalization, their language, and the range of cases or elements that they address.

In addition, different methods may be used to gain data about different aspects of revolutions, or to analyze that data. Again, these different methods, ranging from statistical analysis of large data sets to biographical analysis of particular individuals, produce outputs that differ in their language, and the range of elements and cases that they cover.

While each such theory or methodological effort may illuminate a portion of the complex phenomenon of revolution, another aspect of progress in the theory of revolution is the degree to which diverse theories and methodological analyses can be integrated into a coherent theoretical framework.

At any given time, revolutionary theory is likely making progress on one or more of these fronts. However, progress in one area often leads to regress in another. Increasing the range of events covered often rests on decreasing the number of elements addressed; thus new theories aiming to cover many cases often focus mainly on the causes, or the participants, or the outcomes of revolutions, leaving one or more aspects undertheorized. Similarly, increases in the number of cases covered or elements addressed often leads to new vulnerability with regard to accuracy. And as new theories are advanced to cover more cases, and different methodologies are used to advance accuracy in our understanding of events, the task of integration is often set back. As noted above, progress therefore should be seen as a spiral, rather than a simple upward climb, in which movements in different directions combine to expand the overall area covered by revolutionary theory.

Let us now look at how this advance has taken place.

THE BEGINNINGS OF REVOLUTIONARY THEORY: TOCQUEVILLE, MARX, WEBER

Writers since ancient times had sought to define the "best" form of government, or spoke in general terms of a cyclical rise and fall of states. However, the scientific study of revolutions began only in the nineteenth century, with the work of Karl Marx and Alexis de Tocqueville. These writers made an effort to identify why revolutions occur at certain times and places in history and not others, based on empirical observations of historical cases of revolution and general principles of human action and societal evolution. They also specified the outcomes that could be expected of revolutions in terms of fundamental, long-term social change—such as the growth of capitalism, or of political equality—rather than endless cycles.

Tocqueville focused on the French Revolution of 1789, but also drew on his study of America after its anticolonial revolution against Britain, and on his first-hand knowledge of the French Revolutions of 1830 and 1848. He argued that by the eighteenth century the feudal/aristocratic institutions of Europe were breaking down everywhere, in large part because the growth of centralized royal authority made the aristocracy superfluous. Tocqueville saw a general trend toward the centralization and rationalization of authority, and demands for equal treatment under the law for all, as inevitable. Thus despite their resistance, the aristocracy and the institutions that gave them their privileges would have to be swept aside.

From this starting point, Tocqueville developed several further deductions about revolution:

1. Rulers, seeing the need for change, will try to initiate reforms. However, they are unlikely to overcome resistance to major changes. The result will be to instruct people that change is necessary and desirable, while the current rulers will not be able to provide it. Reforms will thus often accelerate, not reduce or delay, the impetus to revolution.
2. Revolutions may aim at overthrowing political or religious authority, but as new regimes consolidate their power, the growth of centralized state power will continue. Thus new revolutionary regimes will usually be even stronger and more centralizing than the old regimes they replace.
3. Revolutions are driven by desires for equality; but making all equal before the power of the state simply ensures that nothing can protect individuals or minorities from the tyranny of the majority. Thus revolutionary regimes may become even more dangerous to liberty and security than the old regimes that they replaced.

Despite drawing his evidence from relatively few cases, the three major deductions of Tocqueville's theory have held up well, and are incorporated in most modern theories of revolution.

Marx's theory of revolutions centered on class conflicts. Marx argued that revolutions occur only when an economically dominant class is losing ground due to technical changes in the economy. That class then becomes vulnerable to efforts by the subordinate class to wrest away control of the apparatus of government. Revolutions are therefore a necessary and inevitable result of long-term technical change. The details of this theory have not held up well. Today scholars believe that most revolutions involve divisions within classes and cross-class coalitions rather than pitting a rising against a falling class. Nor are revolutions most likely to occur in those countries where the economically dominant class has lost the most ground to competitors; many poor and backward countries such as Russia in 1917, or Cambodia in 1975, have been home to massive revolutions. Nonetheless, two aspects of Marx's theory have been found to be widely valid, and have been incorporated into most modern theories of revolution. First, much of the conflict in revolutions involves the demands of particular economic groups to be free of the domination of other groups. These include peasants and workers seeking greater security of wages, land, and livelihood from landlords, employers, or the state; and middle-class professionals, students, intellectuals, and bureaucrats seeking greater economic and political opportunity in restrictive societies. Second, much of the impetus for revolutions comes from changing economic conditions. These might include any changes in the international or domestic economy that affect the income and opportunities for states, elites, or popular groups.

Marx's and Tocqueville's insights were synthesized and added to early in the twentieth century by Max Weber. Weber granted that economic changes that influenced the relative wealth and status of different groups could lead to contests for political power. He also granted that the long-term rationalization and growth of state authority, which he argued was best shown in the growth of bureaucracy, would not be halted by revolutions. Yet Weber also insisted on the importance of values and leadership for revolutionary change.

Weber argued that all forms of government rested on a set of values that gave their institutions legitimacy—various ancient traditions for monarchies and empires, belief in the rationality of individuals and the value of universal laws for modern democracies. A revolution involved breaking the legitimacy of the old regime, and giving legitimacy to new institutions and values. Weber argued that rare historical individuals, whom he called "charismatic leaders," had the power to inspire people to put their faith in new values, to overturn old institutions, and embody those new values in new principles of social and political organization.

Modern theorists certainly do not consider all revolutionary leaders to be charismatic. However, the key elements of this view—that revolutions involve an attack on old value systems and the effort to build new institutions based on new values, and that leadership is crucial to the success of revolutionary movements—are widely accepted.

Tocqueville, Marx, and Weber are deemed the "classics" or "fathers" of modern sociological theory. This does not imply that they have not been superseded.

In fact, many of their core assumptions about social change have been discarded. We no longer think that revolutions are all about class conflict, or that only charismatic leaders can bring revolutionary change. Rather, their work marks the beginning of a scientific approach to social phenomena such as revolutions. Despite errors in some of their broader assumptions, certain observations and conclusions that they arrived at have proven to be of lasting value. No theory of revolutions today would be seen as wholly adequate unless it had a role for the impact of state reforms, economic change, and leadership among the causes of revolution, and paid attention to the long-term growth of state power, the emergence of state tyranny among revolutionary regimes, and changes in the values underlying political institutions as elements of revolutionary outcomes.

THE EARLY TWENTIETH CENTURY: LENINISM AND THE NATURAL HISTORY OF REVOLUTIONS

Tocqueville, Marx, and Weber wrote before the Russian Revolution of 1917. They were primarily influenced by the French Revolution of 1789, the American Revolution of 1776, and the European Revolutions of 1830 and 1848, although they also were familiar with the English Revolution of the 1640s, and with classical and Renaissance instances of attacks on governments. The Russian Revolution posed a major challenge to theories of revolution. It was made in the name of Marxism, yet in a country where revolution would hardly be predicted by Marx's theory. It was led by workers and made in the name of socialism in a country where capitalism hardly existed. And it introduced a new phenomenon: the party-state.

Leninism and the Vanguard Party

The leader who guided the Russian Revolution, Vladimir Lenin, was also a revolutionary theorist. He modified Marx's theory of revolution in light of the empirical realities he found in Russia. First, Lenin found that workers—who Marx predicted would readily recognize the need to overthrow the government and classes that oppressed them—were far more worried about wages and job security than about overthrowing the authorities. Second, Lenin began to believe that the weakness of capitalism in Russia, which by Marx's theory meant that Russia was not ready for a socialist revolution, might actually be an advantage for revolutionaries. Since capitalism was so weak and capitalists so few in Russia, there were no class obstacles to workers taking control of the country. Thus one might be able to skip over the stage of capitalism altogether, and go directly from a traditional landlord-dominated state to a socialist system, if workers could simply overthrow the traditional Tsarist regime and encourage peasants to drive out the landlords.

To deal with these empirical realities, Lenin (1973) developed the theory of the vanguard party. Lenin argued that while Marx was correct in his overall view of history, in which traditional states would give way to capitalism and then to socialism through class-based revolutions, Marx did not pay enough attention to the need for revolutionary leadership. History itself would not turn workers into enemies of the state; that would require the tutelage of intellectuals—like Marx and Lenin—who understood the direction of history.

The vanguard party would have to train and mobilize workers to take revolutionary action; it would then direct the annihilation of the old regime and its supporters from the dominant classes. Indeed, the power of the vanguard party could be so great as to take advantage of favorable opportunities and allow a society to "skip" stages on the way to the inevitable outcome of socialism.

To an astonishing degree, Lenin and Leninism succeeded. In 1917, with Russia buckling under the strain of its enormous losses in World War I, the Tsar's government faced massive strikes, military defections, and peasant uprisings. The Tsar abdicated and a provisional government of nobles and professionals took power, but this provisional government continued the war and brought neither peace nor economic improvement to Russia. Then, in October of 1917, a combination of workers and mutinous sailors organized by Lenin's Bolshevik Party marched on the Palace in St. Petersburg, deposed the provisional government, and seized power. The Bolsheviks quickly made peace with Germany, and forging a new army from the workers of the capital cities and the remnants of the Tsarist armed forces, set out to conquer all of Russia for communism. The Party succeeded in establishing a communist, party-led regime, with Lenin as its first head of state, that lasted for seventy years.

The Leninist theory of the vanguard party mobilizing the masses for a quick revolutionary "leap" to socialism spread widely among revolutionaries (Colburn 1994). Revolutionary parties modeled on the Bolsheviks sprang up in China, in Southeast Asia, in Africa, and in Latin America. In China in the 1930s, Mao Zedong added yet another wrinkle to Marxism-Leninism, by arguing that one could not only have a socialist revolution without capitalists, one could even do largely without workers. Basing his vanguard party in the countryside after failing in an attempt to create a worker-based revolution in China's cities, Mao argued that rural peasants, if organized for guerrilla warfare, could provide a basis for the revolutionary creation of socialism.

Marxism-Leninism-Mao Zedong thought, as this line of theory is sometimes called, provided a theoretical guide to revolutionaries seeking a means to implement Marx's vision of historical change. As a practical matter, it was an enormous success, with dozens of regimes founded on revolutions led by vanguard socialist parties achieving rule over billions of people by the late twentieth century. However, its appeal for scientific studies of revolution remains limited. Its emphasis on the role of the vanguard party, and the inevitable forces of historical development, tells us little about the actual role of workers, peasants, and nonparty elites. More importantly, it provides few insights into why some such parties succeeded in making revolutions, while others—notably on the mainland of Latin America—failed badly. Finally, it says little or nothing about how communist revolutions are similar to, or different from, the noncommunist revolutions that occurred in America, France, England, and elsewhere around the world.

The effort to place all of these revolutions in some kind of broad theoretical framework led to the first dominant perspective on revolutions in this century, the natural history approach.

The Natural History of Revolutions

Scholars working in this perspective aimed to study revolutions the way biologists studied natural history (that is, the history of life), namely by gathering the specimens, detailing their major parts and processes, and seeking common patterns. These scholars—notably Edwards (1927); Pettee (1938); and Brinton (1938)—compared the English, American, French, and Russian Revolutions, often using biological analogies, and found distinct patterns that reappeared across these cases. They laid out a scheme of events that they believed all major revolutions followed, ranging from causes to outcomes.

They noted that prior to a revolution, the bulk of the "intellectuals"—journalists, poets, playwrights, essayists, teachers, members of the clergy, lawyers, and trained members of the bureaucracy—cease to support the regime, write condemnations, and demand major reforms. Just prior to the fall of the old regime, the state attempts to meet this criticism by undertaking some reforms. However, the actual fall of the regime begins with an acute political crisis brought on by the government's inability to deal with some economic, military, or political problem rather than by the action of a revolutionary opposition.

After the old regime falls, even where revolutionaries had united solidly against the old regime, their internal conflicts soon cause problems. While the first group to seize the reins of state are usually moderate reformers, who often employ organizational forms left over from the old regime, more radical centers of mass mobilization spring up with new forms of organization (such as the Jacobin clubs in France, or Leninist vanguard parties). These radical groups challenge the moderates, and eventually gather popular support and drive them from power. The great changes in the organization and ideology of a society occur in revolutions not when the old regime first falls, but when the radical, alternative, mass-mobilizing organizations succeed in supplanting the moderates.

However, the disorder brought by the revolution and the implementation of radical control usually results in forced imposition of order by coercive rule, often accompanied by a period of state-imposed "terror." The struggles between radicals and moderates and between defenders of the revolution and external enemies frequently allow military leaders to take commanding, even absolute, leadership of the new revolutionary regimes (for example, Cromwell, Washington, or Napoleon). Eventually, the radical phase of the revolution gives way to a phase of pragmatism and moderate pursuit of progress within the new status quo, but with an enlarged and more centralized state.

The natural history school provided a clear and fairly comprehensive picture of the preconditions, dynamics, and outcomes of the revolutionary process. Not only did this schema fit rather well to the cases for which it was developed; it also fit remarkably well to cases that arose decades later, such as the Islamic Revolution in Iran in 1979.

It should be clear that this scheme echoes many of the themes first laid out in the theories of Tocqueville, Marx, Weber, and Lenin, such as the role of state-led reforms before the revolution, the potential tyranny of a revolutionary regime, the role of party organizations, and the growth of the state. However, the natural history school made progress in the following respects: Their theory applied to a broader range of cases than previous theories, encompassing events from the English Revolution of the 1640s to the Russian Revolution of 1917. Their theory dealt with more of the elements of revolutions and revolutionary situations (e.g., the defection of the intellectuals, the initiating role of state crises, the rise of revolutionary state terror, the emergence of military rulers) than previous theories. In large part because of attention to these diverse elements, these theories corresponded more accurately to the historical details of these cases.

At the same time, these theories failed to move forward in relating revolutions to similar events, or to integrate diverse methods and theories. They treated revolutions as quite separate from riots, protests, or other popular movements, and they rested on a single method, the comparison of historical narratives.

Perhaps the most significant drawback of the natural history school, however, is that it failed to present a convincing reason why revolutions should occur at certain times and places but not others. The defection of the intellectuals, and the initiating political crisis, simply appear as historical contingencies. The fall of the old regime then follows as a matter of course.

Some political scientists and sociologists, however, noted a further pattern in the course of revolutions. It appeared to them that revolutions spread through history in step with the process they called "modernization." This process consisted of an attack on traditional authority, the spread of notions of individuality, citizenship, nationalism, and democracy, and the emergence of rapidly growing, free-market economies. Modernization theorists saw this process emerging first in Britain, the spreading to America and France, and then further across Europe and to Asia, Africa, and Latin America. This also seemed to be the pattern of the spread of revolutions from the seventeenth century to the twentieth. Thus the next challenge for theories of revolution was to somehow link them to modernization.

THE MID-TWENTIETH CENTURY: MODERNIZATION AND NEO-MARXISM

Modernization theory spread widely through the social sciences, influenced by the sociological work of Talcott Parsons (1951, 1966). Parsons argued that societies cohered in a systematic manner, so that in a stable social system the economy, the political system, and the value system all rested on the same principles, and all functioned together to support the maintenance of the society. Thus in traditional societies economic exchange, political authority, and religious and cultural precepts would all reflect traditional beliefs oriented to past practices. In modern societies the economy, governance, and culture would all reflect a more rationalized and individualistic view of social life. Theorists of revolution used this perspective to argue that revolutions occurred when societies were in transition from traditional to modern foundations, in particular when different aspects of the social system developed at different rates, creating a dysfunctional situation in society.

The application of modernization theory to revolutions was spurred by new empirical realities as well. In the aftermath of World War II, from the 1940s through the 1960s, a large number of anticolonial and antitraditional revolutions occurred in the developing world. These included anticolonial revolutions in Indonesia, Vietnam, Algeria, and many African countries; communist revolutions in China and Cuba; nationalist revolutions in Egypt and the Arab world; and populist revolutions in Bolivia and Costa Rica. These decades were also marked by a host of guerrilla and peasant revolts ranging from Colombia's *La Violencia* to Kenya's Mau-Mau and the Philippine's Huk revolts. The enormous geographical range and variety of these revolts seemed to call for some broad general force that was causing societies to break down on a global scale. Modernization seemed to be exactly what was required.

Several different theories of revolution were derived from the basic modernization framework. Chalmers Johnson (1966) suggested that in many developing countries, trade, travel, and communications tended to break down traditional values, while economies and political systems changed far more slowly, leading to a dysfunctional breach between values and social organization. Samuel Huntington (1968) focused more tightly on political demands. He noted that developing countries often provided increased education and participation of their people in the market economy while still maintaining a closed, traditional, political system. Unless political participation was also expanded, he believed this imbalance would lead to explosive demands for changing the structure of political authority. Ted Robert Gurr (1970) claimed that even if economies were growing and political systems were developing, imbalances could still arise. If people expected still greater change to occur than they actually experienced, they would feel "relative deprivation." This feeling of frustration could lead to demands for still more rapid and extensive changes, fueling a revolutionary transformation of society.

All these theories were variants of a model in which modernizing changes in traditional societies disrupted established patterns and expectations regarding social and political life.

This may sound similar to Marx's assertion that economic changes lead to revolutionary class conflicts. However, Johnson, Huntington, and Gurr all eschewed class analysis, and argued that economic change had no primacy—changes in values, education, and expectations were part of the social disruption, not merely the result of economic change. These theorists thought more in terms of a conflict between governments and society at large, spurred by unbalanced social change, rather than conflicts among classes, and kept their distance from Marxist theories. They were clearly more hospitable to Weber's concern with changes in values, and Tocqueville's assertions regarding the inevitable growth of equality and the centralized state. They also largely accepted the patterns of revolutionary dynamics developed by the natural history theorists, incorporating the latter's characterization of revolutionary sequences and attempting to extend them to the recent revolutions in developing societies.

The modernization theories made progress in the theory of revolutions on several fronts. By explicitly addressing themselves to the large number of post–WWII revolutions in the developing world, they greatly expanded the range of cases covered. Modernization theory also allowed revolutions to be brought under a single theoretical umbrella with other forms of protest and collective action. Theorists such as Smelser (1963) argued that revolutions were just the largest and most extreme form of the more general phenomenon of collective protest that arose when people felt trapped in a social system that was out of equilibrium. Crime, strikes, riots, and revolutions were all characteristic of societies in which people felt varying degrees of dysfunction in the social system. In addition, these theories made great strides in integrating additional theoretical and methodological approaches. Huntington and Gurr used psychological theories of aggression to ground their theories, and Gurr (1968) used statistical analysis of large data sets to seek support for the hypothesized links between modernization transitions and political violence.

However, on other fronts there was retreat in theory progress. By focusing so heavily on the broad systemic forces that unbalanced modernizing societies, and the universal trends to modern political and economic structures, these theories reduced their examination of many aspects of revolutionary situations, such as leadership, revolutionary organization, and the variety of economic and political outcomes. Also, as we shall see below, their view of revolution as pitting the government against discontented masses, and being rooted mainly in problems of modernization, lacked accuracy when confronted with a full range of historical and contemporary data.

In consequence of these faults, a reaction came from other theorists who felt that modernization erred in rejecting the insights of the Marxist-Leninist tradition. Charles Tilly (1973, 1978) went directly after Huntington and Gurr, arguing that popular discontent could never by itself launch a revolution. In this he elaborated on the insights of Leon Trotsky, who had organized and led the Red Army for Lenin's Bolsheviks in the Russian Revolution, and who wrote a brilliant, theoretically astute chronicle of the Revolution (Trotsky 1959). Trotsky observed that popular misery and frustration never lead to revolution by themselves; if they did, he wrote, the masses would be in revolt at all times and everywhere. As Lenin insisted, it required a revolutionary organization to channel popular discontent into political grievances, and to mobilize the masses for revolutionary action. Trotsky further observed that in the course of a revolution, a critical period of contention occurs between revolutionary forces and the government, during which the government is still in command but is losing popular support, while the revolutionary forces are gaining support and resources but not yet in power. The resolution of this period of "dual power" is the key to the revolution; only if the revolutionary forces are able to build their strength and defeat the forces of the government can a revolution triumph.

Tilly (1978) constructed from these observations a more formal theory of revolutionary mobilization and contention. He argued that only when organized contenders emerge, capable of mobilizing popular support against the government and defeating the government for control of society, can revolution occur. Modernization might lead to the emergence of such contenders, but it would not automatically provide for their success. That required action by the contenders to assemble revolutionary forces, to acquire political, military, economic, and other resources to confront the government, and then to defeat it.

Tilly's theory thus filled in some of the gaps in modernization theories of revolution. It reintegrated key insights from the Marxist-Leninist tradition, and provided a more detailed and accurate depiction of the power struggles that were actually observed during revolutionary situations than the main modernization theories. Tilly also carried forward the other advances of modernization theories of revolution. Tilly too extended his argument to social movements and other forms of protest, claiming that merely pointing to social disequilibrium could not explain them. Rather, all such collective protest required the mobilization of actors and resources to act on discontent. In addition, Tilly and associates (Tilly, Tilly, and Tilly 1975) used quantitative data analysis to test their arguments that modernizing social change per se (such as urbanization) was only poorly related to outbreaks of revolution.

A further challenge to modernization theory came from the work of Barrington Moore Jr. (1966). Moore argued that while modernization might be the fate of all nations, there were in fact several distinct paths to modernization, with very different economic and political outcomes.

Moore highlighted a democratic path, founded on liberal revolutions such as those that occurred in England and France; a communist path, founded on Leninist revolutions such as those that occurred in Russia and China; and a fascist path, founded on nationalist revolutions such as those that occurred in Fascist Italy, Nazi Germany, and Meiji Japan. Which path a particular nation took depended, as Marx had insisted, on their pattern of class relations. Yet while Marx had simplified those classes into landlords, peasants, workers, and capitalists, and postulated a similar historical pattern of class conflict in all societies, Moore argued that patterns of class power and conflict could vary. In some nations, the emerging capitalist elite might unite with the older landlord elite in order to suppress the masses and create fascism; in others it might unite with the masses to overturn the landlords and create democratic capitalism; in still others it might remain so weak that it is overwhelmed by a popular revolution that creates socialism. Moore thus offered a neo-Marxist view, with class conflict still central, but now with a greatly enriched and more flexible view of the pattern of those conflicts and their possible outcomes.

By arguing for several distinctive kinds of revolution with distinct outcomes, and insisting on the importance of class relations, Moore's neo-Marxism posed a greater challenge to modernization theories than Tilly's mobilization theory. Moore advanced the theory of revolution by incorporating still more cases, indeed some cases which many scholars had not treated as revolutionary situations (Nazi Germany, Fascist Italy, the United States during the Civil War). His detailing of distinct and varied revolutionary outcomes greatly advanced our understanding of that element of the revolutionary process, and offered far greater accuracy than theories that pointed only to a modernization or strengthening of state power. Yet in other respects, Moore recapitulated the limitations of prior approaches. His methods rested on comparing historical narratives, with no statistical or formal analysis.

By the late 1970s, the theory of revolutions was in something of a chaotic state, and was again being challenged by new empirical results. Modernization theorists had found it more difficult than they anticipated to measure individual discontent, and such proxy measures as education or urbanization or inequality failed to link up consistently with political violence (Gurr 1980). Tilly's mobilization theory gained acceptance as a key element in any explanation of revolutions and other kinds of social protest. Yet it said little about the causes that produced successful mobilization, or the results that followed. Moreover, Moore had laid down a critical challenge to modernization theory by demonstrating that modernizing revolutions were not all of one sort, but had clearly distinct outcomes.

In addition to these theoretical conflicts, yet another empirical "shock" added to confusion. A closer examination of historical cases of revolution revealed that they had surprisingly little consistency with regard to modernization. The Latin American revolutions of Independence, from 1808 to 1825, occurred in countries with few measurable signs of economic or value modernization. More recently, the separatist revolts in the Congo (Zaire) in the 1960s, the Sudanese Civil Wars, or the Cambodian Revolution also occurred in states where modernization seemed to have hardly begun. In contrast, the revolutions to found communism in Cuba and in Eastern Europe after World War II occurred in countries that, compared to most of the world and certainly compared to England in the 1640s or France in 1789, were already quite well modernized. The transition to modernization per se thus seemed to be a weak reed on which to rest any analysis of why revolutions occurred in certain societies at particular times.

Modernization theories of revolution thus were coming under fatal fire. There was a clear need to somehow improve upon modernization as a causal force in creating revolutionary situations, while also incorporating Tilly's theory of mobilization and Moore's insights regarding the variety of revolutionary outcomes. This challenge was met by the next major step forward in theories of revolution, the social-structural theory of Theda Skocpol.

THE LATE TWENTIETH CENTURY: SOCIAL-STRUCTURAL THEORY AND ITS CRITICS

In 1979, Theda Skocpol published *States and Social Revolutions*, which was immediately recognized as a landmark in the theory of revolutions. Although it was preceded by several other books that took a somewhat similar approach (Paige 1975; Eisenstadt 1978), it was considerably more successful than any other works in resolving the dilemmas in revolutionary theory at the end of the 1970s.

Skocpol did confine her range of coverage, in order to improve on the accuracy of her theory and cover a number of distinct elements of the revolutionary process. She chose to focus on the great social revolutions—namely the French, Russian, and Chinese Revolutions. She then compared these cases with other cases of less extensive or less successful revolutionary change: the English Revolution, the German Revolution of 1848, the Prussian Reform Movement, and the Japanese Meiji Restoration. Skocpol also limited her methodological and theoretical range. She worked almost entirely from comparing historical narratives, and focused on revolutions to the exclusion of any other kind of social protest or collective action. Nonetheless, within these bounds, she was able to make powerful advances in exploring new (or heretofore unappreciated) elements of the revolutionary process, and creating a theory with far greater correspondence to the facts of these great revolutions than was offered by any modernization-based theories.

Skocpol's first step, following the lead of Wallerstein (1974), was to take modernization out of the individual country, and move it to the world-system as a whole. Skocpol argued that it was not the impact of modernizing change within a country that disturbed political stability; rather it was international military and economic competition between states at different levels of modernization that created destabilizing pressures. A regime that faced military pressure, or economic competition, from a neighboring state at a more advanced level of development would have no choice but to seek to increase its own resources by restructuring its financial, military, and economic system. In her cases, eighteenth-century France faced pressure on its trade and colonies from more advanced Britain; Tsarist Russia was overwhelmed by German military might; and China had to deal with a long stream of imperialist incursions from European powers and Japan. Skocpol pointed out that if a state in this situation encountered resistance to reform from powerful elites in its own country, this conflict could trigger a political crisis and precipitate a revolution. Oddly, international pressures had remained largely absent from prior theories of revolution. Adding this new element made revolutionary theory better correspond to observed conditions facing states, and at the same time helped resolve the conundrums presented by modernization theories that focused only on internal change.

Skocpol's second innovation was to highlight the conflicts between state rulers and a country's political and economic elites. Prior revolutionary theories had more or less taken for granted that state rulers and national elites would be natural allies. Even in Moore's nuanced accounts of class conflict, the question was which combination of elites would take state power, not how rulers and elites might themselves come into conflict. Elite theories of politics, such as those of Pareto and Mosca, spoke of the rotation of power among different elites, and conflict between them, but not of an autonomous ruler facing off against elite groups. In pointing out that state rulers have their own agendas and resources, and that the need for rulers to raise more resources could come into conflict with elite claims to those resources, Skocpol presented a scarcely appreciated source of revolutionary dynamics. Harking back to Tocqueville, this aspect of her theory of revolutionary processes corresponded far better with the observed conflicts between the French monarchy and the elite Parlements that led to the calling of the Estates-General in 1789, or with the observed conflicts between the Chinese Imperial rulers and the warlords who took over China after 1911, than did any modernization theories.

If conflict between a state ruler needing to pursue reforms and elites who resisted them could precipitate a crisis, Skocpol nonetheless realized that this would not suffice for a revolution. Following Tilly's mobilization theory, Skocpol argued that an organizational framework was needed that would allow popular groups to take advantage of conflict and crisis at the political center. This could be a Leninist party, as was the case with the Communist Party in China. However, Skocpol also pointed out that where peasants had their own village organizations and leaders, who were accustomed to taking decisions for the village over matters such as taxation or the distribution of land, this village structure could form the basis for local rural uprisings. In countries like eighteenth-century France and twentieth-century Russia, strong local peasant villages could therefore act when the political center was paralyzed by conflict, and launch rural uprisings that would undermine the political and social order.

Skocpol thus presented her theory as laying out three conditions in a country's social and political structure that were necessary and sufficient for a great social revolution: international pressure from a more advanced state or states; economic or political elites who had the power to resist state-led reforms and create a political crisis; and organizations (either village or party) that were capable of mobilizing peasants for popular uprisings against local authorities. Countries lacking one of these conditions might have less extensive or unsuccessful revolutionary events, but they could not undergo great social revolutions.

Skocpol did not rest with an analysis of the causes of revolution. She continued to consider the variation in outcomes. She argued that social structure also constrained outcomes. Where the sources of wealth in the economy were widely dispersed (such as land and small shops and artisanal establishments), no revolutionary regime could seize control of the economy. In such conditions, revolutions would produce new regimes that protected private property (as in England in the 1640s and France in 1789). However, where industrialization had produced great concentrations of economic power in the shape of large factories, electrical power grids, and railroads, a revolutionary regime could (and most likely would) seize those resources in its drive for power, creating a socialist regime with the government commanding the economy. Here, differences in the level of modernization drive differences in revolutionary outcomes, respecting Moore's insights while incorporating modernization theory into an account of revolutionary outcomes, not merely causes.

Other authors also pointed out that revolutionary outcomes were constrained by international economic structures. Eckstein (1982) showed for a number of Latin American revolutions that despite variations in economic policy, revolutions did nothing to change the basic position of poor countries dependent on raw material exports in the world economy.

Skocpol's three-factor theory of revolutionary causes and her account of outcomes appeared as a simple and elegant solution to the problems of prior theory. Even though she covered only a handful of cases, she successfully illuminated new elements—international pressures and state/elite conflicts—that appeared to have wide applicability to other cases. Her treatment of modernization in terms of international competition and constraints on outcomes seemed far more accurate than the claims of prior modernization theories of revolution. At the same time, she successfully incorporated a wide range of insights from prior revolutionary theories, from Tocqueville's claim that state-led reforms often lead to revolutionary crises to Tilly's treatment of mobilization.

Skocpol's social-structural approach became the dominant theory of revolutions for the last two decades of the twentieth century. Yet almost as soon as it was published, the theory was challenged by new empirical events. Revolutions in Iran and Nicaragua in 1979, in the Philippines in 1986, and in the communist countries of Eastern Europe and the Soviet Union raised new questions about the causes, processes, and outcomes of revolutions.

The Iranian revolution soon generated a debate on the applicability of Skocpol's theory (Skocpol 1982). The Iranian state under the shah, far from being pressured by competition from more advanced states, was the most powerful and advanced state in the Persian Gulf region, and had the strong and committed support of the world's leading superpower, the United States.

Yet the shah's government nonetheless provoked the opposition of almost all sectors of the Iranian elites. While there were economic and political reasons for this opposition, a major role was clearly played by ideological conflict, specifically between the shah's advancing of Westernization and elites defending traditional Islamic practices and laws. Skocpol's theory allowed no role for such ideological roots of state crisis, stating that revolutions are not made, but come as a result of external military or economic pressures. In Iran, the revolution did appear to be made by the opposition, and the state crisis seemed to revolve around the escalation of ideologically motivated conflicts (Kurzman 1996; Rasler 1996; Parsa 2000).

Skocpol's theory of revolutionary mobilization also began to seem deficient in light of new events. The Iranian revolution had no peasant revolts, whether party-led or based in rural village organizations. The Philippine Revolution also had no peasant revolts—or rather the revolutionary party that organized rural rebellion played little or no role in driving the dictator Marcos from power. In both Iran and the Philippines it was overwhelmingly urban protestors who provided the popular base for the revolution (Gugler 1982). Shifting attention to urban crowds made it clear that Skocpol had perhaps underestimated the importance of urban protest in her cases of France and Russia, where the critical events in Paris and St. Petersburg were downplayed relative to peasant revolts. Urban revolt was even more undeniably the story of popular protests in the overthrow of communism. Here, neither vanguard parties nor any other formal organizations seemed to play a major role in popular mobilization. Virtually spontaneous protests in Leipzig, Prague, and Moscow, erupting from little more than a public call for protests, grew until the communist regimes lost the heart to suppress them, and collapsed (Opp, Voss, and Gern 1995; Oberschall 1994; Urban, Igrunov, and Mitrokhin 1997).

Finally, Skocpol's theory of structural constraints on revolutionary outcomes seemed at odds with the wide variety of outcomes of the revolutions of the 1970s, 1980s, and 1990s. In Iran, revolutionaries erected an Islamic republic. In Nicaragua, socialist revolutionaries built a state that respected and preserved private property, and where the vanguard Sandinista party surrendered to democratic elections. In the Philippines, revolution also led to democracy, as it did in Eastern Europe and the Baltic states. Yet in Russia and most of the other Soviet successor states, democracy was shaky or absent; and even though all these states had a high degree of concentration of modern industries, most attempted to create free-market economies and undo state control. It appeared that the ideals and programs of the revolutionary regimes, rather than inescapable structural constraints, were dictating the pattern of revolutionary outcomes.

Despite these difficulties, scholars did not quickly abandon Skocpol's social-structural perspective. The key insights regarding the importance of international influences and state-elites conflicts seemed sound, even if the details of recent events departed somewhat from the pattern of Skocpol's historical cases. The treatment of popular protest, it was felt, could be extended to incorporate urban protests. Thus scholars worked to extend Skocpol's perspective to cover a variety of additional cases, including Iran and Nicaragua (Farhi 1990), anti-colonial revolutions (Goodwin and Skocpol 1989), and guerrilla wars in Latin America (Wickham-Crowley 1992).

Nonetheless, the deficiencies in the social-structural approach grew more apparent, especially with the collapse of communist regimes. In these cases, especially in the central case of the Soviet Union, it was not clear that one could even speak of conflict between state rulers and elites, since there were no independent economic or political elites outside the structure of the communist party-state. Rather, it was cleavages within the party, setting reformist against conservative factions of the military and political elites, that led to the fall of the Soviet regime.

New comparative studies of revolution therefore appeared that departed in various ways from Skocpol's specific structural theory, while still incorporating many of the elements of her approach. Goldstone (1991) analyzed revolutions and large-scale revolts in Europe, the Middle East, and Asia from 1500 to 1800. He argued that international pressures would only create state crises if states were already weakened by fiscal strain. Moreover, he pointed out that merely having a conflict between states and elites need not produce a revolution; strong states could overcome elite opposition, while elites that were firmly united against the state could simply insist on a change in rulers or reforms. It was only when elites themselves were severely divided over how to respond to those pressures that a paralyzing revolutionary crisis would occur.

Goldstone also pointed out that both urban and rural protests often had similar roots in declining economic opportunities. In the cities, rising unemployment and falling real wages made workers open to revolutionary mobilization; in rural villages shortage of land and rising land rents similarly disposed peasants to protest action. Moreover, a specific mobilizing agency—whether it be a vanguard party or a village communal organization, was not always necessary. What mattered, Goldstone argued, was that popular groups see the state as vulnerable, and be prompted by elites calling for change and claiming that it was necessary. Popular groups could then call on a wide array of existing social networks—villages, neighborhoods, workplaces, occupational groups, religious congregations—to mobilize for protest action. Work by Glenn (1999); Gould (1995); Osa (1997); Parsa (2000); and Pfaff (1996) made it clear that no one form of formal organization was needed for protest mobilization; rather a wide variety of formal and informal networks could fulfil that role.

By adding attention to domestic fiscal strains and intra-elite conflicts, as well as the economic basis for urban and popular revolt, Goldstone was able to make several further advances in the coverage and accuracy of revolutionary theory. First, in looking for some causal factor that could simultaneously cause state fiscal strain, intra-elite conflicts, and economic pressure on popular groups, Goldstone was led to the role of sustained population growth in relatively inflexible preindustrial economies. He noted that where a population's demands for food, housing, and manufactured goods pressed on the ability of the economy to supply them, the usual result was inflation, particularly inflation focused on the most inflexible and crucial resource in agrarian economies, namely land. For preindustrial states with relatively fixed taxation mechanisms, this inflation tended to erode state revenues, leading to efforts by the state to increase its resources, usually at the expense of elites. Yet the elites themselves were sharply divided between those who managed to profit from this inflation and those who were hurt by it, at the same time that ever-larger numbers of aspirants for elite positions pressed their demands on the state. Finally, population growth and land scarcity created hardship both for workers, whose real wages tended to decline, and for peasants, who faced rising rents. This combination—fiscally strapped states in conflict with more numerous and divided elites, presiding over an increasingly strained population of workers and peasants—was highly volatile. Should either a section of the elites call for popular protest to support their claims on the state, or should some elites take advantage of popular uprisings over land or wages to press their attack on the state or rival elites, a revolutionary situation would quickly arise.

The most striking finding of Goldstone's work is that revolutions and major rebellions across Europe and Asia from 1500 to 1800 did in fact correspond to the pattern of population growth and decline across those centuries. From 1500 to 1650 population increased, and a wave of revolutionary conflicts grew from the late 1500 through the 1660s in Europe, the Ottoman Empire, and China. From 1650 to 1730, population growth receded, and revolutions were rare.

But from 1730 to 1850 population growth resumed, and revolutionary conflicts again spread all across Europe, the Middle East, and China from the late eighteenth century through the 1840s and 1850s. Showing how population growth could affect the key mechanisms of state crisis, elite conflicts, and popular unrest allowed an explanation of this wave pattern across three centuries. In addition, it extended the coverage of revolutionary theory to new cases of state breakdown, such as regional revolts in the Ottoman Empire and the collapse of the Ming Dynasty.

Goldstone also suggested a major change from Skocpol's theory of revolutionary outcomes. He noted that the great revolutions in Europe and the major revolts and state breakdowns in Asia seemed to have very similar economic and political origins; they also led to substantial institutional changes. Yet in Europe, these changes were often accompanied by a major shift in values and a condemnation of the old regime as obsolete and in need of replacement; in Asia, these changes were usually accompanied by little or no shift in values, and a condemnation of the old regime as flawed for its failure to live up to traditional values and ideals. Goldstone therefore argued that social-structural conditions alone could not account for the different character of revolutionary outcomes; rather, the revolutionary breakdown of the former regime offers a uniquely fluid situation in which the new revolutionary leadership has choices as to how to present itself, and how to rebuild the social and political order. The ideology of the new revolutionary regime can therefore, he argued, be decisive in determining the outcome and trajectory of the postrevolutionary state.

Goldstone's revisions of Skocpol's approach thus continued the progress of the theory of revolutions. The range of historical cases covered by Goldstone and Skocpol now ranged from the absolutist states of Europe to the great empires of the Middle East and China. The elements of the revolutionary process were now expanded to include international pressures, fiscal strain, intra-elite conflict, a wide range of popular protest and mobilization, underlying population pressure on resources, and coordination between opposition elites and popular protest to produce revolutionary situations, as well as the pivotal role of revolutionary ideologies in guiding outcomes. Correspondence to empirical events continued to improve, as various details of state actions, elite conflicts, and popular action could be grounded in revolutionary theory. The ability of that theory to provide an explanation for the wave pattern of revolutionary crises all across Eurasia in the late preindustrial period was particularly striking.

Skocpol and Goldstone also made considerable strides in integrating new theories and methods, in that principles from international relations theory and economic history were now integrated into the theory of revolutions. Goldstone, following the pioneering treatment of peasant revolutions by Paige (1975), supplemented historical narratives with statistical analysis to demonstrate the correspondence between such variables as population growth, price increases, state revenue shortfalls, elite mobility, land rents, and real wages, thus providing more formal and concrete grounding for the theory. Skocpol's emphasis on international factors opened the way for a major area of research, including works by Armstrong (1993); Walt (1996); Katz (1997); Halliday (1999); and Snyder (1999) showing how the origins, development, and outcomes of revolutions were affected by international forces, and how international relations among states were affected by revolutions. These scholars showed that international wars and shifts in international alignments were highly likely to follow revolutions, since revolutionary regimes tended to distance themselves not only from old regime domestic policies, but from their international policies and alliances as well.

Yet deficiencies in the theory of revolutions still remained. It was highly problematic to apply Skocpol or Goldstone's approach to modern revolutions, where the limits of traditional agrarian economies no longer applied. In addition, their revolutionary theory had no clear relation to other areas of social protest and collective action, where theorists of social movements were busy building their own theory of movement origins and actions based on such concepts as political opportunities, mobilization structures, and framing (McAdam, McCarthy, and Zald 1996).

While Goldstone had greatly increased the role of ideology in guiding revolutionary outcomes, critics of structural theory further insisted that ideology must be given a far greater role in the origins of revolutions, in shaping the opposition and guiding revolutionary mobilization (Sewell 1985; Foran 1992; Emirbayer and Goodwin 1994; Selbin 1993; Katz 1997; Mahoney and Snyder 1999). In particular, they noted that structural accounts gave far too little role to leadership and conscious decision making by both rulers and revolutionaries. It may have been true, as Skocpol argued, that Lenin's precise designs for communism in Russia could not be implemented. Yet it is hardly credible to go from that observation to theorizing as if Lenin's decisions and actions were wholly irrelevant to the development and outcome of the Russian Revolution. Several scholars therefore undertook important studies of modern revolutions that demonstrated the key role of ideology and leadership at multiple stages in revolutionary processes (Foran 1997a; Katz 1997; Goodwin 1997; Parsa 2000; Selbin 1993).

Finally, an entirely separate line of theorizing regarding revolutions was developing among political scientists using game theory (also called "rational choice analysis"). Instead of studying empirical cases in detail, rational choice analysts created formal mathematical structures whose logic was held to embody the choices faced by actors in revolutionary situations. Oddly, these formal models predicted that revolutions should not happen at all. Olson (1965) and Tullock (1971) showed that for any individual who contemplated joining in a revolutionary action, the risks and efforts of protest that he or she faced were normally quite considerable, while their contribution to the success of that protest was usually small. In fact, for most individuals their contribution was so modest that the outcome for society—whether or not the revolution succeeded—would likely be the same whether they joined or not. Thus for any individual, the logical incentives were strongly in favor of not joining a revolutionary protest, as they faced substantial risks but were unlikely to change the outcome.

This paradox of collective action was held to show a major deficiency in sociological theories of revolution based on analysis of large-scale, national revolutionary trajectories. Without showing how the paradox of collective action was overcome, rational-choice theorists accused sociological theorists of offering theories that lacked solid foundations in individual behavior (Kiser and Hechter 1991).

At the dawn of the twenty-first century, revolutionary theory had made enormous strides in its coverage of cases, in the range of elements in revolutions treated, in its historical accuracy, and its integration of diverse theories and methods. Yet for all its triumphs, the social-structural approach was under severe assault. It was unclear how to apply the theory of revolutions to the suddenly large number of new and surprising revolutions from Iran and the Philippines to the collapse of communist regimes. Critics had shown that the theory did not give enough play to the role of ideology in the origins and unfolding of revolutions. Theories of social movements and protest action were forging ahead in apparently unrelated directions. And political scientists armed with formal models of individual rational action claimed that the theory of revolutions had no grounding in the behavior of individuals. These were formidable challenges indeed.

INCORPORATING RATIONALITY AND IDEOLOGY INTO REVOLUTIONARY THEORY

As has happened before when revolutionary theory was confronted with new empirical and theoretical challenges, theorists have risen to the occasion. While it is too soon to identify a new dominant perspective on revolutions, the building blocks for that new perspective are already apparent. Older theorists such as Goldstone and Tilly, and younger scholars such as Foran, Gould, Lichbach, Goodwin, Wickham-Crowley, and Parsa are laying out new principles for understanding a still broader range of revolutionary events.

Let us begin with the challenges posed by rational choice theory. Mark Lichbach (1995) has led the way in showing how the collective action problem can be overcome. He has identified over a dozen different mechanisms by which opposition groups can motivate people to join revolutionary movements, consistent with rational action. Whether through contracts, incentives, prior commitments, or exercising preexisting authority over individuals, opposition movements have a variety of tools available to promote mobilization. The key to these approaches is to realize that individuals do not make isolated choices on whether or not to join revolutionary protests, as the early rational-choice theorists suggested. Rather, individuals come to social interaction already bound up in a web of social connections and obligations. It is through building on these extant linkages and commitments that revolutionary mobilization occurs (Opp and Roehl 1990; Goldstone 1994b; Gould 1995).

Attention to processes of mobilization also helped to link revolutionary theory with theories of social movements. As McAdam, Tarrow, and Tilly (1997) and Goldstone (1998a) pointed out, these theories were in fact converging on similar sets of conditions and processes for protest and revolutions. Social movement theory had argued that protest movements arose when three conditions were conjoined: (1) political opportunities, which are brought by state weakness or intra-elite conflicts; (2) active mobilization networks, drawing on preexisting social linkages or organizations; and (3) a cognitive framework showing the need for and effectiveness of protest, created by leaders who "frame" the need for protest in a persuasive ideology (Tarrow 1998). The first two of these conditions were, in effect, already part of the theory of revolutions. The last condition, ideology, clearly needed to be brought into revolutionary theory.

Goldstone (1998a) argued that modernization theories had erred in seeing revolutions simply as "larger" or more extreme cases of social protest movements, but that structural theory also had erred in seeing revolutions and social movements as wholly distinct phenomena. Instead, he suggested an evolutionary relationship between the two. A common set of conditions (e.g., state crisis, intra-elite conflicts, mobilization networks, economic grievances) generate opposition to state authorities. If the authorities treat this opposition as legitimate and give it scope to seek reforms, the result is likely to be a social protest movement with reformist ideology. However, if the authorities treat the protest as illegitimate, and seek to entirely deny or repress it, then moderate elements in the movement are likely to give way to more radical groups, with ideologies calling for more far-reaching change, and challenging the rights and authority of government itself. Thus it appears that when the role of ideology is more fully comprehended in revolutionary theory, a single theory will be able to encompass the development of both revolutions and social protest movements.

McAdam, Tarrow, and Tilly (2001) have gone even farther in showing how a variety of concrete mechanisms of mobilization, elite-popular alliances, and ideological development are found to be equally present in historical cases of revolutions and social movements. Theories of revolution are thus making strong progress on the problem of integrating revolutionary theory with the analysis of other kinds of social protest.

The role of ideology, however, is extremely complex, and still being explored. Selbin (1993) has argued that ideology is linked to leadership, and that effective leadership is needed to both inspire revolutionaries through persuasive ideology, and to build and maintain revolutionary institutions. In this, he echoes Max Weber's theory of revolutions, which argued that while charismatic leaders are needed to challenge status quo institutions, stable and widely accepted new values are required to underlay the construction of new institutions. Foran (1997a) and Wickham-Crowley (1992) have argued that almost all societies maintain a stock of ideologies of protest or rebellion from past conflicts with authority, and that revolutionary leaders need to tap into these memories of conflict experiences in their own societies to construct persuasive and attractive ideologies of rebellion. Wickham-Crowley (1991); Foran (1997a); and Parsa (2000) have argued that it is ideologies that provide the glue for alliances between elites and popular groups. Calhoun (1994) has further pointed out that ideologies carry notions of identity and group commitment, which help sustain and invigorate the social networks that mobilize people for revolutionary action. It is clear that ideologies play so many crucial roles in revolutionary processes that the task of integrating ideology into revolutionary theory is still ongoing.

MANY REVOLUTIONS, MANY CAUSES: THE PROBLEM OF PARSIMONY IN REVOLUTIONARY THEORY

The largest challenge to revolutionary theory is to accurately encompass the major revolutions of the late twentieth century, including anticolonial, nationalist, and antidictatorial revolutions such as those in Cuba, Iran, the Philippines, and the former communist regimes. Here, too, theories of revolution have made significant progress, with efforts by many scholars grappling with different sets of cases.

Foran (1997b); Wickham-Crowley (1992); Goodwin and Skocpol (1989); and Goldstone, Gurr, and Moshiri (1991) have all shown that modern revolutions have common features that they share with the revolutions in agrarian monarchies and empires. Most of those features were already laid out in the social-structural approach. International pressures, state crises, intra-elite conflicts, and popular mobilization remain key components in the development of revolutionary situations even in modern regimes. However, these broad factors need to be modified to gain accurate correspondence with the events observed in modern revolutions, and a role needs to be added for ideology as well. Although these scholars overlap to a good degree in identifying the factors important to modern revolutions, they do not agree on precisely which conditions should comprise the core of revolutionary theories.

International pressures, for example, are not sufficiently described in terms of international military or economic competition. Increasingly, direct foreign intervention and support—or withdrawal of that support—are common. In Cuba, Iran, Nicaragua, and the Philippines, the pattern of initial U.S. support for dictators, followed by reduction or withdrawal of that support, contributed to the outbreak of revolutionary conflicts (Halliday 1999; Snyder 1999). Moreover, revolutionary ideologies, organizations, and events often have strong international influences and linkages, leading to spreading "waves" of revolutions, as occurred with Arab nationalist revolutions in the Middle East, and the anticommunist revolutions throughout Eastern Europe (Katz 1997).

State crisis is also not merely a problem of states running into elite resistance to reforms. In modern states, the relationships between rulers and elites are quite varied. Elites may oppose rulers because of failures of patronage, problems in economic development, exclusion from political power, or lack of progress on nationalist goals. Goodwin (1994); Goldstone (1994b); Wickham-Crowley (1992); and Snyder (1998), all building on the key work of Dix (1983, 1984), have argued that one type of modern dictatorship—the personalist, or neopatrimonial dictatorship, in which a single individual has amassed great power and gains elite loyalty mainly by dispensing favors and positions—is especially vulnerable to social revolutions. This kind of regime can appear quite strong when the dictator is able to keep elites factionalized and dependent on his favor. Yet when economic or international political pressures weaken the dictator's ability to control the elites, there are no other traditional or institutional supports for his regime. Such regimes can thus fall with remarkable swiftness when they lose elite support. In addition, because the dictator has no established organizations or institutions to enlist and maintain popular support, beyond the repression of the police and military, elites can fairly easily encourage popular opposition if the repressive institutions appear weakened or unwilling to defend the regime. This pattern of neopatrimonial regime collapse can be identified in the revolutions in Cuba (1959), Nicaragua (1979), and Iran (1979), and was expected—and in fact occurred—in the Philippines (1986), Indonesia (1998), and Zaire (1998). In contrast, dictatorships linked to and strongly supported by a particular social group, be it the military, landed elites, industrialists, or a political party organization, are more stable.

The study of modern revolutions has also shown that if intra-elite conflicts are necessary to create conditions favorable to revolution, a strong revolutionary movement generally requires cross-class coalitions linking elite and popular groups. This is particularly true where revolutionary movements take the form of guerrilla war against the government. For such movements to succeed, the rural guerrillas must find allies among elites and urban groups; otherwise they remain isolated in rural rebellion (Wickham-Crowley 1991, 1992).

Goodwin (1994) and Goldstone (1998b) have demonstrated that the collapse of communist regimes can be brought within the scope of revolutionary theory. In Goldstone's explanation of the collapse of the U.S.S.R., he points out that international competitive military and economic pressure from the West led a faction of Soviet elites led by Gorbachev to seek major reforms in the communist regime (Glasnost and Perestroika). However, by the time of those reforms, a sharp contraction in Soviet economic growth had already weakened the state's ability to provide continued employment improvement and higher living standards for its population. The stagnation of professional employment produced a large number of educated elites (technicals) with college degrees who were stuck in blue-collar jobs and excluded from political or economic advancement. Economic decline, along with grievous pollution and inefficient health care, had also produced a marked decline in life expectancy since the mid-1970s. Health and safety concerns were particularly strong in those areas with the most polluting and dangerous factories and mines.

The technical elites, urban workers, and miners saw Gorbachev's reforms as an opportunity not merely to reform, but to throw out communist control over political and economic life. They supported the reformist faction, led by Yeltsin in Russia and by other nationalist leaders in the Baltic, Caucasus, and Central Asian Soviet Republics, and pressed for the withdrawal of communist authority, mobilizing vast urban demonstrations in cities around the U.S.S.R. At the same time, more conservative military and political leaders became alarmed at the prospect of the communist party's loss of authority, and planned a coup d'etat against Gorbachev. The coup was able to seize Gorbachev while he was out of the capital. However, the coup leaders failed to seize the parliament and TV and radio stations, due to lack of elite support and widespread popular opposition. As a result, supporters of Yeltsin were able to take control of Parliament and the media. Deprived of access to the centers of power and with its supporters in disarray, the communist regime collapsed, as did Soviet control over the various republics, which soon declared their independence. The key elements in this process—international pressure, state weakness, intra-elite conflicts, cross-class coalitions among elite reformers and popular groups facing depressed living conditions, and ideologies of rebellion (democracy and nationalism) that united regime opponents and inspired rebellion—are precisely those found in other major revolutions. Goldstone thus argued that as in most other major revolutions, struggles for power would likely continue, and in the absence of leaders strongly committed to democracy—an absence felt in most former communist regimes except for a few in Eastern Europe and the Baltics—democracy was not likely to develop, whatever the hopes of Western aid contributors and well-wishers.

Goodwin (1994) further pointed out that differences in the way that anticommunist revolutions unfolded reflected differences in state structure. Romania's revolution against the neopatrimonial Ceaucescu regime was most like the sudden and violent overthrow of other personalist dictators, while the limited resistance put up by the communist regimes in East Germany and Czechoslovakia meant that these events unfolded more like social protest movements.

While these efforts have shown how revolutionary theory can be modified and applied to explain modern revolutions, they have also created their own problem in the complexity that resulted from the extension of theory to cover more cases. In the course of these efforts, the earlier goal of identifying a short and consistent list of causes that lead to revolution seems to have been lost. For example, while state weakness or crisis is a condition of revolution, what are the causes that produce that condition? Scholars have enumerated such causes as military defeat or competition, economic downturns, excessive state debt or fiscal strain, long-term demographic pressures, uneven or unsuccessful economic development, strains on colonial powers' resources or domestic support, rulers' departures from religious or nationalist principles, foreign interventions, shifts in state resources due to changing export or import prices, ethnic conflicts, erratic or excessive repression by rulers, shifts in international standards for human rights, harvest failures or other natural disasters (including earthquakes, flood, and droughts), with no two revolutions having precisely the same causes. Similarly, intra-elite conflicts may arise from ethnic divisions, political exclusion, state actions that favor a particular group, religious divisions, conflicts over resources or economic development, or shifts in social mobility that produce new elite aspirants or that undermine the continuity of existing elite families.

In short, it has become more difficult to look behind the "conditions" of revolution—such as state crisis or elite conflicts—for concrete historical causes. The latter are simply too diverse, and vary too greatly across cases, to serve as the foundation for general theory. Moreover, there is a realization that the unfolding of revolutions has emergent properties; once a revolutionary situation has begun, the actions and decisions of rulers and revolutionaries influence further events. Certain mechanisms persist across revolutionary situations—popular mobilization, leadership, ideological framing, building cross-class coalitions, confronting authorities with mass actions—but they may develop in different ways in different cases. Thus simply listing conditions for revolution does not tell us how revolutions develop, because these conditions combine and concatenate in different ways. For example, in Russia intra-elite conflict was not important until after WWI produced a collapse of the Tsar's military; Lenin and Trotsky's leadership and mobilization of workers then proved critical in the ensuing intra-elite struggles for control of the post-Tsarist state. In Iran, by contrast, the military was never weakened by international conflicts. Rather, intra-elite conflicts precipitated protests over the shah's religious policies and alliance with the United States; these protests then led to more constrained U.S. support and a decision by the shah's military to withdraw from defending the shah against mass opposition. In other cases, revolutions develop through guerrilla wars; in still others through relatively peaceful strikes and protests. A list of "conditions" of revolution is thus too static to capture the reality of the revolutionary process, in which conditions enter in different combinations and temporal patterns, interacting with the decisions of rulers and revolutionaries to produce varied revolutionary trajectories.

A NEW STAGE IN REVOLUTIONARY THEORY—PROBLEMATIZING STABILITY, NOT JUST REVOLUTION

Goldstone (2001) has suggested a way out of this impasse by turning the problem of revolutionary causation around. Theories of revolution have generally proceeded as if states have a huge variety of ways to operate normally, but only a small and particular set of conditions is sufficiently disruptive to produce revolutions. However, over a century of empirical events and investigations now suggests that may not be so. Instead, it appears that a huge variety of events are involved, in various combinations, in producing different varieties of revolutionary situations. Goldstone therefore suggested that instead of treating stability as unproblematic, and piling up a large set of conditions that lead to revolution, we should consider stability as the key problem that states continually face, and see revolutions as the result of the loss or undermining of conditions that maintain stability. The different ways this happens will generate different trajectories leading to various processes and outcomes of protest and/or revolution.

The conditions for stability are more easily enumerated, by inverting the much longer list of revolutionary conditions. They are: (1) rulers (or ruling organizations) that are widely perceived as both effective and just; (2) elites that are united and supportive of the regime; and (3) popular groups that are able to secure their customary standard of living in a reliable manner. States that meet these conditions are reliably stable; the more that states fall short of meeting these conditions the more likely they are to experience conflict, protest, and revolution.

Departures from the conditions for stability then create situations in which revolutionary leaders can begin to mobilize oppositions, and rulers to plan their response. The decisions and actions of rulers and revolutionaries, the particular elite cleavages and groups that are mobilized, the specific ideologies used to generate support, and international reactions then generate the variety in the pattern of protests and revolutions that we observe—some involving guerrilla warfare, some involving the sudden collapse of a state, some occurring in neopatrimonial dictatorships, some in one-party states, some in democracies.

By focusing on the loss or undermining of conditions of stability, revolutionary theory can allow much greater scope for dynamic processes such as leadership, mobilization, and decision making by rulers and revolutionary opponents, and for the interplay of these processes to vary over time. In addition, specifying conditions for stability allows for the enormous range of specific concrete factors shown to be important in revolution—such as military or economic failures, failures to uphold religious or nationalist principles, or excessive or inadequate repression or response to disasters, to name a few—to play a role without having to specify the same set of causal factors being involved in all revolutions. In this way, those specific factors specified by Skocpol—military pressure that undermines state effectiveness, state reforms that undermine elite unity and support for the state, and village communal organizations facing more onerous taxes and rents—become simply one particular set of conditions undermining state stability. The demographic pressures noted by Goldstone in late preindustrial societies, and the ways that personalist dictatorships may decline in effectiveness or forfeit elite loyalty, similarly become special cases subsumed under the broader theory of regime stability. The ineffectiveness of the Weimar regime that led to the Nazi revolution and of the Chinese imperial court, the court/country divisions in seventeenth-century England and the reformist/conservative blocs in the Communist Party of the Soviet Union in the late twentieth century, the impact of demographic pressures and of commercialized agriculture on peasants across time and space, all can be brought into a common framework of factors that undermine the conditions of state stability. When all three of those conditions of stability are simultaneously lost, by whatever means, a revolutionary situation is the result.

Harking back to Weber's view of revolutions as requiring the institutionalization of new values, the process and outcomes of revolutions can then be conceptualized as an ongoing effort to re-create the conditions of stability. Revolutionary leaders use ideological struggles and mobilization to secure elite support for the revolution, while building a stronger state is essential to gain effectiveness for the new revolutionary regime. Securing a stable material existence for the population is often the most difficult condition to meet, and thus it is normal to expect recurrent popular protests as part of the revolutionary process. Indeed, the difficulty of rebuilding stable conditions implies that revolutionary struggles will often last years, or even decades, and that the fall of the old regime will generally not, in itself, bring a society to popular prosperity, elite loyalty, and effective and just governance (Stinchcombe 1999).

CONCLUSION

Starting from the insights of the founding fathers of sociology, theories of revolution have continually developed over time in response to new events, expanding to incorporate new cases and additional details of the revolutionary process. A focus on state crises, elite conflicts, and popular mobilization has helped bring events from the French Revolution to the collapse of the Soviet Union into a common framework. This framework is currently being further expanded to cover additional elements in the revolutionary process, including the role of ideology, leadership, rational action, and international linkages. Treating the conditions for stability, rather than of revolution per se, as the central problematic holds out the possibility of greater parsimony in understanding the causes of revolutions, and their relationship to other varieties of collective action and political change.

Lest we end on too triumphal a note, we should be clear that important further challenges for revolutionary theory still remain. Though receiving increasing attention, the role of women and gender issues in revolution has yet to be adequately theorized (Moghadam 1997; Tétreault 1994; Wasserstrom 1994). Although rational choice theory has offered some guidance, no mathematical formalization of revolutionary processes is widely accepted. Macro-level theories of revolution still need to be harmonized with social-psychological theories of individual behavior. As in any fruitful field of research, further frontiers of theory development yet await.

REFERENCES

Arjomand, Said A. 1988. *The Turban for the Crown: The Islamic Revolution in Iran.* New York: Oxford University Press.

Armstrong, David. 1993. *Revolution and World Order: The Revolutionary State in International Society.* Oxford: Oxford University Press.

Berger, Joseph, and Morris Zelditch Jr., eds. 1993. *Theoretical Research Programs: Studies in the Growth of Theory.* Stanford, CA: Stanford University Press.

Brinton, Crane. 1938. *The Anatomy of Revolution.* New York: Norton.

Calhoun, Craig. 1994. "The Problem of Identity in Collective Action." Pp. 51–75 in *Macro-Micro Linkages in Sociology,* edited by Joan Huber. Newbury Park, CA: Sage.

Colburn, Forrest D. 1994. *The Vogue of Revolution in Poor Countries.* Princeton: Princeton University Press.

Dix, Robert. 1983. "The Varieties of Revolution." *Comparative Politics* 15:281–95.

———. 1984. "Why Revolutions Succeed and Fail." *Polity* 16:423–46.

Eckstein, Susan. 1982. "The Impact of Revolution on Social Welfare in Latin America." *Theory and Society* 11:43–94.

Edwards, Lyford P. 1927. *The Natural History of Revolutions.* Chicago: University of Chicago Press.

Eisenstadt, S. N. 1978. *Revolution and the Transformation of Societies.* New York: Free Press.

Emirbayer, Mustafa, and Jeff Goodwin. 1994. "Network Analysis, Culture, and the Problem of Agency." *American Journal of Sociology* 99:1411–54.

Farhi, Farideh. 1990. *States and Urban-based Revolution: Iran and Nicaragua.* Urbana: University of Illinois Press.

Foran, John. 1992. "A Theory of Third World Social Revolutions: Iran, Nicaragua, and El Salvador Compared." *Critical Sociology* 19:3–27.

———. 1997a. "The Comparative-Historical Sociology of Third World Social Revolutions: Why a Few Succeed, Why Most Fail." Pp. 227–67 in Foran 1997b.

———, ed. 1997b. *Theorizing Revolutions.* London: Routledge.

Forster, Robert. 1980. "The French Revolution and the New Elite, 1800–1850." Pp. 182–207 in *The American and European Revolutions, 1776–1850,* edited by J. Pelenski. Iowa City: University of Iowa Press.

Garton Ash, Timothy. 1989. "Revolution in Hungary and Poland." *New York Review of Books* 36 (August 17): 9–15.

Glenn, John K. 1999. "Competing Challengers and Contested Outcomes to State Breakdown: The Velvet Revolution in Czechoslovakia." *Social Forces* 78:187–212.

Goldstone, Jack A. 1991. *Revolution and Rebellion in the Early Modern World.* Berkeley: University of California Press.

———. 1994a. "Is Revolution Individually Rational?" *Rationality and Society* 6:139–66.

———. 1994b. "Revolution in Modern Dictatorships." Pp. 70–77 in Goldstone 1994c.

———. ed. 1994c. *Revolutions: Theoretical, Comparative, and Historical Studies.* 2d ed. Fort Worth, TX: Harcourt Brace.

———. 1998a. "Social Movements or Revolutions? On the Evolution and Outcomes of Collective Action." Pp. 125–45 in *Democracy and Contention,* edited by Marco Guigni, Doug McAdam, and Charles Tilly. Boulder, CO: Rowman & Littlefield.

———. 1998b. "The Soviet Union: Revolution and Transformation." Pp. 95–123 in *Elites, Crises, and the Origins of Regimes*, edited by Mattei Dogan and John Higley. Boulder, CO: Rowman & Littlefield.

———, ed. 1998c. *The Encyclopedia of Political Revolutions.* Washington, DC: Congressional Quarterly Press.

———. 2001. "Toward a Fourth Generation of Revolutionary Theory." *Annual Review of Political Science* 4:139–187.

Goldstone, Jack A., Ted Robert Gurr, and Farrokh Moshiri, eds. 1991. *Revolutions of the Late Twentieth Century.* Boulder, CO: Westview Press.

Goodwin, Jeff. 1994. "Old Regimes and Revolutions in the Second and Third Worlds: A Comparative Perspective." *Social Science History* 18:575–604.

———. 1997. "The Libidinal Constitution of a High-Risk Social Movement: Affectual Ties and Solidarity in the Huk Rebellion, 1946 to 1954. *American Sociological Review* 62:53–70.

———. 2001. "Is the Age of Revolutions Over?" Pp. 272–83 in *Revolution: International Dimensions,* edited by Mark Katz. Washington DC: CQ Press.

Goodwin, Jeff, and Theda Skocpol. 1989. "Explaining Revolutions in the Contemporary Third World." *Politics and Society* 17:489–507.

Gould, R. V. 1995. *Insurgent Identities: Class, Community, and Protest in Paris from 1848 to the Commune.* Chicago: University of Chicago Press.

Gugler, Josef. 1982. "The Urban Character of Contemporary Revolutions." *Studies in Comparative International Development* 17:60–73.

Gurr, Ted Robert. 1968. "A Causal Model of Civil Strife: A Comparative Analysis Using New Indices." *American Political Science Review* 62:1104–24.

———. 1970. *Why Men Rebel.* Princeton, NJ: Princeton University Press.

———, ed. 1980. *Handbook of Political Conflict.* New York: Free Press.

Halliday, Fred. 1999. *Revolution and World Politics.* London: Macmillan.

Huntington, Samuel P. 1968. *Political Order in Changing Societies.* New Haven: Yale University Press.

Johnson, Chalmers. 1966. *Revolutionary Change.* Boston: Little, Brown.

Katz, Mark. 1997. *Revolutions and Revolutionary Waves.* New York: St. Martin's Press.

Kiser, Edgar, and Michael Hechter. 1991. "The Role of General Theory in Comparative-Historical Sociology." *American Journal of Sociology* 97:1–30.

Kuhn, Thomas S. 1996. *The Structure of Scientific Revolutions.* 3d ed. Chicago: University of Chicago Press.

Kurzman, Charles. 1996. "Structural Opportunity and Perceived Opportunity in Social-Movement Theory." *American Sociological Review* 61:153–70.

Lenin, Vladimir Ilich. 1973. *What Is to Be Done? Burning Questions of Our Movement.* Translation of the 1st ed. of 1902. Peking: Foreign Languages Press.

Lichbach, Mark I. 1995. *The Rebels' Dilemma.* Ann Arbor: University of Michigan Press.

Mahoney, James, and Richard Snyder. 1999. "Rethinking Agency and Structure in the Study of Regime Change." *Studies in Comparative International Development* 34:3–32.

McAdam, Doug, John D. McCarthy, and Mayer N. Zald, eds. 1996. *Comparative Perspectives on Social Movements.* Cambridge: Cambridge University Press.

McAdam, Doug, Sidney Tarrow, and Charles Tilly. 1997. "Toward a Comparative Perspective on Social Movements and Revolution." Pp. 142–73 in *Comparative Politics: Rationality, Culture, and Structure,* edited by Mark Lichbach and Alan S. Zuckerman. Cambridge: Cambridge University Press.

———. 2001. *Dynamics of Contention.* Cambridge: Cambridge University Press.

Moghadam, Val M. 1997. "Gender and Revolutions." Pp. 137–67 in Foran 1997b.

Moore, Barrington Jr. 1966. *Social Origins of Dictatorship and Democracy.* Boston: Beacon Press.

Oberschall, Anthony. 1994. "Protest Demonstrations and the End of Communist Regimes in 1989." *Research in Social Movements, Conflict, and Change* 17:1–24.

Olson, M., Jr. 1965. *The Logic of Collective Action: Public Goods and the Theory of Groups.* Cambridge, MA: Harvard University Press.

Opp, Karl-Dieter. 1994. "Repression and Revolutionary Action: East Germany in 1989." *Rationality and Society* 6:101–38.

Opp, Karl-Dieter, and Wolfgang Roehl. 1990. "Repression, Micromobilization, and Political Protest." *Social Forces* 69:521–47.

Opp, Karl-Dieter, Peter Voss, and Christianne Gern. 1995. *Origins of a Spontaneous Revolution: East Germany, 1989.* Ann Arbor: University of Michigan Press.

Osa, Maryjane. 1997. "Creating Solidarity: The Religious Foundations of the Polish Social Movement." *East European Politics and Society* 11:339–65.

Paige, Jeffrey M. 1975. *Agrarian Revolution*. New York: Free Press.

Parsa, Misagh. 2000. *States, Ideologies, and Social Revolutions: A Comparative Analysis of Iran, Nicaragua, and the Philippines*. Cambridge: Cambridge University Press.

Parsons, Talcott. 1951. *The Social System.* Glencoe, IL: Free Press.

———. 1966. *Societies: Evolutionary and Comparative Perspectives.* Englewood Cliffs, NJ: Prentice-Hall.

Pettee, George S. 1938. *The Process of Revolution.* New York: Harper and Row.

Pfaff, Steven. 1996. "Collective Identity and Informal Groups in Revolutionary Mobilization: East Germany in 1989." *Social Forces* 75:91–110.

Rasler, Karen. 1996. "Concessions, Repression, and Political Protest in the Iranian Revolution." *American Sociological Review* 61:132–52.

Selbin, Eric. 1993. *Modern Latin American Revolutions.* Boulder, CO: Westview Press.

———. 2001. "Same as It Ever Was: The Future of Revolution at the End of the Century." Pp. 284–98 in *Revolution: International Dimensions,* edited by Mark Katz. Washington, DC: CQ Press.

Sewell, William Jr. 1985. "Ideologies and Social Revolutions: Reflections on the French Case." *Journal of Modern History* 57:57–85.

Skocpol, Theda. 1979. *States and Social Revolutions.* Cambridge: Cambridge University Press.

———. 1982. "Rentier State and Shi'a Islam in the Iranian Revolution." *Theory and Society* 11: 265–303, with responses by Nikki Keddie, Walter Goldfrank, and Eqbal Ahmed.

Smelser, Neil J. 1963. *Theory of Collective Behavior.* New York: Free Press.

Snyder, Richard. 1998. "Paths out of Sultanistic Regimes: Combining Structural and Voluntarist Perspectives." Pp. 49–81 in *Sultanistic Regimes,* edited by H. E. Chehabi and J. J. Linz. Baltimore, MD: Johns Hopkins University Press.

Snyder, Robert S. 1999. "The U.S. and Third World Revolutionary States: Understanding the Breakdown in Relations." *International Studies Quarterly* 43:265–90.

Stinchcombe, Arthur L. 1999. "Ending Revolutions and Building New Governments." *Annual Review of Political Science* 2:49–73.

Tarrow, Sidney. 1998. *Power in Movement: Social Movements and Contentious Politics.* 2d ed. Cambridge: Cambridge University Press.

Tétreault, M. A., ed. 1994. *Women and Revolution in Africa, Asia, and the New World.* Columbia: University of South Carolina Press.

Tilly, C. 1973. "Does Modernization Breed Revolution?" *Comparative Politics* 5:425–47.

———. 1978. *From Mobilization to Revolution.* Reading, MA: Addison-Wesley.

Tilly, C., L. Tilly, and R. Tilly. 1975. *The Rebellious Century, 1830–1930.* Cambridge, MA: Harvard University Press.

Trotsky, Leon. 1959. *The Russian Revolution.* Edited by F. W. Dupee, translated by Max Eastman. New York: Doubleday/Anchor Books.

Tullock, G. 1971. "The Paradox of Revolution." *Public Choice* 1:89–99

Urban, M., V. Igrunov, and S. Mitrokhin. 1997. *The Rebirth of Politics in Russia.* Cambridge: Cambridge University Press.

Wallerstein, Immanuel. 1974. *The Modern World System.* Vol. 1. New York: Academic Press.

Walt, Stephen M. 1996. *Revolution and War.* Ithaca, NY: Cornell University Press.

Wasserstrom, Jeffrey N. 1994. "Gender and Revolution in Europe and Asia." *Journal of Women's History* 5:170–83, 6:109–20.

Wickham-Crowley, Timothy. 1991. *Exploring Revolution: Essays on Latin American Insurgency and Revolutionary Theory.* Armonk, NY: Sharpe.

———. 1992. *Guerrillas and Revolution in Latin America.* Princeton, NJ: Princeton University Press.

V

INSTITUTIONAL STRUCTURES

9

The Development and Application of Sociological Neoinstitutionalism

Ronald L. Jepperson

Sociological neoinstitutionalism is one of the most broad-ranging "theoretical research programs" (TRPs [Berger and Zelditch 1998]) in contemporary sociology and one of the most empirically developed forms of institutional analysis. This program, centered around the work of John W. Meyer and his collaborators (but now extending beyond this group), has produced an integrated and extensive body of research about the nation-states, individuals, and organizational structures of modern society. The central concern of this institutionalism is the embeddedness of social structures and social "actors" in broad-scale contexts of meaning: more specifically, the consequences of European and later world culture for social organization (Meyer, Boli, and Thomas 1987:31).

This institutionalism originated in a set of theoretical papers in the 1970s by Meyer, and in concurrent research in the sociology of education, where the program has remained central. The program expanded into full-blown research efforts concerning organizations, the world system, and individual identity. Applications continue to proliferate. For instance, this institutionalism now supports one of the most extensive lines of research on current "globalization"—for example, John Boli and George Thomas's work on the extraordinary recent increase in international nongovernmental organizations (Boli and Thomas 1997)—as well as new efforts on collective identity, sexuality, law, and for that matter even financial accounting. These efforts are now found across the sociological community at many of its major research sites.

This chapter surveys and analyzes the development of this TRP. It explicates its intellectual core, surveys its interrelated applications in different substantive domains, and analyzes the growth of these applications over time.[1] The primary concern is how this institutionalism has been used to generate substantive insights—that is, both new observations and new explanations of the social world.[2]

INTELLECTUAL CONTEXT

Meyer worked out a number of the core theoretical ideas by 1970.[3] A set of fundamental papers, developing and consolidating main ideas, appeared in print between 1977 and 1980: on the "effects of education as an institution" (Meyer 1977), on "institutionalized organizations" (with Brian Rowan [Meyer and Rowan 1977]), and on "the world polity and the authority of the nation-state" (Meyer 1980).[4]

In developing his ideas, Meyer was reacting to the enduring individualism of American sociology, the manifest empirical difficulties of its associated "action" and "socialization" theories (including Talcott Parsons's variant, emphasizing action guided by internalized norms), and the persistent attempt by much American social theory especially to analyze modern society as a "society without culture" (Meyer 1988).[5] Asked to characterize the development of his thinking, in an interview in *Sozusagen* (a publication of the Bielefeld Department of Sociology), Meyer indicates that he did not think of society as fundamentally constituted by "actors," or of people or structures as primarily actors (Krücken 2000). He "took less seriously the actorhood of individuals than American sociologists would normally do" (ibid.:58): "I did not think individuals were the fundamental units of society, nor did I think they were tightly organized 'hard-wired' structures. I thought society was made up of knowledge and culture" (Meyer 1999b). Accordingly, in his work (the interview continues), Meyer tried to reconceptualize the sociology of education to "give it a less individualistic picture. It is less a matter of socializing raw individuals, but more about labeling, credentialing, and creating categories—more institutional in a word. . . . In organization theory, I did the same, and also in my work on the nation state, which I see as structures embedded in a broader meaning system and less as autonomous actors" (Meyer in Krücken 2000:58).

By seeing society as institutionalized "knowledge and culture," Meyer (then others) work from an analytical imagery as basic as the actor-and-interest imagery of more conventional sociology: namely, the "construction" of structures and actors within broad institutional frameworks, and the cultural "scripting" of much activity within these frameworks. By focusing upon the broad institutional frameworks of society (including world society), sociological neoinstitutionalism then *de*focalizes "actors" *on purpose*. The whole point of this TRP is to find out what can be gained by seeing actors (and interests and structures and activity) as in many respects derivative from institutions and culture. This idea is pursued in order to envision features of the social world not easily captured—or not captured at all—when focusing upon actors (Meyer and Jepperson 2000).

A clear research agenda has followed from this intellectual thrust. There is a background historical argument about the evolution of modern society within the institutional matrices and cultural schemas provided by Christendom (see

Meyer 1989; Meyer, Boli, and Thomas 1987; Meyer and Jepperson 2000). There is an additional background argument about the long-term reconstruction of modern society around a world system of national states, the latter units constituted as societies of organizations and of citizen-individuals. The three main research clusters of the program then follow directly. National states are seen as embedded in a world polity and culture, and the common cultural contents and trends of these states are sought. Organizations are seen as embedded in national (and increasingly world) institutional environments, and their externally institutionalized features are sought. People are seen as enacting elaborate doctrines of individualism, rather than acting in some more generic fashion; these doctrines have both world cultural sources and distinctive national variations, and both are studied. In each research area, many basic features of the entities examined—national states, organizations, individuals—are shown to be constructions of institutionalized cultural environments, rather than being "hardwired" and pregiven outside the social system.

TWO BACKGROUND THEORETICAL ARGUMENTS: AN INTRODUCTION VIA THE SOCIOLOGY OF EDUCATION

Questioning the Role of the "Socialization" in Producing and Reproducing Social Order

The American sociology of education of the 1950s and 1960s—and American sociology generally—tended to assume a picture of society as made up of and produced by highly socialized individuals, the educational system then central in the reproduction of society in large part via its socializing activities. But empirical studies presented anomalies for this theoretical picture. Notably, many studies showed small "socializing" effects of American colleges on student attitudes, and only small differences in these effects across colleges, despite the big differences among colleges. Studies of medical schools found it difficult to isolate much "socialization," but did incidentally pick up dramatic shifts from medical students thinking of themselves as merely students to thinking of themselves as doctors.

In reflecting upon these results, and in conducting research on student college and occupational choices (e.g., Meyer 1970b), Meyer and colleagues developed the following interpretation (reflected in Meyer 1970b, 1972, 1977; Kamens 1977). Seen as institutions, what schools do primarily is produce graduates and bestow the identity "graduate." If the social status and role of graduates in society is largely the same—as is the case in egalitarian American society, but not in many more status-stratified European ones—then the schools will largely have similar effects on individuals, because individuals are enacting a largely singular identity. (In Germany, in contrast, there are more differentiated categories of "graduate," and hence different identities [and attitudes] for individuals to enact.[6]) Relatedly, medical schools confer the identity "doctor": medical students learn they are doctors and people in the social environment learn this too, and these are large effects. David Kamens added the fundamental observation that schools develop formal structures that dramatize their advertised effects on students (Kamens 1977). For example, colleges emphasize their selectivity, or their "residential education," or their putatively rigorous requirements. In so doing schools "create and validate myths" concerning both the college experience and "the intrinsic qualities that their graduates possess" (Kamens 1977:208).

Two basic theoretical points are reflected here. First, the truly fundamental "socialization" is the construction and certification (the "chartering") of identities (Meyer 1970a), and this particular socialization can occur without any especially deep or common inculcation of values or attitudes (or knowledge, for that matter). Second, the "socialization" is as much of *others* in the social environment as of those directly involved in an institution: for instance, the medical profession teaches others about the identity "doctor" as well as medical students; colleges teach others about their graduates. In a word, the socialization is "diffuse" as well as direct (Meyer 1970a).

In making these arguments, this institutionalism was one of a number of lines of thought emerging in opposition to Talcott Parsons's and Robert Merton's emphasis on the internalization of "norms" as the foundation of social order. Instead, the "phenomenological" counterargument (shared by and developed within this institutionalism) was more cognitive and collective in character, in two respects. First, the fundamental "socialization" according to phenomenological sociology is the learning of broad collective representations of society—pictures of what society is and how it works—and the acceptance of these pictures as social facts. Peter Berger and Thomas Luckmann referred to learning "recipe knowledge" about the social system, and about being inculcated into a "symbolic universe" (1967); Meyer referred to learning about "symbols" (like the general symbol "school"), or to learning basic "myths" (i.e., broad cultural accounts) of society (Meyer 1970c, 1977). People learn highly abstract and symbolic accounts of society more than detailed empirical information; hence this learning coincides with people's well-known low levels of actual information about their social environment, even about matters of substantial import to them (such as schooling or job markets or marriage networks).

Second, the causality of social rules and "myths," argued Meyer, inheres "not in the fact that individuals believe them, but in the fact that they 'know' everyone else does" (Meyer 1977:75). That is, the truly fundamental beliefs for reproducing a social order are people's beliefs about *others'* behavior and beliefs; the basic "myths" of society operate primarily by establishing beliefs about what others think and expectations about how others will behave. Further, in this phenomenological line of argument, social order depends more upon the degree to which the basic myths of the system are taken for granted—accepted as realities, grounded in common expectations—than upon personal belief in them (Meyer 1977:65, 1970b).[7] In clarifying this point (and a number of related ones), Morris Zelditch distinguished between the *validation* of myths versus the *endorsement* of them (Zelditch 1984; Zelditch and Walker 1984): social order, contra Parsons and Merton, depends more on the degree of validation of collective reality—the pragmatic acceptance of rules and accounts as in place and binding—than upon the endorsement of it. This point has remained fundamental to institutionalism as it has developed.

Elaborating the Nature and Effects of Institutionalization

In the 1970s, scholars in the sociology of education were considering how education worked to "reproduce" societies over time. Addressing this issue, Meyer developed the argument that the educational system embodies a "theory of knowledge and personnel" of society, as well as socializing individuals and channeling them to social positions. That is, it is a primary institutional location for consolidating the knowledge system of society, and for defining and legitimating the specific identities of both elites and democratic citizens (Meyer 1972, 1977). Changes in educational curricula end up "restructur[ing] whole populations" by creating new categories of authoritative knowledge and then entirely new roles (new professions, new elites, new ideas about citizenship) (Meyer 1977:55). "Not only new types of persons but also new competencies are authoritatively created" by education as an evolving institution (ibid.:56). For example, the field of demography was codified within the education system, subsequently chartering and producing demographers, and eventually enabling and encouraging population control policies (Barrett 1995; Barrett and Frank 1999). In a formula, "institutionalized demography creates demographers, and makes demographic control reasonable," that is, legitimate and conventional.[8]

Note that the causal connections posited in this example are *collective-level* and *cultural* in nature—they feature processes occurring within and between institutions (within the educational system, broadly considered, and between the educational system, professions, and the state). These processes are of course produced via the behavior of people, *but* (in this example) the people implicated are various educators and scholars and state elites, hence occupants of highly institutionally constructed roles, operating more in their cultural and professional capacities—that is, as *agents* of the cultural system—than as generic individual "actors" bearing only simple or private interests. Also, the causal linkages involved in these collective processes are far removed from the aggregation of simple social behavior, or from individual socialization and its aggregate effects, or even from the social network processes presented in educational stratification arguments. Attention to collective-level and cultural processes is the main distinguishing feature of this institutionalism, as we'll see.

ORGANIZATIONS IN INSTITUTIONAL ENVIRONMENTS[9]

Background: Questioning the Integration and Boundedness of Organizations

The institutionalist contribution to organizational analysis followed directly from the 1970s research on school organizations,[10] as well as from research on evaluation processes in organizations by W. R. Scott and Sanford Dornbusch (Dornbusch and Scott 1975), and from Scott's research on health care organizations. Meyer and Brian Rowan (1977) argued that schools survive in the first instance not because of tight organizational controls—or because of any particular effectiveness in schooling—but because of conformity with highly institutionalized categories and myths in the broader society (the basic idea of what a school is, or what mathematics is, or what "second grade" is). The emergent institutionalist idea was that these features might be general characteristics of organizations, at least far more so than generally acknowledged. Sociological neoinstitutionalism was "but one of several theories that developed in reaction to prevailing conceptions of organizations as bounded, relatively autonomous, rational actors" (Scott and Meyer 1994:1). As in other application areas, the institutionalist effort was to question the assumed naturalness of organizations, seeing them instead as "(a) connected to and (b) constructed by wide social environments" (Meyer and Scott 1992:1), as opposed to being prior realities external to the cultural system (Meyer, Boli, and Thomas 1987:22).

Three Core Ideas about Formal Organizing

In developing this line of argument, a starting idea was that the *building blocks* for formal organization were institutionally constructed and were "littered around the societal landscape" (Meyer and Rowan 1977:345). More specifically, the ongoing "rationalization"[11] of social life creates new organizational elements, and new social nodes around which formal organizations can form. Meyer and Rowan gave the following examples: the development of psychology certifies new professionals and creates new specialized agencies and departments; the expansion of professional research stimulates R&D units within organizations; the movement of sexuality into the public sphere new therapies and their associated organizations (ibid.:344). This rationalization has been a continuing process: "A wider range of purposes and activities becomes legitimate grounds for organizing: child care; leisure activities and recreation; even finding a compatible marriage partner" (Scott and Meyer 1994:114).[12]

A second core idea, also in Meyer and Rowan (1977), was that "the formal structures of many organizations in postindustrial society . . . dramatically reflect the myths of their institutional environments instead of the demands of their work activities" (341). By "formal structure" the authors referred to a "blueprint for activities," including the table of organization and an organization's explicit goals and policies (342). Formal structure is in many respects "ceremonial" in function: it often demonstrates adherence with currently predominant myths (i.e., cultural models)—including, in postindustrial environments, myths of rationality. Such adherence "signals rationality" to internal and external groups, and hence can enhance internal and external legitimacy, access to resources, and ultimately organizational survival (352–353, 355; also Scott and Meyer 1994:115).

Third, Meyer and Rowan (and then Meyer and Scott) stressed one particular structural consequence of the linkage of organizational elements to broad institutional structures. This linkage produces organizational forms that are often "sprawling"—loosely integrated and variously "decoupled." Formal structure and rules are often decoupled from actual activities; programs are often decoupled from organizational outcomes; internal organizational sectors are often decoupled from one another; and organizational decision-making activity is often decoupled from actual organizational action (e.g., Meyer 1983/1992:239; Brunsson 1989). The decoupling of formal and informal activity was long observed in the organizational literature; this institutionalism now offered a more general explanation of it and made the observation central. "Stable organizing requires and results from external legitimation and may be quite consistent with a good deal of internal looseness" (Scott and Meyer 1994:2).

Different Types of Organizations

In contextualizing their arguments, Meyer and Rowan provided two reasons to think that institutional effects on organizations should be ubiquitous. First, they argued that the "rise of collectively organized society" had "eroded many market contexts," thus expanding the range of organizations subject directly to institutional forces (1977:354). Second, they added that even "[o]rganizations producing in markets that place great emphasis on efficiency build in units whose relation to production is obscure and whose efficiency is determined, not by true production functions, but by ceremonial definition" (ibid.:353).

Later, Scott (1987:126) and Scott and Meyer (1991:122–124) began to distinguish different sorts of institutional effects on organizations. In order to do so, they distinguished stronger and weaker "technical environments" from stronger and weaker "institutional environments": some organizations are subject to strong versions of both (utilities, banks), some weak versions of both (restaurants, health clubs), and some exist in one of two mixed patterns (e.g., general manufacturing organizations exist in a weaker institutional but stronger technical environment, while schools and mental health clinics exist in a weaker technical but stronger institutional environment). With this classification of environments at hand, Scott and Meyer, and independently Lynne Zucker, presented arguments about the conjoint effects of the varying environments on different sorts of organizations, concentrating upon variations in organizational structures and on patterns of success and failure (Scott and Meyer 1991; Zucker 1983; Zucker 1987).

An Elaboration: The Institutional Construction of the "Ground Rules of Economic Life"

These institutionalists insisted that even markets themselves are highly "institutionally constructed": thinking for example of all the legal, political, and social definitions involved in the coevolution of American society and the automobile market. This emphasis is not distinctive to this institutionalism but rather follows a general institutionalism going back to Max Weber. Recently this particular literature has begun to elaborate the idea of the institutional construction of "organizational fields," strategies, and doctrines (reviewed by Dobbin 1994a). First, scholars have pursued the "interdependence of state regulatory policies, organizational fields, and management strategies" (Scott 1995:99). In a formidable piece of research, Neil Fligstein studied the evolution of the largest American firms from the 1800s to the present (Fligstein 1990). Among other things, he found (in Frank Dobbin's admirable epitomization) that "the Sherman Antitrust Act of 1890 made mergers the favored business strategy at the dawn of the 20th century *and* popularized a new theory of the firm that reinforced horizontal integration. Then after World War II, the Celler-Kefauver Act, amending Sherman, made diversification the favored American business strategy *and* helped to popularize finance management and portfolio theory" (Dobbin 1995:280, emphasis added).

Dobbin has stressed the theoretical implication of this line of work: the economic environment, far from being generic or natural, is partly constituted and re-constituted by public policies and ideologies (Dobbin 1994b, 1995). Public policies alter "the ground rules of economic life" (ibid.). New business strategies emerge under each policy regime, and eventually new theories emerge justifying the efficiency of the new strategies. Drawing upon his own historical and comparative research (Dobbin 1994b), Dobbin asks: "How did Americans arrive at the conclusion that rivalistic state mercantilism was the most effective means to growth? How did they come to believe that approach was wrong, and support cartels? How did they decide to crush cartels and enforce price competition?" (Dobbin 1995:282) Dobbin's answer (in brief) is that Americans altered earlier policies when the policies came into perceived conflict with institutionalized precepts of American democracy—especially the opposition to concentrated power. So, when new forms of concentrated power were perceived, reform efforts ensued and the rules of the game were eventually changed. After some further lag, economic doctrines adjusted to find the changed rules to be efficient (Dobbin 1995:301; 1994b). The institutionalist point: even the principles of rational organizing are themselves socially constructed and reconstructed.

Effects of Variation in Institutional Environments (1): Cross-National Variation

If formal organizing is interpenetrated with institutional environments, it follows that different institutional environments will construct different sorts of formal organizations. Most of the initial institutionalist research was U.S.–centric, the primary exception being study of cross-national variation in educational organizations. In 1983 Meyer offered an explicit comparative framework, contrasting "statist," "corporatist," and "individualist" variants of modern institutional environments (and associating the historical trajectories of France, Germany, and the United States with these variants [Meyer 1983b]). He then linked this institutional variation to variation in the amounts, types, and structure of formal organizing, in a set of propositions. For example, Meyer argued that statist environments (such as France) are likely to suppress formal organizing relative to other environments, and to construct organizational structures that are simpler, more highly formalized, and sharply bounded (Meyer 1983b:276–277). Individualist environments (notably the United States) are likely to produce more formal organizing, with the organizations showing more formal structure, weaker boundaries, more functions, and (accordingly) less formal rationality than organizations elsewhere (ibid.:275–276). Elaborating this analysis, Jepperson and Meyer (1991) drew upon the existing empirical literature on cross-national variation in organizations, and pointed out that this variation does appear to cluster by polity types. In an extensive research program on organizational variations in East Asia, Gary Hamilton and colleagues developed broadly parallel arguments. They found that the institutionalization of different models of authority powerfully affected the kinds of economic organizations that emerged in different countries (e.g., Hamilton and Biggart 1988; Orrù, Biggart, and Hamilton 1991). Despite the obvious import of this area of work, research on cross-national organizational variation within this institutionalism, testing and developing such ideas, has only recently begun to expand.[13]

Effects of Institutional Variation (2): Variation over Time

If formal organizing is interpenetrated with institutional environments, it also follows that changes in institutional environments will lead to changes in formal organizing. Here more work has been done—again, with most reference to the United States—organized around three sets of observations.

First, Meyer, Scott, and colleagues have focused upon the recent (post-1950s) and rapid institutional centralization in the United States (a centralization that remains "fragmented" in character when compared to the more statist systems). A correlate is that organizations are increasingly embedded in systems having a vertical structure, "with decisions about funding and goals more highly centralized and more formally structured today than in the past" (Scott and Meyer 1983/1992:150). One consequence is a "*trend toward societal sectoralization*": the formation of "functionally differentiated sectors whose structures are vertically connected with lines stretching up to the central nation-state" (Scott and Meyer 1983/1992:150). Because of the continued fragmentation of this institutional environment (for instance, many governmental agencies at many levels, many professional authorities), administrative structures become more complex and elaborate (Scott and Meyer 1994:117 and section II). A consequence: many organizational systems are now "better viewed as loosely related collections of roles and units whose purposes and procedures come from a variety of external sources, not a unitary internal superior" (ibid.:117).

Second, the ongoing rationalization of social structure around formal organizations—creating "societies of organizations" everywhere (Perrow 1991; Coleman 1974)—has also lead to the *increasing standardization* of formal organizing. Organizations are now socially *depicted* as instances of formal organization rather than more specifically as schools or factories or hospitals (Meyer 1994b:44). "[O]ne can discuss proper organization without much mentioning the actual substantive activities the organization will do." Standardized management accompanies standardized organizations: "An older world in which schools were managed by educators, hospitals by doctors, railroads by railroad men now recedes into quaintness. All these things are now seen as organizations, and a worldwide discourse instructs on the conduct of organization" (ibid.).

Third, the increasingly *expanded individualism* of contemporary societies "creates organizational work" (Scott and Meyer 1994:211 and section III). Organizations must deal with people carrying far more complex "educational, occupational, and psychological properties" (Scott and Meyer 1994:209). Existing organizations expand their structures to accommodate them: including, developing structures of "organizational citizenship," such as due process and grievance mechanisms and affirmative action (and programs of employee "development") (Dobbin et al. 1988). New categories of organizations arise to "create and modify individuals": new schooling, therapeutic, counseling, physical health, religious, and cultural organizations (Scott and Meyer 1994:211). Further, expanded individualism contributes to the *de-bureaucratization* of organizations: true bureaucracies and many tight systems of technical control (e.g., Taylorist ones) decline—so that over time, fewer people actually give and receive orders (ibid.:212).

Linkages between Institutional Environments and Organizations

Meyer and Rowan (1977), Meyer, Scott, and Deal (1981), and Scott and Meyer (1983/1992) discussed a wide range of processes linking institutional environments and organizations, although these were not especially highlighted or typologized. In 1983 Paul DiMaggio and Walter Powell presented such a typology in an influential analysis that helped to secure the standing of institutionalism as a main approach to organizational analysis (DiMaggio and Powell 1983).[14] Reviewing the literature, they asserted that "organizational isomorphism"—similarities of form and structure—can occur due to coercive processes (rooted in political control and in legitimacy-seeking), mimetic processes (rooted in the development of standard responses to uncertainty), and normative processes (rooted especially in professionalization). They then developed a number of propositions about organizational isomorphism and change, referring to these processes, and in addition discussed how these processes related to ones highlighted by other schools of organizational analysis. The typology has subsequently been generalized in a fundamental way by Scott (1995), in an analysis that has yet to take proper hold in the literature.[15]

David Strang and Meyer later added a general point specifically about the diffusion of organizational forms and practices: that the highly theorized nature of contemporary societies tends to heighten greatly the diffusion of organizational forms and practices (Strang and Meyer 1993). Strang gives the example of the prominent, rapid, and highly theorized diffusion of (perceived) Japanese organizational practices in the U.S. context (Strang 1994). Meyer and Scott discuss the earlier diffusion and conventionalization of modern personnel administration (Meyer and Scott 1992:1–2) in this connection.[16] In highly institutionalized (and theorized) environments, policies and programs tend to evolve and change in a highly "contextual" way. That is, reform ideas emerge and evolve within a dense (national, increasingly world) policy culture; local organizations sample from this culture in an often haphazard and decoupled fashion.[17]

NATION-STATES IN A WORLD POLITY AND CULTURE[18]

Background: Questioning "Modernization"—and the Hard Reality of States

Some of the same issues were eventually raised about states in the world system. In this research area, Meyer and Michael Hannan and their collaborators[19] in the 1970s were curious about the claims of a then highly conventionalized theory of societal "modernization." The research group was aware of a seemingly extreme gap between the strong claims of this literature, and a lack of serious evidence—in two senses. First, in scholarship, the empirical literature was very primitive, consisting largely of a cross-sectional (i.e., not longitudinal) correlational literature, plus scattered case studies. Second, in the world, scholars and advisors and elites from core-countries were encouraging more peripheral states to do things like expand education systems to mimic American or European ones—without basing such recommendations upon any plausible evidence. Hence both the research and the reality seemed highly ideological.

Thus motivated, the research group assembled available quantitative data on country characteristics in a "panel" format (that is, for many countries at regularly spaced time points)—such data had not been much assembled and analyzed, to the group's surprise—as well as coding additional cross-national material to create new measures.[20] As ideas and research designs consolidated, the group began to focus upon direct institution-to-institution connections within the world system—that is, the specific interrelations of political, educational, and economic structures and outcomes (ibid.:5–6).[21]

The initial wave of research produced numerous findings (the studies were collected in Meyer and Hannan 1979c), but the overall patterns of particular interest for institutionalism were the following. First, the research documented an "explosive expansion of national systems of education"; the sources of this expansion appeared "to lie outside the properties of particular countries and to reflect exigencies of global social organization whose logics and purposes are built into almost all states" (ibid.:13–14). Second, in parallel fashion "[s]tates tend to expand their power and authority within society in all types of countries through the modern period" (ibid.:14). Third, in general, "[t]he world as a whole [during 1950–70] shows increasing structural *similarities of form* among societies without, however, showing increasing *equalities of outcome* among societies" (ibid.:15). The authors noted that this pattern may be "quite specific to a period of great economic expansion and extension of markets" and that "[a] period of sustained world-wide economic contraction or a long-term stabilization, might alter the picture considerably" (ibid.:15).

To take a specific example, the studies of educational systems and curricula showed that both were changing substantially over time, but in a very similar way across countries: there was truly remarkable "isomorphism" (Meyer, Ramirez, and Boli-Bennett 1977; Ramirez and Rubinson 1979; Meyer and Ramirez 1981). This pattern presented a major anomaly (if initially a little-noticed one) for the sociology of education, which was functionalist[22] in its basic theoretical imagery. In a functionalist scheme, educational structures should have clear political or economic functions; hence, the large national economic and political variations of societies should be accompanied by big educational variations (since the educational and politico-economic variations should be adaptations to and facilitators of one another). Empirically, however, this co-variation was not present: educational systems were more and more alike.

The interpretation that emerged, only fully consolidated after an extended period of work, was the following. It appeared that education was being constructed more for an imagined society than for real societies (at least in the post–WWII period of educational expansion). This argument reflects the general institutionalist idea that people in modern societies are constantly developing, redeveloping, and enacting *models* of society: modern social worlds are highly theorized, hence "imagined."[23] Further—a crucial point—while actual societies are very different, it appears that *imagined* societies are pretty much alike (at least for those countries with some connection to world institutions). So, the education seen as appropriate for world-imagined society is quite standardized: models of both imagined society and education appear to change over time at a (nearly) world level.[24] In fact, educational curricula are now explicitly organized around ideas of a global society and culture, and ideas of a globally standard individual (Meyer, Kamens, and Benavot 1992; McEneaney and Meyer 2000; Meyer and Ramirez 2000; Meyer 2000a).

A "World Polity" and World Culture as Well as a World Economy

During the same period, other scholars had also broached ideas of a broad "world system." Immanuel Wallerstein had initiated his pioneering historical studies of a world economy and stratification system (Wallerstein 1974), Charles Tilly and colleagues had initiated long-term studies of the development of European states (Tilly 1975), and a separate literature on economic "dependency" had posited effects of world network positioning on developmental paths. The distinctive institutionalist intervention, worked out in conjunction with the above-sketched research, was the argument that the world system was not limited to a world economy or geomilitary system. The world system also comprised a world "polity" and world culture—institutional features originating in Christendom. Further, Meyer and collaborators called particular attention to the specific configuration of the "modern world system": a "relatively unified cultural system and a densely linked economy. . . without a centralized political system" (Meyer and Hannan 1979a:298; also Meyer, Boli, and Thomas 1981). This configuration was highlighted as a cause of many of features of modern social and political development, as we will see.

By 1980, pressing his theoretical line, Meyer wished to qualify and contextualize Wallerstein's account of the Western state system, primarily by reminding that the "Western state also developed in part as a project under the aegis of the now invisible universal Western Church and was legitimated by broad cultural mechanisms" (Thomas and Meyer 1984:470). "All the European societies in the modern period were deeply embedded, not only in a world commodity economy and system of exchange, but also in a constructed world collectivity—a society and a stateless polity" (Meyer 1981:899). In a review of Wallerstein's second volume of *The Modern World System*, Meyer argued that a number of features of the modern world could not be well accounted for without invoking this "wider cultural polity." To give the flavor of the argument:

> The presence of this wider evolving culture provided a legitimating base for the unusual world Wallerstein writes about. It is a world in which long-distance exchange makes sense and can properly be incorporated and adapted to, in which such exchange can be extended to the furthest strange lands with which one has no direct political linkage, in which techniques are of general utility and can be copied, in which rationalized social structures and policies are not only competed with but quickly copied, in which the nominally ultimate state political authorities are legitimately seen as subordinate to wider purposes, in which these purposes are shared across units, and in which a shared orientation integrates disparate desiderata into a single value standard (monetarization) across units (international currency) (Meyer 1982:266).

The Embedding of Nation-States within a World Polity

The core ideas about a "wider cultural polity" were not deployed historically, however, but rather directed to the contemporary period. They were developed by Meyer in his paper on "the world polity and the authority of the nation-state" (Meyer 1980). Following the general institutionalist imagery, Meyer presented nation-states as "embedded in an exogenous, and more or less worldwide, rationalistic culture" (1999a:123), a culture "located in many world institutions (in "interstate relations, lending agencies, world cultural elite definitions and organizations, transnational bodies" [(Meyer 1980:117]). In particular, this culture was composed of "world definitions of the justifications, perspectives, purposes, and policies properly to be pursued by nation-state organizations" (ibid.:120).[25]

Without invoking this world polity, Meyer argued, it seemed impossible to account for a number of basic features of the system of nation-states. First, its very existence: there is far more similarity in political forms in the world than one would expect if one attends primarily to the great differences in economic development and internal cultures.[26] And there is far more stability in forms than one would anticipate: the nation-state form has been a sticky one (Strang 1990).

Second, state structures and policy domains have continued to expand rapidly over time, and notably in formally similar ways across countries. More and more countries have more of the same ministries and the same broad policy programs. This "isomorphic expansion" has occurred even in the peripheries—if in a pronounced "decoupled" way in these zones. (Peripheral countries often adopt currently common ministries and plans, without implementing actual policies.[27]) All this standardization appears to develop within and be propelled by trans-country discourses and organizations—for example, in what have now been labeled as "epistemic communities" (scientific and professional), "advocacy networks," and international governmental and nongovernmental organizations.

The Long-Term Buildup of a "World Society" Carrying "Models" of Political Form and Responsibility

In reflecting upon the initial wave of research collected in Meyer and Hannan (1979c), the authors noted a methodological limitation of their studies: that "[s]imple panel analyses of the relationships among features of national societies provide no information on larger system processes affecting *all* subunits. . . . This takes us in the direction, not of causal comparative analysis (for we really have but one case evolving over time), but toward historical description and time series analysis" in order to "attempt to describe features of the whole system" over a longer period of time (ibid.:12–13, 298). As research efforts continued, various scholars developed these research designs during the 1980s and 1990s.[28]

Some studies tracked the consolidation of the nation-state form itself: for instance, David Strang studied the decline in dependent and external territories in the world system, and showed that once units become sovereign states, they rarely exit that form (Strang 1990). Other scholars documented the consolidation of a basic formal model of a nation-state, seeing such a model reflected in formal applications for UN membership (McNeely 1995), in the development of standardized data systems across countries (ibid.), and in the development of more standard population censuses (Ventresca 1995). Increasing commonality in state activities and policies was clearly documented in various longitudinal research: commonality in (among other areas) science policies (Finnemore 1996a), welfare policies (Strang and Chang 1993), population control ideas (Barrett 1995), women's rights (Berkovitch 1999a, 1999b), environmental policy (Frank 1997; Meyer et al. 1997). Common changes in national membership and citizenship models was found as well: apparent in constitutional rights (Boli 1987a), and in the changing status accorded to women, ethnoracial minorities, sexual minorities, and labor migrants (e.g., Ramirez and Cha 1990; Bradley and Ramirez 1996; Frank and McEneaney 1999; Soysal 1994).

As this research consolidated, Meyer, John Boli, George Thomas, and Francisco Ramirez integrated the findings via a tightened theoretical argument, focusing upon the idea of a "world society," and specifically upon the idea that "[m]any features of the contemporary nation-state derive from *worldwide models* constructed and propagated through global cultural and associational processes" (Meyer et al. 1997:144–145, emphasis added). These processes have intensified in part due to the continuing "statelessness" of the world system, a background cause once again invoked (ibid.:145). This configuration continues to generate an extensive transnational elaboration of collective agendas—within international organizations, scientific communities, and professions—agendas worked out for nation-state actors. Scientific, professional, and other international nongovernmental organizations have been institutionalized worldwide (documented and studied in Boli and Thomas 1997, 1999b), as have global consulting industries of various sorts, promoting recipes for economic, political, organizational, and individual development (Meyer 2000b). In this connection, Strang and Meyer argued that the culture of this world system provides substantial impetus for extensive diffusion of ideas, given its underlying assumptions of the ultimate similarity of societies and of common human actorhood (Strang and Meyer 1993). Further, as nation-states try to act, while taking on increasingly elaborate forms and responsibilities, they come to depend more and more upon the increasingly elaborate consulting machineries, a dynamic that in turn generates more and more responsibilities (Meyer 2000b).[29]

In such a context, entire institutional complexes diffuse across the world system, leading to some striking departures from standard ideas about the adaptiveness of institutions. For instance: both the relative expansion of higher education within countries, and the relative development of scientific research organizations, show modest *negative* effects on countries' economic growth, at least in the short run (Meyer, Schofer, and Ramirez forthcoming). This pattern has largely been neglected by social scientists because it has not made much sense when seen from dominant standpoints (including in this case neoclassical economics). The institutionalist interpretation, pursued in current research, is that countries tend to construct broad-spectrum higher education and science institutions, not ones tightly linked to economic development (ibid.; also Schofer 1999). Accordingly, the presence of these institutions tends to be correlated with forms of world-cultural participation—for example, with the presence of human rights and environmental organizations—but negatively correlated with growth in the short term, probably due to the investment costs involved (Shenhav and Kamens 1991).

The theoretical idea is that conformity processes are also found at the level of entire institutional complexes within world society. Higher education and science appear to a kind of "turnkey" social technologies, imported into societies but in forms linked more to broad ideas about a progressive society rather than to narrower social objectives such as economic growth.

Transformative Processes

Some of the systemic processes at work may be transformative ones; institutionalists have called particular attention so far to three. First, it seems that the processes above are transforming the very nature of states. As "enactors of multiple dramas whose texts are written elsewhere," states increasingly are both expanded organizational forms, but also "sprawling, weakly integrated," fragmented ones (Meyer 1999a:136–139, 1994a:51–53). This line of argument provides one theoretically principled account for now-common impressions of state decomposition or "disarticulation" (e.g., Smelser with Badie and Birnbaum 1994).

Second, in 1980 Meyer had argued that with the post–WWII buildup of the state, individuals had become more embedded in states, losing standing as autonomous actors (1980:132). However, with the intervening buildup of world society, there may be a trend shift: Meyer and David Frank say that "the society to which the individual human belongs has also importantly globalized" (Frank and Meyer 2000). Earlier Yasemin Soysal had isolated the core issue: an emergent and partial move beyond the nation-state model, via a "reconfiguration of citizenship" from a model based upon nationhood to a more transnational one based upon personhood and human (rather than citizen) rights (Soysal 1994:137 and ch. 8). An emergent "post-national membership"—particularly apparent in Europe and surrounding issues of labor migration—"transgresses" the national order (ibid.:159). This disruption is apparent in the rise of multicultural politics, in the loosening of citizenship restrictions and obligations (e.g., voting, military), and in expansion of multiple citizenship arrangements.

Third—an even longer-term transformation—as basic cultural models change, the evolution has produced new logics for the actors of the system, including states, social movements, foundations, and consultants. For example, David Frank argues that a new cultural account of the humanity-nature relationship, picturing humans as embedded in the natural world via a long evolutionary chain, has generated the two dominant types of environmental movements: one that defines nature as part of society to be managed, and one that defines nature as sacred and requiring protection (Frank 1997; Frank et al. 1999). Deborah Barrett argues that the current "neo-Malthusian" orientation in population policy is rooted in the evolution of theories representing population growth as a constraint upon economic growth (and in the displacement of earlier theories associating population growth with state power) (Barrett 1995; Barrett and Frank 1999).

Multiple Modernities and Their Logics: Seeing the Modern Polities as Organizing around Distinct Variants of a Common Cultural Model

In another distinct line of argument, Meyer and others have depicted the different modern polities as distinct variants of a common Western cultural model. In this effort, initial direction was provided by Guy Swanson's conspectus of different types of polities within early modern Europe (1967, 1971). In this analysis, Swanson distinguished polities depending upon their primary locations of collective authority and agency: in a state apparatus; in remnants of a feudal community; and in individuals pictured as having direct ties to god (Thomas and Meyer 1984:471). Attempting to generalize such ideas, Meyer sketched a typology of modern polity types, distinguishing between statist, corporatist, and individualist orders (loosely capturing France, Germany, and the United States in their broad historical trajectories) (Meyer 1983b). This idea subsequently has received some elaboration and modification, and some empirical exploration (Jepperson and Meyer 1991; Jepperson 2000).[30]

It has been natural to argue that the different polity forms are responsible for a number of additional cross-national differences. For example, the arguments about the effects of varying polity-organization upon formal organizations, discussed above, have this character (i.e., Meyer 1983b; Jepperson and Meyer 1991). There have been other deployments of this sort. For instance, in a central book-length development using similar ideas, Yasemin Soysal showed that different types of European polities established different regimes for incorporating labor migrants into society (Soysal 1994). Similar arguments have been adduced for variations in constructions of family violence and child protection (e.g., that child or spouse abuse are less likely to emerge as public issues in more corporate polities [Meyer et al. 1988]), for cross-national variation in legal strategies (e.g., that statism and governmental centralization both appear to affect individual recourse to legal activity [Boyle 1998]), and for cross-national variation in voluntary associations (e.g., that different institutional orders construct different types of membership organizations and are more or less encouraging of individual participation in them [Schofer and Fourcade-Gourichas 1999]). Needless to say, these are just illustrative examples.[31]

In a powerful illustration and deepening of this line of argument, Frank Dobbin documented long-lasting historical effects of variations in basic political models (Dobbin 1994b, 1995). In his book on railroad development and industrial policy formation in the United States and Europe (especially France), Dobbin shows that very different interpretations were given to railroad development in (statist) France and the (liberal) United States, despite surprisingly similar actual public sector involvements. Similar state activities were "concealed" as state actions in the United States while "revealed" and accentuated in France. The different interpretations were generated from the different preexisting political cosmologies of France and the United States, and then the interpretations themselves were powerfully consequential (Dobbin shows) for the subsequent divergent development of industrial policies.[32]

INDIVIDUAL IDENTITY WITHIN INDIVIDUALISM[33]

Background Argument: The Political Reconstruction of Society around Individualism

Much of the development of national polities has been "channeled into an intensification of individualism, rather than taking other forms, so that it is easy to view the secularization and elaboration of individualism as a main theme in Western history" (Meyer 1986b:200). Institutionalism emphasizes that this individualism is an evolving public theory: a public political theory (citizenship), a public economic theory (markets), a public religious and cultural theory (the soul, the private self) (Meyer 1986b:200). As such, doctrines of individualism are central to the basic Western cultural models of society.

The research on the "world educational revolution" mentioned above was pursued in part in its connection with the production of modern individuals (including, citizen-members of nation-states) (Meyer, Ramirez, and Boli-Bennett 1977; Meyer, Ramirez, and Soysal 1992). John Boli's book on the emergence of mass schooling in Sweden is precisely about the institutionalization of schooling as the dominant approach to childrearing (and individual formation) (Boli 1989), as were Francisco Ramirez's and Boli's related surveys of comparative-historical material about the relations of states and schools (Ramirez and Boli 1987b) and of available comparative data on the development of schooling systems (Ramirez and Boli 1987c). Boli showed in detail that the "social imperative" of mass schooling developed before the urban and industrial takeoff of the 1860s and 1970s. Instead it was rooted in an earlier-developing Europe-wide social movement, in which European states, both competing with and imitating one another, attempted to construct nations of citizen-individuals (Boli 1989).[34]

Individualism as a Collective-Level Construction and Individual-Level Enactment

Standard ideas about the development of individualism have pictured it as an outcome of social-psychological, especially experiential, processes. For example, scholars have often depicted individualism as an outcome of people's reactions to their experience of markets or cities or industrial work. The causal imagery, often implicit, is one of people experiencing a market system individually, reacting to it largely individually (or maybe with others in households or local communities), and then through their aggregate reactions eventually producing a large-scale cultural commonality—individualism.

This picture has been almost axiomatic for many scholars. For example, in their survey-based study of the development of "individual modernity" in developing countries, Alex Inkeles and David Smith argued that "exposure to modern institutions produces modern persons," focusing in particular upon exposure to modern factories (Inkeles and Smith 1974:307). Presumably if enough people are exposed long enough, an individualist ("modernized") context is produced: that is, via an individual-level experiential process, and via aggregation of the common individual effects. Many other studies shared this imagery. However, the evidence produced by these same studies did not well support such interpretations. For instance, in the Inkeles and Smith data the best predictors of an individual's relative "modernity"[35] were his education level, then nationality, then mass media exposure—all reflecting highly ideological forces. To Inkeles and Smith's apparent surprise, other variables, including those better capturing people's social experience—for example, years of factory work, occupation, urban vs. rural origins, family background—were far less salient.

In response to such empirical patterns, Meyer offered a reinterpretation of individualism, featuring (once again) collective-level processes (Meyer 1986a, 1986b, 1990). In this alternative imagery, individualism is "*not* centrally the product of human persons organizing their experience for themselves," but rather in the first instance a doctrine worked out by "various bodies of professional officials—religious ideologues, their secular counterparts (for example, psychologists, teachers, lawyers, and administrators)—and by other institutions of the modern state" (Meyer 1986a:212, emphasis added). People are then aggressively tutored in such doctrine (in families, schools, the polity) and come to enact it as part of their basic identity. In this account, a different set of causal processes is featured: collective-level scripting together with individual enactment. From this account it would follow that the relative "modernity" of people (for instance) would vary depending more upon a person's relative immersion in the ideologies of individualism—in the education system, for instance—than upon their actual social experience. And this is what empirical research tends to show (Meyer 1990; Jepperson 1992).

In such arguments, Meyer and other institutionalists were not so much reacting to specific research programs but more to a general analytical imagery: the almost automatic rendering of societal outcomes in individual-level terms. For instance, James Coleman seemed to insist that the effect of Protestantism upon European society must be theorized as an aggregation of the changed behaviors of individuals resocialized by Protestant churches and sects (Coleman 1986).[36] Sociological institutionalists depart from both the methodological individualism and from the specific substantive sociological claim. Instead, they would argue that Protestantism in the first instance modified collectively dominant models of society.[37] In so doing it also reworked the identity and status of the individual in these models, giving the individual dramatically enhanced metaphysical and public centrality. Over time individuals began to enact this new expanded identity, tutored by church, legal, and pedagogic scripts. This enactment can proceed concurrently with more experiential effects such as Max Weber's postulated "salvation anxiety," but may in fact be the more fundamental process involved in large-scale transformation. This argument is representative of the institutionalist challenge to individual-level processes and actor-centric explanation.

Construction of the Self Relative to an Institutionalized "Life Course"

In the same papers, Meyer argued that basic features of the self are as much affected by highly institutionalized scripts for assembling an individual identity than by any untutored, unscripted, "experiences" (Meyer 1986b:199). People "work out selves with a great deal of institutional support" (ibid.). In particular, a distinctive personal identity is worked out relative to a highly standardized and institutionalized "life course": "carefully sequenced age-grade systems of childrearing, education, work, and retirement" (ibid.:200). Much of a life is highly institutionally assembled and organized: for example, most middle-class people in the United States (for example) "know" that they will go to school, have a family and career and leisure, retire, and so on (ibid:207).

Because of this extensive structuring, Meyer hypothesizes, measures that tap people's subjective experience of the institutionalized life course—for instance, their consciousness of their education and occupation—will understandably show high prominence and high continuity over time. Other features of consciousness or personality closely linked to major life course statuses should also appear central and stable: for instance, cognitive competencies, values and tastes, knowledge, and perceived efficaciousness—qualities all linked to formal education. As a corollary, however, those aspects of subjectivity *less* directly tied to core life course statuses might be expected to show less stability over time: for instance, measurements of individuals' needs for achievement or power or intimacy, or measures of self-esteem or self-control. Stability in these features of the subjective self may be suppressed, precisely because modern society "strips definite and fixed role-related content from the self, leaving it free to find motives, needs, expectations, and perceptions appropriate to the situation" (ibid.:209).

In such a context, Meyer adds, researchers can easily form impressions of a general "instability" of the self, but this is misleading. This impression is partly due to scholarly definition: that is, their conceptualization of the self as precisely those features of personal identity *not* institutionally and structurally stabilized (Meyer 1986b:208). "The whole mass of material connected to the rules of the life course tends to be excluded" from research definitions of the self, and, in fact, people generally "may use the term 'self' to capture only the transitory aspects of their identity" (ibid.). The point: isolating cultural parameters of the self can help to account for otherwise anomalous features.

The Different Individualisms and Hence Different Individual Identities of the Modern Polities

The previous arguments were general arguments about individualism, and about individual identity within individualism. But this institutionalism also encourages one to look for variation: specifically variation in the kinds of individualism constructed in the different Western polities.

In initial formulations Meyer had distanced himself from "national character" (and related) ideas about cross-national variations in individual identity. For instance, reflecting upon the findings of *The Civic Culture*, Gabriel Almond and Sidney Verba's famous comparative study (1963), Meyer addressed the finding that people in Germany (in the late 1950s) tended to report a lower sense of political efficacy than individuals elsewhere. Meyer argued that this outcome as likely reflects features of the German political system than any uniquely German "characterological" deficiencies in ego-strength or self-esteem—that is, it is more likely that the German respondents were simply reporting the rather inefficacious status accorded to them, in the rather elitist and statist German democracy of the time (Meyer 1970c). The underlying idea, articulated later, is that modern nation-states are all "variously committed to individualism," but institutionalize different forms of it—forms that people learn to enact in their behavior and report in their talk (Frank, Meyer, and Miyahara 1995:362; Jepperson 1992). The United States represents a historically extreme form of individualism, given that it was originally constituted in an individualist and associational way (and fundamentally Protestant way) (Meyer 1983b, 1986a:214–215). In connection with this historical atypicality, in comparative studies Americans tend to get *high* scores in measures of self-direction and felt efficacy. In Meyer's argument, Americans respond this way more "because they think they are Americans, rather than because of any extraordinary individuation in their experience"—that is, because they are enacting the basic model of the American polity, a model that stresses individual agency and responsibility (Meyer 1990:54). The various European individualisms in contrast have all tended to embed the individual in more communal social structure of one sort or another (family, locality, other communities, the state). Accordingly, Meyer argues, one would expect Europeans relative to Americans to report less sense of autonomy and less felt social efficacy–which they in fact do in survey responses and interviews (Meyer 1986b:214; Jepperson 1992).

These institutionalist ideas have as yet only partly been pursued in research. Jepperson (1992) pursued and elaborated them some in a dissertation synthesizing available cross-national survey material, showing their utility in comprehending cross-national variation in individual attitudes and identities. Relatedly, David Frank, Meyer, and David Miyahara studied national variation in the size of the psychology profession worldwide, finding that the size of the profession (incorporating various controls) tended to covary roughly with the individualism of the polity (for example, Protestant countries were high) (Frank et al. 1995). This result accords with the idea that the greater the individualism of the polity, the greater the prominence of professionalized psychology—due to the greater public salience of issues of individual psychological identity in the more individualistic cultural settings.

General Changes in Individual Identity as Individualism Has Evolved

Meyer and others deployed the same basic ideas historically, to grasp some general West-wide changes in individual identity over time. "Individualism, like other central elements of Western doctrine, is continually being 'reconstructed'" (Meyer 1986a:212). Here less work has been done, but three ideas seem especially central.

First, the scope of individualism has continued to expand, both within and across societies—just as early Christian conceptualizations greatly expanded the number of morally relevant "souls" in the world. To reference just one line of research, Francisco Ramirez and colleagues have been innovative and persistent in tracking empirically the worldwide cultural reconstruction of women into citizen-individuals, focusing especially upon the movement of women into higher education—a movement long-in-coming but then rapid and nearly worldwide once initiated, even in countries (like some Islamic ones) that otherwise maintain high levels of gender segregation (Ramirez and Weiss 1979; Ramirez and Cha 1990; Bradley and Ramirez 1996).[38] Even more broadly, and obviously, ideas of basic "human rights" extend individuality (and a kind of world citizenship) to all humans (Boli and Thomas 1999a).[39]

A second general change: as more previously private issues and domains have become public over time, producing an expanded public domain across the modern nation-states, the private sphere has been correspondingly reconstructed. For instance, as sexuality has moved more into the public culture (and hence out of a more purely private realm), the private self is reconstituted. Over time, this private self is less sexed: more a "sexless figure for whom sexuality is a technique of proper linkage to the world, not an intrinsic element" (Meyer 1986a:224). In related research, David Frank and Elizabeth McEneaney studied changes in the legal regulation of sexuality. As individuals have replaced families as the basis of societies, sexuality has moved out of family control into a public sphere in which sexuality becomes a matter of public rights, and hence eventually less subject to legal control (Frank and McEneaney 1999).

Third, the long-term and ongoing deconstruction of previous corporate and collective identities (hypernationalisms, castelike identities, family-based identities, collective religious identities), together with the concurrent buildup of equal personhood as a central public identity, are root causes of the "contemporary identity explosion" (Frank and Meyer 2000). The former process creates new available sources of personal identity (for instance, the taming of ethnicity in the United States creates newly available "symbolic ethnicity" for individuals). The second element creates a newly dominant node of identity to which all kinds of qualities and tastes can be attached. These ideas are being pursued in current institutionalist writing and research.[40]

SOCIOLOGICAL NEOINSTITUTIONALISM AS A THEORETICAL RESEARCH PROGRAM

Contributions of the Program

The contributions of sociological neoinstitutionalism have been of three main sorts. First and foremost, like any truly basic analytical imagery, this institutionalism makes *new observations* possible—just as actor-centric imagery (its "rational choice" form) illuminated "collective action" (Olson 1965) and principal/agent relationships (Kiser 1999). Institutionalism too directs attention to different features of the social world, fundamental features that were otherwise unnoticed or disregarded. For instance, because of their focus upon possible effects of a broader world frame, institutionalists brought out the homogeneity in structure among nation-states. This homogeneity is striking, and remarkable given the great differences in country resources and cultures, but before institutionalism it had not been much problematized. In organizational analysis, institutionalists brought out the extraordinary world-spanning rationalization and standardization of organizational forms, as well as the transformation of organizational forms to accommodate the "expanded individuals" of contemporary society. Regarding individualism, institutionalists brought out (for example) the variation in professional psychology across countries, in its connection to differently constructed individualisms. In each of the application areas discussed above, the truly fundamental contribution of institutionalism has been to call attention to features of the social world that were largely *unobserved* before, let alone theorized.

Second, institutionalism also has offered *new explanations*—either about its new observations, or about established observations. For instance, sociology had long observed the ubiquitous decoupling of formal structures from informal arrangements and practical activity. The institutionalist literature gave this decoupling centrality and offered a more general explanation of it, linking it to conformity with institutionalized environments. Sociology had also obviously long observed the increasing individualism of modern society. Institutionalism offered new explanations, including the very basic argument that individualism was unlikely just an outcome of people's aggregated social experiences, but rather a collective doctrinal construction and individual enactment. Such ideas had certainly been voiced before—a root source is Emile Durkheim's discussion of the modern "cult of the individual" (Collins 1992:ch. 2)—but the institutionalist interventions have isolated the core analytical issues much more clearly.

Third, the concentration upon institutionalized cultural models enables this institutionalism to produce *reflexive contributions*, by endogenizing features of social science in its explanations. For instance, institutionalism offers not only a distinctive set of observations and explanations about modern educational systems. It also offers a theory of the sociology of education itself: namely, how this field has largely accepted the cultural myths of education, its research agenda then historically rather narrowly organized around the ways in which educational realities fail to live up to these myths. Or how the literature on social stratification has similarly been organized around broader cultural myths of individualism and egalitarianism (focusing resolutely on specific forms of individual inequality and missing more organizational forms of it as well as overly backgrounding the extraordinary egalitarian dynamic of the contemporary period) (Meyer 1994a). Or how the literature on "international relations" has sustained its arch realism about states only by constantly redefining its turf so as to maintain a narrow focus on continuing forms of interstate conflict and disorder in the system, editing out a broader world polity and culture (Jepperson, Wendt, and Katzenstein 1996).

In principle, the contributions of sociological neoinstitutionalism should be complementary with insights generated by other basic analytical imageries. However, the whole issue of complementarity is rarely taken up, given sociology's sectlike segmentation and propensity to reify theories.[41]

The Main Source of the Program's Contributions

Actor-centric imagery, as in James Coleman's most basic explication (Coleman 1986), "backgrounds" context and the historical construction of actors in a context, and foregrounds (1) largely taken-for-granted actors in their interest-driven choices and strategic interactions; and (2) the aggregations of these choices, or the outcomes of their strategic interaction games. The various utilitarian, exchange, and (many) network sociologies all build upon this basic imagery, if in differing ways.

In contrast, if one foregrounds cultural institutionalization, the picture of modern actors—organizations, states, individuals—as tightly integrated, highly bounded, autonomously acting entities, hardwired outside of society, is problematized. In fact, as empirically observed, these entities appear to be open, interpenetrated with institutional environments, and hence loosely coupled and varying in particular construction. Because of these qualities, actors from this institutionalism's standpoint are seen as rather derivative, for analytical purposes. For instance, if actors are highly open, rather than tightly bounded, they are then subject to many context effects: ranging from the initial contextual construction of modal actor identities, to the collective scripting of activity for identities, to actors' ongoing dependence upon consultation with "others" for managing identities and making (already highly scripted) choices. These context effects accordingly occupy institutionalist attention.

The task of causal analysis for this institutionalism is then different. It becomes the study of the construction and institutionalization of the cultural model that both defines identities *and* scripts the main lines of activity for identities. Thus, the modeling and enactment processes that transmit and reproduce these scripts are focalized, and the choice processes that occur within highly institutionalized frames and identities become of secondary interest. For example, the institutionalist interest is more in why and where markets are created, rather than market behavior, and why (and where) elections exist, rather than why people vote the way they do.[42] Similarly, the institutionalist interest is more in the nonchoice (the taken-for-granted routine) of going to college for most middle-class American high school students, and less in the choice of which college to attend. There is fundamental interest in how contemporary individuals believe (and often pretend) they are making unscripted and autonomous choices—and in how researchers go along with the pretense—when more usually people are enacting models and scripts of broad collective construction and reach.

One upshot of institutionalist research is that modern actors only exist with a lot of institutional scaffolding and support; but then with this support they are not really actors in the senses often imagined. The "middle-class students" just mentioned (or their parents) can talk with much more elaboration and clarity than their forebears (or than, say, peasants). But much of their talk (as well as their menus of choice) are highly scripted and institutionally organized. They are thus more actorlike in some respects, but arguably less actors (than their forebears, or peasants) in other respects. In any case they are not plausibly the exaggerated actors marching around the metatheory of actor-centric social science. The bite of this institutionalism is its exposure of the hypocrisies of modern actorhood—and its related insistence that one needs to do anthropology about modern "actors" as much as about peasants (Meyer and Jepperson 2000).

While defocalizing actors in order to problematize them, *people* and *activity* are nevertheless thoroughly invoked in institutionalist arguments. But the people who are invoked are not usually actors, and the activity invoked is not usually action—at least in the sense of generic humans engaging in highly informed, reflective, deliberative, and autonomous choice-making in pursuit of relatively private interests.[43] Instead the people invoked in this institutionalism are usually ones operating as *agents* of the collectivity (like professionals or state elites or advocates), formulating or carrying broad collective projects. Or, they are "*others*," in G. H. Mead's sense—that is, social responders and consultants, asserting the basic expectations and standard practices of society (Meyer 1994b, 1996). Collective agency and othering provide the primary microfoundations for this institutionalism.

Evolution and "Growth" of the Program

Pattern of Growth

Seen in ecological terms, the program gives the impression of pursuing a highly stable specialist strategy—in this respect like other basic imageries such as rational choice or population ecology (although unlike rational choice it has no pretense of being a self-sufficient or all-purpose imagery). In Joseph Berger's and Morris Zelditch's terms (Berger and Zelditch 1998), the pattern of growth has been the "proliferation" of substantive applications over the domains defined by the main socially constructed "actors" of modern society—organizations, states, individuals. In each domain, as we've seen, the same basic logic is applied: the formation of actor-structures within institutional environments. As we've also seen, the specific substantive applications were also motivated by empirical anomalies (or theory-empirics gaps) apparent in the research literature.

Sources of Growth

The proliferation of the program has been propelled primarily by what Berger and Zelditch call a "substantive working strategy" and a "methodological working strategy" (ibid.) The substantive strategy is the theoretical imagery discussed throughout. The methodological strategy has been to study historical and comparative variations among contexts—due to the highly contextual nature of the core theoretical ideas. Institutionalists have especially sought to study the basic cultural models of social systems, and their effects; this concentration follows from the basic argument that the actors and "others" in modern social environments are constantly elaborating and taking up models for organizing and acting. Such studies have been fostered by a set of research designs in what someone half-seriously labeled "quantitative macro phenomenology"; these have been worked out by Meyer and colleagues (like Mike Hannan, Dick Scott, and Nancy Tuma), and deployed in many doctoral dissertations especially. These designs have often involved finding comparative or historical quantitative data—or materials that can be coded as counts—and using standard techniques of statistical inference, although often employed in exploratory and interpretive ways that cannot be described here.[44]

Over time research designs have become more diverse. Quantitative analyses have diversified beyond regression-based strategies, following the field. And the program has become less exclusively based in quantitative designs, especially with greater comparative historical work (for example, by Boli, Dobbin, Soysal, and others). Evidence and measurement strategies have continued to broaden, to include coding of (for example) yearbooks of international organizations (for study of the buildup of world culture [Boli and Thomas 1997]), college curricula (for study of changes in the knowledge system [David Frank, in preparation]), history and civics texts (for study of changing collective identities [Frank et al. 2000; Soysal 1998]), and conferences and discourse of international nongovernmental organizations (about women, environment, science) since the nineteenth century (for study of changing cultural models [Boli and Thomas 1999b]).

In connection with these developments, the inferential strategies for showing institutional effects have become more direct. In initial research institutionalists sought mainly to demonstrate the existence of unexpected isomorphisms and decouplings, and then secondarily to infer, indirectly, the existence of institutionalization as a cause of them. This was an "inputed effects" strategy (Schneiberg and Clemens forthcoming): the *absence* of standard (for example, organizational) correlations was taken as indirect evidence of the *presence* of institutional forces. In analysis of educational organizations, this inferential strategy worked well, since readers were informally quite familiar with the institutional classifications involved (grade-levels, standard curricula, etc.). In analysis of nation-states, the absence of major economic effects (say, on some feature of political structure) plus the presence of isomorphism, plus some evidence on world society processes, were used to infer institutionalization.

As research has expanded, there have been more direct demonstrations of institutional effects. For example, the research on the effects of "world society" contain a number of such more direct studies of the effects of change at the institutional level: David Frank et al. 1999 on changes in constructions of the environment, and their effects; Deborah Barrett on changes in ideology about population growth and control, and their effects (Barrett 1995; Barrett and Frank 1999); Nitza Berkovitch (1999a, 1999b) on changes in doctrines about the identity and status of women, and their effects. (Boli 1999 summarizes some of this research.)

It seems fair to say that the research fertility of the program does *not* appear to be based in any of the following possible sources of theoretical innovation and growth. There are no special methodological tools or claims. There is no special theoretical formalization. There is no special epistemology or logic of explanation—beyond an insistence on multilevel analysis and hence an unwillingness to go along with the very special epistemology of methodological individualism. There is no exotic topical concentration: the program has generated applications in the historically core domains of sociology, and has published in standard general outlets. The fertility and distinctiveness of the program is based almost exclusively in its different theoretical imagery, and in the aggressive empirical deployment of this imagery in different domains using a set of similar research designs. Almost all energy has been put into identifying and exploring interesting substantive issues, new sources of data, and different possible explanations, with metatheoretic issues (for good or for ill) largely put aside.[45]

CONCLUSION

In its research fertility, theoretic integration, and continued expansion, sociological neoinstitutionalism seems a very substantial success. However, institutionalism has been less successful in receiving full acknowledgement of these achievements, at least as yet. Two factors appear to account for this interesting disjunction. First, one should not underestimate a standard factor: the highly segmental ecology of the field sustains intellectual diversity but also produces little encouragement for actual interchange or recognition (or for that matter, for broad reading—there is often little incentive to know about others' work, even though the myth of mutual awareness and interest is maintained).

Second, probing a bit more deeply, the intellectual culture of American sociology is still predominantly individualist and realist in construction, and institutionalism maximally deviates by being both structuralist and phenomenological. Due to this deviance, it predictably has received feigned and real incomprehension—for instance, easy labeling as a dispensable concern for myth and symbols, or for other "superstructural" fluff. (Some neoinstitutionalist writings have played into these characterizations.) The fundamental institutionalist concern with the basic matrices of modern society is thereby elided. In this way, this institutionalism as yet is not firmly conventionalized as a line of truly basic social theory.[46]

However, the segmental ecology and intellectual culture of sociology have also facilitated institutionalism, internally—as one line of truly basic social theory. The worldwide social scientific reification of actorhood continues to give sociological institutionalism a lot of space to defocalize actorhood, and produces far fewer near-competitors, and far less real criticism, than should be present. In this space, this institutionalism continues to develop as a theoretical program, both expanding and deepening its research applications.

NOTES

This chapter draws upon recent conversations or correspondence with John Boli, John Meyer, Thomas Risse, Evan Schofer, and Marc Ventresca and upon comments from this volume's editors. Meyer endured multiple queries about the research program during the preparation of this chapter, and Boli provided repeated commentary. The author appreciates the support of the Robert Schuman Centre for Advanced Studies, European University Institute, Florence.

1. There are few treatments of sociological neoinstitutionalism as an integrated TRP. Krücken and Hasse (1999) is a monograph in German reviewing sociological neoinstitutionalism generally, starting with organizational analysis. The most important general theoretical statement is Meyer, Boli, and Thomas (1987). A consideration of conceptual issues is offered in Jepperson 1991. Other reviews concentrate upon parts of the program. DiMaggio and Powell (1991) concentrate upon organizational analysis. A book-length survey of the whole range of neoinstitutionalist ideas and research in organizational analysis is provided by Scott (1995).

2. The scope of this chapter is intentionally restricted in the following three ways:

   1. The chapter limits itself to the sociological neoinstitutionalism associated especially with John Meyer, and does not attempt to provide an overview of the various institutionalisms present in sociological theory. Scott (1995) and DiMaggio and Powell (1991) provide more general overviews, as does Hall and Taylor (1996) for political science. It is probably safe to say that the sociological neoinstitutionalism surveyed in this chapter has been the version most developed as a "theoretical research program" in the specific sense analyzed by Berger and Zelditch (1998).
   2. Within this restricted focus, there is particular attention to Meyer's work, for straightforward reasons: many of the core ideas and innovations in the program come from his individual work or from his collaboration with colleagues (such as Michael Hannan and W. R. Scott) and with students and ex-students.
   3. Due to this volume's focus, and to space constraints, this review concentrates upon expositing the development of ideas within the research program. While it refers constantly to the program's empirical studies, it is not able to convey them with proper vividness and detail. Nor is it able to offer a critical evaluation of the program.

3. For instance, an unpublished memo on "institutionalization" bears that date (Meyer 1970c; ideas discussed with Morris Zelditch Jr., among others), as does Meyer's article offering an institutional reinterpretation of the nature of "socialization" in schools (Meyer 1970a, to be discussed).

4. In a concurrent development, Lynne Zucker's "The Role of Institutionalization in Cultural Persistence" (1977) demonstrated experimentally that presenting a situation as an institutionalized formal organization has substantial effects upon individuals' expectations and behavior. (Zucker had studied at Stanford and had worked with a number of the sociologists and social psychologists there.)

5. Meyer was taking off most immediately from the general interest in contextual and structural thinking prominent at Columbia University in the 1960s, as well as from phenomenological ideas then developing in the sociological environment (including ethnomethodology, Peter Berger's [and Berger and Luckmann's] work, Erving Goffman's social psychology). These ideas were emerging partly in response to Talcott Parsons's and Robert Merton's focus upon norms, internalization, and socialization—a focus increasingly seen as excessive and empirically problematic. Meyer was also influenced directly by Daniel Bell (viz., Bell's general macrohistorical concerns), and by Paul Lazarsfeld (viz., Lazarsfeld's concern for multilevel analysis). Meyer was a lecturer in a program led by Bell, and was a research assistant for Lazarsfeld.

6. In Germany, the educational system has been far more differentiated by types of schools, with the different tracks associated with different occupations and social status. Hence in Germany

the identity "graduate" has not been a singular one: people have received one of a number of different identities from their participation in a particular segment of the educational system.

7. "Even Weber's idea that institutions require *legitimacy* can be reinterpreted to mean not that people must approve of them or like them, but that they must acknowledge that they are actually binding—that they do actually organize social responses to the actor" (Meyer 1970c).

8. Meyer, personal communication, July 2000.

9. Meyer and W. Richard Scott offer their own narrative of the emergence and development of this institutionalism in organizational analysis (Meyer and Scott 1992:1–17)—an account adhered to here. See Scott 1995 for an extended (book-length) and definitive treatment. See also Strang 1994 for a particularly effective characterization of the elaboration of research ideas in this area, as well as DiMaggio and Powell 1991 (esp. good on intellectual context); Zucker 1987 (for many substantive examples); and Dobbin 1994a (esp. good on phenomenological aspects of the program).

10. By Meyer, Elizabeth Cohen, Terrence Deal, and Brian Rowan, among others.

11. The idea, originating in Max Weber's work, that European (later, world) society reflects the following fundamental cultural and institutional dynamic: (1) continuing efforts to systematize social life around standardized rules and around schemes that explicitly differentiate and then seek to link means and ends; (2) the ongoing reconstruction of all social organization—both social activities and social actors, including the nation-state itself as an actor—as means for the pursuit of collective purposes, these purposes themselves subject to increasing systematization (Meyer, Boli, and Thomas 1987:24; Scott and Meyer 1994:3). More concretely, "through rationalization, authority is structured as a formal legal order increasingly bureaucratized; exchange is governed by rules of rational calculation and bookkeeping, rules constituting a market, . . . [including] such related processes as monetarization, commercialization, and bureaucratic planning; cultural accounts increasingly reduce society to the smallest rational units—the individual, but also beyond to genes and quarks" (Meyer, Boli, and Thomas 1987:25).

12. Institutionalists have mostly focused upon the contemporary expansions of formal organizing and their institutional sources. Scott and Meyer stated in 1994 that they have not tried to offer a "general macrosociological model of long-term organizational change" (1994:8), and neither they nor others in the immediate literature have pursued this task. Fligstein (1990) is a partial exception.

13. Some appears in Scott and Christensen 1995.

14. As did their edited volume, Powell and DiMaggio 1991.

15. Organizations respond to environments via three logics, Scott suggests: instrumentality, appropriateness, and orthodoxy (Scott 1995:35 and ch. 3). Instrumentality is based in expedience (awareness of possible legal sanctions, for example); appropriateness is based in social obligation (awareness of moral norms, for example); orthodoxy is based in taken-for-grantedness (perceived conceptual correctness, for example). This typology would seem to have quite general utility for social theory.

16. That is, modern personnel administration developed as a broad ideological movement, and eventually was "institutionalized as standard operating procedure—defined sometimes in law, but often in custom, professional ideologies, and doctrines of proper organizational management—and thus appears in many contexts. These procedures flow from organization to organization, sector to sector, and even country to country, as a collection of culturally defined categories and procedures, and as institutionalized packages supported by a variety of processes. Ultimately, they are taken-for-granted by individuals and organizations as the right way to do things" (Meyer and Scott 1992:1–2).

17. For this reason, "reform" waves sweep through organizational systems—"management by objectives," Japanese quality control ideas, "new math" in schools—but with haphazard, seemingly unpredictable, patterns of actual adoption in practices over various local settings (Meyer 1983a). The likelihood of implementation at any location is often hard to predict from local conditions and interest alignments.

This institutionalism paints a picture of a "society of organizations," but not of autonomous and bounded ones: "Although organizations may have absorbed society, as Perrow claims society has not less absorbed organizations" (Scott and Meyer 1994:4). In fact, this institutionalism has come to picture organizations as sufficiently interpenetrated with institutional environments, such that, analytically speaking, "organizations tend to disappear as distinct and bounded units" (Meyer and Rowan 1977:346).

18. For fuller reviews of this application area, see especially: Meyer et al. 1997; Meyer 1999a; Meyer 2000b.

19. The collaborators included John Boli[-Bennett], Christopher Chase-Dunn, Jacques Delacroix, Jeanne Gobalet, François Nielsen, Francisco Ramirez, Richard Rubinson, George Thomas, and Jane Weiss.

20. For example, features of national constitutions, "information load of exported products," number of cabinet posts in governments (Meyer and Hannan 1979b:6).

21. Surprisingly, few studies had done this. Most available studies had pursued relationships among individuals, or among groups, within one or more societies, rather than studying macrosociological connections directly (Meyer and Hannan 1979b:4–5).

22. As used here, "functionalism" does not refer to any specific theory, such as the "structural-functionalism" of classical anthropology or Parsons. Rather it refers to a general imagery: that of a highly bounded and tightly coupled social "system," with its structures existing, or having the form that they do, because they are tightly adapted to and facilitative of one another. In the sociology of education, functionalist ideas tend to represent educational structures as filling various needs or requirements (or legitimating requirements) of stratification systems, or (in the neomarxian variant) of specific social classes (Meyer 1986c). From methodological discussions it has become clear that functional imagery is empirically and logically suspect, but that functional arguments of a more narrow-gauged sort, meeting certain analytical requirements, may be legitimate in some cases (Stinchcombe 1968; Elster 1983: ch. 2).

23. The language of "imagined society" was imported into the research program later, borrowed from Anderson (1991).

24. One striking example: UNESCO codified the tripartite (6/3/3) categorization of school grade levels to simplify and regularize data collection. This data collection scheme was then implemented as actual organizational structure in many school systems in the world.

25. Later Meyer referred more fully to "a set of models defining the nature, purpose, resources, technologies, control and sovereignty of the proper nation-state" (1999a:123).

26. That is, how is it that in spite of "the differentiating power of the world economy, the state system expands?" (1980:115). Relatedly, the legitimacy of other political forms, such as ethnic or religious polities, or polities based solely in economic associations, has weakened (ibid.:120).

27. For instance, emphasis on national planning is especially common in *less*-developed countries. Further, sometimes planning cannot realistically be accomplished in these settings, but elites may nevertheless load up constitutions with currently dominant principles and programs—even if these are not to be enacted in practice (Meyer et al. 1997:155).

28. Reviewed especially in Meyer 1999a and Meyer et al. 1997.

29. Writing about these "scripts" for nation-states, Francisco Ramirez adds that "[m]uch of what is articulated is advisory and much of the advice is sufficiently abstract to allow for cross-national variation in interpretation and implementation. However, it would be difficult to explain the growing isomorphism among nation-states were one not to postulate the common models or blueprints that guide their formation" (Ramirez 2000).

30. However, as with organizational analysis, the macrohistorical side of sociological institutionalism has received less development than one would expect.

31. Jepperson 2000 provides more.

32. The underlying institutionalist idea is that states too are interpenetrated with their institutional environments. They appear to be "at least as fraudulent as functional creatures as organizations, schools, and persons"—a perspective at odds with the arch realism of much "theory of the state" in sociology and political science (Meyer, personal communication, August 2000).

33. See Meyer 1986a for a partial overview of ideas in this research area.

34. Further, in an attempt to study the consolidation and institutionalization of standard life-stages of an individual—core to the construction of a standard individualist identity—Boli studied the incorporation of ideas about child protection and development into the political and ideological systems of many societies. He did so in part by coding references to children in the political constitutions of nation-states, using these references as indicators of the consolidation of a transnational ideology of childhood and individuality (Boli and Meyer 1978).

35. In this project, "individual modernity" referred to a syndrome of "attitudes, values, and dispositions to act," especially "a thrust toward more instrumental kinds of attitudes and behavior" (Inkeles and Smith 1974:301, 291). The syndrome included an ideal of informed participant citizenship, an efficacious self-image, values of independence and autonomy, and openness to new experience and ideas (ibid.).

36. In Coleman's version, a change in the social context (the Protestant Reformation movements) resocializes individuals, who then behave differently (reflecting "salvation anxiety" and then greater economizing), and then, in aggregate, produce a further change in the context (eventually a more marketized social system) (Coleman 1986). Coleman seems to insist that the effects of Protestantism must take this form, or that the *major* effect of Protestantism would necessarily take this form, or that one must in any case theorize Protestantism in this form. Each of these claims seems arbitrary and quite problematic. For instance, the institutionalist explanation sketch is an entirely plausible alternative, in many respects a much more plausible one, yet it does not take the Coleman-prescribed form. (See Collins 1980 for a more collective-level reading of Weber's argument.) However, in principle the institutionalist explanation sketch could be either complementary to or competitive with the Coleman sketch. The point is that this is an empirical matter, not a matter for methodological fiat.

37. In this picture, in changing the dominant theory of collective purpose and progress, Protestantism reworked both the roles and the objectives of priests and lawyers and state elites, who, operating as agents of the changed theory, changed various rules of the societal game. (For example, rich people could subsequently use their money as capital investment, rather than having to buy status and protection.)

38. Ramirez and colleagues have also focused upon the expansion of women's suffrage in the world system, studying how a highly contested issue became a taken-for-granted feature of political life. (They find that between 1870 and 1940, the extension of voting rights to women is related to domestic features of countries: for instance, the degree of "Westernization" of, and strength of women's organizations within, a country. However, after this period, such factors appear much less important; instead, external factors seem to be at work: the policies of other countries in a region and in the world at large [Ramirez, Soysal, and Shanahan 1997; Ramirez 2000 for review].)

39. And to some degree, to nonhumans: conceptions of "animal rights" accord a kind of individuality, and quasi-social membership, to a widening range of "charismatic fauna" (for instance, whales).

40. This institutionalism casts individuals in the same light as modern society's other "actors": their actorhood is highly constructed and scripted. In this line of argument, basic features of individual identity have been reinterpreted as a consequence of collective-level cultural processes: in this case, the collective project of individualism.

41. A longer version of this chapter discusses this institutionalism's relations with other theoretical programs (e.g., population ecology, rational choice) (Working Paper, Robert Schuman Centre for Advanced Studies, European University Institute, Florence, 2001).

42. Thomas and Meyer point out relatedly that "[w]e have better studies of why people vote the way they do than of why there are elections, or of market behavior rather than of why markets are created" (Thomas and Meyer 1984:462).

43. John Boli helped with this characterization of "action" (personal communication).

44. See Schneiberg and Clemens (forthcoming) as well as Meyer and Hannan 1979c.

45. John Boli stressed this feature (personal communication).

46. Or even disregarded: for example, Randall Collins can leave the program out of his impressive overviews of sociology's intellectual capital (Collins 1988, 1994). A longer version of this chapter provides a more elaborate "sociology of knowledge" of this institutionalism's intellectual position within sociology (Working Paper, Robert Schuman Centre for Advanced Studies, European University Institute, Florence, 2001).

REFERENCES

Abell, Peter. 1995. "The New Institutionalism and Rational Choice Theory." Pp. 3–14 in *The Institutional Construction of Organizations*, edited by W. Richard Scott and Søren Christensen. Thousand Oaks, CA: Sage.

Almond, Gabriel, and Sidney Verba. 1963. *The Civic Culture.* Princeton, NJ: Princeton University Press.

Anderson, Benedict. 1991. *Imagined Communities.* 2d ed. London: Verso.

Barrett, Deborah. 1995. *Reproducing Persons as a Global Concern: The Making of an Institution.* Ph.D. dissertation, Stanford University.

Barrett, Deborah, and David Frank. 1999. "Population Control for National Development: From World Discourse to National Policies." Pp. 198–221 in *Constructing World Culture: International Nongovernmental Organizations since 1875,* edited by John Boli and George M. Thomas. Stanford, CA: Stanford University Press.

Berger, Joseph, and Morris Zelditch Jr. 1998. "Theoretical Research Programs: A Reformulation." Pp. 71–93 in *Status, Power, and Legitimacy,* edited by Joseph Berger and Morris Zelditch Jr. New Brunswick, NJ: Transaction.

Berger, Peter, and Thomas Luckmann. 1967. *The Social Construction of Reality.* New York: Double Day.

Berkovitch, Nitza. 1999a. *From Motherhood to Citizenship.* Baltimore: Johns Hopkins University Press.

———. 1999b. "The International Women's Movement: Transformations of Citizenship." Pp. 100–126 in *Constructing World Culture: International Nongovernmental Organizations since 1875,* edited by John Boli and George M. Thomas. Stanford, CA: Stanford University Press.

Boli, John. 1987a. "Human Rights or State Expansion? Cross-National Definitions of Constitutional Rights, 1870–1970." Pp. 133–149 in *Institutional Structure: Constituting State, Society, and the Individual,* edited by George Thomas, John W. Meyer, Francisco O. Ramirez, and John Boli. Newbury Park, CA: Sage.

———. 1987b. "World Polity Sources of Expanding State Authority and Organization, 1870–1970." Pp. 71–91 in *Institutional Structure: Constituting State, Society, and the Individual,* edited by George Thomas, John W. Meyer, Francisco O. Ramirez, and John Boli. Newbury Park, CA: Sage.

———. 1989. *New Citizens for a New Society.* Elmsford, NY: Pergamon.

———. 1999. "World Authority Structures and Legitimations." Pp. 267–300 in *Constructing World Culture: International Nongovernmental Organizations since 1875,* edited by John Boli and George M. Thomas. Stanford, CA: Stanford University Press.

Boli, John, Francisco Ramirez, and John W. Meyer. 1985. "Explaining the Origins and Expansion of Mass Education." *Comparative Education Review* 29:145–168.

Boli, John, and George M. Thomas. 1997. "World Culture in the World Polity: A Century of International Non-governmental Organization." *American Sociological Review* 62:171–190.

———. 1999a. "INGOs and the Organization of World Culture." Pp. 13–49 in *Constructing World Culture: International Nongovernmental Organizations since 1875,* edited by John Boli and George M. Thomas. Stanford, CA: Stanford University Press.

———, eds. 1999b. *Constructing World Culture: International Nongovernmental Organizations since 1875.* Stanford, CA: Stanford University Press.

Boli-Bennett, John, and John W. Meyer. 1978. "The Ideology of Childhood and the State." *American Sociological Review.* 43:797–812.

Boyle, Elizabeth Heger. 1998. "Political Frames and Legal Activity: Anti-Nuclear Power Litigation in Four Countries." *Law & Society Review* 32:141–174.

Bradley, Karen, and Francisco Ramirez. 1996. "World Polity Promotion of Gender Parity: Women's Share of Higher Education, 1965–85." *Research in Sociology of Education and Socialization* 11:63–91.

Brunsson, Nils. 1989. *The Organization of Hypocrisy: Talk, Decisions, and Action in Organizations.* New York: Wiley.

Carroll, Glenn R., and Michael T. Hannan. 1989. "Density Dependence in the Evolution of Populations of Newspaper Organizations." *American Sociological Review* 54:524–548.

Chase-Dunn, Christopher. 1989. *Global Formation: Structures of the World Economy.* Cambridge: Basil Blackwell.

Coleman, James S. 1974. *Power and the Structure of Society.* New York: Norton.

———. 1986. "Social Theory, Social Research, and a Theory of Action," *American Journal of Sociology* 91:1309–1335.

Collins, Randall. 1979. *The Credential Society: A Historical Sociology of Education and Stratification.* New York: Academic Press.

———. 1980. "Weber's Last Theory of Capitalism: A Systematization." *American Sociological Review* 45:925–942.

———. 1988. *Theoretical Sociology.* Orlando, FL: Harcourt Brace Jovanovich.

———. 1992. *Sociological Insight.* New York: Oxford University Press.

———. 1994. *Four Sociological Traditions.* New York: Oxford University Press.

DiMaggio, Paul, and Walter W. Powell. 1983. "The Iron Cage Revisited: Institutional Isomorphism and Collective Rationality in Organizational Fields." *American Sociological Review* 48:147–60.

———. 1991. "Introduction." Pp. 1–40 in *The New Institutionalism in Organizational Analysis*, edited by Walter W. Powell and Paul DiMaggio. Chicago: University of Chicago Press.

Dobbin, Frank. 1994a. "Cultural Models of Organization: the Social Construction of Rational Organizing Principles." Pp. 117–142 in *The Sociology of Culture: Emerging Theoretical Perspectives*, edited by D. Crane. Oxford: Basil Blackwell.

———. 1994b. *Forging Industrial Policy: The United States, Britain, and France in the Railway Age.* New York: Cambridge University Press.

———. 1995. "The Origins of Economic Principles: Railway Entrepreneurs and Public Policy in 19th-Century America." Pp. 277–301 in *The Institutional Construction of Organizations*, edited by W. Richard Scott and Søren Christensen. Thousand Oaks, CA: Sage.

Dobbin, Frank, John R. Sutton, John W. Meyer, and W. Richard Scott. 1993. "Equal Opportunity Law and the Construction of Internal Labor Markets." *American Journal of Sociology* 99:396–427.

Dobbin, Frank, John R. Sutton, John W. Meyer, W. Richard Scott, and Ann Swidler. 1988. "The Expansion of Due Process in Organizations." Pp. 71–100 in *Institutional Patterns and Organizations: Culture and Environment*, edited by Lynne G. Zucker. Cambridge, MA: Ballinger.

Dornbusch, Sanford M., and W. Richard Scott, with the assistance of Bruce C. Busching and James D. Laing. 1975. *Evaluation and the Exercise of Authority.* San Francisco: Jossey-Bass.

Elster, Jon. 1983. *Explaining Technical Change.* Cambridge: Cambridge University Press.

Finnemore, Martha. 1996a. *National Interests in International Society.* Ithaca, NY: Cornell University Press.

———. 1996b. "Norms, Culture, and World Politics: Insights from Sociology's Institutionalism." *International Organization* 50:325–347.

Fligstein, Neil. 1990. *The Transformation of Corporate Control.* Cambridge: Harvard University Press.

Frank, David. 1997. "Science, Nature, and the Globalization of the Environment, 1870–1990." *Social Forces* 76:409–435.

Frank, David, Ann Hironaka, John Meyer, Evan Schofer, and Nancy Tuma. 1999. "The Rationalization and Organization of Nature in the World Culture." Pp. 81–99 in *Constructing World Culture: International Nongovernmental Organizations since 1875*, edited by John Boli and George M. Thomas. Stanford, CA: Stanford University Press.

Frank, David, Ann Hironaka, and Evan Schofer. 2000. "The Nation-State and the Natural Environment over the Twentieth Century." *American Sociological Review* 65:96–116.

Frank, David, and Elizabeth McEneaney. 1999. "The Individualization of Society and the Liberalization of State Policies on Same-Sex Sexual Relations, 1985–1995." *Social Forces* 77: 911–944.

Frank, David, and John W. Meyer. 2000. "The Contemporary Identity Explosion: Individualizing Society in the Post-War Period." Unpublished paper, Harvard University.

Frank, David, John W. Meyer, and David Miyahara. 1995. "The Individualist Polity and the Centrality of Professionalized Psychology." *American Sociological Review* 60:360–367.

Frank, David, Suk-Ying Wong, John W. Meyer, and Francisco Ramirez. 2000. "What Counts as History: A Cross-National and Longitudinal Study of University Curricula." *Comparative Education Review* 44:29–53.

Frank, David, Suk-Ying Wong, Francisco Ramirez, and John W. Meyer. 2000. "Embedding National Societies: Worldwide Changes in University Curricula, 1895–1994." *Comparative Education Review* 44:29–53.

Hall, Peter, and Rosemary Taylor. 1996. "Political Science and the Three New Institutionalisms." *Political Studies* 44:952–73.

Hamilton, Gary, and Nicole W. Biggart. 1988. "Market, Culture, and Authority: A Comparative Analysis of Management and Organization in the Far East." *American Journal of Sociology* 94 (Supplement):S52–S94.

Hannan, Michael T., and John Freeman. 1977. "The Population Ecology of Organizations." *American Journal of Sociology* 82:929–964.

______. 1989. *Organizational Ecology.* Cambridge: Harvard University Press.

Inkeles, Alex. 1983. *Exploring Individual Modernity.* New York: Columbia University Press.

Inkeles, Alex, and David H. Smith. 1974. *Becoming Modern.* Cambridge: Harvard University Press.

Jepperson, Ronald L. 1991. "Institutions, Institutional Effects, and Institutionalism." Pp. 143–163 in *The New Institutionalism in Organizational Analysis*, edited by Walter W. Powell and Paul J. DiMaggio. Chicago: University of Chicago Press.

______. 1992. "National Scripts: The Varying Construction of Individualism and Opinion across the Modern Nation-States." Ph.D. dissertation, Yale University.

______. 2000. "Institutional Logics: The Constitutive Dimensions of the Modern Nation-State Polities." Working Paper RSC No. 2000/36, European University Institute, Florence, Italy.

Jepperson, Ronald L., and John W. Meyer. 1991. "The Public Order and the Construction of Formal Organizations." Pp. 204–231 in *The New Institutionalism in Organizational Analysis*, edited by Walter W. Powell and Paul J. DiMaggio. Chicago: University of Chicago Press.

Jepperson, Ronald L., Alexander Wendt, and Peter Katzenstein. 1996. "Norms, Identity, and Culture in National Security." Pp. 33–78 in *The Culture of National Security*, edited by Peter Katzenstein. New York: Columbia University Press.

Kamens, David H. 1977. "Legitimating Myths and Educational Organization: The Relationship Between Organizational Ideology and Formal Structure." *American Sociological Review* 42:208–219.

Katzenstein, Peter J., ed. 1996. *The Culture of National Security.* New York: Columbia University Press.

Kiser, Edgar. 1999. "Comparing Varieties of Agency Theory in Economics, Political Science, and Sociology: An Illustration from State Policy Implementation." *Sociological Theory* 17:146–170.

Krücken, Georg. 2000. "An Interview with John W. Meyer." *Sozusagen* (Dept. of Sociology, Bielefeld) 7:58–63.

Krücken, Georg, and Raimund Hasse. 1999. *Neo-Institutionalismus.* Beilefeld: Transcript Verlag.

McEneaney, Elizabeth, and John W. Meyer. 2000. "The Content of the Curriculum: An Institutionalist Perspective." Pp. 189–211 in *Handbook of Sociology of Education*, edited by M. Hallinan. New York: Plenum.

McNeely, Connie. 1995. *Constructing the Nation-State.* Westport, CT: Greenwood.

McNeill, William. 1963. *The Rise of the West.* Chicago: University of Chicago Press.

Meyer, John W. 1965. "Working Paper on Some Non-Value Effects of Colleges." BASR, Columbia University.

______. 1970a. "The Charter: Conditions of Diffuse Socialization in Schools." Pp. 564–578 in *Social Processes and Social Structures*, edited by W. R. Scott. New York: Holt.

______. 1970b. "High School Effects on College Intentions." *American Journal of Sociology* 76:59–70.

______. 1970c. "Institutionalization." Unpublished paper.

______. 1971a. "Comparative Research on the Relationships between Political and Educational Institutions." In *Politics and Education*, edited by M. Kirst and F. Wirt. Boston: D. C. Heath.

______. 1971b. "Economic and Political Effects on National Educational Enrollment Patterns." *Comparative Education Review* 15:28–43.

______. 1972. "The Effects of the Institutionalization of Colleges in Society." Pp. 109–126 in *College & Student*, edited by K. Feldman. New York: Pergamon.

______. 1977. "The Effects of Education as an Institution." *American Journal of Sociology* 83:55–77.

______. 1978. "Strategies for Further Research: Varieties of Environmental Variation." Pp. 352–68 in *Environments and Organizations*, edited by M. Meyer. San Francisco: Jossey-Bass.

______. 1980. "The World Polity and the Authority of the Nation-State." Pp. 109–137 in *Studies of the Modern World-System*, edited by Albert Bergesen. New York: Academic Press.

______. 1981. "Review Essay: Kings or People." *American Journal of Sociology* 86:895–899.

______. 1982. "Political Structure and the World Economy" (review essay on Wallerstein). *Contemporary Sociology* 11:263–266.

———. 1983a. "Innovation and Knowledge Use in American Public Education." Pp. 233–260 in *Organizational Environments*, by J. Meyer, W. R. Scott, et al. Beverly Hills, CA: Sage.
———. 1983b. "Institutionalization and the Rationality of Formal Organizational Structure." Pp. 261–282 in *Organizational Environments: Ritual and Rationality*, by J. W. Meyer, W. R. Scott, et al. Beverly Hills, CA: Sage.
———. 1986a. "Myths of Socialization and Personality." Pp. 212–225 in *Reconstructing Individualism*, edited by T. Heller, M. Sosna, and D. Wellbery. Stanford, CA: Stanford University Press.
———. 1986b. "The Self and the Life Course: Institutionalization and Its Effects." Pp. 199–216 in *Human Development and the Life Course*, edited by A. Sorensen, F. Weinert, and L. Sherrod. Hillsdale, NJ: Erlbaum.
———. 1986c. "Types of Explanation in the Sociology of Education." Pp. 341–59 in *Handbook of Theory and Research for the Sociology of Education*, edited by J. Richardson. Greenwood, CT: Westport.
———. 1988. "Society without Culture: A Nineteenth Century Legacy." Pp. 193–201 in *Rethinking the Nineteenth Century*, edited by Francisco Ramirez. New York: Greenwood Press.
———. 1989. "Conceptions of Christendom: Notes on the Distinctiveness of the West." Pp. 395–413 in *Cross-National Research in Sociology*, edited by Melvin Kohn. Newbury Park, CA: Sage.
———. 1990. "Individualism: Social Experience and Cultural Formulation." Pp. 51–58 in *Self-Directness: Causes and Effects throughout the Life Course*, edited by J. Rodin, C. Schooler, and K. Schaie. Hillsdale, NJ: Erlbaum.
———. 1992a. "From Constructionism to Neo-institutionalism: Reflections on Berger and Luckmann." *Perspectives* 15:11–12. Washington, DC: American Sociological Association.
———. 1992b. "The Social Construction of Motives for Educational Expansion." Pp. 225–238 in *The Political Construction of Education*, edited by B. Fuller and R. Rubinson. New York: Praeger.
———. 1994a. "The Evolution of Modern Stratification Systems." Pp. 730–737 in *Social Stratification in Sociological Perspective*, edited by David B. Grusky. Boulder, CO: Westview Press.
———. 1994b. "Rationalized Environments." Pp. 28–54 in *Institutional Environments and Organizations*, by W. Richard Scott, John W. Meyer, et al. Newbury Park, CA: Sage.
———. 1996. "Otherhood: The Promulgation and Transmission of Ideas in the Modern Organizational Environment." Pp. 241–252 in *Translating Organizational Change*, edited by B. Czarniawska and G. Sevon. Berlin: de Gruyter.
———. 1999a. "The Changing Cultural Content of the Nation-State: A World Society Perspective." Pp. 123–143 in *State/Culture: State Formation after the Cultural Turn*, edited by George Steinimetz. Ithaca, NY: Cornell University Press.
———. 1999b. Memo to H. Fujita. Stanford University, September 1999.
———. 2000a. "Globalization and the Curriculum: Problems for Theory in the Sociology of Education." *Journal of Educational Sociology*, Japan Society of Educational Sociology, 66.
———. 2000b. "Globalization: Sources, and Effects on National States and Societies." *International Sociology* 15:235–250.
Meyer, John W., John Boli-Bennett, and Christopher Chase-Dunn. 1975. "Convergence and Divergence in Development." *Annual Review of Sociology* 1:223–245.
Meyer, John W., John Boli, and George M. Thomas. 1981. "Rationalization and Ontology in the Evolving World System." Paper presented at the meeting of the Pacific Sociological Association.
———. 1987. "Ontology and Rationalization in the Western Cultural Account." Pp. 12–38 in *Institutional Structure: Constituting State, Society, and the Individual*, by George M. Thomas, John W. Meyer, Francisco O. Ramirez, and John Boli. Newbury Park, CA: Sage.
Meyer, John W., John Boli, George Thomas, and Francisco Ramirez. 1997. "World Society and the Nation-State." *American Journal of Sociology* 103:144–181.
Meyer, John W., David Frank, Ann Hironaka, Evan Schofer, and Nancy Tuma. 1997. "The Structuring of a World Environmental Regime, 1870–1990." *International Organization* 51:623–651.
Meyer, John W., and Michael Hannan. 1979a. "Issues for Further Comparative Research." Pp. 297–308 in *National Development and the World System*, edited by John W. Meyer and Michael Hannan. Chicago: University of Chicago Press.

——. 1979b. "National Development in a Changing World System: An Overview." Pp. 3–16 in *National Development and the World System*, edited by John W. Meyer and Michael Hannan. Chicago: University of Chicago Press.

——, eds. 1979c. *National Development and the World System.* Chicago: University of Chicago Press.

Meyer, John W., and Ronald L. Jepperson. 2000. "The 'Actors' of Modern Society: The Cultural Construction of Social Agency." *Sociological Theory* 18:100–120.

Meyer, John W., David Kamens, and Aaron Benavot, with Yun-Kyung Cha and Suk-Ying Wong. 1992. *School Knowledge for the Masses: World Models and National Primary Curricular Categories in the Twentieth Century.* London: Falmer Press.

Meyer, John W., and Francisco O. Ramirez. 1981. "Comparative Education: Synthesis and Agenda." Pp. 215–238 in *The State of Sociology*, edited by J. Short. Newbury Park, CA: Sage.

——. 2000. "The World Institutionalization of Education." Pp. 111–132 in *Discourse Formation in Comparative Education*, edited by J. Schriewer. Frankfurt: Peter Lang Publishers.

Meyer, John W., Francisco O. Ramirez, and John Boli-Bennett. 1977. "The World Educational Revolution, 1950–1970." *Sociology of Education* 50:242–258.

Meyer, John W., Francisco O. Ramirez, Richard Rubinson, and John Boli-Bennett. 1977. "The World Educational Revolution, 1950–1970." *Sociology of Education* 50:242–258.

Meyer, John W., Francisco O. Ramirez, and Yasemin Soysal. 1992. "World Expansion of Mass Education, 1870–1970." *Sociology of Education* 65: 128–149.

Meyer, John W., Francisco O. Ramirez, Henry Walker, Sorca O'Connor, and Nancy Langton. 1988. "The State of the Institutionalization of Relations between Women and Children." Pp. 147–158 in *Feminism, Children, and the New Families*, edited by Sanford M. Dornbusch and Myra Stroeber. New York: Guilford Press.

Meyer, John W., and Brian Rowan. 1977. "Institutionalized Organizations: Formal Structure as Myth and Ceremony." *American Journal of Sociology* 83:340–363.

——. 1978. "The Structure of Educational Organizations." Pp. 78–109 in *Environments and Organizations*, edited by M. W. Meyer. San Francisco: Jossey-Bass.

Meyer, John W., and Richard Rubinson. 1975. "Education and Political Development." *Review of Research in Education* 3:134–162.

Meyer, John W., Evan Schofer, and Francisco O. Ramirez. Forthcoming. "The Effects of Science on National Economic Development, 1970–90." *American Sociological Review.*

Meyer, John W., and W. Richard Scott. 1983a. "Centralization and the Legitimacy Problems of Local Government." Pp. 199–215 in *Organizational Environments*, by J. Meyer and W. R. Scott. Beverly Hills, CA: Sage.

——. 1983b. *Organizational Environments: Ritual and Rationality.* Beverly Hills, CA: Sage.

——. 1992. "Preface to the Updated Edition." Pp. 1–6 in *Organizational Environments*, rev. ed., by J. W. Meyer and W. R. Scott. Newbury Park, CA: Sage.

Meyer, John W., W. Richard Scott, and Terrence E. Deal. 1981. "Institutional and Technical Sources of Organizational Structure: Explaining the Structure of Educational Organizations." Pp. 157–178 in *Organization and the Human Services*, edited by Herman D. Stein. Philadelphia: Temple University Press.

Mizruchi, Mark S., and Lisa C. Fein. 1999. "The Social Construction of Organizational Knowledge: A Study of the Uses of Coercive, Mimetic, and Normative Isomorphism." *Administrative Science Quarterly* 44:653–683.

Olson, Mancur. 1965. *The Logic of Collective Action.* New York: Schocken Books.

Orrù, Marco, Nicole Woolsey Biggart, and Gary G. Hamilton. 1991. "Organizational Isomorphism in East Asia." Pp. 361–389 in *The New Institutionalism in Organizational Analysis*, edited by Walter W. Powell and Paul J. DiMaggio. Chicago: University of Chicago Press.

Perrow, Charles. 1985. "Review Essay: Overboard with Myth and Symbols." *American Journal of Sociology* 91:151–155.

——. 1986. *Complex Organizations: A Critical Essay.* 3d ed. New York: Random House.

——. 1991. "A Society of Organizations." *Theory and Society* 20:725–762.

Powell, Walter W., and Paul J. DiMaggio, eds. 1991. *The New Institutionalism in Organizational Analysis.* Chicago: University of Chicago Press.

Ramirez, Francisco O. 2000. "Women in Science/Women and Science: Liberal and Radical Perspectives." Unpublished paper, Stanford University.

Ramirez, Francisco O., and John Boli. 1987a. "Global Patterns of Educational Institutionalization." Pp. 150–172 in *Institutional Structure*, by G. M. Thomas, J. W. Meyer, F. O. Ramirez, and J. Boli. Newbury Park, CA: Sage.

———. 1987b. "On the Union of States and Schools." Pp. 173–197 in *Institutional Structure*, by G. M. Thomas, J. W. Meyer, F. O. Ramirez, and J. Boli. Newbury Park, CA: Sage.

———. 1987c. "The Political Construction of Mass Schooling: European Origins and Worldwide Institutionalization." *Sociology of Education* 60:2–17.

Ramirez, Francisco O., and Y.-K. Cha. 1990. "Citizenship and Gender: Western Educational Developments in Comparative Perspective." *Research in Sociology of Education and Socialization* 9:153–174.

Ramirez, Francisco O., and John W. Meyer. 1980. "Comparative Education: The Social Construction of the Modern World System." *Annual Review of Sociology* 6:369–399.

Ramirez, Francisco O., and Richard Rubinson. 1979. "Creating Members: The Political Incorporation and Expansion of Public Education." Pp. 72–84 in *National Development and the World System*, edited by J. W. Meyer and M. T. Hannan. Chicago: University of Chicago Press.

Ramirez, Francisco O., Yasemin Soysal, and Suzanne Shanahan. 1997. "The Changing Logic of Political Citizenship: Cross-National Acquisition of Women's Suffrage Rights, 1890 to 1990." *American Sociological Review* 62:735–745.

Ramirez, Francisco O., and Jane Weiss. 1979. "The Political Incorporation of Women." Pp. 238–249 in *National Development and the World System*, edited by J. Meyer and M. Hannan. Chicago: University of Chicago Press.

Schneiberg, Marc, and Elisabeth S. Clemens. Forthcoming. "The Typical Tools for the Job: Research Strategies in Institutional Analysis." In *How Institutions Change*, edited by W. W. Powell and D. L. Jones. Chicago: University of Chicago Press.

Schofer, Evan. 1999. "Science Associations in the International Sphere, 1875–1990: The Rationalization of Science and the Scientization of Society." Pp. 249–266 in *Constructing World Culture: International Nongovernmental Organizations since 1875*, edited by John Boli and George M. Thomas. Stanford, CA: Stanford University Press.

Schofer, Evan, and Marion Fourcade-Gourinchas. 1999. "State Structures and Voluntary Associations." Paper presented at the annual meeting of the American Sociological Association.

Scott, W. Richard. 1983/1992. "Introduction: From Technology to Environment." Pp. 13–17 in *Organizational Environments*, rev. ed., by J. W. Meyer and W. R. Scott. Newbury Park, CA: Sage.

———. 1987. *Organizations: Rational, Natural and Open Systems*, 2d ed. Englewood Cliffs, NJ: Prentice-Hall.

———. 1995. *Institutions and Organizations*. Thousand Oaks, CA: Sage.

Scott, W. Richard, and Søren Christensen. 1995. *The Institutional Construction of Organizations*. Thousand Oaks, CA: Sage.

Scott, W. Richard, and John W. Meyer. 1983/1992. "The Organization of Societal Sectors." Pp. 129–153 in *Organizational Environments: Ritual and Rationality*, rev. ed., by John W. Meyer and W. Richard Scott. Newbury Park, CA: Sage.

———. 1991. "The Organization of Societal Sectors: Propositions and Early Evidence." Pp. 108–142 in *The New Institutionalism in Organizational Analysis*, edited by Walter W. Powell and Paul J. DiMaggio. Chicago: University of Chicago Press.

Scott, W. Richard, John W. Meyer, et al. 1994. *Institutional Environments and Organizations*. Thousand Oaks, CA: Sage.

Shenhav, Yehuda, and David H. Kamens. 1991. "The 'Costs' of Institutional Isomorphism: Science in Non-Western Countries." *Studies of Science* 21:527–545.

Skocpol, Theda. 1985. "Bringing the State Back In." Pp. 3–37 in *Bringing the State Back In*, edited by Peter B. Evans, Dietrich Rueschemeyer, and Theda Skocpol. Cambridge: Cambridge University Press.

Smelser, Neil, with Bertrand Badie and Pierre Birnbaum. 1994. "The Sociology of the State Revisited." Pp. 59–75 in *Sociology*, edited by Neil Smelser. Oxford: Blackwell.

Soysal, Yasemin Nahoglu. 1994. *The Limits of Citizenship.* Chicago: University of Chicago Press.

———. 1998. "Identity and Transnationalizaton in German School Textbooks." *Bulletin of Concerned Asian Scholars* 30:53–61.

Stinchcombe, Arthur. 1968. *Constructing Social Theories.* New York: Harcourt, Brace, and World.

Stone Sweet, Alec, Wayne Sandholtz, and Neil Fligstein, eds. Forthcoming. *The Institutionalization of Europe.* Oxford: Oxford University Press.

Strang, David. 1990. "From Dependency to Sovereignty: An Event History Analysis of Decolonization, 1870–1987." *American Sociological Review* 55: 846–860.

———. 1994. "Institutional Accounts as a Form of Structural Analysis." *Current Perspectives in Social Theory* 1994, Supplement 1:151–174.

Strang, David, and Patricia Chang. 1993. "The International Labor Organization and the Welfare State: Institutional Effects on National Welfare Spending, 1960–1980." *International Organization* 47: 235–262.

Strang, David, and John W. Meyer. 1993. "Institutional Conditions for Diffusion." *Theory and Society* 22: 487–511.

Sutton, John, Frank Dobbin, John Meyer, and W. Richard Scott. 1994. "Legalization of the Workplace." *American Journal of Sociology* 99:944–971.

Swanson, Guy. 1967. *Religion and Regime.* Ann Arbor: University of Michigan Press.

———. 1971. "An Organizational Analysis of Collectivities." *American Sociological Review* 36:607–624.

Thomas, George M., and John W. Meyer. 1984. "The Expansion of the State." *Annual Review of Sociology* 10:461–482.

Thomas, George M., John W. Meyer, Francisco O. Ramirez, and John Boli. 1987. *Institutional Structure: Constituting the State, Society, and the Individual.* Newbury Park, CA: Sage.

Tilly, Charles. 1984. *Big Structures, Large Processes, Huge Comparisons.* New York: Russell Sage.

———. 1992. *Coercion, Capital, and European States.* Cambridge: Basil Blackwell.

———. 1997. *Roads from Past to Future.* Lanham, MD: Rowman & Littlefield.

———. 1999. "Epilogue: Now Where?" Pp. 407–419 in *State/Culture,* edited by George Steinmetz. Ithaca, NY: Cornell University Press.

———, ed. 1975. *The Formation of National States in Western Europe.* Princeton, NJ: Princeton University Press.

Ventresca, Marc. 1995. "Counting People When People Count: Global Establishment of the Modern Population Census, 1820–1980." Ph.D. dissertation, Stanford University, Department of Sociology.

Wallerstein, Immanuel. 1974. *The Modern World-System.* Vol I: *Capitalist Agriculture and the Origins of the European World Economy.* New York: Academic Press.

———. 1991. *Geopolitics and Geoculture: Essays on the Changing World System.* Cambridge: Cambridge University Press.

Zelditch, Morris Jr. 1984. "Meaning, Conformity, and Control." *Journal of Mathematical Sociology* 10:83–90.

Zelditch, Morris Jr., and Henry A. Walker. 1984. "Legitimacy and the Stability of Authority." Pp 1–27 in *Advances in Group Processes: Theory and Research,* vol. 1, edited by E. Lawler. Greenwich, CT: JAI.

Zucker, Lynne G. 1977. "The Role of Institutionalization in Cultural Persistence." *American Sociological Review* 42:726–743.

———. 1983. "Organizations as Institutions." Pp. 1–47 in *Research in the Sociology of Organizations,* vol. 2, edited by S. Bacharach. Greenwich, CT: JAI.

———. 1987. "Institutional Theories of Organization." *Annual Review of Sociology* 13:443–464.

———. 1989. "Combining Institutional Theory and Population Ecology: No Legitimacy, No History" (comment on Carroll-Hannan, 1989). *American Sociological Review* 53:542–545.

———. 1991. "The Role of Institutionalization in Cultural Persistence: Postscript." Pp. 103–106 in *The New Institutionalism in Organizational Analysis,* edited by W. W. Powell and P. J. DiMaggio. Chicago: University of Chicago Press.

10

The Selectorate Model: A Theory of Political Institutions

Bruce Bueno de Mesquita, James D. Morrow, Randolph Siverson, and Alastair Smith

We endeavor here to summarize the main theoretical and empirical features of our collective research program. That research program is designed to address fundamental questions about politics, especially related to how political institutions shape the incentives leaders have to enhance or diminish public welfare. In the research discussed here, as well as in prior research programs pursued by us as individual researchers, we strive to embed the analysis we do within the constraints imposed by the scientific method. That method, of course, requires a logically coherent explanation for presumed causal links among explicitly specified variables and assumptions. It also requires independent evidence as the means to evaluate the reliability of the explanatory or causal claims that are made. Within the very broad strictures of the scientific method, we focus on the use of game theory as a tool around which to construct testable theories of social behavior. Before turning to an examination of our collective research, therefore, we take a moment to discuss the fundamental assumptions of game theory and to review why we believe it is an especially advantageous tool from which to construct theories of social behavior.

A GAME THEORETIC RESEARCH PROGRAM: INTERNATIONAL CONFLICT

Game theory is a powerful analytic tool for studying the problems associated with international or interpersonal conflict and policy formation, the subjects of our earlier research. Its power derives from the fact that it requires transparent logic and it focuses attention squarely on patterns of strategic interaction. That is, game theory concerns individual or collective choices that are made in a contingent environment. One of the central contingencies is the expectations each decision maker or chooser has about how others will respond to alternative actions that could be taken. Actions are chosen and strategies formed by each player with an eye to doing that which the player believes will maximize her or his welfare in the situation the game models. So, players are rational in the limited, instrumental sense that they are trying to do what they believe is in their best interest. Because of uncertainty about the intentions of others or about their own welfare at the end of the game, players can end up making choices that turn out badly for them, but their ex ante decisions always are based on what they believe is their best response to the expected actions of others. The players do what they think will be best for them, given what they know and believe at the time they must make a decision. Game theory allows no hindsight to enter into analysis, while it strongly emphasizes counterfactual reasoning about alternative states of the environment.

A game consists of a set of players, choices (actions), information, and outcomes. A strategy is a complete plan of action for every contingency (i.e., combination of choices) that can arise in the game. Information surrounds the preferences each player has for each possible outcome of the game and knowledge of the history of play up to the point at which a given choice is being made. Players can be uncertain about payoffs (costs and benefits) to others or to themselves. They can also be uncertain about the choices players made in prior stages of the game so that they do not know the complete history of play up to the moment of their current choice. Players can hold beliefs about prior actions and can learn by observing behavior and evaluating its logical consistency with their beliefs about the actions or preferences of other players. Such learning generally is done in accord with Bayes's Rule that tests the consistency between beliefs and actions by evaluating the probability of observing particular actions conditional on prior beliefs. Thus, game theory provides a parsimonious set of tools for evaluating strategic interaction among competing or cooperating decision makers (Morrow 1994).

Game theory provides several advantages in the investigation of politics and especially international affairs. First, game theory is a body of reasoning designed explicitly to attend to the logic of strategic interaction. It is difficult to imagine constructing any falsifiable, explanatory theory of international relations without thinking explicitly about the interdependencies between events and individual choices. Non–game theoretic points of view often assume away or greatly simplify the most interesting features of strategic interaction or rely on knowledge of how things turned out to construct a rationale for why people behaved in a particular way. Of course, constructing a rationale after learning the outcome uses information people in the situation could not possibly have had available to them when they made their choices. Thus, such methods greatly diminish and perhaps preclude the possibility of reliable prediction and overlook the complex patterns suggested by strategic maneuvering. Game theory models, by contrast, embrace the idea of strategic maneuvering and, as noted earlier, do not rely on knowledge of how things turned out to construct explanations of actions. In that sense, game theory seems like an approach particularly well suited for studying social behavior.

Second, game theory provides tools for dealing with many of the concerns and assumptions of structural, behavioral, and psychological theories and so can help integrate the important knowledge derived from these other approaches. Structure is a central element in games of sequential decision making in which choices are constrained by the situation decision makers find themselves in. Through a strategic analysis of the prior history of play, preferences, and beliefs, game theory provides a means to examine attitudes, perceptions, uncertainties, and learning on the part of decision makers. At the same time, game theory provides a systematic means of analyzing and predicting behavior across large classes of events whether they involve sincere behavior, bluffing, or other forms of strategic decision making. These are all crucial elements in the study of international affairs and, indeed, virtually all social situations. Other approaches may take these features into account, but game theory is the only method that explicitly requires attentiveness to all of these concerns. Having said that, we should keep in mind that there is not a single game theory of politics or of international relations. Rather, game theory is a mathematical foundation from which to construct different, even competing theories. As such, game theory is an axiomatically based theory of decision making that insures that certain crucial factors, including the ones just enumerated, are taken into account.

A third reason for focusing on game theoretic approaches to international relations is that they have enjoyed particular success in the area of prediction. As John Gaddis (1992) noted, structural, behavioral, and psychological perspectives failed to yield clear, specific, and detailed predictions of important events. Regrettably, he did not review the accomplishments or predictions based on rational choice theories, including game theory models (Ray and Russett 1996). These models, as he has now agreed, have a significant track record of success in forecasting accurately complex social interactions in situations as diverse as decisions about war and peace, decisions about domestic policies, and so forth (Bueno de Mesquita 2002, 1993).

Game theorists accept the relevance and importance of cultural, temporal and contextual considerations as means to understand past or future events (Bates et al. 1998; Rabushka and Shepsle 1972; Bueno de Mesquita 1981). They strive to embed such factors within logically transparent and consistent theoretical constructs in which these factors serve as variables. In that way, game theory facilitates the incorporation of seemingly idiosyncratic factors that often form the focus of other research programs.

For the social scientist the events of history are a laboratory against which to test their claims about how variables are associated with each other; to test their theoretical propositions about causation. As such, the social scientist's task is not so much to explain particular events, but to identify relations among critical variables that explain classes of events or phenomena. Game theory provides an explanation that often can be tested against actual behavior and so is susceptible to falsification. As it derives hypotheses from first principles rather than from known patterns in the data, it more readily lends itself to empirical tests where the hypotheses are independent of the evidence used to evaluate them. In fact, we emphasize four aspects of the study of politics and social interaction from a game-theoretic perspective. These four aspects include (1) endogenous, strategically made choices and their implications for path interdependence; (2) selection effects in theory and in data and how they can distort inferences in empirical analysis; (3) the importance of independence between arguments and the evidence used to evaluate their merits if we are to distinguish between description, explanation and prediction; and (4) prediction as a means of evaluating the potential of scientific inquiry to help improve future international affairs. These four items: endogeneity, selection effects, independence between argument and evidence, and prediction represent areas where game theoretic inquiries have proven to be helpful in clarifying problems that frequently arise in other modes of analysis. These four areas provide organizing principles behind the research program reviewed here (Bueno de Mesquita 1996, 2000).

THE SELECTORATE PROJECT

We are concerned with how political institutions shape the incentives under which leaders function. Civic-minded leaders can be turned to emphasizing venality and greed if they operate under certain political arrangements. Similarly, even the most corrupt individuals can be found acting like paragons of civic virtue if the institutions under which they function reward civic-mindedness and punish corruption, cronyism, and kleptocracy. Leopold II, king of Belgium from 1865 to 1909 and personal owner and ruler of the Congo Free State from 1880 to 1908, illustrates this claim. In Belgium he was a progressive, powerful constitutional monarch who promoted the right of workers to strike, laws protecting women and children, universal adult male suffrage, improved education, free trade, and so forth. In the Congo, he promoted the murder and maiming of workers (and children) who failed to meet their rubber quota, stole the country's wealth and did little, if anything, to promote education, representative government, or any other measure designed to improve public welfare. Leopold merely illustrates the power of political institutions. The puzzle is how and why institutions shape incentives.

Starting early in the 1990s, we have been developing a theory of how institutions influence political incentives. The earliest work in this project, by Bruce Bueno de Mesquita and Randolph Siverson (1992 [with Woller], 1995b, 1997), focused on the consequences for leadership survival in office of fighting and winning or losing wars. That research was motivated by the observation that studies of the causes of war rarely examined the consequences of war.[1]

Yet, many explanations of the causes of war relate to the pursuit of specific political goals without assessing whether war helped leaders achieve those goals. In the course of the early efforts in this project, we uncovered a new theoretical explanation for the disproportionate propensity for democracies to win the wars in which they become embroiled. Whereas earlier accounts attributed this known empirical regularity to better organization, more efficient decision-making, or greater popular support for war efforts in democracies, Bueno de Mesquita and Siverson concluded that the cause of the regularity was a selection effect. Specifically, they concluded that democracies, because of their institutional makeup, would only fight in wars they were confident of winning. The reason was straightforward. Democratic leaders are much more likely to be deposed following military defeat than are autocratic leaders. Subsequent empirical research on virtually all wars since 1815 strongly supports the theoretical conclusion (Reiter and Stam 1998). Our early research in this project also uncovered other empirical regularities regarding international conflict and war outcomes, including, most notably, the greater propensity for democratic victors rather than autocratic victors to remove foreign adversaries from office, imposing leaders more to their liking. The early studies found that war helped achieve certain objectives (such as removing troublesome adversaries), but that it did so as a function of the type of regime involved on each side.

The theoretical implications of the earliest studies in this project led Bueno de Mesquita and Siverson to pursue a more general account of leadership incentives and their relationship to domestic political institutions. They realized that their theoretical results did not depend specifically on assumptions tied to international relations, but rather depended on a theory of policy choices tied to the assumption that leaders are motivated by their own interests rather than the welfare of the society they lead. With the addition of James Morrow and Alastair Smith to the project, the team was complete and prepared to venture on an effort to construct a general, albeit preliminary and greatly simplified, theory of politics. The team of Bueno de Mesquita, James D. Morrow, Randolph M. Siverson, and Alastair Smith quickly came to be known within the political science community as BdM2S2, the shorthand that will be used throughout the rest of this chapter. Whereas the earliest studies in the project focused exclusively on international conflict (Bueno de Mesquita and Siverson 1992, 1995a and b, 1997; BdM2S2 1999a, 2001), subsequent theoretical and empirical developments broadened the horizons to examine domestic politics as well as foreign policy (BdM2S2 1999b, 2002, 2003; Bueno de Mesquita 2000). The theory was expanded to account for the allocation of public and private goods to the society as a whole and to critical individual backers of the incumbent.

Our effort is designed with two primary objectives in mind. First, we want to establish hypothetical links between variables based on an explicit, axiomatic mathematical structure. Second, we want to establish whether the record of history is consistent with our logically derived deductions. We believe these two prongs—explicit, formal theorizing and rigorous statistical testing on a large and diverse data set—are essential elements of progress in any science. That is not to say that inductive methods do not lead to progress, for surely they do. Nor is it to suggest that individual case histories do not contribute to progress.

Rather, it is to say that whether one begins inductively or deductively, confidence in the causality of an argument is advanced by establishing a logical, deductive structure that provides an explanation for observed empirical regularities, while suggesting novel hypotheses.

Formal models, like hunches, statistical patterns, case histories, or any other foundation for hypotheses, are inevitably based on empirically informed assumptions, but the implications of the combination of those assumptions often lead to theoretical surprises. We believe that is true of the theory proposed below. Said differently, deductive models provide a basis for making predictions that are independent of the data used to test them. Purely statistically derived models or case studies tend to describe the data, without then having a separate, independent database with which to test the previously described regularities. As the account of the data or case history in inductive research usually is drawn from the data, the account is not an explanation of any reputed regularities. Formal models derive regularities from logic rather than from data, thereby weakening the link between test data and hypothesis formation. The logic provides an explanation, while the data analysis affords a genuine test of the theory's explanation in light of the empirical record.

Rigorous statistical tests establish that the deduced relationships among variables are or are not consistent with the broad patterns of history. Individual case histories can highlight subtle details of theoretical expectations and can help illustrate how a theory works, but alone they are rarely sufficient to establish the credibility or falsity of a theory in the social sciences. The reason for this is straightforward. Social science theory generally is probabilistic rather than deterministic. When probabilistic predictions are made (as when, for instance, there are multiple equilibria), then historical tests need to be evaluated against the predicted statistical distribution of outcomes. A single case is insufficient to evaluate the distribution of relationships among variables and, of course, it is the relations among variables that test a theory's reliability. If a strong association exists that supports or refutes the predicted relations among variables, still seeming counterexamples will exist. One or even a few case studies can mislead the analyst with regard to the strength of association. After all, if a correlation of zero exists between the independent variables and the dependent variable, then about half the cases will show a positive association and half, a negative association. Only a large number of test cases can reveal the general strength, or weakness, of association between a theory's nondeterministic predictions and outcomes.

THE MODEL

Every political system depends in part on two institutions. One is the size of what we call the selectorate and the other is the subgroup of the selectorate who form the winning coalition that keeps the incumbent in power. The selectorate is the set of citizens who have a prospect of becoming members of an incumbent's winning coalition. In a universal adult suffrage political system, such as prevails in most democracies (and in some rigged-election autocracies), any citizen has some chance of rising to political influence. In monarchies, military juntas, and many autocracies, by contrast, only a small portion of the population has any chance to become influential in politics or to gain access to the benefits that involvement in politics can bring.

The winning coalition is made up of a portion of the selectorate. The winning coalition has two special qualities. First, its support is essential for the incumbent to stay in office. If members of the winning coalition defect to a rival and new members cannot quickly be added to replace them, then the incumbent is deposed and the rival comes to power. Second, members of the winning coalition are accorded a privilege not available to those outside this group. Specifically, they share in any of the private benefits that the leadership distributes. Keeping the loyalty of the winning coalition is crucial for any political leader. Whether it is best to do so by giving them special private privileges (private goods in the vocabulary of economics) or by producing public policies intended to raise the welfare of the whole society depends on the size of the selectorate and the size of the winning coalition.

Governments raise resources through taxation. These resources then are allocated by the political leadership in a way designed to help them stay in office by retaining support from the members of the winning coalition. Leaders can invest resources in the production of public goods or they can invest resources in providing private benefits for their supporters, or in any mix of the two. Public goods are enjoyed by all members of society, whether they belong to the winning coalition, the selectorate, or they are disenfranchised residents with membership in neither group. Government-provided private goods are enjoyed only by members of the winning coalition. We can think of the allocation decision between public and private goods as reflecting either a shopping basket of some mix of goods of each type or as a basket of mixed goods, with different degrees of emphasis on the private or public elements of each good that was chosen.

The incumbent leader decides how much public policy to purchase and how many private goods to generate given the available resources. This decision is made with an eye toward staying in office. Members of the current winning coalition continue to support the incumbent leader provided the benefits they receive outweigh those they expect to receive if a challenger replaces the incumbent. That expectation depends, in part, on how much the challenger can credibly offer. Of course, this is limited by the available budget of resources, which is no larger for the challenger than it is for the incumbent. However, it also depends on how readily a member of the winning coalition can believe that he will be essential to a new government and so continue to get private benefits if he defects. This risk of exclusion from benefits is closely linked to the size of the selectorate and the size of the winning coalition, as well as any idiosyncratic affinity an individual feels for the incumbent.

When the selectorate is made up of a large number of people, then the pool from which to draw supporters is big and so any individual's chance of being essential is smaller than when the selectorate is small. By contrast, when the required winning coalition is large, as in an electoral democracy, then many supporters are needed and so each individual's chances of getting access to the winning coalition is better than if that coalition needed only to be small. For example, in majoritarian democracies, the selectorate is very large and the winning coalition equals about half of the people in the selectorate (suitably adjusted for voter turnout). In a rigged-election autocracy, the selectorate is typically very large, although unlike in democracy, very few make it into the winning coalition. Thus, an individual from a family without influence, like Stalin, Khrushchev, Brezhnev, or Gorbachev could rise to prominence in the Soviet Union, but only with a minuscule probability. Tens of millions of Chinese citizens are members of the Communist Party, which offers special advantages not available to those not in the Party, but even these tens of millions are a small portion of the 1.3 or 1.4 billion Chinese. As such, the selectorate is still very big relative to the size of the winning coalition needed to keep the incumbents in office. This means that a defector in an autocracy runs a high risk of losing access to the private benefits provided by the leadership. In a democracy, the risk of losing such access is small, equaling about one half.

The allocation of resources that maximizes the incumbent's chances of political survival drives the degree to which she emphasizes good public policy or cronyism and corruption. When the winning coalition is small, a leader only needs the support of a few individuals. Suppose that under these circumstances, the leader decided to allocate the majority of resources into private goods. Since the winning coalition is small, each supporter receives a relatively large proportion of the available resources. By concentrating on private goods, leaders with small winning coalitions can really enhance the welfare of their supporters. However, as the winning coalition increases in size, each member's share of the private goods allocation shrinks because these goods are distributed to a greater number of individuals. This reduces the welfare of members of the winning coalition. As the size of the winning coalition increases, the provision of private goods is no longer an efficient mechanism through which to enrich supporters. Rather than continuing to focus on private goods, as the winning coalition grows, leaders are better able to enrich their supporters by investing a greater proportion of available resources in public goods. Of course, the increased provision of public goods benefits all in the society and not just the members of the winning coalition. The logic is straightforward. When the winning coalition is large, leaders perforce must be more concerned with the provision of public goods, not out of civic-mindedness, but because the provision of such goods is compatible with their desire to stay in office. When the winning coalition is small, the same leaders would be more inclined to provide more private goods and fewer public goods because that is the allocation that would then be compatible with their interest in remaining in power. In this circumstance, a leader who emphasizes good public policy over bribing supporters is likely to lose to a challenger as members of the winning coalition defect to get a better deal. So, large winning coalitions, such as exist in democracy, encourage attention to the quality of public policy. Small winning coalitions, such as typify autocracies, discourage attention to good public policy because such attention raises the risks the incumbent will be turned out of office.

Suppose that one or more members of the current winning coalition defects and the incumbent is removed from office. Because members of the coalition have defected, the challenger now has the opportunity to form a new government. The challenger must draw enough supporters from the selectorate. Since the winning coalition is always smaller than the selectorate, the defectors cannot be certain of making it into the new winning coalition. Many of the defectors may be weeded out, proving to be inessential to forming a new winning coalition. Consequently, there is a risk and a cost associated with political defection. Defection to the camp of the incumbent's political rival involves the chance of exclusion and the cost entails being cut off from a future stream of private goods conditional on being excluded from the successor winning coalition. As the size of the winning coalition becomes smaller, or the size of the selectorate becomes larger, challengers are less likely to use the support of any particular individual when forming their winning coalition. Hence, if either the size of the winning coalition shrinks or the size of the selectorate grows, then defection becomes riskier.

When the selectorate is large and the winning coalition is small then individuals who defect from the current winning coalition are especially unlikely to gain access to private goods in the future as compared to defectors when the coalition is large relative to the selectorate. Consequently, systems, like many autocracies, in which the winning coalition is small and the selectorate is relatively large induce a norm of loyalty toward the incumbent leadership. Large selectorates and small winning coalitions helps keep supporters loyal by making defection from the current winning coalition unattractive. As the size of the winning coalition grows relative to the selectorate, the degree of loyalty to the incumbent declines because the cost and risk of defection declines. This norm of loyalty is a powerful force in autocracy. It insulates leaders from being turned out of office just because they do a poor job on public policy. They are protected as long as they do not "squander" resources on public welfare, keeping those resources to use as bribes to their few essential supporters instead. In democracy, the value of individual private goods is small because they must be divided among so many people and so leaders do not enjoy the same loyalty from their backers. Consequently, they must compete over the provision of successful policies; they do not have a sufficient loyalty advantage through cronyism and corruption. The consequence is that democrats work harder at producing effective policies, enjoy less loyalty, and so get turned out of office more frequently than their autocratic counterparts. For autocrats, bad policy often is good politics because their focus on cronyism and corruption ensures their stable leadership. That is almost never true for democrats.

The model examines the resource allocation of the incumbent, followed by the proposed allocation promised by the incumbent's political rival. Following that promise, the members of the selectorate choose to retain the incumbent or depose her, replacing her with the challenger.

COMPARATIVE STATIC RESULTS

The role of institutions in influencing the action in the game is plain. As the winning coalition (W) increases, public goods make up a larger proportion of policy provisions. As the winning coalition size increases, survival becomes harder for incumbents, who must spend a higher proportion of the available resources in order to meet the incumbency criterion; namely that the expected benefits to the winning coalition from remaining loyal exceed the benefits coalition members can credibly expect to get from switching to the political challenger. The size of the winning coalition affects policy provision on two dimensions. First, the larger W, the weaker the loyalty norm and hence the greater the total quantity of resources expended on policy provision. Second, as W gets larger so does the relative importance of providing public goods compared to private goods.

Selectorate size (S) also influences policy provision. As S increases leaders reduce their expenditures (other than for their own discretionary purposes), although the strength of this relationship depends heavily on the size of the winning coalition. Selectorate size does not influence the relative importance of public or private goods in determining the policy mix that the incumbent provides, but it does help determine the risk of exclusion from future coalitions. The probability of inclusion in the long-term coalition of the challenger is (W/S). So, as S increases each individual's chance of gaining access to future private goods declines. When W is large most rewards are provided via public goods and so exclusion from a future coalition is not too costly. Under this circumstance, an increase in S has only a modest effect on loyalty. When W is small, the majority of rewards are private in nature and the relative difference in welfare between those inside and those outside the coalition is large. In this case, exclusion from future coalitions is extremely costly and, therefore, increasing S sharply increases loyalty, allowing leaders to skim off more resources for their own discretionary use.

The size of the available pool of resources and the relative patience of the citizens, that is the degree to which they discount future benefits as compared to current benefits, also influences the effort level of the incumbent. The more resources that are available, the greater the challenger's best credible offer and, therefore, the more the incumbent must offer to retain incumbency. Consequently, when the resource pool is larger, so is the total expenditure on the optimal mix of private and public goods. This finding, that rich societies enjoy higher levels of policy provision than poor societies, is unsurprising. More surprising is the result that the more patient citizens are, the lower the level of policy provisions they receive. This result is best explained by reference to the incumbency criterion; that is, the logical rule that assures the incumbent of reselection as detailed in Bueno de Mesquita, Morrow, Siverson, and Smith (2002) and Bueno de Mesquita, Smith, Siverson, and Morrow (2003).

In equilibrium, the incumbent spends m resources on the coalition in each period. In making his best credible bid for power, the challenger offers to spend everything in the first period. Of course in subsequent periods, having learned the affinity selectors have for him and so having settled on a coalition of backers who are relatively loyal, the challenger behaves as the current incumbent does, spending m resources on a coalition of size W. As we have noted, the larger W is, the larger m must be and the less that is left over for the leader's personal use or to help save the leader's incumbency on a rainy day.[2] In that regard, m provides a measure of the difficulty of surviving in office. The higher m must be to stay in office, the lower the leader's welfare.

When individuals choose between leaders, they are uncertain as to whether they will be included in the challenger's long-term coalition. Effectively this means the challenger can only promise private goods probabilistically while the incumbent promises them with certainty to her current coalition. With regard to future payoffs, the incumbent can promise more than the challenger because the incumbent's coalition is made up of individuals with relatively strong affinity for the incumbent. If the challenger succeeds in toppling the incumbent, the challenger's transition coalition, made up in part of defectors, is well compensated. But, in the post-transition stage of the selectorate theory's game, and over time in reality, the former challenger and selectorate members learn their affinity for the challenger. Naturally, the challenger then drops coalition members who do not have high affinity and replaces them with individuals whose affinity makes them more likely to be loyal, mimicking the loyalty characteristics of the previous incumbent (though with different individuals). The discount factor weights the importance of future, post-transition payoffs relative to payoffs today. When citizens are patient, the incumbent's inherent advantage in providing future private goods weighs heavily in a current supporter's calculations. This means that in the current period the incumbent can offer only a low level of reward relative to what the challenger is currently offering and still look like the more attractive leader. When citizens are impatient, heavily discounting future rewards compared to current ones, incumbents must spend more to survive in office. In this circumstance, the incumbent's inherent advantage in providing private goods in the future is worth less relative to rewards in the current period. As a result, the incumbent must spend more resources in order to match the challenger's offer. This deduction stands in contrast to much of the literature on cooperation and regimes (Axelrod 1984; Axelrod and Keohane 1986. For a result related to ours, though in a different context and from a different model, see Powell 1999). If our theory is correct, patience is not a (social) virtue.

The results above address how institutions affect policy provision. We now consider what is implied about the welfare of members of the winning coalition.

In equilibrium, the incumbent can always spend enough to retain office.[3] To do so, she must take into account how institutions influence the equilibrium level of expenditure, m, required for her political survival. Members of the winning coalition receive both public and private goods. In equilibrium, their level of welfare is the value of these goods.

How do changes in W affect the winning coalition's level of benefits? We start by considering W. Of course, no members of the winning coalition want institutional changes that remove them personally from the winning coalition. Having said that, conditional on remaining a member of the winning coalition, it is possible for the membership to prefer to expand or to contract the size of the coalition. Whether altering the size of the winning coalition through institutional change increases or decreases the payoffs to the members depends upon the initial conditions.[4] First, the increase in W means that each member's share of rewards is diluted since the overall number of people who receive rewards has increased. This effect reduces welfare. Second, the increase in W reduces the loyalty norm and therefore forces leaders to spend more resources on keeping their coalition loyal. Such an increase in expenditures improves the welfare of members of the winning coalition. Which of these two effects dominates depends upon the specific conditions. Figure 10.1 shows a plot of the winning coalition's welfare, as a function of the coalition's size. The pattern it illustrates is indicative of the incentives held by members of the winning coalition. When

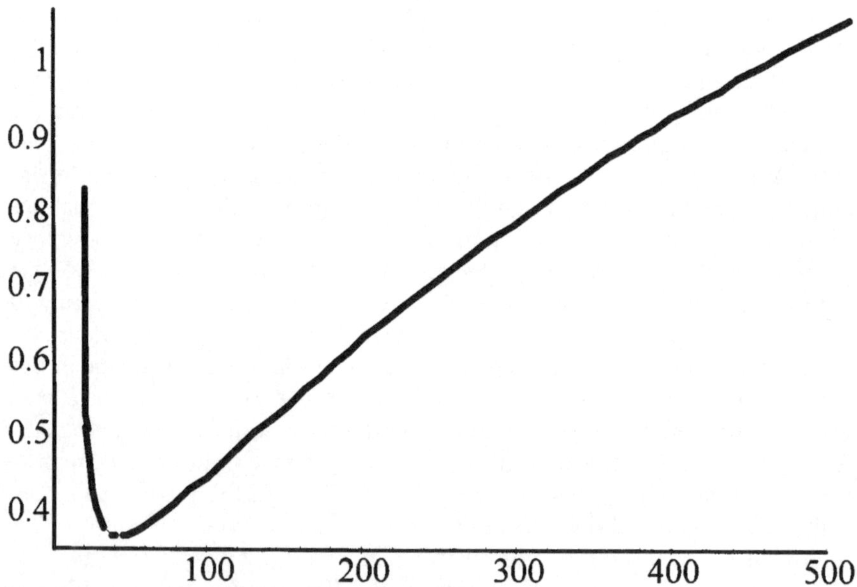

Figure 10.1. Coalition Welfare: Theoretical Expectations

W is small, increases in coalition size diminish the rewards received by members of the winning coalition. Beyond a turning point, as seen in figure 10.1, further increases in W improve the welfare of members of the winning coalition, although at a diminishing marginal rate. This happens because the increases in W from this point forward improve the odds of being in a successor coalition faster than they decrease the value of private goods. As the probability of being in a successor coalition improves, the loyalty norm is weakened and so the incumbent must try harder, spending more to satisfy her supporters.

In contrast to coalition members, the incumbent never wants to expand the size of the winning coalition. Given their druthers, leaders, like Leopold II in the Congo, prefer arrangements that strengthen the loyalty norm, diminish how much they must spend on their backers, and maximize the resources available for their own discretionary use. A small coalition with a large selectorate is the preferred institutional arrangement from an incumbent's point of view. Therefore, incumbents, when they can, seek to purge people from the winning coalition and seek to establish rigged electoral systems with universal suffrage.

Those in the selectorate, but not in the winning coalition, and those who are disenfranchised always prefer to expand the coalition and, to the extent possible (since W≤S), shrink the selectorate. This is so because systems with large coalitions emphasize public goods. These are the only benefits from government that those not in the winning coalition can hope to receive. Perhaps this is why populations migrate disproportionately from autocracies to democracies.

EMPIRICAL EXPECTATIONS

We touched on several implications of our model as we developed our argument. Here we pull some of the implications together. In particular we address the questions of leadership tenure, peace, and prosperity. Elsewhere, we explore in much greater depth the degree to which thousands of leaders have or have not complied with the empirical implications of the theory (BdM2S2 2003).

Our model indicates that compared to democrats (i.e., leaders with large winning coalitions), it is easier for autocrats (leaders with small winning coalitions) to survive in office. It also indicates that those with the worst tenure prospects—leaders with large winning coalitions—have the strongest incentive to distribute public goods rather than private goods. They need not be civic-minded to do what is best for the citizens. Enhancing the peace and prosperity of the citizenry certainly falls within the domain of public goods provision, exactly what they must do to maximize their chance of staying in office. By contrast, leaders with the best tenure prospects rely on small coalitions drawn from a large selectorate. Such political arrangements provide incentives to reward backers disproportionately with private goods rather than public goods. Providing peace and prosperity is fine, but if it comes at the expense of retaining sufficient rewards for the coalition members, the leader will be turned out of office. Therefore, leaders in such systems pay less attention to promoting peace and general prosperity and more attention to cronyism and corruption as means to benefit their core constituents. Finally, the welfare of coalition members; that is, per capita expenditures on them, are expected to be distributed like the swish of the Nike symbol when compared to the size of the coalition. We turn to statistical tests of each of these claims. More extensive tests of these and many other propositions that follow from the selectorate theory can be found elsewhere (BdM2S2 1999a, 1999b, 2001, 2003; Bueno de Mesquita 2000a). Figure 10.2 provides a schematic summary of the main empirical expectations. The logical proof for each of these expectations is to be found in Bueno de Mesquita et al. (2002) and Bueno de Mesquita et al. (2003).

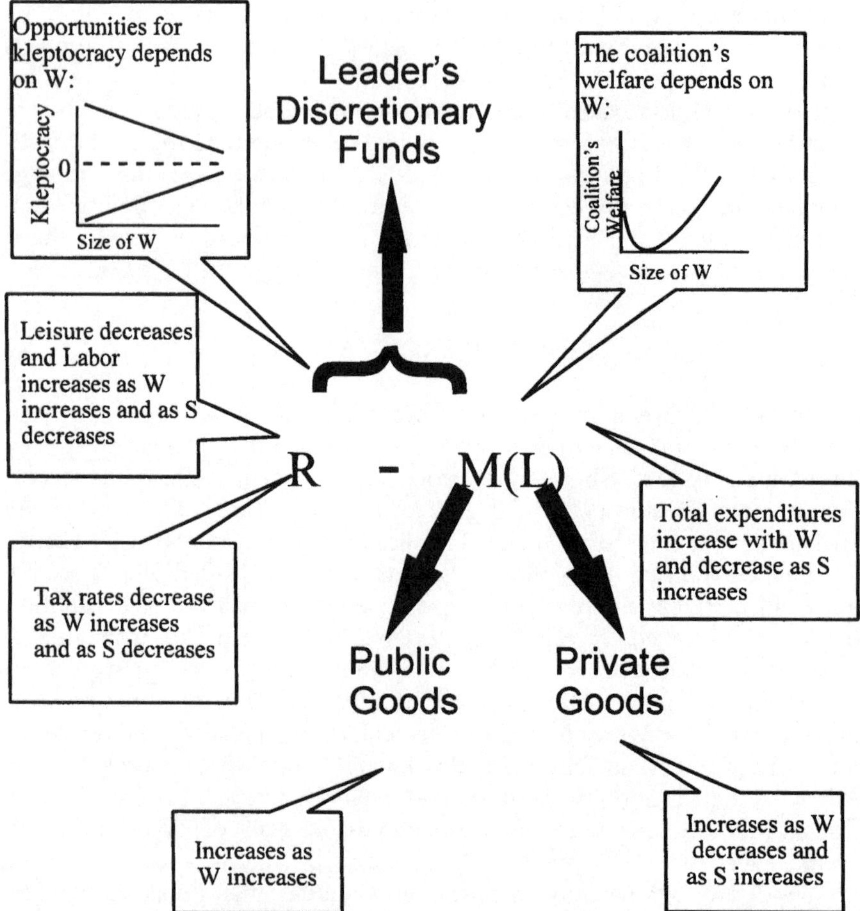

Figure 10.2. Schematic Representation of Theoretical Expectations

Measurement Issues

Reducing any political system to its winning coalition and selectorate obviously oversimplifies reality. Politics is more complex and more nuanced than such a reduction implies. We are well aware of these complexities and make no suggestion that these factors alone explain the major features of governance. However, we think it unlikely that anyone will successfully build a general theory of politics by starting with an all-inclusive model, gradually whittling down the number of variables that need to be addressed. We, in any event, prefer to start with a fairly simple, skeletal view of politics and build up toward greater inclusiveness and complexity as required to account for important phenomena. Therefore, our purpose here is not to maximize the variance explained for any dependent variable, but rather to assess the extent to which the selectorate model contributes meaningfully to a general understanding of the quality of governance and the tenure of leaders. We examine the performance of leaders in providing peace and prosperity as a function of coalition size and then evaluate how these relate to tenure in office.

The unit of analysis in our data set is a leader-year. The data are organized around 2,700 individual leaders of 172 different countries, spanning the years 1763–1992. Although we have data on at least some variables for 16,935 observations, we are plagued with substantial amounts of missing data. For some variables examined here, our data only extend back to 1950 and for no variable do we have data more current than 1992. For still other variables, the data go back only to 1961.

W, W/S

Measurement of selectorate size and winning coalition size is in its infancy. This means that the approximations we propose are crude and primitive. They should be adequate to evaluate whether the central tendencies of politics are aligned with the expectations that follow from the selectorate model, but they certainly are no more than a starting point.

The Polity II data (Gurr 1990) and subsequent updates by Monty G. Marshall and Keith Jaggers (for the most current data and codebook see www.bsos.umd.edu/cidcm/polity/) include a number of institutional variables, four of which provide a reasonable basis for constructing an index of the size of W. A fifth variable, Legislative Selection (LEGSELEC), appears to be an appropriate indicator of S. We discuss the latter first.

LEGSELEC measures the breadth of the selectiveness of the members of each country's legislature. In the Polity data, this variable is coded as a trichotomy, with 0 meaning that there is no legislature. A code of 1 means that the legislature is chosen by heredity, ascription, or is simply chosen by the effective executive. A code of 2, the highest category, indicates that members of the legislature are directly or indirectly selected by popular election. It is evident that the larger the value of LEGSELEC, the more likely it is that S is large. We divide by its maxim value of two so that it varies between 0 and 1. This variable is referred to as S. It should also be evident that in reality the size difference between a selectorate with score zero and a selectorate with score 1 is smaller than the size difference between a score of 1 and a score of 2. Unfortunately, we do not yet have a way to estimate the actual magnitude of selectorate size beyond this rough indicator except for a small subsample of our data. When we investigate corruption, we will be able to evaluate the size of the selectorate by also using data on the actual number of people in the selectorate in each of the 67 countries in our cross-sectional, but not time series corruption data set. We currently are developing an additional dataset that focuses on enfranchisement rules as a means to estimate selectorate size.

To estimate the size of W we construct a composite index based on the variables REGTYPE (in Polity II only, Gurr 1990), XRCOMP XROPEN, and PARCOMP in Polity III and subsequent updates. When REGTYPE is not missing data and is not equal to codes 2 or 3 in the Polity data set, so that the regime type was not a military or military/civilian regime, we award one point to W. When XRCOMP, that is, the competitiveness of executive recruitment, is larger than or equal to code 2 then another point is assigned to W. An XRCOMP code of 1 means that the chief executive was selected by heredity or in rigged, unopposed elections. Code values of 2 and 3 refer to greater degrees of responsiveness to supporters, indicating a larger winning coalition. XROPEN, the openness of executive recruitment, contributes an additional point to W if the executive is recruited in a more open setting than heredity (that is, the variable's value is greater than 2). Finally, one more point can be contributed to the index of W if PARCOMP, competitiveness of participation, is coded as a 5, meaning that "there are relatively stable and enduring political groups which regularly compete for political influence at the national level" (Gurr 1990, p. 18). Again we divide by the maximum value, which is 4. The minimum value, then, is 0 and the maximum is 1. And again it is evident that the progression from 0 to 1 to 2, up to 4 is not linear, as the indicator suggests. Alas, we do not yet have adequate means to know how nonlinear it is. One might readily think of our coarse indicators of W and S as logarithms of some exponential function. For now, this is the best that is available over a long time span and a broad cross-section of polities.

A weak loyalty norm is indicated by the value W/S being large. When the loyalty norm is strong so that W/S is small, then private goods production is in a leader's interest according to the selectorate model. When the loyalty norm is weak (W/S is large), public goods are favored over private goods. Therefore, when we test the theory against the production of public and private goods, we examine both the effects of W and W/S. We therefore construct a variable W/S by dividing W by (S+1)/2. We make this transformation of S to avoid division by zero. In this way we preserve observations without altering any results as this construction is, of course, perfectly correlated with a construction that did not transform S, though for a smaller sample size due to division by zero.[5]

Every cross-sectional, time-series analysis we examine includes the interaction of geographic region and year as a set of fixed effects dummy variables. Because there may be spatio-temporal dependence in our data resulting, for instance, from factors that influence fluctuations in economic growth rates or the persistence of peace in particular parts of the world, all of our statistical estimates include fixed effects for each geographic region each year. In this way we recognize that war, drought, the business cycle and a host of other factors have an impact on government performance at different times in different places. We specify six geographic regions. These are: Europe, South and Central America, North America and the Caribbean, Asia, the Middle East, and Africa. We have also tested our theory against alternative regional specifications that are less geographical and more cultural, economic, or political. Of course, since we are interested in political effects, it makes little sense to reduce these factors to fixed effects. In any event, our results are substantively the same across widely used means of specifying regions. We generally do not discuss the fixed effects as they are strictly statistical corrections of no substantive interest regarding the tests of our theory. Their presence, however, makes our tests especially demanding as we have removed any temporal and spatial factors that might be the actual explanation for shifts in the values of our dependent variables. The number of fixed effects variables can be enormous, so success at finding substantively and statistically significant institutional effects provides considerable encouragement for further refinement and testing of the selectorate theory.

Peace, Prosperity, and the Black Market

The selectorate theory draws our attention to the provision of public and private goods, but does not instruct us as to which particular public or private benefits will constitute the bundle of goods offered by any leader. The specific bundle of goods presumably depends on the personal tastes and needs of the winning coalition, selectorate, and leadership. Therefore, elsewhere we test the theory against a broad array of such social, economic, and political public and private goods. Here we focus on three specific goods as dependent variables. Two are quintessential public goods and one is a fundamental indicator of private goods distribution.

One strong indicator that a government provides lots of public goods for its citizenry is the overall wealth of the country's residents. Therefore, the first public good we examine is real gross domestic product per capita. We use the variable labeled as RGDPC from the March 1997 update of the Penn World Tables. This variable is real GDP per capita in constant dollars based on 1985 international prices. We call the variable Prosperity. Observations on this variable cover the years 1950–92 and includes data on 134 countries.

In testing the effects of W on Prosperity, we control for other factors expected to add or detract from per capita GDP. With a one year lag for W and all other independent variables, we assess the effects of average education level of the labor force, openness of the economy to trade, and the exchange rate premium paid above the official exchange rate for converting the local currency into dollars. The data for Education spans the years from 1961 to 1988 and can be found on the Web, along with a definition at www.worldbank.org/html/prdmg/grthweb/ddfische.htm, where it is referred to as bhkavg. The openness to free trade is referred to as Open and is found at the Web site for the Penn World Tables, the address for which is datacentre.chass.utoronto.ca:5680/pwt/docs/subjects.html. The data for this variable cover the period 1950–1992. Open evaluates the receptiveness of each country's economy to trade.

Peace is based on the hostilities data from the Militarized Interstate Disputes data set (see Peace Science Society [International] Web site at pss.la.psu.edu/MID_DATA.HTM to download these data). Each year that a leader is in office without experiencing participation in a violent international dispute (MIDs variable Hostlev1 not equal to 4 or 5) a one is added to whatever her or his previous number of years at peace was. If a violent conflict interrupts a string of peace, the count starts over again with the year of the dispute counted as zero, the next year also as zero if the dispute continued and counted as 1.0 if the country was no longer engaged in a violent international conflict. The year after the score increases to 2.0 if there is no new violent dispute and returns to zero if there is, and so on. Each score is divided by the number of years the leader has been in office up to that time so that Peace measures, each year, the proportion of the incumbent's ruling period to date that represents a series of years of persistent peace. Peace, of course, is a fundamental public good. The tests concerned with the provision of persistent peace examine the effects of W and W/S, both lagged by one year, as well as the lagged effects of Open and Education and the leader's tenure in office to date. Liberal free trade policies are thought to contribute to national peacefulness. One hopes that a more educated populous is keener to find diplomatic solutions to conflict and, thereby avoid war. Tenure allows us to evaluate whether experience is pacifying or exacerbates the threat of violent conflict.

To assess the provision of private goods we examine the black market exchange rate mentioned earlier. The data for this indicator, which we call Black Market, is found on the World Bank Web site mentioned earlier where it is called exchprem. Data for this variable cover the years 1961–1988. In testing the effects of W and W/S, both lagged by one year, we control for the lagged effects of Prosperity and Open because where the average citizen has a higher income, fewer black market opportunities are expected to exist as personal well-being is presumed to be caused by a less private goods-oriented form of wealth distribution. Likewise, open trade markets operate best when payment can be done above board, which means avoiding black market exchange rates.

To assess the welfare of the coalition, we estimate per capita government expenditures, tested against the size of W and W^2. Recall that the expected shape of the functional relationship is asymmetric and nonmonotonic, looking much like the swish of the Nike brand logo. Expenditures per capita is measures as the logarithm of Polity's variable ngex (national government expenditures) divided by population size.

Leadership tenure is measured as the number of year, months, and days an individual was in office. In testing for peace, we also control for the time in office up to the year of observation.

STATISTICAL EVIDENCE

Table 10.1, columns 1–3, shows the regression analysis that evaluates the effects of coalition size on Prosperity. Columns 4–6 substitute the variable W/S for W, while continuing with the same control variables that are found in column 1. Increasing the coalition size from its minimum to its maximum adds over $1,000 to per capita GDP, an effect that is both substantively and statistically of great significance. When the strength of the loyalty norm is substituted for coalition size, prosperity rises a comparable $838. In both cases, the theory is supported. Additionally, we note that societies that greatly reward black marketeering also significantly undercut general prosperity. Free trade and substantial educational attainment help contribute to prosperity.

Table 10.2 reports the results when the dependent variable is Peace. As with the evaluation of prosperity, we see that persistent peace is reinforced by having a large winning coalition or a weak loyalty norm (i.e., W/S is large). The maximum value that the variable Peace can have is 1.0 as it is the proportion of a leader's tenure that to date has enjoyed uninterrupted peace. Shifting from the smallest to the largest winning coalition system increases the odds of continued peace by nearly 17 percent, or 15 percent if we focus on the loyalty norm instead. In either case, the effect is highly significant and of great importance for promoting a less violent international environment. Free trade policies also help promote persistent peace, while, unfortunately, leadership experience and

Table 10.1. Prosperity, Coalition, and Selectorate Size

Variable	*Coefficent*	*Standard Error*	*Probability*	*Coefficent*	*Standard Error*	*Probabilty*
W	1,052	187	.000			
W/S				838	172	.000
Education	354	27	.000	327	26	.000
Open	3.3	1.3	.013	3.3	1.4	.015
Black Market	−694	113	.000	−739	116	.000
Constant	858	153	.000	957	147	.000
Summary	N=1277	150 FE	R^2=.34	N=1100	132 FE	R^2=.32

FE=Fixed Effects

Table 10.2. Peace, Coalition, and Selectorate Size

Variables	*Coefficent*	*Standard Error*	*Probability*	*Coefficent*	*Standard Error*	*Probabilty*
W	0.167	0.036	0.000			
W/S				0.145	0.004	0.000
Education	−0.220	0.004	0.000	−0.027	0.005	0.000
Open	0.002	0.000	0.000	0.002	0.000	0.000
Tenure	−0.015	0.001	0.000	−0.018	0.002	0.000
Constant	0.577	0.028	0.000	0.631	0.030	0.000
Summary	N=1876	150 FE	R^2=.12	N=1577	132 FE	R^2=.15

high educational attainment in the society raise the risks of violent international conflict. Although these are interesting observations, they are not the central concern here. The central concern is the performance of political systems as a function of coalition size. We find, in keeping with the prediction of the selectorate model, that the public good of peace (and prosperity) is increasingly provided when the coalition is large and decreasingly provided when the coalition is small.

Table 10.3 shows the statistical analysis for Black Market. The analysis again strongly supports the expectations from the selectorate model. Leaders who rule with large winning coalitions or a weak loyalty norm apparently pursue policies that make the use of private benefits through the black market difficult to access. Black market premiums over official exchange rates are diminished by about 20 percent in societies with the largest winning coalitions. The effects are highly significant. Prosperity and openness to trade also help diminish the provision of this private good that helps cronies of the leadership but harms the general welfare.

Before turning to leadership tenure, we now assess table 10.4. Here we evaluate whether the deductively derived, unusual and surprising functional relationship between coalition members' welfare and coalition size is borne out. Indeed it is. The curve that best fits the data statistically is a Nike-like swish. W lies between 0 and 1.0. The minimum expenditure per coalition member arises when W=.33, the high point arises at 1.0 for W, with a local maxima when W=0.

Table 10.3. Black Market, Coalition, and Selectorate Size

Variables	*Coefficent*	*Standard Error*	*Probability*	*Coefficent*	*Standard Error*	*Probabilty*
W	−0.197	0.049	0.000			
W/S				−0.129	0.047	0.004
Prosperity	3.00e-05	7.03e-06	0.000	−5.00e-05	8.01e-06	0.000
Open	−0.002	0.000	0.000	−0.002	0.000	0.000
Constant	0.606	0.032	0.000	0.542	0.031	0.000
Summary	N=1547	168 FE	R^2=.04	N=1234	138 FE	R^2=.06

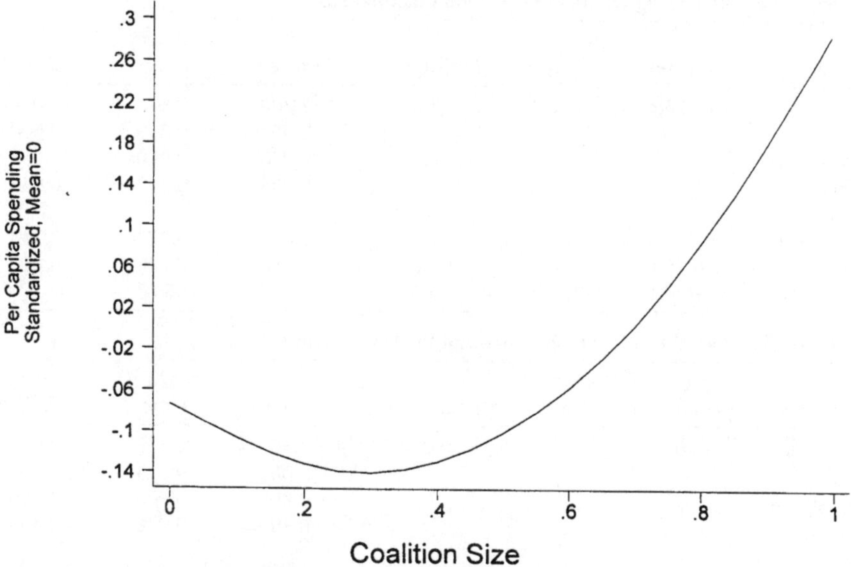

Figure 10.3. Empirical Assessment of Coalition Size and Welfare

Figure 10.3 depicts the empirical relationship. It looks exactly as predicted from our mathematical structure.

We conclude our empirical analysis by examining the relationship between coalition size lagged by one year and the amount of time beyond that point that the leader lasted in office. We repeat this analysis, but adding lagged controls for how long the leader has already been in office, the country's prosperity, peacefulness and black market opportunities. That is, we control for the major public and private goods we previously showed depend on coalition size. The results, reported in tables 10.5a and 10.5b, are quite revealing. We know that large coalitions produce increases in peace and prosperity and decreases in black marketeering. Tables 10.5a and 10.5b shows that, as predicted by the selectorate model, large coalitions also substantially decrease a leader's prospects of remaining in office. Without controls, the largest value for W alone is associated with a diminution of 3.76 years in the time a leader has left in office at any given moment. This result would arise fewer than one time in a thousand samples and is based on nearly 11,000 observations spanning more than a two hundred year period.

Table 10.4. Expenditures per Capita, Coalition Size, and the Nike Swoosh

Variables	*Coefficient*	*Standard Error*	*Probability*
W	−.0008	.0003	.009
W^2	.0012	.0003	.000
Constant	.0009	.0001	.000
Summary	N=4667	576 FE	R^2=.01

Table 10.5a. Remaining Tenure in Office and Coalition Size

Variables	*Coefficent*	*Standard Error*	*Probability*	*Coefficent*	*Standard Error*	*Probabilty*
W	−3.760	0.311	0.000	−2.200	0.536	0.000
Tenure				0.068	0.019	0.000
Prosperity				−0.000	0.000	.052
Peace				−0.028	0.349	0.935
Black Market				0.093	0.273	0.733
Constant	9.160	0.183	0.000	5.480	0.448	0.000
Summary	N=10931	112 FE	R^2=.03	N=1258	168 FE	R^2=.08

Table 10.5b. Remaining Tenure in Office and the Loyalty Norm

Variables	*Coefficent*	*Standard Error*	*Probability*	*Coefficent*	*Standard Error*	*Probabilty*
W/S	–6.08	0.341	0.000	−2.30	0.629	0.000
Tenure				0.085	0.025	0.000
Prosperity				−0.001	0.000	0.000
Peace				0.309	0.456	0.498
Black Market				−0.231	0.418	0.000
Constant	9.530	0.208	0.000	6.720	0.586	0.000
Summary	N=7482	902 FE	R^2=.05	N=957	132 FE	R^2=.10

When we control for other factors, the effect of W remains substantively and statistically extremely strong. Even after controlling for peace, prosperity, black market opportunities and prior tenure, maximizing W decreases a leader's future tenure by 2.2 years. Prior tenure adds to the expected length of incumbency, prosperity diminishes it, and neither peace nor black marketeering have consequential effects. The effects are the same when W/S is substituted for W.

FUTURE DIRECTIONS

Current and future research is pushing the model in new directions. We currently are documenting the empirical evidence that the theory helps account for such diverse factors as economic growth rates, education levels, black market exchange rates, openness to international trade, immigration patterns, quality of health care, tax policy, corruption, kleptocracy, coups d'etat, per capita and gross government expenditures, the decline of monarchy, the rise of democracy, the stability of autocracy, and so forth. We continue to expand the set of dependent variables that the theory helps explain and to expand the generality with which the theory is stated. For instance, we have recently generalized our theory in several directions.

In the earlier formulations of our theory we relied on Cobb-Douglas utility functions. Such functions assume that players prefer a mix of goods (public and private) to receiving all of one type and none of the other. The theory now is generalized so that our proofs hold for all smooth concave utility functions, that is all functions in which utility increases at a decreasing rate. Furthermore, whereas we earlier took tax rates and government revenue as exogenously given, we have recently generalized the theory so that tax rates and government revenues are endogenous, being part of the strategic decision process. We find theoretically and empirically that large coalition systems tend to have low tax rates while small coalition systems tend to have high tax rates that support redistributing income from the poor to the wealthy.

We currently are studying the differences in expected policy choices in systems in which affinity is fairly smoothly and uniformly distributed (as assumed here) and in polities in which affinities are lumpy or correlated along ethnic, religious, or occupational lines (e.g., voting along ethnic lines, by organized groups like trade unions, etc.). We conjecture that lumpy distributions of affinity lead to bloc voting so that such systems appear to have a large coalition requirement, but only require the support of a small set of coalition members who can deliver blocs of votes. It is our conjecture that it is such bloc voting in nineteenth century and some contemporary American cities, in India and elsewhere today, that explains relatively high levels of corruption in some seemingly democratic systems. The extension of our model to situations in which affinities are not uniformly distributed promises to lead to significant new deductions.

Our research is now also focused on expanding our theory to incorporate an explanation of revolutions. Our initial results suggest several intriguing conjectures. We believe that we will prove within the logic of our theory that revolutions always seek to expand the size of the selectorate. We also believe that we will show that the factors that produce emigration are very similar to the factors that produce revolution. In essence, emigration is an exit strategy for those not in the winning coalition when they receive few public goods while revolution or terrorism are internal strategies to give voice to the demand for more public goods. Further, we believe we can explain why some revolutions lead to autocratic, rigged electoral systems (e.g., Castro's Cuba, Marcos's Philippines, Kenyatta's Kenya, Mobutu's Congo), while others produce more democratic forms of governance (the American revolution, Mandela's success in overturning South Africa's apartheid regime, Gandhi's success in winning independence for India, etc.). Finally on the theoretical front, we are now working on applying our theory to differences between proportional representation voting systems, and single-member district systems in a parliamentary setting and in a presidential setting. Our current conjecture is that those three types of democratic polities have different sized winning coalitions. Specifically, we believe proportional representation, list voting systems have the smallest winning coalitions of these three types of democracy while presidential systems have the largest coalitions. This implies higher levels of corruption in proportional representation and parliamentary systems than in presidential systems, as well as other important policy differences. Preliminary evidence supports these expectations.

While striving to expand the range of political phenomena that the theory can explain, we also are looking for ways to improve the estimation of coalition and selectorate size. It is our fervent hope that others will find our results sufficiently intriguing that they will be tempted to assist in developing better estimates of our key independent variables. With improved measures we believe the selectorate theory will also have the prospect of assisting in institutional design in emerging democracies and in underdeveloped economies. If incentives can be correctly modified, changes in behavior can be expected to follow.

CONCLUSION

We presented the essentials of a model that relates political institutions, particularly the size of the selectorate and winning coalition, to the quality of governance and the length of incumbency. We deduced several propositions, five of which were tested here. All were supported by an extensive body of evidence. Perhaps most interestingly, a subtle and surprising functional relationship between coalition size and the welfare of coalition members was deduced, tested, and found to be the shape of the empirical relationship. These results, preliminary though they are, point encouragingly to the ability to explain a broad array of political phenomena from a rigorously deductive theory of institutions and leadership incentives.

NOTES

Bruce Bueno de Mesquita is Silver Professor, NYU, and a senior fellow at the Hoover Institution, Stanford University. James D. Morrow is a professor of political science at the University of Michigan. Randolph M. Siverson is a professor in the Department of Political Science, University of California, Davis. Alastair Smith is an associate professor in the Department of Politics, NYU. The authors would like to thank Marcus Berliant, Ken Judd, Fiona McGillivray, Stephen Morris, Thomas Nechyba, and several anonymous reviewers for their comments and suggestions.

1. Two notable exceptions to this observation are Organski and Kugler 1980 and Starr 1972.

2. That is, the leader retains for her discretionary use whatever leftover resources constitute the difference between the total resources available to the government and the quantity of those resources that must be spent on public and private goods to retain office. In small coalition, large selectorate systems, this difference in available and spent resources is large. It is small in large coalition systems.

3. Of course, if we introduce uncertainty into the model this will not be true. Or interest here, however, is in the comparative static analysis of the allocation of resources and its implications for tenure in office and quality of governance. These are readily addressed theoretically and empirically without complicating the model with uncertainty about the resource pool, etc.

4. An increase in W has two competing effects on the welfare of the winning coalition.
$dv(m^*,W)/dW=(\partial v(m^*,W)/\partial m^*)(\partial m^*/\partial W)+\partial v(m^*,W)/\partial W$.

5. It is worth mentioning how our index W relates to a standard indicator of democracy or autocracy. The Polity data contain ten point indexes of autocracy and of democracy. As is common in the literature, we construct an indicator that equals Democracy-Autocracy. This variable's overall correlation with our indicator W is just above 0.8. This high correlation, however, masks important differences. If we take the Democracy-Autocracy cases at the extremes, for those cases the correlation with W is nearly 1.0. If we look, however, at interior scores, that is, scores for countries that are not fully democratic (e.g., India in the 1970s and 1980s, the United States before the Civil War, Mexico before 2000) or fully autocratic (e.g., Taiwan in the 1950s, 60s, and 70s, the Soviet Union under Gorbachev, Mexico in the nineteenth century), the correlation is only 0.6. In these thousands of interior cases, W appears to discriminate more effectively than standard democracy/autocracy measures. In

fact, about one-quarter to one-third of the relationship we examine are not statistically significant if we focus on democraticness, while virtually all are significant when we focus on coalition size.

REFERENCES

Anderson, Gary M., and Peter J. Boettke. 1993. "Perestroika and Public Choice: The Economics of Autocratic Succession in a Rent-Seeking Society." *Public Choice* 75:101–18.

Axelrod, Robert. 1984. *The Evolution of Cooperation.* New York: Harper Collins.

Axelrod, Robert, and Robert O. Keohane. 1986. "Achieving Cooperation under Anarchy: Strategies and Institutions." In *Cooperation under Anarchy,* edited by Kenneth A. Oye. Princeton, NJ: Princeton University Press.

Baron, David. 1998. "Comparative Dynamics of Parliamentary Government." *American Political Science Review* 92:593–610.

Bates, Robert, Avner Greif, Margaret Levi, Jean-Laurent Rosenthal, and Barry Weingast. 1998. *Analytic Narratives.* Princeton, NJ: Princeton University Press.

Besley, Timothy, and Stephen Coate. 1997. "An Economic Model of Representative Democracy." *Quarterly Journal of Economics* 112:85–112.

Bueno de Mesquita, Bruce. 1981. *The War Trap.* New Haven, CT: Yale University Press.

———. 1993. "The Game of Conflict Interactions: A Research Program." In *Theoretical Research Programs: Studies in Growth of Theories of Group Process,* edited by Joseph Berger and Morris Zelditch, pp. 139–171. Stanford, CA: Stanford University Press.

———. 1996. "The Benefits of a Social-Scientific Approach to Studying International Affairs." In *Explaining International Affairs since 1945,* edited by Ngaire Woods, pp. 49–76. Oxford: Oxford University Press.

———. 2000. "Political Instability as a Source of Growth." Hoover Essays in Public Policy, No. 99.

———. 2001. "Political Survival and International Conflict." In *War in a Changing World,* edited by Zeev Maoz. Ann Arbor: University of Michigan Press.

———. 2002. "Foreign Policy Futures." Hoover Institution.

Bueno de Mesquita, Bruce, James D. Morrow, Randolph M. Siverson, and Alastair Smith. 1999a. "An Institutional Explanation of the Democratic Peace." *American Political Science Review* 93:791–807.

______. 1999b. "Policy Failure and Political Survival: The Contribution of Political Institutions." *Journal of Conflict Resolution,* 43:147–161.

______. 2001. "Political Institutions, Political Survival, and Policy Success." In *Governing for Prosperity,* edited by Bruce Bueno de Mesquita and Hilton Root, pp. 59–84. New Haven, CT: Yale University Press.

———. 2002. "Political Institutions, Policy Choice and the Survival of Leaders." *British Journal of Political Science* (forthcoming).

Bueno de Mesquita, Bruce, and Randolph M. Siverson. 1995a. "Nasty or Nice? Political Systems, Endogenous Norms, and the Treatment of Adversaries." *Journal of Conflict Resolution* 41:175–199.

———. 1995b. "War and the Survival of Political Leaders: A Comparative Study of Regime Types and Political Accountability." *American Political Science Review* (December).

———. 1997. "Nasty or Nice? Political Systems, Endogenous Norms, and the Treatment of Adversaries." *Journal of Conflict Resolution* 41:1 (February):175–199.

Bueno de Mesquita, Bruce, Randolph M. Siverson, and Gary Woller. 1992. "War and the Fate of Regimes: A Cross-National Analysis." *American Political Science Review* (September):638–646.

Bueno de Mesquita, Bruce, Alastair Smith, Randolph M. Siverson, and James D. Morrow. 2003. *The Logic of Political Survival.* Cambridge, MA: MIT Press.

Bueno de Mesquita, Ethan. 2000. "Coalitions, Strategic Voting, and Non-Policy Voting: The Political Causes of Electoral Reform in Israel." *Comparative Politics.*

Campos, Jose Edgardo, and Hilton Root. 1996. *The Key to the Asian Miracle: Making Shared Growth Credible.* Washington, DC: Brooking Institution.

Cox, Gary W. 1997. *Making Votes Count.* New York: Cambridge University Press.

Dixit, A., and John Londregan. 1996. "The Determinants of Success of Special Interest Groups in Redistributitive Politics." *Journal of Politics* 58: 1132–1155.

Downs, Anthony. 1957. *An Economic Theory of Democracy.* New York: Harper and Row.

Ferejohn, John. 1986. "Incumbent Performance and Electoral Control." *Public Choice* 50:5–26.

Findlay, Ronald. 1990. "The New Political Economy: Its Explanatory Power for LCDs." *Economics and Politics* 2:191–222.

Gaddis, John L. 1992. "International Relations Theory and the End of the Cold War." *International Security* 17:5–58.

Grossman, G., and E. Helpman. 1996. "Electoral Competition and Special Interest Politics." *Review of Economic Studies* 63:265–286.

Grossman, Herschel I. 1999. "Kleptocracy and Revolutions." *Oxford Economic Papers* 51:267–283.

Gurr, Ted R. 1990. "Polity II: Political Structures and Regime Change, 1800–1986." Ann Arbor, MI: Inter-university Consortium for Political and Social Research.

Huntington, Samuel. 1968. *Political Order in Changing Societies.* New Haven, CT: Yale University Press.

Laver, Michael, and Norman Schofield. 1990. *Multiparty Government: The Politics and Coalition in Europe.* Oxford: Oxford University Press.

Londregan, John, and Keith Poole. 1990 "Poverty, the Coup Trap, and the Seizure of Executive Power." *World Politics* 49:1–30.

McGuire, Martin C., and Mancur Olson. 1996. "The Economics of Autocracy and Majority Rule: The Invisible Hand and the Use of Force." *Journal of Economic Literature* 34:72–96.

Morrow, James D. 1994. *Game Theory for Political Scientists.* Princeton, NJ: Princeton University Press.

North, Douglass C. 1990. *Institutions, Institutional Change, and Economic Performance.* New York: Cambridge University Press.

North, Douglass C., and Barry R. Weingast. 1989. "Constitutions and Commitment: The Institutions Governing Public Choice in Seventeenth Century England." *Journal of Economic History* 44:803–832.

Olson, Mancur. 1991. "Autocracy, Democracy, and Prosperity." In Richard J. Zeckhauser, ed. of *Strategy and Choice.* Cambridge: MIT Press.

Organski, A. F. K., and Jacek Kugler. 1980. *The War Ledger.* Chicago: University of Chicago Press.

Persson, Torsten, Gerard Roland, and Guido Tabellini. 1997. "Comparative Politics and Public Finance." Centre for Economic Policy Research, Discussion Paper. (November): 1737.

———. 1998. "Towards Micropolitical Foundations of Public Finance." *European Economic Review* 42:685–694.

Persson, Torsten, and Guido Tabellini. 1994. "Growth, Distribution, and Politics." In *Monetary and Fiscal Policy,* vol. 2, edited by Torsten Persson and Guido Tabellini, pp. 243–262. Cambridge: MIT Press.

Powell, Robert. 1999. *In the Shadow of Power.* Princeton, NJ: Princeton University Press.

Przeworski, Adam. 1990. *The State and the Economy under Capitalism.* Chur, Switzerland: Harwood Academic Publishers.

———. 1991. *Democracy and the Market.* New York: Cambridge University Press.

Przeworski, Adam, and Fernando Limongi. 1997. "Modernization: Theories and Fact." *World Politics* 49:155–183.

Rabushka, Alvin, and Kenneth Shepsle. 1972. *Politics in Plural Societies: A Theory of Democratic Instability.* Columbus, OH: Merrill.

Ray, James L., and Bruce M. Russett. 1996. "The Future as Arbiter of Theoretical Controversies: Predictions, Explanations and the End of the Cold War." *British Journal of Political Science* 25:1578.

Root, Hilton. 1994. *The Fountain of Privilege.* Berkeley: University of California Press.

Starr, Harvey. 1972. *The War Coalitions.* Lexington, MA: Lexington Books.

Wintrobe, Ronald. 1998. *The Political Economy of Dictatorship.* New York: Cambridge University Press.

VI

THEORY CONSTRUCTION AND THEORY INTEGRATION

11

Theoretical Integration and Generative Structuralism

Thomas J. Fararo and John Skvoretz

In the last decade of the twentieth century, social theorists have split into two camps. For some, "social theory" means the abandonment of scientific aspirations toward generality and explanatory power associated with postclassical developments in sociological theory. For these analysts, social theory is a body of discursive interpretations of the social world that eschews orientation to rigorous standards of theory construction and theory assessment. Theory does not grow, it simply provides interpretations that may be analyzed and debated within a community of interested readers. For others, however, "social theory" means scientific theory. These analysts, found in various research programs, retain scientific aspirations toward generality. Our orientation puts us in this second camp. We welcome work that involves the construction of general explanatory theories, especially when these are formal and testable. Our distinctive commitments, within this camp, are twofold.

First, for several decades we have pursued theoretical integration. We ignored the "do your own thing" implications of the early phase in the bifurcation of sociological theory—the emergence and advocacy of multiple paradigms of sociological discourse—in favor of "the spirit of unification in sociological theory" (Fararo 1989b). By this phrase, we do not mean the unification of paradigms in one fell swoop, nor do we mean that, over time, entire structures of theories will be brought under a single more comprehensive theory. Rather, we mean a commitment to forming linkages between otherwise disconnected theoretical developments, moving toward more comprehensive, wide-scope theoretical systems. The type of linkage varies with the source theories. When the theories are formally stated, the linkage is similar to the unification that physics has successfully generated. But, the linkage may involve a weaker form of unification whose key accomplishment is a systematic, ongoing basis for articulating concepts and principles associated with the distinct research programs. Wagner and Berger (1985) note that a research program can advance internally through proliferation and integration. We observe that the same processes can occur between programs—they can proliferate and they can be integrated by forging conceptual linkages between them. Any such linkage or integration is an episode in "the spirit of unification."

Our second commitment is to an orienting strategy for theory construction that we have termed "generative structuralism." "Generative" refers to the behavior of actors and, in particular, to how the concatenation (interaction or interdependence) of their actions generates collective outcomes. "Structuralism" refers to the analytic focus on the system, the network of interacting or interdependent actors, and the social patterns and outcomes that emerge and are reproduced through the generativity of the action basis.

Generative structuralism generalizes aspects of our work undertaken in the spirit of unification and developed through episodes of integration. All of our integrative work focuses on social structure, conceived of as stable states of a dynamic interaction process, but varies in level of application from macrostructures of networks and differential population compositions to microstructures of relations in small groups. Further, most of this work postulates formally stated generative mechanisms or rules that refer to the behavior of actors and how their activities interlock to produce and reproduce system-level regularities.[1] In the next three sections of this chapter, we outline three integrative episodes we have worked on and advanced over the past several decades, drawing attention to how they implement both the spirit of unification and the orienting strategy of generative structuralism.[2] For each of these episodes, we describe its background and basic ideas, recent theoretical advances, and relevant empirical tests. We conclude with a general characterization of our work and what makes it distinctive as part of contemporary sociological theory.

E-STATE STRUCTURALISM: AN INTEGRATIVE THEORETICAL METHOD

E-state structuralism builds theoretical models of interaction processes based upon the integration of conceptual components from two paradigms in recent sociology: expectation states theory and social network analysis. Expectation states theory is adumbrated elsewhere by its originators (see, for instance, Berger, Wagner, and Zelditch 1985; see also chapter 3). The foundations of social network analysis have been set out by a number of authors (for instance, Wellman 1983). For our purposes, we would like to call attention to some major comparative aspects of each paradigm (see figure 11.1).

Two common analytic frameworks in social science are the actor-situation framework of social psychology and the multiactor system-environment framework of sociology. In the first framework, what is important is the subjective point of view of an actor on a situation defined by certain fixed aspects. Expectation states theory (EST) is grounded in this actor/situation framework and

Paradigm 1: Expectation States Theory Type: *Actor-Situation Model* Core Concept: *Expectation States* Math Model: *Graph* Interpretation: *Cognitive (Internal)* Strength: *Process theorizing* Problem: *Actor-system logical gap*
Paradigm 2: Social Networks Type: *Social System Model* Core Concept: *Social Relations* Math Model: *Graph* Interpretation: *Objective (External)* Strength: *Structural analysis* Problem: *Structure-process gap*
E-State Structuralism Unification Agenda: *Retain strength of each paradigm* *Solve problem in each paradigm*

Figure 11.1. E-State Structuralism: Unification Logic

posits that the key relation between actor and situation is the expectation state of the actor vis-à-vis a comparison of self and others in the situation with respect to such elements as social status and instrumental ability. To formalize this key relation, EST uses graphs in which points and lines represent mental states such as beliefs. The strength of this actor/situation theory with its mathematical model of expectation states is that it provides a processual account of interaction as involving expectation influenced events such as giving the other an opportunity to speak or accepting influence from another. But any actor/situation theory has a key problem, namely, how to make a transition to the multiactor systemic level of the social process. This key problem stimulated our integrative work. Namely, EST theorized about the actor-situation connection but with the ultimate aim of drawing conclusions about a multiactor system outcome, the emergence of a power and prestige order. Our earliest formulation of generative structuralism suggested closing the gap with a model that represented, simultaneously, the various actor/situation subsystems coupled through an evolving social network.

Hence, we turned to social network analysis (SNA) for the relevant ideas. SNA presupposes a multiactor system/environment frame of reference. Its theoretical spotlight illuminates an entire set of actors standing in various social relations to each other and existing in a sociocultural or ecological environment. The network of social ties among actors is represented by a graph, the same type of mathematical object employed in EST but with (usually) an "objective" interpretation: actors are points and relations (lines connecting points) are objective, externally observable ties. While the strength of EST lies in the realm of process analysis, the strength of SNA lies in structural analysis. The graph representing the social ties among actors is analyzed for the structural properties or forms it exhibits, some obvious and some only apparent after detailed formal analysis, for example, hierarchy, center-periphery, and other structural forms.

But multiactor system/environment theories have a key problem as well: they tend to favor structural analysis of the system and neglect the processual question of system structure emergence. In particular, SNA has developed an impressive armada of techniques for describing structural properties of graphs (Wasserman and Faust 1994). Process takes a secondary position, either in the form of hypotheses about how some structural property varies over time in a group, or how some exogenous process (e.g., diffusion) is shaped by the given network structure. Given even less attention (until recently) are processes by which networks themselves emerge and change.

E-state structuralism emerged in an episode of integration designed to retain the strength of each paradigm but to solve their respective key problems: use SNA to provide the transition from the actor/situation framework of EST to the multiactor system level and use EST to provide understanding, at least within a certain scope, of the emergence and change of networks themselves (Fararo and Skvoretz 1986b). The specific impetus for the episode was the empirical work of Ivan Chase (1982) who, in the context of animal studies, demonstrated that a dyadic model of interaction could not adequately explain how a dominance hierarchy emerges in a group. He proposed a triadic mechanism.

Our E-state structuralist model developed his insight by proposing a bystander effect through which a third party witnessing an interaction between two others could develop expectation-states (or E-states) for deference or dominance vis-à-vis the observed interactants. A specific theoretical model was constructed in which the axioms pertain to the actors in a situation in which, as an initial condition, the E-states for dominance or deference are unformed. As behaviors occur, E-states build up. When an E-state is formed, it then determines behavior. Eventually, all relevant E-states are formed and these determine who dominates whom in the interaction system. In fact, the structure of all such dominance relations tends very strongly toward a hierarchy. Thus, at any point in time, the state of a group of actors is defined by a particular network configuration of dominance ties and over time, the group moves through a "state-space" of such configurations as ties are gradually added. Since the movement from one configuration to another is partly chance-determined, the mathematical model is a probabilistic one.[3] Each tie is a pair of symmetric E-states in which one actor expects to dominate and the other to defer to the partner. Since the E-states govern behavior after they form, in equilibrium, a stable network of social relations exists and governs behavior, having been generated by the processes formulated in the model. In short, using the E-state structuralist method, we have an example of generative structuralism.

To illustrate these ideas, table 11.1 displays one possible realization of the process for a 4-actor group. The first event, A directs interaction to C, results in a dominance tie forming from A to C. Both B and D are bystanders to this event and so potentially could, via bystander effects, develop dominance ties vis-à-vis A and C. However, none of these possibilities materialize after the first interaction. In the second event B directs interaction to D, but no dominance tie from B to D forms, nor do any bystander effects occur. In the third event, B again directs interaction to D and this time a dominance tie forms from B to D. In addition, bystander effects occur: a dominance tie forms from A to D and one forms from C to D. At this point in the group's interaction, four of the six ties possible between pairs of actors have formed: in the internal ranking of the group, A dominates both C and D, and B and C dominate D. The internal orderings of A and B and B and C have yet to be determined. The fourth interaction, B to A,

Table 11.1. A Realization of the E-State Model for Dominance Orders

Interaction	*State of Network*	*Explanation*
A to C	A → C; B; D	A gains dominance over C via the direct interaction effect.
B to D	A → C; B; D	No change in the structure of the dominance order.
B to D	A → C; A → D; B → D; C → D	B gains dominance over D via the direct interaction effect, A gains dominance over D via a bystander effect, C gains dominance over D via a bystander effect.
B to A	B → A; B → C; B → D; A → C; A → D; C → D	B gains dominance over A via the direct interaction effect, B gains dominance over C via a bystander effect.

occasions the formation of these last two ties: first, a dominance tie forms from B to A as a result of direct interaction, and, second, a tie forms from B to C via a bystander effect. The internal dominance order of the group is now complete. The order happens to be a fully transitive linear hierarchy, although this is but one of several possible outcomes. Also, for the purposes of illustration, the order has emerged very rapidly. In actual groups and, of course, depending on the values of the model's parameters, emergence is much less rapid.

Recent Theoretical Advances

We built upon this integrative episode to extend the method's scope and power. We generalized the process of E-state formation to include the possibility of conflicting E-states in which actors in a dyad both expect to dominate (or defer) to the other (Fararo, Skvoretz, and Kosaka 1994), a form of theory elaboration in terms of Wagner and Berger (1985). We explored computer simulations of the model, focusing on the images actors develop of the dominance structures that shape their relations to others (Hummon and Fararo 1995). We demonstrated the importance of the bystander effect in creating social structure, as that concept is defined in the social network literature (Skvoretz, Faust, and Fararo 1996).

Our most far-reaching elaboration was to extend the method to human task groups (Skvoretz and Fararo 1996b) via the unification of the E-state model with the "behavior interchange pattern" concept of Fisek, Berger, and Norman (1991) and with a function proposed by Balkwell (1995) for E-state effects on directed participation in groups. The resulting model offered an explanation for the emergence of internal status orders in task groups that had several advantages over previous models. First, it described the process of status evolution in the group as well as the eventual power and prestige structure; previous models (Skvoretz 1988; Fisek et al. 1991; Balkwell 1991) only described the eventual inequality structure. Second, it formally incorporated the bystander mechanism into the performance expectation process, a component of that process not found in Fisek et al. (1991) or in Balkwell's (1991) model. Finally, it was stochastic and so in principle could explain the development of complete and incomplete hierarchies, and fully or partly transitive structures.

Empirical Tests

As a theoretical method, E-state structuralism does not make empirically testable claims. However, E-state theoretical models—specific theoretical models—lead to empirical claims that can be tested. For example, in Fararo and Skvoretz (1988), we fit the basic E-state model to Chase's data from chicken triads, finding that some predictions were in agreement with some aspects of the data, for instance, there were few cases in which one animal attacked another immediately after the second had attacked the first (attack reversals), but were not in agreement with other aspects of the data, for instance, there were too few instances in which one animal would attack both of the other two animals in succession (double attack). Overall, the conceptual structure of the model, especially the fundamental bystander effect, appeared empirically sound, but the axioms linking states of the evolving dominance network to behavior patterns clearly required reformulation. More recently, Skvoretz, Webster, and Whitmeyer (1999) reported a preliminary assessment of the E-state model for task discussion groups using data gathered from 60 four-person groups. The assessment was favorable in some important ways—triads were more transitive than chance expectations, indicating the presence of a bystander effect, and actors with initially higher external status tended to rank higher in the internal participation distribution, indicating the presence of a status activation effect. More precise model evaluation, however, requires fuller and more complex coding of the discussion data than the simple counts of participation acts used in this report.

INSTITUTIONAL PRODUCTION SYSTEMS: AN INTEGRATIVE MODE OF REPRESENTATION

In the early 1970s, we worked on formal representations of institutions, as that concept was understood in some major conceptual frameworks of sociological and anthropological theory. The mode of formal representation emerged from the revolution in cognitive psychology that emphasized the cybernetic control of action (see figure 11.2).

In sociological and anthropological theory, the concept of action was fundamental to the concept of institution. In sociology, George Herbert Mead emphasized a concept of action that involved both an internal and an external or behavioral aspect. Max Weber addressed the same dichotomy with his distinction between two kinds of subjective meaning we attribute to action: "the what" and "the why."[4] Talcott Parsons adopted the Meadian and Weberian action foundations of sociology and argued that both the internal and external aspects of human action could be united through what he called the *cybernetic control* of action, that is, through the control of external physical activity by the internal goals and objectives of the actor.[5] Hence, Mead's point that action has an internal aspect corresponds to Parsons's idea of cybernetic control.

In anthropology, Nadel (1951:108ff) viewed institutions as "standardized modes of social behavior" and proposed that the standardization resided in the routine following of "if-then" rules specifying that "in such-and-such situations, people of a certain description act regularly in a particular fashion." Sociologists Berger and Luckmann (1966) in their influential theoretical monograph proposed a similar understanding of institutions as bodies of ordinary social knowledge in the form of shared *typification schemes* for social interaction.

These three sets of ideas about the institution concept—those of Parsons, Nadel, and Berger and Luckmann—presuppose the common idea that an institution is an enduring action pattern in a social system. Two related usages of

Conceptual Elements: Institution
Reality construction theory: Typification schemes *Sociological action theory:* Cybernetic control *Anthropological theory:* If-then situations
Formal Elements: Generativity
Grammatical *Dynamical*
Institutions As Production Systems
Hybrid generativity Symbolic cultural space Production rules *Unit institution concept* Distributed subsystems Institutionalized action and choice *Generated normal forms*
Two Recent Episodes of Conceptual Linkage
Blumer's symbolic interactionism *Structured agency theory*

Figure 11.2. Formal Analysis of Institutions

the term "institution" should be distinguished from this usage. In one, a particular collectivity that has some importance in a community is called an institution, for example, a particular bank or university as contrasted with the action patterns replicated in any bank or in any university. In the notation to be introduced below, the latter are <bank> and <university>, respectively, denoting schemes of typification embedded in if-then rules that control conduct in certain situations. In another related usage, an entire economy or polity of a society may be termed an institution. Such a functional subsystem of a social system is a complex of institutionalized action patterns. For instance, the employment contract and the privately owned firm are economic institutions of a capitalist system. In our work, we have used the term "unit-institution" to refer to such a component of an institutional complex. In what follows, we mainly deal with the problem of formally representing any such unit-institution. The integration of unit-institutions to form complexes is dealt with in some of our papers (e.g., Fararo and Skvoretz 1986a).

To illustrate these ideas, consider the criminal trial as an institution. As a typification scheme, it includes such features as typified actors (e.g., judge), typified acts (e.g., setting a date for sentencing), and typified situations in which such typified acts occur (e.g., the jury has reached a decision and it has just been announced). Both actors and observers understand what occurs in an actual trial in such typical terms. We comprehend the actual details through the general terms supplied by the typification scheme. In fact, without such a scheme we may not be able to understand the action we witness. Typification schemes, argued Berger and Luckmann, are legitimated at several levels, but the most fundamental is the simple fact that the institution is part of social reality; it simply "is." The fundamental level of social control, on this view, resides in the fact that people experience the typification schemes in existential terms: institutions define social reality for them and so are legitimated. For instance, criminal trials exist; they are part of our society whatever anyone may think about them.

As theorists our problem was to formalize these ideas about action and its institutionalization. In particular, our point of departure was the cybernetic control concept as implemented by if-then rules for action. The rules are expressed in terms of elements of typification schemes. In this way, our work would help to integrate the action theory of Parsons, grounded in the ideas of Mead and Weber, the social structuralist theory of Nadel, and the social constructionist theory of Berger and Luckmann.

The cybernetic control concept resonated with early phases of the cognitive revolution in psychology, in particular, Miller, Galanter, and Pribram's (1960) notion of a *plan.* A plan was a unit-act combining knowledge and behavior. For instance, hammering a nail is a control process in which the goal-state "get nail flush" governs the overt behavior until the observed state of the nail and the goal-state coincide. Control then passes to some other plan. Being alive, for a human being, is always to be in the midst of some plan. And plans come in hierarchies—"hammering a nail" may be an executable subcomponent of a larger plan "building a chair," which in turn could be a subplan of a grander 0.design "furnishing a house," and so on. The combination of this plan idea with the heritage of ideas about institutions from sociology and anthropology gave us a starting point for the sociological action theory of institutions. Our aim, then, was to find a mode of formal representation in which we could express the basic nature of unit-acts and institutions as involved in systems of such acts in the shifting contexts of if-then situations. The problem was how to represent acts and concatenations of acts in such a way that both the cybernetic control aspect of action and the institutional organization of action through schemes of typifications could find their place.

In addition, we wanted to implement in this context the generative structuralism strategy. In the E-state integrative episode, actions of individual actors generated networks of dominance relations that, in turn, constrained further action by the agents. This form of generativity may be called "dynamical." That is, through a succession of changes of states—each change produced by some specific effect specified in the theory—the structure of relations among actors emerged. In the present context, the generativity may be termed "grammatical"—institutionalized interaction is modeled in such a way as to be able to generate from a finite rule basis all and only the forms of interaction recognized by the actors as "normal" in the institutional sense. The institution constitutes a "grammar" of action from which all legitimate ("normal") forms of interaction can be generated.

Unlike the structure of dominance ties in the previous episode, this episode's structure, an institution, is treated as given rather than emergent in the formal model. Clearly, this modeling approach borrows from the well-known program of Chomsky's generative linguistics. But, unlike a natural language, occasions of interaction involve the simultaneous "execution" of multiple institutions. Also, the grammar model of an institution has its constitutive rules distributed among actors, rather than entirely embodied in each actor, and the more so the more differentiated the action system is into structural roles. Therefore, the integration of the action systems of distinct actors—the coordination of action—was seen by us as a fundamental problem to be addressed in the formal representation.

The representational scheme we developed can be encapsulated in the phrase "institutions as production systems." A production system is a system of if-then rules of the form,

$$\text{Situation} \rightarrow \text{Action}$$

Such rule systems have been employed by cognitive scientists to model the mind, including the plan concept (Newell and Simon 1972; Anderson 1993). Our own published work began with Axten and Fararo (1977) and continued with a variety of published studies, including Axten and Skvoretz (1980). A lengthy overview of the theoretical basis of all this work was provided in Fararo and Skvoretz (1984).

The elementary components of the situation and action parts of a rule are found in the symbolic-cultural space of institutional relevant typifications, that is, the basic actor and action types and situation features recognized by the actors in the system of action. So, for instance, in the criminal trial institution, this space would contain typifications such as <judge>, <defendant>, <defense attorney>, <prosecutor>, <juror>, <plea>, <motion>, and the like. These social constructions form part of the standardized content of this institution.

The production system divides into a system of subsystems of production rules because of structural role differentiation. In our example, we would have subsystems such as JUDGE, DEFENDANT, DEFENSE ATTORNEY, PROSECUTOR, and JUROR, each of which is a system of if-then rules. The legitimate or normal form of action that any one of them takes is contingent on the situation of action. Moreover, such actions may often have optional realizations. In other words, the called-for actions generally leave space for an actor to exercise strategic or other forms of behavior realizing the institutionally called-for mode of action. For example, if the jury announces a "guilty" verdict, the action called for in the JUDGE subsystem may be some form of the action-type SENTENCE. This action will be "parameterized" by the relevant legal code that constrains the judge's choices but also provides for options, for instance, as to length of prison term. On one hand, the judge's action is "determined"—he or she must execute the action-type SENTENCE—and constrained in terms of the parameters of the legal code. On other hand, he or she faces a choice situation that is subinstitutional, that is, not institutionally predetermined. Specifics of the concrete realization of the action-type SENTENCE are left open for the judgment of the particular actor instantiating the institutional identity <judge>.

A production system model of an institution requires specification of the entire set of rules distributed to each of the roles in the system of institutionalized social interaction to be represented. As given, the model constitutes a grammar of action and interaction (Skvoretz and Fararo 1980; Skvoretz 1984). But, as executed on particular occasions by particular individuals, the model produces a dynamic flow of action through time and so implies a form of dynamical generativity. That is, the instantiated production rules are transition rules that move the overall action system from one state to another. When one individual produces a realization of an institutionally called-for action, it changes the situation of action of one or more other actors whose productions respond to the new situation state, one or more of them acting to produce further changes in the situation of action . . . and so forth. A discussion of the interplay of the grammatical and dynamical aspects of these models may be found in Fararo and Skvoretz (1986a).

A highly simplified sketch illustrates the general points. In a criminal trial, an observed partial sequence of action might resemble the following: (1) closing arguments (by prosecution and defense); (2) instructions to the jury (by judge); (3) deliberations and decision (by jury); (4) formal announcement of decision (by clerk); and (5) setting of date for sentencing (by judge). The model-building problem is to generate such sequences. The actual actions will be instances of these typified actions, for example, particular closing arguments by particular lawyers, particular instructions by a particular judge, and so forth. These particulars are not generated; they are inputs from the particular actors as they engage in structural role behavior that is institutionally organized. This institutional organization is the grammar. For instance, the actor <judge> does not set the date for sentencing before instructing the jury! Rather, this actor awaits an instance of <situation> corresponding to the accomplished action (4). The JUDGE production system will include, therefore, a rule that amounts to:

<clerk> announced <guilty decision by jury> → set sentencing date

Note that it is not only that the judge awaits the announcement but also that the latter must satisfy two conditions. First, it must be the decision of the jury; and, second, it must be a guilty verdict. In this way, the setting of the sentencing date is made conditional upon not only the purely grammatical fact that it must await a jury verdict but also it must occur only if that verdict takes a particular (institutionally legitimate) form—an input from the particular jury. In this way, the generative model incorporates both the structure of social action and the agency of the actors, the latter as inputs that enter into the dynamical flow of the realized action sequence.

Recent Theoretical Advances

Two of our most recent elaborations of this integrative episode build conceptual linkages to two research traditions: Blumer's symbolic interactionism and what we call "structured agency theory," our name for key ideas of Giddens and Bourdieu. The first linkage is discussed extensively in Skvoretz and Fararo (1996a) and the second in Fararo and Butts (1999). We discuss each of these briefly, beginning with the latter.

In the example above, the formal representation of institutional action incorporates both structure and agency. The interlocking of these two aspects of social life has been a key theme in the writings of Giddens and Bourdieu. Giddens's (1984) concept of structure as pertaining to largely implicit rules of action corresponds to our production system representation. Whereas Giddens is content to present a discursive presentation of these ideas, our generative structuralist commitment leads us to attempt to develop formal representations. Roughly speaking, it is one thing to talk of objects moving in space through time and quite another to formally represent and derive that movement, as in classical and modern physics. The former is a prelude to the latter. Bourdieu's (1990) concept of habitus pertains to almost automatic modes of behavior adjusted to the actor's position in a social system. Although Bourdieu emphasizes the habitus conditioned by class location, the idea is quite general. The general point is the structure is not only external but also internal. Agency is structured but not fully determined by structure; indeed, it is enabled by structure, as emphasized by Giddens. For instance, the structure of the criminal trial institution enables a whole range of choices that presuppose its existence but are not thereby determined by it. In short, agency and structure together account for the observable orderly character of social action.

The linkage to symbolic interactionism arises in terms of the correspondence of our ideas, as sketched above, to the methodological directives set out by Herbert Blumer (1969:ch. 1). First, human society must be represented as consisting of a system of acting agents. Second, all action takes place in situations through agents' interpretations of the "things" in the situation that they must take into account. Third, other agents in the situation must be represented. Fourth, the organization of human society must use structures of meaning inside of which social action takes place. Fifth, agents must embody structures of knowledge that link typifications to social action. Production systems provide a formal representation that satisfies all these directives and from which situated sequences of interaction mediated by symbolic interpretations can be derived.

Finally, a third recent elaboration turns to the problem of the dynamic emergence and transformation of production systems (Skvoretz and Fararo 1995).

We use a formal model to create an example of how such systems can emerge and evolve through cultural transmission processes.

Empirical Tests

The general principle that institutional structure consists of distributed production systems is not itself directly testable. However, as in the case of E-state structuralism, specific models are testable. We have closely studied the unit-institution governing the relationship between customers and waitpersons in relatively standardized commercial restaurant settings. Our choice was dictated not by functional importance but by ease of observation of a setting with strong institutionalized routines. We view the restaurant as sociology's "fruit fly," an arena of application chosen for its usefulness in advancing theoretical ideas rather than any significance extrinsic to theory growth. We model the grammatical-dynamical structure of the customer-waitperson relationship as a production system with two subsystems that together generate normal forms of interaction observable in restaurant settings. We examined brief slices of activity from several different establishments in our early empirical work (Skvoretz, Fararo, and Axten 1980) and recently reported an analysis of one very long behavior trace (Skvoretz and Fararo 1996a). Both analyses suggested refinements of the specific production system model would be needed to capture the details of even such mundane institutionalized social action.

To summarize this section, we note that the work illustrates the spirit of unification and involves multiple integrative episodes linking ideas drawn from distinct research traditions. There is no attempt to set out a single all-embracing social theory at one fell swoop, as we have emphasized. The work also illustrates generative structuralism. The structuralist aspect is the focus on institutions as basic structures of social life. The generative aspect is the adoption of an action theory foundation embodied in the formalism of production rule systems, which generate institutionalized social interaction.

MACROSTRUCTURAL NETWORK THEORY: A UNIFICATION OF SOCIOLOGICAL THEORIES

Our third integration episode constitutes a deductive theory that began by connecting Peter Blau's macrostructural theory (1977) with a formal model for the formation of social networks known as "biased net theory." Blau set out the basic ideas of his theory with considerable lucidity and he and his colleagues conducted associated empirical work (for instance, Blau, Blum, and Schwartz 1982). The formalization occurred when it became clear that Blau's theory was about the location of social ties in a large-scale social network. Such networks had been the subject of mathematical models in the 1950s and 1960s (Rapoport 1951, 1957; Fararo and Sunshine 1964). Using some ideas from the latter monograph, a first effort to define and study "Blau models" (Fararo 1981) was followed by a major advance in this work (Skvoretz 1983) which, in turn, gave rise to a sequence of extensions and applications of formal macrostructural network theory.

Blau's dependent variable refers to social associations among individuals who belong to different groups or positions. Consider a single dimension that partitions the people into disjoint groups, such as different ethnic groups.[6] A particular social tie, like a particular marriage or a particular friendship, might be between persons in the same ethnic group or between persons in different ethnic groups. Blau's theory seeks to account for variations in the relative frequency of such intergroup social ties, that is, variation in the rate of intergroup association. A key explanatory factor in his theory is how diverse or heterogeneous the overall population is with respect to the partitioning dimension. For instance, the theory asserts that the more ethnically heterogeneous communities will have higher rates of interethnic marriages, that is, will have greater proportions of marriages that are interethnic.

Our formalization assumes the formation of a social tie depends both on chance and on nonchance or bias factors. The bias factors capture how the selection of others for association is systematically influenced by the positions that others occupy along social dimensions that partition the population and by the positions that others occupy in the network of social ties that surrounds an actor. In Fararo and Sunshine (1964), three basic biases were introduced. The names we give them now are homophily, reciprocity, and closure. The first refers to the tendency to select similar others for association at greater than chance levels, a tendency that Blau calls the salience of a structural dimension. For instance, if ethnicity is very salient with respect to marriages, then marriages between co-ethnics are much more likely than chance, indicating that the ethnic homophily bias is strongly positive. The second bias refers to the greater than chance level that a person x directs a tie to a person y, given that y has directed a tie to x. For Blau's theory, this bias is not relevant because its scope is explicitly restricted to associations that are symmetric or reciprocal. The closure bias refers to the greater than chance level of association between two persons y and z, given that both are associated with a common third person x. This bias is called closure because the triad xyz "closes" by adding the y-z tie to the x-y and x-z ties.

The original concern of biased net theory was not with intergroup association but with the connectivity of a network, that is, the expected proportion of a population that could be reached by tracing out along the network's connections from a small subset of starter actors. Sociologically, connectivity is one measure of the degree of a population's social integration. Formal arguments proved that this proportion was a function of how many ties or contacts each person had on average (the element density of the network) and the biases. For instance, a greater proportion could be reached from a small subset in denser networks and in networks with weaker reciprocity biases and with weaker closure biases. These three factors, density, reciprocity, and closure, provided a macroclassification of social networks based upon whether the proportion of the population reached from a small subset of starter persons followed a similar trajectory in both networks.[7] Thus, these three factors provided a way of talking about the equivalence of large-scale social networks.[8]

Blau's theory and biased net theory link up through the homophily bias parameter in the context of different proportional distributions of a population over a set of salient social categories. The homophily bias parameter and the heterogeneity of the population distribution determine the proportional allocation of a social tie such as marriage within social categories or between social categories. After developing this basic linkage between Blau's theory and biased net theory, we then unified our formal macrostructural theory with social network's weak ties theory (Granovetter 1973). While both Blau and social network theory shared common influences from earlier work in the structuralist tradition, notably that of Nadel (1951), they viewed one another as pursuing different theoretical goals in essentially unconnected research programs. Blau treated network analysis as implying microsociology, while network analysts treated the heterogeneity focus as individualistic research based on an aggregation of attributes of persons rather than structural research into the connections between persons. Our work unified macrostructural theory with a central part of the social network model in the current literature, that is, Granovetter's weak ties hypothesis that social integration (e.g., of a community) is facilitated by weak ties that bridge clusters or groups of people connected by strong ties. If there are few weak ties connecting such sectors of a community, its connectivity will be lower, hence information will not get to remote parts of it from any given starting point. Actors will be restricted to information obtained from close ties, so that remote job opportunities, for instance, will remain unknown.

Our work on this problem has been reported in detail elsewhere (Fararo and Skvoretz 1987). Here we want to focus on the logic of the unification episode (see figure 11.3). The opportunity for theoretical integration arises as soon as one sees the complementarity of the two theories through the lens of biased net theory. In one theory, persons are differentiated by memberships in salient social categories and this is a "given" for network formation, while in the other persons are undifferentiated nodes. The theory that differentiates persons views ties as undifferentiated associations, all represented by a single type of tie, or line, while in the other theory, ties are differentiated into weak and strong. In terms of biases, weak ties theory requires formalization in terms of the closure bias. Weak ties exhibit a smaller closure bias than do strong ties, hence the potential for greater connectivity, the network based measure of social integration. Macrostructural theory requires the homophily bias in its formalization to represent the salience of a dimension of differentiation. And it treats social integration as a matter of rates of intergroup association. Our formal unification goes beyond noticing these complementarities. The formal representation of each theory as a biased net model enables the construction of a third, more comprehensive model that (1) captures each of the theories as special cases; and (2) theoretically articulates them in formulas that include concepts from both sources.

Theory 1: Weak Ties Model *Persons:* undifferentiated *Relations:* differentiated *Bias Parameter:* closure *Integration:* connectivity *Axiom:* Closure of weak ties is less than that of strong ties.
Theory 2: Macrostructural Model *Persons:* differentiated *Relations:* undifferentiated *Bias Parameter:* homophily *Integration:* intergroup relation rate *Axiom:* More diversity yields greater intergroup relations.
Unified Theoretical Model Combine corresponding features of each model into a generalized model that includes each as a special case and makes additional statements about the macrostructural network.

Figure 11.3. Logic of an Episode of Theoretical Unification

Recent Theoretical Advances

Among the numerous further advances in this line of theoretical research, we mention two. First, the theory has been extended to the formalization of other significant components of Blau's theory, especially inequality and consolidation (Skvoretz and Fararo 1986). Strictly speaking this advance was limited to formal macrostructural theory prior to its integration with weak ties theory. The second elaboration pertains to the small world problem (Skvoretz and Fararo 1989). This elaboration used the full resources of the integrated theory to calculate mean acquaintance chain lengths in networks in which both nodes and ties were differentiated. This extension then explored how mean chain length was related to seven different model parameters—element density, the homophily bias, strong tie closure bias, weak tie closure bias, strong tie bias for homogeneous links, strong tie bias for heterogeneous links, and the heterogeneity of the population on a salient dimension. For more recent work on the small world problem that draws upon some of these ideas, see Watts (1999a, 1999b).

Empirical Tests

Our empirical tests examine formal macrostructural theory rather than the integrated product. Furthermore, these tests both replicate and go beyond empirical examination of Blau's theory conducted by Blau and his colleagues. The general findings support the theory, but more importantly show that the formalization is essential to properly testing it (Skvoretz 1990, 1998). The empirical focus in all these tests is intermarriage rates calculated over various dimensions of differentiation of metropolitan regions in the United States.

Specifically, in Skvoretz (1990), data on intermarriages from the 1970 U.S. Census for the 125 largest SMSAs are used to estimate both simple and complex equations for the intermarriage rates. For instance in the simple equation for the rate of interethnic marriage in an SMSA, there is but one determinant, namely, the degree of ethnic heterogeneity in the SMSA. The homophily bias turns out to be the effect parameter that calibrates the impact of SMSA heterogeneity on the rate of intermarriage—larger homophily biases producing more attenuation in the effect of population heterogeneity. Thus, for example, the homophily bias estimate for the race dimension is particularly large (.978) while for the occupation dimension, it is rather small (.261). Hence, a change in an SMSA's occupational heterogeneity has a larger impact on the inter-occupational marriage rate than an equivalent change in its racial heterogeneity has on its interracial marriage rate. The complex models take account of whether dimensions like race and occupation are correlated in predicting intermarriage rates on either dimension. In general, these more complex models fit the data better and for the reasons proposed originally by Blau—correlated dimensions produce reinforcing in-group biases that reduce intergroup association.

In closing, we return to the general themes of theoretical integration and generative structuralism in relation to formal macrostructural network theory. Clearly, the focus of macrostructural network theory is social structure. The institution-theoretical analyses described earlier focus on "social culture" that defines and orients role-interaction in standardized situations. Macrostructural network theory takes a Simmelian approach, treating the form and not the content of social relations. The networks it models arise by virtue of the "space" left open by institutions for individual choices, for example, of marriage partners, friends, collaborators, and the like. Put compactly in terms of Homans's (1950) framework, institutional structure provides the external system for interaction and the macrostructural network constitutes the emergent internal system—now at the community level (i.e., relating to a system of groups) rather than the group level.

The generative aspect of macrostructural network theory does not involve either grammatical or, in most cases, dynamical considerations. Moreover, the action of agents takes a back seat to the analysis of constraints. Thus, in this context, generativity resides in the logical deduction of a variety of structural phenomena from the theory. In fact, it is much stronger in deductive fertility than are the programs of E-state structuralism and institutions as production systems. E-state structuralism, through its constructed dynamic models, is generally nonlinear. Deduction is replaced by simulation in generating logical consequences of assumptions. The institution approach, in its general theoretical character, has little by way of theorems and its specific models are analyzed not so much by abstract deduction but by a procedure closely resembling simulation. By contrast, most of our work with macrostructural network theory has a strong deductive component with a variety of deduced formulas. Taken together, we may say that E-state structuralism exhibits nonlinear dynamical generativity, production system models of institutions exhibit a combination of dynamical and grammatical generativity, and macrostructural network theory exhibits deductive generativity.

CONCLUSIONS

Sociologists use the term "theory" to cover a wide range of intellectual activities and their products. In the scientific sense, "theory" is a set of propositions that form a deductive system in which some of them can be empirically tested. Specific theories are usually constructed within a more general frame of reference. The assumptions or unproven propositions of one theory may overlap with those of other theories. In the general case, then, a more comprehensive level of theoretical formulation exists in which specific theories are theoretical models relative to higher-level frameworks' theoretical concepts and principles.

We believe that strong scientific advances can be made if formal representation principles are employed so that logical, mathematical, and/or computational models can be constructed to specify the general theory to particular domains. In contrast to other sociological theorists, we stress the development of formal representations that are particularly appropriate for the theoretical analysis of social phenomena. Moreover, we try to do this in close relationship to contributions by theorists who eschew formal representation.

On the formal side, we have worked out such general formal-theoretical logics as E-state structuralist representations for dynamic interaction process, distributed production system representations for institution analysis, and large-scale network representations for macrostructural analysis. In the development of these three modes of representation, we make contact with and strive for unifying conceptual linkages with many sociological approaches. E-state structuralism synthesizes elements from network analysis and expectation states theory. Institutional production system theory, on its sociological side, synthesizes ideas from distinct traditions of general theory. On its formal side, it synthesizes grammatical and dynamical modes of analysis. Macrostructural network theory partially synthesizes ideas in the traditions of macrostructural theory and social network analysis. In short, all three of our major programs aim toward the specification and application of principles of formal representation in the context of a commitment to integrative sociological theory construction. And the same is true of the three other developments we described more briefly in endnote 2.

Elsewhere, generative structuralism has been interpreted as an example of an orienting strategy (Fararo and Butts 1999). As such, it is superordinate to theoretical research programs and links these in terms of some highly generalized conceptual ingredients. In our case, this orienting strategy implies an invariant focus on social structure as the core analytical focus of sociology. The generativity aspect, as we have seen, appears in our research programs in a variety of different forms: dynamical, grammatical, combined grammatical and dynamical, and deductive. Generative structuralism, despite its metatheoretical generality, is a distinctive approach. For example, as we have pointed out above, formal representation looms large in our strategy. This differentiates it, for instance, from the research program of Bourdieu, whose work involves standard statistical interpretations of abstract concepts rather than the construction of formal-theoretical models. Similarly, when we turn to the analysis of social structure as institutionalized social culture, our approach converges with that of Giddens, as pointed out elsewhere (Fararo and Butts 1999). But the formal representation aspect again differentiates it from the purely discursive elaboration of ideas characteristic of Giddens's work.

In addition, except for a good part of the macrostructural work, our approach orients toward the formal representation of process even as we focus on social structure. For instance, institutional structures are analyzed as latent processes in the same sense that a piece of software is a latent process of symbol processing. This contrasts with the largely hand-waving characterization in sociology in which institutions are either undefined or said to consist of rules, norms, and the like, without a coherent and generalized mode of representation for these concepts. Again, in our variant of social network analysis, the thrust of the work is dynamic, with a formal representation of the process mechanisms. This is in contrast with the largely static and descriptive character of much present-day network analysis.

In conclusion, given our metatheoretical presuppositions as constituting the orienting strategy of generative structuralism and given the implementation of this strategy in the spirit of unification in a variety of integrative theoretical research programs—these together form our contribution to contemporary sociological theory.

NOTES

1. See Fararo and Skvoretz (1993) for a discussion of how generative structuralism relates to philosophical integration of instrumentalist, positivist, and realist philosophical models of theoretical science as well as bridging methodological individualism and methodological holism.

2. These three episodes together are set out in over twenty-five papers or book chapters. We do not have space in this chapter to discuss three of our other, less fully developed integrative episodes, even though they exhibit the basic features of our general approach. The first episode tackles the problem of deviance and social control seeking to integrate numerous discrete theories (Messner, Krohn, and Liska 1989). For this problem we construct a general dynamic network model that combines the key principles of a large number of theories, representing these principles either as specific mechanisms or as parameters of the model. The model employs a micro-macro approach in which the microlevel is described in terms of a set of rational choice axioms and also a self-other "Meadian" interpretive process linked to formal balance-theoretical ideas (Fararo and

Skvoretz 1997; Hummon and Fararo 1995). The second episode seeks to bring together rational choice, exchange theories and neofunctionalism. In this episode, Fararo (1993, 1996) builds a conceptual bridge between the theory template of Coleman, on the one hand, and Parsons, on the other. Then, Skvoretz and Fararo (1992) provide a critical overview of various network exchange theories and explore embedding this work under the umbrella of the Coleman template for exchange. Finally, Fararo and Skvoretz (1993) pursue the principle of adaptively rational action (Fararo 1989a) as a unifying linkage among a set of group process theories, showing how theories of power and bargaining on one hand, and theories of legitimation, justice, equity, and status expectations, on the other, can be viewed as theories about how adaptively rational action plays out in competitive contexts, in the first instance, and in collective contexts, in the second instance.

3. Specifically, the model is a discrete time Markov chain model in which the probability of moving from one state to another is constant at each time point.

4. For instance, wood chopping may be "the what" of some observed behavior: an attribution of meaning to some observable physical activity of an actor. On the other hand, "working for a wage" might be one of "the why" of wood chopping by that actor at that time.

5. Cybernetics deals with the way in which some systems are organized so that some components that use relatively little energy guide or control the activities of other components that generally use higher energy. The link between the two takes the form of goal-oriented information. So cybernetic control is the use of information to guide the direction taken by energy-consuming components of a system. An example is the use of computers to control heating and cooling units. With respect to action, Parsons's point is that physical behavior that one undertakes depends upon one's goals or purposes.

6. For simplicity, we describe the logic of our formalization with reference to the most widely studied element of Blau's theory: heterogeneity.

7. Two social networks are approximately structurally equivalent if and only if they have approximately the same set of "structure statistics," that is, a set of values for the proportion reached at successive steps, starting from a small set of starters. Random net theory provides a formula for the expected values of these structure statistics. In that formula, the key factor is the element density of the network, that is, the number of contacts each person has. The biases in biased net theory effectively reduce the value of the element density, and thus change the structure statistics of the network.

8. Certain extreme cases exhibit the logic of this theoretically-derived classification scheme. If the element density is constant, each person has the same number of ties to others. Then, if reciprocity and closure biases are zero, the network is random, exhibiting no discernible substructure. If reciprocity and closure are at their maximum values, the network consists of a set of disconnected subnetworks, each of the same size (the density plus one). Thus, the vast space of equivalent network structures has two intelligible extremes, the random net and the partitioned or cliquelike net.

REFERENCES

Anderson, John R. 1993. *Rules of the Mind.* Hillsdale, NJ: Lawrence Erlbaum Associates.

Axten, Nick, and Thomas J. Fararo. 1977. "The Information Processing Representation of Institutionalized Social Action." Pp. 35–77 in *Mathematical Models of Sociology,* edited by P. Krishnan. Keele, UK: Sociological Review Monograph 24. Reprinted 1979, Totowa, NJ: Rowman & Littlefield.

Axten, Nick, and John Skvoretz. 1980. "Roles and Role-Programs." *Quality and Quantity* 14:547–583.

Balkwell, James. 1991. "From Expectations to Behavior: An Improved Postulate for Expectation States Theory." *American Sociological Review* 16:461–468.

———. 1995. "Strong Tests of Expectation-States Hypotheses." *Social Psychology Quarterly* 58:44–51.

Berger, Joseph, David Wagner, and Morris Zelditch Jr. 1985. "Introduction: Expectation States Theory, Review and Assessment." Pp. 91–171 in *Status, Rewards, and Influence,* edited by Joseph Berger and Morris Zelditch Jr. San Francisco: Jossey-Bass.

Berger, Peter, and Thomas Luckmann. 1966. *The Social Construction of Reality.* New York: Doubleday.

Blau, Peter M. 1977. *Inequality and Heterogeneity.* New York: Free Press.

Blau, Peter M., Terry C. Blum, and Joseph E. Schwartz. 1982. "Heterogeneity and Intermarriage." *American Sociological Review* 47:45–62.

Blumer, Herbert. 1969. *Symbolic Interactionism.* Englewood Cliffs, NJ: Prentice Hall.

Bourdieu, Pierre. 1990. *The Logic of Practice.* Stanford, CA: Stanford University Press.

Chase, Ivan. 1982. "Dynamics of Hierarchy Formation: The Sequential Development of Dominance Relationships." *Behavior* 80:218–240.

Coleman, James S. 1990. *Foundations of Social Theory.* Cambridge, MA: Harvard University Press.

Coleman, James S., and Thomas J. Fararo, eds. 1992. *Rational Choice Theory: Advocacy and Critique.* Newbury Park, CA: Sage.

Fararo, Thomas J. 1981. "Biased Networks and Social Structure Theorems." *Social Networks* 3:137–159.

———. 1989a. *The Meaning of General Theoretical Sociology: Tradition and Formalization.* ASA Rose Monograph. New York: Cambridge University Press.

———. 1989b. "The Spirit of Unification in Sociological Theory." *Sociological Theory* 7:175–190.

———. 1993. "General Social Equilibrium: Toward Theoretical Synthesis." *Sociological Theory* 11:291–313.

———. 1996. "Foundational Problems in Theoretical Sociology," Pp. 263–284 in *James S. Coleman,* edited by Jon Clark. London: Falmer Press.

Fararo, Thomas J., and Carter T. Butts. 1999. "Advances in Generative Structuralism: Structured Agency and Multilevel Dynamics." *Journal of Mathematical Sociology* 24:1–65.

Fararo, Thomas J., and John Skvoretz. 1984. "Institutions as Production Systems." *Journal of Mathematical Sociology* 10:117–182.

———. 1986a. "Action and Institution, Network and Function: The Cybernetic Concept of Social Structure." *Sociological Forum* 1:219–250.

———. 1986b. "E-state Structuralism: a Theoretical Method." *American Sociological Review* 51:591–602.

———. 1987. "Unification Research Programs: Integrating Two Structural Theories." *American Journal of Sociology* 92:1183–1209.

———. 1988. "Dynamics of the Formation of Stable Dominance Structures," Pp. 327–350 in *Status Generalization,* edited by Murray Webster and Martha Foschi. Stanford, CA: Stanford University Press.

———. 1993. "Methods and Problems of Theoretical Integration and the Principle of Adaptively Rational Action." Pp. 416–450 in *Theoretical Research Programs: Studies in the Growth of Theory,* edited by Joseph Berger and Morris Zelditch Jr. Stanford, CA: Stanford University Press.

———. 1997. "Synthesizing Theories of Deviance and Control: With Steps toward a Dynamic Network Model." Pp. 362–386 in *Status, Network, and Structure: Theory Development in Group Processes,* edited by Jacek Szmatka, John Skvoretz, and Joseph Berger. Stanford, CA: Stanford University Press.

Fararo, Thomas J., John Skvoretz, and Kenji Kosaka. 1994. "Advances in E-state Structuralism: Further Studies in Dominance Structure Formation." *Social Networks* 16:233–265.

Fararo, Thomas J., and Morris Sunshine. 1964. *A Study of a Biased Friendship Net.* Syracuse, NY: Syracuse University Youth Development Center and Syracuse University Press.

Fisek, M. Hamit, Joseph Berger, and Robert Z. Norman. 1991. "Participation in Heterogeneous Groups: A Theoretical Integration." *American Journal of Sociology* 97:114–142.

Giddens, Anthony. 1984. *The Constitution of Society.* Berkeley: University of California Press.

Granovetter, Mark S. 1973. "The Strength of Weak Ties." *American Journal of Sociology* 78:1360–1380.

Homans, George C. 1950. *The Human Group.* New York: Harcourt, Brace & World.

Hummon, Norman P., and Thomas J. Fararo. 1995. "Algorithms for Hierarchy and Balance: For Dynamic Network Models." *Journal of Mathematical Sociology* (Special Issue on Sociological Algorithms, edited by David Heise) 20:145–159.

Messner, Steven F., Marvin D. Krohn, and Allen E. Liska, eds. 1989. *Theoretical Integration in the Study of Deviance and Crime: Problems and Prospects.* Albany: State University of New York Press.

Miller, George A., Eugene Galanter, and Karl H. Pribram. 1960. *Plans and the Structure of Behavior.* New York: Holt.

Nadel, S. F. 1951. *Foundations of Social Anthropology.* New York: Free Press.

———. 1957. *The Theory of Social Structure.* London: Cohen & West.

Newell, Alan, and Herbert A. Simon. 1972. *Human Problem Solving.* Englewood Cliffs, NJ: Prentice-Hall.

Rapoport, Anatol. 1951. "Nets with Distance Bias." *Bulletin of Mathematical Biophysics* 13:85–91.

———. 1957. "Contributions to the Theory of Random and Biased Nets." *Bulletin of Mathematical Biophysics* 19:257–277.

Skvoretz, John. 1983. "Salience, Heterogeneity, and Consolidation of Parameters." *American Sociological Review* 48:360–375.

———. 1984. "Languages and Grammars of Action and Interaction: Some Further Results." *Behavioral Science* 29:281–297.

———. 1988. "Models of Participation in Status-Differentiated Groups." *Social Psychology Quarterly* 51:43–57.

———. 1990. "Social Structure and Intermarriage: A Reanalysis." Pp. 375–396 in *Structures of Power and Constraint: Papers in Honor of Peter M. Blau,* edited by Craig Calhoun, Marshall W. Meyer, and W. Richard Scott. Cambridge: Cambridge University Press.

———. 1998. "Theoretical Models: Sociology's Missing Links." Pp. 238–252 in *What Is Social Theory? The Philosophical Debates,* edited by Alan Sica. Oxford: Blackwell.

Skvoretz, John, and Thomas J. Fararo. 1980. "Languages and Grammars of Action and Interaction: A Contribution to the Formal Theory of Action." *Behavioral Science* 25:9–22.

———. 1986. "Inequality and Association: A Biased Net Theory." Pp. 29–50 in *Current Perspectives in Social Theory,* vol. 7, edited by John Wilson and Scott McNall. Greenwich, CT: JAI Press.

———. 1989. "Connectivity and the Small World Problem." Pp. 296–326 in *The Small World,* edited by Manfred Kochen. Norwood, NJ: Ablex.

———. 1992. "Power and Network Exchange: An Essay toward Theoretical Unification." *Social Networks* (Special Issue on Exchange Networks, edited by David Willer) 14:325–344.

———. 1996a. "Generating Symbolic Interaction: Production Systems Models." *Sociological Methods and Research* 25:60–102.

———. 1996b. "Status and Participation in Task Groups: A Dynamic Network Model." *American Journal of Sociology* 101:1366–1414.

Skvoretz, John, Thomas J. Fararo, and Nick Axten. 1980. "Role Programme Models and the Analysis of Institutional Structure." *Sociology* 14:49–67.

Skvoretz, John, Katherine Faust, and Thomas J. Fararo. 1996. "Social Structure, Networks, and E-state Structuralism Models." *Journal of Mathematical Sociology* 21:57–76.

Skvoretz, John, Murray Webster, and Joseph Whitmeyer. 1999. "Status Orders in Task Discussion Groups." *Advances in Group Process* 16:199–218.

Wagner, David, and Joseph Berger. 1985. "Do Sociological Theories Grow?" *American Journal of Sociology* 90: 697–728.

Wasserman, Stanley, and Katherine Faust. 1994. *Social Network Analysis: Methods and Applications.* New York: Cambridge University Press.

Watts, Duncan J. 1999a. "Networks, Dynamics and the Small World Phenomenon." *American Journal of Sociology* 105:493–527.

———. 1999b. *Small Worlds: The Dynamics of Networks between Order and Randomness.* Princeton, NJ: Princeton University Press.

Wellman, Barry. 1983. "Network Analysis: Some Basic Principles." Pp. 155–200 in *Sociological Theory 1983,* edited by R. Collins. San Francisco: Jossey-Bass.

12

Seven Secrets for Doing Theory

Guillermina Jasso

As always, we begin with first principles. The goal of sociology, and all social science, is to produce reliable knowledge about human behavioral and social phenomena. To reach that goal, we undertake three kinds of activities: theoretical work, empirical work, and, even more basic, we develop frameworks that assemble the main elements which will be used in both theoretical and empirical analysis. Each of these three activities has distinctive goals and distinctive methods. Together they can be represented in the form of a triptych, as in figure 12.1.

This chapter focuses on theoretical work, represented by the left panel of the triptych. Though the chapter is organized as a sequence of steps—or secrets—and this sequence could be thought of as a protocol, the spirit in which it is offered is not so much the spirit of a handbook as the spirit of hints and tips. These hints will make your theoretical work easier and better, and concomitantly easier for you and others to understand it deeply, to build on it, and to devise appropriate tests.

If, later, empirical testing dictates that some of the predictions you derive, or even an entire theory you construct, be rejected, you will still have learned an enormous amount. All the habits of mind you developed in building this theory will assist you in building future theories.

We begin by taking a brief look at the basics of building a theory, focusing on deductive theory (the top subpanel of the theory panel in the triptych). Next we turn to the secrets of theoretical work, beginning with three secrets which provide a foundation for all scientific work (for all the work represented in the triptych in figure 12.1)—and hence labeled and called the zero secrets—and continuing with the secrets of theoretical work proper.

As we proceed, we will illustrate the secrets by drawing on theoretical work in the fields of justice and status. Justice processes and status processes are central to the social life, and understanding them is a central task for sociology. In-

Theoretical Analysis	Framework	Empirical Analysis
Deductive Postulates Predictions ——— *Hierarchical* Postulates Propositions	Questions Actors Quantities Functions Distributions Matrices Contexts	Measure/ estimate terms/relations ——— Test deduced preditions ——— Test propositions

Figure 12.1. Social Science Analysis

deed, the juxtaposition of these illustrations may generate new insights about the multifactor nature of behavioral and social phenomena and, further, about procedures for building theories which model several basic forces jointly.[1]

BASICS OF BUILDING THEORY

A theory begins with an *assumption.* This assumption, alone or with other assumptions, illuminates the behavioral and social world by yielding testable *implications* for a wide range of observable phenomena. Theory is like a tree, all the branches (implications) springing from the same trunk (assumptions). Vast areas of the human experience are linked to a simple and parsimonious set of starting principles.[2]

A theory may be thought of as a list of sentences, a list that can be divided into two parts, the first part containing the assumptions and the second part containing the deduced implications. Figure 12.2 presents a diagram of the structure of a theory. Note that the assumption set is small, while the prediction set is large, and growing (there is no bottom border).

There are two sets of criteria for judging theories. The first is theoretical, the second empirical. Empirical validity is the ultimate test of a theory. But before empirical work is even contemplated, the theory must satisfy the theoretical set of criteria. The assumptions should be mutually logically consistent; there should be a minimum of assumptions and a maximum of predictions. Moreover, a good theory will not only have an abundance of predictions but also the predictions will span many areas of human behavior and will include novel

POSTULATES
PREDICTIONS

Figure 12.2. The Structure of a Theory

predictions, that is, predictions for phenomena or relations not yet observed. Of course, a theory can satisfy all the theoretical criteria and yet be false; empirical evidence is the final arbiter.

Beyond satisfying the criteria by which a theory is judged—and, in particular, raising new questions via its novel predictions—a good theory displays one or more of several useful features: the prediction mix includes both intuitive and counterintuitive predictions; the predictions span all levels of analysis; the theory provides a foundation for measurement; the theory yields a framework for interpretation of rare or nonrecurring events.

THE SECRETS

Secret 0a: Always Know Where We Are Working

Look again at the triptych in figure 12.1. The first of the three underlying zero secrets is to know exactly where we are at all times, in which part of the triptych we find ourselves, precisely. If we are absorbed in the problem of how to frame a question, we are in the framework, in the center panel. If we are grappling with how to collect data to measure a particular concept, we are in the empirical, or right, panel. And if we have settled on a starting assumption and are now ready to deduce its implications, we are doing theory, we are working in the left panel, specifically in the top subpanel of the left panel.

Of course, our minds wander. We may be doing theory, and suddenly we become obsessed with empirical measurement. Or we may be doing empirical estimation, and suddenly we realize that this equation whose parameters we are estimating would make a terrific first postulate for a new theory. That is fine. It is not necessary, or even advisable, to forego the many pleasures—and profits—of following our curiosities. But it is enormously useful to know exactly where we are at all times, where we have been, and where we have arrived.

One way to think about Secret 0a is as a global positioning system, or GPS device. The GPS readout provides the latitude and longitude of the starting point, and visualizes the course we are traveling. It is a good idea to get in the habit of taking stock at the end of the day, tracing the day's adventures across the triptych—and similarly at the end of convenient markers of time, such as the end of the week, month, quarter, year, decade. Perhaps we started in the theory panel but quickly went to the center panel to think again about the questions we are asking, and stayed there for the rest of the day. Or perhaps we walked up and down in the framework panel all week trying to find a mathematical relationship that would serve as the starting assumption for a new theory. Or perhaps we have spent the last three months exclusively in the deductive subpanel of the theoretical panel, deducing implications of a growing theory.

Secret 0b: Keep Handy the List of Questions

It is part of the purpose of the framework to collect the major questions in the topical field. In scientific work, questions are like beacons. They point the way. Wherever in the triptych we are working, it is useful to keep a list of questions handy, perhaps on an index card to carry around with us or as a color slide taped to the refrigerator. Unexplored or neglected issues operate the same way. Keeping them around increases the possibility that when we hit on something potentially useful, we will recognize it. Of course, theoretical analysis yields new questions, opening new avenues for research. These new questions can also be added to the list.

To illustrate, consider the lists of questions in justice analysis and status analysis.

Questions of Justice Analysis

It is currently thought that there are four core questions in the study of justice processes, with each core question encompassing many smaller questions (Jasso and Wegener 1997):

1. What do individuals and collectivities think is just, and why?
2. How do ideas of justice shape determination of actual situations?

3. What is the magnitude of the perceived injustice associated with given departures from perfect justice?
4. What are the behavioral and social consequences of perceived injustice?

As will be seen in the illustrations below, the justice evaluation function, which serves as first postulate for a fruitful justice theory, is the current answer to the third question, and operates to help address the fourth question.

Questions of Status Analysis

A list of unresolved issues is presented in Jasso (2001d:96–97): (1) the emergence of status; (2) how to distinguish between, and measure, the status of persons and the status of characteristics; (3) whether quantitative and qualitative characteristics operate differently; (4) how to measure status gaps between subgroups of a group or society; (5) how to assess the effects of the proportions in different subgroups; (6) how to incorporate multiple bases for status; (7) how status processes differ in small groups and large societies; (8) how status processes differ in task groups and other kinds of groups; and (9) how status is shaped by the degree of correlation among valued personal characteristics.

To our knowledge a set of core questions, similar to the list in justice analysis, has not been proposed. An initial and very tentative list, to which status researchers might add and subtract, might be:

1. What do individuals and collectivities think is worthy of status, and why?
2. How do ideas of status shape determination of actual attainments?
3. What is the magnitude of the status accorded by one person to another? of the status expected by one person from another?
4. What are the behavioral and social consequences of according and receiving status and of discrepancies between expected and received status?

As will be seen in the illustrations below, the S1 status function, which is used as a postulate, represents an answer to the third question and operates to address the fourth question.

Secret 0c: Stay Fixed on the Holy Grail

Beyond the questions of immediate interest there are the larger and fundamental questions. The great goal is to discover the basic forces which govern human behavioral and social phenomena. For these, too, it is useful to keep handy a list of tentative basic forces, perhaps on an index card to carry around with us or as a color slide taped to the refrigerator. Keeping them around, as with the immediate questions, increases the possibility that we will recognize the clues that come our way.

In the spirit of contributing to the search for the Holy Grail, here is a list of four candidates for basic forces: (1) to know the causes of things; (2) to judge the goodness of things; (3) to be perfect; (4) to be free.[3]

As you think of other possibilities for basic forces, add them to your list. And as you take stock of your work, link it to one or more of the candidate-forces on your list.

Secret 1: Think Theoretically

The first secret of theoretical work is to think theoretically. Thinking theoretically represents a radical departure from most of what we learn in college and graduate school. Empirical analysis dominates sociology and many social sciences, and we are taught to think like empirical analysts. In empirical analysis we begin by focusing on an *outcome*—a dependent variable—thinking about what produces it or generates it, shapes it or influences it. These latter factors are the *inputs*, and much of empirical analysis is concerned with discovering the inputs and assessing their effects on the outcome. Symbolically, when we do empirical work we are obsessed with a *Y*, and we seek to learn the identity of the *X*s which produce it and, later, the effects of each *X* on *Y*.

Theoretical thinking is dramatically different. Rather than starting with an outcome, we start with an input—which may itself resemble an *X*-affects-*Y* relation—and focus on this input, investing it with the character of an assumption, and asking what may be its effects or implications, that is, what outcomes it generates. The goal is to discover the outcomes it produces and, later, its effect on each outcome. The input's importance depends on the variety of outcomes it generates and the part it plays in generating them.

Note, moreover, that the implications generated by an assumption will often be in the form of an *X*-affects-*Y* relation. Thus, one may think of an assumption as a *super-input* generating many *super-outcomes*, where each super-input and super-outcome is itself a relation. A fruitful theory will have an abundance of super-outcomes, and the starting point is always the super-input, that is, the assumption generating the predictions.

To illustrate, the justice evaluation function (to be more carefully introduced shortly), when used as an assumption, generates a large variety of super-outcomes, such as:

1. In a society that values wealth, the greater the wealth inequality, the greater will be the amount of conflict between two racial or ethnic subgroups.
2. Post-traumatic stress syndrome is more likely and more severe among veterans of wars fought away from home than among veterans of wars fought on home soil.
3. The parent who dies first is mourned more.

In the foregoing examples, the predictions all have the character of a relation, and thus they are what we are here calling super-outcomes. Note that in each of these super-outcomes, the mini-input—the level of wealth inequality, the war venue, and the timing of death, respectively—does not "cause" the mini-outcome. Rather, the entire relationship embedded in the prediction (in the super-outcome) is "caused" by the entire relationship embedded in the assumption (the super-input, in this case, the justice evaluation function).

Secret 2: Be Willing to Make an Assumption

It is not easy to make an assumption. Part of the attractiveness of science is precisely that it frees us—or rescues us—from ignorance and superstition. There is something concrete to hold on to, a reality against which to test our conjectures. We would feel much safer if we did not have to make an assumption. It would be reassuring to begin with self-evident propositions. And, of course, sometimes we do. But often—perhaps most of the time—the assumption is an idea about human nature and it defies direct test. Thus, in order to assess its validity, we derive its implications and it is the implications that we test. This strategy, invented by Newton and often referred to as the hypothetico-deductive model, makes it possible to learn about human nature by learning about the implications of our assumptions.

Secret 3: Choosing an Assumption

In *Don Quijote*, Cervantes has Don Quijote consider the question of how to choose a husband or wife:

> Anyone starting off on a long trip, if he's sensible, will first try to hunt up some safe and pleasant companions for the road—and why shouldn't you do exactly that, when the trip you're taking is your whole life . . .? (Cervantes 1999:458)

Choosing an assumption may not be as momentous or consequential as choosing a spouse, but for the theorist it comes close. One works day after day, month after month, year after year, with an assumption or set of assumptions. Some assumptions seem to have infinite charms, and if we ask them questions, they reveal themselves, showing astonishing profundity. Others seem shallow, and they soon stop yielding implications.

Unfortunately, it is often difficult to know in advance how an assumption will behave once the theorist goes to work on it. Nonetheless, there are some hints. First, an assumption that is expressed in general terms is likely to be more fruitful than one that is expressed in specific terms. This is because it will apply to many special cases, and each special case will open new avenues of inquiry. Second, an assumption that is mathematically expressed is likely to be more fruitful than one that is expressed only in words. This is due in part to the parsimony of mathematics and in part to the rich variety of mathematical tools that can be applied to deduce the assumption's implications. Moreover, mathematics is the unsurpassed guardian against tautology and other dangers. Third, an assumption that embeds a WHO-WHAT-WHOM form is likely to be unusually fruitful, as it highlights both the actors and the activities involved in the process and as well is amenable to further representations, each of which can be used to yield implications. The "WHO-WHAT-WHOM" label is an abbreviation for "WHO does/thinks/feels WHAT about/with/to WHOM." Note that questions of "how" and "why" are easier to pose and to address if the starting point is in the WHO-WHAT-WHOM form.[4]

The WHO-WHAT-WHOM form highlights the social nature of the phenomena; there are at least two fundamental actors in processes amenable to this representation. Purely individual-level phenomena may be understood via a simpler, intransitive WHO-WHAT form.

Of course, both the simpler WHO-WHAT form as well as the WHO-WHAT-WHOM form may also exhibit attentiveness to the social and temporal context, becoming a WHO-WHAT-WHERE-WHEN form, in the purely individual case, and a WHO-WHAT-WHOM-WHERE-WHEN form in a two-actor social representation.

To illustrate, we look at two assumptions that have been used in building theories, the justice evaluation function of justice analysis and the first-order status function of status analysis.

Justice Evaluation Function

In the justice framework, an observer judges the justice or injustice of a rewardee's holding of a good or bad.[5] For example, the observer may judge the fairness of the rewardee's earnings or prison sentence or grades in school. The rewardee may be the observer him/herself or someone else. This *justice evaluation*, denoted J, is represented by the full real-number line, with zero representing the point of perfect justice, negative numbers representing unjust underreward, and positive nembers representing unjust overreward. Thus, a justice evaluation of zero indicates that the observer judges the rewardee to be perfectly justly rewarded. A justice evaluation of -2 and a justice evaluation of -4 both indicate that the observer judges the rewardee to be unjustly underrewarded, with the rewardee associated with the -4 judged to be more underrewarded than the rewardee associated with the -2. Similarly, a justice evaluation of 2 and a justice evaluation of 4 both indicate that the observer judges the rewardees to be unjustly overrewarded, with the rewardee accorded the 4 judged to be more overrewarded than the rewardee accorded the 2.

The justice evaluation function expresses the justice evaluation J as a function of the discrepancy between the rewardee's actual amount or level of the good or bad—the *actual reward*, denoted A—and the amount or level judged just for the rewardee by the observer—the *just reward*, denoted C. The reward may be cardinal, like wealth, or ordinal, like beauty. The justice evaluation function can be expressed in a number of ways, ranging from a general form to a specific form which embodies a logarithmic specification:

$$J = \theta \ln\left(\frac{A}{C}\right), \tag{12.1}$$

where, as before, J denotes the justice evaluation, A denotes the actual reward, and C denotes the just reward. The form in expression (12.1) also includes the Signature Constant, denoted θ, which captures both the observer's framing of the reward as a good or a bad and the observer's expressiveness. The justice evaluation function was introduced in Jasso (1978) and first used as an assumption in Jasso (1980).[6]

When the good or bad to which the justice evaluation refers is cardinal, the actual and just rewards are measured in the reward's own units, for example, in a monetary currency or as acres of land; and the actual and just rewards are called, more specifically, the actual amount and the just amount. When the good or bad to which justice evaluation refers is ordinal, the actual and just rewards are measured as relative ranks; in this case, the actual and just rewards are called the actual rank and the just rank.[7]

In cases in which the cardinal thing is divided among a set of recipients, the actual amount and just amount are sometimes called the actual share and just share. For example, if the justice evaluation is about income, the terms actual income share and just income share may be used. Of course, the "share" terminology would not be applicable to such things as prison sentences, for years to be spent in prison are not divided among a set of inmates.[8]

In justice analysis, the justice evaluation function is embedded in a system that includes several other functions (such as the just reward function, the allocation function, the perceived-actual reward function, and the justice consequences function).

First-Order Status Function

In the status framework, an observer, sometimes called Self, accords *first-order status*, denoted S1, to a target, sometimes called Other. S1 is represented by positive numbers. Thus, a person receiving S1 status of, say, 3, has substantially greater status than a person receiving S1 of .5.

The S1 status function expresses the individual's status as a function of his or her *rank* on a quantitative characteristic, such as beauty, intelligence, or wealth:

$$S1 = \ln\left(\frac{1}{1-r}\right), \tag{12.2}$$

where r denotes the relative rank (between zero and one) on the valued quantitative characteristic. Sørensen (1979) introduced the status function, applying it to occupations, and used it as an assumption in a theory of occupational status; the status function embodies properties held by Goode (1978) to be important in an individual-level status function, and was used as an individual-level assumption in Jasso (2001d).[9]

Because the relative rank r refers to a person's actual characteristic or holding, it is sometimes called the actual rank, exactly as in the case of the justice evaluation function when the reward is ordinal.

The S1 function is embedded in a system that includes at least two other equations (the S2 and S3 status functions).

Both the justice evaluation function and the S1 status function possess the three desirable properties listed above. First, they are both general functions, applying to a wide number of actors and contexts; for example, the justice evaluation function is applicable to the study of earnings, punishments, grades, and so on, and the S1 status function is applicable to the study of status processes in all kinds of groups. Second, both are mathematically expressed. Third, both embed the WHO-WHAT-WHOM form; for example, in the justice evaluation function, the observer judges the fairness of the reward held by the rewardee, and in the S1 status function, the observer accords status to a target recipient. In fact, both the justice evaluation function and the S1 status function are attentive to the social and temporal context, and thus display the more elaborate WHO-WHAT-WHOM-WHERE-WHEN form.

Again, note that questions of how and why become easier to pose and address. In the justice case, the justice evaluation function leads to consideration of the discrepancy between the actual reward and the just reward and to the mechanisms by which observers form ideas of the just reward (the first core question in the list above). Similarly, in the status case, the S1 status function leads to consideration of the mechanisms by which goods come to be valued and individuals attain their ranks on these goods' distributions (the first and second questions in the provisional list of core questions set forth above). Further, both the J and the S1 functions lend themselves easily to representation via associated distributions and matrices (see, for example, the matrix representations of J in Jasso (1999:136–141) and of S1 in Jasso (2001d:101), thus preparing them for application of a wide variety of tools for deriving predictions.

Secret 4: Getting to Know an Assumption

Before getting to work deriving implications from an assumption, it is useful to learn as much as possible about the assumption's properties and behavior. Of course, there is much one already knows, and usually this knowledge has become part of the framework. Thus, it may be that all that is necessary is to review this knowledge, perhaps making color slides with the main properties or a handy list on an index card to carry around.

When the assumption is a mathematical function, getting to know the assumption begins with characterizing the function. In general, we begin with the following properties of the function: (1) domain; (2) range; (3) monotonicity; (4) convexity; (5) zeros; (6) y-intercepts; (7) extrema.

Of course, functions may be characterized in many further ways that shed additional light on the operation of the proposition chosen to play the part of assumption.

To illustrate, we examine the justice evaluation function and the S1 status function. We begin by placing them side by side, as in table 12.1, and listing some key features.

As shown, initial inspection of the justice evaluation function and the S1 status function reveals that the justice evaluation function represents a substantially more elaborate process than the S1 status function. First, the justice evaluation is a function of two variables—the actual reward and the just reward—while the S1 status function is a function of only one variable—the actual rank. Second, the justice evaluation function distinguishes between cardinal and ordinal rewards, while the S1 status function notices only ordinal properties of goods and bads. Third, the justice evaluation includes an extra parameter, the Signature Constant θ.

Thus, we know at the outset that justice effects will be more tightly linked to contextual features than status effects. While justice effects will differ between societies that value cardinal things (materialistic societies) and societies that value ordinal things (nonmaterialistic societies), status effects will be the same in both. Moreover, amounts of cardinal things will play a part in justice effects but not in status effects; and similarly inequality in the distributions of cardinal things will play a part in justice effects but not in status effects.

Justice effects will thus be more challenging to derive than status effects. Or so it would appear at first blush.

To further contrast the justice evaluation function and the S1 status function, we obtain a special case of the justice evaluation function, which eliminates the

Table 12.1. The Justice Evaluation Function and the S1 Status Function

Justice Evaluation Function	*S1 Status Function*
$J = \theta \ln\left(\frac{A}{C}\right)$	$S1 = \ln\left(\frac{1}{1-r}\right)$
• Two independent variables, the actual reward *A* and the just reward *C*	• One independent variable, the relative rank *r* on an actual characteristic or holding
• Distinguishes between cardinal and ordinal characteristics and rewards	• No distinction between cardinal and ordinal characteristics and rewards
• Includes extra parameter, the Signature Constant θ	• No extra parameter
Both *J* and S1 can accommodate multiple goods or bads; the number and weights may vary across persons.	

extra parameter and expresses J as a function of a single independent variable. First, we restrict attention to the case of a good, thus restricting the Signature Constant θ to positive values. Second, we set the Signature Constant to one, that is, purging the justice evaluation of the observer's expressiveness (a quantity which plays an important part in empirical work but which can be safely deleted in a large fraction of theoretical work). Third, we add the assumption known as the Identity Representation of the Just Reward, whereby the just reward is expressed as the arithmetic mean of the actual reward, multiplied by a parameter θ which captures everything unknown to the theorist about how the observer forms ideas of justice. Fourth, for purposes of this illustration, we let θ equal one, thus representing the just reward by the expected value of the actual reward. The special case of the justice evaluation function obtained by this procedure is written:

$$J = \ln\left(\frac{A}{E(A)}\right), \tag{12.3}$$

where $E(\cdot)$ denotes the expected-value operator.[10]

The special-case version of the justice evaluation function in (12.3), because it has only one independent variable (the just amount being constant in this special case), enables a conventional contrast with the S1 status function. To further sharpen the contrast, we make use of the fact that the rank in the S1 status function is an actual rank, and insert the subscript "A," writing:

$$\text{S1} = \ln\left(\frac{1}{1-r_A}\right). \tag{12.4}$$

Contrasting equation (12.3) and equation (12.4), we see that the functions differ in domain and range. The domain of the justice evaluation function is the set of all positive numbers, while the domain of the status function is the set of positive numbers less than one. The range of the justice evaluation function is the full set of real numbers, while the range of the status function spans only the set of positive numbers. While both functions are increasing in the actual term (the actual amount or the actual rank in the case of J, the actual rank in the case of S1), they differ importantly in convexity. The justice evaluation function increases at a decreasing rate as A increases, but the S1 function increases at an increasing rate as the actual rank increases (this is the property emphasized by Goode 1978).

Of course, there are many further properties to explore in getting to know these two functions. And, of course, the justice evaluation function must be understood in its entirety. For example, the complete two-argument function (as in expression (12.1)), is a symmetric function; it has the properties of additivity and scale-invariance; it is neither convex nor concave (further properties are described in Jasso 1999, 2001a).

Substantively, getting to know the assumption selected for use in building a theory, as in this initial look at the justice evaluation function and the S1 status function, prepares the theorist for the derivations to come. We know already that justice effects and status effects will differ, though we have only the barest intimation about how they will differ or how much or in which contexts.

Secret 5: Distinguish between Small Groups and Large Populations

In sociology, groups are our bread and butter. Groups shape individuals, and individuals shape groups; and the nature of these processes is a central focus. Thus, it will not be a surprise that one of the most useful things for a theorist to do is to take the assumption and immediately express it in two distinct ways, one amenable to small groups and the other to large populations. In general, if a formula contains a group size factor, it is the formula for small groups; otherwise, it is the formula for large populations. Technically, the formula for large populations may be thought of as the limiting case of the formula for small groups, as the group size N goes to infinity.

To illustrate, we now obtain small-group and large-population formulas for the special case of the justice evaluation function obtained above and reported in expression (12.3) and for the S1 status function.

Justice Evaluation Function—Small-Group Formulas

We obtain formulas for both the cardinal case and the ordinal case.

In the case of cardinal goods, the justice evaluation function in (12.3) is rewritten:

$$J = \ln\left(\frac{xN}{S}\right), \tag{12.5}$$

where x denotes the individual's own wealth, S denotes the total group wealth, and N denotes the group size, and the expression makes use of the fact that the arithmetic mean is equal to the total group wealth divided by the group size.

In the case of ordinal goods, the justice evaluation function reduces to:

$$J = \ln\left(\frac{2i}{N+1}\right), \tag{12.6}$$

where i denotes the absolute rank (represented by the sequence of positive integers from 1 to N), the relative rank is represented by $[i/(N+1)]$, and the arithmetic mean of the relative ranks is $\frac{1}{2}$.

Justice Evaluation Function—Large-Population Formulas

In the cardinal case, the formula is merely a restatement of (12.3):

$$J = \ln\left(\frac{x}{E(X)}\right), \tag{12.7}$$

where X denotes the valued good, and, as in the usual notation, lowercase letters are used for an individual amount and uppercase for the variate.

To construct the large-population formula for the ordinal case, let α denote the relative rank (of which the quantity $[i/(N+1)]$ is an approximation), so that we write:

$$J = \ln(2\alpha). \tag{12.8}$$

Note that, as expected, the small-group formulas include the group size N and the large-population formulas do not.

In the same way, we obtain the small-group and large-population formulas for the S1 status function.

S1 Status Function—Small-Group Formula

The S1 status function notices only ranks, and thus the expression is straightforward. Using the same notation as in the case of the justice evaluation function, the formula, derived from formula (12.2), is written:

$$\mathrm{S1} = \ln\left(\frac{N+1}{N+1-i}\right). \tag{12.9}$$

S1 Status Function—Large-Population Formula

For consistency with the notation used for the justice evaluation function, we rewrite expression (12.2) using α to denote the relative rank:

$$\mathrm{S1} = \ln\left(\frac{1}{1-\alpha}\right). \tag{12.10}$$

Note again that N appears in the small-group formula but not in the large-population formula.

It seems like a small, even trivial, thing. Yet, having ready these formulas that distinguish between small groups and large populations will substantially enlarge the scope and vision of the deduced implications. Not only will there be parallel sets of predictions for small groups and large populations, but also there will often be new predictions that contrast the effects in small groups with the effects in large populations.

Secret 6: Techniques for Deriving Implications

This is the exciting part. Look around. There is a multitude of behavioral and social phenomena all around us. People engage in conversation; they react with fear, anger, joy; they make plans. Nations go to war. People give gifts and leave bequests. Individuals get sick; they develop eating disorders, post-traumatic stress disorders, other ailments. Sometimes religious institutions thrive, at other times they shrivel for lack of members. Planes crash and trains derail; the earth quakes and volcanoes erupt.

We now ask: What does this assumption I am working with imply for all these sociobehavioral situations? Is it possible to derive predictions about justice effects in disasters? For gift giving? For theft? For the growth of the Franciscan and Dominican orders in the thirteenth century? What about status effects? Is it possible to derive predictions about status effects in all these situations?

Many years of work on justice theory provide abundant evidence that justice processes have a long reach, touching virtually every area of the human experience. What about status effects?

The work on justice theory has developed three main techniques for deriving implications. The three techniques have come to be called the *micromodel*, *macromodel*, and *matrixmodel* strategies. As well, there is an emergent fourth technique, which though used briefly in the past has not until this chapter been thought of as an independent set of procedures. It is applicable to the study of small groups and networks, and hence we call it the *mesomodel* strategy. This fourth technique may prove useful not only in the study of justice and status but also in the study of power and other small-group processes. We briefly review the four strategies for deriving predictions.[11]

Micromodel Strategy

The micromodel approach begins with investigation of the effects of an event on an individual, where the event may be a human action (such as giving a gift or stealing a radio), or the outcome of a human action (such as receiving a gift or having a radio stolen), or an event not traceable to human agency (such as a natural disaster). The objective is to assess the effects of the event on some characteristic of all individuals in the collectivity. In justice theory, the characteristic of interest is the sense of justice. The micromodel thus makes it possible to ascertain change in the sense of being justly or unjustly rewarded, establishing, for example, who becomes better off and who becomes worse off, and by how much. The basic equation in the micromodel approach is an equation that compares the individual at two points in time. The micromodel uses small-group formulas, but, interestingly, yields effects at all levels of analysis. For example, the micromodel yields the macrolevel prediction that a society is more vulnerable to deficit spending as its wealth increases.

There are two variants of the micromodel strategy, one used for cardinal things, the other for ordinal things. However, most of the work done to date has used the cardinal-good version. In this version, the justice evaluation function is expressed as a function of own wealth, group wealth, and group size (as in expression (12.5), except that the idiosyncrasy parameter ϕ is kept in the formula). A change in any of these three factors will produce a change in the justice evaluation. A change-in-J equation is set up, denoted the CJ equation. It is then possible to assess the effects of any action or event that alters one or more of the three factors. For example, in a theft situation, the theft alters the own wealth of the thief and the victim and may alter the total group wealth if the thief and victim come from different groups. It is also possible to compare the outcomes in insider theft and outsider theft. To illustrate, justice theory yields the prediction that the thief's gain from theft is greater when stealing from a fellow group member rather than from an outsider, and the further prediction that this increment to the gain is itself greater the poorer the group.

In the ordinal-good version of the micromodel strategy, there are only two sources of change, own rank and group size. Preliminary, unpublished work with this model suggests that vulnerability to anorexia, for example, will be greater in large groups than in small groups.

Only the ordinal-good version of the micromodel strategy can be used to study S1 status effects. It will be interesting to see how useful the micromodel strategy will be in deriving predictions in status theory. Concomitantly, using the ordinal version to study status processes may renew interest in its use to study justice processes, thus potentially leading to many new predictions.

Both the cardinal and ordinal versions may prove useful for deriving predictions from a broad range of assumptions, far removed from the study of status and justice.

Macromodel Strategy

The second major technique that has been used in justice theory is the macromodel strategy. The macromodel strategy begins with the distribution of a theoretically based quantity in a collectivity. When the macromodel is used in justice theory, the theorist begins with the distribution of the justice evaluation. Interest centers on parameters of that distribution, and on a variety of other features, such as substantively pertinent subdistribution structures. For example, in justice theory, two kinds of subdistribution structures are studied: (1) the truncated subdistribution structure associated with three subgroups—the underrewarded, the justly rewarded, and the overrewarded; and (2) the censored subdistribution structure associated with splitting the collectivity into subgroups defined by a qualitative characteristic such as race, ethnicity, religion, gender, and the like.

The macromodel strategy uses the large-population formulas, but, like the micromodel strategy, it, too, yields implications at all levels of analysis. For example, it yields the microlevel prediction that the overreward experienced by the most beautiful or most talented person in a collectivity is modest compared to the overreward experienced by the wealthiest person.

In general, there are two main goals in the macromodel approach. The first is to obtain distribution-independent results; the second is to obtain results for a wide variety of distributional forms that can be considered as approximations to real-world distributions of the theoretically based quantities. For example, cardinal goods (and bads) are represented by a wide variety of distributional forms (e.g., the Pareto, lognormal, power-function, and so on). Part of the excitement lies in assessing differences between societies which value cardinal goods and societies which value ordinal goods, as well as, within the set which value cardinal goods, differences by the distributional form of the valued cardinal good.

To illustrate, we draw on a study of subgroup conflict that used this strategy (Jasso 1993a). That study derived the prediction that in societies that value ordinal goods, conflict severity is a decreasing function of the proportion in the disadvantaged subgroup (for example, the disadvantaged race, religion, or ethnicity). However, in societies that value cardinal goods, the direction of the effect of the proportion disadvantaged on conflict severity differs by the distributional form of the valued good. For example, in one kind of distributional form, conflict severity increases as the proportion disadvantaged increases; in a second kind of distributional form, conflict severity is a decreasing function of proportion disadvantaged; and in a third kind of distributional form, conflict severity is a nonmonotonic function of proportion disadvantaged, decreasing to its nadir when the two subgroups are of equal size and subsequently increasing.

Current work is using the macromodel strategy to derive predictions from status theory. One of the first pieces of research investigates conflict severity, setting up a model that parallels the model used to obtain justice effects (Jasso 2002). This work indicates that if conflict severity is a function of the status gap rather than of the discrepancy in the experience of justice and injustice, then conflict severity increases as the proportion in the bottom subgroup increases—opposite the ordinal-good result in the justice case. Indeed, there are further intriguing results. The conflict severity function arising from status processes and the conflict severity function arising from justice processes in the ordinal case are reflections of each other about the vertical line at the subgroup split of .5. Thus, given, say, a subgroup split of 10-90, conflict severity will be substantially greater in a society where individuals are motivated by the sense of justice than in a society where they are motivated by status. In fact, conflict severity in a justice society with a 10-90 subgroup split will be as great as conflict severity in a status society with a subgroup split of 90-10. Meanwhile, a society in which the subgroup split is exactly 50-50 will have the same conflict severity whether justice or status processes are dominant.

As with the micromodel strategy, it is likely that the macromodel will prove useful for deriving predictions in many fields beyond justice analysis and status analysis.

Matrixmodel Strategy

The matrixmodel strategy, as the name suggests, begins with the entire matrix of self-other or observer-rewardee magnitudes. Justice theory has made limited, but productive, use of the matrixmodel strategy to date. Its use seems appealing in status analysis. For example, we can imagine models in which each actor considers the distribution of status he or she receives from all group members, setting in motion a train of individual and social behaviors, including phenomena classically associated with the looking-glass self.

Note that the matrixmodel strategy is uniquely suited for studying consensus processes. This should prove useful in the deeper analyses of justice and status processes still to come.

Note also that the matrixmodel is not limited to study of assumptions in the WHO-WHAT-WHOM form—though this is a natural and appealing application—as it can also be used for studying intransitive WHO-WHAT-WHEN-WHERE forms which incorporate social and temporal context.

Of course, like the micromodel and macromodel strategies, the matrixmodel strategy may prove useful for deriving predictions from a wide variety of assumptions.

Mesomodel Strategy

Recently, a new technique for deriving predictions has emerged. It was used in early work on justice theory (Jasso 1983) and again recently in status theory (Jasso 2001d). This technique begins with an entire small group, characterizing each member by his/her theoretically given quantity—say, the justice evaluation or S1 status—and proceeds to assess the relations among subsets of members. Important areas for investigation include the social distance between adjacent individuals and between the bottom and top members.

In this strategy, we begin with the small-group formulas—for example, equation (12.6) for the justice evaluation function in the case of ordinal goods and equation (12.9) for the S1 status function. From these formulas we derive the formulas for each relation or quantity of interest, for example, for the difference in S1 status between two adjacent individuals, for the average S1 status, and for the distance between the bottom person and the top person. The entire small group can be visualized by graphing the S1 and/or J magnitudes for each group member.

To illustrate, figure 12.3 provides a way to visualize a 12-member group in both the justice (ordinal-good) case and the status case.[12] The S1 status magnitudes and the justice evaluation magnitudes are plotted for each member of the group. Note that while the status scores would be the same for any group of 12 persons which values one good (or several positively correlated goods), the justice scores would differ in groups whose members value cardinal goods.

As shown, for every member of the group, the status score is greater than the justice score. This means that if justice and status are commensurate quantities—if, for example, they contribute to happiness—individuals who care more about status than about justice will be happier persons. The difference, however, is not constant. As shown, the gap between J and S1 is greater for the bottom- and top-ranked group members, and is smallest for the middle ranks.

In a preliminary way, figure 12.3 raises the question whether anhedonia might be a sickness of justice seekers and analgēsia a sickness of status seekers, opening for systematic inquiry a line of thought that stretches back to the ancient Greeks.

Three results obtained using the mesomodel strategy warrant discussion. First, the formulas for the distance between adjacent group members (for example, between the third-ranked and the fourth-ranked) indicate that in groups whose members are dominated by justice concerns, each person is closer to the neighbor above than to the neighbor below, while the opposite occurs in groups whose members are dominated by status concerns (figure 12.3 illus-

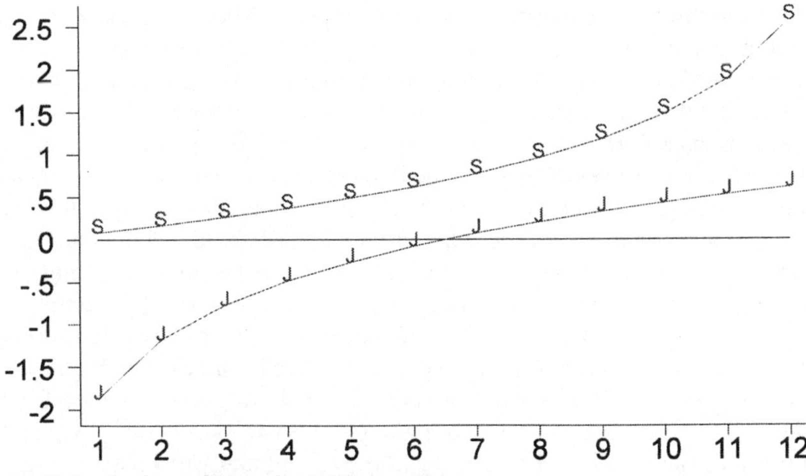

Figure 12.3. Justice and Status in a 12-Person Group

trates this effect for 12-person groups). This prediction is highly suggestive for experiments in small groups and networks.[13]

Second, the group size influences in opposite ways the average status and the average justice evaluation. As group size increases, the average justice evaluation (i.e., the justice index JI1 proposed in Jasso 1999) decreases but the average status increases.

Third, notwithstanding the many differences between the justice group and the status group, the distance between the top and bottom members is the same in both kinds of groups—ln(N)—increasing with group size.

The mesomodel strategy rounds out the four sets of techniques for deriving predictions that have proved useful in justice analysis and, more recently, in status analysis. All four strategies have the potential for wide applicability in a wide range of theories.

Secret 7: Presenting the Theory and Reporting New Predictions

All the work is done. At least for now. You chose an assumption, and you derived predictions from it. Very likely you were surprised by some of the predictions. Some of the predictions were intuitive, but others wildly counterintuitive. Moreover, some of the predictions involved phenomena or relations you quite literally had never heard of—the vaunted novel predictions. You are becoming respectful of the assumption. It has a long reach, touching broad areas of the human experience.

Now you have to tell your colleagues about your work.

As discussed in Secret 1, most training in the social sciences emphasizes empirical work. In the usual social science curriculum there is little preparation for writing a theory paper. Here I provide some hints.[14]

There are three main ingredients in a theory paper. Theory begins with an assumption, and the first ingredient in a theory paper is a description of the assumption or assumptions. The description should be complete enough that any reader can take the assumption(s) and not only replicate your work (that is, derive the predictions reported in the paper) but also derive new predictions. The second ingredient, corresponding to the methods section in an empirical paper, is description of the procedures used to derive the predictions. For example, if you use the macromodel strategy, the description will include the distributional families used to model the distributions of the theoretical quantities in the assumption(s); and the description will mention any special tools used (such as central limit theorems or l'Hôpital's Rule). The final ingredient is, of course, the predictions.

In reporting the assumption(s), it is often useful to summarize them in a table. Tabular presentation has several advantages, including convenience for the reader and potential user of the assumption(s), who need only refer to the table rather than hunting through the text. Moreover, tabular presentation reduces the possibility of confusion; in particular, it eliminates all uncertainty about what is being assumed and what is being deduced.

To illustrate, table 12.2 presents the set of five assumptions currently used in justice theory. As shown, the first assumption is the justice evaluation function, used in this chapter to illustrate the Secrets. The second and third assumptions also played a part in our illustration.

In reporting the predictions, the theorist has several options. The predictions may be arranged in several alternative ways. If the predictions span several topical domains, they may be arranged by subject matter. If the predictions are obtained by several procedures, they may be classified according to the procedure. In a paper highlighting the scientific antecedents of the predictions, the arrangement might be by insights in earlier work. In a paper assessing the structure of the theory, a useful tool is the Merton Chart of Theoretical Derivation, proposed in Jasso (1993b), a spreadsheet-like presentation which not only reports the predictions but also the postulates and provides space for indicating which assumptions were used to generate each prediction. Finally, of course, the list of predictions may be simply presented, with no internal arrangement.

Examples of these various kinds of presentational options include the following: Jasso (2001c) provides a list of predictions obtained via the micromodel strategy, further classified by topical domain; the topical domains include "Gifts," "International Migration," and so on. Jasso (2000) provides a list of predictions which embody insights in Merton's ([1949, 1957] 1968) and Merton and Rossi's (1950) work on reference groups, and these are arranged by the original Merton and Rossi ideas; to illustrate, the headings include "Effects of Group Absolute and Relative Size," "Effect of Stratification Structure," and so on.

A sample blank Merton Chart of Theoretical Derivation is presented in figure 12.4. There is space for the formulas associated with each assumption (in the cells immediately below the heading "Postulates") and, of course, there is space for the predictions. Checkmarks are used to indicate which postulates were used to obtain

Table 12.2. Fundamental Postulates of Justice Theory

A. Individual-Level Postulates

1. Postulate of Logarithmic Specification

$$J = \theta \ln\left(\frac{A}{C}\right)$$

2. Measurement Rule for Holdings

$$A, C: \begin{cases} x, & \text{cardinal good/bad} \\ \dfrac{i}{N+1}, & \text{ordinal good/bad} \end{cases}$$

3. Identity Representation of Just Reward

$$C = \phi E(A)$$

B. Social-Level Postulates

4. Social Welfare

$$SW = E(J)$$

5. Social Cohesiveness

$$Social\ Cohesiveness = -GMD(J)$$

Notes: As described in the text, J denotes the justice evaluation, A the actual reward, and C the just reward. The signature constant θ is positive for goods and negative for bads. For both actual and just rewards, x denotes the amount of the cardinal good or bad, i denotes the rank-order statistics arranged in ascending order, and N denotes the population size. ϕ denotes the individual-specific parameter, $E(\cdot)$ the expected value, and $GMD(\cdot)$ the Gini's mean difference.

each prediction. The Merton Chart enables assessment not only of how many assumptions, and which assumptions, are required to generate each prediction, but also of which assumptions are doing most of the work. Analysis of this type of presentation may lead, for example, to elimination of an assumption. For an example of a filled-out Merton Chart, see Jasso (1993b:240–241); in this example, the postulates are represented by the associated formulas, exactly as given in table 12.2.

If a theory paper focuses exclusively on predictions in one topical domain and if all the predictions are obtained using the same technique, there may be no particular reason to differentiate them. In such case, it is sufficient to list them. For an example, see Jasso (1993a).

Theory: ____________________ *Date:* ____________
Page: ____________

PREDICTIONS	POSTULATES				

Notes:

Figure 12.4. Merton Chart of Theoretical Derivation

Sometimes the predictions are sufficiently elaborate that they require further and sharper tabular presentation. For example, the predictions on the emergence of norms about theft reported in Jasso (2001c) distinguish between homogeneous groups and heterogeneous groups, and they include predictions on strength of various constituencies (thief, victim, members of thief's group, members of victim's group, societal Guardians) for various kinds of norms (general theft norms, punishment norms, etc.).

Finally, sometimes the intent is to provide a flavor for the predictions, and a simple list may be all that is necessary. To illustrate, table 12.3 lists some of the predictions that have been obtained in justice theory. There is no division by topical domain, though predictions for similar types of phenomena tend to be near each other. There is no indication which technique was used to derive them. Such a list is useful nonetheless because it signals the long reach of the underlying process. In this case, table 12.3 indicates that justice processes influence the timing of parental gift giving, play a part in patterns of grief, shape a thief's choice of victim, and are discernible in immigration policy. The theorist becomes eager to find other justice effects.

There is a further importance attached to the list of predictions. Remember, predictions require test, and testing requires prior dissemination of the predictions to the scholars most qualified to design and carry out the tests—the empirical social scientists who specialize in the topical domain of the predictions. It is thus a critical task to communicate with non-theorists and topical specialists (family sociologists, criminologists, health specialists, and so on). The list of predictions—and the abstract—may be the best way to reach them.[15]

Table 12.3. Some Predictions of Justice Theory

1. The problem for new groups is to choose the valued goods.
2. Newcomers are more likely to be welcomed by groups that value cardinal goods than by groups that value ordinal goods, and more likely to be welcomed by groups that play games of chance than by groups that play games of skill.
3. A thing changes value as it, and its owner, move from group to group.
4. Parents of non-twin children will spend more of their toy budget at an annual giftgiving occasion rather than at the children's birthdays.
5. A gift is more valuable to the receiver when the giver is present.
6. Thieves prefer to steal from fellow group members rather than from outsiders.
7. Society loses when rich steal from poor.
8. The norm, "Thou shalt not steal," is not likely to arise unless it is imposed by Guardians; in homogeneous societies it does not arise because most of the population is indifferent, and in heterogeneous societies because there are strong factions both in support and in opposition.
9. A society becomes more vulnerable to deficit spending as its wealth increases.
10. In wartime, the favorite leisure-time activity of soldiers is playing games of chance.
11. Posttraumatic stress is greater among veterans of wars fought away from home than among veterans of wars fought on home soil.
12. In historical periods when wives tend to predecease their husbands (e.g., due to death in childbirth), mothers are mourned more than fathers; but in historical periods when husbands tend to predecease their wives (e.g., due to war), fathers are mourned more than mothers.
13. The death of a child is mourned more than the death of a parent.
14. Societies that welcome immigration must be societies that value at least one cardinal good—that is, materialistic societies.
15. In materialistic societies, emigration is an increasing function of income inequality.

16.1. A necessary condition for origin and destination countries to both oppose, or to both favor, bilateral migration is that they have unequal wealth.

16.2. A necessary condition for the origin and destination countries to both favor the migration is that the origin country be a poor country and the destination country a rich country; a necessary condition for the origin and destination countries to both oppose the migration is that the origin country be a rich country and the destination country a poor country.

17. Vocations to the religious life are an increasing function of income inequality.

18. In materialistic societies, the salutary effect of the cloister differs by the shape of the income distribution.
19. The larger the cloistered subgroup, the greater the benefit conferred by the cloister.
20. Conflict severity is a function of subgroup size and, in a materialistic society, always increases with income inequality.
21. In a conflict situation, the direction of the effect of subgroup size depends on whether the society values cardinal or ordinal goods.
22. In a conflict situation in a materialistic society, the direction of the effect of subgroup size depends on the shape of the income distribution.
23. In societies that value ordinal goods, the larger the group, the lower the average happiness.
24. In a disaster, if there is no property loss but at least one death, then all group members will experience psychological distress.
25. The greater the economic inequality, the greater the sense of injustice.

AFTERWORD

We end as we began—with first principles. The goal of social science is to accumulate reliable knowledge about human behavioral and social phenomena. Theoretical work, represented by the left panel of the triptych in figure 12.1, is critically important for making progress toward our goal.

The seven secrets for doing theory will make your theoretical work easier and better. Your theories will be more beautiful—their assumption set more spartan, their prediction set more abundant. Indeed, even before reaching the end of this chapter, your mind will already be at work. You will derive the formulas for justice and status processes used here as examples, and you will graph them. You will derive new predictions from the assumptions presented here, gaining familiarity with the derivation strategies and tasting the pleasures of new predictions. Later you will suddenly see formulas for other basic processes; you will bring them out of their hiding places, and use them as the first assumptions of new theories.

The seven secrets are signposts on our way to the Holy Grail.

NOTES

1. For fuller and more comprehensive exposition of the ideas in this chapter and the formulas used in the illustrations, see the following sources: (1) on the basics of doing theory, Jasso (1988, 2001b); (2) on justice analysis, Jasso (1999, 2001a); (3) on status analysis, Jasso (2001d); and (4) on basic forces, Jasso (2001c). Of course, this work has a rich foundation. For example, (1) on doing theory, see Berger, Zelditch, and Anderson (1972); (2) on justice analysis, see Berger, Zelditch, Anderson, and Cohen (1972); and (3) on status analysis, see Berger, Fisek, Norman, and Zelditch (1977); Goode (1978); Rossi (1979), Sørensen (1979); and Turner (1984).

2. Here we use the terms *assumption* and *postulate* and *starting principle* interchangeably, and similarly with the terms *implication* and *consequence* and *prediction*. See Jasso (2001b) for discussion of the nuances associated with these terms.

3. Further discussion of the candidate-forces will be found in Jasso (2001c).

4. It is no accident that the WHO-WHAT-WHOM form makes great titles in film and fiction; as examples, consider *Paul Loves Libby* and *When Harry Met Sally*.

5. A quantitative thing of which more is preferred to less is called a good, and a quantitative thing of which less is preferred to more is called a bad.

6. Comprehensive exposition of properties of the justice evaluation function appears in Jasso (1999).

7. This procedure is known as the "measurement rule." It was introduced in Jasso (1980) so that the justice evaluation function, which originally applied only to cardinal things, could be applied as weil to ordinal things. In the usual axiomatization, the measurement rule appears as the second assumption.

8. In empirical justice analysis, the "share" terminology is appropriate only for fixed-pie things divided among a set of recipients.

9. Comprehensive exposition of properties of the first-order status function appears in Jasso (2001d).

10. When the special justice evaluation in (3) refers to cardinal things, the ratio of the actual amount to the mean amount (the quantity in the denominator) is called the relative amount. This is the same relative amount that plays an important part in the measurement of inequality (Firebaugh 1998, 1999).

11. The (cardinal-good version of the) micromodel strategy is comprehensively described in Jasso (2001c), and the macromodel strategy in Jasso (1997). The matrixmodel strategy is of more recent vintage, and the protocol has not yet been fully systematized. The mesomodel strategy, though encompassing a set of procedures that have been used previously (Jasso 1983, 2001d), has also not yet been fully systematized.

12. Twelve-member groups play an important part not only in the real world (as in juries) but also in history and fiction. The mesomodel procedures could be used to analyze, say, relations among the 12 peers of France.

13. This result is a consequence of the convexity properties of the two functions.

14. See also the recent helpful paper by Thomson (1999).

15. It would be useful to think further about mechanisms for disseminating theoretical predictions to empirical topical specialists. One possibility would be for topical journals (e.g., *Journal of Health and Social Behavior*, *Journal of Marriage and the Family*, *Sociology of Education*, and the like) to include a "Theoretical Prediction Department" which would publish a list of predictions submitted by theorists and based on theoretical work published elsewhere. This is a topic that requires further thought.

REFERENCES

Berger, Joseph, Hamit Fisek, Robert Norman, and Morris Zelditch. 1977. *Status Characteristics and Social Interaction: An Expectation States Approach*. New York: Elsevier.

Berger, Joseph, Morris Zelditch Jr., and Bo Anderson. 1972. "Introduction." Pp. ix–xxii in *Sociological Theories in Progress,* Volume 2, edited by Joseph Berger, Morris Zelditch Jr., and Bo Anderson. Boston: Houghton Mifflin.

Berger, Joseph, Morris Zelditch Jr., Bo Anderson, and Bernard P. Cohen. 1972. "Structural Aspects of Distributive Justice: A Status-Value Formulation." Pp. 119–246 in *Sociological Theories in Progress,* Volume 2, edited by Joseph Berger, Morris Zelditch, and Bo Anderson. Boston: Houghton Mifflin.

Cervantes de Saavedra, Miguel. [1605, 1615] 1968. *Don Quijote de la Mancha.* Edited and annotated by Martin de Riquer. Barcelona: Juventud.

Cervantes, Miguel de. (1605, 1615) 1999. *Don Quijote.* Translated by Burton Raffel and edited by Diana de Armas Wilson. New York: W. W. Norton.

Firebaugh, Glenn. 1998. "Measuring Inequality: A Convenient Unifying Framework." Paper presented at the annual meeting of the Population Association of America, Chicago, April.

———. 1999. "Empirics of World Income Inequality." *American Journal of Sociology* 104:1597–1630.

Goode, William J. 1978. *The Celebration of Heroes: Prestige as a Control System.* Berkeley: University of California Press.

Jasso, Guillermina. 1978. "On the Justice of Earnings: A New Specification of the Justice Evaluation Function." *American Journal of Sociology* 83:1398–1419.

———. 1980. "A New Theory of Distributive Justice." *American Sociological Review* 45:3–32.

———. 1983. "Social Consequences of the Sense of Distributive Justice: Small-Group Applications." Pp. 243–294 in *Theories of Equity: Psychological and Sociological Perspectives*, edited by David M. Messick and Karen S. Cook. New York: Praeger.

———. 1988. "Principles of Theoretical Analysis." *Sociological Theory* 6:1–20.

———. 1993a. "Analyzing Conflict Severity: Predictions of Distributive-Justice Theory for the Two-Subgroup Case." *Social Justice Research* 6:357–382.

———. 1993b. "Building the Theory of Comparison Processes: Construction of Postulates and Derivation of Predictions." Pp. 212–264 in *Theoretical Research Programs: Studies in the Growth of Theory*, edited by Joseph Berger and Morris Zelditch Jr. Stanford, CA: Stanford University Press.

———. 1997. "Derivation of Predictions in Comparison Theory: Foundations of the Macromodel Approach." Pp. 241–270 in *Status, Network, and Structure: Theory Development in Group Processes*, edited by Jacek Szmatka, John Skvoretz, and Joseph Berger. Stanford, CA: Stanford University Press.

———. 1999. "How Much Injustice Is There in the World? Two New Justice Indexes." *American Sociological Review* 64:133–168.

———. 2000. "Some of Robert K. Merton's Contributions to Justice Theory." *Sociological Theory* 18:331–339.

———. 2001a. "Comparison Theory." Pp. 669–698 in *Handbook of Sociological Theory*, edited by Jonathan H. Turner. New York: Kluwer Academic/Plenum Press.

———. 2001b. "Formal Theory." Pp. 37–68 in *Handbook of Sociological Theory*, edited by Jonathan H. Turner. New York: Kluwer Academic/Plenum Press.

———. 2001c. "Rule-Finding about Rule-Making: Comparison Processes and the Making of Norms." Pp. 348–393 in *Social Norms*, edited by Michael Hechter and Karl-Dieter Opp. New York: Russell Sage.

———. 2001d. "Studying Status: An Integrated Framework." *American Sociological Review* 66:96–124.

———. 2002. "Comparing the Implications of Justice Theory and Status Theory for Intergroup Relations." Paper presented at the Second Joint Japan–North America Conference on Mathematical Sociology, Vancouver, BC, May–June.

Jasso, Guillermina, and Bernd Wegener. 1997. "Methods for Empirical Justice Analysis: Part I. Framework, Models, and Quantities." *Social Justice Research* 10:393–430.

Merton, Robert K. [1949, 1957] 1968. *Social Theory and Social Structure.* New York: Free Press.

Merton, Robert K., and Alice S. Rossi. 1950. "Contributions to the Theory of Reference Group Behavior." Pp. 40–105 in *Continuities in Social Research: Studies in the Scope and Method of "The American Soldier,"* edited by R. K. Merton and P. Lazarsfeld. New York: Free Press. Reprinted as pp. 225–280 in *Social Theory and Social Structure*, 2d rev. ed., edited by R. K. Merton. New York: Free Press.

Rossi, Peter H. 1979. "Vignette Analysis: Uncovering the Normative Structure of Complex Judgments." Pp. 176–186 in *Qualitative and Quantitative Social Research: Papers in Honor of Paul F. Lazarsfeld*, edited by R. K. Merton, J. S. Coleman, and P. H. Rossi. New York: Free Press.

Sørensen, Aage B. 1979. "A Model and a Metric for the Analysis of the Intragenerational Status Attainment Process." *American Journal of Sociology* 85:361–384.

Thomson, William. 1999. "The Young Person's Guide to Writing Economic Theory." *Journal of Economic Literature* 37:157–183.

Turner, Jonathan H. 1984. *Societal Stratification: A Theoretical Analysis.* New York: Columbia University Press.

VII

REFLECTIONS ON CAREERS IN THEORY

13

Reflections on a Career as a Theorist

Peter M. Blau

This chapter has six sections. The first deals with the field work for my dissertation on a regional office of a federal employment security agency, inspired by Max Weber's work on bureaucracy. The second is a short synopsis of my book on *Exchange and Power in Social Life.* The third is concerned with my analysis with Otis Dudley Duncan of the American occupational structure, with special concern for social mobility. A national study of Employment Security Agencies is briefly analyzed in section four. The fifth section is a very short summary of my theory of population structure. Finally, I conclude with a brief reflection on the paths I pursued in my work.

THE DYNAMICS OF WORK GROUPS IN BUREAUCRACY

Weber's theory of bureaucracy (Weber [1918] 1968) aroused my particular interest, because it is the prototype of the "iron cage," Weber's term for the increasing confinement of individual freedom by the growing rationalization and bureaucratization of modern life. More generally, bureaucracy dramatically illustrates structural constraints—the limits structural conditions impose on individuals' choices and opportunities—which I consider to be the central subject matter of sociology.

I decided to conduct empirical research on bureaucracies for my dissertation, using as a conceptual framework Weber's theory of bureaucracy. A popular research subject at that time was the empirical study of work groups in industry. The best-known example is the study of several groups of manual workers in one of the plants of the Western Electric Company—*Management and the Worker* by Roethlisberger and Dickson (1946). I had taken a course in industrial sociology with Conrad Arensberg, in which studies of work groups in industry were analyzed and a method for systematically recording the social interaction among their members was presented (Chapple and Arensberg 1940). I decided to undertake an equivalent study on bureaucracy. If the operation in a factory can be clarified by studying industrial work groups, one should be able to throw light on operations in a bureaucracy by observing groups of officials at work.

Early during my observation period I noticed that the officials in the federal law-enforcement agency I first studied often discussed problems in their cases with colleagues, although every official worked on different cases and it was officially proscribed to consult anyone but the supervisor (who might refer intricate legal problems to the legal department). This intrigued me because it was similar to the prohibited practices reported among manual work groups such as restriction of output. When I studied it further, however, I found that it was quite different and far more interesting. I discovered unofficial consultations, the informal stratification system it generated, and the diverse consultation practices by which people sought to protect or improve their informal status.

The analysis of unofficial consultation and the informal status structure it produced gave me the idea for the theory of social exchange I later elaborated (1964). Even before I did so, Homans (1961) developed a theory of social exchange based on substantially different assumptions, in which he also used my analysis of unofficial consultation as the prototypical illustration of social exchange processes. Paradoxically, in my field of study of bureaucracy, based on Weber's macrosociological theory of it, I had discovered a kernel of a microsociological theory.

THEORY OF SOCIAL EXCHANGE

We can start with the following idea: A fundamental difference between social life in small isolated communities and that in large complex societies is the declining significance of the groups into which one is born and the growing significance of reciprocated choices between erstwhile strangers for human relations. Dependence on reciprocated choices implies that, if I want to associate with someone, I cannot realize my goal unless I make him interested in associating with me. For our social relations to persist, both of us have to sustain an interest in its continuation.

The idea of social interaction as exchange occurred to me in my fieldwork for my dissertation at a federal agency of law enforcement. I often saw two agents or three in discussions with one another, sometimes at the desk of one, sometimes at the water cooler. Agents often consulted one another when they had a problem with their cases, although they were officially required to consult only their supervisor. But they were reluctant to ask the supervisor for advice for fear it would adversely affect the periodic rating of their performance. Indeed, how could it not, since one item the supervisor was expected to take into account was "independence of decision making." Moreover, most agents considered the competence of the best of their colleagues as superior to their supervisor's, who was a veteran of the First World War. (Promotions to supervisor were not based on merit alone but strongly influenced by veteran status.) Hence, they rarely consulted the supervisor and went to colleagues for advice instead. I had many occasions to observe these unofficial consultations, especially at lunch, which most agents spent in colleague groups, and most of them permitted me to join them.

It occurred to me that both parties must obtain benefits from consultations to motivate participation in this practice. Whyte's (1943) concept of "mutual obligations" in street corner gangs suggested to me that these unofficial consultations must involve an exchange of some benefits. Both parties must benefit from consultations, and both must pay a price. The one asking for advice can perform better without exposing his difficulties to the supervisor. The cost of this is paying respect to the other official's competence, which is implicit in asking for his advice.

The agents regularly consulted pay the cost of devoting time to giving advice and letting it interrupt their work, in return for which they gain prestige in the form of the respect colleagues implicitly pay by recurrently asking for advice. This is how informal status becomes differentiated in work and other groups. As the contributions some make to others and the group itself make them more respected, they gain initially prestige and ultimately also power to influence others, for we are reluctant to antagonize people we respect by disagreeing with their suggestions lest we lost the benefits we gain from consulting them.

Most officials liked being consulted, because it raised their self-confidence and minimized their anxiety over decision making, which may well have actually improved their decision-making skills. Agents who often asked for advice were in a less fortunate position. Their recurrent dependence on colleagues undermined their self-confidence and standing in the group. The cost of advice became prohibitive if the consultant appeared reluctant to give it, by postponing the consultation or being impatient during it. To avoid such implicit rejections, most agents established partnerships of mutual consultation and reserved consulting experts for their most difficult questions. The partnerships neutralized or, at least, minimized the status threat of asking for advice, as it is paid for by recurrently giving it. Since agents often did not need help but only support for a tentative decision by having it confirmed, a colleague who is not more but only equally qualified sufficed for such support.

Expert agents had a different problem. Theirs was that they were reluctant to ask for help for fear that they would lose their colleagues' respect and their superior status as experts. They substituted another practice for requesting help. When worried about the solution of a complex problem, they walked to a colleague's desk to tell her about the interesting problems in the case, or they told a group at lunch about them. Lunch periods were filled with such discussions, despite occasional remarks, "No more shop talk."

Since the situation was now defined as an interesting discussion of issues and not as a request for help, the official raising the issues did not lose respect for requiring help but might even gain some by initiating a good discussion. Yet such "thinking out loud" elicits support for decision making. The attentive listening of fellow experts, their interested questions, appreciative comments, and failure to interrupt help arrive at a correct conclusion.

The basic assumption of the theory of social exchange is that persons establish social associations because they expect them to be rewarding and that they continue them because they do experience them to be rewarding. The exchange of rewards is a starting mechanism of social relations and is not contingent on norms prescribing obligations.

Social relations often get started when both parties attempt to impress the other with their outstanding qualities—their wit, their charm, intelligence, and so forth. This often turns into an exchange of favors, which are expected to be reciprocated. Favors are expected to be discharged at some future date. This contrasts with economic exchange, where terms of exchange are explicit.

The diffuseness of the obligations implies that large-scale social exchange is not likely to occur without formal agreement unless firm social bonds rooted in trust have been established.

While it seems that rationality must play an important role, this is somewhat misleading. Social exchange does imply some rational pursuit of rewards, which is manifest in the obligation to reciprocate. But among friends the prime benefit sought is the rewarding experience derived from the association itself.

A paradox of social exchange is that it occurs among peers but gives rise to differentiation of status. The consultations among formal peers create informal differentiation among them. Exchange implies that both participants gain something and both have to pay a price. By asking for advice, the agent pays his respect the superior proficiency of his colleague. The acknowledgment of inferiority is the cost of receiving assistance.

The principle of marginal utility applies in this sense: those who are most frequently asked for advice experience diminishing gains in informal status and rising cost of interrupted work as the number who ask advice increases.

I can put here the underlying principles of imbalanced and balanced exchange into general terms. Rendering important services or providing valuable benefits is a claim to superior status. Reciprocation denies this claim and excessive returns make a counterclaim. Failure to reciprocate validates the claim. Thus, the contingency that determines whether social exchanges lead to friendships between peers or subordination and super-ordination is whether benefits are reciprocated or not.

I conclude with a synopsis of the gist of my exchange theory, which I derived from a seminal article by Richard M. Emerson (1962). I reconceptualized his scheme of how balance in a social relation can be restored by asking what alternatives there are to becoming dependent on a person who has the resources I need or want.

First, I can give him or her something in return for what I want, if I have anything she or he wants. Second, I can get it from somebody who wants something I have. Both these alternatives lead to an exchange relation. Third, I can take it by force. Fourth, I can do without. But if I cannot or will not do any of these and want or need something from him or her, I have no alternative but to submit to his or her demands. This is, in my opinion, the principle underlying all differences in status and power.

Before my work on exchange appeared, my dissertation was published after several revisions (1955), and Homans (1956) reviewed it. His review was gratifyingly favorable, but he first criticized the title (*The Dynamics of Bureaucracy*), saying that the book was a study not of bureaucracy but of small groups of officials. I had to admit that he was right. I did not study the concepts in terms of which Weber analyzed bureaucracy—large size, division of labor, administrative hierarchy, impersonal decisions—but the informal social processes and status structures in work groups. This is why a micro and not a macro theory emerged from it. But how would one study the issues Weber poses—for instance, whether the attributes he considers to characterize bureaucracy do in fact occur together in formal organizations. Answers would require data on many cases, but how can one survey many organizations if data collection on a few work groups takes a full year? This question had a sleeper effect on me. Right then I could not deal with it, as I was involved in another empirical study.

THE AMERICAN OCCUPATIONAL STRUCTURE

Although I had written only a few papers on the subject, I was a member of the International Sociological Association's Research Committee on Stratification, which in the 1950s had as its objective to encourage its members to conduct national surveys on stratification and mobility in their respective countries. Despite the prominence of U.S. scholars in survey research, no national survey on stratification and mobility had been carried out in this country. I was encouraged to undertake one, and I reluctantly decided to try. I was fully aware that I did not have the statistical competence to analyze a quantitative national survey adequately on my own and that I needed a collaborator who had the necessary methodological skills. I asked Otis Dudley Duncan, who did, whether he would join me in conducting such a survey and he agreed to do so.

The book in which the analysis of our research is published—*The American Occupational Structure*—is generally known, and there is little point in summarizing it here. Suffice it to say that our objective was to obtain data on American stratification and mobility comparable to data from other nations. We wished to ascertain major characteristics that influence differences in people's occupational achievements and in their opportunities to move up from their social origins. For this purpose, we not only analyzed the conventional mobility matrix, cross-tabulating the occupational origins and current occupations of respondents, but we also used another procedure with three new elements.

These three new statistical procedures were introduced by Duncan. First, we used regression analysis, which had been used only very rarely before in sociological surveys except in demography. Second, to use regression analysis we had to convert (detailed) occupations into a measure of occupational status that could be treated as a continuous variable. The measure used was Duncan's (1961) socioeconomic index, based on the prevailing education and income of the members of each detailed occupation. Third, Duncan (1966) introduced path coefficients, employed by Sewall Wright (1960) in his biometric work, into sociological analysis; these enabled us to trace the influences from every independent variable, via possibly various intervening variables, to the dependent variable. After our book's publication in 1967, regression and path analysis became widely used in sociological research on other topics as well as on occupational mobility.

The project was not designed to make a theoretical contribution but to provide a baseline for future trends in the American occupational structure and for comparisons of it with those in other countries. To be sure, we interpreted a number of our findings in theoretical terms. Thus, we pointed out that while we observed no vicious circle of poverty for people generally, we did see one for blacks, as indicated by their cumulative disadvantages in comparison to whites. At each step of their careers, blacks are handicapped even when they have overcome earlier handicaps. Thus, statistical analysis shows that even if blacks had the same educational opportunities as whites, as they do not, they would get less good jobs; and even if they had the same occupations as whites, which they do not, their earnings would be lower.[1] In another connection, we derive some inferences from several findings about expanding universalism in American occupational life. But such ad hoc interpretations do not contribute to a general theory that is testable in research on other subjects.

The main contribution of this study, which made it so popular and influential, consisted of the methodological innovations Duncan introduced. Our long collaboration on this research, which involved repeated disagreements owing to our very different sociological orientations, also furthered progress on my own serpentine path to a macrostructural theory. Used to the Lazarsfeld tradition of statistical analysis based on cross-classifications, I was not familiar with regression analysis; initially I tried to convince Duncan that we should use cross-tabulations instead. But he resisted, and since he was more knowledgeable about quantitative procedures, I had to give in. After I became used to regression analysis, however, I was completely sold on it, owing to its ease of examining multiple influences, their nonlinear and contingent (interaction) effects. I continued to employ it in my subsequent research, including that testing macrostructural theory.[2]

ORGANIZATIONAL DIFFERENTIATION

The major one was an investigation of all state Employment Security Agencies (ESA) to obtain information on their administrative structure. To my own surprise, considering the unusual design, I obtained the grant; I also obtained the cooperation of the U.S. Bureau of Employment Security for such a study. After some preliminary pilot studies including some at ESA regional headquarters, three research assistants visited every state headquarters of the ESA at each state capitol for a few days, collecting extensive information on the formal structure of the entire agency and much more limited data on that of its larger local offices.

Thus, we had detailed data on 53 state agencies (in addition to those in the 50 states, data were collected on three of the four other ESAs—the District of Columbia, Puerto Rico, and the Virgin Islands, but not that in Guam). We also had much sparser data on 1,201 local offices of these agencies. This [53] is a small number for regression analysis, but it is essentially the entire universe of ESAs.[3] We also analyzed 387 major divisions as cases, and the analysis of local offices was based on data from 1,201. During the next decade, quantitative research on a variety of public and private organizations was conducted, each project confined to a single type. Examples of public bureaus studied are public personnel agencies and finance departments. The studies of private and nonprofit organizations included department stores, manufacturing concerns, hospitals, and universities and colleges.

I developed a theory (Blau 1970) to explain the regularities observed in this research on public employment agencies (which are also responsible for unemployment insurance). The basic findings incorporated in the theory are the following: First, the large size of organizations increases their differentiation in various dimensions at decelerating rates. This is the case whether the division of labor, vertical levels, horizontal subdivisions, or other forms of differentiation are examined.

Second, large size reduces administrative overhead (the proportion of administrative personnel), which implies an administrative economy of scale. Third, degree of differentiation, which entails greater structural complexity, is positively related to administrative overhead. Finally, large size directly reduces yet indirectly (mediated by its influence on differentiation) increases administrative overhead since the direct negative exceeds the indirect positive effect on administrative cost, this produces the net negative effect that finds expression in the administrative economy of scale.

The theory seeks to explain why the rate of differentiation with the increasing size of organizations declines for larger organizations. The inference made is that size's direct effect on organizational differentiation and complexity raise administrative costs. To sustain the economy of scale in administrative cost from which large organizations benefit, they must not become so differentiated that the administrative cost of complexity absorbs this economy of scale.

This theory has been corroborated in the research on other organizations. Whatever type we examined, whether public or private, profit or nonprofit, large organizations were more differentiated in various dimensions than were small ones. Yet, administrative overhead was less than that of small organizations, despite the fact that their differentiation (and hence large size, indirectly) raised administrative overhead. This strong supportive evidence for the empirical findings strengthens confidence in the inference that the dampening effect of the administrative cost of complexity can account for the *decline* in the rate at which differentiation increases as size does.[4]

The importance of abstract concepts clearly distinct from any empirical variables implied by them is well illustrated by this theory, as is the importance of theoretical generalizations beyond their empirical manifestations. To be sure, the theory is derived from empirical data and their relationships. But theoretical insights often emerge from empirical research, sometimes unexpectedly (what scientists refer to as serendipity) and at other times from exploratory research designed to search for new theoretical ideas. The concept of differentiation is truly an abstraction from diverse manifestations of it, like division of labor, hierarchical levels and ranks, branch offices in different locations, and diverse subunits of various kinds on different levels. But the case of administrative overhead is different. The distinctive significance of management should be noted. Only senior managers have the authority to organize the work and to order others to perform it. In short, senior managers have power over the life chances of workers.

The only thing an organization's administrative management and staff have in common is that they are not production personnel; they do not directly perform operations that contribute to the organization's objectives. A theoretical abstraction, however, must refer to an underlying common denominator of diverse empirical variables, not simply to nonmembership in a given population segment. Surely, that one is not a ditch digger or not a Supreme Court Justice is not a theoretical abstraction. Whatever the definition of the administrative component, therefore, it is not an abstract theoretical term, but rather one of two alternative ways of defining empirically a component of the personnel of an organization.

Whereas the theory has been supported by a variety of organizations, they all were formal organizations. The reason is not merely that our research program studied only various organizations. It is also that the theory is not testable in groupings of people that have no designated administrative staff. Ethnic groups, social movements, families, corner gangs, social classes, age cohorts, neighborhoods, educational categories, and innumerable other subdivisions of society can be characterized in terms of their differentiation in various respects, but they do not have administrative components, unless they establish or become formal organizations, as exemplified by social movements that become political parties.

Generalizations about diversity, inequality, or other forms of differentiation could be advanced for and tested in these other groupings, but it would not make sense to test generalizations about a non-existing administrative component. In short, the theory based on Weber's scheme is confined to formal organizations, though not to public bureaucracies. Can sociological theories apply to all populations? I seek to answer this question with a case in point.

A THEORY OF POPULATION STRUCTURE

My central interest is the influence of the social structure of a population on people's life chances, not only the opportunities in their careers but also their other opportunities, such as their chances to make certain friends or marry certain spouses. Population structures are characterized by the population distributions in different dimensions, such as ethnic distributions or occupational distributions. Three generic population distributions are distinguished: heterogeneity, the distribution among nominal categories, such as ethnic affiliation; inequality, the distribution along a continuum, such as education or income; and intersection, which is the degree to which differences in various respects are not highly correlated in a population.

Intersection corresponds to Simmel's ([1908] 1923) concept of crosscutting social circles. All three generic differences among populations are abstract concepts in Braithwaite's (1953) sense and also in Simmel's—pure social forms abstracted from their contents. There is no heterogeneity as such, only particular empirical manifestations of it, like religious heterogeneity or diversity in national background, just as there is no competition as such, only economic, political, or some other competition. I consider Simmel's forms to be theoretical in Braithwaite's meaning of the term—theoretical abstractions appropriate for sociological analysis. All three populations characteristics are emergent properties which have no counterparts that refer to individual attributes, whereas a population's mean income, for instance, is not an emergent property but describes the population by an average characteristic of its members.

The theory developed (Blau 1977) deals with the influence of the population structure on chances of intergroup relations, defined as the rate of dyadic relations between persons whose social affiliations differ in any respect. The two basic assumptions refer, respectively, to the dependence of social associations on contact opportunities, and to the oft-demonstrated tendency for ingroup relations to be more prevalent than outgroup relations. The theory is exemplified here by three major theorems. The first assumption and the definition of heterogeneity imply the theorem that heterogeneity promotes intergroup relations. The same assumption and the definition of inequality imply that inequality promotes intergroup (status-distant) relations. (This seems implausible, but tests support it—as shown in note 6). Probability theory is implicated in these two theorems. The second assumption and people's multigroup memberships, which Simmel emphasized, imply that intersections of social differences promote intergroup relations.

After it had been published, the theory was tested by comparing the population structures of the 125 largest American metropolitan areas in 1970 and ascertaining, as implied by the theory, their influence on intermarriage (Blau and Schwartz 1984). This is a severe test, since as profound and lasting a relation as marriage is less likely than casual relations to be influenced by sheer probability. The tests were conducted on numerous empirical manifestations of heterogeneity, inequality, and intersection, as they influenced intermarriage.[5] With rare exceptions, all tests supported the theoretical predictions, as did tests carried out with somewhat improved procedures on the same theorems and some tests that tested different theorems, for example, those on conflict.[6]

This project intersects two major interests of mine, as an academic and as a progressive. Ever since graduate school, I have been fascinated by the effects of the impersonal social structure, like a population's sheer composition, on people's opportunities, a point illustrated by this study. As a political animal, I have been horrified by the recent growth in poverty and inequality in this country and the growing ethnic strife throughout the world. The study shows that multiple diversity of a population promotes tolerance, not merely casual contacts but friendships and even marriage between persons with different backgrounds, which may well portend improving social integration of society's diverse groups and strata.

REFLECTIONS

My career began with empirical observation of the agents of a public employment agency in which unofficial consultations among peers gave rise to an informal system of stratification. To explain it, I constructed an abstract, general theory of social exchange, the basic principle of which was reciprocity. It was unequal exchange that explained the differentiation of status and power.

My basic orientation has always been to develop such abstract, general principles. But the next stage of my career looked, for a time, as if I had suddenly wandered down a different path—one still concerned with stratification, but in a historically particular case, the American occupational structure, with a result, furthermore, better known for a methodological than a theoretical innovation, path analysis.

But the study had been motivated by a desire to contribute to a more general, comparative study of stratification and the same goal drew me back to public employment agencies in a comparative study of 53 of them. Unlike my earlier study of a small group of officials in one public employment agency, the study of 53 of them made it possible to construct a theory in which the actors were complex organizations rather than individual officials described by more, and more general, dimensions of differentiation—division of labor, functional differentiation, and differentiation of levels, as well as hierarchy. In this study, I found economies of scale in administration despite the fact that the indirect effect of size on administration, through its effect on differentiation, was positive: The amount of differentiation of an organization increased with its size and the amount of administration increased with its differentiation. But, in the theory I constructed to explain the amount of administration in organizations, negative feedback from the amount of administration to the amount of differentiation was posited to explain the dampening of its indirect effect, that is, to explain the fact that the effect of an organization's size on its differentiation increased at a decreasing rate; which, in turn, had the effect that the direct negative effect of size exceeded its indirect positive effect; which, in turn, resulted in a net economy of scale in administration.

Although differentiation was a highly abstract variable, administration was a concrete element of concrete organizations. The objective of my theory of population structure, which marked the next stage of my career, was to construct a more fully abstract, general theory of the distribution of a population in a multidimensional space of social categories such as occupation, education, income, race, and ethnicity. The purpose of the theory was to explain the probability of intergroup relations (such as association, friendship, and marriage) in terms of preferences for homophily, the effect of pure number in a category on constraints that limit the capacity of preferences to determine choices, and the effect of the intersection of multiple categories: to the extent they are not perfectly correlated, choices based on preferences for one category create opportunities for intergroup contact with another. Subsequent research has provided empirical support for many hypotheses deduced from this theory.

Thus, the theory of population structure exemplifies an orientation to theory that is abstract, that is, to concepts that have multiple instances; general, that is, to principles that go beyond their original empirical manifestations; deductive, that is, to systems of hypotheses in which many of them follow logically from others; and empirically grounded, that is, to tests of these hypotheses that close the gap between theory and research.

There are two observations that I would like to make, as I reflect back at my own efforts and try to understand what topics fully engaged me in my work and why. While there may be some disillusionment currently with abstract, deductive theory, this approach offers two distinctive advantages. First, because this approach to theory construction requires clearly defined premises and explicit derivations, other researchers can easily scrutinize it for logical errors. Second, it leads to empirical predictions that if falsified will also falsify the theory, but if supported suggests that the theory can be further generalized. I did not always use this approach, but I found it particularly helpful in my work on bureaucracy and intermarriage.

The second observation I would like to make is more personal than scientific. I believe that one main motivation to become a sociologist is scientific, namely to better understand social dynamics and social patterns, but another main motivation is utopian, namely, a hope that one can discover clues about how social conditions can be better to enhance the well being of more people. For example, what fosters fairness in organizations? What are the mechanisms that enhance the chances of social mobility? What are the conditions that promote intergroup tolerance? Questions such as these motivate all sociologists, I believe. These are extra-scientific questions, or, if you like, ones that come from sociology's humanistic traditions.

NOTES

Part of the present chapter, "Theory of Social Exchange," was presented at the meeting of the Theory Section of the American Sociological Association in Washington, DC, in August 2000. In addition, the present chapter includes parts previously published as "A Circuitous Path to Macrostructural Theory" *Annual Review of Sociology* (1995) 21:6–8, 9–14, 17–19.

1. I use the present tense although the data referred to are from 1962, because despite some improvements these statements are apparently still correct.

2. Ironically, at the end of his career Duncan started using log-linear procedures, which though greatly refined, ultimately rest on Lazerfeld's old-fashioned cross-tabulations.

3. I had originally thought that this ESA project was the first quantitative study of formal organizations, but I was wrong. The first one was probably Woodward's (1958) analysis of British industrial firms. Another British one was published by a group at Aston University in Birmingham, about the same time as the ESA study, in a series of articles in the *Administrative Science Quarterly*; the first of a series analyzing research (an earlier one was a literature review) is Pugh et al. (1968).

4. Cross-section studies by others of these relationships in organizations generally support our findings, but studies of changes within organizations were inconsistent and did not support them (Cullen, Anderson, and Baker 1986, who also summarize other studies). Longitudinal studies that pool organizations, rather than examine their internal charges, found that growth reduces administrative overhead, in accordance with my theory, but decline in size does not raise it, contrary to what is implicit in the theory (Freeman and Hannan 1975).

5. Virtually all those available in the PUS of the Bureau of the Census for 1970.

6. To answer the implicit question raised above by the implausible finding on status-distance: Although inequality in education and socioeconomic status makes status more salient and thus indirectly discourages status-distant marriage, this indirect negative effect is overshadowed by a direct positive one, which makes status-distant marriage more likely owing to the greater average status-distance between any two persons implicit in greater inequality.

REFERENCES

Blau, Peter. 1955. *The Dynamics of Bureaucracy.* Chicago: University of Chicago Press.

———. 1964. *Exchange and Power in Social Life.* New York: Wiley.

———. 1970. "A Formal Theory of Differentiation in Organizations." *American Sociological Review* 35:201–18.

———. 1977. *Inequality and Heterogeneity.* New York: Free Press.

Blau, Peter, and Otis Dudley Duncan. 1967. *The American Occupational Structure.* New York: Wiley.

Blau, Peter, and Joseph E. Schwartz. 1984. *Crosscutting Social Circles.* Orlando: Academic Press.

Braithwaite, Richard B. 1953. *Scientific Explanation.* Cambridge: Cambridge University Press.

Chapple, Eliot D., and Conrad M. Arensberg. 1940. *Measuring Human Relations. Genetic Psychology Monographs XXII.* Provincetown, MA: Journal Press.

Cullen, John B., Kenneth S. Anderson, and Douglas D. Baker. 1986. "Blau's Theory of Structural Differentiation Revisited." *Academy of Management Journal* 29:203–29.

Duncan, Otis Dudley. 1961. "A Socioeconomic Index for All Occupations." Pp. 109–38 in *Occupations and Social Status*, edited by A. J. Reiss, P. K. Hatt, and C. C. North. New York: Free Press.

———. 1966. "Path Analysis." *American Journal of Sociology* 72:1–16.

Emerson, Richard. 1962. "Power-Dependence Relations." *American Sociological Review* 27:31–41.

Freeman, John H., and Michael T. Hannan. 1975. "Growth and Decline Processes in Organizations." *American Sociological Review* 40:215–28.

Homans, George C. 1956. "Review of *The Dynamics of Bureaucracy.*" *American Journal of Sociology* 61:490–91.

———. 1961. *Social Behavior.* New York: Harcourt, Brace & World.

Pugh, D. S., D. J. Hickson, C. R. Hinings, and C. Turner. 1968. "Dimensions of Organization Structure." *Administrative Science Quarterly* 13:65–105.

Roethlisberger, Fritz J., and William J. Dickson. 1946. *Management and the Worker.* Cambridge: Harvard University Press.

Simmel, Georg. [1908] 1923. *Soziologie.* Munchen: Duncker & Humbolt.

Weber, Max. [1918] 1968. *Economy and Society,* edited by Guenther Roth and Carl Wittich, translated by E. Fischoff et al. New York: Bedminster.

Whyte, William Foote. 1943. *Street Corner Society.* Chicago: University of Chicago Press.

Woodward, J. F. 1958. *Management and Technology.* London: HMSO.

Wright, S. 1960. "Path Coefficients and Path Regressions." *Biometrics* 16:189–202.

14

The Itinerary of World-Systems Analysis; or, How to Resist Becoming a Theory

Immanuel Wallerstein

The term theory tends to evoke for most people the concept of a set of interconnected ideas that are coherent, rigorous, and clear, and from which one may derive explanations of empirical reality. The term theory however also denotes the end of a process of generalization and therefore of closure, even if only provisional. In the construction of adequate or plausible explanations of complex phenomena, proclaiming that one has arrived at a theory often imposes premature closure on scientific activity, and therefore can be counterproductive. The more complex the reality, the more this tends to be true. What I believe it is often better to do in such cases is to explore empirical reality using spectacles that are informed by theoretical hunches but not bound by them. It is because I believe this is eminently the case in the explanation of historical systems, which are large-scale and long-term, that I have long resisted the appellation of world-systems *theory* for the kind of work I do, insisting that I was engaged instead in world-systems *analysis*. This is thus the story of the itinerary and growth of a non-theory, which I call world-systems analysis.

The story begins for me in the 1950s when I entered the graduate program in sociology at Columbia University. My principal empirical interest was contemporary politics, in the United States and in the world. Columbia sociology at the time was considered to be the center of structural-functional analysis, and the department was particularly proud of pursuing research that combined the theorizing of Robert K. Merton with the methodological approaches of Paul F. Lazarsfeld. What is less often noticed is that Columbia was also the center of a major new subfield of sociology, political sociology.[1] At the time, its faculty (and visitors) included S. Martin Lipset, Daniel Bell, and Johan Galtung, all of whom were prominently associated with political sociology, plus Robert S. Lynd, C. Wright Mills, Herbert Hyman, Ralf Dahrendorf, Daniel Lerner, as well as Lazarsfeld, all of whom in fact did political sociology under other rubrics.

Political sociology was a thriving and growing field. One of the very first research committees of the newly founded International Sociological Association was the one in political sociology. The Social Science Research Council sponsored a multiyear, multivolume project by its Committee on Comparative Politics. I considered it obvious that I would consider myself a political sociologist.[2]

I did have one peculiarity, however. I did not believe the Cold War between the Western "free world" and the Soviet "Communist world" was the primary political struggle of the post-1945 arena. Rather I considered the main conflict to be that the industrialized nations and what came to be called the Third World,[3] also known as the struggle of core vs. periphery, or later still North-South. Because of this belief, I decided to make the study of contemporary social change in Africa my main scholarly pursuit.[4] The 1950s was a period in which the Western world took its first serious look on what was happening outside its own redoubt. In 1955, the Bandoeng conference of Asian and African independent states was the moment of self-assertion by the non-Western world, the moment in which they laid claim to full participation in world politics. And 1960 was the Year of Africa, the year in which sixteen different states became independent; the year also of the Congo crisis, which led to massive United Nations involvement in its civil war, a civil war that was bedeviled by much outside interference.

The year 1960 was also the year in which I came to know Frantz Fanon, an author I had long been reading, and whose theorizing had a substantial influence on my own work. Fanon was a Martinican and a psychiatrist, who went in this latter capacity to Algeria, where he became a militant of the Algerian *Front de Libération Nationale*. His first book, *Black Skin, White Masks* (first published in French in 1952), is about the psychic impact on Blacks of White dominance. It has been widely revived and republished in the 1990s, and is considered highly relevant to the discussions on identity that have become so prevalent. But at the time, it was his fourth and last book, *The Wretched of the Earth* (published in French in 1961 just before his very premature death from leukemia) and prefaced by Jean-Paul Sartre, which made him world-famous. The book became in a sense the manifesto of the world's national liberation movements, as well as of the Black Power movement in the United States.

In the best tradition of both Freud and Marx, Fanon sought to demonstrate that what on the surface was seemingly irrational, notably the use of violence by these movements, was beneath the surface highly rational. The book was therefore not merely a polemic and a call to action but a reflective work of social science, insisting on a careful analysis of the social basis of rationality. I wrote a number of articles at the time, seeking to explain and defend Fanon's work,[5] and I returned to the issue in my discussion of Freud and rationality in my Presidential address to the International Sociological Association in 1998 (Wallerstein 1999c:9–12).

The 1960s was a period of cascading independences in Africa. It was also a period of the first postindependence difficulties—not only the Congo crisis but the beginnings of military coups in a large number of states. Since I was lecturing on and writing about the contemporary scene, I was called upon to explain these multiple new happenings. I came to feel that I was chasing headlines, and that this was not the proper role of a social scientist. During the time that I was doing the fieldwork on the movement for African unity in 1965, I decided to try out a new approach to these issues by expanding the space scope and the time scope of my analyses. I gave three versions of a first cut at this approach at three African universities—Legon in Accra, Ghana; Ibadan in Nigeria; and Dar-es-Salaam in Tanzania.

The interested reception led me to try two things when I returned to Columbia. I created a new course that embodied this expanded scope into the analysis and I found considerable student response to this approach. At the same time, Terence Hopkins and I were asked by the department to give a course on the methodology of "comparative analysis," which we turned into a critique of "the comparative study of national societies." We wrote jointly an article assessing past modes of doing such work (Hopkins and Wallerstein 1967).

At the same time, we undertook a big content analysis project, seeking to extract systematically the propositions to be found in the by then innumerable articles purporting to be comparative in method. We enlisted some twenty graduate students as our readers (in a dozen languages) who were asked to fill in a schedule about each article that we had devised. We never published this gigantic content analysis because we discovered that an extremely large proportion of articles that were "comparative" according to their title compared one somewhat "exotic" country with one the author knew well, since he came from that country (most often the United States). Unfortunately, too many authors compared the data they collected in the exotic country with the remembered or imagined (but not empirically examined) reality of their own. Something, we thought, was very wrong.

About this time, I discovered some wonderful articles by Marian Malowist while roaming through *Africana Bulletin*, an obscure source, since it was the journal of Polish Africanists. Malowist was an economic historian of the fourteenth to seventeenth centuries. He wrote primarily about eastern Europe but he wandered afield to write both about colonial expansion and about the gold trade in the fourteenth to fifteenth centuries between the west coast of Africa and North Africa (Malowist 1964, 1966). The articles had two merits in terms of my further development. They led me to Malowist's other writings. And in the first article, Malowist introduced me to Fernand Braudel's great work on *The Mediterranean*.[6]

It was at this point that my dissatisfactions with the comparative study of national societies combined with my discovery via Braudel of the sixteenth-century world inspired a bad idea which serendipitously turned my work around, and toward world-systems analysis. Since I, along with multiple others, had been describing African and other postcolonial states as "new nations," I said to myself that must mean that there are "old nations." And old nations must at one time have been new nations. So I decided to investigate how old nations (essentially western Europe) had behaved when they were new nations, that is, in the sixteenth century. This was a bad idea, as it was based on premises of modernization theory, which I was to reject so strongly later.[7] Western European states in the sixteenth century were in no way parallel to Third World states in the twentieth century.

Fortunately, I was reading both Braudel and Malowist.[8] What I discovered in Braudel was two concepts that have been central to my work ever since: the concept of the world-economy and the concept of the *longue durée.* What I discovered in Malowist (and then of course in other Polish and Hungarian authors) was the role of eastern Europe as an emergent periphery of the European world-economy in the sixteenth century. I should elaborate on the three discoveries.

What Braudel did in *The Mediterranean* was to raise the issue of the unit of analysis. He insisted that the Mediterranean world was a "world-economy." He got this term from its use in the 1920s by a German geographer, Fritz Rörig, who spoke of *Weltwirtschaft.* Braudel translated this term not as *économie mondiale* but as *économie-monde.* As both he and I were to make explicit many years later, this distinction was crucial: between *économie mondiale* meaning the "economy *of the* world" and *économie-monde* meaning an "economy *that is a* world" (see Braudel 1984, esp. pp. 21–24). The difference was first of all conceptual. In the latter formulation, the world is not a reified entity that is there, and within which an economy is constructed; rather, the economic relationships are defining the boundaries of the social world. The second difference was geographic. In the first usage, "world" equals the globe; in the second usage, "world" means only a large geographic space (within which many states are located), which however can be, and usually is, less extensive than the globe (but also can encompass the entire globe).

I faced one problem immediately. The Romance languages permit making this distinction easily, by using an adjectival noun in place of a true adjective (that is, *économie-monde* as opposed to *économie mondiale*). German doesn't permit the distinction at all orthographically, because one can only use the adjectival noun and it is attached to the noun it is modifying to form a single word. This is why Rörig's usage, which could only be understood contextually, never really received notice. English as a language is in-between. I could translate Braudel's term by inserting a hyphen (thus: "world-economy" instead of "world economy"), the hyphen turning the adjective into an adjectival noun and indicating the indissolubility of the two words which represent thereby a single concept.[9]

I then took Braudel's concept of the "world-economy" and combined it with Polanyi's notion that there were three modes of economic behavior, which Polanyi had called reciprocity, redistribution, and exchange (see Polanyi 1957, 1967, and finally a very clear version, 1977). I decided that reciprocity referred to what I called minisystems (that is, small systems that were not world-systems), and that redistribution and exchange referred to what I called the two varieties of world-systems, world-empires, and world-economies.[10] I then argued that the modern world-system was a capitalist world-economy, that capitalism could only exist within the framework of a world-economy, and that a world-economy could only operate on capitalist principles. I make this case throughout my writings. The earliest (and most widely read) version is Wallerstein (1974b, reprinted in 1979a).

I faced a second problem in orthographics. Both Braudel and I believed that world-economies were organic structures that had lives—beginnings and ends. Therefore, there had to have been multiple world-economies (and of course multiple world-empires) in the history of humankind. Thus I became careful to speak not of world-system analysis but of world-system*s* analysis. This may seem obvious, except that it would become the cornerstone of a fierce attack by Andre Gunder Frank in the 1990s, when he argued that there had been only one world system ever and that it had been covering the Euroasiatic ecumene for twenty-five hundred years at least and the entire world for the last five hundred years (hence no need for either a hyphen or a plural). Obviously, different criteria were being used to define the boundaries of a system. Along with these different criteria came the assertion that the concept of capitalism was irrelevant to the discussion (it either having always existed or never).[11]

If the appropriate unit of analysis of the modern world is that of a world-system, and if there had been multiple world-systems in human history, then Braudel's concept of multiple social temporalities became immediately central. Braudel had built *The Mediterranean* (1949) around an elementary architecture. He would tell the story three times in terms of three temporalities, the short term, the middle term, and the long term. It was only later, however, that he explicitly theorized this fundamental decision in a famous article published in 1958, entitled "History and the Social Sciences: The *longue durée*" (Braudel 1958).[12]

In this article, Braudel speaks not of three temporalities, as we might expect, but rather of four, adding the "*very* long term." He has conceptual names for the four. The short term is *histoire événementielle*, the middle term is *histoire conjoncturelle*, and the long term is *histoire structurelle*. About the very long term he says: "If it exists, it must be the time of the sages" (ibid:76). There are problems with the translation of each of these terms,[13] but the crucial issue to discuss is epistemological. Braudel zeroed in on the fact that, in the last 150 years, the social sciences had seen a split between nomothetic and idiographic modes of knowing, the so-called *Methodenstreit*. Braudel identified this as the split between those who looked only at the eternal truths of social reality (the very long term) and those who thought that everything was particular and therefore non-replicable (the short term). Braudel wished to assert that the crucial social temporalities were in fact the other two, and first of all that of the *longue durée*—which harbored those structural constraints that have three characteristics: they are not always immediately visible, they are very long-lasting, and very slow to change, but they are *not* eternal.

The most immediate impact on me of this Braudelian imperative—about the priorities scholars should give different social temporalities—was in the conception of how I would write *The Modern World-System.* It became not the search for the eternal truths of comparative organizational analysis, which was the norm in post-1945 sociology (including in political sociology), but rather the story of a singular phenomenon, the modern world-system, informed by a mode of explanation I was calling world-systems analysis. Braudel called this *histoire pensée*, which may best be translated as "analytic history." Braudel's insistence on multiple social times would also lead me later to larger epistemological concerns as well.

What Malowist (and then the larger group of east European historians) did for me was to give sudden flesh to the concept of periphery, as had been initially adumbrated by the Latin American scholars grouped around Raúl Prebisch in the Economic Commission for Latin America (ECLA). The term "second feudalism" to describe what took place in Europe "east of the Elbe" in the sixteenth to eighteenth centuries had long been commonplace. What had not been commonplace, perhaps still isn't, is to see that the "second" feudalism was fundamentally different from the "first" feudalism, and that sharing a common descriptor has done a great disservice to analytic thought.

In the "first" feudalism, the manorial units produced largely for their own consumption and perhaps for that of surrounding small zones. In the so-called "second feudalism," the estates were producing for sale in distant markets. The view that such units were part and parcel of the emerging capitalist world-economy became one of the fundamental themes of my book, and of world-systems analysis. Furthermore, the view that the so-called second feudalism was a feature of a capitalist system had important implications for the prior theorizing, both by Marxists and by liberals, about the nature of capitalism. For a long time, capitalism had been defined in terms of an imagery drawn from the history of nineteenth-century western Europe, of wage-workers in factories (often newly proletarianized and not "owning the means of production") receiving wages (which was their entire income) from an employer who was seeking profits in the market. So strong was this imagery that most analysts refused to categorize as capitalist any enterprise organized in any other mode of labor compensation. Hence, it followed that most of the world could not be considered to be capitalist, or rather was said not *yet* to be capitalist.

Rejecting this nineteenth-century view was a crucial step in the development of world-systems analysis. The classic liberal-Marxist view was based on a theory of stages of development that occurred in parallel ways in units of analysis called states (or societies or social formations). It missed what seemed to us the obvious fact that capitalism in fact operated as a system in which there were *multiple* modes of compensating labor, ranging from wage-labor which was very widely used in the richer, more central zones to various forms of coerced labor very widely used in the poorer, more peripheral zones (and many other varieties in-between). If one did one's analysis state by state, as was the classical method, it would be observed that different countries had different modes of compensating labor and analysts could (and did) draw from this the conclusion that one day the poorer zones might replicate the structure of the richer zones. What world-systems analysis suggested was that this differential pattern across the world-economy was exactly what permitted capitalists to pursue the endless accumulation of capital and was what in fact made the richer zones richer.[14] It was therefore a defining structural element of the system, not one that was transitional or archaic.

Did I theorize this insight? In a way, yes, but diffidently, although I was sure I was on the right track. When I completed *The Modern World-System*, I realized that it was replete with analytic statements, and that there were a whole series of architectonic devices, but that they were nowhere systematically laid out. I worried less about the legitimacy of the exercise than about the potential confusion of the reader. So I added a final chapter, which I called a "Theoretical Reprise." This, plus the "Rise and Demise" article (which was largely a critique of the theorizing of others plus an attempt to show how changing a few premises increased the plausibility of the results), constituted my initial theorizing statements in world-systems analysis.

It wasn't enough for my critics. Many reviewers, even some friendly ones,[15] chided me for insufficiently explicit theorizing—I believe the term is "disprovable hypotheses"—and argued that without it my effort was at most interesting narrative.[16] I was also chided for excessively long footnotes, "winding around the page." To me the long footnotes reflected a deliberate strategy of building my analysis around scholarly discussions on empirical issues, attempting to show how recasting the issues (theorizing?) inserted clarity into what had become for most people murky debates.[17]

I should note that not all the criticism was about the absence of theorizing. There were also important debates about empirical issues. Was Russia really an "external arena" in the sixteenth century, as I asserted, or was it rather a "peripheral zone" just like Poland (see Nolte 1982)? How could I have ignored the Ottoman Empire in the analysis of Charles V and his difficulties in constructing a world-empire? Was the Ottoman Empire really "external" to the European world-economy?[18] While I was ready to defend myself on my empirical choices, such criticisms constantly raised definitional (and therefore theoretical) problems. They forced me to refine my position in order to defend it.

There were two kinds of fundamental theoretical attacks. One came from a Marxist stance, arguing that I had grossly understated the fundamental importance of the class struggle and misdefined capitalism. This was the Brenner critique, suggesting that my view had a "market" bias (sometimes called "circulationism") rather than being a properly "class-based" view of capitalism.[19] In his article, Brenner had attacked not only me but Paul Sweezy and Andre Gunder Frank as well. And the three of us decided that we would not write either a joint reply or separate replies to the article, which was widely read and discussed at the time. I decided to take another path in response to Brenner, whose views struck a resonant note among many persons.

At the same time, a second fundamental critique came from what might be called the Otto Hintze camp. Both Theda Skocpol and Aristide Zolberg launched polemics arguing that world-systems analysis puts into a single arena political and economic phenomena, and that analytically they were separate arenas, operating on separate and sometime contradictory premises.[20] Of course, they were right about what I had done, but I did not think this was an error. Rather I considered it a theoretical virtue. This pair of articles also were widely read.

My substantive answer to both theoretical critiques is to be found in Volume II of *The Modern World-System*, which bore the subtitle *Mercantilism and the Consolidation of the World-Economy, 1600–1750* (Wallerstein 1980). I sought to show in it that, contra a Brenner version of Marxism, there were not multiple forms of capitalism—mercantile, industrial, financial—but rather that these referred to alternate ways for capitalists to make profits, which were better or worse for particular capitalists according to conjunctural shifts in the operations of the world-economy. Furthermore, I argued that the itinerary of Dutch hegemony incarnated a necessary sequence. It was made possible by first achieving supremacy (in terms of efficiency) in productive activities, which led to supremacy in commercial activities, which then led to supremacy in the financial arena; and that the decline of the Dutch followed the same sequence. As for the supposed separate logics of the market and the state, I sought to show that, on the contrary, a singular logic operated in the world-system as a whole and in all of its parts—the core zones, the periphery, and the semiperiphery (whether rising or declining).[21]

What I was also trying to do, as a matter of tactics, became clear to me. Each volume and each chapter of the succeeding volumes was moving forward in time, discussing new empirical issues, and raising further elements of an architectonic scheme. One cannot discuss everything at once. And how all the pieces fit together becomes clear (or clearer) only as one works through the complex empirical data. Furthermore, I had decided on a tactic of overlapping time segments. The second volume starts in 1600 whereas the first ended in 1640, and the third starts in the 1730s whereas the second ended in 1750. And so it will continue to be the case in further volumes. In addition, the chapters within the books had each their own chronological limits, sometimes violating those of the overall book. This is because I came to believe firmly that chronological limits, always difficult to set, are a function of the problem being discussed. The same event belongs in two different chronological limits, depending on the issue. Writing a complex story requires an intelligently flexible schema.

By now I was also writing a large series of articles, published all over the place. If one wishes in an article (talk) both to argue the case for world-systems analysis and to discuss a specific issue, one has to balance the presentation between fundamental premises and particular discussion. I tried to make each important article say at least something worth saying that had not been said before by me. But I had of course also to repeat much of what I had already said, or the audience/readers might not have been able to follow my reasoning. Grouping these articles together in collections had the virtue not merely of making them more available, but of elaborating the theoretical skein.

In the early 1980s, I was asked to give a series of lectures at the University of Hawaii. At the same time, a French publisher asked me to do a short book on "capitalism." I replied that I would write such a book, provided I could call it "*historical* capitalism." The adjective was crucial to me, since I wanted to argue that there was no point in defining in our heads what capitalism is and then looking around to see if it was there. Rather, I suggested we should look at how this system actually worked. Furthermore, I wanted to argue that there has only ever been *one* capitalist system, since the only valid unit of analysis was the world-system, and only one world-economy survived long enough to institutionalize a capitalist system. This is of course the same issue as that discussed above in my rejection of wage-labor as the defining feature of a capitalist system. Is the system a *world*-system or are there as many capitalist systems as there are states?

So I gave the lectures at Hawaii on "historical capitalism" and revised them into a short book. Despite its title, the book has very little empirical/historical data in it. It is a series of analytic statements, assertions about how the system has historically worked, and why. Twelve years later, I was asked to give another series of lectures at the Chinese University of Hong Kong, and I used that occasion to make an overall assessment of the capitalist world-system over its history. I called these lectures "Capitalist Civilization," and there now exists a book in print which puts the two sets of lectures together (Wallerstein 1995a). This book is the closest effort I have ever made to what might pass as systematic theorizing. It is not possible here to summarize the book, but it is the only place in which I tried to cover the whole range of issues I had discussed in other books and essays, and I did try to show how the various parts of the whole fit together.

In 1976, I went to Binghamton University to join my collaborator, Terence Hopkins. We established the Fernand Braudel Center for the Study of Economies, Historical Systems, and Civilizations (FBC),[22] of which I have been the director ever since. There are three things to note about the center: its name, its mode of operation, and its substantive activities.

The use of Braudel's name was intended to indicate our commitment to the study of the *longue durée*, that is, of long-term, large-scale social change. But the rest of the name was taken from a modification of the subtitle of the name of the journal, *Annales*. Its subtitle (at the time) was *E.S.C.*, standing for "economies, societies, and civilizations," all in plural form. We changed, however, "societies" to "historical systems." This was a deliberate theoretical stance. The term *society*—fundamental to general sociological orientations (Merton 1957:81–89)—seemed to us to have led social science in a seriously mistaken direction. In practice, the boundaries of the term *society* have been determined by the adjective placed before it. In the modern world, these adjectives are virtually always the names of states—Dutch society, Brazilian society, and so forth. So the term required that the unit of analysis be state-structured, thereby extending present-day states into their (presumed) historical past. German society was to be seen as the society of the "Germanic peoples" over perhaps two thousand years, although the state itself came into existence only in 1871, and then only in boundaries which were contested and were to change several times thereafter.[23] We insisted instead on the term *historical system,* by which we meant an entity that was simultaneously systemic (with boundaries and mechanisms or rules of functioning) and historical (since it began at some point, evolved over time, and eventually came into crisis and ceased to exist). The term *historical system* involved for us a more precise specification of the concept of the *longue durée.*

The mode of operation of the FBC was somewhat unusual. It involved an organizational shift that reflected a further theoretical stance. Almost all organized research has been done in one of two ways. One mode is the research program of one (or sometimes several) individuals, either alone or using assistants who are hierarchically subordinate and whose intellectual function is to carry out assigned tasks. Using assistants is simply the expanded version of the functioning of the isolated scholar. The second is the collaborative format, in which several (even very many) scholars (or research institutes) work together (perhaps under the leadership of one person) on a common problem. The outcome is typically a work of many chapters, individually authored, to which someone writes an introduction attempting to show how they fit together.

The FBC sought to institutionalize not collaborative research but collective, unitary research. The mode was to bring together a potential group around a common concern "coordinated" by one or several persons. These groups are called Research Working Groups (RWGs). Each group spends a considerable amount of time defining the research problem and developing a research strategy, at which point the group assigns to its members research tasks. Assignment makes it different from the collaborative project. The assignment process is collective and not hierarchical. Researchers report back to the group regularly, which criticizes their work and sends them out with new group-defined tasks. The results of such work are thus not collections of individual papers but an integrated book written by many hands designed to be read as a monograph.[24] As should be immediately obvious, this approach is the concrete application of the stance advocated in this paper toward theorizing—the avoidance of premature closure.

In addition, it was combined with the assumption that addressing complex intellectual problems requires multiple hands and multiple skills. More than that, these problems require the intrusion of multiple founts of social knowledge, drawn from the multiple social biographies of the participants. It should be noted that typically such RWGs at the Fernand Braudel Center had researchers coming from across the globe and knowing a multiplicity of languages, a crucial element in accumulating multiple kinds of knowledge, including those that are buried in the unconscious psyches of the researchers.

As for the substantive activities, the RWGs have over the years engaged in research on a wide series of major areas which the logic of world-systems analysis suggested needed exploring. And exploration is the key word. Each of the topics was big. Each had enormous problems of locating, in effect creating, appropriate data to utilize. Each resulted in a small step forward in the specification of the integrated theoretical architecture we hoped to build. None contained carefully delineated disprovable hypotheses. Rather each contained somewhat novel conceptualization and the utilization of incomplete and inadequate data (but the best we have presently at our disposition, or at least so we believed). And each sought to rewrite the received canons of presumed theoretical knowledge.

Not every group succeeded even that far. Some research projects had to be abandoned. But those carried through to completion and thereupon published included: the relationship of cyclical rhythms and secular trends of the world-system; the functioning of trans-national commodity chains; hegemony and rivalry in the interstate system; regionality and the semiperiphery; incorporation of the external arena and consequent peripheralization; patterns of antisystemic movements; creating and transforming households; the tension between racism-sexism and universalism; the historical origins and development of social science; the trajectory of the world-system, 1945–2025; the origins of the two cultures and challenges to the epistemology; and currently, a massive project on what others call globalization but which we perceive as "crisis, stability, or transformation?"[25] Each project typically required three to ten years of collective work.

The FBC, like other research structures, constantly sought funds to permit its operation, and therefore submitted projects to multiple foundations. We discovered that when we applied to NSF or even to NEH, we typically received outside evaluations that were evenly balanced between enthusiasm and panning. Few reviewers seemed neutral. Sometimes we got the money and sometimes we didn't. But the panning would always center on methodological questions, on the degree to which the research mode we suggested was insufficiently positivist and therefore in the view of some reviewers insufficiently scientific. We realized some twenty years ago that if one wished to reconstruct the way the analysis of the contemporary world was done, it was insufficient to present data, or even to present data undergirded by a solid theoretical explanation. We had to tackle the question of how one knows what one purports to know, or more properly the appropriate epistemology for social science.

In the 1980s, a second challenge to our work raised its head, coming from that broad current some call cultural studies and others postmodernism or post–other things. For these critics, it was not that we had too few disprovable hypotheses, but that we had far too many. World-systems analysis was said to be just one more "grand narrative," to be cast into the dustbin however recently it had been constructed. We may have had the illusion that we were challenging the status quo of world social science; for these critics we incarnated that status quo. We were said to have committed the fatal sin of ignoring culture.[26]

I turned my attention to these issues, as did the Fernand Braudel Center. I could argue that this was just a matter of our unfolding agenda (one can't do everything at the same time) but no doubt it speeds up the pace of one's agenda when one has the fire beneath one's feet. I suppose it was therefore fortunate, but then there are really no accidents in intellectual history, that it was at this time that I discovered Ilya Prigogine. I heard him speak at a conference in 1981 (not having even known his name before that) and was amazed to hear someone formulate so clearly what I had long been feeling in a confused fashion. And to find that this someone was a Nobel Prize in Chemistry was, to say the least, astonishing, or at least so it was to me at that time.

Prigogine is a chemist by training. The historic relationship of chemists to physicists is one in which the physicists reproached the chemists for being insufficiently Newtonian, that is, for being in fact insufficiently positivist. Chemists were constantly describing phenomena in ways, such as the second law of thermodynamics, that seemed to contradict the premises of classical dynamics, for example, by seeming to deny time-reversibility. Physicists argued that these descriptions/laws must be considered interim formulations, essentially the result of incomplete knowledge, and that eventually what the chemists were analyzing would come to be described in more purely Newtonian terms. Prigogine received his Nobel Prize in 1977 for his work on "dissipative processes" but more generally in fact for being a leader in the analysis of the physics of nonequilibrium processes, central to the emerging large field of "complexity studies." What is more, as he has continued his work, Prigogine has gotten bolder. He is no longer merely saying that nonequilibrium processes exist *as well as* equilibrium processes. He is now saying quite clearly that equilibrium processes are a very special, an *unusual* case, of physical reality, and this can be demonstrated in the heartland of classical physics itself, dynamical systems.[27]

I shall not review the details of his arguments here.[28] What became central for my own analysis, and in my opinion for social science as a whole, are two interrelated elements of the Prigogine construct. The first is the fundamental indeterminacy of all reality—physical and therefore social. One should be clear what one means by indeterminacy. It is *not* the position that order and explanation do not exist. Prigogine believes that reality exists in a mode of "deterministic chaos." That is, he takes the position that order always exists *for a while*, but then inevitably undoes itself when its curves reach points of "bifurcation" (that is, points where there are two equally valid solutions for the equations), and that the choice actually made in a bifurcation *intrinsically* cannot be determined in advance. It is not a matter of our incomplete knowledge but of the *impossibility* of foreknowledge.

I have since argued that Prigogine's position is the call for an "unexcluded middle" (determined order and inexplicable chaos) and is, in this regard, absolutely parallel to that of Braudel, who also rejects the two extremes presented as the exclusive antinomies of particularism and eternal universals, insists on orders (structural time) that inevitably undo themselves and come to an end (Wallerstein 1998b). Prigogine's position had two consequences for world-systems analysis: one was psychologico-political, and the second was intellectual.

The psychologico-political one is not to be underestimated. Nomothetic social science is based on the absolute legitimacy of the Newtonian verities, as a model and a constraint. To have a physical scientist challenge these verities in a plausible way, and to see this challenge become a central part of a serious and substantial knowledge movement within the physical sciences itself undermines the intimidating effect so pervasive within the social sciences of arguments put forward by those who hold on to outmoded scientific methodologies (for example, methodological individualism) when the physicist progenitors of these methodologies are in the process of rethinking them, or rather (as I have insisted) *unthinking* them, that is, of removing them from our internalized and now subconscious assumptions.[29]

The intellectual consequence is nonetheless still more important. Prigogine's work has immediate implications for how one does world-systems analysis, and indeed how one does any kind of social science. It enables one to place precise referents to the concept of the "normal" development of a structure, when the laws of that structure hold and when processes tend to return to equilibrium (what we call the "cyclical rhythms" of the world-system), and to distinguish this period of "normal" development (the development taking the form of "secular trends") from the moments of structural crisis. The moments of structural crisis are those in which the system has moved "far from equilibrium" and is approaching the bifurcation. At that point, one can only predict that the existing system cannot continue to exist, but not which fork it will take. On the other hand, precisely because at a bifurcation the swings of the curve are more violent, every input has more significant impact, the opposite of what happens during "normal" periods, when large inputs result in small amounts of change.

We were now able to take this as a model of transformation of the most complex of all systems, social systems. We could argue, with both Braudel and Prigogine, that such systems have lives—beginnings, normal development, and terminal crises. We could argue that, in terminal crises, the impact of social action was much greater than in periods of normal development. We could call this the period in which "free will" prevails.[30] And we could then apply this to an analysis of the modern world-system. Thus, in the collective work of the Fernand Braudel Center, we argued, on the basis of an analysis of six vectors of the world-system between 1945 and 1990 that the world-system was in structural crisis and was facing a bifurcation (Hopkins and Wallerstein 1996).[31]

The second contribution of Prigogine was to insist that time reversibility was absurd—absurd not only where it seemed obviously absurd, as in heat processes or social processes, but in every aspect of physical reality. He adopted the forgotten slogan of Arthur Eddington, "the arrow of time," and argued the case that even atoms were determined by an arrow of time, not to speak of the universe as a whole. Here, too, he joined forces with Braudel, and here too it was crucial that this theme was coming from a physical scientist. Of course, it added plausibility to our insistence that social systems were *historical* systems, and that no analysis, at any level, can omit taking into account the arrow of time.[32]

We had been thrust into the maelstrom of epistemological debates, which in the end are philosophical as well as scientific questions. These issues moved to the center of world-systems analysis. What we could contribute is to understand the evolution of these debates as a process of the modern world-system, as an integral reflection of its geoculture. I discussed these issues in *Unthinking Social Science.* And in 1993, with a grant from the Gulbenkian Foundation, we set about convening an international commission to study the historical evolution of the social sciences and to look into its possible restructuring.

Constructing the Commission was a key part of the task. We decided to keep it small, in order that it be workable—hence ten persons. We decided we wanted persons from different disciplines in the social sciences. We decided we also wanted to have some physical scientists, and some persons from the humanities. We ended with quotas of 6-2-2. We also decided we wanted persons from all over the world (all five continents), and from different linguistic traditions (we managed four). With a ten-person limit, we couldn't include everything, but we came close. We also wanted persons who had shown prior interest in the large epistemological issues.[33]

The committee's report, *Open the Social Sciences,*[34] contains four chapters. The first is on the historical construction of the social sciences from the eighteenth century to 1945 (Wallerstein et al. 1996). The second deals with three major debates since 1945: the validity of the distinctions among the social sciences; the degree to which the heritage is parochial; and the reality and validity of the distinction between the "two cultures." The third chapter asks, what kind of social science shall we now build? and discusses four issues: humans and nature; the state as an analytic building block; the universal and the particular; and objectivity. The final chapter is a conclusion on restructuring the social sciences.

Aside from the contribution the report tried to make to the understanding of the historical construction and current intellectual dilemmas of the social sciences, it also pointed (albeit in a minor way) to the historical construction of the more enveloping schema, the "two cultures." It seemed to us the next step for world-systems analysis to take was to understand how the very categories of knowledge had come into existence, what role such categories played in the operations of the world-system, and how they shaped the emergence of world-systems analysis itself. Here I can only report on an a work in progress at the FBC, which has taken as its object of its study just that: the reasons why the distinction between "philosophy" and "science" became so central to modern thought in the eighteenth century, for it is easy to show that before then most thinkers thought the two concepts not only were not antagonistic but overlapped (or were even virtually identical). We are also studying why a series of challenges emerged in multiple fields to this distinction in the post-1945 and especially the post-1970 period. We are trying to tie these challenges to the structural crisis of the world-system.[35]

In the Giddens-Turner (1987) volume, I wrote an article on "world-systems analysis," calling for a debate about the paradigm. It opens with the sentences: "'World-systems analysis' is not a theory about the world, or about a part of it.

It is a protest against the ways in which social scientific activity was structured for all of us at its inception in the middle of the nineteenth century."[36] In 1989, I gave a talk on "World-Systems Analysis: The Second Phase" (Wallerstein 1990, 1999a).[37] In that article, I outlined a number of tasks unfinished. I said that the key issue, and "the hardest nut to crack" was how to overcome the distinction of three social arenas: the economic, the political, and the sociocultural. I pointed out that even world-systems analysts, even I myself, although we proclaimed loudly the spuriousness of separating the three arenas that are so closely interlinked, nonetheless continued to use the language of the three arenas and seemed unable to escape it. And in a millennium symposium of the British Journal of Sociology in 2000, I called for sociologists to move forward to the construction of a new and reunified discipline I call "historical social science" (Wallerstein 2000b).

I continue to believe that world-systems analysis is primarily a protest against the ways in which social science is done, including in theorizing. I continue to believe that we must somehow find modes of description that dismisses the very idea of the separation of the three arenas of social action. I continue to believe that the historic categorizations of the disciplines of the social sciences make no intellectual sense any more. But if we continue to protest, it is because we remain in a minority. And if we cannot solve the "key" theoretical conundrum, perhaps we deserve to be. For without solving it, it is hard to convince many of the irrelevance of our consecrated disciplinary categories.

Hence I continue to believe that we are in an uphill battle, but also that this battle is part and parcel of the systemic transformation through which we are living and which will continue for some time yet. Consequently, I continue to believe that it is very worth trying to do what we are doing. But we must be open to many voices and many critics if we are to go further. And that is the reason I continue to believe it is premature to think of what we are doing as a theory.

NOTES

1. For a very brief statement of the cultural importance of this subfield, see Wallerstein (1995b).

2. My M.A. thesis in 1954 was entitled "McCarthyism and the Conservative." My Ph.D. dissertation in 1959 was entitled "The Role of Voluntary Associations in the Nationalist Movements in Ghana and the Ivory Coast." It was later published as *The Road to Independence: Ghana and the Ivory Coast* (Wallerstein 1964). At the first ISA meeting that I attended in Stresa, Italy, in 1959, I spent my time at the meetings of the Committee on Political Sociology. Later, I attended one of the conferences of the SSRC Committee in Frascati, Italy in 1964 and contributed a paper to the volume resulting from the conference (see Wallerstein 1966).

3. See my look backward as of 2000 in Wallerstein (2000a).

4. My first two books, aside from the published dissertation, were *Africa: The Politics of Independence* (Wallerstein 1961) and *Africa: The Politics of Unity* (Wallerstein 1965). In 1973–74, I was elected president of the African Studies Association.

5. See my entries on Fanon (Wallerstein 1968, 1970, 1979b).

6. *La Méditerranée et le monde méditerranéan à l'époque de Phillippe II* was first published in 1949 with a revised edition in two volumes in 1966 (Braudel [1949] 1966). Its English translation, based on the revised version did not appear until 1972 (Braudel 1972).

7. My "manifesto" is found in Wallerstein (1976) delivered in 1975, appearing originally in *The Uses and Controversy of Sociology* and reprinted in Wallerstein (1979a).

8. I acknowledge my debt to both of them in Wallerstein (1974a).

9. I discuss the issue of the hyphen in Wallerstein (1991b).

10. Note the hyphen in all of these formulations. "World empire" (and *Weltreich*) is a term that others have used before me. I felt however that since none of these structures was global, in English the hyphen was required by the same grammatical logic that made it requisite in the case of world-economy.

11. By now Frank has published these arguments in many texts. See especially the early version, Frank (1990), and the mature version, Frank (1999). For my critique of *ReOrient*, see Wallerstein (1999b). The same issue of *Review* also contains critical reviews of Frank by Samir Amin and Giovanni Arrighi.

12. This was republished in Braudel (1969). This has appeared in English in at least four different versions. The reader must beware of the most accessible translation, that found in *On History* (Braudel 1980) since it is inaccurate at points crucial for this discussion.

13. I discuss how best to translate them into English in Wallerstein (1991b).

14. This view is argued in many of my writings. See in particular part 1 of Wallerstein (1979a).

15. See, for example, Hechter (1975:221), who tempers his praise with a critique of shortcomings, two of which revolve around theorizing. "[T]here is no theory to account for the triumph of the European world-economy in the sixteenth century. . . . There is a certain lack of conceptual precision which mars the analysis."

16. See the marvelous discussion of the criticism that Wallerstein has "only one case" in Wulbert (1975).

17. One of the few persons to remark favorably upon this technique, and to explicate clearly the strategy, is Franco Moretti (2000:56–57): "Writing about comparative social history, Marc Bloch once coined a lovely 'slogan,' as he himself called it: 'years of analysis for a day of synthesis'; and if you read Braudel or Wallerstein you immediately see what Bloch had in mind. The text which is strictly Wallerstein's, his 'day of synthesis,' occupies one third of a page, one fourth, maybe half; the rest are quotations (fourteen hundred, in the first volume of *The Modern World-System*). Years of analysis; other people's analysis, which Wallerstein synthesizes into a system."

18. "Is there good reason for considering Poland part of the periphery within Europe's world-economy and regarding the Ottoman empire as part of an external arena?" (Lane 1976:528).

19. "Thus the correct counterposition cannot be production for the market versus production for use, but the class system of production based on free wage labour (capitalism) versus pre-capitalist class systems" (Brenner 1977:50).

20. Theda Skocpol (1977:1079) suggests, like Brenner, who acknowledges seeing her article before publication, that I have ignored the "basic Marxist insight that the social relations of production and surplus appropriation are the sociological key to the functioning and development of any economic system." However, her more fundamental critique has to do with the relation of the economic and political arenas: "[The] model is based on a two-step reduction: first, a reduction of socioeconomic structure to determination by world market opportunities and technological production possibilities; and second, a reduction of state structures and policies to determination by dominant class interests" (ibid:1078–79).

Aristide Zolberg (1981), in his critique of my work specifically recommends Hintze as a more "fruitful avenue for theoretical reflection." He says that Hintze "remains one of the very few scholars who identify the interactions between endogenous processes of various kinds and exogenous *political* processes as a *problématique* for the analysis of European political development." Note the italicization of "political." For Zolberg, as for Skocpol, as indeed for Brenner, I am too "economistic."

21. Core-periphery as an antinomy to be applied to the analysis of the world-economy was first made famous by Raúl Prebisch and his associates in the U.N. Economic Commission of Latin America in the 1950s, essentially to replace the then dominant antinomy of industrialized and agricultural nations. Prebisch was implicitly using a world-systems perspective by insisting that what went on in the two sets of countries was a function of their interrelations more than of social structures internal to

each set of countries. The Prebisch framework was further developed, particularly in its political implications, by what came to be known in the 1960s as dependency theory. In my book *The Modern World-System*, vol. 1 (Wallerstein 1974a), I insisted on adding a third category, the semiperiphery, which I claimed was not merely "in-between" the other two but played a crucial role in making the system work. What the semiperiphery is, and how exactly it can be defined, has been a contentious issue ever since. An early attempt by me to spell this out may be found in Wallerstein (1979a:95–118).

22. See the website: fbc.binghamton.edu.

23. See my discussion of this issue, precisely using the case of Germany to make a general theoretical point, in "Societal Development, or Development of the World-System?" (Wallerstein 1986). This was an address to the *Deutsche Soziologentag* and was published first in *International Sociology* and then republished in *Unthinking Social Science* (Wallerstein 1991a).

24. I have discussed a bit of this organizational history and philosophy in "Pedagogy and Scholarship" (Wallerstein 1998a).

25. The story from 1976–91 can be found in a pamphlet, *Report on an Intellectual Project: The Fernand Braudel Center, 1976–1991*. It is now out of print but can be found on the Web: fbc.binghamton.edu/fbcintel.htm. The annual story since then can be found in the newsletters of the FBC, also on the Web: fbc.binghamton.edu/newsletter.htm.

26. The bulk of the article attacks the uses of "systems theory" for its nomothetic bias, and then draws this inference: "Ideologies of legitimation, questions of cultural domination, etc. take on little or no importance. . . . Wallerstein sees no need to account for the specific development of hegemonic bourgeois democratic ideologies which are already in the process of formation in the period of capitalism's early rise" (Aronowitz 1981:516).

27. "[O]ur position is that classical mechanics is incomplete, because it does not include irreversible processes associated with an increase in entropy. To include these processes in its formulation, we must incorporate instability and nonintegrability. Integrable systems are the exception. Starting with the three-body problem, most dynamical systems are nonintegrable. . . . We therefore obtain a probabilistic formulation of dynamics by means of which we can resolve the conflict between time-reversible dynamics and the time-oriented view of thermodynamics" (Prigogine 1997:108).

28. The latest and clearest version is to be found in *The End of Certainty*. It should be noted that even here, the issues of orthography intrude themselves. Certainty in the English edition is singular. But the French original is entitled *La fin des certitudes*, and there certainty is plural. I believe the publishers made a serious error in the translation of the title.

29. On the importance of "unthinking" as opposed to "rethinking," see the introduction, "Why Unthink?" to *Unthinking Social Science: The Limits of Nineteenth-Century Paradigms* (Wallerstein 1991a:1–4 and passim).

30. I placed the discussion of "free will" within a fifth social time, not dealt with by Braudel. I called it "transformational time," and suggested that this was the *kairos* discussed by Paul Tillich (1948, esp. pp. 32–51). *Kairos* means "the right time" and Tillich says that "All great changes in history are accompanied by a strong consciousness of a kairos at hand" (ibid:155). See "The Invention of TimeSpace Realities: Towards an Understanding of our Historical Systems," *Unthinking Social Science* (Wallerstein 1991a:146–47), where I specifically tied the concept of transformational time to the discussion by Prigogine of the consequences of "cascading bifurcations."

31. The six vectors are the interstate system; world production; the world labor force; world human welfare; the social cohesion of the states; and structures of knowledge. These six vectors are then summed up in two chapters that I wrote, entitled "The Global Picture, 1945–1990" and "The Global Possibilities, 1990–2025."

32. The importance of the time dimension in the redirecting of sociological theorizing is at the heart of my ISA presidential address (Wallerstein 1999c).

33. The final list of the commission was: Immanuel Wallerstein, chair, sociology, United States; Calestous Juma, science and technology studies, Kenya; Evelyn Fox Keller, physics, United States; Jürgen Kocka, history, Germany; Dominique Lecourt, philosophy, France; V. Y. Mudimbe, Romance Languages, Congo; Kinhide Mushakoji, political science, Japan; Ilya Prigogine, chemistry, Belgium; Peter J. Taylor, geography, United Kingdom; Michel-Rolph Trouillot, anthropology, Haiti. Given the

academic and geographic mobility of scholars, the disciplines listed are those of their doctorates, and the countries those of their identification (via birth or nationality).

34. As of 2002, the report exists in twenty-five editions in twenty-two languages. Others are in process.

35. See a first treatment of this last issue in Richard Lee, "Structures of Knowledge" (1996).

36. The article is reprinted in *Unthinking Social Science* (Wallerstein 1991a). The quote is to be found on p. 237.

37. It was published in *Review*, reprinted in *The End of the World as We Know It: Social Science for the Twenty-first Century* (Wallerstein 1990, 1999a).

REFERENCES

Aronowitz, Stanley. 1981. "A Metatheoretical Critique of Immanuel Wallerstein's *The Modern World-System*." *Theory and Society* 10:503–20.

Braudel, Fernand. ([1949] 1966). *La Méditerranée et le monde méditerranéan à l'epoque de Philippe II*. Paris: Armand Colin.

———. 1958. "Histoire et sciences sociales: La longue durée." *Annales E.S.C.* (October-December):725–53. This was reprinted in *Ecrits sur l'histoire*. Paris: Flammarion.

———. 1969. *Ecrits sur l'histoire*. Paris: Flammarion.

———. 1972. *The Mediterranean and the Mediterranean World in the Age of Phillip II*. New York: Harper and Row.

———. 1980. *On History*. Chicago: University of Chicago Press.

———. 1984. *Civilization & Capitalism, 15th–18th Century: The Perspective of the World*. New York: Harper and Row.

Brenner, Robert. 1977. "The Origins of Capitalist Development: A Critique of Neo-Smithian Marxism." *New Left Review* 104:25–92.

Frank, Andre Gunder. 1990. "A Theoretical Introduction to 5,000 Years of World-System History." *Review* 13:155–248.

———. 1999. *ReOrient: Global Economy in the Asian Age*. Berkeley: University of California Press.

Giddens, Anthony, and Jonathan Turner, editors. 1987. *Social Theory Today*. Cambridge: Polity Press.

Hechter, Michael. 1975. "Essay Review," *Contemporary Sociology* 4:217–22.

Hopkins, Terence K., and Immanuel Wallerstein. 1967. "The Comparative Study of National Societies." *Social Science Information* 6:25–58.

———, coordinators. 1996. *The Age of Transition: Trajectory of the World-System 1945–2025*. London: Zed Press.

Lane, Frederic. 1976. "Economic Growth in Wallerstein's Social System." *Comparative Studies in Society and History* 18:517–532.

Lee, Richard. 1996. "Structures of Knowledge." Pp. 178–206 in T*he Age of Transition*, coordinated by Terence K. Hopkins and Immanuel Wallerstein. London: Zed Press.

Malowist, Marian. 1964. "Les aspects sociaux de la première phase de l'expansion coloniale." *Africana Bulletin* 1:11–40.

———. 1966. "Le commerce d'or et d'esclaves au Soudan Occidental." *Africana Bulletin* 4:49–93.

Merton, Robert K. 1957. "The Bearing of Sociological Theory on Empirical Research." Pp. 85–101 in *Social Theory and Social Structure*, revised and enlarged edition. Glencoe, IL: Free Press.

Moretti, Franco. 2000. "Conjectures on World Literature." *New Left Review* (2d ser.) 1:54–68.

Nolte, H. H. 1982. "The Position of Eastern Europe in the International System in the Early Modern Times." *Review* 6:25–84.

Polanyi, Karl. 1957. *The Great Transformation*. Boston: Beacon Press.

———. 1967. "The Economy of Instituted Process." Pp. 243–70 in *Trade and Market in the Early Empires*, edited by Karl Polanyi et al. Glencoe, IL: Free Press.

———. 1977. "Forms of Integration and Supporting Structures." Pp. 35–43 in *The Livelihood of Man*, edited by Harry W. Pearson. New York: Academic Press.

Prigogine, Ilya. 1997. *The End of Certainty: Time, Chaos, and the New Laws of Nature.* New York: Free Press.

Skocpol, Theda. 1977. "Wallerstein's World Capitalist System: A Theoretical and Historical Critique." *American Journal of Sociology* 82:1075–90.

Tillich, Paul. 1948. *The Protestant Era.* Chicago: University of Chicago Press.

Wallerstein, Immanuel. 1961. *Africa: The Politics of Independence.* New York: Random House.

———. 1964. *The Road to Independence: Ghana and the Ivory Coast.* Paris: Mouton.

———. 1965. *Africa: The Politics of Unity.* New York: Random House.

———. 1966. "The Decline of the Party in Single-Party African States." Pp. 201–14 in *Political Parties and Political Development,* edited by J. LaPalombara and M. Weiner. Princeton: Princeton University Press.

———. 1968. "Frantz Fanon." *International Encyclopedia of the Social Sciences.* Vol. 5:326–27.

———. 1970. "Frantz Fanon: Reason and Violence." *Berkeley Journal of Sociology* 15:222–31.

———. 1974a. *The Modern World-System: Vol. 1, Capitalist Agriculture and the Origins of the European World-Economy in the Sixteenth Century.* New York: Academic Press.

———. 1974b. "The Rise and Demise of the World-Capitalist System: Concepts for Comparative Analysis." *Comparative Studies in Society and History* 16:387–415. Reprinted in I. Wallerstein, *The Capitalist World-Economy.* Cambridge: Cambridge University Press.

———. 1976. "Modernization: Requiescat in Pace." Pp. 131–35 in *The Uses and Controversy of Sociology,* edited by L. Coser and O. Larsen. New York: Free Press. Reprinted in *The Capitalist World-Economy.*

———. 1979a. *The Capitalist World-Economy.* Cambridge: Cambridge University Press.

———. 1979b. "Fanon and the Revolutionary Class." Pp. 250–68 in *The Capitalist World- Economy.* Cambridge: Cambridge University Press.

———. 1980. *The Modern World-System: Vol. 2, Mercantilism and the Consolidation of the European World-Economy 1600–1750.* New York: Academic Press.

———. 1986. "Societal Development or Development of the World-System?" *International Sociology* 1:3–17. Republished in *Unthinking Social Science.*

———. 1988. "The Invention of TimeSpace Realities: Towards an Understanding of our Historical Systems." *Geography* 73:289–97. Reprinted in *Unthinking Social Science.*

———. 1990. "World-Systems Analysis: The Second Phase." *Review* 13:287–293. Reprinted in *The End of the World as We Know It: Social Science for the Twenty-First Century.*

———. 1991a. *Unthinking Social Science: The Limits of Nineteenth-Century Paradigm.* Cambridge: Polity.

———. 1991b. "World System Versus World-Systems: A Critique." *Critique of Anthropology* 11:189–94.

———. 1995a. *Historical Capitalism, with Capitalist Civilization.* London: Verso.

———. 1995b. "The Significance of Political Sociology." Pp. 27–28 in *Encounter with Erik Allardt,* edited by R. Alapuro et al. Helsinki: Yliopistopaino.

———. 1998a. "Pedagogy and Scholarship." Pp. 47–52 in *Mentoring, Methods, and Movements: Colloquium in Honor of Terence K. Hopkins by His Former Students,* edited by I. Wallerstein. Binghamton, NY: Fernand Braudel Center.

———. 1998b. "Time and Duration: The Unexcluded Middle, or Reflections on Braudel and Prigogine." *Thesis* 10:79–87.

———. 1999a. *The End of the World as We Know It: Social Science for the Twenty-First Century.* Minneapolis: University of Minnesota Press.

———. 1999b. "Frank Proves the European Miracle." *Review* 22:355–71.

———. 1999c. "The Heritage of Sociology, The Promise of Social Science." *Current Sociology* 47:1–37.

———. 2000a. "C'était quoi le tiers-monde?" *Le monde diplomatique* (August):18–19.

———. 2000b. "From Sociology to Historical Social Science: Prospects and Obstacles." *British Journal of Sociology* 51:25–35.

Wallerstein, Immanuel, et al. 1996. *Open the Social Sciences: Report of the Gulbenkian Commission on the Restructuring of the Social Sciences.* Stanford, CA: Stanford University Press.

Wulbert, Roland. 1975. "Had By the Positive Integer." *American Sociologist* 10:243.

Zolberg, Aristide. 1981. "The Origins of the Modern World System: A Missing Link." *World Politics* 33:253–81.

Index

About the Contributors

Joseph Berger is Emeritus Professor in the Department of Sociology and Senior Fellow at the Hoover Institution, Stanford University.

Peter M. Blau is Emeritus Professor in the Department of Sociology at the University of North Carolina, Chapel Hill.

Bruce Bueno de Mesquita is professor in the Department of Politics at New York University and Senior Fellow at the Hoover Institution, Stanford University.

Thomas J. Fararo is Distinguished Service Professor in the Department of Sociology at the University of Pittsburgh.

Jack A. Goldstone is professor of sociology and international relations in the Department of Sociology at the University of California, Davis.

Douglas D. Heckathorn is professor in the Department of Sociology at Cornell University.

David R. Heise is Rudy Professor of Sociology in the Department of Sociology at the University of Indiana.

Guillermina Jasso is professor in the Department of Sociology at New York University.

Ronald L. Jepperson is assistant professor in the Department of Sociology at the University of Tulsa.

Michael Lovaglia is associate professor in the Department of Sociology at the University of Iowa.

Barry Markovsky is professor in the Department of Sociology at the University of South Carolina.

Gerald Marwell is the Richard T. Ely Professor of Sociology Emeritus in the Department of Sociology at the University of Wisconsin, Madison.

John D. McCarthy is professor in the Department of Sociology at Pennsylvania State University.

James Morrow is professor in the department of Political Science at the University of Michigan.

Pamela Oliver is professor in the Department of Sociology at the University of Wisconsin, Madison.

Brent Simpson is assistant professor in the Department of Sociology at Texas A&M University.

Randolph Siverson is professor in the Department of Political Science at the University of California, Davis.

John Skvoretz is the Carolina Distinguished Professor of Sociology in the Department of Sociology at the University of South Carolina.

Alastair Smith is associate professor in the Department of Politics at New York University.

Shane Thye is assistant professor in the Department of Sociology at the University of South Carolina.

David G. Wagner is associate professor in the Department of Sociology at the State University of New York, Albany.

Henry A. Walker is professor in the Department of Sociology at the University of Arizona.

Immanuel Wallerstein is professor and director of the Fernand Braudel Center for the Study of Economics, Historical Systems, and Civilizations at the State University of New York, Binghamton.

David Willer is professor in the Department of Sociology at the University of South Carolina.

Robb Willer is a Ph.D candidate in the Department of Sociology at Cornell University.

Mayer N. Zald is Emeritus Professor in the Department of Sociology at the University of Michigan.

Morris Zelditch Jr. is Emeritus Professor in the Department of Sociology at Stanford University.